THE RISE OF THE AMERICAN
CONSERVATION MOVEMENT

THE RISE OF THE AMERICAN
CONSERVATION MOVEMENT

Power, Privilege, and Environmental Protection

DORCETA E. TAYLOR

Duke University Press ◆ Durham and London ◆ 2016

Designed by Courtney Leigh Baker
Typeset in Garamond Premier Pro by Westchester Publishing Services

Library of Congress Cataloging-in-Publication Data
Names: Taylor, Dorceta E., author.
Title: The rise of the American conservation movement : power, privilege, and environmental protection / Dorceta E. Taylor.
Description: Durham : Duke University Press, 2016. | Includes bibliographical references and index.
Identifiers: LCCN 2016009769 (print) | LCCN 2016011250 (ebook)
ISBN 9780822361817 (hardcover : alk. paper)
ISBN 9780822361985 (pbk. : alk. paper)
ISBN 9780822373971 (e-book)
Subjects: LCSH: Conservation of natural resources—United States—History—
19th century. | Conservation of natural resources—United States—History—
20th century. | Environmental protection—United States—History—19th century. |
Environmental protection—United States—History—20th century.
Classification: LCC S930 .T39 2016 (print) | LCC S930 (ebook) | DDC 333.720973–dc23
LC record available at http://lccn.loc.gov/2016009769

Cover art: Carleton E. Watkins, *North Dome, Yosemite*, ca. 1865. Prints and Photographs Division, Library of Congress, LC-DIG-ppmsca-09988.

Duke University Press gratefully acknowledges the support of the School of Natural Resources and Environment and the Office of the Vice Provost for Research at the University of Michigan, which provided funds toward the publication of this book.

Dedicated to my husband, Ian, and
daughters, Justine and Shaina

———————

Siblings Pansy, Seymour, and Ruth

———————

Nieces and nephews Stacey, Jamie, Djanielle,
Jason, Brandon, DeLeon, and Morgan

———————

Grand-niece Salome

———————

Contents

Acknowledgments

I owe an enormous debt of gratitude to my husband Ian and my daughters Shaina and Justine for putting up with the writing of yet another book. It takes special people to put up with the seemingly endless research, references to esoteric facts, and detours to strange places so that I could see something "I wrote about in my book." Thank you for putting up with it.

The students of the University of Michigan have inspired me. They keep asking challenging questions and are curious about the books I write. They want to know more and they push me to write more. Thanks to all of you who have supported me. I really couldn't have done it without all the conversations in my office, over at my house, and all over the Dana Building.

To Maren Spolum, who runs my research program—thank you for helping to make this possible through the wonderful work you do. To all the research assistants and postdoctoral fellows who have worked in my lab in the past years: I appreciate your help and dedication.

Special thanks to the School of Natural Resources and Environment and to the Office of the Vice Provost for Research for providing a book subvention award to help with the completion and publication of this book.

I am grateful to the anonymous reviewers who read the manuscript and provided very useful feedback. Your suggestions helped to improve the manuscript tremendously. Finally, I want to thank the amazing editorial staff at Duke University Press. I have enjoyed working with you. Thank you for your support and your belief in the project.

Introduction

In the United States, many of the initiatives to protect nature began among urban elites. Though several factors contributed to the rise of pro-environmental behavior, the way elites perceived and related to the city was an important dimension of environmental protection. That is, what eventually emerged as the conservation movement in the early twentieth century was built on the activism that began centuries earlier in urban areas. As cities grew, urban elites were ambivalent about them. They developed what could best be described as a love-hate relationship with cities. This is not unusual: the city evokes complex emotions in people. On the one hand, it attracts vast numbers of people who want to live, work, and play in its confines, but on the other, many fear it or are repulsed by it. Some are simultaneously attracted to and repelled by it.

Elites were among the latter group: the city both fascinated and troubled them. Their desire to enrich themselves, build powerful financial institutions, flex their industrial muscles, use their publications to broadcast their messages on the grandest stages, and exert power and control over the masses drew them to the cities. The cities also had the most luxurious homes; influential networks; exclusive social clubs; powerful churches; the most prestigious theaters, museums, libraries, and universities; elegantly landscaped open spaces; and unparalleled opportunities to innovate and execute ideas. Though elites found these aspects of city life appealing, they were appalled and alarmed by what they perceived as its disorderliness and rampant immorality. By the nineteenth century, crime, vice, riots, overcrowding, poverty, diseases and epidemics, premature death, pollution, uncontrolled industrial development, and massive conflagrations were commonplace. The rich and poor rubbed elbows as they went about their daily routines, and racial mixing grew more commonplace in poor neighborhoods as people scrambled to find affordable housing. These conditions led elites to establish a foothold in the city yet to look beyond its boundaries for adventure, beauty, serenity, inspiration, and ways of reinforcing their status. In essence, the desire to establish themselves in the cities was counterbalanced by a strong impulse to move outward and away from it.

It is not surprising that environmentalism started as an urban phenomenon, because many of the reforms that laid the groundwork for the birth of conservationism and preservationism took place in cities before they did in the countryside. Long before outdoor recreationists, wilderness advocates, and wildlife activists began campaigning to protect remote natural spaces, urban environmental activists campaigned for environmental protection and undertook a series of initiatives to improve conditions in the city: urban residents had to decipher how to dispose of their wastes properly, provide clean and adequate water for residents, rid the cities of epidemics, provide safe and affordable housing, reduce air pollution, monitor industries and control where they were sited, reduce fire hazards, monitor the quality of the food supply, alleviate overcrowding, and provide open space and recreational opportunities for their burgeoning populations. I examine these early reforms in greater detail in *The Environment and the People in American Cities* (Taylor 2009).

This book, *The Rise of the American Conservation Movement*, examines the actions and experiences of elites with regard to environmental protection. It traces the outward movement of people from the cities to the countryside and wilderness; it studies the rise of competing bodies of environmental thought as conflicts arose over access to land and resources, industrial development, degradation, resource depletion, governance, and sustainability. These bodies of thought include Transcendentalism, primitivism, frontierism, conservationism, preservationism, and business environmentalism.

The book analyzes the roles of economic, business, political, intellectual, policy, legal, and religious elites in the rise of these ideologies. Yet it also examines the thoughts, actions, and experiences of poor whites and people of color, which are key to understanding how environmental protection evolved in the United States. The book also investigates the relationship between gender and environmental protection. Hence discussions of racism, discrimination, sexism, and classism inform the narrative of this book as it explores themes such as wildlife conservation, wilderness and park preservation, the establishment of hunting and fishing ethics, rural beautification and farmscaping, outdoor recreation and the establishment of sportsmen's clubs, the formation of environmental organizations, and the promulgation of environmental policies.

Overview of the Book

The Rise of the American Conservation Movement examines the activism of the elites behind that rise. Some of those elites moved outward, leaving the cities behind to live in or explore the countryside, wilderness, and other remote areas. Some left the city to settle in the West and pursue entrepreneurial opportunities, while others wanted to escape its ills. Some left the city for health reasons, some out of curiosity; others wanted to test themselves. Whatever the reasons for their outward sorties, the experiences that resulted from the journeys led many to become active in environmental affairs. When one looks at environmental history, one cannot help but notice the significant impact that wealthy urbanites had on the nineteenth- and early twentieth-century environmental campaigns. This book examines how these activists conducted conservation campaigns, crafted environmental policies, and left their mark on the conservation movement.

Though this book is about the rise of conservation thought and action, understanding the urban context from which the activists originated is important. Though some conservationists got involved in environmental issues because of their aversion to the city or the constraints urban life placed on them, others got involved because of the unparalleled opportunities the city provided—the chance to collaborate with like-minded individuals, incubate ideas, and plan campaigns. Furthermore, the urban environmental campaigns gave the budding conservationists valuable experiences and helped to set the stage for activism aimed at preserving and conserving resources. The conservationists and preservationists discussed in this book drew on the tactics, strategies, framing, and models that were successful in early urban environmental campaigns. For instance, in the campaigns to establish national parks and forests, activists drew upon the lessons learned in the urban parks campaign. Moreover, many of the activists continued to live in the cities as they explored the countryside and wildland areas.

The Rise of the American Conservation Movement situates outdoor recreation, wilderness, and wildlife activism in the context of the urban environmental activism that went before it, helping the reader to understand the relationship between these two realms of activism. The book studies the roles of a wider range of activists than earlier works in this genre have done. It examines how social class (wealth, power, and privilege), race, and gender affected the articulation of problems, the development of environmental policies, and the resolution of issues. Like other environmental history books, it looks at how upper- and middle-class white males advocated for environmental protection, but it does not stop there: it also discusses the interactions between the upper, middle, and lower classes; between males and females; and between whites and ethnic minorities. The book examines the indigenous peoples of the West as well as the voluntary and forced migrations of people of color to the West as the country was settled. The book analyzes the social implications of environmental policy formation and the rise of the conservation movement and highlights both the role businessmen played in responding to environmental problems and the challenges produced by their involvement. It dissects the framing of environmental problems and the assignment of blame for environmental degradation, asking how these narratives changed over time and how people responded to those changes.

Finally, the book examines the mixed motives of people who became involved in conservation issues. While it is tempting to portray conservation advocates as either saints or sinners, such a simplistic approach to this complex story is inadequate. Most of the actors got involved in conservation issues for multiple reasons; some of those reasons were admirable, but others bear questioning. Likewise, their tactics and strategies ranged from democratic and populist to exclusionary and autocratic. Thus this book examines the trade-off between public participation in conservation policy making and an elite-driven model of conservation decision making devoid of public representation and input.

Part I of the book (chapters 1 and 2) introduces key concepts that arise throughout the narrative and sets the stage for the early years of the conservation movement. Chapter 1 focuses on the central concepts, which are organized around environmental thought, social dynamics, framing of discourses, institutionalization, power, and privilege. Chapter 2 looks at how conditions in the cities prompted the rise of environmental activism: as urban areas became larger, more crowded, and more industrial, wealthy urbanites began to explore nearby rural areas as well as far-flung destinations, and those explorations heightened their environmental consciousness and stimulated actions to protect nature.

Part II (chapters 3–5) illustrates the ways that sexism, racism, and discrimination affected the rise of the environmental movement and recounts how women and people of color contributed to conservation despite the barriers they faced. By looking at the recreational pursuits of upper-class men and women and how their interests influenced their participation in conservation activities, it explores the interactions between elites, the working class, and minorities as activists sought to define sporting ethics, identify problems of resource degradation, and set about monitoring and managing said resources. Chapter 3 examines the cult of manhood and the impetus for men to explore beyond the boundaries of cities and engage in outdoor recreation. Chapter 4 discusses the cult of true womanhood and the way that construct constrained and framed women's experiences, while chapter 5 looks at class dynamics as well as the experiences of people of color in the wilds.

Part III (chapters 6–8) analyzes efforts to protect wildlife, particularly birds, big game, and fish. It examines the relationship between hunting, overfishing, and the decimation of wildlife stocks, describing the rising awareness about environmental degradation and resource depletion and identifying activists and organizations that emerged to lead the nature protection campaigns. It also looks at some of the class, gender, and racial conflicts that arose during the emergence of explicit conservation discourses, the development of a conservation ethic, and the articulation of clear conservation ideologies. Finally, it discusses the impact of social class, race, gender, and wealth on the framing of those discourses, on policy formation and the enactment of conservation laws, and on responses to resource scarcity.

Part IV (chapters 9–12) studies the emergence of the preservationist perspective and the rise of wilderness and national park preservation. Both men and wealthy white women played important parts in efforts to beautify rural areas, propagate the spread of pastoral landscapes, and conserve forests and other open spaces, but there were clear differences in gender roles. This section of the book discusses those differences and analyzes the role of race, class, and gender in the major preservationist battles of the early twentieth century and in the social construction of the emerging conservation and preservation discourses. It compares conservation and preservation ideologies and looks at their relation to the establishment of the national forest and park systems, respectively. It also explores how corporate interests intersected with conservation and preservation.

Tying together the major points presented in the preceding chapters, the conclusion summarizes the characteristics of the early conservation movement through the lenses of class, race, and gender.

Other Books in This Series

This book is the second in a series. The first book, *The Environment, and the People in American Cities: 1600s–1900s,* is a detailed account of environmental change, policy making, reform, and activism in American cities from the seventeenth to the twentieth centuries. The book examines the responses of elites and ordinary citizens as they struggled to enhance morality, civility, culture, and social order in the cities.

The third book in the series, *Toxic Communities: Environmental Racism, Industrial Pollution, and Residential Mobility*, examines the issue of siting of hazardous facilities in minority and low-income rural and urban communities. It investigates the historical and contemporary policies and practices that help to account for the siting patterns as well as the responses of people of color to the presence of hazardous facilities in their communities.

PART I
THE IMPETUS FOR CHANGE

I

KEY CONCEPTS INFORMING
EARLY CONSERVATION THOUGHT

The conservation movement arose against a backdrop of racism, sexism, class conflicts, and nativism that shaped the nation in profound ways. Though these factors are not usually incorporated into environmental history texts, they are incorporated into this narrative because they are critical to our understanding of how discourses about the environment were developed, policies formulated, and institutions organized. Hence, this chapter identifies seven key concepts that recur in the book: (1) race relations; (2) colonialism; (3) nativism; (4) gender relations; (5) the evolution of environmental ideologies; (6) power elites and environmental governance; and (7) the creation of an environmental identity.

Race Relations in the Environmental Context

Four aspects of race relations that had considerable impact on the transformation of the environment are defined here: the appropriation of Native American land and resources; the enslavement of blacks; the seizure of Latino territories; and the containment of Asians.

The role that race played in the formative experiences of early environmental activists and their subsequent formulation of environmental ideologies has been understudied, but race issues—relationships between Europeans and non-Europeans—were critical to the development of environmental discourse and activism in the United States. For instance, the American government and European settlers battled Indians for centuries to gain control over the land and other resources. These conflicts played significant roles in the crafting of policies that had lasting impacts on indigenous peoples and the environment.

During the battles to control land and resources, Native Americans were overpowered militarily and decimated by diseases. Tribal lands were seized as war bounties or through treaty making and breaking. Furthermore, Indians were repeatedly expelled (or removed) from their homelands, forced to live in reservations located on marginal lands, and allotted small parcels of land on which to subsist. Over time, federal Indian policies evolved to focus on the control of land, water, and mineral resources; the extermination and containment of Indians; forced assimilation, the transformation of Indians into farmers and urban low-wage laborers; and restrictions on religious and cultural expression (Nabokov 1991; Taylor 2009, 2014).

The first commercial trade between Indians and whites in North America probably occurred in the eleventh century, when Nova Scotia Indians traded gray fox and sable pelts for Viking knives and axes. During the fifteenth and sixteenth centuries, as timber, fur-bearing animals, and other natural resources were depleted in Europe, Europeans explored the Americas for raw materials. Consequently, the French, English, and Dutch competed with each other to trade with Indians. In exchange for trinkets, metal objects, liquor, and guns, Indians traded raw materials such as salt, tobacco, wood, fish, fur, and hides. However, as trade increased Indians found themselves competing with each other to extract natural resources and trade them as rapidly as possible (Nabokov 1991: 32–35; R. Thornton 1987: 11–12).

Despite the long history of commercial relations, whites and Indians had vastly different views and attitudes toward the land. Whites viewed Indian worship of animal spirits, rocks, and rainbows as pagan rituals to be purged. Hence, by the 1630s numerous Spanish missions were established in the South and thousands of Indians were Christianized; those who refused baptism were beaten or executed. In the Southwest, in what is now New Mexico, the Spanish established a feudal system (the *encomienda*) sustained by the perpetual servitude of the native inhabitants. When British soldiers took over the territory in the 1700s, they sold thousands of the Indian converts into slavery (Hannan 2001; Nabokov 1991: 50–52, 70; U.S. Commission on Human Rights 1992: 13–31).

Native Americans and whites had differing views of the land, and this led to many conflicts and the disenfranchisement of indigenous peoples. Indians viewed themselves as custodians and stewards of the earth, not as masters with dominion over it. By contrast, white settlers saw the land as a commercial product best suited for private ownership and exploitation; consequently, they cleared forests for cultivation and the development of towns, and private property was essential to their entrepreneurial ventures. Whites were also disdainful of the Indian custom of sharing undeveloped, common land. These differences formed the philosophical basis of the Euro-American seizure of Indian lands.

The justification for seizing land was articulated early on when the first governor of Massachusetts, John Winthrop, expressed a view that was typical of the European perspective on Indian land-use practices. He questioned the communal living arrangements and seasonal migration patterns of Native American tribes. He also articulated and rationalized a colonialist ideology of conquest that paved the way for the appropriation of Indian land and resources. In so doing, Winthrop distinguished between two rights to the land—a natural right and a civil right. He argued that Native Americans had a natural right to the land, but Europeans in settling and developing the land had a civil right to it. The civil rights, in his view, superseded the natural rights. In 1629, Winthrop argued that the earth was the "Lord's garden" and that the earth was given to the "sons of Adam to be tilled and improved by them" (Winthrop [1629] 1846: 272–276).[1] Winthrop justified the taking of Indian lands by arguing:

> That which is common to all is proper to none. This savage people ruleth over many lands without title or property; for they enclose no ground, neither have they cattle to maintain it, but remove their dwellings as they have occasion . . . And why may not Christians have liberty to go and dwell among them in their waste lands and woods, (leaving them such places as they have manured for their corn,) . . . there is more than enough for them and us. (Winthrop [1629] 1846: 275–276)

John Locke also promoted individual ownership of land and resources in his writings about natural and property rights. In 1689, Locke argued that humans had a right to self-preservation, therefore they had a right to food and drink to subsist on as provided by nature. He stated, "The earth and all that is therein is given to men for the support and comfort of their being." However, Locke made an important argument about the appropriation of resources for individual use. He contended that though the bounties of the earth are given to humans in common, there must be a way to "appropriate them some way or other before they can be of any use, or at all beneficial, to any particular men" (Locke [1690] 1824: 144–145).[2] Raising the question of native peoples' common use of resources, Locke argued that they had a natural right to resources, but postulated that once an individual added his or her labor to bring about the improvement or development of a particular resource, then that person gained individual rights to it and can claim it as individual property. Locke argued,

> The fruit or venison which nourishes the wild Indian, who knows no enclosure, and is still a tenant in common, must be his . . . Every man has a "property" in his own "person." This nobody has any right to but himself. The "labour" of his body and the "work" of his hands, we may say, are properly his. Whatsoever, then, he removes out of the state that Nature hath provided and left it in, he hath mixed his labour with it, and joined to it something that is his own, and thereby makes it his property. (Locke [1690] 1824: 145–146)[3]

Locke assumed that resources were bountiful; consequently, he argued that one can remove resources from the communal pool as long as one leaves adequate resources of good quality for others. That is, privatization should not result in the taking of something from someone else. In addition, one should not take excessive amounts, only what one can use without causing spoilage. However, since mineral resources did not rot, one could accumulate as much as one wanted. To avoid spoilage of resources that tended to degrade, one could sell them before they rotted (Locke [1690] 1824: 147–150). These arguments provided a rationale for privatization and trade in or aggregation of resources to generate wealth that had a strong influence on American thought.

Over the years, the courts were asked to rule on the primacy of agricultural and industrial land uses over communal land use and subsistence activities such as hunting and gathering. At first the courts were reluctant to decide. For instance, in *Johnson v. McIntosh* (1823), the court balked at taking sides. Chief Justice John Marshall argued, "We will not enter into the controversy, whether agriculturalists, merchants, and manufacturers, have a right, on abstract principles, to expel hunters from territory they possess, or to contract their limits. Conquest gives a title which the Courts of the conquerer cannot deny." However, five years later James Kent, an expert on American jurisprudence, argued decisively that the "cultivators of the soil" should be given priority over hunters vis-à-vis their property rights (J. Kent 1828: 312).

Although Indians were enslaved in the United States, enslavement wasn't the primary means by which tribes were suppressed. European settlers overpowered native tribes through warfare, the appropriation of land, treaties, and the control of natural resources. By contrast, blacks were subjugated primarily through forced migration from Africa and enslavement on American soil.

Historical records indicate that Africans had been visiting the American shores since the early 1500s and that African slaves were brought to Spanish Florida in the 1560s. The colonists who established St. Augustine in 1565 brought black slaves with them to help in the building of the settlement (Reynolds 1886: 20–105). However, blacks were not systematically enslaved until the seventeenth century. In 1619, about twenty Africans from Angola arrived in Virginia on a British pirate ship. The census shows that in 1623 there were twenty-two blacks in Virginia. Shortly thereafter blacks were enslaved in response to chronic labor shortages in the region (L. Bennett 1993: 5–12, 66–75, 84–90; D. B. Davis 2006: 124; Franklin and Moss 1994: 57; Parish 1989: 12–26; U.S. Census Bureau 1864: xiv). Roughly 12.5 million slaves were put on ships sailing from Africa to the Americas from the sixteenth century to the nineteenth; about 10.7 million Africans arrived alive in the Americas—the remaining 1.8 million died at sea. Estimates are that 389,000 of the Africans who survived the Transatlantic crossing were brought to the United States (Eltis and Richardson 2010: 4, 17–18; Sublette and Sublette 2016: 10–11; U.S. Census Bureau 1975: 1168).[4]

The slave population in America increased rapidly. The 1790 census of southern states indicated that there were 650,000 slaves; the total population of the United States was 4 million at the time. By 1830 the number of slaves had increased to more than 2 million, even though the importation of slaves had been banned in 1808 (table 1.1). The slave population continued to rise. However, as opposition to slavery mounted, slaves were increasingly concentrated in fifteen slaveholding states. In the intercensal period between 1850 and 1860 the white population in slaveholding states increased by 27.3 percent, while the slave population in those states increased by 23.4 percent. In 1860, slaves accounted for almost 4 million of the 12.2 million people residing in the slaveholding states. There were also 251,000 free blacks living in those states (L. Bennett 1993: 101–102; Parish 1989: 12–26; U.S. Census Bureau 1864).[5] Nationwide, slaves comprised roughly 31 percent of the labor force in 1800 and about 23 percent in 1860 (Lebergott 1966: 117–204; U.S. Census Bureau 1864, vii). Table 1.1 also shows that rate of growth of free blacks slowed dramatically

TABLE 1.1. Census of Slaves and Free Blacks: 1790–1860

Year of Census	Number of Free Blacks	% Increase	Number of Slaves	% Increase	Total Number of Blacks	% Increase
1790	59,466		697,897		757,363	
1800	108,395	82.3	893,041	28.0	1,001,436	32.2
1810	186,446	72.0	1,191,364	33.4	1,377,810	37.6
1820	233,524	25.2	1,538,038	28.8	1,771,562	28.6
1830	319,599	36.9	2,009,043	30.6	2,328,642	31.4
1840	386,303	20.9	2,487,455	23.8	2,873,758	23.4
1850	434,449	12.5	3,204,313	28.8	3,638,762	26.6
1860	487,970	12.3	3,953,760	23.4	4,441,730	22.0

Source: U.S. Census Bureau. 1864. *Population of the United States in 1860, Compiled from the Original Returns of the Eighth Census*. Department of the Interior. Washington, DC: Government Printing Office.

over time, and only about 9 percent of the blacks living in America in 1860 were free.

Some slaves were highly skilled in a variety of trades. Though there is a tendency to view the slave as an unskilled plantation worker or a worker taught a trade by his or her master, some slaves brought skills developed in Africa with them on the slave ships. When the Europeans explored the African shores, they encountered people already skilled in mining and metalwork. West African craftsmen manufactured farm implements and handicrafts (Genovese 1972: 388–392). Most of the slaves brought to North America came from agrarian societies in West Africa, so they were experienced farmers and cattle producers (Blassingame 1979: 5). Rice cultivation was one such job: Africans skilled in growing the crop were brought to the Carolinas as slaves to cultivate it. Plantation owners were willing to pay high prices for slaves from Sierra Leone, Gambia, Liberia, Senegal, Ghana, and other rice-growing regions of Africa. By the 1690s the Carolinas became the largest supplier of rice in the world. As was the case with the Carolinas, Africans being transported to New Orleans took rice seedlings with them (Alpern 2013: 35–66; P. A. Bruce 1895: 331; Carney 2001; Littlefield 1991; Sublette and Sublette 2016: 170–171; Wood 1975: 36). Africans also brought indigo to the United States; sesame seeds were also brought for agricultural and medicinal uses (Bedigian 2013: 67–120; Sublette and Sublette 2016: 171).

Initially, Latinos were incorporated into the United States through military conquest as territory was appropriated from Mexico during the first half of the 1800s. The period of conquest began with the 1836 Battle of San Jacinto and ended with the 1853 Gadsden Purchase. In 1819, Mexico permitted foreigners to settle in the area now known as Texas. By 1830, a year after Mexico abolished slavery, about twenty thousand Anglos (mostly southerners) and about two thousand "freed" slaves (who had been forced to sign lifelong contracts with their former owners) lived in the territory. Soon a number of factors—feelings of racial superiority, anger over Mexico's decision to abolish slavery, defiance of the order to pledge allegiance to the Mexican government and convert to Catholicism (both of which were required of residents in Mexican territory), a rise in the number of European settlers pushing for independence from Mexico, and the failure of diplomatic efforts—resulted in the Texas Revolt of 1835–36 (Aguirre and Turner 1998: 143; Anna 1978; Archer 2003; Estrada et al. 1981: 103–131; Hamnett 1986).

The creation of the Republic and the granting of statehood in 1845 provided the pretext for further U.S. expansion into Mexican territory, thereby setting the stage for the Mexican-American War, which was fought between 1846 and 1848. Under the 1848 Treaty of Guadalupe Hidalgo, which ended the war, Mexicans living in the Southwest were considered U.S. citizens. The treaty also guaranteed that Mexicans could retain their political liberty; whatever property they owned; and the Spanish language, as a recognized and legitimate language. However, by the end of the war Mexico lost about half of its territory, while the United States increased its territory by a third.[6] The United States acquired more land in 1853 with the Gadsden Purchase, when Mexico sold over forty-five thousand square miles of territory in what is now Arizona and New Mexico to gain an infusion of cash to rebuild its war-ravaged economy. The United States purchased the land so it could build railroads to California (Archer 2003; Estrada et al. 1981: 103–131; Hamnett 1986).

Treaties notwithstanding, violations of the civil and property rights of Latinos were widespread. In Texas, the transfer of land (by fraud, intimidation, violence, and force) from Mexicans to Anglos began with the Revolt and accelerated after the war ended. Though Mexicans could defend their property rights in court, the financial costs were staggering, hence, it was not economically feasible for them to defend their land ownership rights through the legal system. Those who went to court ended up selling their land to pay their legal bills. As they took over land, Anglos adopted Mexican mining, ranching, and agricultural techniques. Consequently, whites in Texas expanded the cattle and sheep ranches as well as the cotton plantations, while Mexicans were relegated to the low-wage labor pool. Essentially, this resulted in a transfer of power that resulted in the ascendency of white power brokers and the downward mobility of Mexicans (Estrada et al. 1981: 103–131).

Mexicans were dispossessed of land more slowly in New Mexico than in Texas. Native Americans and Mexicans organized to defend the territory from the few whites who ventured in. New Mexico had communal villages with communal grazing and water rights in the more densely populated north, and privately owned haciendas in the south. It took a military occupation of the area to open up the territory to white cattlemen and farmers, and it was only in the late 1800s, when the railroads were built, that many whites moved into the territory. The land transfers accelerated then. Arizona (originally a part of New Mexico) was also very sparsely populated by Indians who successfully resisted Christianization. The army fought the tribes in the 1880s, and this helped Anglos gain control of the land. Meanwhile, Latinos became low-wage laborers and were forced to live in segregated mining and railroad towns (Estrada et al. 1981: 103–131).

From the eighteenth to the early nineteenth century, Spain sent colonizers of the Franciscan Order to California to build missions on large tracts of land, convert Native Americans to Catholicism, and teach the indigenous people agriculture. Mexican artisans were brought to the missions in the 1790s to facilitate the aims of the missions. Regardless, the missions were not self-sufficient, and by the 1830s the system collapsed and the Franciscans left California (J. E. Bennett 1897a: 9–24; 1897b: 150–161; Estrada et al. 1981: 103–131; Vallejo 1890).

Between 7,500 and 13,000 Mexicans lived in California in 1848, and some were power elites, but within fifty years they were a powerless minority. After the Texas Revolt, large numbers of whites started flooding into California. This migration accelerated during the gold rush. Thousands of Chinese and some Chileans also joined the influx of new settlers. Whites took control of the goldfields and declared that all nonwhites were foreigners who could not own land or become citizens. Taxes were imposed on foreign miners, and even though they were citizens Latino miners were taxed. Taxes were also levied against the vast landholdings of Latinos and they were forced to show titles to prove their land claims. Prior to this, Latinos were taxed on the basis of the amount they produced, not on the acreage of the land. Litigation costs were high and lawyers usually charged a contingency fee of one quarter of the land in question. By the time the lawsuits were settled, most Latinos were left landless.

More land was lost when white squatters organized associations that succeeded in keeping land taken from Latinos illegally (Estrada et al. 1981: 103–131; Jibou 1988a: 23–25).

ASIANS: RESTRICTING OWNERSHIP,
USE, AND OCCUPANCY OF LAND

Cities began experimenting with zoning as a mechanism for constraining the land uses of racial and ethnic minorities in the 1880s. The Chinese were the target of early discriminatory land-use ordinances. They were also the target of the earliest racially restrictive zoning ordinances. In the late nineteenth century, California cities such as San Francisco and Modesto began to ban the construction of laundries in "Caucasian" neighborhoods or the operation of laundries in wooden buildings. In San Francisco, 310 of the 320 laundries were constructed of wood; 240 of the laundries were owned by Chinese. More than 150 of the Chinese-owned laundry owners were prosecuted under the ordinance, while non-Chinese owners were spared prosecution. Though the statute appeared to be race-neutral on the surface, the enforcement of it had a discriminatory effect on the Chinese (Weinberg 1999; *Yick Wo v. Hopkins* 1886).

Further restrictions were afoot. In 1890, Chinese residents of San Francisco were arrested for violating Order No. 2190, the so-called Bingham Ordinance, which specified where the city's more than twenty thousand Chinese residents could reside and conduct business. The ordinance, which went into effect on February 17 of that year, stated, "It is hereby declared to be unlawful for any Chinese to locate, reside, or carry on a business within the limits of the city and county of San Francisco, except in that district of said city and county hereinafter prescribed for their location." The ordinance also stipulated the length of time (sixty days) that Chinese residents had to comply with the new ordinance. Any Chinese who did not comply was found guilty of a misdemeanor and jailed for up to six months (*Federal Reporter* 1890; In re Lee Sing 1890).

The ordinance passed even though the 1868 Burlingame Treaty between the United States and China stipulates that "Chinese subjects, visiting or residing in the United States, shall enjoy the same privileges, immunities and exemptions in respect to travel or residence, as there may be enjoyed by the citizens or subjects of the most favored nation" (Burlingame Treaty 1868). In deciding the Lee Sing case, circuit court judge J. Sawyer argued that "the gross inequality of the operation of this ordinance upon Chinese, as compared with others, in violation of the constitutional, treaty, and statutory provisions cited, are so manifest upon its face, that I am unable to comprehend how this discrimination . . . can fail to be apparent to the mind of every intelligent person" (*Federal Reporter* 1890; In *re Lee Sing* 1890).

The earliest racially restrictive covenants (limitations in the deed of a property specifying what an owner can or cannot do with it) were also directed against Chinese residents living in California. As with racially restrictive zoning, the conflicts that arose from the use of racially restrictive covenants were often decided in the courts. One early case, *Gandolfo v. Hartman*, was decided in 1892. It involved the violation of a covenant that was signed in 1886 regarding a lot on East Main Street in San Buena Ventura, California. The covenant specified that the parties and their heirs and assigns could not rent any buildings or grounds "to a Chinaman or Chinamen" without the parties' consent to the agreement. The defendant in this case, Hartman, purchased the property from one of the original signers of the covenant and then leased the property to two Chinese men, Fong Yet and Sam Choy. A lawsuit was brought against Hartman for violating the terms of the covenant. Judge Ross decided that the covenant violated the Fourteenth Amendment as well as the 1880 treaty with China that offered Chinese residents in America the protections afforded those from a "most favored nation" (*Gandolfo v. Hartman* 1892; Groves 1950–51; Ming 1949). Later courts ignored this ruling.

Punjabi immigrants were also targeted by racially restrictive covenants in the early part of the twentieth century. An influx of Punjabi farmers into California's Imperial Valley resulted in the passage of an ordinance barring the sale of land to "Hindoos." The Punjabi farmers—who were mostly male—circumvented the restrictions by marrying Mexican women living in the area, as these women were not prohibited by law from taking possession of land. More than five hundred such marriages are recorded (Leonard 1994; Majumdar 2006–7).

Private racially restrictive covenants were also widely used in Seattle. Many still appear in the deeds to homes. The first of these covenants was penned in 1924 by the Goodwin Company; it covered three tracts of land in the Victory Heights neighborhood in North Seattle (Silva 2009). From the 1920s through the 1940s neighborhoods in North Seattle, West Seattle, South Seattle, and the suburbs across Lake Washington had deed restrictions on the homes that barred Ethiopians, Africans, and other blacks; Mongolians, Chinese, Japanese, Malays, and other Asians; and Jews from acquiring or residing in homes in these areas. The restrictive covenants also targeted Native Americans, Pacific Islanders, and those of Mexican ancestry. In addition to the Goodwin Company, neighborhoods covered by racially restrictive covenants were developed by the

South Seattle Land Company, Seattle Trust Company, Puget Mill Company, Crawford & Canover Real Estate Partnership, and the Boeing Aircraft Company (Chin 1992; Majumdar 2006–7; Pettus 1948; Silva 2009).

Colonialism

Colonialism is an important force that influences the relationship between settlers, indigenous, and other marginalized peoples. Robert Blauner (1969) defines colonialism as the process by which one country controls the political activities and economic resources of another less developed and less powerful country. He writes that the colonization complex has four main components: (1) forced entry of one country into the territory of another country, (2) alteration and destruction of the indigenous cultures and patterns of social organization of the invaded country, (3) domination of indigenous peoples by members of the invading country, and (4) development of elaborate justifications for the invasion and subsequent behavior of the invaders. Veracini (2010, 2011) argues that this form of exogenous domination is characterized by two elements—displacement of people and unequal relations between the colonizer and those predating them. The unequal relations arise because the colonizers are able to dominate the occupied territories.

European settlement of America occurred through colonial expansion. For example, even before Winthrop migrated to the United States, he envisioned economic and political ascendancy and articulated a logic for taking Indian lands and transferring them to European colonizers (Winthrop [1629] 1846: 272–276). Other settlers plotted their strategies and achieved these goals through warfare, genocide, and other forms of conquest (Fenelon and Trafzer 2014).

INTERNAL COLONIALISM

The term *internal colonialism* is used to describe the conditions and experiences of people of color in the United States. The term is also used to refer to territorial relations within a political entity. Scholars argue that the same dynamics that operate in the external colonial context operate with internal colonialism. In addition to overseas colonial expansion, countries seek to bring their hinterlands or peripheral regions under the control of the central government. Such moves toward internal colonization result in tensions or conflict between the country's core or center and its periphery. The core develops exploitive relations with the periphery, using the hinterland's natural resources and cheap labor to enhance or sustain the development or expansion of the core. If the periphery has indigenous or culturally distinct peoples, the core often discriminates against them. The core monopolizes trade and commerce, thus forcing the peripheral region to develop as a complementary economy of the core. The economy of the internal colony typically relies on one or a few exports. The movement of laborers in the periphery is determined by forces outside of the region. Economic dependence of the internal colony is reinforced by legal, political, and military measures. The periphery is often characterized by lower levels of service and lower standards of living than the core (Blauner 1969, 1972, 1982; Hechter 1994; Horvath 1972; Taylor 2014).

The frame of internal colonialism is also applicable to Native American reservations because these entities arose out of military conquest and subsequent military domination. The reservations are entities that are geographically defined, and their location was chosen by the federal government. Indigenous populations were placed in these designated territories. The reservation system was one of the tools of military conquest that settlers used to get the upper hand over native tribes. The designation of fixed territories for indigenous peoples by invading groups is a common feature of the colonial model. There is a long history of military operations occurring adjacent to reservations. In fact, the U.S. War Department was created in 1789, in part to handle Indian affairs. Even after the Bureau of Indian Affairs (BIA) was created in 1824, Indian matters remained under the aegis of the War Department. The BIA was transferred to the newly created Department of the Interior in 1849 (Bureau of Indian Affairs 2012).

SOVEREIGNTY

The question of sovereignty is also tied to colonial relations. Native American tribes are sovereign nations: they are autonomous and have a legal right to govern and to determine how their lands are used. However, the notion of sovereignty is nebulous when it comes to the appropriation of Indian land for conversion to parks and forests, the extraction of valuable resources, and operation of hazardous facilities. As later discussions show, tribal wishes are usually ignored when decisions are made about designating federal and state parks, forests, wildlife refuges, and so on. While sovereignty allows the tribes greater decision-making power, it also leaves room for manipulation by government appointees and corporate interests.

SETTLER COLONIALISM

Some scholars distinguish between colonialism as described above and settler colonialism. In the American context colonialism was characterized by warfare, appropriation of territory, slavery, the removal and relocation of subjugated peoples, the reservation system, coercive assimilation, and the denial of education. Scholars argue that settler colonialism differs from this form of colonialism in that settler colonialism persists long after obvious forms of colonialism and their structures are dismantled (Veracini 2010, 2011; P. Wolfe 1999). For instance, slavery has been abolished in America for more than a century, yet elements of the logic on which it was built (the belief that whites were superior to blacks, for example, and the fact that whites receive privileges based on race) still persist in society today. Similarly, Native Americans are no longer forced to live on reservations, but the reservation system and all the inequities that go with it are still intact.

Scholars contend that inherent in American settler colonialism is the desire to replicate Anglo-American societies in the wilderness, conquer and corral indigenous peoples, stimulate swift economic growth through mineral extraction and processing, and create political apparatuses based on racial exclusion (Ngai 2015: 1085). The study of such settler colonialism investigates the entrenched and impervious structures and systems that perpetuate inequities arising from the colonizer-colonized relationship. It also examines how rhetoric is used to erase and diffuse claims of inequities between settlers and subjugated peoples. For example, the use of concepts and terminology such as *frontier* and *pioneer* not only erases the presence of indigenous peoples but also establishes the settler as the "first" people to see, do, or experience whatever is being described on "empty" land. It grants settlers ownership and control of land and other resources and gives primacy to their claims. The settler discourse also transforms places like Indian reservations from sites of forced relocations to sovereign homelands. This complicates the claims of the colonized and gives the colonizer opportunities to suggest that equity has been achieved and past harms redressed (Fenelon and Trafzer 2014; L. Russell 2001; Veracini 2010, 2011, 2013; P. Wolfe 1999). Hence, Veracini (2011) argues that while colonialism has an end point, settler colonialism is characterized by its permanence.

Nativism

The rise of nativism, a belief system that influences race and ethnic relations, in the nineteenth century coincided with and influenced the emergence of pro-environmental thought and actions. The term *nativism* refers to organized efforts by some members of a society to improve their quality of life or hold on to remnants of the past by attempting to exclude or eliminate particular groups of people or ideas, beliefs, customs, and objects from a society. It also describes attempts by elites to limit immigration to select racial groups, as nativists revile racial mixing. Nativist movements flourished in the United States during the nineteenth and twentieth centuries, particularly during economic depressions. Nativism was strongly associated with promoting Anglo-Saxon heritage and securing greater privileges for whites. Nativism can arise from economic, cultural, or status conflicts sparked by increased immigration or the competition for jobs, commercial opportunities, housing, outdoor space, and so on. It can also be triggered by one social group's discomfort with the lifestyles of others. In addition, nativism can arise if one group perceives that it has lost status or power vis-à-vis another group. For instance, nativism was rampant in cities like New York in the 1840s. Consequently, as the competition for customers intensified during the 1842 depression, native-born merchants were angered by immigrant peddlers selling wares on the sidewalks of Lower Manhattan and in the streets in front of their stores. Immigrants were seen as invading what was once the exclusive space of the native-born merchants. Those merchants expressed their frustrations by stereotyping the Irish, organizing efforts to exclude immigrant peddlers from upscale commercial districts, and working to restrict immigration (Bradley 2005: 388–389; Spann 1981: 40–41). Likewise, the declaration that Mexicans and other nonwhites were foreigners subject to taxation and devoid of any rights to own land was part of the nativist ideology that grew commonplace in the United States.

Gender Relations

During the time when attitudes were shifting and environmental consciousness was inchoate, social norms prescribed different and rigid roles to men and women. These gender roles influenced the way each interacted with the environment. Many of these influences are explored in the book through the lens of true manhood and true womanhood. These concepts are defined in this chapter and elucidated further below, particularly in chapters 4 and 7.

THE CULT OF TRUE MANHOOD

Gender roles were very structured in nineteenth-century America. Scholars who study the cult of true manhood identify several characteristics of that cult that is evident among the activists discussed in this book. According to this thesis, male honor is rooted in the performance of dangerous tasks, risk taking, daring, and the harsh socialization of men. Men also tended to pursue their own self-interest. While the cult of true womanhood or the cult of domestic-ity associated middle- and upper-class women with the home and domestic sphere, the cult of manhood associated men of similar social classes with the public sphere of economic competition, military conquest, and politics (Gilmore 1991; Merchant 2010: 4; Mosher 1994: 601–605; Winter 2003: 120–122). This is manifested in the stories (recounted below) of male outdoor enthusiasts who routinely left their fiancés, pregnant wives (at a time when there was a high risk of women dying during childbirth), young children, and ailing parents for lengthy periods of time while they went on expeditions. Manhood was also rooted in land ownership. This had gender and racial implications: white males controlled land. They dispossessed indigenous peoples of land and developed policies that made it illegal for slaves and ethnic minority immigrants to own land. In some cases males made major financial decisions—such as purchasing property—without consulting their wives. Men also felt they had to be physi-cally fit; prove their toughness, courage, virility, and dominance over women; and attempt to recover their primitive masculinity.

THE CULT OF TRUE WOMANHOOD

During the first half of the nineteenth century, the epitome of the American woman was defined through the social construct of "true woman." The defini-tion of "true womanhood" arose from the interrelationship between religiosity and civic responsibilities, which had four main tenets: piety, purity, submis-siveness, and domesticity. Because women were thought to be endowed with the virtues of piety and purity, they were perceived as the guardians of moral-ity. In addition, true women were expected to be versed in domestic affairs, as they were charged with caring for and creating a warm and nurturing environ-ment for the family. The true woman was also expected to submit to the will of her husband, family, and the demands of society (Crouse 2005: 259–279; Merchant 1984: 57–85, 2010: 5–6; Rabinovitch 2001: 354–355; Welter 1966: 151). However, true women managed their households rather than doing the actual tasks that made it function. They did not work outside the home, and inside they had slaves or servants to do the housework for them. They were also heavily involved in charitable work.

This definition of womanhood arose at a time of increasing social in-equality, breakdown of social order, and fragmentation of the family. In their attempts to restore social order, elites created rules and norms that set upper- and middle-class men and women apart from the masses. True womanhood was one such idea. Barbara Welter believes true womanhood was such a potent construct that "anyone, male or female [who] dared to tamper with the complex virtue which made up true womanhood was damned immediately as an enemy of God, of civilization, and of the Republic" (Welter 1966: 152).

The Evolution of Environmental Ideology

Environmental consciousness arose during the time of slavery, Native American wars, and the conquest of Mexico. The ideas and actions of early environmental activists were shaped by these events and other social conditions. Later discussions in the book will illustrate their relation to environmental thought and advocacy, which had six influential tenets: Transcendentalism, romanticism, frontierism, conservation, preservation, and business environmentalism.

TRANSCENDENTALISM

One of the earliest manifestations of collective environmental consciousness is found in the rise of Transcendental thought in New England in the 1830s. Transcendentalists believed there was a spiritual relationship between humans, nature, and God. The earliest American Transcendentalists were generally the children of Puritans and liberal Unitarian ministers. Transcendentalists believed in the existence of a reality or truths beyond the physical. In other words, they believed there was a body of knowledge innate within humans that transcended what the senses could convey. They believed that divinity was inherent in the human soul, that a person's perceptions and intuition provided knowledge of the Divine, and that this knowledge was the basis of truth and moral judgment. Transcendentalists argued that there is a parallel between the higher realm of spiritual truths and the lower one of material objects; for them, natural objects are important because they reflect universal spiritual truths. People's place in the universe was divided between object and essence. Their physical existence rooted them in the material portion of their being, while their soul gave them the ability to transcend their physical conditions. Hence they were aware of a God that was both immanent and transcendent. For Transcendentalists, the wilderness was the place where spiritual truths were most pronounced (Bode [1947] 1982: 16–18; Walter Harding 1992: 62–63; Le Beau 2005: 806–808; Nash 1982: 84–86). Transcendentalists placed a premium on individual autonomy and freedom. They also believed the best route to social reform was through individual or personal reform (Richardson [1986] 1996: 74–75, 100–101).

The idea of transcendence comes from the work of the German philosopher Immanuel Kant. While John Locke believed that all knowledge and understanding is gained through sensory experiences, Kant argued that certain concepts, such as time and space, are "transcendental"—that is, they are innate categories of the mind and are known intuitively. Transcendentalists were also influenced by the writings of English thinkers Samuel Taylor Coleridge and Thomas Carlyle, Swedish mystic Emanuel Swedenborg, and French philosopher Victor Cousin. Transcendentalists were influenced by Hindu writing too. Some of the most prominent members of the movement were Ralph Waldo Emerson, Frederic Henry Hedge, Bronson Alcott, George Ripley, Henry David Thoreau, and Margaret Fuller. This group formed the Transcendental Club in 1836; most of its members lived in and around Boston. They met periodically at Emerson's house during the 1840s. Other important Transcendentalists include the three Peabody sisters—Elizabeth, Sophia (who married Nathaniel Hawthorne,) and Mary (who married Horace Mann). The Transcendentalists published *The Dial* from 1840 to 1844. Margaret Fuller, a women's rights advocate, was *The Dial*'s editor, Elizabeth Peabody its publisher (Emerson 1883: 161–188; Walter Harding 1992: 62–63; Le Beau 2005: 806–808; M. Marshall 2005; Nash 1982: 84–86; Paul 1952; Thoreau 1893).

ROMANTICISM

Romanticism connotes an enthusiasm for the strange, remote, solitary, and mysterious. Romantics, particularly those in the second half of the nineteenth century, showed a preference for wild, untamed places like the American wilderness, where they could express their freedom. They disdained tamed and manicured landscapes and wrote about the wildlands in positive terms. This made many want to see these landscapes and protect them. It should be noted that to the earliest generation of American romantics, such as Ralph Waldo Emerson, who wrote about this in the 1830s, "wild" meant the pastoral and picturesque settings of large urban parks or rural towns. Early American romantics were influenced by Jean-Jacques Rousseau, who believed that the lives of the urban poor would be improved if they could experience pastoral beauty and rural charms. They were also influenced by William Wordsworth. However, by the 1860s romanticism was associated with wilder, more remote areas (Lovejoy 1955; Nash 1982: 47).

The Sublime. Romantic landscapes were also considered sublime. The sublime, a ubiquitous cultural construct, is one of the most significant expressions of romanticism. The sublime refers to the belief that in wild places the supernatural was near at hand. One was most likely to realize one's spirituality and commune with the Divine in the wilds, especially in those vast, powerful landscapes that evoke a person's insignificance and mortality. Sublime landscapes triggered strong emotions—fear, excitement, awe, and a sense of wonder. Sublime landscapes were described as sacred; one worshipped them but did not linger in their presence. In the works of the romantics wild places were transformed from satanic abodes to sacred temples (Cronon 1995: 72–75; Lovejoy 1955; Muir [1911a] 1972; Nash 1982: 45–51; Thoreau 1982; Wordsworth 1936: 536).

Primitivism. Primitivism, related to both romanticism and frontierism, advocated that the best cure for the ills of the modern, industrial world was a return to simple, basic living. In nineteenth-century America, Thoreau and Muir were ardent proponents of this view (Rousseau [1761] 1880, [1762] 1974; Thoreau 1893).

FRONTIERISM

Frontierism is both rooted in American thought and influenced by European thinking. Instead of endowing the frontier with sacred qualities, Turner maintained that European immigrants, in moving to the wilds, shed the trappings of civilization; rediscovered their independence, vigor, and primitive drives; reinvented democratic institutions; and displayed a creativity that was the source of democracy and national character. Roosevelt argued, in a similar vein, that the immigrants endowed the frontier with liberating and invigorating qualities. He claimed that if he hadn't been a frontier rancher in the West, he wouldn't have ascended to the presidency (Ambrose 1996: xxvii; Roosevelt [1885] 1996, [1888] 2000, [1893] 1996; Turner [1893] 1953: 22–27).

The 1890 U.S. census signaled the end of the frontier era. The census showed a population distribution that spread from coast to coast. It enumerated 325,464 Native Americans, 7,470,040 blacks, 107,475 people of Chinese descent, 2,039 Japanese, and 54,983,890 whites (Department of the Interior 1895: 396–400; Gibson and Lennon 1999: 4). The census, framed in the discourses of settler colonialism, Manifest Destiny, and westward expansion, triumphantly declared that the United States had witnessed a "century of progress and achievement unequalled in the world's history." Where there was only a group of "feeble settlements" in 1790, a "great and powerful nation" stood a century later. Here Native American communities are seen as fleeting and vanishing, while strength and permanence is bestowed on Euro-American settlements. According to the census, as settlements spread across the continent and the population increased, land was "redeemed from the wilderness and brought into the service of man" (Department of the Interior 1895: xxvii).

It should be noted that though the terms *conservation* and *preservation* are used interchangeably today, at the beginning of the twentieth century the words had different meanings. Conservation implied a utilitarian view of natural resources: that is, they should be developed and used for the current generation. Preservation implied saving resources for their own sake or their intrinsic value. The needs of future generations played a major role in the decision to preserve resources (Nash 1982: 129–139, 222–224).

The term *conservation* was first used to describe reservoirs built to retain floodwaters that were used in dry seasons. In this context, conservation implied planning and efficiency. The term was later expanded to mean the planning and management of rangeland and water supplies in forested areas. In 1907, Gifford Pinchot and Overton Price popularized the term, which they used to mean the wise use of resources. Pinchot thought *protection* and *preservation*, by contrast, meant that resources would be withdrawn from use in perpetuity (Fox 1981: 128–130; Hays [1959] 1999: 5–6, 135; Trefethen 1975: 126–127). According to Pinchot, "the first principle of conservation is development . . . the use of natural resources now existing on this continent for the benefit of the people who live here now" (cf. Turner 1985: 303).

BUSINESS ENVIRONMENTALISM

This book describes a form of environmentalism that I label *business environmentalism*. I argue that business environmentalism is an amalgam of utilitarianism, preservationism, conservationism, and capitalist interests. This form of environmental activism arose during the late nineteenth and early twentieth centuries. It manifested itself through the tight coupling of business and environmental interests: that is, business executives and corporations played significant roles in environmental affairs.[7] Business environmentalism was seen as a win-win situation for conservationists, preservationists, and corporations. Environmentalists were able to protect the environment, while corporations could generate profits from pro-environmental activities. Astute corporate executives realized that the sale of arms, ammunition, gear, and other equipment to the burgeoning ranks of outdoor recreationers was profitable. They also recognized that environmental protections were necessary to ensure that the public continued to participate in outdoor activities. Outdoor recreationers were also in need of transportation to their destinations, and railroad magnates were only too happy to support efforts to preserve scenic wonders so that they could build the rail lines to facilitate access to the wonderlands, along with lodging and food services. Likewise, hoteliers and restauranteurs had a stake in environmental affairs, as they, too, competed to house and feed travelers.

Power Elites

Understanding, using, and protecting the environment was envisioned as a delicate balancing act that was vital to nation-building efforts and long-term sustainability. Power and privilege are critical elements of such efforts. Hence, power brokers orchestrated the emergence of the conservation movement and guided it to prominence. These advocates are referred to as the *power elite*. I explore this concept throughout the book as I examine the significant roles that wealth, power, and privilege played in the early conservation movement.

This discussion is also informed by power-elite theory. It contends that environmental discourses and policies were conceptualized and orchestrated by elites in accordance to upper- and middle-class values and interests. In the context of this discussion, elites can be viewed as the people who run things—that is, the key actors or inner circle of participants who play structured, functionally understandable roles in the formation and execution of environmental policies. Elites are those who obtain most of what there is to get in the institutionalized sector of the society; by exercising institutional power, they enhance and consolidate their own power. Hence, at every stage of any decision-making process, elites will inevitably accumulate disproportionate amounts of valued attributes such as money, esteem, power, or resources that people desire and try to attain. Power-elite theory helps us to identify six types of power elites who helped to shape the events discussed in this book: ideological, innovative, planning, implementing, economic, and political. The theory also helps us to understand the role environmental advocates assume as guardians of the nation's natural resources (Czudnowski 1983; Giddens 1994: 170–174; Mills 1994: 161–169; Prewitt and Stone 1973: 84–85; Schneider-Hector 2014: 645; Taylor 2009: 581).

Environmental Governance

Environmental activists and their supporters were frequently faced with the challenge of responding to political leaders and governance structures that lacked efficacy and legitimacy (Habermas 1975; Ingram 1987: 155–160; Pusey

1993: 92–110). Hence, activists and government entities developed policies and laws to govern resources as environmental awareness spread. These policies generated questions about environmental governance that had significant implications for the integrity of the nation-state. Consequently, environmental conflicts erupted over the question of public versus private ownership of resources such as land, water, wildlife, fisheries, timber, and minerals. There were questions about what constituted a violation of policies, what the appropriate punishment would be, and who had the right to enforce the policies and administer the punishments. Questions also arose about the government's role in the ownership and administration of said resources. Some asked whether the government had a responsibility to provide public goods and services (such as parks, clean water, etc.) for its citizens. The issues of privatization and the protection of national treasures also generated debates: If resources are publicly owned, can and should they be privatized, by whom, and under what conditions? How should these resources be treated, and what exactly did protection mean?

The activities described in this book were as much about winning environmental campaigns as they were about establishing fundamental principles of governance. They were about establishing principles regarding the way people understood and related to the environment. They were also aimed at instilling the idea that the populace had a civic and moral duty to protect the environment. The environmental campaigns also established the concepts of stewardship and sustainability and the notion that future generations ought to be considered in environmental decision making. Probably the most important result was that this activism demonstrated that individual actions were tied to larger environmental actions and outcomes that people should be conscious of.

Though some of these issues still arise in contemporary environmental conflicts, the nature and the implications of the questions are different, because until the early twentieth century there was little or no precedent to draw on when the questions arose. Thus the decisions reached at that point laid the groundwork for what followed. So in the nineteenth century, activists drafted bills and lobbied government bodies to pass legislation to establish hunting seasons, protect migratory species, and conserve forests. However, as soon as laws were put in place, opponents challenged them in court by questioning whether the government owned the resources in the first place or had the right to regulate them. Today citizens generally accept the notion that government entities have the authority to set and regulate hunting and fishing seasons. So though there might be challenges to specific aspects of natural resource policies and regulations, the fundamental questions of whether governments have any right to administer and regulate such resources are not being challenged. In fact, we now see government entities being sued for failing to protect the environment.

Likewise with questions regarding setting aside national forests, parks, and monuments, and so on: while there might still be conflicts over the size and the nature of what's being set aside, the national parks and forests are generally accepted as legitimate. Questions of whether such entities should exist are not being debated or challenged extensively. It is also generally accepted that these entities will be public.

Creating an Environmental Identity

This chapter concludes with a brief discussion of identity formation in the context of pro-environmental advocacy. Activists such as those in the conservation movement articulate their grievances and create identities that attract supporters and facilitate movement building. People are more likely to become active in issues they identify with and are passionate about. Such individuals are likely to join with others of like mind in collective endeavors (Stryker 1968: 558–564, 1981: 23–24). The upper- and middle-class mobilization around the environment occurred because people who spent time in the outdoors found such issues salient. Activists did not expend energy on mass appeals; instead they focused on recruiting individuals who had an attitudinal affinity for the issues addressed by the organizations and campaigns and who were motivated to act on their concerns (Brubaker 2009; Klandermans and Oegema 1987: 519–531; Yamamoto 2015). To sway potential converts, activists employed rhetorical idioms of loss of nature and calamity, and their rhetorical motifs conjured up images of mass slaughters of animals, the frivolous use of dead birds, or the logging of giant ancient trees (Best 1987: 101–121). These claims were effective in appealing to naturalists, wildlife advocates, outdoor recreationers, and country-life enthusiasts. Appeals for support and movement participation were also framed in terms of rectitude. That is, not only were salient identities engaged, but potential supporters were also told that they had a moral obligation to help and that it was their civic duty to do something about the perceived social problems. In addition, they were told how to fix the problem. For instance, in creating the identity of true sportsmen, activists evoked salient and prized roles—that of the naturalist and steward of the earth—and made them essential dimensions of being a sportsman. Sportsmen not willing to embrace these new identities had no credibility with their peers and were ostracized as game hogs, dandies, and depredators.

Thus collective identities are not fashioned from scratch. They are formed by appropriating and co-opting existing roles and expanding and crafting them to suit the needs of the new collective identity (Eder 2009; Friedman and Mc-Adam 1992: 156–173; Thomas, McGarty, and Mavor 2009). As conservationism and preservationism spread, it became evident that it was no longer all right to wear hats festooned with birds or go hunting, birding, mountaineering, fishing, trapshooting, and so on without having a concomitant concern about the indiscriminate slaughter of wildlife, diminishing wildlife stocks, environmental degradation, and deforestation. Both the cultural nationalist and frontierist identities were also incorporated. Cultural nationalists and frontierists were expected to act to either create landscapes or protect existing ones to be cherished. In any case, concern was most appropriately expressed through participation in environmental activities. In essence, the identities associated with the aforementioned recreational pursuits, lifestyles, and sentiments were appropriated and expanded both to recruit a pool of people who were very interested in the issues and to motivate them to act on their interests. Moreover, a collective identity is a public declaration of status. Individuals adopting a collective identity value that identity. By embracing it, adherents are also committing themselves to the principles, values, behaviors, and attitudes the group promotes. Consequently, the individual identities of nature lovers, outdoor recreationists, cultural nationalists, and country-life enthusiasts were redefined to include an activist agenda built around a variety of environmental issues.

WEALTHY PEOPLE AND THE CITY

An Ambivalent Relationship

Urban Environmental Reforms: The Stimuli

POPULATION GROWTH AND RISING INCOME INEQUALITY

Population growth and rising social inequality were two factors that influenced how elites felt about the city. The changing dynamics and increasing complexity of American cities made elites more conscious of where and how they lived. Until the eighteenth century American cities were compact. For instance, most of New York City was confined to the area below City Hall on the island of Manhattan (Burrows and Wallace 1999; Jackson and Dunbar 2002). Boston was so small that the Common was once on the fringes of the city (Karr 2005a: 212–213; Krieger 2001: 156). New Haven, Connecticut, was built around a green and a tight collection of nine squares (T. J. Farnham 1981: 12–14; Sletcher 2004: 65).

In terms of population, too, cities were still relatively small until the nineteenth century—in fact, only twenty-four municipalities had a population exceeding 2,500 in 1790 (U.S. Census Bureau 1998). For example, in 1694 New York City—then the country's second largest municipality, behind Boston—had a population of roughly 5,000 people; that population reached about

25,000 in 1776 (Janvier [1894] 2000: xvi, 25, 31). At the time of the Revolution, Baltimore had 6,000 residents (Olson 1997), while Philadelphia's population reached 51,000 in 1793 (Nord 1997: 21). By 1830, New York had a population of 202,589, Baltimore's had reached 80,620, and Philadelphia's 80,460. Rounding out the top five cities in terms of population, Boston had 61,392 residents, and 46,082 people dwelled in New Orleans. St. Louis had fewer than 80,000 residents as late as 1850, and San Francisco had about 150,000 residents in 1870 (see table 2.1) (U.S. Census Bureau 1998).

The largest cities were east of the Mississippi River, and the country's wealthiest people had residences in them. In such cities, the rich and poor, free and enslaved, lived relatively close together. Because merchants lived above or beside their businesses, while the poor and recent immigrants who worked in such businesses inhabited shabby dwellings within walking distance, the cities' wealthiest residents found themselves living in close proximity to the destitute. However, in early American cities, the wealthiest person wasn't that much richer than the poorest one.

Social inequality was relatively low until the end of the eighteenth century, when the wealth of many cities began to be concentrated in the hands of a few. But in places like New York City, the concentration of wealth could be observed much earlier. In 1664, 10 percent of the city's merchants controlled 26 percent of the wealth. By 1676, the richest 10 percent of the taxpayers owned 51 percent of the wealth. The five richest residents of the city owned 40 percent of the wealth, and the richest man alone owned 14 percent of the wealth. Despite the growing size of the tax rolls, in 1730, the richest 10 percent of New York's population held almost half of the taxable wealth (Burrows and Wallace 1999: 88, 144; Jackson and Dunbar 2002: 18).

The concentration of wealth was evident elsewhere too. In Boston, for instance, in 1771, 15 percent of the property owners owned 66 percent of the taxable wealth, and the top 5 percent controlled more than 44 percent of the taxable wealth. At the same time, 29 percent of the population did not own any property. Conditions were similar in other parts of New England. In Portsmouth, New Hampshire, 10 percent of the residents owned half of the taxable wealth, while 10 percent of the population of Newburyport (Massachusetts) owned 57 percent of the taxable wealth in 1770 (Macieski 2005: 191).

The disparities between the rich and poor increased even more rapidly after 1790: the nineteenth century ushered in a wave of financiers, merchants, industrialists, bankers, and other tycoons who became millionaires. At the same time multitudes of people slid deep into poverty. The nineteenth century was also a time of greater heterogeneity in American cities, as people from a wide variety of

TABLE 2.1 Populations of the Ten Largest Urban Areas, 1790–1900

City and state	1790	1800	YEAR 1810	1820	1830
New York (NY)	33,131	60,515	96,373	123,706	202,589
Philadelphia (PA)	28,522	41,220	53,722	63,802	80,462
Boston (MA)	18320	24,937	33,787	43,298	61,392
Charlestown (SC)	16,359	18,824	24,711	24,780	30,289
Baltimore (MD)	13,503	26,514	46,555	62,738	80,620
Northern Liberties Township (PA)	9,913	10,718	19,874	19,678	28,872
Salem (MA)	7,921	9,457	12,613	12,731	
Newport (RI)	6,716				
Providence (RI)	6,380	7,614			
Marblehead (MA)	5,661				
Southwark District (PA)	5,661	9,621	13,707	14,713	20,581
Norfolk (VA)		6,926			
New Orleans (LA)			17,242	27,176	46,082
Albany (NY)			10,762		24,209
Washington, D.C.				13,247	
Cincinnati (OH)					24,831
Brooklyn (NY)					
St. Louis (MO)					
Spring Garden (PA)					
Chicago (IL)					
Buffalo (NY)					
San Francisco (CA)					
Cleveland (OH)					

Source: Compiled from U.S. Bureau of the Census. 1998. "Population of the Largest 100 Cities and Other Urban Places in the United States: 1790–1990." Prepared by Campbell Gibson, et al. Population Division Working Paper # 27. Released June 15. Retrieved on November 23, 2008 from http://www.census.gov/population/www/documentation/twps0027/twps0027.html.

1840	1850	1860	1870	1880	1890	1900
312,710	515,547	813,669	942,292	1,206,299	1,515,301	3,437,302
93,665	121,376	565,529	674,022	847,170	1,046,964	1,293,697
93,383	136,881	177,840	250,526	362,839	448,477	560,892
29,261						
102,313	169,054	212,418	267,354	332,313	434,439	508,957
34,474						
102,193	116,375	168,875	191,418	216,090		
33,721	50,763					
46,338	115,435	161,044	216,239	255,139	296,908	325,902
36,233	96,838	266,661	396,099	566,663	806,343	
	77,860	160,773	310,864	350,518	451,770	575,238
	58,894					
		112,172	298,977	503,185	1,099,850	1,698,575
		89,129				352,387
			149,473	233,959	298,997	342,782
					261,353	381,768

racial and ethnic backgrounds lived near and mingled with each other. There was really no precedent for this in the world. Tensions rose in the cities as the different racial and ethnic groups who either had limited knowledge of each other or brought long-standing stereotypes, grievances, and competitive histories with them from Europe found themselves packed cheek-to-jowl in decrepit neighborhoods and struggling with each other for scarce resources. As immigrants flocked to the cities, the elites seeking to separate themselves from the congestion and poverty began segregating themselves in upscale downtown neighborhoods or on the periphery of urban centers. As a result, the poor became concentrated in neighborhoods that gradually became deplorable slums. The depression caused by the Panic of 1819 accelerated this process. By the mid-nineteenth century, the cities were characterized by severe overcrowding; substandard housing; homelessness; noise; pollution; disease, epidemics, illness, and premature death; filth and poor sanitation; crime; vagrancy; corruption; and rioting (Bauman 2000: 5; Blackmar 1989: 14–43; Boyer 1978: 4–11; Bridges 1984; Spann 1981).

DISORDER AND LACK OF CONTROL

Urban elites grew concerned about cities as urban areas became increasingly violent and disorderly. In addition to epidemics that frequently disrupted life and made it difficult for municipalities to function, crime, vice, vagrancy, and rioting steadily increased. As rioting grew more frequent, the tenor and targets changed: by the nineteenth century, the wealthy found themselves the targets of attack during riots. Civic leaders struggled to maintain control as the violence escalated and cities became more disorderly (Boyer 1978: 4–11; Spann 1981; Taylor 2009).

Over time the nature and causes of rioting changed. During the eighteenth century, urban riots arose from dissatisfaction with taxes, treaties, or other government policies; revolts against the British; and town-and-gown tensions. For instance, in 1709 food prices skyrocketed in Boston as the city experienced a serious food shortage. Poor residents who did not own land were devastated by the crisis. As this was happening, wealthy merchants like Andrew Belcher were shipping grain out of the port to be sold overseas. Hence, in 1710, a group of about fifty men attacked one of Belcher's cargo ships that was loaded with wheat. The men were arrested but were released without being charged because of the widespread support they received from locals. The next year, in October 1711, there was a riot in the city after a fire left more than one hundred families homeless. A third uprising occurred in May 1713, when more than two hundred people assembled on the Boston Common to protest high bread prices. Once again, Andrew Belcher's ships came under attack. In addition, rioters broke into Belcher's warehouses in search of corn. The bread riot resulted in the passage of laws prohibiting the export of grain during food shortages, the control of grain and bread prices, and the establishment of a public granary (Zinn 1995: 51–52).

The 1765 Stamp Act also triggered riots in Boston, Newport (Rhode Island), and New Haven (Gilje 1995; Sletcher 2004: 30–31). However, during the nineteenth century, as rapidly growing cities became more economically, racially, and ethnically diverse, tensions increased. Consequently, a number of social, political, economic, and religious factors triggered riots. In 1834 Boston was the site of an interethnic and religious conflict that resulted in the burning of the Ursuline Convent in Charlestown (Bradley 2005: 389; Halter and Hall 2005: 330–337).

Class and religious riots grew more common during the nineteenth century. For instance, a religious riot broke out in New York City's Sixth Ward on December 25, 1806, between Irish Catholics and native-born Protestants. There were also violent labor strikes in the city between 1825 and 1828 (Gilje 1995). A class riot occurred on New Year's Eve 1827 that heightened concern among elites. That evening, several thousand working-class men and boys marched over to the Battery and vandalized the park and surrounding homes. At the time, wealthy merchants and their families lived in elegant homes flanking the park. Only the wealthy could afford to live around the few park spaces in American cities. The rioters also tried to attack wealthy revelers leaving a formal ball at the City Hotel (Burrows and Wallace 1999: 473; Taylor 2009: 43–68).

In other riots in New York City, political rivalries led to the fight between Whigs and Democrats during the election on April 9–10, 1834 (Gilje 1995), while religious and racial animosity led to the Anti-abolitionist Riot on June 12, 1834 (Anbinder 2001: 7–12). Economic depressions often resulted in clashes such as the Flour Riot, which was caused by the Panic of 1837. On February 12 of that year, people leaving an antipoverty meeting broke into Eli Hart's warehouse, seized flour, and gave it away. Two other warehouses were also ransacked (Gilje 1995). Interethnic gang warfare added to the sense of chaos in the city. Between 1834 and 1844, there were over two hundred major gang wars in New York City alone. These gang wars continued into the 1850s. The Five Points gang war occurred in 1857; so did the Kleindeutschland Riot, which took place in a German neighborhood. The Civil War was another catalyst for violent confrontations. The Draft Riot, which lasted from July 13 to 17, 1863, began as a class riot and escalated into a race war. Rioting started when poor Irish residents protested a law exempting anyone who paid three hundred dollars from being drafted into the war. At first the mob focused their attention on the symbols of power and privilege by ransacking and burning police stations, arsenals, and the homes of the wealthy. However, as the rioting spread, the crowds began assaulting, lynching, and mutilating blacks; the homes of blacks and of institutions serving them were also destroyed. Estimates of the death toll range from 105 to 1,000 (Blackmar 1989: 175; Boyer 1978: 69; Brands 1997: 15; Gilje 1995; Spann 1981: 67–91, 205–241).

There were food riots in Philadelphia during the early eighteenth century. In 1726, poor residents of the city rioted around the High Street market. Food riots continued into the 1730s and 1740s. In 1738, a law prohibiting the use of fish weirs and racks in the Schuylkill River touched off a riot by working-class residents who thought the law curtailed their access to fish. High bread prices also led to rioting in 1741 and 1742 (Bronner 1982: 60).

Religious and political animus led to an election riot in which Anglicans sought to break the political dominance of the Quakers in Philadelphia in 1742 (McCoy 2007). During the nineteenth century, racial tensions became the catalyst for several riots because the city's black population grew rapidly, increasing by about 40 percent between 1810 and 1830. This led to heightened racial tensions, which in turn led to several race riots; the first of these occurred in 1829. Race riots were commonplace during the 1830s and 1840s. During these riots, blacks were usually assaulted and their homes burned (Du Bois [1899] 1996: 28–30; Wainwright 1982: 295–296).

Labor strife and religious conflicts also led to riots in Philadelphia in the 1840s. For instance, the weavers struck and rioted for a wage increase in 1842. Striking weavers ransacked the homes and destroyed the looms of weavers who did not strike. There were also white-on-white interethnic religious conflicts in Philadelphia, where in 1844 armed skirmishes between Irish Catholics and Protestants resulted in the burning of the homes of thirty Irish families. St. Michael's Catholic Church, the Female Seminary of the Sisters of Charity, and St. Augustine's Church were also burned (Burrows and Wallace 1999: 473; Geffen 1982: 337–338, 353).

Social tensions also manifested themselves in riots that swept through Baltimore. A wave of violence, rioting, and arson engulfed the city from 1829 to 1835. These conflicts coincided with worsening economic times. Riots sometimes broke out over wage disputes or when contractors tried to cut wages or delay paying their workers. The 1829 riot among railroad workers resulted in one casualty and several injuries. Racial conflicts between black and Irish workers escalated into a riot in August 1831. Five people were killed in 1834 when rival gangs of canal workers battled each other. This riot had both racial and interethnic dimensions. Though President Jackson dispatched army units from Fort McHenry to restore calm, white laborers from different ethnic groups attacked each other or black workers. Beginning in February 1835, a three-month wave of arson destroyed factories, law offices, a library, the athenaeum, a church, a female orphan asylum, and an engine house. Quite frequently, Baltimore's wealthiest citizens were the victims of arson. For instance, during the Monument Square riot, the homes of well-to-do residents were torched (Olson 1997: 98–100).

Riots were part of the fabric of life in New England towns too. A "town and gown" riot occurred in New Haven in 1812 when Yale students armed with clubs and knives clashed with city residents (Schiff 1981: 101; Sletcher 2004: 113). The city was engulfed in violence again in 1831 when a proposal was made to build a "Negro college" in New Haven. The mayor, university professors, and students responded to the proposal by rioting outside the homes of activists favoring the idea. A few weeks later, blacks were attacked; so were whites suspected of befriending blacks (Lipson 1981: 42; Sletcher 2004: 58, 62). The Hard-Scrabble and Snow Hill riots that occurred in Providence, Rhode Island, in 1831 arose from racial conflicts between white and black laborers. During the nineteenth century there were also strikes and riots in towns like Pawtucket (Rhode Island), Dover (Massachusetts), and Manchester (New Hampshire) (Macieski 2005: 198).

Riots occurred in southern cities as well. A riot broke out in Memphis on May 1, 1866, when Irish policemen began fighting with black Union soldiers. The violence lasted for three days as it escalated into a generalized antiblack riot (Capers 1939: 177–178, 181; Ellis 1992: 23). A similar incident occurred in New Orleans in 1866: white rioters and the police attacked and killed 34 blacks and injured 119 others (Ellis 1992: 23). Riots also occurred in midwestern cities like Cincinnati (H. L. Taylor 1993: 29) and Chicago (Einhorn 2005) in the 1840s and 1850s and in western cities such as Tacoma and Seattle in the 1880s (Crowley 1998: 2–4). The Great Migration of blacks to urban areas triggered riots in cities all across the country in the early twentieth century (Taylor 2014).

DISEASE AND SANITATION

Urban elites also feared the diseases and epidemics that ravaged cities regularly. Maladies such as yellow fever, smallpox, and cholera killed thousands of people annually. The epidemics crippled cities, often overwhelming medical personnel, social services, undertakers, and political leaders. At times business ground to a halt, as anyone who could afford to leave fled the cities at the first word of an outbreak. Furthermore, each disease could easily spread from one city or town to another in any given year. Epidemics were so commonplace that the wealthy planned summer sojourns away from the city well in advance. If an epidemic hit while they were still in the city, they were among the first to flee (Ellis 1992; McMahon 1997; Powell [1949] 1993; Rosenberg 1987). It was their regular trips to their country estates or exclusive resorts in the Poconos, Adirondacks, and Green Mountains, at Newport Beach, and on Mackinac Island or the islands off the coast of Maine that exposed the upper and middle classes to landscapes and forms of recreation they couldn't or didn't experience in the city. As later discussions will show, these vacations helped fuel among the elites the desire for more adventure.

Early on, reformers linked disease and epidemic outbreaks to poor sanitation, immorality, and irreligiosity. However, reformers willing to look beyond the habits of the poor realized that structural and environmental factors played critical roles in the spread of epidemics. For instance, the development of infrastructure in cities did not keep pace with their rapid population growth; consequently, garbage was routinely dumped in the streets, sewage systems were nonexistent or inadequate, and waterways were contaminated by household and industrial wastes. Thus progressive activists focused on making environmental reforms rather than trying to convert the poor to Christianity (McMahon 1997: 104; Powell [1949] 1993: 91; Rosenberg 1987).

To add to the heightened anxiety about disease, sanitation, and ill-health, in 1841 Lemuel Shattuck—a Boston publisher and founder of the American Statistical Association—conducted a study of the city's vital statistics for the period 1810–1840. The study found that there was increasing mortality and illness in the city (Ellis 1992: 8–9; Rosenkrantz 1972: 14–22). A physician and health reformer, John Griscom, conducted a similar health study of New York City in 1845. These studies caught the attention of merchants because statisticians estimated that in 1853 alone, illness cost New York City about $6,692,640. Griscom argued that about 60 percent of the costs incurred stemmed from substandard sanitation and ineffective public health services (Griscom 1845, 1855). A similar study conducted in New Orleans found excessive mortality (Ellis 1992: 35). The focus on inordinate illness and premature deaths made elites believe they were at risk for contracting diseases as long as they lived in the city or close to poor neighborhoods. The wealthy also felt that they were bearing the brunt of the economic burden that resulted from widespread illness and early death. They chafed at the fact that because of these preventable occurrences, they were left paying to feed and clothe the ill, or for sick laborers who underperformed at work. This led rich urbanites to undertake or push for reforms to reduce illness and mortality (Taylor 2009: 69–112).

Water Pollution. Though cities had ample freshwater supplies early on, as they grew it became more difficult and expensive to find reliable sources of clean and safe drinking water, because urban residents and industries had a habit of polluting their drinking water supply. For example, in the 1650s Boston's civic leaders instructed residents to toss their trash into the Mill Creek instead of piling it in the streets (Corey 2005: 620–621). This practice became commonplace in cities and led to the despoliation of many urban waterways. By 1675 the canal Heere Gracht in Manhattan was such a foul inlet that New Yorkers filled it in and paved it over to create Broad Street (Burrows and Wallace 1999: 85; Janvier [1894] 2000: 25).

Filling in Heere Gracht did not stop New Yorkers from degrading other water sources. Close to the neighborhood that became known as Five Points was a body of water known as the Collect or Fresh Water Pond. The sixty-foot-deep, spring-fed, forty-eight-acre pond was also known by its Dutch names, the *kolch* (a small body of water) or *kalch-hook* (lime shell point). Before being driven from the area by European settlers, Native Americans collected oysters from the pond and deposited the shells on its banks. Just northeast of the Collect, a promontory, Bunker Hill, rose to a height of more than one hundred feet. From Bunker Hill picnickers could view the wildlife around the pond. Blacks established a community on the southern marshy shores of the Collect during the time of Dutch rule (Anbinder 2001: 14–15; Burrows and Wallace 1999: 32–33; Goldstein and Izeman 1995: 1244–1246; Groneman 1995: 250; Jackson and Dunbar 2002: 17, 28; Janvier [1894] 2000: 53–55).[1] The Collect (located in what is now Foley Square) was one of the city's earliest sources of water. However, by the 1780s the water quality of the pond had declined noticeably because city residents dumped garbage, sewage, and the carcasses of dead animals in it (Goldstein and Izeman 1995: 1244–1246).

Industrial pollution also played a major role in compromising the water quality of the Collect. When Governor Edmund Andros expelled the stinky factories and other noxious facilities from the central city in the 1670s, they relocated in areas such as the Collect. Private slaughterhouses and tanneries clustered along the pond's southern and eastern edges. Soon the Collect stank from the pungent wastes of the breweries, carcasses, and chemicals used to tan the hides. By the end of the eighteenth century, the Collect, which was still the drinking water source for poor city residents (the wealthy purchased their water from private water companies), was transformed into a foul cesspool. It was around this time that Pierre L'Enfant proposed cleaning up the pond, encircling it with a park, and making it a focal recreational amenity around which the city could grow. The plan was abandoned when industrialists owning land in the vicinity of the Collect refused to sell their properties to make way for the park. In 1802, the Common Council decided to fill the pond in with earth obtained from the leveling of Bunker Hill. The Collect was filled in between 1803 and 1811, and within a few decades a notorious slum neighborhood—Five Points—enveloped the site of the former pond (Anbinder 2001: 14–15; Burrows and Wallace 1999: 72–85; Corbett 1995: 745–746; Groneman 1995: 250).[2]

Atlanta's water was also polluted. By the 1870s well-to-do Atlantans bought drinking water from Ponce de Leon and other springs. However, the majority of city residents, unable to afford to buy springwater, continued to drink the contaminated water. An 1883 study showed that many of the city's public wells were polluted (Ellis 1992: 142).

Air Pollution. Urbanites lived in fear of drinking the water and breathing the air. Those with the ability and means to escape began to consider living in less polluted environs. Urban air pollution was a nuisance and a health hazard. Burning coal caused enormous pollution as industrial facilities constantly disgorged heavy black smoke and particulate matter. Fine coal dust coated and corroded buildings and statues, irritated the eyes and lungs, and resulted in increased incidence of pulmonary diseases. Soot was also ubiquitous (Nye 1998: 84). Pittsburgh, the epicenter of the iron and steel industry, was so occluded it was nicknamed "the Smoky City." In 1791 an observer complained the city was "kept in so much smoke as to affect the skin of the inhabitants" (Dewey 2000: 22; Grinder 1973: 27–29). Lucy and John James Audubon, the renowned bird illustrator, traveled through Pittsburgh in 1808 on their way to Kentucky. Lucy described the city as having "a thick fog" that "is almost constant over the town." According to her, Pittsburgh was "the blackest looking place I ever saw" (L. B. Audubon 1808).

By the early 1820s, St. Louis, a city that rivaled Pittsburgh for smokiness, had depleted its supply of wood and turned to burning soft coal found in nearby southern Illinois. Hence, in 1823 the *Missouri Republican* noted that the smoke was so dense "as to render it necessary to use candles at mid-day," and during the 1840s an anonymous letter to the editor warned that the city could become "an emporium for disease" because of the smoke (Dewey 2000: 23–26; Grinder 1973: 29–30). Other cities, such as Chicago, had serious air pollution problems too. Despite its location on the flat, windy plains of the shores of Lake Michigan, Chicago's air was polluted by the immense amount of smoke that industries spewed into the atmosphere. By the 1880s, the smoke was so thick it was difficult to see across the street (Dewey 2000: 23).

By the mid-nineteenth century, the outward movement of wealthy residents from city centers was commonplace. The rich left their cramped dwellings in or near their business establishments and began living with others of similar racial, ethnic, and social backgrounds in exclusive residential enclaves on the outskirts of cities. The movement occurred in two ways. First there was a clustering of elites in select neighborhoods near downtown, but there was also a noticeable movement of elites away from the downtowns altogether and toward the urban fringes and the countryside (Taylor 2009: 115–130).

The wealthy moved in order to distance themselves from the things and people of the city that made them uncomfortable or threatened their lifestyle. However, homosocial sorting also occurred because of a desire to be exclusive. As Homberger argues, aristocrats have an insatiable appetite for exclusivity in all aspects of their lives. They want to choose where they live, who lives next to them, what institutions they build or belong to, their recreation, schooling, and so on. American aristocrats pursued exclusivity with such zeal that they aspired to be more exclusive than the Europeans they emulated (Homberger 2002: 1–4).

THE RISE OF COUNTRY ESTATES

In New York, the outmigration of elites from the city began in the first half of the seventeenth century. Soon after the second governor, Wouter Van Twiller, arrived in Manhattan in April 1633, he laid claim to a large parcel of land in what is now Greenwich Village for his own private tobacco farm. Van Twiller's farmhouse was probably the first house erected by Europeans on Manhattan outside Fort Amsterdam (Jackson and Dunbar 2002: 19; Janvier [1894] 2000: 85–90; Ramirez 1995: 506–509).

However, the last Dutch governor, Petrus (Peter) Stuyvesant, made a more deliberate move to the countryside. Stuyvesant lived downtown in the governor's house in Fort Amsterdam when he arrived in New Amsterdam in 1647. Though New Amsterdam[3] was a small town with a population numbering around four hundred in 1640, Stuyvesant did not take long to move his residence to the outskirts of town. When Stuyvesant arrived in New Amsterdam, it was described as a settlement that "presented a very dilapidated and deplorable appearance" (Abbott [1873] 2004: 125).[4] Stuyvesant purchased a farm on the East River at Seventeenth Street in 1651 and built an elegant home—White Hall—on it. He made it his official residence in 1658 (Mooney 1995a: 1133–1134). Soon a steady stream of wealthy New Yorkers imitated Stuyvesant by building country estates on hundreds of acres of land on the urban fringe. The city facilitated this process by turning over large plots of land for little or no money to shrewd businessmen or war heroes like Colonel Anthony Rutgers to develop (Blackmar 1989: 34–35; Burrows and Wallace 1999: 178; Janvier [1894] 2000: 192–197; G. Tauber 1995: 679).

The movement of elites to the outskirts of towns could be seen in other municipalities too. By 1760, the countryside around Boston was dotted with the country estates of the wealthy, in nearby hamlets such as Danvers, Medford, Middleborough, and Brookline. Influential industrialists like the Cabots, Lowells, Lawrences, and Amorys built their estates in Brookline. The country seats were designed to show off the owners' wealth, status, and refinement (Karr 2005b: 214–215; Macieski 2005: 193; P. Thornton 2005: 42).

EXCLUSIVE URBAN ENCLAVES

American aristocrats also cloistered themselves around public open space such as Bowling Green and Battery Park in New York and the Common in Boston. When these spaces grew scarce, affluent urbanites built private parks such as St. Johns and Gramercy in New York and Louisburg Square in Boston (the latter two are still private today) (Taylor 2009: 231–235). American elites did not invent this form of urban living. From the late seventeenth century to the mid-nineteenth, European aristocrats began greening the squares in the most prestigious neighborhoods. From about 1650 to 1850, the residential square was the primary mechanism used to incorporate rural elements into urban landscapes in England. Though London's first square, Covent Garden, was built in 1630, it was a paved open space. Lincoln Inn Fields was also developed in the 1630s but was left as an open undeveloped field surrounded by buildings. However, in the 1660s Leicester Square was developed by residents in the surrounding homes; they planted rows of elm trees in it. By the end of the seventeenth century several squares were laid out with trees and gardens. Beginning with Hanover Square in 1713, all new squares in London were planted with grass. Later this practice was adopted by urbanites in cities such as Dublin, Munich, and Paris (Lawrence 1993: 90–95).

In England, residential squares became a way of demarcating affluent urban neighborhoods from poor ones. The squares were used as instruments to enhance the property values of surrounding homes. Residential squares were also used to stimulate development of new upscale neighborhoods. The earliest residents of residential squares in London were all rural gentry with vast landholdings in the countryside; these landholdings were the primary sources of their wealth. They used their city home as a base from which to participate in the "social season." However, by the mid-eighteenth century, the landed gentry were spending longer periods of time in the city, and in some cases their town homes became their primary residences. Thus the residential squares gradually became spaces in which aristocrats sought to imitate country life in the city. Increasingly, the squares were fenced and locked to separate them "from mankind in general" (Corfield 1990: 132–174; Cruickshank and Burton 1990: 99–133; Lawrence 1993: 95–104).

American aristocrats developed and used residential squares in a similar fashion. The parks and squares around which the aristocrats built their homes served as places to glimpse nature and as resorts for genteel recreation (Homberger 2002: 57). The squares were an indicator of high status and prestige, so elites landscaped and privatized them, built fences around them, and padlocked them. From the outset, American urban elites had a strong stake in the squares and small parks. Unlike their European counterparts, the Americans derived most of their wealth from their entrepreneurial activities in the city. For this reason, their primary residences were in the city and they had a profound interest in the appearance and safety of the squares.

Urban Parks Spur Early Conservation Efforts

Some of the earliest efforts to conserve open spaces occurred in the cities and grew out of the desire to develop and protect the commons and small parks. It began in Boston when Governor John Winthrop purchased forty-five acres of Reverend Blaxton's (Blackstone) farm to create the Boston Common in 1634. Winthrop wanted "The Commonage" to be preserved for "Common use"; this was codified in a 1640 law. Each household was charged six shillings to help purchase land for the Common (City of Boston 1990; Kreiger 2001: 156; Macieski 2005: 188; Warner 2001: 3). During the 1720s Boston took the first step in transforming the Common and surrounding thoroughfares into parklike settings by planting trees along Tremont Street to form the Mall. Boston's tree-planting efforts continued for several more decades, and from 1816 to 1836, tree-lined promenades were developed along Beacon, Charles, Park, and Boylston streets. By 1860, the Common was covered with trees. Elites protected it by defeating proposals to crisscross it with roads and streetcar lines (Karr 2005a: 212–213).

New Haven emulated Boston by setting aside public lands and undertaking park development. However, New Haven didn't just set aside open space on its periphery. Its green was in the center of the city, which had been laid out around it in 1641. Tree planting began when one prominent resident, James Pierpont, planted two trees on his property in 1686. The city began a more concerted effort to plant trees in 1759, planting 250 buttonwood and elm trees around the Green. Trees were then planted along Temple Street. In 1790 the city created a committee to develop bylaws for "preserving trees for shade and ornament" in the city. At this time, James Hillhouse began planting trees around the city. In 1798, the city passed an ordinance to protect the Green from unruly geese and college students (Chiff 1981: 104; Sletcher 2004: 65, 109–111).

Similar conservation efforts were initiated in New York. Lawn bowling was a popular pastime among the Dutch. Beginning in 1626, they held lawn bowling matches in the open space that was later named Bowling Green. Bowling Green, the city's first park, began to take shape during the 1670s. When Fort James was being restored, "the Plaine afore the Forte" was designated. This multiple-use open space was the site of parades and the annual fair where cattle, grain, and produce were sold. Bowling Green was officially laid out in 1733 and rented out to three residents for a nominal fee. A statue erected in the park in 1770 was toppled by rioters six years later. New York had a park called The Common (renamed City Hall Park) that was used for turkey shooting (Burrows and Wallace 1999: 85; Latimer 1995: 132; Lewison 1995: 657).

The Need for More Open Space

Despite these park-building efforts, American cities still had a paucity of park space during the nineteenth century. Moreover, as late as the 1840s, the existing urban parks were very small and quite inadequate to meet the needs of rapidly growing cities. Also, by this time wealthy males in particular had begun to tire of the tiny parks. They longed for larger open spaces where they could hunt, fish, go horseback riding, take carriage rides, and generally engage in more vigorous, challenging outdoor pursuits regularly that were still genteel and exclusive in nature. There was also a desire for safe genteel spaces that well-to-do ladies could enjoy.

During the nineteenth century, upper- and middle-class Americans took regular sojourns to Europe and other parts of the world. In Europe, they encountered elegant urban parks as well as expansive, pastoral rural ones. In medieval Europe, open spaces were maintained exclusively for the use of the ruling classes. The English began landscaping their gardens during the early part of the sixteenth century. These early parks were characterized by broad stretches of greensward (lawn) framed by sparsely distributed trees. The form and functions of parks evolved over time, and in the seventeenth century Europeans began developing public parks. For instance, in 1652, London's Hyde Park was opened to the public, but users had to pay to enter. By the late eighteenth century, landscaped parks were being built in other cities too (Chadwick 1966: 163–220; Olmsted 1861: 768–775; Olmsted, Vaux and Company 1866a; Rogers 1987: 7; Rosenzweig and Blackmar 1992: 3–4; Runte 1987: 2; R. Williams 1973: 122–125).

Americans traveling abroad compared the open spaces in Europe with those available in their own cities and found the latter wanting. American elites also found the lack of open space in American cities irritating because as they built their country estates farther afield or visited distant resorts for the summer, they craved the fresh air and active lifestyle when they returned to the city. They wanted to be able to engage frequently in outdoor recreation while in the city. Consequently, groups of elites emerged as park advocates who campaigned to build large landscaped parks in New York and other cities.

Hence, in the 1840s William Cullen Bryant, Andrew Jackson Downing, and other park advocates began urging New York and other cities to build public parks. Activists had campaigned for parks earlier, but these requests were largely ignored (Chadwick 1966: 166–220; Roper 1973: 124–155; Spann 1981: 2). New York received the most pressure to build an elegant park befitting a first-class modern city. The 1811 city plan originally designated 450 acres of open space in Manhattan, but by 1838, the acreage of the city's seventeen public and private parks totaled a mere 144 acres. Moreover, much of that acreage was undeveloped (*Journal of Commerce* 1851b: 2; Spann 1981: 161).[5] By the 1840s, the open acreage was deemed inadequate to meet the needs of the growing city. However, despite a sustained effort by park enthusiasts to get the city to build a large landscaped park, the pleas of activists were ignored, in part because when the parks campaign began to gain momentum in the early 1840s, New York and other cities were just recovering from the Panic of 1837, and such public works projects were deemed economically impractical. But in the early 1850s New York was booming economically, and the city's business class grew interested in the park movement (Rosenzweig and Blackmar 1992: 24; Taylor 2009: 251–337).

In 1851 a group of businessmen took control of the reins. Spearheaded by a prominent banker, Robert Minturn, who had just returned from a lengthy trip to Europe, the group—without much input from the public but claiming to act on its behalf—decided to pick a site for the park, set about acquiring the property, proposed a tax structure to pay for the park, and secured passage of the park bill through the Common Council. The Minturn Circle, as I call the group, originally picked a 150-acre parcel of land on the East River called Jones Wood. However, park advocates such as Downing lobbied for a larger parcel of land that was at least five hundred acres. The Jones Wood proposal got bogged down in legal wrangling over tax assessments and the acquisition of property (Jones Wood was located close to the country estates of powerful families, two of which—the Joneses and Schermerhorns—refused to sell their land to turn their estates into a public park). The proposal drew many critics opposed to the idea of levying a general tax on city residents to pay for the park. As the Jones Wood proposal became embroiled in controversy, a group of wealthy Upper West Side residents wanting a large park to anchor their upscale community proposed the development of a more centrally located park that was much larger than Jones Wood. The Central Park proposal levied some general taxes, but taxed those living close to the park heavier than the remainder of the population. After much political maneuvering, the bill approving the 778-acre Central Park was passed in 1853 (Jones Wood was not built). The Minturn Circle held a design competition, and the landscape architects Frederick Law Olmsted and Calvert Vaux won. Construction began in 1856. Their model was quickly copied across the country as other cities clamored to build elegant landscaped parks designed by the landscape architects of Central Park fame (Bryant 1844; Downing 1851: 147–153; Homberger 2002: 238–242; *Journal of Commerce* 1851a: 2; 1851b: 2; Rosenzweig and Blackmar 1992: 20–26, 33–35, 55–59; Taylor 2009: 223–337).

The development of large landscaped parks satisfied the quest for more recreational space in the city and genteel recreation for elites—but not for long. By the late nineteenth century, elite men began to take lengthy trips to the western frontier, scale high peaks, trek, and take on conservation issues. Conservationism also grew out of the participation in sport such as fishing, hunting, and birding. Outdoor recreation activities and adventures also became a forum for women to undertake conservation activities.

PART II
MANLINESS, WOMANHOOD, WEALTH, AND SPORT

3

WEALTH, MANLINESS,
AND EXPLORING THE OUTDOORS
Racial and Gender Dynamics

In the fifteenth century, at a time when women were not expected to speak with authority about outdoor leisure pursuits, a female English writer named Dame Juliana Berners hypothesized about the things that made men happy. She argued that four pastimes—hunting, hawking, fishing, and fowling—were good and honest sports that helped men lead long, happy lives. She associated these sports with the nobility and the elites (Berners 1496).[1] Berners addressed her book to men and framed sports and leisure as endeavors that were good for their longevity. It is striking that Berners did not address women, youth, or the poor and their need for outdoor recreation.

Berners's views and the perceptions of others like her are relevant to this discussion as English attitudes toward recreation and sports were very influential in American thinking. For instance, the pastimes identified by Berners became popular among American male aristocrats. As American elites sought to distinguish themselves from the masses and appear more refined and genteel in the seventeenth century, wealthy men took part in angling, hunting, horseback riding, and other sports favored by European nobility. In the American context, such men were able to work when they pleased, or not at all, and assume the trappings of the leisured class.

As a result, two sports—horseback riding and racing—grew immensely popular. Elites were so smitten with horse racing, also known as the "sport of kings," that in 1665 Governor Richard Nicholls established the New Market Track at Salisbury Plain (now Hempstead, Long Island). He supervised the first race held at the track. Another racetrack, the Church Farm Course, operated in Manhattan from 1725 to 1750 (S. D. Bruce [1868] 1898; Reiss 1995: 557–559; Sheridan 1971: 18).[2] Thoroughbred racing was introduced to America in 1745, when Governor Samuel Ogle of Maryland organized a race at Annapolis. Philadelphia's horse racing enthusiasts formed the Jockey Club in 1766. Horse racing became so popular that a North-South Challenge held in 1823 at the Union Course in Long Island drew sixty thousand spectators (Longrigg 1972; Tinkcom 1982: 121–122). During the 1830s horse racing increased in popularity in the Philadelphia area at venues like Nicetown Hunting Park. John Craig built his own racetrack and had a large collection of racehorses at Carlton, his Germantown estate. General Callender Irvine owned thirty-eight thoroughbreds at the time of his death in 1841 (Tinkcom 1982: 121–122; Wainwright 1982: 292). As the sport grew, documentation became a priority, hence the *American Stud Book* made its first appearance in 1868.

Hunting emerged as an elite pastime too. In the 1740s New York's rich and powerful merchant Gerard Beekman, wishing to appear more cultured, made a conscious effort to display a refined lifestyle. He began wearing only the finest silk stockings (instead of the more common linen ones) and acquired a "Genteel fowling Piece" from London so he could pursue the "Glorious sport" of hunting. In one morning's carriage ride around Manhattan, he shot fifteen braces of plovers (Burrows and Wallace 1999: 172–173). Beekman's behavior epitomizes an emerging culture in which corporate moguls participated in early-morning recreational hunts before heading off to the office.

Around the time rich American men were taking an interest in hunting, only wealthy men hunted legally in Europe because the masses were usually denied the right to own hunting rifles and hunting dogs. As late as the nineteenth century, only about 0.01 percent of English men were eligible to hunt legally. Extreme violence was used to prevent ordinary people from hunting; commoners who tried to hunt were penalized severely. In some instances, those poaching deer, boar, or other animals were killed. To create hunting preserves for aristocrats, whole villages were burned and the inhabitants relocated to make way for the game. It wasn't until 1880 that English commoners gained the right to hunt rabbits (Herman 2001: 247–248; Hummel 2004: 460–464; Marsh [1864] 1965: 280–284).

Foxhunting grew in popularity among affluent American urban dwellers as well. In the 1760s, James DeLancey and Lewis Morris purchased large packs of hounds. Soon after DeLancey returned from England, where he had acquired horses as well as the foxhounds, the two combined their packs. DeLancey's manager organized weekly hunts in the Bronx, Brooklyn, and Queens. Smaller packs of hounds were used on hunts in Manhattan, but by 1822 all the Manhattan hunts were moved to Long Island or Westchester (Mooney 1995b: 435–436). A foxhunt was also organized in Philadelphia in 1766 (Tinkcom 1982: 121–122; Wainwright 1982: 292).

Clearly, hunting, fishing, and racing could be conducted on the fringes of American cities, and John James Audubon's experience illustrates the ease with which one could still hunt in New York City itself in the early 1800s. Audubon clerked there from 1806 to 1807. Realizing that the city did not extend much beyond Washington Square, he wandered around Manhattan hunting and collecting bird specimens that he killed and later illustrated (Rhodes 2004: 41).

These recreational activities led participants to become increasingly aware of emergent environmental problems and take an active role in crafting policies and solutions to ameliorate conditions. The remainder of this chapter highlights several prominent men who were vanguards in early efforts to understand and protect the environment. They represent a range of postures and experiences, from naturalists and explorers to woodsmen, Transcendentalists, frontierists, activists and organizers, and policy makers. Their awareness of the environment varied with the times. Moreover, there were similarities and differences in how they dealt with the major social issues confronting society. The stories of these men are important because they illustrate the wide range of ways that nineteenth-century American men of elite upbringing or aspirations thought about nature and the outdoors. Their stories also illustrate the extent to which the notion of manliness was infused into their lifestyles and give us a glimpse into how men who engaged in these activities related to their families, particularly the women.

Early Explorers

By the early nineteenth century, urban intellectuals and affluent men began to roam beyond the cities and small towns for recreation and adventure. Some of the explorations were military expeditions meant to open areas to commercial trade, map the country, identify the location of strategic minerals, and collect statistics on Native American tribes. These were political, economic, and military missions that fueled westward expansion and helped to facilitate Manifest Destiny. It was in this spirit that Meriwether Lewis (Thomas Jefferson's personal secretary) and William Clark went on a high-profile government-sponsored expedition. Both Lewis and Clark were military men. Their overland expedition, which lasted from 1804 to 1806, captivated the nation. Congress appropriated $2,500 for the Corps of Discovery, as the expedition team was called. They mapped a route to the Pacific, identified rivers and other geological features along the way, and collected and identified plant and animal specimens (Clark and Lewis 2003). The Corps of Discovery was also organized to facilitate the expansion of commerce and more systematic and intensive data collection on Native Americans. Expedition leaders were asked to decipher how to increase trade with Indian tribes, document native cultural habits, and create a dictionary of common words in the tribal languages they encountered (R. J. Miller 2006). Throughout the nineteenth century there were similar expeditions, such as the 1819 Long Expedition to the Rocky Mountains, the 1869 John Wesley Powell Expedition into the Grand Canyon, and the 1870 Washburn-Langford-Doane Expedition in and around Yellowstone. These expeditions will be discussed in more detail later on. The remainder of this section of the chapter will examine the experiences of two solo explorers who espoused important conservation ideas in the early nineteenth century.

JOHN JAMES AUDUBON:
ARTIST, BIRD ENTHUSIAST, AND WOODSMAN

Reports documenting the explorations of the hinterlands stimulated interest in traveling beyond the confines of eastern cities and towns and led some men to venture into the American frontier on their own. Unencumbered by the military expectations and nation-building goals of government-sponsored expeditions, some of the solo explorers paid attention to changes in the environment and chronicled signs of degradation, overexploitation, pollution, and so on. These individuals also espoused ideas about nature protection that became the foundation of the conservation and preservation movements.

John James Audubon was one of these explorers. Audubon, a French immigrant who established himself in Philadelphia, began exploring the outdoors because of his interest in art, bird illustration, and hunting. Audubon was born in Saint Domingue (renamed Haiti) in 1785. He moved to France with his father, a plantation owner, after the slave revolt in Haiti and remained in Nantes until he was eighteen. He then left Nantes for America because his father decided that he wanted his son to migrate there. Unfortunately for

Audubon, he landed in New York in 1803 in the middle of a yellow fever epidemic and contracted the disease shortly after his arrival. As a result, he was transported to Philadelphia and placed in the care of two Quaker women who nursed him back to health. Once he recovered, Audubon went to live in Mill Grove, a short distance from Philadelphia (Rhodes 2004: 3–5).[3]

Audubon loved the countryside around Mill Grove. He occupied his time with hunting, fishing, art, music, and the courtship of Lucy Bakewell. It was here that he developed a keen interest in studying and illustrating birds (Rhodes 2004: 7–17). In 1804, he decided that he wanted to draw birds accurately—that is, with more precision than in existing illustrations. He wrote, "Nothing after all could ever answer my enthusiastic desires to represent nature, than to attempt to copy her in her own way, alive and moving!" (Audubon 1999: 760). He carried out the first bird-banding experiments in 1804 and conducted a bird census in Louisville shortly after moving there in 1808 (Audubon 1835: 126ff; Rhodes 2004: 10–11, 37, 60).

In the early nineteenth century, Audubon was a proto-conservationist operating on the rugged frontier. He is not the typical East Coast urban intellectual or elite that will be the subject of later discussions. Audubon and his wife Lucy ping-ponged between affluence and bankruptcy as they moved from one location to the next and as one business venture after another either succeeded or failed. They operated stores and other small businesses in frontier towns such as Louisville and Henderson, Kentucky. They also lived in Cincinnati, New Orleans, and Natchez (Mississippi) before moving to England and finally settling in New York. Though they were living on a shoestring budget when they first moved to Henderson and opened their store in 1810, within two years their business was thriving and they were living the life of the rural gentry. Buoyed by the unpaid labor of the slaves they owned and traded in and profits from their business, they had ample time for recreation. Lucy was somewhat different from East Coast women of means in that she engaged in active outdoor leisure pursuits with her husband; as later discussions will show, the lines of distinction that separated male and female work, household tasks, and recreation in eastern cities and towns were often blurred on the frontier. The Audubons rode together each morning, played their musical instruments, and swam regularly in the Ohio River. Audubon hunted frequently; he also participated in target shooting. At a time when few could afford it, he had a fowling piece, a duck gun, a double gun, and a smooth rifle. The village held derby days in which Audubon raced his horses down the main road. Audubon also fenced. On one occasion he cracked the shin of a visitor who bragged about being an expert fencer and challenged Audubon to a duel (Rhodes 2004: 114–115, 125).

Manliness was a frontier virtue that was asserted when deemed necessary. Though he was gentle and shy in polite company and while navigating high society in New York and Europe, Audubon—a self-described woodsman—didn't back down from a fight or take kindly to threats to his masculinity while living on the frontier. Thinking that a sheriff's deputy in Henderson was not being aggressive enough in searching for a river pirate who had robbed a flatboat, Audubon volunteered to accompany the deputy to search for the alleged thief. When the belligerent pirate threatened his would-be captors, Audubon grabbed an oar and fractured the man's skull with it, promptly arrested him, and transported him back to Henderson to be jailed (Rhodes 2004: 114–115, 298). On another occasion Audubon—whose businesses were on the verge of collapsing in the Panic of 1819—went from Henderson to New Orleans to collect on a debt that was owed him. The debtor reneged, and Audubon returned home empty-handed to face his creditors and the collapse of this business. Audubon sought revenge by spreading a rumor that the debtor, Samuel Bowen, was a crook. Bowen responded by vowing to track down Audubon and kill him. Back in Henderson, the two men got in a fight. Audubon was injured, but he stabbed Bowen and had to go to court to clear his name (Audubon 1999: 790–791).

Until 1819, Audubon was an avid bird collector and illustrator intent on perfecting his illustrations but with no great desire to publicize his work. Though the people viewing his sketches, including noted ornithologist Alexander Wilson, told him that his sketches were superior to any available on the market, Audubon did not actively seek to publish his work. However, in 1819 the Long Expedition changed all that. Members of the expedition, who stopped in Cincinnati on their way to explore the Rockies, were amazed at the quality of Audubon's sketches on display in the museum. Audubon then realized the extent to which the government was interested in expeditions, scientific collections, and documentation of the natural environment. It dawned on him that if he were to gain greater recognition, he needed to branch out beyond the Midwest and collect and draw specimens from other regions of the country. This experience intensified Audubon's desire to travel widely and perfect his sketching skills. Audubon sought financial backing from the government to mount an expedition to the West, but was unsuccessful, so he ended up financing his trips on his own. Audubon eventually traveled through the Deep South and Southeast, New England, the American West, and into Labrador (Canada) to collect and illustrate birds (H. E. Evans 1997: xi–xii; Rhodes 2004: 148–151).

The Audubons lived in several places in the United States and Europe during the 1820s and 1830s before finally settling in New York. They returned to the United States from Europe in 1839. Following a well-worn path of artists and intellectuals who once lived in Lower Manhattan, they began building a home in a rural area on the banks of the Hudson River in what is now Washington Heights. In 1841 they purchased a fourteen-acre property and built their home, Minniesland, on it (Lucy was affectionately known to the family as Minnie—a Scottish term of endearment meaning "mother"). Within a few years, Audubon and his sons had bought additional tracts of land to enlarge the property to twenty-four acres. Though he continued to finance his own expeditions, Audubon took on the life of a gentleman farmer at Minniesland. With the help of his son, John, he planted an orchard containing several types of fruit trees and raised farm animals on the property (Grinnell 1927; Rhodes 2004: 416; Spady 2007).

GEORGE CATLIN: PAINTER OF NATIVE TRIBES AND WESTERN SCENERY

Like Audubon, George Catlin was an illustrator from the Philadelphia area who traveled to the West to paint. Catlin was born in 1796 in Wilkes Barre, Pennsylvania. The year following George's birth, the Catlins bought a plantation in New York State and moved across the border to live there. George's father, Putnam, was a lawyer who cultivated the life of a gentleman farmer and sportsman on the wooded property, hence Catlin grew up horseback riding and hunting. He also enjoyed fishing and searching the woods for Indian artifacts. While still a young boy, he snuck a rifle out of the house and hid it in the woods so that he could satisfy his desire to hunt and kill a deer. Though he failed to kill any on his first try, he continued to hunt deer into his adult life. Young Catlin was riveted by his mother's stories of how she and her mother were held captive by Native Americans in Pennsylvania during the Wyoming Valley Massacre, which took place about twenty years before Catlin's birth. The family moved to Hop Bottom, Pennsylvania, in 1808 to live on another plantation. Catlin became a lawyer and practiced briefly in Wilkes Barre. However, by 1821 he had moved to Philadelphia, where he began a career in painting. He became an accomplished portrait painter. While in Albany, New York, to paint a portrait of Governor DeWitt Clinton, he met Clara Bartlett Gregory, whom he married in 1828. Clara came from one of Albany's wealthy merchant families (Dippe et al. 2002; Haberly 1948: 1–35).

Two years after he was married, Catlin left his sick wife to take his first trip to the West when he accompanied General William Clark up the Mississippi

River (Haberly 1948: 30–35). Catlin gave up his portrait studio business in Philadelphia in 1832 after meeting an Indian delegation. The thirty-six-year-old decided to move to Nebraska to paint Native Americans and general scenery. While in Nebraska, Catlin began to think and write about the preservation of nature and culture. Catlin brought his sketches back to the East and exhibited them in Pittsburgh, Cincinnati, and Buffalo. The New York show mounted in 1837, *Catlin's Indian Gallery*, was a huge success and helped to stimulate interest in the "Wild West." Catlin also exhibited his works in Washington, Philadelphia, Baltimore, Boston, and London. He chronicled his experiences in a two-volume book in 1844 (Catlin [1844] 1973; Sheldon 1914: 59).

Intellectual Elites, Transcendentalism, and Nature

By the 1830s the effects of industrial growth were quite apparent in cities. As a result, a group of intellectual elites emerged to critique the condition of cities; they urged people to escape to the countryside to commune with nature and renew themselves. The Transcendentalists were among the most ardent proponents of this viewpoint. They were also among the earliest of the budding preservationists and conservationists to clearly articulate the belief that nature had healing powers that counteracted the effects of the city.

Transcendentalism arose, in part, as a response to the growing industrialization of America. Transcendentalists were concerned about loss of nature and decreasing quality of life in the cities. They were also concerned about the relationship between humans and the industrial world. Though Transcendentalists like Ralph Waldo Emerson urged people to go to the countryside to renew themselves, he did not settle very far away from Boston. Living in places such as Concord, the Transcendentalists had ample opportunity to observe the growth of industrial towns all around them, and they provided social and literary commentary on what they saw.

Even in Concord, a small town of two thousand in 1837, creeping industrialism threatened village life. Concord, Massachusetts, roughly twenty miles west of Boston, had a manufacturing base that was on the rise. The town contained several factories, including a five-story cotton mill. By the 1830s, most of the woods around Concord had been cleared; only about a sixth of the land remained forested. This led Henry David Thoreau to comment that one could not walk around Concord during the daytime without hearing the sound of axes (Richardson [1986] 1996: 14–16).

Emerson's home was a center of Transcendental thought. The home operated on a loose communitarian model: fellow Transcendentalists lived with Emerson and his wife, Lydia, for months at a time. People who lived with the Emersons at various times included Thoreau, Margaret Fuller, Elizabeth Hoar (Charles Emerson's fiancée), and Lucy Brown (Lydia's sister) (A. B. Brown 2005; Richardson 1995). Some Transcendentalists were attracted to attempts to blend industrialism, utopianism, and communitarianism the way it was practiced in places such as Hopedale (Chomsky 2008: 19; Malloy, Malloy, and Ryan 2002; Morris and Kross 2004: 140; National Park Service-National Register n.d.). However, Transcendentalists like Thoreau were critical of the economic policies that drove the industrial revolution so evident around him. Some well-known Transcendentalists tried to establish a direct link between Transcendental ideas and social change. For instance, Bronson Alcott (father of Louisa May Alcott) taught the children enrolled in his Temple School to learn through open discussion and responding freely to the Bible, while George Ripley established a utopian community at Brook Farm on a 160-acre property in West Roxbury on the border of Newton (Le Beau 2005: 806–808; Richardson [1986] 1996: 33, 100–103). Brook Farm began in 1841, and two years later Alcott and Charles Lane started Fruitlands, a short-lived utopian community located on Prospect Hill in Harvard, Massachusetts (Walter Harding 1992: 125–126).

Transcendentalists were drawn to the utopian communitarianism espoused by François Charles Fourier. Fourier argued that social problems could be solved by developing small, planned communes or garden cities organized as cooperatives in which people and industry coexisted harmoniously. He saw poverty as the source of disorder in society and thought that high wages for those who worked and a minimum wage for those who couldn't was the solution to social problems (J. Beecher 1996; Cunliffe and Erreygers 2001: 461; Frothingham 1888: 307–308; Richardson [1986] 1996: 101). These utopian communitarian experiments were the closest Transcendentalists came to reforming the workplace or reducing poverty.

Ripley expanded on Fourier's ideas about poverty and wealth. He saw Brook Farm as a collective effort intended to reform agricultural practices and the distribution of land. He invited Emerson and Thoreau to participate in the experiment, but both men declined. Thoreau was also asked to join Fruitlands, but he spurned that offer too. However, Nathaniel Hawthorne and his wife, Sophia Peabody, were among the first people to take up residence at Brook Farm. Hawthorne spent only a few months there. At its peak, Brook Farm had about one hundred residents (Walter Harding 1992: 125–126; Richardson [1986] 1996:

101–103). The societal transformation Ripley and Brook Farm residents hoped to achieve did not materialize.

Collective social reform or the building of a mass movement wasn't the central aim of the Transcendentalists. Most of them focused on individual transformation through the ideas that emerged from their discussions, writing, thinking, and lecturing. This approach earned them a reputation of having their heads in the clouds (Richardson [1986] 1996: 72–74). For instance, in "The Celestial Railroad," Nathaniel Hawthorne wrote about the "Giant Transcendentalist." As Hawthorne—who lived in Concord from 1842 to 1852—described the figure, "We caught a hasty glimpse of him, looking somewhat like an ill-proportioned figure, but considerably more like a heap of fog and duskiness. He shouted after us, but in so strange a phraseology that we knew not what he meant, nor whether to be encouraged or affrighted" (Hawthorne [1845] 1860: 6). Though Hawthorne became good friends with Thoreau, married a Transcendentalist, and lived among them in Concord, he remained ambivalent about the group.

Nonetheless, the contributions of Transcendentalists should not be underestimated. Their preservationist ideas, concern with nature, and writings about humans in relation to nature contributed to greater awareness about the environment by the end of the nineteenth century. In addition, Thoreau's essay "Civil Disobedience," which argues that individuals have a right to oppose the state when the state is morally wrong, has been very influential (Alves 2005b: 1004–1006; Baker 2005: 1032–1033; Bode [1947] 1982; Emerson 1883; Walter Harding 1992: 137; Paul 1952; Thoreau 1893). Moreover, some Transcendentalists, including Emerson, Theodore Parker, and Thoreau, were antislavery advocates. As later discussions will show, Transcendentalists such as Elizabeth Peabody actively campaigned on behalf of Indians and for park preservation in the second half of the nineteenth century (Richardson [1986] 1996: 32–33).

Though they were sometimes critical of Transcendentalism, Nathaniel Hawthorne and Herman Melville sided with Transcendentalists in their critique of industrialization. Hawthorne spoofed industrialism in "The Celestial Railroad," while Melville depicted the leisurely life of the bachelors and the degradation of the female factory workers in "The Paradise of Bachelors and the Tartarus of Maids" in 1855 (Alves 2005b: 1004–1006; Baker 2005: 1032–1033; Hawthorne [1845] 1860: 1–10; Melville 1855: 671–678).

RALPH WALDO EMERSON: RURAL LIFESTYLE

Ralph Waldo Emerson was one of the earliest thinkers to begin writing about and urging Americans to leave the city and take up residence in the countryside. Born in 1803 in Boston, Emerson followed his father's footsteps and became a minister. He was also a poet, philosopher, social critic, and Transcendentalist who began writing about nature during the 1830s. A believer in gentle exercise, he was a lifelong rambler who was drawn to nature at a young age. Emerson was following a well-established tradition of sauntering popularized by the likes of Lewis and Clark, whose two-year expedition of more than five thousand miles required trekking much of the way. Audubon was also a well-known rambler. Emerson was twenty years old when his family moved from Boston to the rural Canterbury section of Roxbury in 1823. However, the family still lived close enough to Boston for him to walk to the city daily. At times he carried a hunting rifle as he rambled through the woods. The rural charms of Roxbury appealed to Emerson; he described it as "a picturesque wilderness of savin, barberry bush, catbrier, sumach, and rugged masses of pudding stone" (E. W. Emerson 1889: 29; Gilman et al. 1960–1982: 184; Richardson 1995: 45; D. C. Smith 1997: 3).

Emerson came from a modest background but inherited his first wife's (Ellen's) estate and earned enough money later on from speaking engagements to live very comfortably for much of his adult life. Emerson, who had an epiphany while visiting the Jardin de Plantes (the old King's Garden) in Paris in 1833, became interested in plant taxonomy, order in the natural world, the beauty of gardens, and pastoral settings. Following his visit to Jardin de Plantes, he began incorporating more ideas about the natural world in his writings. Emerson was also interested in rural life, the cultivated nature of European formal gardens, and in orchards such as the one he developed on his property in Concord. On leaving Europe, Emerson returned to Boston. After living there for several years, he left the hectic city behind for good and settled in Concord in 1835 with his second wife, Lydia Jackson. Emerson was familiar with Concord: he had lived there briefly with his grandparents when he was eleven years old. The newlyweds settled on a two-acre property that sloped toward Mill Brook (Emerson acquired more property in Concord later on). Emerson considered Concord and Bush (the name of his estate) a refuge from "the compliances and imitations of city society." He liked the "lukewarm milky dog-days of common village life." Emerson loved sauntering around Concord. He took daily walks in the woods around Walden Pond and went on longer hikes to Cape Cod, the Connecticut Valley, and Maine. These experiences provided the context in which Emerson wrote about the natural world and encouraged others to embrace a rural lifestyle. Emerson wrote one of his most influential pieces, *Nature*, in 1836 (Richardson 1995: 3–5, 138–142, 206–209, 283; quote on 208).[4]

HENRY DAVID THOREAU:

RUGGED INDIVIDUALISM AND SIMPLE LIVING

Thoreau was born in 1817 in Concord, Massachusetts, to a family of modest means. Though the family had once owned property in Boston and Concord, by the time Thoreau was an infant they had lost both because of indebtedness. Consequently, the family bounced from one rented home to another in Concord, Chelmsford, and Boston's South End during Thoreau's childhood. Thoreau was descended from French and Scottish immigrants, and protest and social criticism ran in his family: he was the grandson of Asa Dunbar, who in 1766 instigated the Butter Riot at Harvard College—the first recorded student protest in the United States. Thoreau graduated from Harvard in 1837. After college he taught at the Concord Academy with his brother until 1841, then for a time worked on and off at his father's trade—manufacturing lead pencils. Thoreau won critical acclaim for his inventions with the pencil (Bode [1947] 1982: 14–15; Buettner 2004: 14; Emerson 1862; Walter Harding 1992: 3–6, 11–13, 157–158, 177–178; Richardson [1986] 1996: 1–3, 28).

While Thoreau was away at college, Emerson purchased and settled in the Coolidge House (later renamed Bush), half a mile outside Concord, in 1835. The two met each other that year, and Emerson became Thoreau's mentor. Thoreau also met other writers and thinkers, such as Ellery Channing, Bronson Alcott, Margaret Fuller, and Nathaniel Hawthorne (all of whom lived in Concord at some point). In 1843 Thoreau left Ralph Waldo Emerson's house, where he had been living and working as a handyman since 1841, and moved to Staten Island to become a tutor to the three children of Judge William Emerson, Ralph Waldo's brother. Thoreau was also the family's gardener. While in New York he met Horace Greeley. Thoreau returned to Concord in 1844 (Bode [1947] 1982: 14–15, 19, 28–29; Walter Harding 1992: 60–61, 145–148; Richardson [1986] 1996: 14–15; 18–19, 23).

New York simultaneously fascinated and appalled Thoreau. Arriving by boat at a wharf near Castle Clinton (Battery Park), his first impression of the residents was that of "a confused jumble of heads and soiled coats, dangling from flesh-colored faces—all swaying to and fro, as by a sort of undertow" (Thoreau [1958] 1974: 99). He also wrote to Emerson, "Everything there disappoints me but the crowd." Sometime later he described his feelings about the city: "I don't like the city better, the more I see it, but worse" (Thoreau [1958] 1974: 101). Nonetheless, he was fascinated enough by the city to leave rural Staten Island and make the trip to Manhattan four or five times in the first month he was there (Richardson [1986] 1996: 125–127).

Thoreau, one of America's earliest and most fervent Transcendentalists, believed in solitude and simple living (Bode [1947] 1982: 1–27; D. C. Smith 1997: 1–5; A. I. Tauber 2001: 1–22). On returning to Concord, he expressed this in his desire to live alone at Walden Pond, about a mile from Concord, to experience the workings of nature. Thoreau wrote, "I want to go soon and live away by the pond where I shall hear only the wind whispering among the reeds—It will be a success if I shall have left myself behind." When asked why he wanted to live in solitude, Thoreau replied, "Will it not be employment enough to watch the progress of the seasons?" (Thoreau [1906] 1962: December 24, 1841).

Lacking the financial wherewithal to realize his dream, Thoreau had bided his time. He jumped at the opportunity to live at Walden Pond when Emerson purchased property there in October 1844. The next spring Thoreau put up a one-room cabin on the fourteen or fifteen acres of land Emerson had bought. He moved into his new abode on July 4, 1845, and remained there until 1847. Though Thoreau's retreat to Walden is often portrayed as a solitary one, he wasn't entirely alone: poor whites and former slaves also lived in cabins around the pond. From Walden Thoreau sauntered long distances, studied plants, farmed two and a half acres, and wrote about nature. He visited town regularly, and friends such as Emerson, Hawthorne, and the Alcotts made frequent visits to his cabin. With Horace Greeley's help, Thoreau published *The Maine Woods* in 1848. *A Week on the Concord and Merrimack Rivers* was published in 1849 and *Walden* in 1854 (Bode [1947] 1982: 21–33; Walter Harding 1992: 3, 151–152, 180–188; Richardson [1986] 1996: 101–104, 147–149, 151; Thoreau 1893). Thoreau's retreat to Walden can be understood as three kinds of reform: (1) a reform of the individual through more in-depth reflection and realization of self, (2) a reform of social norms through ascetic living and communion with nature, and (3) achieving self-sufficiency through farming.

DOWNING, GENTILITY, AND RURAL CHARMS

Like Thoreau and Emerson, Andrew Jackson Downing spent his time between the city and the ruralized suburbs. A leading advocate of tasteful and genteel rural living, Downing was born in 1815 in Newburgh, about sixty miles north of Manhattan. His father was a prosperous wheelwright, nursery man, and real estate investor. Downing attended exclusive boarding schools, where he learned the craft of drawing. He did not want to take over his father's nursery; he began running that business in 1837, but by then he had cultivated wealthy friends among New York's elite, and a year later he married Caroline Elizabeth DeWint, daughter of a wealthy land speculator and investor in rail and ferry lines. The couple built an elegant Gothic revival home on land donated by Downing's parents and with financing from Caroline's father. Downing used his own estate to demonstrate the landscaping techniques he wanted his clients and others to emulate (D. Hayden 2003: 26, 34; Schuyler 1996).

Downing, too, urged people to leave the cities and move to the countryside. He advocated rural living because he thought the rural lifestyle would combat the excitements and anxieties that accompany urban living. His 1841 publication, *A Treatise in the Theory and Practice of Landscape Gardening*, helped to establish him as the country's premier landscape architect. Though Downing's *Treatise* was heavily influenced by J. C. Loudon's *The Suburban Gardener, and Villa Companion*, the American gentry viewed Downing's work as a fresh way to look at and interact with rural American landscapes. Downing was savvy enough to speak directly to elites trying to emulate and cultivate taste and style at their rural residences. He used the book to demonstrate how to convert a farm into an elegant country estate. Downing suggested using ample lawns, curving driveways, and strategically placed trees and bushes in the front of the property. He urged estate owners to cultivate orchards in the rear of their property. Downing also suggested that estate owners remodel their farmhouses to make them look more elegant. He recommended accentuating the roof-lines and chimneys and adding Gothic elements and porches. To facilitate the transformation of rough-and-tumble farms into estates, Downing developed a nursery and mail-order business to ship plants to aspiring gentleman farm-ers and gardeners all over the country. He also urged rural property owners to make farm life more appealing. He believed that a more comfortable home life would encourage men to settle down and reduce the urge to migrate. Eventu-ally Downing had to sell his nursery, as he did not have the financial resources to keep up his Hudson River estate. In the end, the bickering and legal tug-of-war between him and his father-in-law forced him to sell the nursery to pay off his debts (Beveridge and Schuyler 1983; Bryant 1844; Downing 1848, [1841] 1860; D. Hayden 2003: 26–27, 34; Jackson and Dunbar 2002: 173; Loudon 1838; Roper 1973; Schuyler 1996: 88).

JOHN MUIR: MOUNTAIN MAN AND EXTREME ADVENTURER

John Muir was a second-wave Transcendentalist who embraced Thoreau's ideas and pushed the boundaries much further than Thoreau or any of the original Transcendentalists ever did. While the first-generation Transcendentalists ex-perimented with establishing farms and communes and living in solitude, John Muir was trying his utmost to escape the rigors of pioneer farming and the bru-tality of his father, a relentless taskmaster and zealous Christian. Muir believed in instinct and intuition as necessary components of understanding nature. He also believed in the connection between nature and spirituality. Muir decided to practice, on a more elaborate scale than Thoreau attempted, the idea of living on the bare essentials in nature (see, for example, Muir [1911a] 1972, 1913, 1916; Nash 1982: 122–140).

Born in Scotland in 1838, John Muir migrated to the United States in 1849. At Fountain Lake farm northeast of Portage, Wisconsin, Muir lived very close to the Winnebago and Menominee Indians. When the Muirs established Fountain Lake, their property was on the frontier; their closest white neighbor was four miles away, but they were within a mile of a well-used Native American trail. Even before leaving Scotland Muir had read about Native Americans and had learned to fear them (Muir 1908a: 32; J. Stewart 1975: 15). Once in America, Muir was curious about the Native Americans he encountered but wary of them (Fleck 1985: 85). Muir also had an intense curiosity about the natural world around the family's farm. He noted that they didn't often see deer, though their tracks were evident (Muir 1913: 169–170).

Muir left home in 1860 to display his inventions at the Wisconsin State Fair; he won prizes and some acclaim there. Four months after the fair he enrolled at the University of Wisconsin. He was a student in his mid-twenties during the Civil War. He was worried he might be drafted, and his family kept him apprised of local news of the draft and the war. He lived in a part of Wisconsin filled with recent immigrants, many of whom had left Europe to escape famines. Like many others around him, Muir did not see himself as an American or feel any strong desire to participate in the war (Muir 1862; Rhodes 2004: 38).[5] He didn't even become an American citizen until April 1903, when he was sixty-five years old, and then only because he was about to travel around the world and needed a passport (Fox 1981: 42; Muir 1903).[6] Instead of taking part in the Civil War, in 1863 Muir left the university and went to the Wisconsin Dells and Iowa. The next year he went to Canada to "botanize" (Fox 1981: 41–47, 92–114; Muir 1863; 1908b: 242–243; Ross 1977: 13; Turner 1985: 91–120; Wolfe 1945: 81).

Muir believed there was unity in nature and that unity revealed the nature of God. Within a year of returning to the United States, Muir—then twenty-nine years old—embarked on a thousand-mile walk from Indianapolis to Florida. The walk helped him to understand the meaning of nature, the place of humans in nature, and his moral obligations to the environment. It was on this walk that Muir took the first steps toward developing his own unique ideas about how people could and should relate to nature. His philosophy of nature and wilderness was influenced by Emerson, Thoreau, George Perkins Marsh,

Charles Darwin, Swiss-born naturalist and glaciologist and Harvard professor Louis Agassiz, and the German naturalist and explorer Alexander von Humboldt. In addition, Ezra Slocum Carr, a professor at the University of Wisconsin, and his wife, Jeanne Carr, were very influential in Muir's life and understanding of nature (Cohen 1984: 20, 172; H. F. Smith 1965: 27; Wolfe 1945: 76, 82–83). Although Muir was strongly influenced by Thoreau and Emerson, his brand of nature philosophy differed substantially from each of these men's. For instance, Muir incorporated Darwinism into his philosophy—a dimension missing from the philosophies of Thoreau and Emerson (Agassiz 1887; Fleck 1985; Oelschlaeger 1991; Sachs 2006; H. F. Smith 1965: 27–28).

Muir made it all the way to Cuba, then sailed back to New York. From there he sailed to California, arriving in San Francisco in 1868. Once in San Francisco, he immediately headed for Yosemite, spent several weeks there, then returned to the lowlands, where he did odd jobs for the rest of the year. In his spare time he undertook geological and botanical studies. He worked as a sheep hand in the Sierra Nevadas for three summers (Muir 1911a, 1916, 1938; Teale 1954). After spending several years studying the flora, fauna, and peaks of the Sierras and traveling across the West, Muir went farther afield. Shortly after his engagement to a well-to-do doctor's daughter, Louisa Strenzel of Martinez, California, he set out on his first voyage to Alaska. He returned shortly before the wedding but left for another voyage shortly after the nuptials, leaving his pregnant wife at home. He did not return until after the birth of his first daughter. He made several voyages to Alaska between 1879 and 1899. Muir managed the Strenzels' thriving orchard and turned it into a profitable business in between trips to Alaska and the Sierras. By the end of the nineteenth century, he had emerged as one of the nation's leading ecologists and experts on the nation's western landscapes. He became influential in environmental policy making, was appointed to presidential commissions, and was invited to travel on prestigious scientific expeditions (Muir 1909a, 1911b, 1915, 1917).

Craving More Excitement

Eventually elite men began to tire of the rural suburbs, their country estates, downtown mansions, and the landscaped city parks. By the time Central Park was completed in 1876, prosperous men were bored with slow trots around the park and hunting in the limited confines of their private estates. To make matters worse, it was becoming more difficult to find open spaces to hold horse races or take hounds hunting in and around the cities. A number of foxhunts were established in locales close to the big cities, and Theodore Roosevelt explained that men enjoyed an afternoon's ride across the country chasing foxes. As Roosevelt saw it, "A single ride across the country . . . will yield more exercise, fun, and excitement than can be got out of a week's decorous and dull riding in the park [Central Park]" (Roosevelt [1893] 1996: 686–687).

Because they craved more challenging recreational opportunities, genteel urban men found the frontier enticing. It emerged as the perfect place for silk-stocking-clad men of wealth and power to explore and experiment with the pioneer lifestyle. The frontier was fascinating because though the likelihood of engaging in combat with Native Americans was vastly diminished, the possibility that such encounters might occur added a sense of excitement and danger to the trips that intrigued the explorers. As a result, their explorations were quasi-military operations. Stories were also circulated among easterners that Indians were fearful of whites; this emboldened would-be explorers to think that if they did encounter Native Americans they would have an advantage. In addition, the Civil War was over, and large herds of animals still roamed the West. In the post–Civil War era, it became increasingly common for men to demonstrate their masculinity, wealth, and upper-class status by undertaking conquest-oriented outdoor activities such as hunting big game in the West. It was also fashionable to adorn one's home with the trophies: Roosevelt's home, Sagamore, was crowded with heads, hides, and antlers from his hunting trips. Guests were frequently regaled with tales recounting how the skin rugs on the floor or the stuffed animals over the mantelpiece got to their final resting place (Brands 1997: viii; P. Burroughs 1995: xiii). Furthermore, some elite men, such as Roosevelt, fellow Harvard grad Caspar Whitney, and George Bird Grinnell, took up ranching in the West (Roosevelt [1893] 1996: 639).

It was in this spirit that increasing numbers of heavily armed elite white men headed west for new adventures. In 1828, Josiah Gregg described how much he and his fellow travelers feared Native Americans. Referring to the indigenous peoples as "savages," Gregg wrote that adventurers might "be set upon by marauding Indians, but if well armed and of resolute spirit" one could travel unmolested. Consequently, he urged adventure seekers and traders not to explore the prairies without "a sufficient supply of arms" (Gregg 1851: 26–28). Likewise wary of Native Americans, renowned writer Washington Irving described how his party prepared to sleep at night: he noted that "as the twilight thickened into night, the sentinels were marched forth to the stations around the camp, an indispensible precaution" (Irving 1835: 59–60; see also Irving 1873). Audubon expressed similar sentiments. He wrote about "the constantly impending danger of being murdered, while asleep in their encampments, by the prowling and ruthless Indians" (Audubon 1832: 291).

Samuel Bowles, editor of the *Springfield Republican* (Massachusetts), recounts similar fears among members of his party in 1865 and 1866, when he traveled with a group of men to the Sierra Nevadas and the Pacific Northwest. Bowles describes how fearful and apprehensive of Native tribes he and others in his party were as they rode across the Plains. He reports being forced to hide in "dreary cabins" until they could replace their stolen horses and get "soldierly protection" to continue the journey (Bowles 1869: 151–175). Other travelers obtained military protection before embarking on their trips. For instance, Gustavus Doane noted in his account of the 1870 Yellowstone expedition that they were well armed and accompanied by soldiers. There were one hundred rounds of ammunition per man, and the party was accompanied by the Second Cavalry. However, Doane was of the opinion that Indians feared whites and that his party was safe. He wrote that members of the Snake tribe "ran from the sight of a white man or from any other tribe of Indians" (Doane 1871: 1, 8, 26).

With reports like these filtering out, parties of easterners made sure they were armed and had military escorts when they embarked on their adventures. One group of men from New York's sports clubs left Grand Central Depot in September 1871. The group, composed of the "fastest society set," was headed for Fort McPherson, Nebraska, to hunt buffalo. The supply train awaiting them in Nebraska consisted of sixteen wagons filled with tents, food, ice, wine, and champagne. In addition, three hundred troops from the Fifth Cavalry traveled with the group to protect them from the Native American tribes these wealthy easterners feared. William "Buffalo Bill" Cody also awaited them. The New Yorkers hunted bison with Buffalo Bill by day and dined on the meat and fine spirits around the campfire by night. They were so enamored by Buffalo Bill that they invited him to New York for a six-week stay. Treating him as a trophy as well as a human curiosity, they feted and paraded him from one society party to another. Born in Iowa in 1846 as William Coyle, Cody had gained notoriety among New York's elite even before his visit: New Yorkers became curious about him when Ned Buntline featured him in an 1869 novel. At the time Buntline's book was published, Cody was a twenty-three-year-old working-class market hunter who grew famous because of the enormous number of buffalo he killed each year. Consequently, he was lionized by New York's gentry, and his visit and party-hopping stimulated much interest and excitement (Buntline [1869] 1974; Burrows and Wallace 1999: 955; Library of Congress 2004).

As later discussions show, many American luminaries who became conservationists and preservationists or played prominent roles in protecting nature—

including William Cullen Bryant, Ralph Waldo Emerson, Frederick Law Olmsted, Albert Bierstadt, George Catlin, John Muir, Theodore Roosevelt, George Bird Grinnell, and John James Audubon—traveled to the West to explore the natural wonders, live, work, or paint the landscape. These men were following a well-worn path blazed by other early naturalists and wilderness explorers, such as the botanist John Josselyn, who climbed Mount Washington in 1663 (Josselyn [1672] 1865: 56), and William Byrd II, who admired the Appalachian Mountains as he surveyed the boundaries of Virginia and North Carolina in 1728 (Byrd 1901). The botanist William Bartram traveled about five thousand miles in the Southeast between 1773 and 1777 (Bartram 1958: 212–213). Harvard graduate Thaddeus Mason Harris explored the upper reaches of the Ohio Valley in 1803 (T. M. Harris 1805: 14, 21, 60). A New Hampshire lawyer named Estwick Evans embarked on a four-thousand-mile "pedestrious tour" to the West in 1818. According to Estwick, he set out on his tour in the winter to "experience the *pleasure* of suffering and the *novelty* of danger" (E. Evans 1819). Thomas Cole traveled in and painted the Catskills in the 1820s (Nathan 1940: 24–62). Washington Irving longed to see buffalo, and did so in 1832 on a trip to Kansas and Oklahoma. New York writer and editor Charles Hoffman journeyed through the Mississippi Valley in 1833 (Hoffman 1835), and the editor and landscape painter Charles Lanman explored Maine and Minnesota in the 1830s (Lanman 1847: 105–171). Benjamin Bonneville explored the Rocky Mountains in the 1830s, and Josiah Gregg explored the Santa Fe area in 1839 (Gregg 1851: 2: 156–158). Boston Brahmin and Harvard graduate Francis Parkman explored New England and Canada. He described his motive for taking an excursion to the White Mountains in 1841 as follows: "My chief object in coming so far was merely to have a taste of the half-savage kind of life . . . and to see the wilderness where it was as yet uninvaded by the hand of man" (Parkman 1947: 31; see also Nash 1982: 44–83, 141–160, for descriptions of adventures).

The remainder of this section focuses on three additional explorers, adventurers, sportsmen, and environmental activists—George Bird Grinnell, Theodore Roosevelt, and Gifford Pinchot. Their travels in the West in the second half of the nineteenth century illustrate how men with inherited wealth related to nature and the environment. Those travels also influenced their subsequent environmental activism.

GEORGE BIRD GRINNELL

Grinnell, born in Brooklyn to a wealthy Huguenot family in 1849, was the son of a successful textile merchant and investment banker. Like other prosperous New Yorkers, the Grinnells lived in several locations before building their home in Upper Manhattan. They lived on Twenty-First Street in the mid-1850s and took sleigh rides in Central Park soon after construction began on it (Reiger 1972: 8). Grinnell remembered the park as a "wilderness of rocks and pasture land" when he first began visiting it. Grinnell believed that his father moved from Lower Manhattan to safeguard the health of his five children. At the time the Grinnells moved from Lower Manhattan, poor European immigrants were flooding into nearby slum areas such as Five Points. In response, wealthy residents around Bowling Green, the Battery, and other prestigious neighborhoods began moving to exclusive Midtown and Uptown addresses. The Grinnells also moved as epidemic outbreaks occurred, crime increased, and rioting became commonplace in Lower Manhattan. After leaving Lower Manhattan, the Grinnells lived briefly in Weehawken, New Jersey, on the edge of the Palisades. In Weehawken Grinnell learned to ride the horse his father kept in a pasture behind the house (Grinnell 1915: 4).[7]

When he was eight, Grinnell and his family moved to Audubon Park (John James Audubon's property, about six miles from Lower Manhattan). By this time the Audubons had built three houses on their property. Because of recurring financial problems, they rented out the houses and sold off some of their land. As newcomers moved into the neighborhood, Minniesland and the surrounding properties became known as Audubon Park. After leasing one of the houses, the Grinnells purchased some of the land and built a large Victorian home, the Hemlocks, on their property overlooking the Hudson River. Grinnell, who moved to Audubon Park six years after John James Audubon died, was tutored by his widow, Lucy, who ran a small school to help meet expenses. At Audubon's home Grinnell was exposed to his illustrations and vast collection of trophies. However, Grinnell first came in contact with trophy collections at his grandfather's house in Greenfield, Massachusetts, when he spent his summers there. Grinnell's uncle, Thomas, who was in his twenties, hunted, collected, and preserved the animals at his grandfather's house. Among his collection was said to have been the last wild turkey killed on Mount Tom (Massachusetts) in 1849. Thomas filled Grinnell's head with stories of hunting and fishing adventures. Grinnell was captivated and began hunting, collecting, and mounting birds by the time he was eleven or twelve years old; he became an expert taxidermist. From the roof of his house, he shot and killed passenger pigeons as they flew overhead. He, Audubon's grandsons, and other boys living in Audubon Park also hunted in the nearby woods and swamps, where they shot many birds. The boys also went camping and hunting in the Palisades (P. Burroughs 1995: xvii–xviii; Fox 1981: 151–152; Grinnell 1927; Reiger 1972: 6–9, 11, 17–22, 57; Spady 2007).[8]

Despite his poor academic performance in college and his suspension for hazing, Grinnell was able to join Professor Othniel C. Marsh, a renowned paleontologist, on a five-month fossil-collecting trip to Nebraska, Utah, and Wyoming right after graduating from Yale in 1870. Well-known men like John Reed Nicholson, the chancellor of Delaware; James W. Wadsworth, a New York Congressman; and Eli Whitney, inventor of the cotton gin, were also on the expedition. Sixteen cavalry and two Pawnee scouts escorted the twelve expedition members. The men on the expedition each carried a Henry repeating rifle, a pistol, cartridges, and a Bowie knife. The fear of being attacked by Native American tribes led expedition members to stop in what is now downtown Omaha, Nebraska, set up targets and practice shooting their rifles before proceeding further (P. Burroughs 1995: xix–xxii; Punke 2009; Reiger 1972: 29–30, 32).

Grinnell met Buffalo Bill, whom he admired. Grinnell described Bill Cody, who accompanied the expedition part of the way, as "a tall, well-built, handsome man who wore his blonde hair long and was a striking figure; above all on horseback . . . his splendid physique made very noticeable." Grinnell also noted that "shooting from the ground with a rifle, Cody was an ordinary shot . . . but he was the finest horseback rifle shot ever known." He was "skill[ed] in killing buffalo on the run" (Grinnell n.d.; see also Reiger 1972: 32, 35). By the time Grinnell met Buffalo Bill, his mystique was so great that for an eastern tenderfoot like Grinnell, simply being in Cody's company must have been a thrill.

While on the expedition, Grinnell hunted elk traveling in herds of between 200 and 250 but did not succeed in killing any. Though Grinnell was developing a fascination with Native American culture (a fascination that led him to study and write about Indians later on), he openly expressed his fear of being attacked by indigenous people while on the expedition. The expedition members collected more than a hundred species of extinct vertebrates hitherto unknown to scientists (Reiger 1972: 37–71).

Grinnell worked in his father's firm when he returned to New York in late 1870, but he longed to return to the West. He considered the buffalo hunt the crowning glory of the western adventure and wanted to experience it, so he joined another expedition in 1872 for a buffalo hunt in southern Nebraska. The young men who went on the hunt rode to the West in style on luxury train cars. Grinnell was able to secure free passes for the train ride. This time Grinnell's party did ride into an ambush, but neither the Native Americans nor the ambushed hunters attacked (P. Burroughs 1995: xxii; Fox 1981: 151–152; Reiger 1972: 1–4, 58, 80).[9]

Grinnell was a hunter who exalted in the pursuit of game. He hunted elk in Nebraska in 1873 and described the thrill of hunting in the West for readers in *Forest and Stream*. He was just as thrilled with killing the first elk as he was with his first buffalo kill. However, Grinnell's admiration for the countryside and excitement about the hunt was tempered by his fear of Native Americans. He wrote, "We were not without apprehensions that we might encounter some small band . . . but we wanted game more than we feared the Indians, and therefore we decided to take the risk" (Grinnell 1873a: 116).

Grinnell rode with Custer in the Black Hills in 1874 when gold was discovered there. At the time Grinnell was pursuing a doctorate at Yale; he went on the expedition to collect fossils. Grinnell was also on a reconnaissance mission with Captain William Ludlow and the Army Corps of Engineers as they mounted an expedition into Yellowstone in 1875. When the Ludlow Expedition got to Yellowstone, the group saw animals being slaughtered in the park, trees being felled, and anything of value being removed from the park (P. Burroughs 1995: xxii; Fox 1981: 151–152; Reiger 1972: 80–81, 100, 109, 117–118).

Grinnell was appalled at what he saw and wrote a letter of protest that was inserted in the official report of the expedition. In the letter Grinnell criticized the market hunters for killing game for the sole purpose of taking and selling their hides. Grinnell also noted that big game were being killed without regard for their age, gender, or the time of year. He mentioned that the females were being killed in the spring just before giving birth to the young. He estimated that about three thousand elk were killed during the winter of 1874–75, and only their hides were taken. Though there were game laws in the western states, these were inadequate to stop the slaughter. Grinnell objected neither to sport and trophy hunting nor to pot hunting; however, he was quite opposed to market hunting because he believed that the market hunters were the most wasteful and were responsible for the decimation of the herds (Grinnell 1876: 61; Reiger 1972: 118–119). Though Grinnell was developing a consciousness about the indiscriminate killing of animals, he still enjoyed being a sport hunter: in the summer of 1876 he reported riding, botanizing, and killing "a good many woodcock[s]" on his family's property in Milford, Connecticut (Grinnell 1915: 77).

Grinnell returned to the West in 1878, 1879, and 1881. He went on fossil collecting and hunting trips in the Rockies. Though Grinnell despised market hunters, he worked on Buffalo Bill's ranch in western Nebraska for a while. In 1883, Grinnell decided to become a gentleman rancher. That year he purchased a 1,100-acre ranch in the Shirley Basin in southeastern Wyoming—one of his old hunting haunts that was not yet overrun by homesteaders and prospectors. The ranch had about three thousand sheep on it when Grinnell bought it. After losing about a third of the sheep in the first year alone (at an elevation of about 7,500 feet it was difficult to raise animals on it), Grinnell sold the remainder of them the second year and invested in horses and cattle. Despite pouring vast sums of money into the ranch, Grinnell took little interest in actual ranching activities. From his base at the ranch, he explored the remaining frontier, delighting in the solitude and exploring places where other whites had not been before. Grinnell explored the area that later became Glacier National Park and gave the area many of the Anglo names it boasts. Grinnell sought out the remote areas because he thought the charm and independence was expunged from settled locales (Reiger 1972: 130–133, 150–151; [1975] 2001: 148–149).

Grinnell didn't marry until he was fifty-three years old. In 1902 he married twenty-seven-year-old Elizabeth Kirby Curtis. Elizabeth accompanied Grinnell on his explorations and documentation of the Cheyennes in Montana and Oklahoma. She was the official photographer for the trips, while Julia Tuell was her assistant. Some of Curtis's and Tuell's photographs—housed in the Smithsonian Museum collection—depict Native American women in the environment doing everyday chores (Grinnell 1923; Nebraska State Historical Society 2010; Smithsonian Institution Research 2010).

THEODORE ROOSEVELT

Like Grinnell, Theodore Roosevelt was a wealthy New Yorker who longed for the West. In 1858 Roosevelt was born in New York into a prominent Dutch family. His grandfather, Cornelius Van Schaack Roosevelt, one of New York's ten millionaires in 1868, made his fortune in real estate and merchandising plate glass. As a child, Theodore Roosevelt lived in a brownstone in Lower Manhattan on East Twentieth Street among other elites. He played in the Gramercy Park–Madison Square neighborhood. Theodore Roosevelt was introduced to conservation politics at an early age. His uncle, Robert Roosevelt, was very active in efforts to preserve the shad runs on the Hudson and a leader of the pioneering New York Sportsmen's Club (Auchincloss 2001: 9; Brands 1997: 5, 9, 16).

Like other wealthy families, the Roosevelts spent time in Europe. It was during an 1869 excursion that Roosevelt, then eleven years old, was introduced to the lifestyle of strenuous and vigorous activities. He was a frail, sickly asthmatic boy with poor eyesight; nevertheless, whenever he was healthy enough, he hiked in the Alps. Roosevelt was excited by his physical accomplishments and that awakened in him an interest in using outdoor activities to test the limits of his capabilities. He went camping with friends in Maine at age fourteen, learned to shoot, and took up boxing (Brands 1997: 25–32).

As he embraced the strenuous lifestyle, he also took an interest in birds. He spent long hours exploring the woods and fields, fishing, and hunting. From the time he received his first gun at age fourteen, he began chasing and shooting wild animals. He also learned how to preserve and stuff the specimens he killed. While on a family trip to Egypt in the 1870s, Roosevelt found the time to go hunting. A highlight of the trip was meeting Ralph Waldo Emerson, who was also touring Egypt at the same time. Roosevelt also went hunting for birds, rabbits, and jackals while in Syria. When the family stopped off in Dresden, Roosevelt went hunting for local birds and small animals as often as he could (Brands 1997: 31–40).

Like other New York patricians, the Roosevelts moved uptown to West Fifty-Seventh Street in the early 1870s. Roosevelt explored, hiked, rode, and skated in Central Park, which was located only two blocks from his house. When Roosevelt entered Harvard University in 1876, he adorned his room with his stuffed birds. While his outdoor activities were somewhat constrained during the school year, in the summers Roosevelt and his well-heeled friends (like the Minots) explored the Adirondacks and the Maine woods. Roosevelt spent the summer of 1878 in Maine. There he and a guide, Bill Sewall, canoed, tramped through the woods, went hunting and fishing and swimming, chopped wood, and skinned and cooked what they caught. They lived off the land. They slept under the pines and got soaked by rain and chilled to the bones by the winds. Roosevelt was so delighted by the trip that he returned to Maine the following spring (Brands 1997: 31–32, 34–36, 40).

Roosevelt went on his first hunting trip to the American West in 1880, after his graduation from Harvard and right before his impending nuptials to Alice Lee. He also departed for this trip right after surviving a bout of cholera. He and his brother, Elliott, camped and hunted for six weeks in Illinois, Iowa, and Minnesota. In 1883, he traveled further afield, to the Dakotas, to hunt buffalo and antelopes (Ambrose 1996: xiii; Brands 1997: 105–107; Roosevelt [1885] 1996: 34–35). The quest for grand trophies piqued Roosevelt's interest. When Roosevelt had trouble finding any buffalo to hunt, he sent a letter to his pregnant wife back in New York lamenting, "I haven't killed anything, and am afraid the hall [in their new Oyster Bay, Long Island, home] will have to go without horns for this trip at least." Notwithstanding his disappointment with the hunting, Roosevelt decided that he wanted to become a cattle rancher and promptly wrote a check for fourteen thousand dollars to begin a ranching operation. He bought Chimney Butte ranch located near Medora (on the Little Missouri River running through the Badlands). Before the end of his trip his luck changed, and he successfully hunted and killed a buffalo. He scribbled a quick note to his wife: "Hurrah! The luck has turned at last. I will bring you home the head of a great buffalo bull" (quoted in Brands 1997: 151, 154–158). Roosevelt's wife died on Valentine's Day 1884, shortly after giving birth to a girl named Alice (Roosevelt's mother died earlier that same day). Within months of his wife's and mother's deaths and the birth of his daughter, Roosevelt returned to Chimney Butte to manage the ranch, acquire a second (Elk Horn), and hunt and shoot his first grizzly. The ranches were costly, and by the end of 1886, he had spent about eighty thousand dollars on them (Brands 1997: 172–175, 180–181, 205).

Roosevelt soon found out that cattle ranchers faced a common problem. All, including Roosevelt, grazed their cattle on public lands on a first-come-first-serve basis and were keenly aware of the potential for overgrazing, or for one person to monopolize the common resources to the detriment of the others. Soon after Roosevelt acquired the Chimney Butte and Elk Horn ranches, he added about a thousand head of cattle, increasing his herd more than fivefold. This led a local rancher to hire a reputed hit man named Paddock to try to scare Roosevelt off the range and away from his ranches. One day Paddock and a group of ruffians showed up at Roosevelt's ranch unannounced and demanded that Roosevelt stop grazing his cattle on the range or pay the rancher who claimed he owned the grazing rights to the range. They also urged Roosevelt's ranch hands to tell their boss (who was not around when Paddock showed up) to get out of town. Paddock allegedly bragged about wanting to shoot the New Yorker at the first opportunity. Like Audubon, Roosevelt did not back down from threats. On hearing Paddock's message, Roosevelt loaded his guns and rode over to Paddock's place. There he announced he was ready for the shooting to start. Paddock backed off, claiming that he had been misquoted (Brands 1997: 183, 186).

However, the Paddock incident made Roosevelt more aware of the need to organize the local cattlemen. When Roosevelt increased the size of his herd, local ranchers feared that Roosevelt might use more than his fair share of the common resources. That provoked Paddock's visit. Realizing this, Roosevelt decided to form a stockmen's association in the Little Missouri region to deal with issues of overgrazing, governance of the commons, and other local concerns. He spent several weeks riding from ranch to ranch recruiting potential members. In December, Roosevelt called to order the first meeting of the Little Missouri Stockmen's Association. Roosevelt was selected as the association's president and charged with writing its constitution. The group focused on the theft of cattle, diseases, branding strays, and the importation of new cattle into the region (Brands 1997: 186).

When he was not organizing cattlemen, Roosevelt continued to enjoy hunting. He wrote to Henry Cabot Lodge (one of his Harvard professors), "I am very fond of hunting and there are few sensations I prefer to that of galloping over these rolling, limitless prairies, rifle in hand" (as quoted in Ambrose 1996: xiv). Roosevelt experienced a "keen delight" in "hunting in lonely lands" feeling "the joy of a horse well ridden and the rifle well held . . . crowned at the end with triumph" (Roosevelt [1893] 1996: 329–330). Roosevelt, once a sickly boy, was obsessed with manliness, which he felt hunting promoted. He wrote that the chase "is among the best of all national pastimes; it cultivates that vigorous manliness, for the lack of which in a nation, as in an individual, the possession of no other qualities can possibly atone" (Roosevelt [1893] 1996: 329).

Other early environmental activists agreed with Roosevelt. For instance, George Perkins Marsh had expressed a similar sentiment about the chase decades earlier. Marsh wrote, "The chase is a healthful and invigorating recreation, and its effects on the character of the sportsman, the hardy physical habits . . . the courage and self-reliance, the half-military spirit . . . are important elements of prosperity and strength in the bodily and mental constitution of a people" (Marsh 1857: 8–9). Audubon too thought a strenuous frontier life and hunting brought out manly qualities that effete eastern gentlemen should embrace (Audubon 1999: 62–63). Washington Irving argued, "We send our youth abroad to grow luxurious and effeminate in Europe: it appears to me that a previous tour of the prairies would be more likely to produce that manliness, simplicity, and self-dependence" that the nation needs (Irving 1835: 55–56).

Roosevelt idealized the life of the gentleman rancher as "the pleasantest and healthiest life in America" (Roosevelt [1885] 1996: 26). He bragged about the large numbers of animals he killed and his expertise in doing so (Roosevelt [1885] 1996: 42). Despite his growing understanding of conservation practices, Roosevelt was not averse to hunting and killing species nearing extinction. In fact, sport hunters of his ilk took some pleasure in bagging a trophy of the last living specimen of a particular game animal. Roosevelt bragged, "I killed an elk near my ranch; probably the last of his race that will ever be found in our neighborhood" (Roosevelt [1885] 1996: 286). Roosevelt also hunted bison assiduously as the last herds roamed the Plains (Roosevelt [1893] 1996: 567–572). Industrialist John M. Phillips of Pittsburgh behaved similarly. While hunting with his friend Hiram Frost in Elk County, Pennsylvania, Phillips and Frost began tracking a deer. They tracked it for two days and finally came upon a buck the morning of the third day. On killing the deer Phillips said to his friend, "I fear I have killed the last deer in Pennsylvania" (quoted in Warren 1997: 48).

Roosevelt shared Grinnell's distaste for market hunters. However, he also opposed those who hunted solely for the mere sport of it. In addition to bringing out his manliness, Roosevelt hunted to put food on the table. He and his camping buddies and ranch hands ate most of the animals they hunted and killed (Ambrose 1996: xix). He considered life on the frontier analogous to life in the wilderness. Roosevelt wrote, "For a number of years much of my life was spent either in the wilderness or on the borders of the settled country." He lionized the "free, self-reliant, adventurous life, with its rugged and stalwart democracy; the wild surroundings, the grand beauty of the scenery, the chance to study the ways and habits of the woodland creatures—all these unite to give the career of the wilderness hunter its peculiar charm" (Roosevelt [1893] 1996: 329).

Roosevelt also admired frontiersmen such as Daniel Boone and Davy Crockett. He admired their ability to capture, privatize, and develop the land. He argued, "Where they [Boone and his fellow hunters] pitched their camps and built their log huts or stockaded hamlets, towns grew up, and men who were tillers of the soil, not mere wilderness wanderers, thronged in to take and hold the land" (Roosevelt [1893] 1996: 336). Roosevelt held Boone in high regard because he was an Indian fighter. Roosevelt saw Boone as the ideal hunter and trekker. He thought that Boone was a true pioneer and stood at the head of that class of Indian fighters, game-hunters, forest-fellers, and backwoods farmers who facilitated westward expansion. Roosevelt also saw Boone as "self-reliant, fearless, and possessed of great bodily strength and hardihood" (Roosevelt [1891] 2000: 33–34). Roosevelt held frontier men in high esteem because he considered their lifestyle an affirmation of manhood as well as an expression of primitivism and simple living—the antithesis of industrialism (Roosevelt [1888] 2000: 6). Roosevelt also admired Andrew Jackson, whom he considered the "greatest of all the backwoods leaders" because of the war he waged against the Creeks (Roosevelt [1893] 1996: 337).

Roosevelt admired frontier men's ability to take matters into their own hands and control their destiny. Conversely, he expressed his disdain for the men who did not (Roosevelt [1888] 2000: 55–56). As the Paddock incident illustrates, Roosevelt did not allow anyone to challenge his authority. In an incident that mirrored Audubon's response to river piracy, Roosevelt responded swiftly and decisively when his boat was stolen by three men during the frigid winter of 1886–87. Roosevelt's boat was the only one on the river at the time; therefore, determined to find his boat and bring the thieves to justice, Roosevelt and his ranch hands built a flat-bottomed scow and rowed it downriver for three days, until they caught up with the robbers. Roosevelt recovered his boat, captured the thieves, and took them back to the sheriff's office, where they were placed into custody. Roosevelt, who traveled about three hundred miles to catch the thieves, also collected a fee of about fifty dollars for the arrests (Roosevelt [1888] 2000: 111–128).

Unlike early nature protectors like George Perkins Marsh and John Muir, who saw animals as creatures with intrinsic worth, Roosevelt saw some animals as dangerous or noxious and, like the New Englanders who advocated eradicating birds they viewed as pests, Roosevelt felt that it was lawful to shoot animals like the bear, cougar, or wolf. He thought animals could be killed when their death benefited humans—for instance, when they could be consumed or used as trophies (Ambrose 1996: xx; Judd 1997: 79–80, 83).

GIFFORD PINCHOT

Gifford Pinchot, like Roosevelt and George Perkins Marsh, grew up as a sickly boy. Pinchot was born in 1865 in Simsbury, Connecticut, at the summer home of his maternal grandfather. Pinchot's grandfather made his fortune speculating on and logging stands of timber in and around Milford (northwestern Pennsylvania). Pinchot's father moved to New York, where he became rich by developing a successful interior furnishing and design company. Pinchot shuttled back and forth between the summer homes of his grandparents in Simsbury and Milford, and between the Manhattan residences of his parents and maternal grandparents. The Pinchots toured Europe for three years in the early 1870s, visiting England, France, Germany, and Italy (C. Miller 2001: 8, 30, 41, 58).

During the winter of 1883–1884 Pinchot withdrew from Exeter because of failing eyesight. His parents sent him to the Adirondack Mountains in the hope that fresh air and vigorous exercise might improve his health. Pinchot went to the Saranac Lake region, a resort area frequented by wealthy New Yorkers looking for a restorative stay. Though a tutor accompanied him, Pinchot spent most of his time in the Adirondacks hiking and snowshoeing. He wrote to his parents, telling them that he had done what he went to the woods to do—get strong. He also told them, "I find that I can with perfect ease stand a day in the woods, even with the mercury near zero." Pinchot also took a keen interest in hunting while at Saranac Lake. He informed his parents that he had killed seven rabbits, the largest number a local guide could recall anyone killing in a day. Pinchot also bragged that another guide said Gifford shot better than any other sportsman he had known. This led Pinchot to proclaim that by the time his parents saw him again he would be a combination of Davy Crockett and John L. Sullivan (C. Miller 2001: 64–65).

One of the early influences on Pinchot's life was George Perkins Marsh. His father gave him a copy of Marsh's book *The Earth as Modified by Human Action: A New Edition of Man and Nature* in 1882. The book helped Pinchot to become more aware of natural resource issues; it also prompted his father to begin reforesting the hillsides around Grey Towers (Marsh [1864] 1965; C. Miller 2001: 55–56).[10] Pinchot's father encouraged his son to pursue a profession in forestry, so when Gifford graduated from Yale in 1889, he announced that he would undertake graduate studies in that field in Europe (C. Miller 2001: 72).

However, once bitten by the hunting bug in the Adirondacks, Pinchot hunted when the opportunity presented itself. For instance, while traveling for the Forestry Commission in 1896, Pinchot took time off to hunt for grizzlies in the Rockies with Harry Graves. Unlike Roosevelt, whose writings often focused on the mechanics of hunting and the thrill of the chase and kill, Pinchot mixed policy with recreation when possible. Though he did not shoot a bear during his hunting trip with Graves, he was still so keenly aware of his natural surroundings that the trip resulted in the creation of the Flathead Forest Reserve, part of which later became Glacier National Park. Similarly, Pinchot continued to hunt alone with a Blackfoot Indian guide after Graves returned to Michigan on business, and the hiking and hunting they did in the Swan River and Kootenai Mountains resulted in the creation of the Lewis and Clark Forest Reserve. Pinchot eventually killed a bear and a deer. He and his guide were out of food for several days and subsisted on the animals they killed (Pinchot [1947] 1982: 97–99).

Pinchot was married to Cornelia (Leila) Bryce. Born in 1881 into a wealthy Newport, Rhode Island, family, Bryce had enjoyed frequent travel to Europe as well as hunting and polo. Her father was the editor of the *North American Review*, while her mother's father was Peter Cooper, an inventor who founded the Cooper Union. Bryce, who had strong family ties to New York, became involved in social reform issues early on. She was a suffragist, women's rights advocate, and labor reformer. She served as the fire inspector for the Committee on Safety that was formed after the 1911 Triangle Shirtwaist Factory fire, which killed more than a hundred people, most of them young female garment workers. Bryce married Pinchot in 1914 in the midst of his first senatorial campaign; she was thirty-three at the time, and he was forty-nine. She urged Pinchot to incorporate social justice concerns into his conservation message (Furlow 1976: 328–346; Pinchot n.d.; Severance n.d.; for more information on the Triangle Shirtwaist Factory fire, see Taylor 2009: 407–434).

Though Pinchot was an avid hunter and angler, he did not focus as much on his hunting activities or prowess in his writings as Audubon, Grinnell, or Roosevelt did. After serving two terms as the governor of Pennsylvania and three unsuccessful bids for a senate seat, Pinchot published the book *Just Fishing Talk* in 1936. In *Breaking New Ground* he wrote about his experiences as a forester.

The above discussion illustrates a variety of ways that elite men responded to pressures to embrace manliness. Being rugged and vigorous was a characteristic many embraced. Emerson practiced this through long rambles, while Thoreau, Muir, and Audubon combined strenuous hikes with survival in difficult and desolate terrain. Thoreau, Muir, and Roosevelt mixed rugged living with simple living—surviving on the bare essentials. Catlin overcame his fear of native tribes and lived and hunted among them for an extended period of time. Elite men who came of age in the post–Civil War era were under intense pressure to embrace the cult of true manhood. That culture placed a strong emphasis on masculinity and equated masculinity with strength, power, stamina, physical endurance, self-reliance, and fearlessness. However, the culture also expected upper- and middle-class men to be refined. Though they weren't members of the upper class, the frontier heroes of the time—Buffalo Bill, Daniel Boone, Davy Crockett, and so on—were strong, muscular men who had triumphed over challenges in nature and had the physical presence to impose their will on others.

Elite men did not admire or want to emulate working-class urban men or slaves who gained their strength from manual labor in the factories and fields. Though slaves conquered the elements and transformed the landscape through their labor, they were a racially subjugated group; they were not free, were not masters of their fate, and were not in a position to impose their will on others. Although some aspects of Native American interactions with nature were admired, by and large this wasn't the lifestyle that elite men regarded as an ideal. After all, Native Americans as a group lost much of their land and culture to European conquest. Moreover, black, Native American, Latino, and working-class white men toiled alongside their female counterparts. The upper-class notion of manliness was one in which women were frequently left at home as caregivers and caretakers of the domestic sphere while men engaged in outdoor pursuits as solitary explorers or in all-male groups. The social construction of womanhood will be discussed in more detail later.

For wealthy men coming of age in the late nineteenth century, masculinity was a major concern. They hadn't created farms from scratch on the frontier, logged or mined their way to riches, or built industrial complexes the way their grandfathers did. They were also too young to have proven themselves on the battlefields the way their fathers and earlier generations had. Hence, to get a taste of the rugged lifestyle, many rich young men shunned the staid and predictable rhythms of their cloistered neighborhoods, elite universities, and inherited corporations and headed for challenges awaiting them in the West during the latter part of the nineteenth century. There they had ample opportunities to grow physically fit and muscular, dominate indigenous people and the poor, conquer wild animals, and wrestle with the elements. Thus their quasi-military explorations served as a stand-in for war.

Some men of the Gilded Age, such as Theodore Roosevelt, eventually got a chance to prove themselves on the battlefield by volunteering to be a part of the Rough Riders and going to fight in Cuba in 1898 (Walker 1998). Though the notions of manliness and strenuous lifestyle appear more prominently in the writings of Roosevelt and Grinnell, other environmentalists also express aspects of this cult. Audubon articulated such concerns in his writings in the 1820s. Muir and Thoreau, both of whom came of age in the early to mid-nineteenth century, went to the wilderness. They weren't in the wilderness to hunt, like Pinchot, Grinnell, and Roosevelt; however, while there they demonstrated their self-reliance and showed their ability to withstand severe physical challenges. Both Thoreau and Muir saw self-reliance as a virtuous trait because they thought it would help people learn to live more simply. A simpler lifestyle meant less destruction of the environment (for example, see Muir [1894] 1991, [1911a] 1972, 1915; Thoreau 1982: 57–227, 258–572).[11] Roosevelt's writings are also replete with the notion of self-reliance, but for Roosevelt, self-reliance is quite intimately linked with manliness. Roosevelt's espousal of a simple life was situational. Though he practiced simple living while on the frontier, he lived the lavish lifestyle of an aristocrat while in New York.

Thoreau and Muir—neither of whom grew up as a wealthy urbanite—explored the wilderness and frontier differently than Roosevelt, Grinnell, and Pinchot. Thoreau hovered on the brink of poverty but managed to live a comfortable life as a New England writer and intellectual by staying with friends. He traveled to the woods to go hiking and canoeing. Hunting and trophy collecting was not his goal. He traveled alone or with small groups. While exploring, he lived off the land as much as possible. He often used his time in the woods to contemplate nature. Muir was a similar type of wilderness explorer. Muir, who came from a middle-class Wisconsin frontier farming family and lived the life of a wealthy orchard farmer after marrying at the age of forty-two, often hiked great distances alone with very little food. He subsisted off the land or on what he begged along the way. He did not hunt or collect trophies, but he did collect plant specimens for scientific classification purposes. Muir was interested in being in the outdoors for the sake of reveling in the experience and developing a closer bond with nature. He also wanted to learn how natural systems worked and what caused certain landforms to emerge. He mixed scientific inquiry and explorations of nature with advocacy to protect natural wonders (Muir [1894] 1991, [1911a] 1972, 1915; Thoreau 1982: 57–227, 258–572).

Thoreau's and Muir's styles of exploration were not typical of the era. Many nineteenth-century genteel men preferred to travel and explore in a way that allowed them to bring all the creature comforts and trappings of wealth with them. Instead of traveling alone or relying on the elements for food, they traveled with trainloads of food and spirits, gourmet chefs, and entourages to take care of their every need.

4

WEALTH, WOMEN, AND OUTDOOR PURSUITS

Upper- and middle-class white women were not granted the same leeway to undertake expeditions; travel in the wilds; forsake spouses, children, and parents; and participate in outdoor activities as their male counterparts. The forests and wilderness were seen as places for the manly pursuits of recreation and activism; nonetheless, some of these women defied traditions and embarked on a range of outdoor activities. And though some women did get involved in a variety of outdoor pursuits and nature protection activities, their contributions to the field of conservation are often overlooked.

The history of American women's relationship to wildlands is very complex and worthy of further investigation. Women wanted to explore beyond the boundaries of their cities and towns. Some upper- and middle-class white women did just that, while others found themselves living or working in wild areas. Some female explorers documented their trips and received some acclaim. Other women who did not venture too far afield lived vicariously through male explorers. For instance, Jeanne Carr, wife of Ezra Slocum Carr (one of Muir's professors) and lifelong friend and mentor of John Muir, lived vicariously through Muir's experiences (Muir 2001).

It isn't only white females whose activities are understudied; not enough attention has been paid to the environmental experiences of people of color either. This neglect is striking when one considers the environmental accomplishments and experiences of people of color. In the annals of environmental history, little space has been allotted to the journeys of people of color, such as Sara Winnemucca, Sacagawea, York, Biddy Mason, Harriet Tubman, Sojourner Truth, or the tribes that survived the Trail of Tears. However, people of color used tremendous environmental knowledge, skills, and instincts to survive forced treks, slavery, and the reservations. The experiences of people of color will be discussed in more detail in chapter 5.

Women and the Wilds

For much of the nineteenth century, most of the women encountering wilderness did not do so as tourists or explorers. Rather, most of the women in the wildlands were Native American women subsisting on the land or trekking thousands of miles when their tribes were forcibly relocated. In addition, black women's slave labor helped to transform the southern wilderness and build the infrastructure of eastern cities. Black women were also forced to trek long distances as slaves were moved from one part of the South and West to another. Black women trying to escape slavery also walked hundreds of miles through the wilderness to freedom. Similarly, Latinas in the Southwest subsisted on the land or worked as low-wage laborers as the West was settled, and Asian women too worked as low-wage laborers in the West. Poor white women who lived on the frontier or worked as low-wage laborers also encountered wilderness daily as they helped to transform crude settlements into towns and cities. Though these women's experiences should have provided ample evidence that women were capable of undertaking strenuous activities and surviving the rigors of the wilds, the achievements of women of color and low-income white women were all but ignored in popular conceptions of women. Not until frail, wealthy, educated, and cultured white women undertook successful excursions to the wilds were skeptics quieted.

Middle- and upper-class white women, like their male counterparts, were active in efforts to protect nature during the nineteenth century. They also wrote about nature in compelling ways. Though women's efforts have been slighted, recent feminist environmental scholarship has brought some of these achievements and experiences to light. Hence, there is now more documentation of women's explorations of the American frontier. The accounts show that women have been among the early mountaineers, hikers, explorers, and travelers to the wilderness and to national parks and forests, and the documentation of their experiences has helped to publicize these places.

However, unlike Native American, black, Latina, Asian, and working-class white women, upper- and middle-class white women's lives were much more privileged and constrained. While working-class white women and women of color were not spared the back-breaking labor or any of the indignities meted out to their male counterparts, affluent white women were set apart from their male counterparts and from other women. Wealthy white women were perceived as delicate and incapable of undertaking strenuous activities. If these women pursued strenuous activities too vigorously, they risked having their womanhood questioned. So even though most American women did not fit this stereotype, ideal womanhood was defined by the standard set for affluent white women. Still, some white women traveled to the wilds as the spouses, daughters, mothers, and sisters of explorers; others mounted expeditions on their own. Women undertook these trips to challenge conventional stereotypes of womanhood, for political empowerment, to experience the romantic wilds, and to renew their health.

THE CULT OF TRUE WOMANHOOD

While the nineteenth-century cult of true manhood urged genteel men to tramp through the woods, hunt, skin, and stuff animals, leave their families for extended periods of time to explore the wilderness and other faraway places, and push themselves to the limits by undertaking strenuous activities, this was not expected of or encouraged in their female contemporaries. Quite the contrary: upper- and middle-class women were expected to remain tethered to the home, tend to domestic affairs, immerse themselves in charitable activities, and be chaperoned when they ventured out of the house. Genteel recreation for these women was anything but strenuous. It typically involved lavish balls, sewing circles, recitals, carriage rides, sauntering in local parks, botanizing, gardening, and similar kinds of leisure activities (Taylor 2009).

Though some women accompanied their spouses, fathers, and brothers on expeditions or embarked on them with other women, they were exceptions to the rule, and their actions were often frowned upon. For example, Sarah Kemble Knight encountered shocked hosts who rebuked her for riding through the woods late at night accompanied by only a guide on her trip from Boston to New Haven in 1704 (Knight [1704] 1838: 8). However, the achievements of the women who challenged traditional expectations helped to change the way women were perceived and paved the way for greater environmental activism by women in the twentieth century.

As mentioned before, the norms that applied to middle- and upper-class women were norms that white working-class women or women of color could not attain. Working or slaving away outside the home barred them from consideration. Furthermore, black women who were routinely raped or bred to produce young slaves were considered neither pure nor pious (Stansell 1987; B. Stevenson 1996; White 1987). Scholars have also identified regional differences in the likelihood of women attaining true womanhood (Pease and Pease 1990). As Dunlap found, elite women traveling to the West found it difficult to live up to the standards of womanhood they were accustomed to in the East (Dunlap 1995). For instance, after returning from a lengthy trip to the East, Caroline Kirkland described at length—and with some humor—the attempts of her neighbor on the Michigan frontier to keep up appearances in table manners and the look of her house and garden (Kirkland 1842: 52–54). However, as time went on, frontier and western women transformed their framing of womanhood to conform more closely to the realities of life on the frontier. Despite the differences in women's lives and the improbability that most could live up to the standards of true womanhood, it was the ideal to which all American women were expected to aspire.

ECOLOGY AND THE CULT OF DOMESTICITY

Several nineteenth- and early twentieth-century movements that women played key roles in, such as the municipal housekeeping and rural beautification movements, placed women squarely in the domestic realm. The rural life movement inspired Catharine Beecher to write books on suburban home design. Beecher's books described good sanitation practices and contained illustrations of efficient home designs with the latest time- and space-saving devices. Writing in the 1840s, around the same time Andrew Jackson Downing was advocating improved taste in rural residences, Beecher urged women to keep their homes neat and clean and to plant gardens around them (C. Beecher 1842; Beecher and Stowe 1869).

Beginning in the 1850s, Ellen (Swallow) Richards, a Vassar graduate and the first female to attend Massachusetts Institute of Technology, applied the concept of *oekologie* (ecology) to her work (Worster 1994: 192).[1] However, some of her most significant contributions to our understanding of the environment came in the field of municipal housekeeping and sanitary reform. Using her background in sanitary chemistry and nutrition, Richards focused on the home environment—sanitation, waste, home economics, and food chemistry.

Richards was also concerned about air and water pollution and wrote extensively about the causes of pollution. Richards's work also contributed to the consumer nutrition and home economics movements (R. Clarke 1973; Gottlieb 1993: 216–217).

Other women, such as Mildred Chadsey, also played key roles in the municipal housekeeping movement (Chadsey 1915: 53–59). The 1880s saw a proliferation of groups like the Ladies' Health Protective Association of New York, which pushed for sanitary homes and cities. Newly established housekeeping and home decoration journals also promoted domesticity. The journals instructed women on cooking and food safety techniques, home design and decoration, and general fashion tips. Journals such as *McCalls*, the *Ladies' Home Journal*, and *Good Housekeeping* were widely distributed and very influential. For instance, in 1900 the *Ladies' Home Journal* had a monthly circulation of almost 1 million (Doughty 1975: 15).

Rural Life and Nature Study

Women were also very active in the rural life and nature study movements. This was particularly true of the New England female gentry who extended their interest in domesticity to encompass concerns about making village life more appealing. Many of these women expanded their interest in gardening and their love for birds and other wildlife to include nature study and natural history. Unlike the male naturalists, outdoor enthusiasts, conservationists, and preservationists who left their families behind for lengthy sojourns, several of the women who became active in nature protection movements engaged in conservation activities while rearing children. The women differed from the men in that they traveled with their children and studied nature without resorting to shooting, mounting, and stuffing the animals they were interested in. Though some collected wildflowers, the wildlife trophy hunting so common among men was not a typical feature of women's study and appreciation of nature. Five women who exemplify the rural life and nature study tradition are profiled below: Susan Fenimore Cooper, Sarah Orne Jewett, Edith Matilda Thomas, Genevieve Jones, and Anna Botsford Comstock.

SUSAN FENIMORE COOPER

Susan Fenimore Cooper is reminiscent of Emerson in that she lived in a rural village in New York, not far from a city. She was a rambler who observed and commented on village life from a naturalistic perspective. She also reveled in the outdoors. In statements such as "Delightful day; first walk in the woods, and what a pleasure it is to be in the forest once more!" she expresses how joyful she is to be engrossed in nature and making her interactions with nature part of her regular routine (Cooper 1850: 30).[2] Cooper was born in Scarsdale, New York, in 1813. She was the second-born child of renowned novelist and naturalist James Fenimore Cooper, but the oldest to survive childhood. The Coopers moved to live in Paris in 1826 and remained there for a decade, after which they returned to the United States and settled in Cooperstown, New York. Susan's grandfather had founded Cooperstown in 1789. In 1873, Susan founded an orphanage in Cooperstown; she also founded the Friendly Society in 1886 (Anderson and Edwards 2002: 34; Johnson and Patterson 2002: vii–xviii).

Susan Fenimore Cooper was an accomplished naturalist and writer in her own right. She wrote about the rhythms of rural life. Her second book, *Rural Hours* (1850), predated some of the more famous pieces of nature writing done by the likes of Thoreau and Muir. In *Rural Hours* she discussed climate change, noting that the summers were warmer and springs more uncertain and that some plants were becoming scarcer. Cooper described plentiful fish in village waterways and large flocks of pigeons that nested in nearby hills (Cooper 1850: 2, 16–18). A recurrent theme in Cooper's writings is the diminishing number of birds and other wildlife. In the essay "Ostego Leaves I: Birds Then and Now," she argued that the number of birds had declined precipitously between the 1850s and the 1870s and that some species were on the brink of extinction (Cooper 1878a: 529). Her concern for birds led her to become one of the early bird-protection advocates.

Cooper also examined the ecology of invasive species. She argued that the most abundant noxious weeds came from Europe and as far away as Asia. She noted that the imported species were much more prolific than native species and harder to eradicate (Cooper 1850: 109). Though much of the credit for raising awareness of the decimation of birds goes to men (as later discussions make clear), women were also vanguards in the bird-protection movement. In fact, Cooper was one of the first bird-protection activists to implore boys to stop shooting birds and to criticize the use of bird feathers to decorate women's hats (Cooper 1878a: 530).

SARAH ORNE JEWETT

Like Susan Fenimore Cooper, Sarah Orne Jewett was a rambler who wrote about rural life and the environment in and around her community. Jewett was born in 1849 in South Berwick, Maine, and spent most of her life there. Her father was a doctor, and her mother belonged to a prominent family that helped to settle Exeter, New Hampshire. Jewett first fell in love with the outdoors when she was sent on frequent walks as a youngster to combat the rheumatoid arthritis that she had developed. She made frequent trips to Boston. Jewett, like Susan Fenimore Cooper, never married. She died in 1909 after being paralyzed in a carriage accident (Cary 1962: 1–30; Shute 1877: ix–xiii).

In the preface of her 1877 book, *Deep Haven* (a fictional town patterned after South Berwick), Jewett bemoans the passing of village life; she believed that the influx of immigrants was causing overcrowding, the rapid expansion of towns, and sprawl. She also noted that the rapid increase in wealth and poverty in the post–Civil War era had given rise to a class of people who owned homes in the city and countryside; she complained that the increasing number of summer residents led to overcrowding and expressed the fear that urbanites and rural residents could not coexist amicably. She also argued that country people lived much closer to nature than city dwellers (Jewett 1877a: 1–3, 186). Jewett also bemoans the loss of traditional village life and the changing character of small New England towns in her book *Country By-Ways*. She noted that the front yards were disappearing from many homes (Jewett 1881: 116–127). As later discussions will show, Jewett was foreshadowing some of the later conservation battles that would erupt between urban elites summering in the countryside and permanent rural residents. She also foreshadows the anti-immigrant hysteria that influenced some conservation policies in the early twentieth century.

Jewett was intrigued by the forest and marveled at what she saw as the tenacity and nobility of the trees. She noted that trees have a "natural vitality and bravery" (Jewett 1881: 167–171). Young girls, too, were central figures in her nature writing. One example is Sylvia, a young girl fascinated by birds, in her short story "A White Heron" (Jewett 1877b: 1–15). Jewett wondered whether it is possible to get so close to nature that one is a piece of nature. She thought one could do this by "following a primeval instinct with perfect self-forgetfulness and forgetting everything except the dreamy consciousness of pleasant freedom" (Jewett 1896: 220).

EDITH MATILDA THOMAS

Becoming one with nature was a theme in Edith Matilda Thomas's writing too. Thomas was a naturalist and nature writer who was born in Chatham, Ohio, in 1854. The daughter of a teacher, she began writing for local newspapers at an early age. She moved to New York with her uncle in 1881, and he introduced her to Helen Hunt Jackson. Jackson encouraged Thomas to submit her work to prominent periodicals. As a result, she published in the *Century* and other national magazines. Thomas settled permanently in New York in 1888 (Anderson and Edwards 2002: 91; Howe 1896: 221).

Thomas believed that one understood nature better by communing intently with it. She begins the essay "Nature and the Native" by claiming that nature is more welcoming and yielding of her secrets when one locates oneself in it. That is, a person has to stay in nature long enough for this to happen; those who try to engage with nature through fleeting contacts are unlikely to have truths revealed to them (Thomas 1886: 5). Thomas, who was influenced by Emerson and other romantics, spoke of the "music of nature," arguing that nature excites the expectations of those who are its friends (Thomas 1886: 53, 172, 240).

GENEVIEVE JONES

Genevieve Jones, who grew up in Circleville, Ohio, has been called "the female Audubon." Born in 1847, she developed an interest in birds by tramping around the woods with her father, a medical student and amateur ornithologist. She became fascinated with illustrating in the 1850s after finding an unusual bird's nest that she and her family could not identify. In 1876 she saw an exhibition of John James Audubon's work at the Centennial World's Fair in Philadelphia and noted that even he did not highlight the nests and eggs in his illustrations. That year, her parents—who forced her to call off her engagement—encouraged her to compile her illustrations into a book. Jones and a childhood friend, Eliza Shulze, embarked on a project to illustrate 130 species of birds that nested in Ohio. To fund the project, they sold subscriptions to the book. They sent the first three lithographs to reviewers in 1878 and were praised for them (Jones et al. 1879–1886; Kiser 2012; Rea 1961–1962: 98–100, 119).

The renowned ornithologist William Brewster commended the work highly (Brewster 1878). Elliott Coues, another prominent ornithologist, said of the work, "I had no idea that so sumptuous and elegant a publication was in preparation, and am pleased that what promises to be one of the great illustrated works on North American Ornithology should be prepared by women." He went on to say that no other work since Audubon's had showed such skill and scientific accuracy (Coues 1882: 112). President Rutherford B. Hayes and Theodore Roosevelt (then a student at Harvard) subscribed to the book. Unfortunately, Jones contracted typhoid fever and died in 1879. Upon her death Coues wrote that Jones's work "rivals in beauty and fidelity of illustration the productions of Audubon's pencil and brush." Her mother, Virginia, learned lithography, and the family continued to work on the project; they completed it in 1886 (Coues 1880: 39; Howard Jones [1931] 1970: 14–19; Jones et al. 1879–1886; Kiser 2012).

Anna Botsford Comstock, who grew up studying flowers, trees, and insects with her mother, was born in 1854 in Otto, New York. The only child of prosperous farmers, Anna was also a first-rate scientific illustrator. She began studying at Cornell University in 1874 but left after two years.[3] She married John Henry Comstock, an entomology faculty member at Cornell, in 1878. Anna met John when she enrolled in his invertebrate zoology course, and the two spent time studying the flora and fauna of the Finger Lakes region of upstate New York. Through John, she developed an interest in insect illustration. As with many women of her time, Comstock's labor was harnessed to further the career of her husband. However, Comstock honed her drawing skills as she illustrated her husband's publications and eventually developed an independent career. She continued to illustrate her husband's works even after he was appointed the chief entomologist at the U.S. Department of Agriculture from 1879 to 1881. Her illustrations appear in the 1880 *Report of the Entomologist* on citrus insects and in her husband's 1888 book, *Introduction to Entomology*. She got formal training in engraving at the Cooper Union, and her engravings—in all, more than six hundred plates—are found in several different books. The Comstocks, who lived in Washington, DC, and Germany for a while, had no children (Comstock Publishing Associates 1953; Jacklin 1971: 367–369; E. H. Smith 1976: 1–26).

Anna Comstock was at the center of the nature study movement that began in the state of New York in the 1890s. In 1895, she was named to the Committee for the Promotion of Agriculture. The committee was sponsored by a group of philanthropists who were seeking to improve farming conditions and halt the migration of people from farms to the cities. The committee also sought to get children more interested in farming through nature study. Comstock created the leaflets and other curricular materials for the project. Eventually she joined the faculty at Cornell, becoming its first female professor. She took her students outdoors to study nature (Comstock Publishing Associates 1953; Jacklin 1971: 367–369; E. H. Smith 1976: 1–26).

Comstock thought nature study made young people healthier because of their exposure to the outdoor air. In her seminal book, *The Handbook of Nature Study* (1911), she says that "a study of nature ... consists of simple, truthful observations that may, like beads on a string, finally be threaded upon the understanding and thus held together as a logical and harmonious whole" (A. B. Comstock 1911: 1). Comstock authored several other books, including *Ways of the Six-Footed* (1903), *How to Know the Butterflies* (1904), *How to Keep Bees* (1905), and *Trees at Leisure* (1916).

Women were also attracted to the teachings of Transcendentalism and sought to explore nature by venturing deep into the wilds. Two such women, Margaret Fuller and Elizabeth C. Wright, are profiled below.

MARGARET FULLER

Margaret Fuller was named Sarah Margaret Fuller at birth. She was born on May 23, 1810, in Cambridge, Massachusetts. Her earliest educator was her father, Timothy Fuller. She later attended the Port School in Cambridgeport and the Boston Lyceum for Young Ladies. She went on to become the first editor of *The Dial*—the Transcendentalist journal (Baker 2003: 130). Female Transcendentalists such as Margaret Fuller repaired to the wilds to deepen their understanding of nature. When she was thirty-three years old, Margaret Fuller went on such a trip from June to September 1843. She toured rural and urban parts of the Great Lakes, making stops in Buffalo, Cleveland, Chicago, Milwaukee, Sault Sainte Marie, and Niagara Falls. She recorded her adventure in *Summer on the Lakes*, published in 1843 (Anderson and Edwards 2002: 20; Fuller 1843).

Fuller's writing is replete with romantic and sublime prose that portrays the landscape in positive imagery. She wrote of nature's complexity and its ability to generate intricate designs. She also wrote of the wonderment and "solemn awe" that "imperceptibly stole over" her as the "deep sound of the ever-hurrying rapids prepared . . . [her] mind for the lofty emotions to be experienced" at Niagara Falls (Fuller 1843: 11). Fuller's response to the prairie was more ambiguous. At first she recoiled from the vast, flat landscape because she felt that scenery derived its spiritual power from mountains. However, she grew to love the sunsets and the sense that one could travel through the prairie unobstructed (Fuller 1843: 34).

Later in the trip she wrote about the attractiveness of the undulating plains and how they triggered different sensations than travel through the mountains. The very vastness she at first found daunting became a source of sublimity as she grew accustomed to the landscape. She wrote, "I think it would impress you, as it does me, that these scenes are truly sublime. I have a sensation of vastness which I have sought in vain among high mountains. Mountains crowd one sensation on another, until all is excitement, all is surprise, wonder, enchantment. Here [the prairie] is neither enchantment or disappointment, but expectation fully realized" (Fuller 1843: 78–79). So by familiarizing herself with a landscape other than what she was used to, Fuller realized that one could experience wonderment in different ways and from unexpected sources.

In 1844, Fuller went to New York to work as a literary critic at Horace Greeley's *New York Tribune*. She was sent to Europe on assignment in 1846. There she met an Italian marquis, Giovanni Angelo Ossoli, who was disinherited by his family. The two cohabited and bore a child, Angelo Eugene Philip Ossoli, in 1848. In 1850, Fuller decided to return to America with her partner and child. However, the three perished in a tragic accident when their ship crashed on a sandbar less than a hundred yards off the coast of Fire Island, New York (Baker 2003: 130; P. McFarland 2004: 170–171).

ELIZABETH C. WRIGHT

Though little is known of Elizabeth C. Wright and she published only one book, it was an important piece of nature writing that bridged the discourse between ecology and Transcendentalism. She was born in New York in 1831 or 1832 and married Henry C. Wright, a book dealer. The Wrights lived in Dunkirk, New York, with their two children. The Wrights also lived in Illinois in the late 1850s and St. Louis in the 1880s (Patterson 2008: 400–406).

Elizabeth Wright was a nature writer who—like Susan Fenimore Cooper—lived in upstate New York and was critical of the general disregard for the environment she perceived and of the environmental degradation evident around her. However, Wright was strongly influenced by Transcendentalist thinking. She took Emerson and Thoreau's instructions to heart and escaped to the woods for renewal and refreshment. Indeed, she begins her 1860 book by declaring, "We were tired and wanted a holiday, so we went off into the woods, out of the way of finery and etiquette, and conventional rubbish, where we should escape from fashionable twaddle, gossips, and flirts—from humbugs and household botheration, and be free to rest and refresh ourselves at leisure" (E. C. Wright 1860: 9).

Wright and her camping party immersed themselves in the freedom of the woods. She proclaimed that "it was utterly delightful to let ourselves loose, and live freely," unencumbered from the mores and strictures of society. She proclaimed that to "do what pleased us best was paradisiacal enough." Wright, who had grown up in the woods, relished being outdoors. To her "the mountain echoes were ravishing music" that was "played by the wind on a wilderness of harps" (E. C. Wright 1860: 17–19). Wright also adhered to the Transcendentalist view that nature revealed truths beyond the obvious—and that most people are not aware of such truths even though they are everywhere in nature (E. C. Wright 1860: 112).

She was a saunterer, an advocate of outdoor leisure who extolled the virtues of exercise. Like Theodore Roosevelt and Gifford Pinchot, she believed that regular walks could cure one's maladies and restore one's health (E. C. Wright 1860: 56–78). She argued that nature cures not only the body but also the mind. In "The Nature Cure—For the Mind," Wright argues, "As soon as you begin to enter into the arcane of nature, you feel the shackles of outward customs grow loose, and the liveries of many servitudes drop off, as a bird moults its feathers. Nothing is done suddenly, for Nature has plenty of time—all the time there is—and is never in a hurry" (E. C. Wright 1860: 91). However, she is also similar to Frederick Law Olmsted (codesigner of Central Park in New York) in her views on the optimal way nature stimulates the mind: Olmsted believed in the gentle exercise of the mind that occurred when one strolled through picturesque scenery; he thought the overstimulation of the mind that resulted from rough-and-tumble exertion was counterproductive (Olmsted 1865; Taylor 2009: 264–267). Wright expresses this idea when she says, "Nature forbids over activity as well as sloth" (E. C. Wright 1860: 68).

Women on the Frontier

During the middle of the nineteenth century large numbers of people moved to the West. Between 1841 and 1867, around 350,000 people used wagons to travel to California and Oregon (Jeffrey [1979] 1998: 3). Though this form of travel was grueling, many women accomplished it, and these arduous trips and rustic living conditions hastened the process by which women defied convention and had experiences that were outside the norm for the period. Regardless of social class, frontier women were often unconventional, escaping the "true womanhood" mold. The frontier was a place where the meaning of that ideal was tested and redefined. Rich or poor, frontier women ranged from pious ladies to tomboyish girls and gun-toting women. Clothing was one area in which frontier women did not or could not follow convention: many women traveling west with their families found pants more appropriate than long dresses and hoop skirts (Dunlap 1995: 2–3, 59–63).

Such women found they had to do tasks traditionally considered "men's work" in addition to the usual domestic chores. Their daughters wore pants rather than dresses, played and worked with boys, hopped fences, rode astride, and did a wide range of tasks around the homestead regardless of the gender usually assigned to those tasks (Dunlap 1995: 2–3, 59–63; Jeffrey [1979] 1998: 6). Caroline Kirkland noted that the division of labor between men and women as well as between the different social classes was blurred on the frontier (Clavers 1839: 123–124).[4] This is borne out by the recollections of Matilda Paul, who reported that when she was a child she had to collect wood for cooking, fetch water, and feed the calves in addition to her regular household chores (Riley 1980: 261). Molly Dorsey, tired of ripping her long skirt, responded by devising more practical clothing for her lifestyle. She said, "It occurred to me how much easier I could get through the tangled underbrush if I were a man! and without letting anyone know of my project, I slipped out into the back shed, and donned an old suit of Father's clothes" (cf. Faragher 1979: 53).

Margaret Fuller described the juxtaposition of gentility and the rugged world of frontier living she encountered when she visited the Illinois home of an "English gentleman" whose bookcases were overflowing and whose daughters were schooled in the fine arts. Fuller found that though the young women were musicians who spoke French fluently, they also had to take care of the milk room and kill the rattlesnakes that preyed upon their poultry (Fuller 1843: 38).

Many of the women who traveled to the West were middle-class women who regarded themselves as the guardians of refinement and civility and saw themselves as missionaries charged with enhancing the culture and civility of frontier settlements. They brought the cult of domesticity with them. Catharine Beecher was a proponent of the view that females were integral to the propagation of these values in the West. Consequently, from 1835 onward she worked through the American Lyceum to send groups of young white females to the West to teach (Jeffrey [1979] 1998: 20).

However, even before the middle- and upper-class women reached their destinations, some of the traditional norms and expectations fell by the wayside. Realizing that riding sidesaddle on rocky, weather-beaten trails was nigh impossible, they rode astride. They hunted to augment their food supply and drove the wagons when circumstances necessitated it. Some women loathed this experience, while others exulted in their newfound freedoms (Dunlap 1995: 9–12). Mrs. A. M. Green reviled the Great Plains, which she described as "those dreadful, hateful, woeful, fearful, desolate, distressed, disagreeable, dusty, detestable, homely, and lonely plains" (M. M. Allen 1972: 116). However, Alice W. Rollins relished her experience there. She described the Plains as "the great breathing space . . . where your horizon comes absolutely to the ground in every direction" (M. M. Allen 1972: 116).

Even in the East, women had mixed reactions to the wilds. Anne Bradstreet, in an earlier time period, had used positive imagery to portray nature in such poems as "The Four Seasons of the Year" (Bradstreet 1678: 59–68) and "As Spring the Winter Doth Succeed" (Bradstreet [1657] 1898: 53). Likewise, in 1802 Charlotte Ludlow described Ohio as "those beautiful extended plains" with "lofty forests" and "clearest streams" (see Myres 1982: 18). But Sarah Kemble Knight wrote about the "dolesome" and "lonesome" and "surly" river and the "clownish" and "boisterio's" trees. She also expressed her fear of river crossings on her Boston to New Haven trip in 1704 (Knight [1704] 1838: 16–17). Elizabeth House Trist, who traveled from Philadelphia to New Orleans in 1783–1784, found the forests she traversed overwhelming. She wrote, "I felt oppress'd with so much wood towering above me in every direction and such a continuance of it . . . My spirits were condanc'd to nothing; my head began to ache and I returned to town quite sick." Eliza B. Glitherall, traveling in 1784 from Wilmington, North Carolina, to the Great Smoky Mountains, had similar reactions (quoted in LaBastille 1980: 14). Lucy Audubon described the eastern mountains as "very stony and disagreeable" after traveling to Kentucky with her husband, John James Audubon, in 1808 (L. B. Audubon 1808).

Class and race influenced how affluent white women positioned themselves on the frontier. Despite having to expand the framing of womanhood to reflect the more varied experiences they were having on the frontier, upper- and middle-class white women sought to separate themselves from the poor white women and women of color whom they encountered in rural areas. Like their male counterparts, upper- and middle-class white women did not want to emulate the lifestyles of poor white women and women of color living on the frontier (Jeffrey [1979] 1998: 7). According to Caroline Kirkland, life on the frontier was a struggle of "leveling upwards." Frontier settlers found this more appealing than "leveling downwards" (Clavers 1839: 310).

Elite white women often regarded people of color with loathing. For instance, Caroline Kirkland referred to the Native Americans she encountered in disparaging terms such as "desperate looking savage" (Clavers 1839: 52). However, Margaret Fuller distinguished between the way white men and white women viewed Native Americans. She argued that while white men felt hatred toward Indians, white women felt disgust and loathing (Fuller 1843: 183). The remainder of this chapter will profile women living on the frontier, including mountaineers, explorers, entrepreneurs, botanists, and ornithologists.

CAROLINE MATILDA KIRKLAND

Caroline Matilda Kirkland, a cultural nationalist and urban park advocate, wrote about life in Michigan (Taylor 2009: 235–237). She straddled the realms of urban park advocacy and romanticism. Kirkland was born into a middle-class family in New York City in 1801. Her father was a publisher and her mother a writer. Kirkland taught briefly in Clinton, New York. She married William Kirkland, a tutor at Hamilton College, in 1828. The couple founded a school for girls in Geneva, New York. In 1835 the Kirklands moved to Detroit, where they headed the Detroit Female Seminary. The Kirklands were entre-preneurs who dreamed of founding a city on the Michigan frontier, so two years after moving to Detroit, they purchased eight hundred acres of land and founded the village of Pinckney. The Kirklands returned to live in New York in 1843, and William died in 1846 in a drowning accident. Caroline and William had seven children (Fetterley 1985; Osborne 1972).

Kirkland wrote about frontier life while living in Pinckney. In 1839 she pub-lished *A New Home, Who'll Follow?* (Clavers 1839). Unlike Margaret Fuller, who was at first repulsed by the flat midwestern landscape, Kirkland described the setting of the new town in romantic imagery. She wrote, "When I made my first visit to these remote and lonely regions, the scattered woods through which we rode for many miles were gay in their first gosling-green suit of half-opened leaves, and the forest odours which exhaled with the dews of morning and evening, were beyond measure delicious to one" (Clavers 1839: 10).

In her 1842 book, *Forest Life*, she expressed the desire that people cared more about aesthetics and that women and children had greater access to out-door recreation. She advocated for parks in rural settlements as well as the city. While in Pinckney, during a time period when the urban park movement was just getting under way, Kirkland argued for planned outdoor recreation spaces. She also advocated for recreational access for females and children years before renowned park advocates like Olmsted did (Kirkland 1842: 41; see also Taylor 2009: 245–247).

Other women wrote in a similar vein. For instance, Eliza Farnham, another writer and cultural nationalist who promoted the West, said the West should be "preferred over all other portions of the earth. Its magnitude, its fertility, the kindliness of its climate, and the variety and excellence of its production are unrivalled in our country, if not on the globe" (E. Farnham 1846: iii).

MARY HUNTER AUSTIN

Unlike Kirkland, who migrated from the city to the frontier, Mary Hunter Austin spent virtually all of her life on the frontier. She was born in Carlin-ville, Illinois, in 1868. Her father, a captain in the Civil War, died of malaria when she was ten years old. Austin began writing poetry at this age and said she drew on a deep inner spirit when she wrote. Her mother moved the family to California to establish a homestead in the Owens Valley in 1888—the same year she graduated from Blackburn College. Three years after arriving in Cali-fornia, Mary married Stafford Austin, a native of Hawaii and graduate of the University of California at Berkeley. Stafford was a grape grower. He was also the manager of an irrigation project that failed in 1891, causing the couple great financial hardship. To exacerbate matters, their daughter, Ruth, was born with mental disabilities. The Austins went their separate ways, and their daughter was placed in a mental institution. Mary Austin studied and wrote about the natural environment as well as the Native American tribes in the region. She was also an advocate of Native American and Latino rights in California (Doyle 1939; James, James, and Boyer 1971: 67–69). In 1903 Austin published *Land of Little Rain*, a book on desert ecology.

Mountaineering, Wilderness, and Solitude

HANNAH TAYLOR KEEP AND ESTHER JONES

The negative perceptions of the wilds that some elite women had were countered by the exhilaration others felt in the wilderness. As early as the 1840s, well-to-do white women undertook difficult mountain climbing expeditions. In 1849—the same year Harriet Tubman fled from slavery to freedom—Hannah Taylor Keep and Esther Jones were among a group of five women who ascended Mount Katahdin in Maine (now the northern terminus of the Appalachian Trail). Keep, who lived in Burlington, Maine, was the daughter of a colonel. She married Marcus Keep in 1849. He was a missionary, amateur geologist, and guide who took tourists to Mount Katahdin (Hazen 1881: 118). In 1855, six young females were accompanied by women's rights advocate Thomas Wentworth Higginson as they scaled Pamola (the lower eastern peak of Mount Katahdin). Sporting bloomers, the women used the climb to promote clothing reform and healthful exercise for women. They announced, "Our moral is that there is more real peril to bodily health in a week of ballroom than in a month of bivouacs" (Waterman and Waterman 1989: 122–124, 162).

These white women's ascent of Katahdin is important because of the mountain's place in romantic, Transcendental, and primitivistic lore. Keep, Jones, and their companions climbed the mountain three years after Thoreau's famous climb. When Thoreau climbed Katahdin, he found it daunting and shocking. He wrote that it was "even more grim and wild than . . . [I] had anticipated, a deep and intricate wilderness" and that the landscape was "savage and dreary." Thoreau said he "felt more lone than you can imagine" on the mountain. The wilderness seemed to him "a place for heathenism and superstitious rites—to be inhabited by men [Indians] nearer of kin to the rocks and wild animals than we." The climb decreased Thoreau's enthusiasm for primitivistic ideology; he began espousing a philosophy of balancing the wildness and hardiness that comes from forays into the wilderness with periods of exposure to intellectual refinement and civility (Nash 1982: 90–94; Thoreau 1893).

John Muir expressed a similar feeling of desolation on a trip to Hetch Hetchy. Muir wrote, "To one unacquainted with the hidden life and tenderness of the high Sierras, the first impression is one of intense soul-crushing desolation" (Muir 1873). But unlike Thoreau, Muir reveled in this sensation and enjoyed his time alone in the wilderness. The admissions of Thoreau and Muir show that men were able to express feelings of desolation, aloneness, sensations of being overwhelmed by the landscape, without running the risk of being stereotyped as incapable of handling outdoor adventures. Women did not get this benefit of the doubt.

While elite women slowly broke with the convention of heavy, restrictive clothing and began to wear Yosemite suits (knee-length bloomers worn under the skirt), working-class women of the West wore men's pants regularly in the latter half of the nineteenth century without fanfare. For example, Calamity Jane (Martha Jane Cannary), a white woman, and Stagecoach Mary (Mary Fields), an African American woman, dressed in men's long pants. Stagecoach Mary sometimes wore skirts, but always wore pants underneath (Dunlap 1995: 35–40; Katz 1992: 80–83; LaBastille 1980: 69). As later discussions will show, Harriet Tubman also wore pants on her expeditions to free slaves and guide them to the North (Bradford [1869] 1981).

HELEN BRODT, ANNA MILLS JOHNSTON, AND ANNA DICKINSON

In the West, women also made highly publicized climbs of significant mountain peaks. For instance, in 1864 Helen Brodt climbed the Lassen Volcano (now Lassen Volcanic National Park) with Major Reading. Brodt, who is recorded as the first white woman to climb Lassen, was a landscape artist. She lived in New York, but moved to Red Bluff, California, in 1863. She worked as a schoolteacher at the same time that she practiced her art, and her paintings were exhibited at the 1893 Chicago World's Fair. Lake Helen on Mount Lassen is named after Brodt (Mount Shasta Companion 2001; National Park Service 1941: 1).

Sheriff Mulkey's wife and daughter accompanied him on a climb of Mount Langley in August 1872. At that time the peak, ascended by Clarence King a year earlier, was thought to be Mount Whitney—the highest peak in the Lower Forty-Eight states. The first ascent of Mount Whitney was made in 1873. Four women climbed the peak (now a part of Sequoia National Park) in 1878. Anna Mills Johnston, one of these four, kept a record of the trip. The other three women were Hope Broughton, Mary Martin, and Mrs. Redd. The trip was arduous, but the women persisted. Johnston wrote, "My horse took a notion to jump over a small stream, very unexpectedly to me, and my back was so severely injured that I could hardly step without experiencing severe pain. Having been lame from early childhood, everybody said it would be utterly impossible for me to climb to the summit of Mt. Whitney. But I was not easily discouraged." She continued, "The supreme joy I felt when I realized that . . . I was at last really standing on the summit of Mount Whitney, knew no bounds" (Farquhar 1969: 173–188).

Another notable mountaineer was Anna Elizabeth Dickinson. Born in 1842 in Philadelphia to Quakers, she was an antislavery activist and suffragist. Her father died when she was two years old, leaving the family in poverty. Dickinson was educated at the Friends School. She climbed several of Colorado's "fourteeners" (mountains over fourteen thousand feet high). In 1873 she became the first white woman to climb Longs Peak (now in Rocky Mountain National Park) in Colorado—five years after the first white male made the ascent. Dickinson, who climbed with the editor of *Rocky Mountain News* and a member of the U.S. Geological Survey, named the peak "Lady Washington" as a counterpart to Mount Washington in New Hampshire, which she had ascended twenty-seven times. Reflecting on the Longs Peak ascent, Dickinson said, "One goes to the top of a mountain for emotions, not descriptions" (A. E. Dickinson 1879: 251–271, quote on 251; Gallman 2006: 74–109, 120–130, 258; Kaufman 1996: 14–15; LaBastille 1980: 46–49, 73–74).

ISABELLA BIRD: THE QUEST FOR SOLITUDE

A few weeks after Dickinson's climb, Isabella Bird also ascended Longs Peak. Bird, born in 1831 in England into an upper-middle-class family, was the first female member of the Royal Geographic Society of England. She traveled to the United States in 1854 and again in 1872. Bird enjoyed solitude and, like John Muir, frequently traveled alone (Bird [1879] 1893; Federal Writers' Project 1941: 99; Stoddart 1907: vi, 8, 28, 77). When she climbed in the Rocky Mountains, she wrote about their sublimity and beauty; she also felt the mountain scenery energized her. Bird's accounts of her explorations are replete with romantic and Transcendental imageries. She said, "The scenery up here is glorious, combining sublimity with beauty, and in the elastic air fatigue has dropped off from me." She also describes "monstrous protuberances" that "inflame the imagination and elevate the understanding." Her narrative is sprinkled with phrases such as "Scenery satisfies my soul." She regarded the mountains as magnificent and the air as "life-giving" (Bird [1879] 1893: 6, 63). Bird was at a loss for words after her ascent of Longs Peak. She declared, "No sort of description within my powers could enable another to realize the glorious sublimity, the majestic solitude, and the unspeakable awfulness and fascination of the scenes" (Bird [1879] 1893: 97).

At several points during her travels Bird reflected on solitude and what it meant to her during her explorations of the wilds. Like other explorers who hiked alone, at times she felt overwhelmed by the isolation. She described the solitude as somber, eerie, awful, vast, and oppressive, but also as glorious and majestic (Bird [1879] 1893: 22, 42, 46, 72, 92, 97, 204, 229, 238). Despite the drawbacks of being alone in the wilds, she concluded that "solitude is infinitely preferable to uncongeniality, and is bliss when compared to repulsiveness, so I was thoroughly glad when I got rid of my escort and set out upon the prairie alone" (Bird [1879] 1893: 157–158).

EXPLORING THE HEIGHTS AND DEPTHS OF YOSEMITE

Yosemite and Yellowstone were big attractions for female explorers and settlers. The first whites might not have seen the valley until 1851 (Bunnell [1880] 1990: x–xi).[5] Tourists began to visit Yosemite in 1855, and the first whites settled in the valley the following year. In May 1857, two young teachers from San Francisco, Harriet Kirtland and Anna Park, donned long skirts and rode sidesaddle into Yosemite Valley. Mrs. Denman and Mrs. Holmes were also on the trip; they were the wives of James Denman, superintendent of the San Francisco high school where Kirtland and Park worked, and L. Holmes, editor of the *Mariposa Gazette*. James Hutchings's articles and accounts, along with all the stories being told about the valley, stimulated intense interest in Yosemite. News reports of white women traveling safely in Yosemite encouraged other white women to venture into the Sierras and other wilderness areas. By 1870, women were wearing the Yosemite suit and riding astride in rugged terrain (Farquhar 1965: 120; Kaufman 1996: 3–5). British viscountess and explorer Thérèse Yelverton visited Yosemite in 1870. She wrote a novel, *Zanita*, about her trip. The male character, Kenmuir, is loosely based on John Muir (Yelverton 1872). New York writer Sarah Jane Lippincott, who wrote under the pen name Grace Greenwood, visited Yosemite in 1871 and chronicled her adventure in *New Life in New Lands* (1873).

Helen Hunt Jackson. Helen Hunt Jackson also explored California and Colorado in the 1870s. Jackson was born in 1830 in Amherst, Massachusetts. Her mother died of tuberculosis in 1844 and her father, an Amherst College professor and orthodox Calvinist minister, died of dysentery three years later. She was schooled at the Ipswich Female Seminary. She went to live in Albany, New

York, with relatives in 1851. There she met Captain Edward Hunt, a graduate of West Point; she married him in 1852. One of her sons died in infancy, the second died of diphtheria at age nine, and her husband died during the Civil War. A doctor ordered the young widow to visit the Rockies in order to revive her health. There she met and married a prominent Colorado Springs banker, William Jackson. Helen was a classmate and lifelong friend of another Amherst native, Emily Dickinson (Phillips 2003: 11–17, 25–26; Sky 2009).

Jackson traveled to Yosemite Valley in 1872 along with her friend Sarah Woolsey (Susan Coolidge) of New Haven, Connecticut. Jackson criticized Lafayette Bunnell both for orchestrating a massacre of Indians in Yosemite and for popularizing the name Yosemite over the older Indian name, Ah-wah-ne. Though she traveled in Yosemite years after it had been designated a state park, the degradation from mining activities was still apparent. Jackson described the defunct mining operations along the roadside as dismal and ghastly, with masses of excavated rocks and gravel visible everywhere. She also described loggers felling trees that were hundreds of years old (H. H. Jackson 1872; 1878: 87–97, 105–114). In an article written for *The Century*, Woolsey discussed the enormous expense involved in mounting the trip (Coolidge 1873: 25–31).

Jackson published *Bits of Travel at Home* in 1878 (Federal Writers' Project 1941: 99; H. H. Jackson 1878). She became an Indian rights advocate and drew attention to the plight of the tribes in her book *Ramona*, published in 1884. She was part of a special commission in 1883 that investigated the status of the Mission Indians in California. This led her to write a scathing report criticizing Indian policies and detailing atrocities perpetuated against Native Americans (H. H. Jackson 1883, 1890).

Other Women in the Sierras. In 1877 several women, including Anna Dickinson and Elizabeth Cady Stanton, rode into Yosemite. Dickinson and Olive Logan rode astride, but Stanton, finding the ride uncomfortable, walked to the valley from Tamarack Flat—a distance of about twenty miles (Perkins 1877: 5; Russell [1959] 1992: 52–53). Yosemite became such an important symbol of women's emancipation that women's rights leaders Stanton and Susan B. Anthony wrapped up their California suffrage campaign by making a stop in Yosemite. Noticing the number of trees named for men, women attending Stanton's lecture wrote the names of "a dozen leading women" on cards and tacked them on unnamed trees (Greenwood 1873b: 5; Kaufman 1996: 6–7).

Some men were fascinated by the women's decision to ride astride. As the guide for the Dickinson-Stanton party reported, "You ought to have seen Anna Dickinson . . . Why, Anna got on like a man—rode astride." When the skeptical listener asked, "Now honestly, guide, did Anna really ride astride or is this a California lie?" The guide replied, "Yes, Sir, she did ride up and down those mountains like a man" (Perkins 1877: 5).

Women were among the early entrepreneurs in the Yosemite Valley; they worked as proprietors, managers, and guides. Mrs. Neal moved to Yosemite with her husband John to run the Lower Hotel in 1859. Beginning in 1864, Elvira Hutchings and her mother, Florantha Sproat, helped to run the Hutchings Hotel. Elvira gave birth to two girls, Florence and Gertrude (Farquhar 1965: 158).[6] In 1866 another woman, Mrs. Leidig—George Leidig's wife—moved to the valley to take charge of the Lower Hotel (Russell [1959] 1992: 99).

In March 1864, Mary Olmsted, wife of Frederick Law Olmsted, moved from New York to Bear Valley (in the Yosemite region) to join her husband at the Mariposa Mining Company. Mary Olmsted was known to take hikes with her husband and travel without male escorts. Just before they left the region to return to New York in 1865, she and her children traveled to Yosemite to hear Olmsted present the first management report of the valley to his fellow commissioners. Two of Mary's children were girls, nine-year-old Charlotte and two-year-old Marion. Mary did not have the usual male escorts, but two men in charge of the pack mules traveled with her (Olmsted 1864a, 1864b; Ranney, Rauluk and Hoffman 1990: 171–208; Roper 1973: 287).

Women and the Mountaineering Clubs. Mountaineering clubs such as the Appalachian Mountain Club (founded in 1876 in Boston), Sierra Club (founded in 1892 in San Francisco), Mazamas Club (founded in 1894 in Oregon), the Mountaineers (founded in 1907 in Seattle), and the Colorado Mountain Club (founded in 1912) encouraged and popularized women's climbing. Through the club outings, hundreds of women climbed mountains from the East Coast to the West. By the early 1900s, women accounted for about a third of the people making successful climbs (Kaufman 1996: 19–21).

GOLD MINERS

Some women became miners. Two young women and their slave were among the forty-niners who went to California to try their hand at gold mining. They staked out a claim in an isolated area, about thirty miles from any other miners. They quickly found about seven thousand dollars' worth of gold dust. Their goal was to amass about ten thousand dollars' worth of gold before leaving (Sprague 1940: 115–116). One enterprising group of nine "strong minded women," the Woman's Lode Mining Claim, registered a claim in Bingham, Utah, in 1864. The women were the wives of soldiers, and each placed her husband's military rank after her own name (Dunlap 1995: 50; James and Taylor 1978: 136–150; Zanjani, 1997: 118–119).

Many other women were involved in mining in one way or another (Zanjani 1997). Mrs. E. C. Atwood of Colorado invested in the mining activities of her acquaintances. After losing ten thousand dollars in one investment, she began studying mineralogy. Shortly afterward, she became the vice president and general manager of the Bonacord Gold Mining and Milling Company. Theora Ailman owned a mine with her husband in Georgetown, California. She did the company's bookkeeping. Lillian Weston Hazen of Gilt Edge, Montana, was also a bookkeeper for a mine (Dunlap 1995: 50).

PIONEERING BOTANISTS

Women were pioneers in the emerging field of American botany as well. Some female naturalists who stayed close to home made significant contributions in the field of botany. Jane Colden, the earliest female naturalist in North America, studied plants around Newburgh, New York, where she lived in the mid-1700s. She discovered the gardenia and corresponded with Carl Linneaus, and her work earned her an international reputation (LaBastille 1980: 72).

In the West, women were at the forefront of early botanical explorations. While John Wesley Powell is famous for his expeditions along the Colorado River, less is known about his sister Ellen Powell, who accompanied him on the second expedition from 1871 to 1872. Ellen, a botanist, discovered several new species of plants (Greenwood 1873a; B. S. Smith 1994: 104–131). Another female botanist, Rebecca Merritt Austin, moved to the gold mines of Plumas County, California, in 1865. She found several rare plants when she began collecting specimens. She displayed the plants in a soapbox herbarium case. When her family moved to Butterfly Valley, she began studying the pitcher plant, genus *Darlingtonia*. She corresponded with European botanists about her studies and published some of her findings. New California species were named for both Austin and her daughter, C. C. Bruce (B. S. Smith 1994: 104–131). Sara Plummer was another pioneering female botanist. She worked alongside her husband J. G. Lemmon collecting plants in the Mount Shasta region and the San Bernardino Mountains. In the 1880s, other women such as Kate Curran Brandegee and Alice Eastwood became well-known botanists (Slack 1993: 221–223).

BIRD CONSERVATIONISTS

Many women were ardent bird-protection advocates. Two of the most vocal women on this topic—Susan Fenimore Cooper and Elizabeth Wright—were discussed above. Now the chapter moves on to three additional bird-protection advocates: Harriet Mann Miller, Mabel Osgood Wright, and Florence Merriam Bailey.

Harriet Mann Miller (Olive Thorne Miller). Harriet Mann Miller, who wrote under the nom de plume Olive Thorne Miller, was born in 1831 in Auburn, New York, where her father was a banker. The family moved to Ohio in 1842, when Harriet was eleven years old. She married Watts Todd Miller in 1854. The Millers lived in Chicago for almost twenty years before moving with their children to live in Brooklyn, where they stayed until Watts's death. Between 1883 and 1903 Harriet studied birds all over the country. Miller was a mother of four when she wrote her first bird book in 1885. Among her hundreds of publications were eleven books on birds. She became a member of the American Ornithological Union in 1887. She moved to Los Angeles in 1904 and died there in 1918 (Bailey 1919: 163–169).

Miller, who explored Colorado in 1892 to conduct painstaking bird studies, viewed nature from a Transcendentalist perspective. She was influenced by the works of Emerson, William Wordsworth, and Thoreau, hence she perceived nature as a healer. She believed that one should go to the woods to be refreshed and to counteract the agitations of everyday life. In this respect she is also similar to Elizabeth Wright. Miller tells the reader at the beginning of her book *A Bird-Lover in the West* that "the sole and simple secret of rest, is this: To go to our blessed mother Nature, and to go with the whole being, mind and heart as well as body." She argued that to make a half-hearted attempt to enjoy nature—with one's body physically present in nature but with one's mind occupied with everyday concerns—defeats the purpose of becoming truly rejuvenated. Hence Miller argued that it was liberating for her to leave her worldly cares behind and go to the woods (O. T. Miller 1894: 4). She began her book *Upon the Tree-Tops* by declaring that in going birding in the Green Mountains, she was turning away from the world of people and the din of the city. She declared, "How refreshing is the heavenly stillness of the country!" (O. T. Miller 1897: 4).

Miller wrote her ornithological studies at a time when the bird protection movement was in its infancy. Along with Susan Fenimore Cooper and several other female nature writers and amateur ornithologists, she was among the early activists speaking out about the slaughter of birds and the use of their feathers to adorn women's hats (O. T. Miller 1885: 22; 1899: 127). At a time when detractors perceived birds as noxious and a threat to farming because they consumed crops, Miller argued that birds were beneficial to the economy (O. T. Miller 1887: 187).

Mabel Osgood Wright. Mabel Osgood Wright was born in New York City in 1859. She published her first essay on nature in the *New York Post* when she was sixteen, and she married James Osborne Wright in 1884. She was the founder and president of the Connecticut Audubon Society (1898). Her rise to prominence in the National Audubon Society will be discussed in more detail in chapter 7. Mabel Wright also founded the Birdcraft Museum and Sanctuary in Fairfield, Connecticut. The preserve was such a significant habitat that by 1914 it had more than ten thousand visitors. By the 1940s, the sanctuary had 153 different nesting species (Connecticut Women's Hall of Fame 2010; Forbes and Jermier 2002: 458–465). Mabel Wright penned her opposition to the use of birds' feathers in women's fashion in *Birdcraft* in 1895. Her objections grew more strident in later years (M. O. Wright 1895: 271; Wright and Coues 1898: 370–371). She wrote several other books, including *The Friendship of Nature* (1894), *Citizen Bird* (1898), *Four-Footed Americans* (1898), *Flowers and Ferns in Their Haunts* (1901), and *The Garden, You, and I* (1906), which was written under the sobriquet "Barbara."

Florence Merriam Bailey. The naturalist Florence Merriam Bailey is another in a long list of New York women who studied bird life and became active in bird conservation. She was born in 1863 in Locust Grove in Lewis County. She grew up on her family's ample estate, Homewood. Her brother, C. Hart Merriam, was the first chief of the U.S. Biological Survey (1885–1910), and her father was a longtime friend of John Muir (the two met in Yosemite in 1871). Her father was a merchant and banker in New York City but moved the family to Locust Grove around the time of Florence's birth. Florence attended Smith College from 1882 to 1886 but did not earn a degree (the college granted her one in 1921). While at Smith, Florence organized the Smith College Audubon Society. She organized a group of one hundred students to send out ten thousand flyers publicizing the plight of birds. She also wrote newspaper articles opposing birds' slaughter. Florence became the first female associate of the American Ornithological Union in 1885. She and her mother joined her brother on a tugboat trip to Neah Bay in the Pacific Northwest in 1889; the trip was taken, in part, to improve Florence's health. She later moved to Washington, DC, to live with her brother. She was a founding member of the District of Columbia's Audubon Society. She married Vernon Bailey, a naturalist at the Biological Survey, in 1899. Together they made several lengthy trips to the West (AAUW 2010; Busman 2005: 20; Kofalk 1989; Oehser 1952: 26).

Following the success of her first book—*Birds through an Opera Glass* (1889), a collection of articles she had written for the *Audubon Magazine*—she wrote several others. The books *My Summer in a Mormon Village* (1894), *A-Birding on a Bronco* (1896), and *Birds of Village and Field* (1898) chronicle her experiences in Utah, Arizona, and California. She wrote about the decimation of birds for their use on women's hats (Bailey 1902: 8; 1928: 92, 218). She also published *Among the Birds in the Grand Canyon National Park* (1939).

FEMALE TRAVELERS AND ENTREPRENEURS IN YELLOWSTONE
Women were among the earliest white travelers to Yellowstone. In 1871, the year before the park was designated, Mrs. Stevenson and Elliott accompanied the Hayden Expedition into Yellowstone. Emma Stone also made the journey with her husband and two young sons in 1872 four months after the park was established. In 1880, Sarah Marshall and her husband opened a hotel in the park. As the national parks established concessions, young women traveled to these areas for adventure and work (Bunce 1872a: 300–301; Kaufman 1996: 9–13).

FEMALE LANDSCAPE PAINTERS IN THE WILDS
Landscape painting drew women to the wildlands too. Like the male landscape painters, female artists helped publicize the national parks through their paintings. Women were sometimes hired by the railroads to paint landscapes that would broaden the appeal of national parks and other natural wonders and encourage entire families to visit the wilderness. For instance, Abby Williams Hill was hired by the Great Northern and the Northern Pacific Railways to paint remote and inaccessible locations in the northern Cascades. Traveling with her two children, Hill camped in the Cascades and painted for the railroads from 1903 to 1906 (Kaufman 1996: 22–23).

The Great Northern Railroad also took an interest in Mary Roberts Rinehart. In 1915, Rinehart took a three-hundred-mile horseback tour of Glacier National Park. Half of the forty-two riders on this tour were women. Rinehart, already a well-known writer and war correspondent, wrote a pamphlet and two books about her experiences. Like Helen Hunt Jackson, Rinehart developed an interest in the plight of the Indians. She befriended several members of the Blackfoot tribe. Shocked at conditions on the reservation, she made a personal appeal to the secretary of the interior to take steps to improve conditions (Kaufman 1996: 24; Rinehart 1916, 1918). Also like Helen Hunt Jackson and Harriet Vaille in Colorado, Rinehart urged the government to retain the use of Native American place-names in the national parks rather than having "obscure Government officials" and "unimportant people … memorialize themselves on government maps." In her criticism of the settler colonial mentality she exhorted, "The white man came, and not content with the eliminating the Indians he went farther and wiped out their history" (Rinehart 1916: 66–69; 1948: 202–205).

The Blackfeet also lobbied on their own behalf to stop the practice of changing Indian place-names in parks. A delegation of Indians led by Curly Bear and Wolf Plume met with the two most powerful people in the parks bureau, Stephen Mather and Horace Albright, in 1915 to discuss the matter. The Native Americans protested the substitution of European names for lakes, streams, mountains, and so on that had Indian names. As Tail-Feathers-Coming-Over-The-Hill argued, white men used "foolish names of no meaning whatever" to name the physical features of the park. Mather promised to use Indian language and translations in the future, but the National Park Service did not honor this promise (Keller and Turek 1998: 51).

IN THE SWAMPS

While many people despair of swamps, Harriet Beecher Stowe—who had one in front of her Florida cottage—wrote, "It is a glorious, bewildering impropriety. The trees and shrubs in it grow as if they are possessed; and there is scarcely a month in the year that it does not flame forth in some new blossom. It is a perpetual flower-garden, where creepers run and tangle; where Nature has raptures and frenzies of growth; and conducts herself like a crazy, drunken, but beautiful bacchante . . . Verily, it is the most gorgeous of improprieties, this swamp" (Stowe 1873: 138–139). Women like Stowe were being exposed to nature in a variety of ways and taking lessons from it.

PEOPLE OF COLOR

Access to and Control of Resources

This chapter examines a broader context in which westward expansion, Manifest Destiny, the expeditions, explorations, and resource exploitation discussed above took place. It provides a brief history of the relations between whites and various ethnic minority groups and the conflicts that ensued as the country was settled. It also offers an additional framework through which to understand the colonial and settler colonial practices, social relations, politics, and economic forces at work when elite white males and females began exploring the frontier and examines some well-known expeditions through the lens of the ethnic minority participants.

Expeditions and the Role of People of Color

The experiences of pioneering explorers such as Lewis and Clark are documented extensively elsewhere. In addition, the critical acclaim, benefits, and financial rewards from explorations usually went to elite men, though people of color and women participated in these ventures too. Minorities are not usually chronicled as explorers or environmental activists, yet the historical records show that they were a part of expeditions, resided and worked on the frontier, founded towns, and were educators and entrepreneurs. In short, people of color were very important actors in westward expansion. Environmental history accounts usually focus on the valor of the explorers, efforts to conserve or preserve landforms, the identification of new or unique specimens, the discovery of minerals, and so on. In the process these accounts often ignore or downplay the experiences of people of color.

It is difficult to document the contributions of people of color in expeditions, as they did not leave written records and more often than not were referred to in the diary entries of elites by generic and disparaging terms such as "the negro," "the Indian," "the slave," "the Chinaman," or "the Mexican." However, people of color participated in explorations and other activities aimed at facilitating westward expansion that was organized by elites as well as by middle- and working-class whites. Ethnic minorities served in a variety of roles and were present when discoveries were being made. However, it is not only the lax way of identifying people of color on these explorations that impairs our ability to find out about them but also the way narratives and discourses about discovery are constructed and propagated. While historical records are replete with accounts of European Americans being led to unique and wondrous landforms by Native Americans, the mantle of "discoverer" is usually attributed to European Americans. Euro-Americans exacerbate matters by expunging and supplanting the place-names used by indigenous peoples. So the credit for seeing, using, and being stewards of places such as Yosemite or Yellowstone tend to go not to Native American tribes, but to the first white explorer to lay eyes on them.

Native Americans

SACAGAWEA

Sacagawea, a woman of color who participated in the Lewis and Clark Expedition, exemplifies the roles that people of color often filled on these missions and the way their contributions were diminished or erased outright. Though her name is well known and often referenced, there are competing narratives about Sacagawea and the part she played in the Corps of Discovery. A Lemhi Shoshone woman, she was one of thirty-three people on the expedition. She was an interpreter and sometimes assumed the role of expedition guide. She gained some fame in the early twentieth century after the National American Women Suffrage Association made her a symbol of independent womanhood.

Sacagawea was born in 1788 in Idaho but was kidnapped when she was about twelve and taken to Hidatsa and Mandan villages near present-day Bismarck, North Dakota. When she was thirteen, Toussaint Charbonneau, a Quebecois trapper of French and Métis (Indian) ancestry, took her as his wife; Charbonneau also had another Indian child-bride as a second wife. Lewis and Clark interviewed several trappers in their quest to find someone who could guide them up the Missouri River. They settled on Charbonneau when they discovered he had a Shoshone wife who could speak the language. Charbonneau left his second wife behind and brought Sacagawea—who was pregnant at the time—to join the expedition at its winter quarters in Fort Mandan in November 1804 (I. W. Anderson 1999: 3–7; Clark and Edmonds 1979: 15; Fresonke and Spence 2004; Kastor and Valenčius 2008: 285–286; Moulton 1983–2001).

At a time when women (or at least upper- and middle-class white women) were considered too frail to engage in strenuous outdoor activities, the teenage mother set off with the expedition a few months after giving birth and made the roundtrip journey of hundreds of miles with her baby strapped to her back. Sacagawea was critical to the success of the expedition. Not only did her presence signal to tribes that it was a peaceful party; she also helped secure additional guides and horses to make it over the treacherous passes in the Rocky Mountains, where she was reunited with her own tribe and family members (Clark and Edmonds 1979: 15; R. J. Miller 2006). When the expedition was low on food supplies, she used traditional food-gathering techniques to find camas roots to supplement their diet. At one point, Sacagawea gave up her beaded belt to Lewis and Clark, who traded it for a fur robe they wanted to present to President Jefferson. On the return trip for the expedition in 1806, Sacagawea found a pass through the Rocky Mountains that is now named Gibbons Pass (Montana). She also advised the expeditioners to cross into the Yellowstone River basin at what is known as the Bozeman Pass. This pass was later chosen as the best route for the Northern Pacific Railroad to traverse the Continental Divide. A tributary of the Musselshell River in Montana was named after Sacagawea in 1805 (I. W. Anderson 1999: 3–7; Fresonke and Spence 2004; Moulton 1983–2001).

Sacagawea did not receive any compensation for her participation in the expedition, but her husband received five hundred dollars for his services. In 1807, Congress authorized double pay and land grants for expedition members. After the expedition, Charbonneau and Sacagawea returned to live among the Hidatsa, where Lewis and Clark first met them. In 1809 the couple moved to St. Louis at the invitation of Clark, who adopted their son, Jean-Baptiste, and enrolled him in the St. Louis Academy. Sacagawea is said to have had a daughter, Lizette, in 1812. Records indicate that Sacagawea died of a fever in 1812 at Fort Manuel, South Dakota, where Charbonneau was a trader. However, one story claims she separated from Charbonneau, returned to her tribe in the West, and lived until 1884 (I. W. Anderson 1999: 3–7; Clark and Edmonds 1979: 16; Fresonke and Spence 2004; Kastor and Valenčius 2008: 287; Moulton 1983–2001).

TERRITORIAL CONFLICTS AND THE
CHANGING STATUS OF NATIVE AMERICANS

The quest to explore, discover, and open up territories is intimately linked to development and ownership. As I pointed out in chapter 1, European settlers made a distinction between natural rights and civil rights to land: civil rights implied private property rights and superseded natural rights. Hence, the notion that those who labored and "developed" the soil and other natural resources had civil rights to the resources drove white-Indian relations and resulted in Indians being dispossessed of vast swaths of their territory.

Moreover, those who developed the land became the primary decision makers, while native people became marginalized. Early in the nineteenth century, Marshall, in his famous trilogy of cases, defined the status of Indian tribes and outlined the nature of the relationship between the tribes, federal, and state governments. Marshall's thinking is still relevant to Indian–government relations today. In addition to the *Johnson v. McIntosh* (1823) decision discussed above, Justice Marshall also asserted in *Cherokee Nation v. Georgia* (1831) that the tribe was a "distinct political society" akin to a "domestic dependent nation": in other words, the relationship of the tribe to the federal government was one of a ward to a guardian. In the third case, *Worcester v. Georgia* (1832), Marshall argued that state law could not interfere with the relationship between the federal government and the tribes.

Though Native Americans outnumbered European settlers for some time after colonization began, whites were still able to dominate the tribes. Estimates of how many Indians lived in the United States during the fifteenth and sixteenth centuries vary widely, ranging from 1 million to 18 million. Estimates of the size of the Indian population improved as the nineteenth century progressed, and by 1890, when the last of the "Indian wars" or "wars of conquest" ended, the census indicated there were 325,464 surviving Native Americans (Catlin [1844] 1973: 6; Department of the Interior 1895: 396–400; Gibson and Lennon 1999: 4; Nabokov 1991: 90–93; Richter 2001: 8; R. Thornton 1987: 16–35; Yenne 2005).

There is also a vigorous debate about the impact of European colonization on the Native American population (Larsen 1994; O'Fallon and Fehren-Schmitz

2011; R. Thornton 1997). While historical documents point to dramatic declines resulting from warfare, enslavement, epidemics, and so on (Crosby 2004; Dobyns 1993), recent scholarship using genetic sequencing of ancient and contemporary mitochondrial DNA found insignificant levels of population decline five hundred years ago (Bolnick and Smith 2003; Shook and Smith 2008; Wang et al. 2004). However, O'Fallon and Fehren-Schmitz (2011), who utilize both historical documentation and genetic sequencing techniques, found evidence of significant population decline caused by widespread mortality during the same time period.

Native Americans lost land and other resources as well as political power through warfare. Between 1500 and 1900, there were numerous outbreaks of hostilities between whites and Indians and between various tribes as Native Americans resisted encroachment on and seizure of their land. Three major periods of warfare between whites and Indians are identifiable. First, resistance to Spanish occupation lasted from the arrival of Columbus until the Spanish conquered the Pueblo Indians in New Mexico in 1692. Veteran Spanish soldiers were used to overrun and destroy Indian communities in Florida, California, and the Southwest and to enslave the inhabitants.

From 1622 to 1812 a second major period of warfare unfolded, this one between Native Americans of the Southeast and the British and French. During and after the Revolution, the United States punished Indian tribes that collaborated with the British. In 1779, American troops launched a scorched-earth campaign that burned forty Iroquois towns to the ground. The third major series of Indian–white wars began in the 1790s and ended a century later with the massacre at Wounded Knee, South Dakota. From 1849 to 1892 the campaign against the Navajo and Apaches engulfed New Mexico, Arizona, and northern Mexico and spread to include other western tribes from Texas to the Canadian border and westward to the Pacific. The prolonged period of warfare decimated the most experienced and respected Indian leaders. Handpicked "Indian leaders" who were less critical of U.S. government policies and had little or no grassroots support in their tribes were installed as replacements for traditional leaders (G. T. Morris 1992: 63; Nabokov 1991: 90–93; Stiffarm and Lane 1992: 23–30; R. Thornton 1987: 50; Vogel 1992: 55–56).

TREATY MAKING AND COLONIAL EXPANSION

Colonial powers had a significant impact on the U.S. Indian policy through the treaty-making[1] process (*Cherokee Nation v. Georgia* 1831; Office of American Indian Trust 2000a, 2000b; *Worcester v. Georgia* 1832). Ironically, Native Americans lost more land by signing treaties than by warfare. Indeed, some of the conflicts occurred because Indians insisted on receiving the land promised in treaties. While the Dutch acquired land by purchase (they "purchased" Manhattan for twenty-four dollars' worth of beads and other trade goods), the French settled in villages, married Indian women, and became administrators of the villages and the new trading posts. However, treaties—which originated with the sixteenth-century Spanish court—came to dominate the relationship between the colonists, the American government, and Native Americans. The British sought to centralize and monopolize contact with the Indians and publicly advocated a policy of land acquisition by purchase, so under the earliest British policies the settlers negotiated with native people for land. Nonetheless, British settlers also acquired land through conquest. The U.S. government followed British policies in negotiating treaties with tribes. These treaties usually called for Indians to vacate their homes and relocate to infertile, marginal land or to "Indian Country" (Oklahoma), subdivide their holdings into single-family farms, and sell excess land to white speculators. Whites reserved the right to build roads, railroad tracks, trails, and so on, across Indian lands, but the treaties also stipulated that tribes should be paid annuities, money, or goods (Jaimes 1992: 124; Nabokov 1991: 117–120; P. Young 1997: 95).

The American government negotiated the first treaty with Indians during the Revolutionary War: in 1778, the Delawares were promised statehood if they helped to defeat the British. However, eighteen treaties later the Delawares did not have statehood and were dispersed from Canada to Oklahoma. The Northwest Ordinance of 1787 sets forth principles for governing landholdings west of the Appalachian Mountains. Despite the promises of the ordinance,[2] Native Americans lost millions of acres of land by signing treaties. The last of 374 treaties was signed with Native Americans (Nez Perce) in 1868. Three years later, the Congress passed the Indian Appropriation Act, which formally ended treaty making (Jaimes 1992: 124; Nabokov 1991: 117–120; Office of American Indian Trust 2000a: 1; P. Young 1997: 95).[3]

A system of reservations was also established for the Native Americans to live on. Initially, reservations were established as an alternative to completely annihilating the tribes. They were intended to be temporary establishments to house Indians while they were in the process of being acculturated. It was thought that once the acculturation was complete, then Native Americans would be fully absorbed into mainstream society. As a commissioner of Indian affairs stated in 1850, the reservation would "civilize" the Indians because they would be "compelled by sheer necessity to resort to agricultural labor or starve." To achieve this goal, Indian agents forbade Native Americans to leave the reservations, hunt, or trade without a permit. Thus Native Americans were forced to be dependent on government rations or the products of their farms (Ambler 1990: 9; Prucha 1986: 108–121). The reservations were also seen as a way to segregate whites from Indians and place Indians in smaller territories, where they could be controlled more easily. Referring to the reservation system, J. Bausman, writing the opinion in *State v. Towessnute* (1916), argued, "The main purpose of the government was to separate the Indian from the white man and to care for the Indian in a more confined district."

REMOVAL AND RELOCATION

The removal of Indian tribes from their homelands began shortly after the European settlers arrived in New England. The settlers created "praying towns" for Christianized Indians. Indians were also encouraged to migrate west (R. Thornton 1987: 50). For instance, New Haven was founded in 1638, and life changed quickly for the Quinnipiacs after the approximately 150 Europeans settled the area. The Quinnipiacs—which numbered about 150 people at the time—gave up their lands around New Haven harbor for cloth, spoons, knives, hatchets, hoes, porringers, and scissors. They ceded several parcels of land beginning in 1638. In return they were placed on the nation's first Indian reservation—a 1,200-acre parcel located on the eastern side of the harbor. Within a short time, other reservations were established in Connecticut for various bands of Quinnipiacs on what was formerly their territory. Between 1700 and 1750, some Quinnipiacs were relocated to Stockbridge, Massachusetts, while others were relocated to Farmington, Connecticut, in 1768. The original New Haven reservation was encroached on repeatedly. Consequently, Indians complained that they had no land on which to practice agriculture. In response, New Haven's Proprietors of the Common and Undivided Land reserved thirty acres for the tribe in 1764 that English settlers should not disturb. This did not stop the encroachment. Finally, in 1773—when the tribe consisted of about thirty-eight people—the last of what had been reserved as Indian lands was sold off (Schiff 1981: 96; Sletcher 2004: 11, 50–54; Townshend 1900: 11, 21, 54, 67–68, 72).

At first Europeans looked askance at Indian farming techniques because women were more often than not the farmers and mixed cropping techniques were frequently used. Notwithstanding, many New England towns were established on lands that Indian tribes had already cultivated, and settlers used the cleared and tilled land. More than sixty of the towns established before 1650 were settled in such a manner (J. R. Garrison 2005: 4–5; Snow 2005: 23–24).

Thomas Jefferson was a fervent proponent of the idea that Native Americans should be assimilated into mainstream culture. Jefferson thought that with adequate resources and coaxing, tribes could be socialized to live in harmony with whites, so the social-control mission of reform organizations was expanded to include acculturation of the Indians. Benevolent societies and missionary organizations were asked to administer socialization efforts, and a Civilization Fund that received annual appropriations from Congress was established in 1819. During the removal and relocation period, missionary stations were moved and reestablished west of the Mississippi as the Indian population was driven westward (U.S. Commission on Human Rights 1992: 20).

Under Andrew Jackson, a president who grew up on the frontier fighting Indians and believed in acquiring land by conquest, there was a dramatic increase in the number of Native Americans forced to relocate. Jackson believed that Indian tribes could be used as pawns of foreign powers seeking to wage war against the United States, and he concluded that corralling Indians in areas where they could be monitored and controlled more easily was in the best interest of national security. Indians who were forced to relocate starved or succumbed to diseases as they trekked west taking with them only what they could carry on their person. Moreover, relocating tribes were often attacked by hostile whites or enemy tribes along the way. The forced relocations peaked in the 1830s with the passage of the Indian Removal Act of 1830 and the Preemption Act of 1830 (which gave white squatters first rights to purchase Indian land they had been squatting on). The removals continued through the end of the nineteenth century. Between 1816 and 1850, 100,790 Native Americans from more than twenty tribes were scheduled to be relocated west of the Mississippi. In 1838 agents report that 81,082 Native Americans had already been moved west of the Mississippi River. Thousands of Indians died on the journeys (Carlson and Roberts 2006: 486–504; Nabokov 1991: 145–150; Office of Indian Affairs 1836: 15–16; 1838: 470; Prucha 1975: 48–52; Remini 2001; R. Thornton 1987: 50–51; Whalen 2013).

Assimilation and Removal. Even the Five "Civilized" Tribes (Cherokees, Choctaws, Chickasaws, Creeks, and Seminoles) were subject to removal. These tribes had sizable mixed-race populations (which arose, in part, from the tribes' extensive involvement in the eighteenth-century deerskin trade) and partially acculturated elites living among them. Several factors led to their removal, including the discovery of gold in Georgia,[4] the desire of cotton growers to gain access to fertile Indian land, and pressure from homesteaders in Arkansas and Georgia to remove all Native Americans from those states. The campaign to remove tribes to lands west of the Mississippi River resulted in boisterous debates in Congress regarding which type of land use should be given priority—

farming or hunting. Euro-American agriculturalists and their supporters won the debates and votes. The removal of the tribes occurred even though the Cherokees, Choctaws, Chickasaws, and Creeks had heeded the American government's advice to assimilate. They had developed court systems, drafted laws and constitutions, farmed, bred herds, held slaves, opened missionary schools, and adopted the customs of their white neighbors in response to the 1819 Civilization Act. Though tribal members were portrayed as merely hunters in the debate over the Removal Act, the reality is that they were established agriculturalists by the time the Removal Act was passed (Carlson and Roberts 2006: 493–496; Champagne 1992: 195–213; Gregg and Wishart 2012: 423; Nabokov 1991: 148; Perdue and Green 2005: 5).

Resisting Removal. The Choctaw tribe was the first of the five to make the journey. A War Department census showed that the tribe had 17,963 Indians, 151 whites, and 521 slaves in 1830. The first wave of about four thousand left Mississippi in the winter of 1831. Barefoot, starving, and weakened by cholera, they did not fare well in the snow, blizzard, and subzero temperatures they encountered. The second wave of removals involving 6,000 to 7,500 Choctaws occurred in 1832; rations were decreased and transportation provided for only those who were very young or very ill. The last wave of about a thousand Choctaws were relocated in 1833. Some Choctaws refused to move; hence, between four thousand to six thousand Choctaws remained in Mississippi after the removal operations ceased. The tribe ceded about eleven million acres of land in Alabama, Arkansas, Mississippi, and Louisiana; in 1834 they occupied approximately fifteen million acres west of the Mississippi River—but they had to allow other tribes to settle among them. Newspapers describe scenes of hundreds of white settlers gathering to cheer as the Huron and other boats left Mississippi loaded with Choctaws. An estimated two thousand five hundred Choctaws died while being relocated (Akers 1999: 63–76; W. L. Anderson 1991; DeRosier 1970: 137, 148–158; Faiman-Silva 1997: 19–20; Kilpinen 2004: 492; *Niles' Weekly Register* 1832; Office of Indian Affairs 1832: 21; Satz 1986: 7–8; U.S. House of Representatives 1834: 118).

The Creeks, who once lived in present-day Mississippi, Louisiana, Alabama, Georgia, and Florida were farmers and ranchers. As white settlers encroached on their land and usurped access to the wildlife, the Creeks tried to protect their resources but found themselves in violent confrontations with the newcomers during the 1830s. This led to the signing of the Cusseta Treaty of 1832, which forced the Creeks to cede 5.2 million acres of land. An 1833 census indicates that the Upper Creek settlements had 14,142 residents (this includes

445 slaves) and the Lower Creek settlements had 8,557 people (including 457 slaves) living in them. Despite signing the Cusseta Treaty, fewer than seven hundred Creeks had moved to Oklahoma by 1835; tribal members complained of fraudulent land deals and refused to leave their homeland before these were settled. As conflict in Creek Country escalated, about two thousand five hundred Creeks moved into Oklahoma in December 1835 to avoid the turmoil. The situation deteriorated and war broke out in Creek Country in early 1836. The Creeks were expelled from Alabama in 1836; many were in chains. An overloaded steamboat carrying one group sank, killing 311 Creeks. Thousands of Creeks died during the relocation. The mass eviction of the Creeks from their homeland was largely over by 1837 (W. L. Anderson 1991; Ellisor 2010: 2, 18–21, 42–47, 56–57, 113, 160–161, 182–263; Ethridge 2003: 14–15, 21, 140–174; Gregg and Wishart 2012: 425; Haverman 2008: 14, 19; Kilpinen 2004: 492; Nabokov 1991: 149–150; Perdue and Green 2005; Prucha 1986: 241; Schneider 1994: 98–99; Whalen 2013).

The Chickasaws, who lived in Tennessee, Mississippi, and Alabama, grew crops, raised cattle, and managed horses. The Treaty of Doaksville—signed in 1837—resulted in the loss of five thousand acres of land and an expedited removal of the tribe. The first wave of emigrants consisted of about four thousand five hundred tribal members. Most of the exodus was completed in thirteen months—in all seven thousand were relocated west of the Mississippi River. Only about five hundred Chickasaws remained in their original territory after that. The final group of 143 tribal members migrated in 1850 (Atkinson 2004: 183, 231–234; Hogan 2015: 122–123; Lewis 1981: 2, 182; Paige et al. 2010; Walls 2015: 2–4, 169).

The Cherokee—who lived in Georgia, South Carolina, North Carolina, Tennessee, Texas, Arkansas, and Alabama—resisted removal by taking their case to the Supreme Court in 1831 and winning. In 1835, leaders of the Cherokee resistance refused to sign the Treaty of New Echota[5] because they felt the small group of 100[6] people negotiating the treaty—which paid out $5 million for 7,882,240 acres of tribal lands east of the Mississippi River and provided 13.8 million acres of land west of the Mississippi—was not representative of the Cherokee people or their wishes.[7] John Ross, Principal Chief of the Cherokee tribe during the removal period, collected the signatures of 16,000 tribal members who opposed the treaty. Ross also estimated that the Cherokee land was worth about $7.23 million. However, President Jackson was firm in belief that the tribes should not remain east of the Mississippi (T. A. Garrison 2002; Gregg 2009: 320–335; Gregg and Wishart 2012: 425, 438; A. Jackson 1835: 40–43). Frustrated by the seemingly slow pace of Indian acculturation, suspicious of their ability to function effectively in white society, and concerned about dwindling wildlife stocks, Jackson wanted to accelerate the pace of removals. This is reflected in a notification he sent to the Cherokees in 1835. It read,

> Most of your people are uneducated . . . With strong passions, and without those habits of restraint which our laws inculcate and render necessary . . . the game has disappeared among you, and you must depend upon agriculture and the mechanic arts for support. And, yet, a large portion of your people have acquired little or no property in the soil itself . . . How, under these circumstances can you live in the country you now occupy? . . . you will ultimately disappear, as so many tribes have done before you. Of all this I warned your people, when I met them in council eighteen years ago. I advised them to sell out their possessions east of the Mississippi, and to remove to the country west of that river . . . I am sincerely desirous to promote your welfare. Listen to me, therefore, while I tell you that you cannot remain where you now are. Circumstances that cannot be controlled, and which are beyond the reach of human laws, render it impossible that you can flourish in the midst of a civilized community. You have but one remedy within your reach. And that is, to remove to the West and join your countrymen, who are already established there. And the sooner you do this, the sooner you will commence your career of improvement and prosperity . . . Why, then, should any honest man among you object to removal? The United States have assigned to you a fertile and extensive country, with a very fine climate adapted to your habits . . . Deceive yourselves no longer. Do not cherish the belief that you can ever resume your former political situation, while you continue in your present residence . . . you cannot drive back the laws of Georgia from among you. Every year will increase your difficulties. Look at the condition of the Creeks. See the collisions which are taking place with them. See how their young men are committing depredations upon the property of our citizens, and are shedding their blood. This cannot and will not be allowed. Punishment will follow, and all who are engaged in these offences must suffer. (A. Jackson 1835: 40–43)

At the time of this notification the War Department conducted a census that found 16,542 Cherokee living in Alabama, Georgia, North Carolina, and Tennessee. These tribal members held 1,592 slaves; an additional 201 people had married into the tribe (T. A. Garrison 2002; McLoughlin 1986; Office of Indian Affairs 1836: 5). The removal was a three-step process. The Treaty of New Echota called for voluntary removal within two years of signing. Sensing the inevitable, the pro-treaty group and others amounting to about 10,000 tribal members moved westward between 1835 and 1837 (W. L. Anderson 1991).

Some prominent citizens objected to the removals. Ralph Waldo Emerson was one of them. Though Emerson resorted to disparaging portrayals of the Cherokees, he expressed his repulsion of the idea of forcibly relocating tribes. In April 1838 Emerson wrote a letter to President Van Buren (who succeeded Jackson) in which he implored the president to rethink the removal policy. Emerson said,

> We have learned with joy their improvement in the social arts. We have read their newspapers. We have seen some of them in our schools and colleges. In common with the great body of the American people, we have witnessed with sympathy the painful labors of these red men to redeem their own race from the doom of eternal inferiority, and to borrow and domesticate in the tribe the arts and customs of the Caucasian race . . . The newspapers now inform us that, in December, 1835, a treaty contracting for the exchange of all the Cherokee territory was pre-tended to be made by an agent on the part of the United States with some persons appearing on the part of the Cherokees; that the fact afterwards transpired that these deputies did by no means represent the will of the nation; and that, out of eighteen thousand souls composing the nation, fifteen thousand six hundred and sixty-eight have protested against the so-called treaty. It now appears that the government of the United States choose to hold the Cherokees to this sham treaty, and are proceeding to execute the same. Almost the entire Cherokee Nation stand up and say, "This is not our act. Behold us. Here are we. Do not mistake that handful of deserters for us"; and the American President and the Cabinet, the Senate and the House of Representatives, neither hear these men nor see them, and are contracting to put this active nation into carts and boats, and to drag them over mountains and rivers to a wilderness at a vast distance beyond the Mississippi. And a paper purporting to be an army order fixes a month from this day as the hour for this doleful removal. In the name of God, sir, we ask you if this be so. Do the newspapers rightly inform us? Men and women with pale and perplexed faces meet one another in the streets and churches here, and ask if this be so. We have inquired if this be a gross misrepresentation from the party opposed to the government and anxious to blacken it with the people. We have looked in the newspapers of different parties and find a horrid confirmation of the tale. We are slow to believe it. Such a dereliction of all faith and virtue, such a denial

of justice, and such deafness to screams for mercy were never heard of in times of peace and in the dealing of a nation with its own allies and wards, since the earth was made. Sir, does this government think that the people of the United States are become savage and mad? . . . The soul of man, the justice, the mercy that is the heart's heart in all men, from Maine to Georgia, does abhor this business. (Emerson 1838)

Despite letters from people like Emerson, the second phase—forced removal—began in May 1838. That month seven thousand soldiers began rounding up about four thousand eight hundred Cherokees and forcing them to move. About a thousand members of the tribe escaped and hid in the mountains (Duncan and Riggs 2003: 273–276). Tribal members were interned in eleven camps.[8] It is estimated that 353 people died of dysentery and other illnesses in the camps. Resigning themselves to the inevitable, the Cherokees also organized their own journeys. Beginning in fall 1838 the third phase—the reluctant removal—occurred under the supervision of John Ross. Roughly one thousand Cherokees were relocated in this round (W. L. Anderson 1991; Duncan and Riggs 2003: 273–276; B. Jones 1984: 74–81).

John Ross estimated in 1838 that the total cost of removing the Cherokee amounted to $13.9 million. This considered the cost of ceded land, losses for private property, transportation, and subsistence costs. Recent estimates that consider the factors Ross based his calculations on puts the figure at $19.7 million. Estimates of the social costs of Cherokee removal is $9.24 million in 1838 dollars (Gregg and Wishart 2012: 425, 438). It is estimated that between four thousand and five thousand Cherokees died during the round ups, in the internment camps and on the 2,200-mile trek. The routes along which the tribes traveled is called the "Trail of Tears" (T. A. Garrison, 2002; Prucha 1986: 241; Thornton 1991; 75–93).

The Seminoles—which numbered approximately five thousand members—were the smallest of the five tribes being discussed, yet they engaged in a protracted opposition to removal. In 1832 tribal members signed a treaty at Payne's Landing that stipulated their removal from Florida. They ceded their land and cattle as conditions of removal (Lancaster 1986: 1, 15–17; Office of Indian Affairs 1832: 160–161; 1836: 3–4; U.S. House of Representatives 1834: 63–64).

Not all of the Seminoles relocated. In Florida, a group of Seminoles—the Miccosukees—avoided forced relocation by hiding in the Everglades. They protested removal by squatting on their homeland for more than 130 years. The Seminoles further angered plantation owners and the government by taking in runaway slaves and interbreeding with them. Although these Seminoles resisted the relentless attacks of the army, by 1842 almost four thousand had been relocated to Oklahoma, and by the end of the Second Seminole War only about five hundred Seminoles remained in the Everglades. In 1861, about two hundred Seminoles were forcibly removed from Florida and relocated in Oklahoma, leaving about three hundred in the swamps. The Seminoles never agreed to any peace accords until the mid-1960s. Finally, the state of Florida agreed to create a small reservation for the Seminoles, and Congress approved it in 1982 (Churchill 1992: 151; Coulter 1978: 22–27; Florida Indian Land Claim Settlement Act 1982).

FORCED FARMING AND LAND REDISTRIBUTION

After the Civil War the crusade to reform the Bureau of Indian Affairs attracted many former antislavery advocates. At this time, there were about three hundred thousand Native Americans. The reformers believed that Indians should be assimilated into white American ways—that is, they should be Christianized, speak English, learn vocational skills, wear European-style clothing, become single-family farmers, and strive toward full American citizenship. This view drove Indian policy making for several decades. Though the notion of allotting Indian lands was a part of early treaties, that idea was a critical part of Indian policy in the 1860s. The policy of "allotment in severalty" was intended to force Indians to become family farmers and weaken the tribal government system. In addition, assimilationist policies initiated and enforced measures aimed at destroying native languages and traditions, while some cultural and religious activities were criminalized (Bureau of Indian Affairs 1999: 41; Nabokov 1991: 232–233).

Congress passed the General Allotment Act (or the Dawes Act) in 1887 as a mechanism to speed up the partitioning of Native American lands. When Senator Henry L. Dawes introduced the bill, he argued that it would be a mighty pulverizing force that could be used to dismantle the tribal system and pave the path for the "civilization" of the "savage." He also thought private land ownership would be the best means of assimilating Indians (Dawes Act 1887; Office of American Indian Trust 2000a). Dawes disdained the practice of communal land ownership. Before sponsoring the Dawes Act, he visited five tribes. Though one tribal chief told him that everyone in the tribe owned their homes, no one was poor, and the tribe owed no money and had built its own schools and hospital, the senator argued that the tribal system was defective. He said the tribes had not progressed as much as they could because they owned their land in common and thus individuals had no incentive to make their homes better than those of their neighbors. He argued that selfishness was the foundation of civilization and that there was none evident in the tribes he observed (Board of Indian Commissioners 1902: 90–91).

Under the Allotment Act, Native American families were offered deeds to property that were either individually or family owned. If anyone refused the deed, a local agent accepted it on their behalf. The Allotment Act gave the allottee full rights to the timber and minerals on the land (Ambler 1990: 42).[9] Indians who were allotted land had to show documentation certifying that they had one-half or more Indian blood to receive title to the land. The allotments were held in trust for twenty-five years, during which time the owners could not sell the land without the consent of the government. At the end of the twenty-five years, the owner received a clear title to the land. After Indian families received their allotments, the remaining portions of the reservations were sold to the highest bidders. This resulted in Indian landholdings being broken up in a checkerboard pattern, as a substantial number of whites purchased land and resided within former reservation boundaries. Some of the Indian lands were also converted into national parks, forests, and grasslands. For instance, Theodore Roosevelt took 2.5 million acres of Indian timber lands—including the mineral rights—and converted them into national forests during his tenure (Ambler 1990: 12, 42; Jaimes 1992: 126, 130; McChesney 1992: 112–113; Nabokov 1991: 188–189, 232–233; National Academy of Public Administration 1999: 7).

Though the allotment policy was intended to convert Indians into family farmers, the number of acres farmed by Indians actually fell as the policy was implemented. Only a small percentage of the Indian allottees were able to retain their homes or establish farms. Indian families who found it difficult to farm on their small allotments sold their land cheaply. This left them destitute, landless, and with no tribal support network around them. In the meantime, groups such as the Indian Rights Association, the National Indian Association, and the Lake Mohonk Conference supported the allotment system and lobbied for its expansion (Carlson 1981: 128–154; Nabokov 1991: 234–238, 256–258).

The allotment policy amounted to a massive redistribution of land from Indians to whites. Almost all tribes lost land through the implementation of this policy. For example, after parcels were allotted to Indian families, Iowa Indians lost 90 percent of their reservations. Likewise, the Cheyenne, Arapaho, and Plains Indians lost about 81 percent of their territories. The Crow reservation in Montana was originally 2.5 million acres; today only about half of that remains in trust. In addition to drastically reducing the Indians' land base, the Dawes Act also cut food rations and other supplies promised in old treaties. Hence, once the Dawes Act was implemented, Indian families found themselves on the most isolated and barren corners of former reservations, often with little or no access to water. Furthermore, Indians lacked the resources needed to farm these challenging parcels, so they went bankrupt. By the 1890s, Congress passed a series of laws that enabled Indians to lease their property to whites—usually for a pittance. The result was that destitute Indians became absentee landowners barely subsisting on the fringes of white society and were once again dependent on the government for food (Nabokov 1991: 258–259; National Academy of Public Administration 1999: 8).

In 1902, Congress allowed heirs to sell parcels before the twenty-five-year limit originally stipulated in the deeds had expired. Within three years, more than a quarter million acres of Indian land was sold off. In Oklahoma, in particular, fraudulent wills were drafted for dead Indians or for people who never existed, whites appointed themselves "guardians" for Indian children who were set to inherit land from their parents, and heirs were bribed and in some cases murdered to obtain their land. The continual transfer of land from Indians to others meant that by 1920 an estimated one hundred thousand Indians were landless (Nabokov 1991: 259–260; Schneider 1994: 104).

Blacks

YORK

As the above discussion indicates, Indian tribes moved their slaves with them when they were relocated to Oklahoma (Office of Indian Affairs 1832; 1836; 1838). Slaves were also moved to the West with their masters or taken on explorations and expeditions as part of the westward expansion and Manifest Destiny. In the West they worked in the fur trading business, mining, agriculture, and ranching, and as guides, cooks, stable hands, and porters. Clark brought his slave, York, who was roughly the same age as Clark, on the Corps of Discovery expedition. Clark inherited York when his father died in 1799. York, who was born around 1770 on the Virginia plantation Clark's family owned, used his incredible skills in hunting, fishing, and collecting greens to provide food for expedition members. He also used his knowledge of field medicine to care for expedition members. York helped to construct the fort and cabins; he was a member of the advanced scouting unit and assumed the task of befriending and entertaining Indian tribes they met along the way. At a time when slaves were not allowed to carry firearms, York was entrusted with a gun that he used to kill buffalo and other animals. His physical strength and prowess reportedly astonished and fascinated Native Americans and enhanced the prestige of the white explorers with the tribes they encountered. York was the primary caregiver to those who fell ill on the trip. York is believed to be the first black male to cross the continent north of Mexico (Betts 1985; C. G. Clarke 1970; Franklin and Moss 1994: 107; D. Jackson 1962; Millner 2003: 302–333; Moulton 1983–2001; National Park Service 2009a; Ronda 1984).

Though York participated as a full member of the expedition, he received neither land nor cash for his services. He requested his freedom on returning from the trip, and Clark refused; Clark even refused to let York join his wife who was in Louisville (York was married before embarking on the expedition). Eventually, in November 1808, he was allowed to visit his wife and in 1809, when he returned and demanded his freedom, he was beaten severely and jailed by his irritated master. Clark considered York insolent for making such demands. York was emancipated more than a decade after the expedition (Clark's grandson reports that York was still Clark's slave thirteen years after the expedition). York's eventual fate is unclear. Some accounts have him returning to the West, where he became a chief of an Indian tribe; another report claims he went into the freighting business in Kentucky and Tennessee and died of cholera in 1832. Yet another report indicates that he escaped slavery to become a free man (Betts 1985; C. G. Clarke 1970; Franklin and Moss 1994: 107; D. Jackson 1962; Millner 2003: 302–333; Moulton 1983–2001; National Park Service 2009a; Ronda 1984).

FORCED RELOCATIONS OF SLAVES

York's forced movement across the country is not unique among slaves. Like Native Americans, African American slaves were forcibly relocated to different parts of the country. With the removal of Indians from the territories of Alabama and Mississippi, cotton plantations dominated the region, so slaves were moved to work on these plantations. Mass movement of slaves accompanied the spread of plantations. The 1850 census showed that most of the 2.5 million slaves in the country worked in cotton, tobacco, sugar, rice, and hemp cultivation. Slaves were also used as scouts in the campaign to open up Indian lands to whites during the westward expansion (L. Bennett 1993: 96; Parish 1989: 21–31).

Trafficking in slaves was commonplace. About a million slaves were forced to move to the South and West between 1790 and 1860. Originally, most of the slaves were moved from Maryland, Virginia, and the Carolinas to Tennessee and Kentucky. However, after 1810 slaves were relocated to Georgia, Alabama, Mississippi, Louisiana, and Texas to supply the labor needed for cotton production. Slave owners were the drivers of this internal migration, which is sometimes referred to as the Second Middle Passage. Breaking up slave families and selling them off was such a common practice that by 1820, a slave child had about a 30 percent chance of being sold and sent to the South. Though many slaves were forced to walk to their new locations, some were transported by ships and railway freight cars. On his first trip to the South in 1859, J. Pierpont Morgan claimed to have witnessed "1000 slaves on a train." Relocated slaves, often weakened from hunger and the long treks, faced a frontier life of forced labor at their new locations. Accustomed to growing tobacco and wheat, these slaves were sent to the South to grow cotton and sugarcane. They had to clear the forests and cultivate crops in virgin fields. Many worked near mosquito-infested swamps and riverbanks that exposed them to malaria and other diseases. During the growing season, slaves worked up to eighteen hours per day (Berlin, Reidy, and Rowlands 1982: 161–180; Blassingame 1979: 250–251; Strouse 1999: 88; Sublette and Sublette 2016: 9).

The slaves who did not work in the fields labored as domestics, skilled artisans, cowboys, and ranch hands around the plantation. Some of the larger plantations were organized like industrial villages. Between 5 and 10 percent of the slaves were hired out by their masters to cities, towns, the southern railroads, factories, and small farmers. The hiring-out system gave the slaves a measure of autonomy because they could bargain for wages and keep some of their wages; some eventually used this income to purchase their freedom (Genovese 1972: 388–392).

THE LIVING CONDITIONS OF SLAVES

Slaves lived in deplorable conditions, but from the late 1830s to the 1860s there was a concerted effort to improve the quality of slave housing. Slave owners had an incentive to improve slave quarters because once the importation of slaves was banned it became more expensive to replace slaves. Hence, southern agricultural journals ran articles imploring plantation owners to improve housing in order to protect the health and reproductive capacity of the slaves, contribute to the maintenance of the social order, and improve the moral standing of slave masters. The articles argued that overcrowding was unhealthy and resulted in conflict and sexual immorality (Blassingame 1979: 254–255; Genovese 1972: 524–525).

While some plantations had two-room log cabins for the families, others had one room with no windows. Many slave owners crammed two families into each cabin, hence four to twelve people shared a cabin (Blassingame 1979: 254–255). When in use, the poorly ventilated cabins' fireplaces generally filled the rooms with smoke, exposing the slaves to indoor air pollution. The cabins were suffocating in the summer and drafty in the winter. John Brown wrote, "The wind and rain will come in and smoke will not go out" (J. Brown 1855: 191). Austin Steward, who was enslaved in Virginia, recalled, "We lived in a small cabin, built of rough boards, with a floor of earth and small openings in the sides of the cabin substituted for windows. The chimney was built of sticks and mud; the door, of rough boards; and the whole was put together in the rudest possible manner" (Steward 1857: 13).

As the nineteenth century progressed, slaves pressured their masters to allow them to build their cabins amid the trees and flowers and beautify them somewhat. However, slaves were able to exert little influence over the way their living quarters were constructed. Plantation owners used slave labor to build the cabins, but the cabins were built to the exact specification of the master. Slave owners tore down cabins that were constructed in traditional African style. A few chimneys in these cabins were made of brick, but most were constructed from tabby (a mixture of oyster shells, lime, and sand), mud, clay, and sticks. Because the fireplace was the only source of heat in the winter, the chimneys were a major fire hazard (Genovese 1972: 524–525, 528).

Slaves relied on nature and the wilderness for their sustenance and survival. Household chores were divided along gender lines. The men collected firewood; the women collected plants (for medicine and consumption), made the fire, and designed candles. The women took tallow from cow innards, boiled out the fat, and inserted a string to make the candles. Some raised bees for the wax. Women also whitewashed the cabins, kept them clean, and decorated them with flowers. While some owners were content to provide planks of wood for bedding, slaves collected moss, scalded it to kill any insects it contained, and molded it into bedding. Some slave masters did provide lumber for bed-making or cotton for bedding. Men who hunted decorated the cabin walls with the skins of the opossum and raccoons they killed. They converted the skins of cattle into rawhide to make their chairs. Slaves went fishing too; they also collected and used oyster and mussel shells for spoons and knives. The slaves collected bottles and stoneware, and they raised gourds they could dry and use as bowls, dishes, ladles, and jugs. Slaves improved their diet and earned money by cultivating vegetable gardens, growing cotton and tobacco, raising pigs and chickens, and selling the surplus. Many of the women did the gardening, dyeing of fabric, quilting, weaving, and sewing (Bedigian 2013: 67–120; Blassingame 1979: 106–108; Genovese 1972: 525–527, 530–531, 535; Sublette and Sublette 2016).

Trappers and Traders. Blacks could be found on the western frontier as fur traders, trappers, miners, and in a variety of other occupations. Blacks were very important in the fur trade and had been involved in it since the Dutch West India Company began importing slaves to work in the industry in the early seventeenth century (Wilson and Greene 1995: 112–115). In 1673, when fur traders Louis Joliet and Father James Marquette paddled down the Mississippi River, five Africans accompanied them (Katz 1971: 28). The Lewis and Clark Expedition opened the West to even greater trade in fur than had existed beforehand, and black trappers functioned as liaisons between white entrepreneurs and Indians. In the 1820s a black man named Edward Rose worked for the Missouri Fur Company as a guide, hunter, and interpreter. Several blacks rose to prominence as trappers in the Minnesota Territory. Peirre Bonga, the slave of a Canadian fur trapper working for the North West Company, was an interpreter who negotiated with the Chippewas on behalf of the company. Bonga's son George, who lived at Fort Michilimackinac in Michigan, also became a well-known trader and voyageur for the American Fur Company. George also worked as an interpreter and assistant for Michigan governor Lewis Cass and eventually grew quite wealthy from his endeavors (Drenning 1950: 65–67; Franklin and Moss 1994: 107; *Journal of Negro History* 1927: 41–54; Katz 1971: 29–33, 39–41; Porter 1971).

Reese, a servant of Francis A. Chardon, was a trader with the Blackfoot tribe in and around Fort Chardon in the early 1840s. Other black fur traders and trappers named in historical accounts include Davy Jackson's slave, Jim, who went on an expedition to California. Mose was a black man who worked as a fur trader at Fort Sarpy, while Auguste operated from Fort Berthold. Several black traders were reported as operating from the Fort Union Trading Post between 1847 and 1848. Many of the trading posts had blacks working in the capacities of horse wranglers, cooks, interpreters, hunters, traders, and trappers (Gwaltney 1994).

Founders and Town Planners in Oregon and Washington. The United States based its successful claim to the Oregon Territory—in part—on the settlement of the region by an Irish immigrant, Michael Simmons, and his black companion, George Washington Bush. In 1820 or 1821 Bush made his first trip to the Pacific on horseback as a member of the party for one of the fur companies in St. Louis. The first major migration along the Oregon Trail occurred in 1843, when almost one thousand people headed westward. The following year, when Michael Simmons wanted to move thirty-two people to Oregon, he called on

Bush because of his mountaineering experience. Bush was the son of an Irish servant and a black father. He was an experienced frontiersman, skilled farmer, voyageur, and trapper. Bush decided that instead of just guiding the party, he would emigrate also. He sold his farm and possessions and was able to amass about two thousand dollars to take with him on the journey. He used some of this money to finance the journeys of others who could not afford the cost. The Bush-Simmons party joined a larger group of about eight hundred people at St. Joseph, Missouri, and from there traveled west. Bush was accompanied by his German wife, Isabella, and their five sons. In 1845, he settled near Turnwater in what is now Bush Prairie, Washington. When the Bush-Simmons party reached Oregon in 1844, they encountered laws that prevented blacks from settling south of the Columbia River. Consequently, Bush and his party settled north of the river. They spent the winter of 1844–45 near Washougal, about twenty miles east of present-day Portland, Oregon, on the Hudson Bay Company's land; they built a more permanent settlement in 1845. Bush trapped for the Hudson Bay Company and farmed the 640 acres he staked claim to. He almost lost his land after the 1846 treaty extended the Oregon Territory to the Forty-Ninth Parallel; with that treaty came the Black Codes prohibiting blacks from settling in the territory. Because Bush had helped so many of his fellow travelers and newcomers to the region, an exemption was made that allowed him to keep his land and continue living where he had settled (Hult 1962; Katz 1992: 68–71; *Museum Gazette* 1999; Oldham 2004).

Another black pioneer, George Washington, is credited with founding the town of Centralia, Washington. The son of a slave and a white mother, George Washington was born in Virginia in 1817. Washington was adopted by a white family—the Cochrans—with whom he traveled to the Oregon Territory in 1850. Washington worked as a lumberjack and acquired some wealth by the time he was in his thirties. Washington too encountered the Black Codes of the Oregon Territory, so when he staked a claim to 640 acres, the land had to be placed in the name of his adopted father. Washington grew cereal and vegetables on his land and raised cattle. When the laws were changed to allow blacks to own land, the property was transferred to Washington's name. The land was located at the confluence of the Shookumchuck and Chalis Rivers, where Centralia, Washington, later emerged as a city. The Northern Pacific built a line across Washington's property in 1872, so in 1875 he and his wife, Mary, drew up a plan and established the town of Centerville (later renamed Centralia). To jump-start things, Washington sold lots for ten dollars to anyone agreeing to build a house worth at least three hundred dollars on the land they purchased. Washington envisioned a town with open space. He donated land for parks, a cemetery, a school, and churches. The two-acre park in the center of town still bears his name (City of Centralia 2009; Katz 1992: 64–67; Oldham 2003; Rigg [1942] 1975: 193–222).

California: Ranching, Mining, and Mountaineering. California was a magnet for blacks moving to the West, and they played important roles in the founding and building of some cities. For instance, twenty-six of the forty-four people who founded Los Angeles in 1781 were black. Some blacks were able to acquire property and build wealth in the state. Maria Rita Valdez, a granddaughter of two of Los Angeles' black founders, owned Rancho Rodeo de las Aguas (better known as Beverly Hills). The San Fernando Valley was owned by Francisco Reyes, another black resident (Katz 1992: 72–73; Lapp 1977: 2).

Slaves were used to mine gold in the Georgia and North Carolina gold rushes, but from 1848 onward, they were moved to California to mine gold for slave owners wanting to cash in on that gold rush. Free blacks from the Northeast and from other countries also made their way to California to search for gold. They mined gold in places such as Spanish Flat and Auburn Ravine. Some slaves used the gold they found to buy their freedom, while those who were already free used the money to secure the freedom of their relatives. Others used their newfound wealth to build schools, churches, and establish newspapers. All told, black gold miners in California were collectively worth about $5 million in 1863 (Katz 1992: 71–75; Lapp 1977: 44–49; Magagnini 1998; Q. Taylor 1999: 27–189).

News of men like Reuben Ruby—a black resident of Portland, Maine, who amassed six hundred dollars in four weeks of digging in the Stanislaus River—encouraged more blacks to migrate to California. An all-black mining company made their way from New York to California. Frederick Douglass even called on the American Colonization Society to settle blacks in California instead of Liberia. Black sailors also deserted their ships as soon as they reached port and made their way to the gold mines. Blacks operated the Sweet Vengeance mine in Yuba County. Blacks were also a part of the Klondike gold rush in Alaska. Lucille Hunter, who accompanied her husband to Alaska, continued to work their claim long after her husband died (Lapp 1977: 13–19, 50–54; Magagnini 1998).

James Beckwourth (Beckwith), one of the best-known black explorers and trappers of the American West, was born in 1798 in Fredericksburg, Virginia. Beckwourth, who was mixed race, left St. Louis to work for the Rocky Mountain Fur Company. In 1823 he accompanied William Ashley on an expedition into the Upper Missouri River Valley. He became a skilled wilderness fighter and in 1824 was adopted by the Crow Indians, who gave him the name Morning Star. Beckwourth married the daughter of the chief, led the tribe on many raids, and eventually became chief ("Bloody Arm"). He served as a scout in the Third Seminole War in Florida. He was also a trapper who joined the California gold rush. He built a cabin and trading post in the state in 1850. He is credited with discovering, in 1850 or 1851, the pass in the Sierra Nevadas that bears his name. The pass identified by Beckwourth is less treacherous than the Donner Pass (Bonner 1856: 29, 423–424; Franklin and Moss 1994: 107–108; Gwaltney 1994; Katz 1992: 29–32; Q. Taylor 1999: 48–49).

Beckwourth was a keen observer of nature. While searching for a pass through the American Valley, he made an observation that is noteworthy because there is limited documentation of people of color's perceptions and appreciation of nature during this time period.[10] Beckwourth wrote about nature using romantic imagery:

> The valley was already robed in freshest verdure, contrasting most delightfully with the huge snow-clad masses of rock we had just left. Flowers of every variety and hue spread their variegated charms before us; magpies were chattering, and gorgeously plumaged birds were caroling their delights of unmolested solitude. Swarms of wild geese and ducks were swimming on the surface of the cool, crystal stream, which was the central fork of the Rio de las Plumas, or sailed the air in clouds over our heads. Deer and antelope filled the plains, and their boldness was conclusive that the hunter's rifle was to them unknown. (Bonner 1856: 424)

Beckwourth lived in a small valley at the mouth of the Beckwourth Pass for about ten years; he raised cattle, guided people through the pass, and in 1851 paid for the construction of a road through the pass that led to Marysville. Beckwourth then moved to Colorado, where he worked as a government agent who negotiated with Native American tribes. He died in Colorado in 1864 (Bonner 1856: 423–430).

There were several other black pioneers living in the West. For instance, Peter Raney was a black fur hunter who traveled to California with Jedediah Smith in 1826. Allen Light, also known as the "Black Steward," was a crew member on the *Pilgrim*. He deserted the vessel in 1835 in Santa Barbara and became an otter hunter. He became skilled at fighting illegal otter hunters and was commissioned by Governor Alvarado in 1839 to stop otter poaching off the Santa Barbara coast (Lapp 1977: 4–6). Jacob Dodson and Sanders Jackson, free men, went on the 1848 expedition with John C. Frémont to California. Beginning in 1843, eighteen-year-old Dodson actually went on three expeditions with Frémont to California and Oregon (Durham and Everett Jones 1965: 5; Franklin and Moss 1994: 107–108; Gwaltney 1994; Katz 1971: 32–39; Lapp 1977: 7; Magagnini 1998; Q. Taylor 1999: 48–49).

William Alexander Leidesdorff became a very successful trader and entrepreneur while living in California (Gwaltney 1994). Born in 1810 Leidesdorff, who was of Danish and St. Croix heritage, left New Orleans and settled in San Francisco in 1841. He smuggled coffee into San Francisco, built the city's first hotel, helped establish its first school, built its first steamship, and staged its first horse race. He made shipping runs between San Francisco and Honolulu. Three years after settling in San Francisco, he owned the biggest house in the city, a warehouse on the waterfront, and about thirty-five thousand acres of land called Rio del Rancho Americana on the southern bank of the American River in Folsom (he acquired this property by becoming a Mexican citizen). He built a cattle ranch there and hired blacks, Chinese, and whites to work on it. He was appointed as U.S. vice consul to Mexico and treasurer of San Francisco. Leidesdorff, a millionaire, never married and bore no children. After he died of typhus fever in 1848, his mother—Anna Marie Sparks, a creole living in St. Croix (Virgin Islands)—was coerced into selling his property for seventy-five thousand dollars. Samuel Smith, an African American, found gold on the property in 1849, but the windfall from this discovery did not go to Leidesdorff's relatives despite the fact that his mother sued and contested the sale (Katz 1971: 32–39; 1992: 71–75; Lapp 1977: 9–11; Magagnini 1998; Q. Taylor 1999; Thurman 1952: 3–4).

Biddy (Bridget) Mason was a slave whose master forced her to walk from Mississippi to California. The Smiths, her owners, converted to Mormonism in 1847 and took her and her three daughters to the Utah Territory. Then, in 1851, they forced Mason to accompany them when they moved to the Mormon's California outpost at San Bernardino. As she trekked behind her master's three hundred wagons, the thirty-two-year-old slave had to keep the livestock together, perform midwifery duties, cook, and tend to her master's children as well as her own. On gaining her freedom in 1856, Mason moved to Los Angeles, where she practiced as a midwife and nurse. She purchased a house and a sizable property in 1866. Over time she amassed a small fortune of about three hundred thousand dollars and purchased several additional parcels of prime real estate. In 1884 she built a commercial building that had rental spaces. She helped to found a travelers aid center, a school, and an African Methodist Episcopalian church in the city. She donated the land on which the church was built (Katz 1992: 88–89; J. K. Williams 2006: 9–15; Women in History 2009).

Stagecoach Mary (Mary Fields), a former slave living on the frontier in Cascade County, Montana, dressed in men's long pants. Fields, born in Hickman, Tennessee in 1832, moved to Montana to work with Ursuline nuns in the 1880s. She worked at the convent for Native American girls doing heavy work such as hauling, stonework, wood chopping, and carpentry. After she was dismissed from her job at the convent in 1894, she was hired to drive a delivery wagon and managed a mail route. She was the first black woman to work in this capacity for the U.S. Postal Service. On one occasion when wolves attacked her wagon and scared off her horses, Fields spent the night alone holding the wolves at bay with a rifle and a pistol (Dunlap 1995: 35–40; Katz 1992: 80–82; LaBastille 1980: 69; Shirley 2011: 5).

Cowboys and Ranch Hands. Slaves were also used to tend cattle on ranches in the West. In 1792, Texas had a population of roughly 2,992 people, 34 of whom were black and another 414 mixed race. The earliest blacks herding cattle in the region worked in the Goliad and Nagodoches areas. Free blacks lived in Texas and herded cattle, but during the 1820s and 1830s the slave population grew rapidly, outpacing the population of free blacks. Some slaves from Gambia and other African countries came from regions where they were accustomed to driving and managing large cattle herds. Slaves from these areas were sought after by ranchers for their cattle-management skills. These slaves started out working on cattle plantations in the tall grass and pine barrens of South Carolina and other parts of the South. As the cattle ranches spread westward, ranchers forced slaves to march from the Southeast to Texas chained or tied together with ropes. The life of the black cowboy was difficult. They drove millions of head of cattle on arduous trails from Texas to Kansas, the Dakotas, Colorado, and Wyoming. Though some estimates list as many as nine thousand black cowboys in the West, the 1890 census indicated that the total number of nonwhite cowboys in the West that year was sixteen hundred. Black cowboys did the hardest work around the ranch and on the cattle drives. They were most common in the eastern part of Texas, where all-black crews were common. One free black male, Aaron Ashfort, owned 2,570 heads of cattle in 1850 (Barr 2000: 1–10; McRae 1996; Q. Taylor 1999: 56, 160; U.S. Census Bureau 1897: 532–626).

Forest Management. Blacks were engaged in conservation work on the frontier as well. Jean-Baptiste-Pointe DuSable, best known for being the first non-Indian to settle in Chicago, was a mixed-race frontiersman, farmer, trader, and trapper. He was of Haitian and French descent. When he arrived in New Orleans in 1765, he was almost enslaved because he had lost his identification papers.

He left New Orleans and traveled to Peoria, Illinois, where he settled and prospered; eventually he owned more than eight hundred acres of land. He married a Potawatomi woman, had two children with her, and became a member of the tribe. Between 1773 and 1779, he settled on the marshy shores of Lake Michigan in a place Native Americans called Eschikagu. He built a home on the north bank of the Chicago River and established a fur trading post. DuSable sided with the Americans during the Revolutionary War and fled with his family to Michigan City, Indiana. He was arrested and imprisoned at Fort Michilimackinac in 1779. After the war he was sent to manage the Pinery, a large tract of land on the St. Clair River south of Port Huron in the eastern part of Michigan. He managed the Pinery from 1780 to 1784. DuSable returned to Chicago in 1784 to reclaim his property and reestablish his trading post. In 1800, he sold the property and left Chicago. He spent his last years in St. Charles, Missouri (Cortesi 1972; S. Graham 1953; Katz 1992: 11–12; Lindberg 1999: 166–168; Meehan 1963: 439–453).

ECOLOGY, SPIRITUALITY, RESISTANCE, AND SELF-DETERMINATION

Even when enslaved, blacks sought to chart their own course and determine their own fate. Hence, slaves rebelled by running away and making their way to the North or West. In response, the Congress enacted the Fugitive Slave Law of 1793, which made it a crime, punishable by a five-hundred-dollar fine, to harbor runaway slaves (L. Bennett 1993: 122–123; Drake and Cayton [1945] 1993: 32). Running away was either an individual or collective act. Some slaves ran away alone and fended for themselves, while others used the vast network of the Underground Railroad to aid them. Though some slaves tried to escape in large groups, it was impractical because of the difficulty of remaining undetected, and most of those who tried to escape this way were captured (Blassingame 1979: 206–209).

Harriet Tubman in the Wilds. The following section discusses Harriet Tubman, one of the most renowned runaway slaves and conductors on the Underground Railroad. Harriet Tubman decided to run away at a time when efforts to expel blacks from northern cities was gaining momentum. The discussion illustrates how Tubman's individual prowess was augmented by a well-established network of antislavery activists. The discussion also highlights the ecological knowledge and awareness necessary to accomplish the things Tubman did. Tubman, like other slaves and free blacks, also used the wilderness as a site for healing and a place to express their spirituality and connections to the earth.[11]

Environmental Recognition and Celebration. One of John Muir's more popular books, *A Thousand Mile Walk to the Gulf* (1916), details his journey from Indiana to Florida in 1867. Readers marvel at his feat—walking an estimated one thousand miles with only the clothing on his back, a plant press, a satchel containing a few books, and a few dollars in his pocket. Within environmental circles, this and Muir's other journeys are revered, emulated, and celebrated as great accomplishments. Trails, parks, monuments, and historic sites are named in honor of Muir's explorations and achievements.

However, conservationists and preservationists have not similarly recognized and celebrated the journeys of Harriet Tubman, York, Biddy Mason, Sacagawea, Sara Winnemucca, or other people of color who undertook feats similar to or exceeding that of Muir's. Women's rights advocates have brought Sacagawea's accomplishments to light, and she has been commemorated for her participation in the Lewis and Clark expedition. But environmentalists aren't the only ones to blame for this oversight. Though Tubman is widely recognized by African Americans for her genius in liberating slaves, her achievements are recognized and celebrated primarily in that context. Until the 1990s when minority activists prodded the National Park Service to designate sites on the Underground Railroad as National Park historic sites, African Americans hadn't recognized or celebrated the environmental accomplishments of Tubman and others like her either.[12] This book argues that the forays of Tubman, if read from an ecological perspective, are as remarkable as any in the field and worthy of greater attention.

Harriet Tubman, born Araminta Ross, grew up in the swampy southeastern tip of Maryland close to the Chesapeake Bay and what is now known as the Blackwater National Wildlife Refuge. She was born on the Thompson plantation below Tobacco Stick in Peters Neck in 1822 and grew up on the Brodess (sometimes referred to as Brodas) plantation near Bucktown in Dorchester County (Blockson 1987: 117; Bradford [1869] 1981: viii, 108; K. C. Larson 2004: 16; Lowry 2008: 44–46). In 1849, Tubman decided that she would rather die than spend any more time in slavery. She wanted to be free. Tubman decided, "There's one of two things I had a right to, liberty or death. If I could not have one, I would have de oder; for No man will take me back alive" (Bradford [1869] 1981: 29; McMullan 1991: 37).

Tubman was exposed to the atrocities of slavery early on. When she was very young, two of her sisters were sold to another plantation owner. By the time she was seven or eight, she was forced into field labor, and when she was about thirteen, an unfortunate incident helped seal her fate. Her master, trying to stop a slave from running away, hurled a two-pound weight in the direction of the fleeing slave. The weight missed its target and hit Tubman in the forehead; she was knocked unconscious by the blow and remained in a coma for months. The blow left her with a prominent scar on her forehead (an easy identifying mark for slave catchers) and a lifelong illness that made her fall into deep slumber at any moment and remain in a semiconscious state for anywhere from a few minutes to several hours (in which state she was very vulnerable to slave catchers). She also had epileptic seizures, headaches, and visions. The fits of unconsciousness made many think of Tubman as a simpleton (Blockson 1987: 118; Bradford [1869] 1981: 108–110; Burns 1992: 22; *Commonwealth* 1863; *Freeman's Record* 1865: 34–38; K. C. Larson 2004: 22–23; McMullan 1991; Sernett 2007: 16–17).

After attempts to turn her into a house slave failed, Tubman was sent to work on the Cook plantation, where she waded through frigid waters to check the muskrat traps. She was later placed under her father's tutelage in the fields. Tubman's father was considered a "trusted slave" and was placed in charge of the timber-harvesting operations on the plantation. In the fields, Tubman felled trees, hauled and split logs, milked cows, drove oxen, and worked with the plow. Tubman's prowess saved her master money because he didn't have to hire more expensive male slaves to do the work she did: a male slave of similar skills would have cost about two and a half to three times as much as Tubman did. Tubman became so strong and adept that the master allowed her to "hire her time"—that is, she could take on extra jobs from other plantation owners for a fee. She turned over a part of her income to her master and was allowed to keep the remainder (about fifty dollars per year) (Bradford [1869] 1981: 14–15; Burns 1992: 20, 25; K. C. Larson 2004: 38).

Despite the harshness of fieldwork, Tubman began to learn about and from the environment. While in the fields, she watched the sky and learned to predict the weather. She learned from her father how to find the North Star and use it to navigate through the woods. Her father also taught her how to move silently though the forest, imitate bird calls, and use bird sounds to communicate to others. He also taught her how to feel the barks of trees for moss—the moss grew more heavily on the north side of the trees and thus pointed the way north. Armed with that knowledge, she later used the trees to help her navigate on dark, starless nights. Her dad taught her about edible fruits and berries, and her mother taught her how to collect plants and boil them to make medicines. Her father also taught her that dogs could not follow her scent in the water. As she worked outdoors, she developed an intimate knowledge of the swamps and the plant life that thrived therein (Bradford [1869] 1981: 72–73).

Aware of her owner's attempts to sell her, on September 17, 1849, Tubman and two of her brothers (Ben and Henry) ran away from the plantation. The plantation owner, Eliza Brodess, placed a notice in the newspaper offering a reward of one hundred dollars for each slave if caught in Maryland and fifty dollars if captured and returned from outside the state (Brodess 1849; K. C. Larson 2004: 78–80). Her brothers had second thoughts, and the three returned to the plantation. Soon thereafter, though, Tubman packed a small amount of food and her favorite quilt and headed out on her own toward freedom. She followed an Underground Railroad route she would use later on as she made repeated forays to free other slaves. Tubman followed the Choptank River north to the Delaware-Maryland border, followed the road to Camden, then continued on to Wilmington and finally to Philadelphia. Runaway slaves from the region traveled through Delaware because many of the rivers were navigable, so they could pilot a canoe for much of the way. Furthermore, Delaware had a large number of free blacks, so a black person wasn't automatically assumed to be a runaway slave. During her quest for freedom, Tubman walked alone by night, and at daybreak she dug a hole in the underbrush and covered herself with leaves to avoid detection. At other times, she hid in the hollows of trees. Years before middle-class white women began experimenting with wearing pants or bloomers under their dresses and skirts during their wilderness treks, Tubman donned men's garb to disguise herself. In the years after her escape, she wore pants regularly as part of her disguise. She also wore pants because they made it easier for her to move around in rugged terrain. In fact, when Amelia Bloomer designed the suit with a jacket and a short skirt worn over full trousers in the early 1860s, Tubman dictated a letter to a friend who then sent it on to Bloomer. In the letter Tubman called the suit "a sensible costume for females" and requested that Bloomer and her friends send her some new outfits made from sturdy material (Bradford [1869] 1981: 21; Burns 1992: 35, 45–46; K. C. Larson 2004: 78–80; McMullan 1991: 51, 69, 91–92).

Tubman's Sixth Sense. Tubman had special attributes that made her so successful. Like a Transcendentalist, she was spiritual, believed in solitude, and relied on her sixth sense and instincts to guide her on her forays through the woods. Though she made some of her trips with other runaway slaves in tow, she reveled in solitude and used it as a space for contemplation when she was alone in the woods. Tubman is reminiscent of Isabella Bird in her solo travels into the woods. She is also like two noted nineteenth-century male environmental philosophers who believed in instinct and the sixth sense: Thoreau and Muir. Thoreau subscribed to the belief that there was knowledge to be gained from human intuition. He believed in the sixth sense, or instinct, which provided valuable insights into the workings of nature and helped us to develop a deeper connection with the natural world. He believed that intuition was superior to the information gained from our five senses: that is, intuition transcended tuition. He also thought that spirituality deepened one's connection to nature and was superior to the quest for material things (Bode [1947] 1975: 1–27; Nash 1982: 84–95). Muir too viewed instinct and intuition as necessary for fully understanding nature and believed in the connection between nature and spirituality (Muir 1911a, 1916; Nash 1982: 122–140). On two separate occasions while he was in Yosemite, Muir's sixth sense gave him important messages: first that his old professor was lost and wandering in the valley below; and then that his mother was dying, so he should gather his brothers and make haste to her bedside in Wisconsin (Muir 1911a: 178–180; 1954).

Tubman experienced and used her sixth sense during her attempt to escape. As she hurried toward freedom just south of the Pennsylvania border (which the slave catchers watched intently), Tubman had a feeling that something was amiss. Though this was her first time in the unfamiliar terrain and she was alone, she followed her instinct and dashed off to hide deep in the woods. Within minutes she heard horses galloping along the road (McMullan 1991: 47). Tubman's solo flight to freedom is remarkable, since most of the slaves who ran away successfully were young men (Blassingame 1979: 201–202).

In Philadelphia, Tubman took one of the few jobs open to black women at the time: she worked as a cook or maid and saved her money to finance further antislavery activities. By the next year she did the unthinkable—she returned to the South to begin leading her friends and family to freedom. With a large bounty on her head and with every slave catcher wanting her as a prize, she made numerous trips and freed scores of slaves. She often had to traverse rugged terrain and vary her route to avoid slave catchers. Tubman worked with other blacks in organizations such as the Vigilance Committee that collaborated with the Quakers and other sympathetic whites to organize and run the Underground Railroad (Bradford [1869] 1981: vi, x, 33, 111–112; McMullan 1991: 50).

Tubman used her knowledge of farming and logging to her advantage. She stashed runaway slaves on the floor of wagons and piled them high with potatoes or onions. Runaway slave parties also hid in the swamps. Tubman used opium or opium-based medicines to put babies to sleep while the families made their way to freedom. The runaway slaves sent signals to each other by imitating the call of the owl or whippoorwill. Tubman learned how to tell the approximate time of night so that she knew when to begin searching for a hiding place; runaway slaves could not afford to be caught wandering about during daylight (Blockson 1987: 120–121; Bradford [1869] 1981: 41–43, 54–55, 72–73).

After a new version of the Fugitive Slave law was passed in 1850, Tubman's activities grew more treacherous. Since free blacks and runaways like her could be returned to the South, slave-catching intensified in the North. Thus the ninety-mile trip from Maryland to Philadelphia turned into a five-hundred-mile one-way trip to Canada. From 1851 to 1858 Tubman lived in St. Catherines in Ontario, Canada. The hungry, frostbitten, and sometimes naked ex-slaves survived in St. Catherines by chopping wood for locals. Tubman made her last conducting trip to the South in 1860 (Blockson 1987: 120; Bradford [1869] 1981: 112–113; Burns 1992: 47; McMullan 1991: 60, 66).

Escaping the Plantation. Tubman used the rhythm of the plantations and daily and seasonal cycles of rural agrarian life to her advantage. She launched her raids during the winter, when the nights were longer—thereby allowing slaves to cover more ground at night. She began the journeys on a Saturday night. Slaves were often allowed to go to market, visit friends, and go to church on the week-ends, so many masters did not realize a slave was missing until Monday morning or afternoon. By then, the runaways were two nights ahead of the search parties. People were more inclined to stay at home on winter nights, so that meant less likelihood of detection. The slave masters were also more likely to be indoors, not roaming around on the plantation. In addition, station masters on the Underground Railroad were also more likely to be in and around their home and be ready to help the runaway slaves. Tubman was deeply religious and often spoke of "consulting with God." Before launching a raid, Tubman did what Henry David Thoreau and John Muir did when they wanted to intensify their connection to the earth: she lay alone in the forest all night. Tubman reported that on such occasions, her whole soul would be filled with the awe of a mysterious, unseen presence that thrilled her with such emotion that her fear vanished. In those moments she knew she could go ahead with the raid (Blockson 1987: 120–121; Clinton 2004: 91; *Commonwealth* 1863; *Freeman's Record* 1865: 34–38).

Spirituality. Tubman's actions should be understood in the context of how slavery constrained the activities of blacks in the wilds. Notwithstanding, slaves found ways to use the wildlands to enhance their spirituality. Hence, slaves embedded in their songs and verses the notion of "Steal[ing] Away to Jesus" and encouraged each other to "Go in de Wilderness" (Dixon 1987: 12–13). This is evident in the following song:

> If you want to find Jesus, go in de wilderness
> Go in de wilderness, go in de wilderness.
> Mournin' brudder, go in de wilderness
> I wait upon de Lord. (Allen, Ware, and Garrison 1867: 14)

Slaves were cognizant that the wilderness offered a type of freedom that couldn't be realized on the plantation, hence they sang:

I found free grace in de wilderness,
In de wilderness, in the wilderness,
I found free grace in de wilderness
For I'm a-going home. (Butterworth 1887: 242)

The wetlands were also an integral part of subterfuge used to undermine slavery. The wetlands also served as sanctuaries, spaces for religious freedom, and sites for connecting blacks to nature. For instance, Peter Randolph (1893), a former slave, described how they worshipped secretly during slavery. He writes:

Not being allowed to hold meetings on the plantation, the slaves assemble in the swamps, out of reach of the patrols. They have an understanding among themselves as to the time and place of getting together. This is often done by first one arriving breaking boughs from trees, and bending them in the direction of the selected spot. Arrangements are then made for conducting the exercises. (Randolph 1893: 202)

PHILLIS WHEATLEY AND CHARLOTTE
FORTEN GRIMKÉ: TWO ROMANTICS

Born in Senegal/Gambia in 1753, Phillis Wheatley was brought to America on the slave ship, the *Phillis*, and sold to a wealthy Boston family in 1761. Her slave masters, the Wheatleys, kept her in bondage until 1773. Phillis Wheatley learned to read and write and began composing poetry by the age of 13; she is the first African American woman to publish a book. Though she gained critical international acclaim for her work and traveled to London, Wheatley died in abject poverty in Boston in 1784 (Carretta 2011; O'Neale 1986: 144–165; Shields 2010: 45–47, 55).

Phillis Wheatley is considered one of the most well known poets of pre-nineteenth-century America (O'Neale 1986: 144–165). Wheatley is also considered one of the earliest American poets to show strong romantic influences in her works. In fact John Shields (2010: 85) argues that there is "demonstrable evidence that Wheatley's salient texts (those most heavily laden with romantic qualities) did, in fact, participate substantially in the flow of thought that evolved into romanticism. Shields compares Wheatley's writings with that of Kant and finds several similarities in the use of the imagination and the sublime. Shields also argues that Samuel Coleridge might also have encountered Wheatley's works and may have been influenced by them (Shields 2010: 85–115).

The romantic influence is quite strong in Wheatley's poem "On Imagination." In the following excerpt Wheatley writes,

> We on thy pinions can surpass the wind,
> And leave the rolling universe behind:
> From star to star the mental optics rove,
> Measure the skies, and range the realms above.
> There in one view we grasp the mighty whole,
> Or with new worlds amaze th' unbounded soul.
> Though Winter frowns to Fancy's raptur'd eyes
> The fields may flourish, and gay scenes arise;
> The frozen deeps may break their iron bands,
> And bid their waters murmur o'er the sands.
> Fair Flora may resume her fragrant reign,
> And with her flow'ry riches deck the plain;
> Sylvanus may diffuse his honours round,
> And all the forest may with leaves be crown'd,
> Show'rs may descend, and dews their gems disclose,
> And nectar sparkle on the blooming rose.
> Such is thy pow'r, nor are thine orders vain,
> O thou the leader of the mental train:
> In full perfection all thy works are wrought,
> And thine the sceptre o'er the realms of thought.
> Before thy throne the subject-passions bow,
> Of subject-passions sov'reign ruler thou;
> At thy command joy rushes on the heart,
> And through the glowing veins the spirits dart.
> Fancy might now her silken pinions try
> To rise from earth, and sweep th' expanse on high:
> From Tithon's bed now might Aurora rise,
> Her cheeks all glowing with celestial dies,
> While a pure stream of light o'erflows the skies.
> The monarch of the day I might behold,
> And all the mountains tipt with radiant gold,
> But I reluctant leave the pleasing views,
> Which Fancy dresses to delight the Muse;
> Winter austere forbids me to aspire,

And northern tempests damp the rising fire;
They chill the tides of Fancy's flowing sea,
Cease then, my song, cease the unequal lay. (Wheatley 1783: 61–63)

Similar descriptions of nature are found in other Wheatley poems such as "Thoughts on the Works of Providence," "To a Lady on the Death of Her Husband," and "To a Lady on her Remarkable Preservation in an Hurricane in North Carolina" (Wheatley 1783: 1816; 1830). Despite being an established romantic, Wheatley is overlooked in analyses of the rise of romanticism and its influence on environmentalism in America. She is not recognized or referenced as having influenced that school of thought in America. However, recent scholarship by Shields (2010) is likely to correct that oversight.

In contrast to Harriet Tubman and Phillis Wheatley, Charlotte Forten Grimké was a free and wealthy woman of color. She was born in Philadelphia in 1837. She was the only child of Robert Forten and his first wife, Mary. Charlotte's mother passed away when she was three years old. Her grandfather apprenticed as a sailmaker and became quite skilled at the trade. He eventually bought his own company and made his fortune from it. Her family used their wealth to promote social change; they were very active in the movement to abolish slavery and obtain equality for blacks. Charlotte moved to Salem, Massachusetts, in 1853 to complete her schooling; she was the only nonwhite student in a class of two hundred. She had private tutors because her father did not want her to attend the racially segregated, poorly equipped schools designated for black children in Philadelphia. Charlotte aspired to be a teacher, and Salem had a well-respected normal school that prepared her for that career. While in Salem she lived at the house of a family friend and fellow black abolitionist, Charles Lenox Remond. Charlotte was one of the first black teachers to go teach in the South (on St. Helena Island in South Carolina); she began teaching there in 1862. She married a Presbyterian minister, Francis Grimké, in 1878. Charlotte was familiar with the Transcendentalists and romantics and was influenced by Margaret Fuller and Emerson (B. Stevenson 1988: 3–56).

Grimké kept a diary as a teenager, and even at that young age, the romantic influence in her writing was evident. The journal entries discussed below were written between 1854 and 1858, when she was in Salem and on St. Helena Island. Like the Transcendentalists who influenced her, Grimké enjoyed rambling. She liked to walk on the Sabbath because "all is so peaceful; the noise and labor of every-day life has ceased; and in perfect silence we can commune with Nature." Her diary makes several references to her observations of nature. She wrote, ' "Summer looks pale and weak but still bears the unmistakable stamp of 'nature's nobleman'" (Grimké 1988: 63, 113, 208, 274, 279). In describing the New Year she said, "Nature wears a robe of spotless white in honor of his birth" (Grimké 1988: 147). Here she sees nature as masculine rather than feminine.

She described pastoral scenery that conveyed a positive image of nature. For instance, she wrote about "a magnificent panorama, painted by Nature with a skill that could never be rivaled by art. We gathered many beautiful wild flowers." She also admired the sweet sounds of birdsong (Grimké 1988: 106, 308). While teaching in South Carolina, Grimké walked a mile each way to the schoolhouse and back, "part of the way through a road lined with trees,— on one side stately pines, on the other noble live-oaks, hung with moss and canopied with vines. The ground was carpeted with brown, fragrant pine-leaves; and as I passed through in the morning, the woods were enlivened by the delicious songs of mocking-birds, which abound here" (Forten 1864: 596).

Latinos

Like Native Americans and blacks, Latinos resisted the attempts of white settlers to suppress their rights and freedoms. This was manifested most openly in the land rights struggles that occurred in the Southwest. This section discusses two such conflicts—the Las Gorras Blancas and the Sangre de Cristo land struggles. The land grant fights also revolved around the issue of the common usage of land versus privatization and development. By the time these struggles erupted, political, economic, and legal elites were firm supporters of the idea of private property rights and systems were in place to defend and enforce such rights.

LAND RIGHTS CONFLICTS

Las Gorras Blancas. The Spanish implemented a very complex land tenure system in the American West. It involved a mixture of individual and communal land rights. That is, though an individual might own a piece of land, communal rights were still paramount. Consequently, all lands were subject to communal grazing, hunting, gathering, and irrigation. So while individuals could benefit from their property, the system guaranteed that the well-being of the entire community was looked after. The Spanish also did not apportion land by the grid method; instead they marked property boundaries by using natural landscape features such as mountains, hills, rivers, mounds, and clusters of trees. The earliest European American settlers adopted the Nuevomexicano lifestyle and land apportionment methods, but things began to change after the

Mexican-American War ended. Across the Southwest, Latinos began to lose access to their land grants because they did not have paper titles and could not identify which land they owned individually, and because the Spanish method of designating land did not correspond readily to the way the new American government platted and recognized individual property (Bowden 1969: 1–50; Rosenbaum 1981: 3–18).

The arrival of the Atchison, Topeka, and Santa Fe Railroads in 1879 brought a new wave of settlers and speculators, who began buying up land in and around Las Vegas, New Mexico, and the rest of the Southwest. The new landholdings were fenced in and grazing, and hunting and gathering rights were transferred to private landowners. Consequently, Latinos and Native American tribes living in the region before the arrival of the European settlers lost access to communal lands—even though the Treaty of Guadalupe Hidalgo promised to honor preexisting land grants. The heightened tensions arising from the land and resource grabs prompted three Latino men, Juan José Herrera and his two brothers Pablo and Nícanor, to form the group Las Gorras Blancas (the White Caps) in April 1889. Juan Herrera studied American law and was a member of the Knights of Labor. Members of Las Gorras Blancas, who sought to restore traditional land rights, mounted nighttime raids in which they cut down fences; scattered livestock; and burned the crops, barns, and other property acquired by white ranchers. Las Gorras Blancas had the support of the Latino community, and in less than a year the group had five hundred members. The district attorney, Miguel Salazar, tried to discredit the organization, calling it "anarchical, revolutionary, and communistic." Wealthy Latinos, Anglo politicians, and large landholders in the region condemned Las Gorras Blancas because the group threatened to undermine their power base and sources of wealth. Members of the group were indicted in 1890, but charges were dropped because of a lack of witnesses to testify against them. The Las Gorras Blancas grew and formed a separate Knights of Labor chapter named the Caballeros de Labor. They also formed a new populist party known as El Partido del Pueblo Unido (the United People's Party). They ran for elections, and in 1892 four members of the group were elected to office. They eventually left their government positions because they were unable to pass the populist legislation they campaigned on. In 1903, the Court of Private Land Claims granted a patent to the town of Las Vegas, which ceded ownership of disputed lands to the city. This essentially ended the campaigns for the restoration of communal lands to claimants (Aragón y Ulibarrí 1999; Bowden 1969: 1–50; Knowlton 1980: 12–21; M. Miller 2004; Rosenbaum 1981: 3–18; Schlesinger 1971: 87–143).

Sangre de Cristo. Settlement of the San Luis Valley, a high alpine desert in southern Colorado, dates back to 1843 and the Sangre de Cristo Land Grant. The land rights struggles of the area have their roots in the Latino land-grant movement from this period. The Sangre de Cristo Land Grant, which comprised almost 1.4 million acres, was issued to Narcisco Beaubien and Stephen Louis Lee of Taos in 1843. Both men were naturalized Mexican citizens who had married into Mexican families. The San Luis Valley, which contained rivers and abundant wildlife, was the traditional spring and summer hunting grounds for the Utes, Apaches, and other tribes. Both land grantees were killed in the Taos Pueblo Uprising of 1847. As a result, Lee's family sold his half of the grant to Beaubien's father, Charles. The elder Beaubien forcibly evicted people who tried to settle on his land without his permission. Instead he recruited settlers (*pobladores*) of his own choosing from the Taos Valley. He also invited French and German merchants to build trading posts around the Costilla and Culebra Rivers between 1849 and 1853. Latinos—most of whom migrated from New Mexico—began to settle in the valley in 1851 with the establishment of La Plaza de San Luis de la Culebra. The settlers received private riparian long-lots (*varas*) in the bottomlands of seven major creeks, but the majority of the land, including woodlands, forests, and parks, were set aside as an *ejido* or commons (Colorado State Archives 2001; Mondragón-Valdéz 2010; Pena and Gallegos 1993: 146–147; Stoller 1980: 22–39).

In 1858, the first territorial governor of Colorado—William Gilpin—bought one-sixth share in the land; he purchased the remainder of it five years later. Gilpin was a second lieutenant in the Seminole wars and one of the members of John Frémont's expedition, which searched for a route across the Continental Divide. When Beaubien sold the land in 1863, he signed a covenant that granted easement to any *pobladores* who allowed settlers to use the slopes for grazing and collecting wood. The covenant recognized the community commons that existed near villages; it also deeded to settlers long-lots extending from rivers to foothills. However, Gilpin did not honor the Beaubien covenant. Gilpin and his financiers (the U.S. Freehold Land and Emigration Company) subdivided the tract and sold it off to investors. The company seized the private and communal lands of the *pobladores* and treated the Latino settlers as if they were trespassers. Gilpin thought the land contained valuable minerals, so between 1864 and 1865 he hired mining companies to assess the mineral potential of the land. Gold was discovered in the area, but only a limited amount of mining occurred in the region until the late 1800s. Up to this point, Latinos remained the primary users of the common lands. However, by the 1890s speculators began enclosing common lands. Filing claims as absentee owners, they tried to sue local Latinos who were using the lands for grazing, hunting, and fuel-wood collection. Undaunted, Latinos continued to settle in the region and use the common lands for subsistence purposes. Speculators also tried to appropriate and manipulate water rights in the Culebra. Latinos responded by occupying the land and using as much water as they could in order to avoid losing their water rights, since nonuse of water was interpreted as forfeiture of water rights. The commons were not effectively enclosed until 1960, when a North Carolinian named Jack Taylor bought the "Mountain Tract." Since then, Latinos have tried to reclaim the tract. There have been armed confrontations, and fences and barricades erected by the owner have periodically been destroyed (Colorado State Archives 2001; Mondragón-Valdéz 2010; Pena and Gallegos 1993: 146–148; Rosenbaum 1981: 3–18; Stoller 1980: 22–39; 1985: 12–17).

LOW-WAGE LABOR AND WESTWARD EXPANSION

Though westward expansion is often viewed as a one-way east to west movement of settlers and laborers to populate the country and exploit its resources for development and nation building, this is not always the case. Westward expansion was a west to east movement also (Austin 2007: 58–84; Limerick 1992: 1021–1049). In some cases it involved the eastward movement of Latinos from the west to the mountain states. In the process they were dispossessed of land and converted into low-wage agricultural and industrial laborers.

Mexicans. The construction of the railroads and the expansion of agriculture stimulated demand for low-wage labor. By 1908 the Southern Pacific and the Atchison, Topeka & Santa Fe railroads were each recruiting over a thousand Mexican laborers each month to lay and maintain the tracks (Estrada et al. 1981: 103–131). Large numbers of Mexican workers were also employed in the fruit, vegetable, cotton, and sugar beet industries. Mexican laborers were used to undercut the wage demands of Japanese workers in California's Central Valley and German and Russian laborers in Colorado. Mexican workers were also employed in New Mexico and Arizona in copper, lead, and coal mines (Dubofsky 1996: 3; Jibou 1988a: 21–22). Until the 1920s, movement across the border between Mexico and the United States was informal and largely unrestricted. The migrants were offered some of the worst jobs at the lowest wages. They were often paid less to do the same jobs as Anglos. This split labor market was further divided by gender: Latinas were assigned worse jobs than Latinos and received lower wages for their work (Dubofsky 1996: 13; Takaki 1993: 318–319).

About the same time the Southwest was demanding an increased pool of cheap labor to fuel its development, World War I and the 1924 National Origins Act drastically reduced the supply of labor from Europe and Asia. Therefore, employers in the Southwest resorted to recruiting Mexicans and southern African Americans to fill the void. Mexicans were exempt from the immigration quotas of the National Origins Act (Acuna 1988: 141–143; Grebler, Moore, and Guzman 1970: 63–65).

Workers of Mexican ancestry were excluded from some unions. Thus, from the late 1920s onward, Latinos formed their own unions and played significant roles in organizing mining and agricultural workers (Estrada et al. 1981: 182–184; Jibou 1988a: 23; R. B. Taylor 1975: 45–46). D. Mitchell (2012) argues that the *bracero* ("arm" or "field hand") program, introduced in 1942, was designed to provide California growers with a malleable, contingent labor force that was used to undercut domestic workers' wages, work conditions, and union demands.

Under the bracero agreement between the United States and Mexico, laborers (primarily poor men from rural Mexico) were issued contracts to work in the United States for specific periods of time. The program grew, and by 1960 braceros supplied 26 percent of the nation's seasonal farm labor. Growers paid the braceros less than American-born workers. Though most braceros were hired as farmworkers, about one hundred thousand of them worked on the railroads. The program ended in 1964, by which time about 4.5 million Mexicans participated in it (Jibou 1988a: 23; Moses 1993: 164–165; R. B. Taylor 1975: 67–68; Vialet 1980).

The bracero program did little to protect the rights of Mexican Americans and Mexican immigrants. Despite the formal arrangements of the program, American citizens of Mexican ancestry were subjected to successive waves of deportations in the quest to reduce "illegal immigration." During periods of heightened deportations, there were "sweeps" and raids of the barrios, homes, and businesses that violated Mexican and Mexican Americans' civil, human, and legal rights (Aguirre and Turner 1998: 147; Grebler, Moore, and Guzman 1970: 521; D. Mitchell 2012).

Puerto Ricans. Like Mexicans, many Puerto Ricans migrated to the United States as a cheap source of labor. Puerto Rico became a U.S. territory in 1898 and the first wave of immigrants moved to Hawaii to work on the sugar plantations after a hurricane devastated Puerto Rico's plantations in 1899. Puerto Ricans gained U.S. citizenship in 1917 but immigration was slow until the 1940s. Since then Puerto Ricans have settled in the urban centers of the East Coast, working in factories and the unskilled service sector. During the 1950s, recruiters went to the island to recruit Puerto Ricans to work in the garment and sugar-cane industries (Aguirre and Turner 1998: 133, 156; Library of Congress n.d.; Rodríguez n.d.).

Cubans. Cubans are another group of Latinos who have a long history of migration to the United States; they too have played a role in agriculture and the development of the country. Cubans have been migrating to the United States since the sixteenth century. When St. Augustine was established in 1565, there were frequent contacts with Cuba, as the Spanish governor for the Americas was stationed in Cuba. The Florida missions and churches were overseen by the bishop in Cuba, and Cuba also supplied the Spanish settlements in Florida with rum, supplies, and soldiers. Consequently, hundreds of Cuban soldiers and their relatives left Cuba and settled in St. Augustine. St. Augustine's stone fort (Castillo de San Marcos) was designed by a Cuban engineer, and hundreds of Cuban soldiers helped to construct the fort. Cubans also migrated to Louisiana and Texas during the late eighteenth and early nineteenth centuries. Another wave of Cubans settled in Florida during the Ten Years' War (1868–78). Beginning in 1868, Cuban cigar manufacturers and thousands of tobacco workers began migrating to the United States because tariffs were crippling the Cuban tobacco industry. Thus by the 1870s, Key West's twenty-nine cigar factories were producing 62 million cigars annually. At the beginning of the twentieth century, the 150 cigar factories in West Tampa and Ybor City produced more than 11 million cigars a year. Cubans also worked on American tobacco plantations (Florida Department of State n.d.: 2–4, 34, 46; Library of Congress n.d.; Reynolds 1886: 20–85).

Asians

Asians were an integral part of westward expansion. They helped to populate the country from west to east; they were also part of the low-wage agricultural and industrial labor pool. They played key roles in extractive industries and construction projects that aided nation-building efforts. However, their economic ascendancy threatened the settler colonial power structure and made them a target of discrimination and exclusion. Consequently, Asians were subject to forced removals and relocations to curtail their activities and increase surveillance. In the process Asians were prohibited from owning land, dispossessed of what they owned, and denied American citizenship and entry into the United States. The remainder of this chapter will discuss five of the earliest groups of Asian immigrants to inhabit the United States—the Filipinos, Asian Indians, Chinese, Japanese, and Koreans.

Filipinos were the first Asian migrants to settle in the United States; they established their first permanent settlement in America in the eighteenth century. They first arrived on the Gulf and Pacific Coasts during the late 1500s, on Spanish galleons on which they had been forced to build and serve as crew members. These Filipinos jumped ship in Mexico and Louisiana and settled in the swampy bayous, establishing villages outside New Orleans in 1763. These settlers subsisted by shrimping and fishing (Agbayani-Siewert and Revilla 1995: 134–136; Bankston 1995: 180–182; Cordova 1983). One group of Filipino men settled in the village of Saint Malo, south of New Orleans, in the early 1800s (an 1883 *Harper's Weekly* article describes the village as being about fifty years old). These men built their homes on stilts and survived by fishing in the bayous (Hearn 1883: 98). Saint Malo was destroyed by a hurricane in the 1890s. The group established a new village near the mouth of the Mississippi River about forty miles from New Orleans. In 1933, that village had about 1,500 residents (Bankston 1995: 182).

Filipinos did not arrive in large numbers in the United States until 1903, the year after the Spanish-American War. Under the *pensionado* plan, the first wave of Filipinos were students (funded by the United States) who matriculated at elite American universities; upon graduating they returned home to occupy high-level government positions. The students formed organizations, published pamphlets, and sent home letters filled with glowing reports of the opportunities in the United States. Around 1906, thousands of Filipino field laborers migrated to Hawaii and California. Unlike the pensionados, most were poorly educated, young, single men fluent in neither English nor Spanish (Agbayani-Siewert and Revilla 1995: 137–139; Bankston 1995: 182–183; Jibou 1988a: 49–51).

Soon the Filipinos (*sakadas*) comprised a growing share of the sugar plantation workers, rising from 19 percent of the workforce in 1915 to 70 percent in 1932 (Kitano and Daniels 1995: 87; Posadas 1999: 13–15). Filipino field laborers were organized in the padrone system and were exploited by the labor contractors. Filipino padrones settled for lower wages than Japanese workers in order to win contracts. They also undercut the bids of Mexican laborers, who contracted with employers on an individual basis (Agbayani-Siewert and Revilla 1995: 137–139; Cordova 1983; Jibou 1988a: 49–51). Filipinos were prohibited from owning land in the United States, but some were able to lease land vacated by interned Japanese during the 1940s. Other workers resented the Filipinos for undercutting wages; consequently, Filipinos were chased out of the Yakima Valley in Washington State and were mobbed and beaten by whites in Watsonville, California (Agbayani-Siewert and Revilla 1995: 140).

ASIAN INDIANS

The first Asian Indians arrived in North America around 1750; a few who worked on merchant marine ships came to America and were sold into indentured servitude or slavery by the ships' captains. Between 1820 and 1870, 196 Asian Indians came to the United States, but by 1910 the number had reached 5,000. The Asian Exclusion Act reduced migration to about 100 Asian immigrants per year. These early immigrants were students, elites, political refugees, farmers, and laborers (Helweg and Helweg 1990: 1–25; Sheth 1995: 170–171).

CHINESE

The Chinese began migrating to Hawaii to work on the sugar plantations in the 1830s. Between 1852 and 1900 about fifty thousand migrated to work on the plantations. The migrants were primarily male (Jung 1995: 6, 19, 293; Takaki 1983: 32, 76–77; Tong 2000: 25–26). From the mid-1800s onward, the Chinese migrated to work as low-wage laborers to help in the opening and exploitation of the West. They took part in the gold rush; they also worked in mining, building the railroads, farming, fisheries, sugar plantations, and factories (Aguirre and Turner 1998: 179; Jibou 1988a: 34; Wong 1995: 58–59).

The first Chinese miners in California were a group of about sixty men who began working in the goldfields in Tuolumne County in 1849 under the supervision of Mexicans from Sonora. Blacks (slaves and freed men), Miwok Indians, Hawaiians, and Chileans also worked alongside whites in the goldfields. In the beginning, whites learned gold-washing techniques from the Chileans and Mexicans, but as competition intensified and gold became scarcer, nativist rhetoric and sentiment resulted in the expulsion of non-Europeans from the goldfields (Ngai 2015: 1086).

Most of the Chinese gold miners came from China's southern region, particularly Guangdong Province (Ngai 2015: 1087). Within a few years of the discovery of gold in California, twenty-four thousand Chinese worked in the mines, where many performed menial tasks. Because of the inflation resulting from the gold strikes and the shortage of women in the West, some Chinese men found a temporary economic niche working as cooks and launderers. In the early 1850s, Chinese men took to the hills in search of gold. They also worked the gold mining claims that white miners had stopped working (Tong 2000: 32–33; Wong 1995: 73–74). When the claims played out, white gold miners sold their old claims to Chinese miners. As the California gold rush ran its course, the percentage of Chinese miners steadily increased. In 1850, Chinese miners accounted for 1 percent of all miners; by 1870, more than 50 percent (Jibou 1988a: 34; Wong 1995: 73).

The Chinese were also hired in large-scale hydraulic mining. They served on the construction crews that built the hydraulic system as well as the work crews that did the actual mining. Some of these mining operations hired as many as eight hundred Chinese in semi-skilled and unskilled positions and three hundred whites as skilled laborers (Ngai 2015: 1095).

Chinese miners made only a small profit, but that was enough to incur the wrath of white miners. Consequently, legal means were used to drive the Chinese out of gold and quartz mining. In 1852, a Foreign Miner's Tax was passed and many districts passed ordinances to expel Chinese miners from their jurisdictions. Violence was also used to expel Chinese workers from mining areas. White miners robbed, beat, and threatened them, and burned their property (Ngai 2015: 1099–1100; Tong 2000: 32; Wong 1995: 73–74).

The Chinese were discriminated against and stripped of some of the basic rights accorded whites (Friday 1994: 2–7, 51; Wong 1995: 59, 63). The animus between the Chinese and whites was so intense that by 1852 anti-Chinese laws were being passed. In that year California passed a law placing a fifty-five-dollar head tax on Chinese passengers arriving by ship. In 1855, California enacted a capitation tax of fifty dollars on passengers who were aliens ineligible for citizenship. Three years later another law was passed that prohibited Chinese from immigrating to California (Aguirre and Turner 1998: 180; Wong 1995: 60).

In 1862, when Congress authorized the construction of the transcontinental railroad, Central Pacific had labor problems. There wasn't a large pool of white laborers in the Pacific region who were willing to work on the railroads, so Central Pacific recruited twelve thousand Chinese laborers from the goldfields, farms, and cities, and from China. Most were acquired through labor contracting firms. The Chinese laborers were paid two-thirds of what white laborers earned. With the hiring of Chinese, whites moved up the occupational ladder to whites-only jobs such as foreman, supervisor, and skilled craftsman. The Chinese were left to tunnel through the mountains, dig through dangerously deep snowbanks, and dangle in baskets along sheer cliff faces while they planted explosives. Many Chinese lost their lives building the tracks across the Sierras. One snowslide in the winter of 1866–1867 took the lives of twenty-two Chinese men (Jibou 1988a: 34–35). After the completion of the transcontinental railroad in 1869, the Chinese took other railroad construction jobs in the West and South. Northern Pacific hired fourteen thousand Chinese, and Southern Pacific's lines in California were built almost entirely by Chinese labor. From 1869 to 1878, Chinese workers laid almost eighteen hundred miles of railroad tracks in California and other western states (Tong 2000: 33).

During the 1870s the Chinese also worked as low-wage seasonal farmworkers (Melendy 1984: 49; Tong 2000: 32). They also did extensive reclamation work. Thousands of Chinese were employed in reclaiming the land on which San Francisco is built. In addition, the California delta of the Sacramento and San Joaquin Rivers was transformed by levees, drainage ditches, and irrigation systems built by the Chinese. Although the Chinese were excluded from salmon fishing by restrictive legislation, by 1880 they fished for sturgeon, shrimp, and abalone. By the end of that decade, Chinese shrimp camps were common on the shores of San Francisco Bay (Sung 1971: 42–57; Wong 1995: 75).

An environmental catastrophe provided some reprieve for the Chinese. The 1906 San Francisco earthquake and fire destroyed most municipal records, including Chinese immigration and citizenship records. The Chinese used the opportunity to take advantage of a legal loophole: they developed a "slot racket" or "paper son" immigration trail. American law stated that children of American-born fathers inherited their father's citizenship. In the slot racket, a Chinese resident would claim American birth, and—since there was no way to disprove this—this "American-born" Chinese would visit China and report the birth of a son, thereby creating an immigration entry slot. Years later, that slot could either be used by a relative or sold to someone else. The purchaser, the "paper son," would enter the United States under the assumed identity of the alleged son (Wong 1995: 63–64). These paper sons lived under a cloud of suspicion for decades. Finally, the Refugee Escape Act of 1957 protected paper sons from deportation. During a ten-year amnesty period from 1959 to 1969, the San Francisco District Office of the Immigration and Naturalization Service received more than eight thousand applications from paper sons seeking to legalize their status in the United States (Melendy 1984: 64).

JAPANESE

The first Japanese in the United States found their way to Hawaii after being shipwrecked and rescued; this occurred in 1841 and 1850. In 1855, 943 Japanese migrated to Hawaii to work on the sugar plantations (Lee 2003: 3–31). Another group of 149 workers left Japan to work on the sugar plantations of Hawaii in 1869, but they were so badly treated that the Japanese government returned some of them to Japan and halted further immigration to the United

States. Also in 1869, a small group of Japanese political refugees from the Meiji Restoration arrived in the United States. They established the Wakamatsu Tea and Silk Colony in El Dorado County near Sacramento, but it was disbanded after ten years because they lacked the funds to finance it. Immigration from Japan to Hawaii began again in 1884. Nearly thirty thousand plantation laborers came from Japan in the next decade; conditions were still so bad that only about half of them stayed (Daniels 1988: 101; Kitano 1969: 12–13; Nishi 1995: 96–97).

Some of the early Japanese immigrants were students, professionals, or farmers with entrepreneurial backgrounds, hence they migrated with skills that helped them to establish businesses. The Japanese immigrants were mostly men; in 1900 only 5 percent were women. Immigration from Japan increased after the Chinese Exclusion Act went into effect in 1882 (Glenn 1986; Ichioka 1988; Lee 2003: 3–31). The Japanese took the railroad and domestic service jobs left vacant by the Chinese. In 1909, ten thousand Japanese worked on the railroads and about fifteen thousand were domestic servants. They also worked in the sugar beet industry in the mountain states, where they were in direct competition with Mexican labor (Jibou 1988a: 42; Nishi 1995: 111). From the 1870s to the 1930s, a small elite group of Asian labor contractors recruited and managed Japanese, Chinese, and Filipino cannery workers (Friday 1994: 2–7, 51).

The Japanese also gravitated toward farming. They grew fruits and vegetables successfully on marginal lands in California. By 1910, thirty thousand Japanese in the United States were involved in agriculture. Most were field hands working under the padrone system, in which a Japanese labor contractor (*Dano-san*) organized a group of Japanese laborers (as much as one hundred) and contracted with farmers to work the fields. The Dano-san work groups functioned as quasi unions (Jibou 1988a: 42–43). However, the contractors were a source of conflict within and between Asian groups. Studies of the Japanese labor contractors show that they exploited the workers for their own gain (Ichioka 1988). Some Japanese immigrants were able to purchase and operate farms. In 1900 there were 39 Japanese farmers, but by 1909 there were 13,723 (Jibou 1988a: 42–43).

As the number of Japanese farmers grew and their success became evident, they became targets of discriminatory campaigns organized by unionized laborers, white workers, and white supremacists. In 1907, steps were taken to curtail the number of Japanese workers entering the country. Japan agreed to limit the number of emigrants. Under the agreement, the second wave of young men leaving were allowed to marry and bring their wives because women were not considered workers. Hence, from 1908 to 1924, Japanese immigration consisted primarily of picture brides and the wives and children of male Japanese workers already in the country (Glenn 1986; Ichioka 1988; Kitano and Daniels 1995: 55–56; Lee 2003: 3–31).

Though most of the farms owned by Japanese growers were small, their success spurred the passage of the Alien Land Act of 1913 in California. The act prohibited Japanese from buying land. A similar act was passed in Arizona in 1917 and in Washington in 1921. This bill declared aliens ineligible for citizenship and, therefore, ineligible to own land. However, Japanese farmers forestalled the seizure of their properties by transferring the title of their land to their American-born children (Jibou 1988b: 357–359; Nishi 1995: 102, 111–112). The discrimination escalated, and by 1920 California passed laws that prohibited Japanese residents from leasing land or being guardians to their American-born children who owned land. The Japanese filed lawsuits challenging their designation as aliens ineligible for citizenship. In the landmark 1922 case *Ozawa vs. U.S.*, the courts maintained that the Japanese were not eligible for U.S. citizenship because they were neither white nor black. Japanese and other Asians were not eligible for U.S. citizenship until the passage of the McCarran-Wallace Act in 1952 (Nishi 1995: 102).

Notwithstanding, the Japanese continued to enter the agricultural business. By the 1940s, the Japanese dominated a small but important segment of California (and West Coast) agriculture. By then about 45 percent of the Japanese residents were directly involved in farming and related businesses. On the eve of World War II, Japanese farmers on the West Coast operated roughly 6,000 farms covering 260,000 acres and worth about $73 million. In addition, urban Japanese dominated the contract gardening industry. Utilizing coethnic links, the Japanese dominated the growth, distribution, and sale of vegetables. They marketed their produce, bought supplies, and transported produce to market by using Japanese-owned businesses developed through mutual credit associations. The Japanese, who introduced the poling method of catching tuna, were also successful in that industry. By 1923, 50 percent of the tuna fishermen in the United States were Japanese (Jibou 1988a: 43; Nishi 1995: 111–112; Park 2008: 447–483).

The Japanese were poised to make a significant impact on the agricultural sector by the 1940s, but World War II intervened in dramatic fashion. Life for Japanese Americans changed dramatically after the bombing of Pearl Harbor in 1941. By the summer of 1942, almost the entire West Coast Japanese American population was interned in relocation camps located in California, Arizona, Idaho, Wyoming, Colorado, Utah, and Arkansas. Blood quantum levels were used to determine who would be interned; anyone who was at least one-eighth Japanese was relocated. Of the approximately 127,000 people of Japanese descent in the United States at the time, about 112,000 were interned. Two-thirds of the internees were American citizens, and many of the others were longtime legal residents (Jibou 1988a: 46–47; Nishi 1995: 103–104; Park 2008: 487–488).

Consistent with the experiences of Native Americans and African Americans, the first people to be arrested in sudden sweeps of Japanese American communities were the community leaders. Families got no word of what happened to their loved ones. The mass evacuations (second wave of internment) began in January 1942. Because they were given only twenty-four hours to prepare for the forced relocation, many families abandoned their homes, farms, businesses, and belongings. Those who could sell their property did so at bargain basement rates—usually about five cents on the dollar. The forced relocation resulted in Japanese lands being transferred to non-Japanese residents. The interned took to camp only what they could carry. Every family was assigned a number that each member wore on a tag. The internment devastated the Japanese community emotionally and psychologically. It eroded the economic position of the Issei (first generation) and weakened their position in the family and community. This was particularly true of the male heads of household (Aguirre and Turner 1998: 183; Espiritu 1997: 42–43; Jibou 1988a: 46–47; Kitano and Daniels 1988: 64, 567; Nishi 1995: 103–104; Park 2008: 487–488).

The concentration camps or "assembly centers," built mainly on racetracks and fairgrounds, were enclosed by barbed-wire fences, guarded by towers outfitted with searchlights, and surrounded by armed soldiers. Between seven thousand and eighteen thousand people were placed in these temporary camps. Families were housed in horse stables and flimsy tar-paper barracks. Families hung sheets from the ceilings for privacy. Even the latrines and showers were open. The internees had to eat unfamiliar mass-produced meals served in army-style mess halls. It was also rare for families to eat together. On average, families stayed in these assembly centers for one hundred days before being moved to relocation centers run by the War Relocation Authority (Clausen and Nishi 1983: 9–12; Hayashi 2004: 1–2; Nishi 1995: 104–105).

The ten relocation centers were located on isolated tracts of public desert lands and Indian reservations. In the case of the reservations, lands were appropriated to establish the relocation centers. The intent of the internment was to move Japanese residents away from the West Coast and place them in locations where they could be under constant watch. The barracks were partitioned in such a way that a family of five or six lived in a twenty- by twenty-five-foot compartment. They were provided with cots and blankets but no running water or cooking facilities. Two to three hundred internees shared these facilities (Clausen and Nishi 1983: 9–12; Hayashi 2004: 1–2; Nishi 1995: 104–105).

Though the relocation of the Japanese was described as a "military necessity" in Executive Order 9066, the Japanese living in Hawaii—the site of the bombing—were not relocated. Critics and scholars argue that they were too vital to the agricultural sector to be removed (Takaki 1989: 360–362). This has also led some to argue that the internment was driven by economic, agricultural, and land interests rather than military necessity. The internment camps—which operated under the auspices of former employees of the Department of Agriculture—were expected to be self-sustaining. Hence, the internees—many of whom were ripped from their agricultural jobs and business ventures—had to farm the reservations on which they were placed. The centers had agricultural programs that produced about sixty-one varieties of crops for sale and for the internees to consume; the internees also produced feed crops, and raised five types of livestock. In essence, the Japanese were used to prepare the lands within the internment centers for post-war production and settlement (Austin 2007: 58–84; Lillquist 2010: 74–104).

Frustrated internees rioted in some camps and gave the guards the silent treatment in others. Anti-American graffiti were scrawled on banners and buildings. Matters got worse when the army decided to establish a Nisei combat team composed of volunteers who passed a loyalty review. Adult inmates were administered a questionnaire requiring a "Yes" or "No" declaration of their complete loyalty to the United States. The internees were placed in a very difficult position: on the one hand they were angry at the unjust treatment, but on the other hand they feared the outcome of a "No" response. Many internees wanted to be accepted and reintegrated into American society. The decisions shattered families, frayed nerves, increased tensions, and at times manifested itself in violent outbursts. The renunciants and their dependents were segregated and sent to the Tule Lake camp; some went to Japan from there (Clausen and Nishi 1983: 10–12). Three Japanese Americans who challenged the constitutionality of the military orders were convicted. The Supreme Court upheld these rulings in *Hirabayashi v. United States* (1943). The three convictions were finally overturned between 1983 and 1987 (Aguirre and Turner 1998: 183; Nishi 1995: 105).

The internment lasted until 1945, and the last internment camp closed in March 1946. Numerous anti-Japanese hate crimes were directed against internees who tried to resettle in their old communities (Hayashi 2004: 1; Park 2008: 472–473). After the internment, activism in the Japanese American community revolved around reparations and citizenship. In 1948, the U.S. Congress passed the Japanese American Evacuation Claims Act, which earmarked $131 million for compensation. Claims were limited to a maximum of $2,500, and claims had to be filed within eighteen months of the passage of the act. It took seventeen years to process all the claims. However, a 1983 fact-finding Commission on Wartime Relocation and Internment of Civilians estimated losses in the range of $1.2 to $6.4 billion. Finally, in 1988, the Congress passed the Civil Liberties Act, which authorized the payment of $20,000 to living survivors of the internment camps (Aguirre and Turner 1998: 183–184; Nishi 1995: 106–107, 123–124).

KOREANS

As early as 1885, Korean political exiles began settling in the United States. The first wave of about seven thousand Koreans immigrated to Hawaii between 1903 and 1905. In 1905, there were about one thousand Koreans living in California. The Koreans were admitted as contract laborers indentured to their employers for seven years. They worked for wages lower than those paid to Americans. Because wages and housing conditions were so poor, the Korean government banned immigration to the United States. The Japanese government also played a role in Korea's decision to stop Korean immigration to Hawaii. As a result of the Russo-Japanese War, Korea became a protectorate of Japan. Hence, in 1905 Japan had significant influence on Korean policies. The large numbers of Koreans moving to Hawaii eliminated the Japanese workers' monopoly on plantation labor. As conditions worsened for the Japanese, many moved to California. Japanese diplomats in the United States worried that large influx of Japanese on the West Coast would result in anti-Japanese movements similar to the ones resulting in the exclusion of the Chinese thirty years earlier. It was thought that halting Korean immigration would protect Japanese residents both in Hawaii and on the mainland (by curtailing Japanese migration from Hawaii to California). Korean immigration did not reach noticeable numbers again until 1965, with the passage of the Immigration and Naturalization Act (Aguirre and Turner 1998: 181–182; Kitano and Daniels 1995; Min 1995: 200–201).

PART III
WILDLIFE PROTECTION

6

SPORT HUNTING, SCARCITY, AND WILDLIFE PROTECTION

A Business Mogul on the New Frontier:
The Harriman Expedition

During the second half of the nineteenth century slavery ended and the Native American wars drew to a close. Railroads crisscrossed the country and Manifest Destiny was within reach. Though the wildlands of the West had become more accessible to travelers, the wildlife had become scarcer. Nonetheless, the frontier continued to intrigue. Hence, by the end of the century, wealthy men went to greater extremes to have thrilling yet genteel recreational experiences: the Gilded Age had produced numerous millionaires, and this group of nouveaux riches emulated and tried to outdo the conspicuous consumption of patricians like the Roosevelts and Grinnells. The parvenus built ostentatious mansions, threw lavish balls, rode in large and luxurious carriages, wore the most expensive clothing, attended high-society events, belonged to the most exclusive clubs, bought the highest-priced pews in the most prestigious churches, and traveled extensively (for example, see Burrows and Wallace 1999: 1071–1088).

Big game hunting was still a prestigious and highly desirable pastime, and men of new wealth like Edward H. Harriman wanted to experience it. But as opportunities to hunt big game grew scarcer in the West, wealthy men sought out more far-flung destinations like Alaska to test their masculinity and prowess. It was in this context that Edward Harriman launched one of the most lavish and highly publicized expeditions in 1899. Harriman's expedition differed from previous explorations in that it combined the luxury of an all-expenses-paid vacation with frontier exploration and scientific inquiry. While expeditions undertaken by other explorers and naturalists were either solitary wanderings or all-male sojourns, Harriman built his voyage around a family trip that included his wife and children. This expedition was also unusual in that the idea did not germinate among the participants or organized by them; unbeknown to them, they were handpicked and invited to go on an odyssey with a benefactor they were not acquainted with.

The Harriman Alaska Expedition illustrates the cross-fertilization that existed between business, conservation, and preservation in the late nineteenth century. Edward Henry Harriman, a wealthy industrialist and railroad tycoon who dropped out of school at age fourteen to go to Wall Street as a quotations boy, was the president of Union Pacific Railroad (P. Burroughs 1995: xiii) and also controlled the Southern Pacific Railroad. Despite his business acumen, Harriman, the son of an Episcopal minister, was not completely accepted into Wall Street's elite inner circle because of his lack of education, brusque style, and crude manners. Aware of his outsider status, Harriman was always on the lookout for new business ventures and ways of enhancing his prestige in upper-class circles. Thus in 1899 when his doctor ordered him to take a break from work, he decided to take a trip to the West to hunt game. However, Daniel Elliot of the Chicago Field Museum persuaded him to abandon his plans to hunt in the West and take a trip to Alaska, the American frontier that had just become the new "hot" tourist destination for the wealthy (Curry 1995: 529; Goetzmann and Sloan 1982: 5–7).

Not content with an ordinary vacation, Harriman decided to organize and finance a scientific expedition. In many ways Alaska was an intriguing place to mount an expedition: much of the region's flora and fauna was uncatalogued, there were plentiful opportunities to hunt magnificent megafauna, and the publicity from the trip would encourage more people to travel to the region. To get to Alaska, many people had to travel by rail to the West Coast on Harriman's rail lines. Harriman also thought the two-month cruise could be organized as a philanthropic undertaking that could garner great publicity and bring him greater acceptance among New York's social, business, and scientific elites.

The trip was being planned at a time when social pressure was mounting on those who were wealthy to donate some of their fortune to enhance the public good. To this end, other moguls and "robber barons" like Andrew W. Mellon and Andrew Carnegie were already contributing to public libraries and to prominent institutions such as the National Gallery of Art to gain respectability (Cannandine 2006; Nasaw 2006).

Science and the environment emerged as prestigious outlets for charitable giving, so Harriman's expedition was framed, first and foremost, as a scientific mission. To build the expedition roster, Harriman invited two leading scholars or practitioners in each field to accompany him (P. Burroughs 1995: xiii–xiv; Goetzmann and Sloan 1982: 6–8, 208–209; Wyatt [1901] 1995: xxxvii–xxxix). Though it was challenging at first, Harriman organized the expedition quickly. Despite his enormous wealth and power, he was not well known outside the circles of high finance, so when he appeared uninvited in C. Hart Merriam's office at the Biological Survey in late March 1899, Merriam did not know who he was. Merriam listened to Harriman's plan with some skepticism, but a quick background check of Harriman showed that he was who he claimed to be. Within a few hours of Harriman's visit, Merriam was sold on the idea and agreed to select the people who would be invited to go on the all-expenses-paid expedition (Goetzmann and Sloan 1982: 8–9, 12, 207–216; Muir 1909a, 1915, 1917, 1993; Wilkins 1995: 248). With the exception of Harriman's wife and children, women were not invited even though many women, such as those discussed above, had distinguished themselves in the emerging conservation field.

In all 126 people (including the Harrimans and the crew) went on the expedition. Those traveling with Harriman included C. Hart Merriam, several members of the Cosmos Club and the National Academy of Sciences in Washington, John Muir, the nature writer John Burroughs, the bird illustrator Louis Agassiz Fuertes, the photographer Edward Curtis, Henry Gannett of the U.S. Geological Survey, and George Bird Grinnell (P. Burroughs 1995: xiv–xvi; Goetzmann and Sloan 1982: 12–15; Nash 1982: 282; *New York Herald* 1899; Wyatt [1901] 1995: xxxix). Guests of the Harrimans first traveled to Seattle on Harriman's private luxury train, which had five palace cars loaded with the finest food, wine, and cigars. Along the way, members of conservation and preservation groups such as the Mazamas in Portland and the Rainier Club in Seattle hosted and feted the travelers (P. Burroughs 1995: xiv–xvi; Goetzmann and Sloan 1982: 17, 28–29; Wyatt [1901] 1995: xxxix).

Though there were activists on the trip, expedition members were not critical of activities that had negative environmental impacts. For instance, as Harriman's train whisked cruise members to Seattle, where they would board the *Elder*, Burroughs noted that the lands through which railroad tracks had been cut were eroding badly. In his final report on the expedition, he noted that "in places the country looks as if all the railroad forces of the world might have been turned loose to delve and rend and pile in some mad, insane folly and debauch" (Burroughs 1902: 6). Though Harriman made his fortune from the railroads, Burroughs did not implicate or criticize Harriman for the devastation.

Members of the expedition collected thousands of plant and animal specimens. They trapped, shot, hunted, caught, and otherwise gathered specimens without regard for the rarity of the species (Goetzmann and Sloan 1982: 101, 119, 147–150). For instance, when Louis Agassiz Fuertes spotted what he thought to be a Bonaparte gull on St. Matthew Island, his rowing companion, ornithologist A. Fisher, said to him, "Pot that, it is a Sabine." Fuertes immediately shot the rare white gull (Fuertes 1956: 52). The bird illustrator and ornithologist also took birds' eggs from the island, and they killed adult birds, leaving young chicks to starve (Wolfe 1938: 411).

After several unsuccessful attempts to kill a bear, Harriman set sail for Kodiak Island because he heard that bear were abundant there. To ensure that he shot a bear, Harriman's hunting companions drove a female bear and her young cub down into a narrow gorge where Harriman waited with a powerful rifle. Just in case the bear attacked Harriman, a group of hunters with enough firepower "to tear the bear to pieces" was stationed near the tycoon. Harriman killed the bear with one shot. The cub was also killed. The expedition's taxidermist skinned both bears, and volunteers dragged the trophies back to the ship. Though the bear was not as big as some of those Harriman had seen adorning his friends' parlors, the Kodiak bear would suffice (Goetzmann and Sloan 1982: 119–122; Wolfe 1938: 402).

Harriman did not practice the art of the pure chase that hunters like Theodore Roosevelt, Grinnell, and Marsh describe and that upper-class hunters had established as ethical more than a century earlier. Rather than tracking the animals painstakingly and taking a shot where the prey had a fair chance of escaping, the crew drove the bears into a gorge, where Harriman ambushed them. There is no evidence that Grinnell criticized Harriman's hunting method during the expedition. Before leaving Seattle, expedition members announced that they intended to bring Kodiak bear specimens back with them. They planned to kill, stuff, and mount bears for the National Museum in Washington, DC.

They also intended to send specimens to Paris, London, and Berlin (*Washington Post* 1899a: 19).

Though Muir was somewhat repulsed by the hunting and specimen collecting activities of Harriman and other expedition members, his disapproval—even in his journal entries—was muted. He did not criticize Harriman or the scientists for their actions in the genteel atmosphere of the cruise (Wolfe 1938: 399–402). However, on his 1880 Alaska voyage Muir had openly criticized, reprimanded, and threatened his Native American crew and guides for shooting a bird (Muir 1915: 235). Muir's 1880 traveling companion, Samuel Hall Young, also wrote that Muir was indignant, cursed at, and threatened an Indian crew member who shot several mountain goats (S. H. Young [1915] 1990: 170–171).

RUMMAGING THROUGH A DESERTED INDIAN VILLAGE

Shortly before the expedition came to an end, the *Elder* stopped at Cape Fox, a deserted Indian village. Though the stop at Cape Fox was meant to be only an impromptu visit before returning to Seattle, expedition members spent the better part of two days pillaging the settlement without any consideration for the Native American tribe that had once inhabited it. They dug up and removed ornately carved totem poles, monuments, religious masks, baskets, carvings, and other cultural and religious artifacts. They ransacked the homes, which seemed to have been hastily abandoned, and removed items of worth. Harriman took two carved wooden bears that were guarding a grave site. Other objects too, such as a Chilkoot blanket that was placed over a grave site, were removed from the burial ground (Goetzmann and Sloan 1982: 163–168).

Social Class and the Ethics of Hunting

Despite Harriman's crude hunting behavior, American sport hunters and anglers have been concerned about the ethics of hunting since the eighteenth century. In 1783 *The Sportsman's Companion*[1] outlined an ethical basis of hunting. Its author expressed sympathy for the quail being pursued and introduced the idea that the game had inherent "rights" that sportsmen should honor. The book instructed sportsmen to hunt only in the proper season, and to search for the game they shot to prevent the animals from suffering a prolonged and painful death (Bell [1783] 1791: 118–119; Phillips and Hill 1930; Reiger [1975] 2001: 8). The descriptions in chapter 4 of the hunting practices of John Phillips, Theodore Roosevelt, and George Bird Grinnell illustrate that the men adhered to sportsmen's codes: good sport hunters empathize with the animals they kill, walk slowly to the downed quarry, take a moment to appreciate the animal, and make sure it is dead. By contrast, Harriman did not stalk the prey, give it an opportunity to escape, or show appreciation for it after he killed it.

In 1827 another seminal book, *The American Shooter's Manual*, was published "by a Gentleman of Philadelphia County." In it Jesse Kester—the author to whom this work is attributed—implored hunters to teach youngsters the proper sportsmen's code, care for hunting dogs, search for wounded game, and kill it humanely. Kester also urged sportsmen to become more than just killers. He framed hunting as an intellectual pursuit in which hunters had a responsibility to become naturalists by studying the habits of the game and environments in which they live (Kester 1827: ix–x).[2] John James Audubon exemplified this approach in his studies (Audubon 1832, 1835, 1999). By expanding the framing of the hunter and tapping into the preexisting and prestigious identities of naturalists and intellectuals, Kester was expanding the hunter's identity. Kester hoped that by encouraging hunters to become naturalists and intellectuals, he could lead them to broaden their interest and become more concerned about a wider array of environmental issues.

Kester was very concerned about the lack of game-protection laws and the rampant destruction of wildlife. He hoped his book would help to infuse in hunters genteel sporting ethics that would help to reduce the slaughter. Kester wrote that America was a "country destitute of game laws and almost without any legal restriction in regard to its [game] destruction." He noted that though most males hunted, very few were worthy of being called sportsmen. According to Kester, most hunters were mere "game killers, and nothing more." Consequently, he wanted to "diffuse throughout the community a taste for genteel and sportsman-like shooting, and to abolish the abominable poaching, game destroying, habit of ground shooting, trapping, and snaring which prevails throughout our country in the neighborhood of all cities and large towns" (Kester 1827: 13–15). *The American Shooter's Manual* also sought to increase awareness about hunting seasons and the environment (Bell [1783] 1791).

Kester was trying to discourage hunting excesses such as the ones Audubon described in 1810. Even as a naturalist and bird enthusiast Audubon participated in shooting sprees (L. B. Audubon 1869: 36–37). Audubon also described a massacre of passenger pigeons he witnessed in Kentucky in 1813. During the shooting, he tried to tally and record how many birds were flying overhead and how many were killed, but the numbers were so staggering that it was impossible to make an accurate count (Audubon 1832: 320–321). Robert Roosevelt, a prominent member of the New York Sportsmen's Club, also recognized that excessive angling led to declines of fish in the Hudson River and in streams in the Bronx (R. B. Roosevelt 1884: 184).

Other publications reinforced the notion that wildlife stocks were declining because of rapacious hunting and angling and that sportsmen should not condone such practices. In 1830, Doughty described a true sportsman as someone who "always respects the rules and seasons for shooting, and most heartily despises the man who destroys the unfledged brood, or the protectors which Nature has provided for them" (T. Doughty [1830] 1930: 7). In the ongoing effort to distinguish between sportsmen who were purists and those who flouted the rules, John Davis defined what constituted true sportsmen in 1835. He also outlined how such men differed from the pretenders who were trying to claim that appellation (J. Davis 1835: 7). Davis identified two groups of pretenders—the market hunter and the dandy. According to Davis, the market hunter "hunts like a vagabond, because he is averse to all regular employment," and the dandy is an aspiring sportsman who hunts "because he wishes to be fashionable." Someone like Edward Harriman would be considered a dandy. As Davis saw it, sportsmen were not confined to a particular class, but a true sportsman hunted only "because he has an innate and ardent love for healthful exercise, and the . . . sports of the field." A true sportsman was also deliberate in his actions; he "*does nothing at random*." The true sportsman studies the habitat and habits of the game. Even after a kill, the true sportsman is calm and in control: "He does not run himself out of breath to get ahead of his companion, but walks coolly up to his dogs; and when the birds spring, singles out his victim with deliberate and *deadly* precision" (J. Davis 1835: 9–10; italics in original).

The ideas about limiting the hunting season, sparing rare species, and conducting the hunt in a gentlemanly fashion gained currency among the elites. This led sport hunters to develop a "Code of Sportsmen," which Hummel (1994: 13) summarizes as follows:

> The sportsman should practice proper etiquette in the field—not crowding other hunters, not claiming more than a fair share of shooting opportunities, not taking more game than can be consumed by the sportsman.
> Do not pursue any game species to the point of extinction.
> Develop skill with the weapons of the hunt so that they can deliver a humane coup-de-grace to the prey species.
> Acquire extensive knowledge of the prey species and its habitat.
> Allow the prey a fair opportunity to escape by use of its natural defense/

flight mechanisms. Meet the prey in its own environment and master it by "fair means."

Possesses an appreciation for the sport in order to be its model representative to the non sporting public and pass it on to future generations.

As the above discussion makes clear, some elite sportsmen had difficulty with the second rule. Theodore Roosevelt, Thomas Grinnell, John Phillips, and Hiram Frost were all wealthy sportsmen who reported hunting game to the point of extinction. Later discussions will show that William Hornaday, a renowned zoologist, behaved similarly.

Early advocates of the American sporting ethic adopted English hunting values, wherein sportsmen were considered gentlemen. They also sought to distinguish gentlemen hunters and anglers from commoners who were classified as market and pot hunters. The market hunters were most reviled because they were perceived as killing excessively for commercial gain. Pot hunters were subsistence hunters trying to feed themselves and their families, but this group was perceived as lacking the requisite understanding of the game and appreciation for the sports of hunting and angling to be considered either gentlemen or true sportsmen. Though sportsmen ate some of what they killed (some of it was also stuffed and mounted for display), they placed themselves in a different category from the pot hunters because sportsmen did not have to rely on the quarry they hunted to provide food and they took the quarry in an "appropriate" manner (Reiger [1975] 2001: 7).

Elite hunters blamed the decimation of wildlife on those who weren't considered true sportsmen. For instance, Robert Roosevelt blamed diminishing fish on those of new wealth and pot hunters (R. B. Roosevelt 1884: 185). Henry William Herbert[3] expounded on the nature of the true or genuine sportsman by distancing sportsmen from wanton destruction. He denounced poachers and market hunters, whom he thought wreaked havoc on game and went unpunished (Forester 1849: 24).

However, the hunting practices of some sportsmen indicated that elite men also hunted in ways that destroyed large numbers of wildlife. To halt these practices, Robert Roosevelt implored true sportsmen to take action to preserve game birds and fish. He argued that the expansion of the railroads provided increased access to the hunting grounds and that real and pseudo sportsmen were decimating wildlife. He implored real sportsmen to commit to halting the destruction. He called on sportsmen because he thought they had the greatest stake in the matter and should do something about it if they wanted to "retain for their old age and leave to their children the best preserver of health, a love of field sports, they must protect game-birds and fish." Consequently, he instructed sportsmen to "discourage, by their conservation and example, all infringement of the law or any cruel or wasteful prosecution of what should be sport." He also urged sportsmen to shun and expose those who broke hunting laws or killed wildlife simply for the purpose of destroying it (R. B. Roosevelt 1884: 186).

As Reiger argues, by adopting the self-imposed code, sportsmen were in effect establishing a contract with their quarry. The one-sided agreement meant that sportsmen would pursue game only by sportsman-like methods and would not pursue and kill game during the breeding season, waste killed game or sell it for profit, or kill in excessive numbers. Thus true sportsmen were thought to exhibit generosity (allowing the quarry a fair chance to escape) and empathy (killing the quarry swiftly and in the most humane way possible) toward the game. By adopting the sportsmen's code, upper-class hunters and anglers saw themselves as superior to others who hunted and fished. At first the adoption of the code was voluntary and enforced by peer pressure, but later on sportsmen made sure it was codified into law (Reiger [1975] 2001: 6–7, 12).

Like fellow aristocrats in the Northeast, William Elliott, a Harvard-educated South Carolinian slave master and owner of nine plantations, decried American hunting practices that allowed the poor as well as the rich to hunt. He was particularly averse to market hunters. In 1846 he published *Carolina Sports by Land and Water*, a book that criticized commercial trade in wildlife, because he thought the epicurean tastes of the wealthy had fueled demand for venison and other wild meat that kept the market hunters in business. He argued that because of this new demand professional hunters were decimating wildlife. For Elliott, the problem of wildlife destruction arose in part because in America the general public had the right to hunt and could do so at their discretion (Elliott [1846] 1859: 284–285).

Theodore Roosevelt was another genteel sportsman who was very concerned about hunting ethics. He wrote disparagingly about hunters, particularly eastern urban sportsmen, who flocked to the Adirondacks to practice "murderous and unsportsman-like forms of hunting." He disdained those who used hounds to drive animals into deep water, where they could be shot at close range from a boat; he expressed disapproval of snowshoeing and trapping animals in snowdrifts, clubbing animals over the head, killing them with axes, jacking,[4] or fire hunting. Roosevelt also opposed hounding, where dogs were used to drive animals like white-tailed deer past stations where hunters lay in wait for them (Roosevelt [1885] 1996: 157, 366–368; [1893] 1996: 676–677). In fact, on the whole Roosevelt didn't like hunting whitetail deer because they usually had to be "killed by stealth and stratagem, and not by fair, manly hunting" (Roosevelt

[1893] 1996: 365). Roosevelt, who had killed a deer in the Adirondacks by jacking when he was a boy, disparaged this form of hunting and thought that fire hunting was useful only to see the wilderness by torchlight at night. However, Roosevelt did not regret having experienced killing an animal in this manner at least once (Roosevelt [1893] 1996: 366).

Thus the image of the American recreational hunter evolved as an amalgam of English elite sporting values combined with the evolving image of frontier heroes like Daniel Boone and explorers and naturalists like Meriwether Lewis, William Clark, and John James Audubon (Hummel 2004: 460–464). In their quest to define the true sportsman, sportsmen weren't only trying to distinguish themselves from the commoners; they also sought to make a distinction between patrician sportsmen or of those of old wealth like the Roosevelts and Grinnells and the nouveaux riches like the Rockefellers and Harrimans. There was a feeling among the patrician class that their hegemony in defining the sports and codes of conduct was being threatened by men who could ingratiate themselves into high society rather than being born or bred into it. The parvenus did not always adhere to the ethical codes established by the old upper class, so the patricians took it upon themselves to ensure that the new rich too adhered to these norms (Reiger [1975] 2001: 52–53).

Early Game-Protection Efforts

It was clear by the late eighteenth century that the indiscriminate hunting of game was decimating wildlife. In August 1787, twenty-year-old John Quincy Adams went hunting in the marshes near Newburyport, Massachusetts. When the future president failed to bag anything, he took time to reflect on the tensions between game laws, individual liberties, and regulating the taking of game. He argued that game laws might violate people's liberties and may have been carried too far in parts of Europe, but where none existed, the game was decimated. Adams went on to say that there was a tension between having laws where only a few could hunt and enjoy the spoils versus having no game laws and allowing game to be hunted to extinction. In the latter scenario, no one would have anything to hunt (J. Q. Adams 1903: 23).

By the time Adams began writing about game protection in his diaries, game laws were already on the books in many eastern states. However, not everyone saw the necessity for these laws or understood the balance that governments had to strike between governance, resource protection, and individual liberties. Game-protection laws began appearing on the books in the late seventeenth and early eighteenth centuries. For instance, Massachusetts had a closed season for white-tailed deer as early as 1694. In 1708, New York declared a closed season on the heath hen (Eastern prairie chicken), wild turkey, bobwhite quail, and ruffed grouse. Despite efforts to save the heath hen, it went extinct in 1832 (Bell [1783] 1791: 118–119; Matthiessen [1959] 1995: 69; Palmer 1912: 14). New York also outlawed battery shooting in 1834. This form of hunting, in which hunters hid in a box or "battery" while it floated amid nesting birds, took a heavy toll on birds. From inside the battery, hunters had an easy shot at unsuspecting waterfowl that approached the decoys stationed around it (Reiger [1975] 2001: 15–16).

However, these early wildlife protection laws did little to stem the rampant destruction of animals, and as the nineteenth century progressed, it became apparent that wildlife was declining rapidly. For instance, the last woodland caribou was seen in Maine in 1902. Moose was also devastated in the nineteenth century; by the 1890s, only small herds of moose lived in remote parts of New England. The states took action: Maine restricted the hunting season for moose in 1897 and later, beginning in 1916, instituted a four-year moratorium on moose hunting. This helped the herds to recover. Similarly, the deer were nearly wiped out by hunting, logging, and forest clearance early in the nineteenth century. As a result, Vermont banned deer hunting in 1865, and in 1878 New Hampshire closed nine of its ten counties to hunting to allow the animal to rebound (Judd 1997: 209–210).

By the middle of the nineteenth century many New England towns had begun to craft laws to protect game and other wildlife. As resources dwindled, states also began to regulate out-of-state hunters. For instance, in 1843 Maine citizens petitioned the legislature to restrict the activities of out-of-state hunters, who were largely blamed for the decimation of the moose and deer populations. In addition, Maine residents also began putting moral pressure on voracious hunters by ostracizing those who killed more than they needed to subsist on. When a hunter named Casswell set out one winter to kill one hundred moose, taking only the hide, and almost succeeded, townspeople described him as worthless and wasteful. Vermonters also tried to restrict the activities of out-of-state hunters (Judd 1997: 49; *State v. Solomon Norton* 1873).

Private Hunting Preserves and Sportsmen's Clubs

This piecemeal approach to wildlife protection was less than satisfying to the growing cadre of wildlife advocates. So in the absence of effective local, state, or federal laws to protect wildlife, private citizens began to take collective action to protect wild animals. They began to build private, multipurpose game parks that were intended to (a) conserve animals, (b) ensure that targets were available for members to hunt and fish, (c) provide financial gain for the owners, (d) exclude nonmembers from gaining access to protected wildlife, (e) promote wildlife policies beneficial to owners and members, (f) promote genteel leisure activities, (g) standardize and enforce sporting ethics, (h) develop breeding and stocking programs, (i) promote sustainability, and (j) cultivate conservation concern.

Private wildlife preserves have flourished in the United States since the seventeenth century. One of the earliest American game preserves, Augustine Herman's Bohemia Manor, was built in Cecil County, Maryland, in 1661. The fenced deer park was of considerable size. Similar game parks founded by English Royalists and other wealthy foreigners were built in Virginia and the Atlantic states. Farmers in these states also have a long tradition of leasing the hunting rights on their land to wealthy sportsmen and clubs (Walcott 1914: 202–203).

Early on, wealthy urban men formed sports clubs so they could fish, hunt, and participate in other outdoor activities close to home. During the eighteenth century angling clubs sprung up in and around cities, since the waterways still had plenty of fish and local forests still had game. In Philadelphia, for example, affluent sportsmen in 1732 founded the Schuylkill Fishing Company, the oldest angling club in America. The club, which is still in existence today, was founded by twenty-eight of the city's most powerful men (many of whom emigrated with William Penn) but began limiting its membership to twenty-five men in 1737. Members of the club also hunted wild fowl along the Schuylkill River. In 1747 Philadelphians formed the Fort St. David's Fishing Company, another club for recreational anglers who represented the "nobility of those days." A third fishing club composed of prominent Philadelphians, the Mount Regale Fishing Company, also operated on the Schuylkill (Burrows and Wallace 1999: 955; *New York Times* 1905a; *Pennsylvania Magazine of History and Biography* 1903: 88; Tinkcom 1982: 121–122; Wainwright 1982: 292; Watson and Hazard 1884: 291–300).[5]

Similar clubs were formed in other cities. In 1806, sportsmen formed the New York Sporting Club. The club tried to institutionalize and enforce game laws and the sportsmen's code of ethics. In 1832 the Carroll's Island Club was formed in Maryland, and similar clubs began sprouting up around New England and the Mid-Atlantic region. In 1836, a group of sportsmen from New Jersey founded the Trenton Club, an organization dedicated to the preservation of game. William Porter, editor of *The Spirit of the Times*, wrote an editorial about the club in which he urged sportsmen in New York and Long Island to form similar clubs (Bittner 2008: 10–11; Reiger [1975] 2001: 34–35, 40; Trefethen 1964: 1–20).

As wildlife stocks declined, hunters, birdwatchers, and anglers formed private clubs that focused on managing natural resources as well as decreeing and enforcing game laws. In an effort to have a ready supply of game for members to shoot or catch, sports clubs also began to develop breeding and stocking programs. This was deemed essential, since not all men could make long trips to the West to hunt; wealthy men also wanted access to fish and game close to home, and the private clubs with breeding and stocking programs provided those opportunities. Five such clubs—the New York Sportsmen's Club, Caton's Preserve, Blooming Grove Park, the Bisby Club/Adirondack League Club, and South Fork Fishing and Hunting Club—are profiled below.

THE NEW YORK SPORTSMEN'S CLUB
AND UNIFORM GAME LAWS

On May 20, 1844, a new type of sports club, the New York Sportsmen's Club, was formed. Inspired by articles written by Henry William Herbert and others decrying the rapid decline in wildlife species that appeared in leading sportsmen's journals such as *The Spirit of the Times* and *American Turf Register and Sporting Magazine*, eighty influential men formed the club (Forester 1857, 1859, 1881; *New York Times* 1858: 1). The organization's members, whose stated goal was the protection and preservation of game, focused more on conservation issues than on socializing and hunting. The New York Sportsmen's Club campaigned against the sale of game for market consumption, spring shooting of game birds, and lax game laws. In 1846, after states turned over the responsibility for wildlife conservation to counties, club members drafted a model game law that passed in New York. The law mandated a closed season on deer, fish, and several species of game birds, and prohibited their sale during closed season. Most of the club's members were prominent attorneys, thus they relied heavily on legal strategies to achieve conservation goals. They successfully sued poachers, dealers, and hotel proprietors for possessing game killed out of season. Their success led to the formation of similar sportsmen's clubs elsewhere. The New York Sportsmen's Club held a sportsmen's convention in Geneva, New York, in 1859, and created the New York State Fisheries Commission in 1868. In 1869, the club voted to allocate one thousand dollars of its funds to pay informants and detectives who helped to prosecute those breaking the game laws (Hallock 1878: 61–68; *New York Times* 1869: 2; 1874: 2; Trefethen 1964: 1–20; 1975: 72–75, 110).

Under the leadership of Robert Roosevelt, the New York Sportsmen's Club evolved into a statewide organization with a new name—the New York Association for the Protection of Game. The name change occurred in 1874. Five years later, the New York Association for the Protection of Game helped pass a law to protect moose, deer, birds, fish, and other game. This law provided a uniform state game code that superseded the myriad of county and local laws already on the books. However, despite their impressive victories, the club's activism waned over time and members shifted their attention to marksmanship and trap shooting. By 1890 the annual meetings were little more than trap shooting contests (*New York Times* 1869: 2; 1874: 2; Trefethen 1964: 1–20; 1975: 72–75, 110).

CATON'S AND OTHER INDIVIDUALLY OWNED RESERVES

To satisfy the demand of hunters wanting access to game, individuals and groups began establishing a new genre of game reserves in the second half of the nineteenth century. In this vein, in 1858 Chicago's Judge John Dean Caton established a two-hundred-acre preserve near Ottawa, Illinois, that he stocked with white-tailed deer, elk, and other game. Caton's preserve differed from older game parks in that he conducted scientific studies of the animals' habits and published his findings in *The Antelope and Deer of America* (Caton 1877: ix, 44). Caton believed that a sportsman should be knowledgeable about the game being hunted. As he wrote in the preface of his book, "He who would enjoy the full measure of field sports must have a good knowledge of the natural history of the objects of his pursuit, and the more complete that knowledge the more complete will be his enjoyment" (Caton 1877: ix).

Austin Corbin of Newport, New Hampshire, also built a private game preserve around his boyhood home in 1886. His 27,000-acre preserve, Blue Mountain Forest Park, held an estimated four thousand big game, including buffalo, wapiti (elk), deer, and boars. Rutherford Stuyvesant began raising game birds on his 8,000-acre estate named Tranquility, located in Warren County, New Jersey, in 1887. He also reared deer, mule, and wapiti. He tried breeding bison and cows without much success. Edward H. Litchfield of Brooklyn also developed a private 10,000-acre preserve near Tupper Lake in the Adirondacks that he stocked with big game. Mr. C. Dieterich had a 3,000-acre fenced park near Millbrook in Dutchess County, New York. Chester W. Chapin built a private park in Sullivan County, New York. Charles C. Worthington created an 80,000-acre bird sanctuary in New Jersey, while Henry Ford had a 2,100-acre bird sanctuary near Detroit (Walcott 1914: 205–208). The private parks in the Adirondacks will be discussed in greater detail later.

Some game parks were built by organized groups of sportsmen. The Blooming Grove Park Association, for example, established the Blooming Grove Park in 1871. The park was located in Pike County in eastern Pennsylvania, about 120 miles from New York City. The association wanted to preserve, import, breed, and propagate birds, fish, and game animals so that their members could hunt and angle on the grounds of the park year-round. They also constructed cottages for members' use (*American Sportsman* 1873: 85; *New York Times* 1899d: 14; Palmer 1910). In 1899, the Blooming Grove Park Association owned eighteen thousand acres of land and leased another ten thousand acres. The bag limits were high; each member could catch as many as forty-two trout per day from the park's well-stocked streams and lakes. Members hired gamekeepers to patrol the park and keep it under constant surveillance (*New York Times* 1899b: 5).

Blooming Grove's founders were Charles Hallock; Fayette Giles, a wealthy jeweler; and Genio Scott, a member of the New York Sportsmen's Club. Giles, who had lived in France for six years, was enthralled by the forests of Fontainebleau and the Grand Duchy of Baden; Blooming Grove was modeled on European forests of this nature. The conservation idea of sustainable yield was at the core of Blooming Grove's operations. The founders envisioned "a grand park or enclosure . . . where game might be bred and protected." They bred and managed game, ran a fish-culture program, and managed their forests. The founders perceived that "the cultivation of forests . . . and the selling of timber and surplus game . . . compensate[d] in some degree for the frightful waste which is annually devastating our forests and exterminating our game" (Hallock 1873: 225–226).

Although the park was in Pennsylvania, its offices were located on Broadway in New York City. The Blooming Grove Park Association played by its own rules. It set and enforced its own game laws, including the length of the hunting season. The park's hunting season varied from the hunting season set by the state of Pennsylvania. The charter under which the organization operated stated that the game laws of Pennsylvania were not applicable to property owned or leased by the association. When comprehensive game laws were passed nationally, the club faced questions about compliance with those laws (N. S. Smith 1903: 14).

Blooming Grove is important because it can be viewed as a transitional type of park that was much larger than the landscaped urban parks of the time. Parks such as Central Park and Prospect Park in New York were designed as "rural" parks intended to capture the romantic wilderness imagery and vistas within the bounds of a city. They allowed horseback riding, sledding, and other genteel sports. But such parks did not accommodate hunting and angling (Taylor 2009: 221–337). Blooming Grove was a rural park in the true sense of the word, and it provided a more masculine space for hunting and fishing activities under controlled conditions. Though there was still an element of uncertainty about how much quarry the user could bag at the end of the day, the fact that the park developed its own stocking program ensured users that there would be game to hunt and fish to catch. It dealt with the anxieties sportsmen were feeling about the scarcity of game, rapidly disappearing wildlife, and the difficulty in hunting or catching them by developing a space and programs to ensure success in outdoor pursuits. Park operators also understood the concept of sustained yield and instituted it as an antidote to unregulated hunting and fishing.

Blooming Grove was innovative in another way too: the park managed its stands of timber with an eye toward using them as a source of income to help maintain the park. This activity preceded similar kinds of practical forest management techniques in the United States by decades. For instance, it wasn't until 1892 that Gifford Pinchot began managing the stands of timber at the Biltmore Estate for profitability (Pinchot [1947] 1998: 49). As Theodore Cart argues, Blooming Grove was the first place to provide a large-scale demonstration of integrated natural resource management in the country. It blended outdoor recreation with forest, fish, and game management (Cart 1971). As later discussions will show, while Yosemite had been set aside and placed under the jurisdiction of the state of California seven years before Blooming Grove was established and had a management plan that was written by Frederick Law Olmsted, the Yosemite Reserve was poorly managed and supervised. Likewise, although Yellowstone National Park was designated the year after Blooming Grove was established, it did not have an effective management and supervision plan until 1894.

The organization changed its name to the Blooming Grove Hunting and Fishing Club between 1903 and 1909. In 1909, when a devastating conflagration consumed the clubhouse and living quarters, which had rooms to house sixty guests, the club occupied roughly forty thousand acres and had two hundred members, most of whom were from New York (*New York Times* 1909a: 20). The Blooming Grove Hunting and Fishing Club currently owns more than nineteen thousand acres of land. Members still hunt ruffed grouse, turkey, and a variety of other birds, white-tailed deer, and bear. The streams are still stocked with more than sixteen thousand trout annually (Blooming Grove Township Comprehensive Plan 2008: 14-1–14-3).

The Clove Valley Rod and Gun Club was modeled after Blooming Grove; however, it took its operations a step further. Located in Dutchess County, New York, Clove Valley became the first sportsmen's club to use the Bayne Law, which allowed for the sale of mallards reared in captivity to turn a profit. The club reared and marketed four thousand mallards and made a profit of $2,500 from their sale (Walcott 1914: 206).

Another club modeled after Blooming Grove is the Bisby Club. The idea for the Bisby Club came about when General "Dick" Sherman fished on Bisby Lake for the first time in 1875. The Bisby Club was established in the Adirondack Mountains two years later because its founders were frustrated that the state of New York had not built a "grand park" in the "vast wilderness" to protect the forest (*New York Times* 1890: 12).

Consequently, a group of prominent sportsmen—most of whom were residents of Utica, Syracuse, and New York City—leased a large tract of land in Herkimer County to create the park. The club's charter limited the membership to twenty-five members; membership was nontransferable. However, widows of deceased members could enjoy membership privileges if they paid assessments. In 1882, the Bisby Club owned or leased about nine thousand acres of land containing nine lakes and several smaller water sources. Members built a clubhouse, a lodge that could accommodate seventy-five persons, and a fish hatchery and stocked the lakes with fish. They also planted wild rice to attract waterfowl (Cookingham 1883: 172; *New York Times* 1890: 12; *Utica Morning Herald and Daily Gazette* 1880; *Utica Weekly Herald* 1888: 7). Members could either live in the lodge or construct their own "handsome and commodious" log camps. They fished and hunted voraciously. One member, Mr. Barber, and his guests killed twenty-seven deer in the fall of 1886 (*Utica Weekly Herald* 1886: 12). Others, like General Husted, who was in the habit of inviting friends to the lakes and entertaining them with rare wines, had enough fish to send a box of fish caught on the lakes to his dear friend Chauncey Depew (*New York Times* 1890: 12).

A similar club, the Adirondack League Club, was founded in 1890. Members of the club purchased the Anson Blake tract of land that contained about one hundred thousand acres with lakes and valuable timber for about five hundred thousand dollars. Immediately club members sought to extend the Herkimer, Newport & Poland railroad into the preserve. They also wasted no time posting signs all over the preserve that forbade hunting, fishing, and trespassing on the property. The signs also warned nonmembers that violators would be "prosecuted according to law." More than twenty guards were hired to patrol the grounds and apprehend trespassers (Adirondack League Club 1890, 1894; Comstock and Webster 1990: 12, 58; *Rome Semi-Weekly Citizen* 1890). The Adirondack League Club instituted a practical forestry program and constructed lodges for its members. The club's adviser was Bernhard E. Fernow, chief of the Division of Forestry in the U.S. Department of Agriculture. The Adirondack League Club had a membership of two hundred but sold five hundred shares in the corporation, hence some members held multiple shares (E. Comstock 1990: 33–34; Cookingham 1883: 172; *New York Times* 1890: 12; *New York Tribune* 1893: 22; Reiger [1975] 2001: 89–90; Stoddard 1893: 213–214; *Utica Morning Herald and Daily Gazette* 1880). By 1893, the Adirondack League Club controlled about 175,000 acres of land containing merchantable timber valued at more than $1 million. The club made about $30,000 annually from logging spruce more than twelve inches in diameter (*New York Tribune* 1893: 22). The Bisby Club transferred all of its property to its neighbor, the Adirondack League Club, in 1893, and the name Adirondack League Club was used from then on to describe the merged entity. The merger meant the Adirondack League Club had property covering almost 200,000 acres, a chain of lakes, and numerous clubhouses stretching for about twenty-five miles (*Boonville Herald* 1893).

Comstock argues that the Adirondack League Club as well as several other private preserves played a critical role in the establishment and maintenance of the Adirondack State Park. He also noted that because the fishing and hunting laws were either stricter in the private reserves than on public forests or were in place earlier on private preserves, these private preserves were often refuges for animals driven from the public domain by hunting pressures (E. Comstock 1990: 34–35).

SOUTH FORK FISHING AND HUNTING CLUB: A DISASTER WAITING TO HAPPEN

Pittsburgh elites founded sportsmen's clubs too. The South Fork Fishing and Hunting Club was founded by Henry Clay Frick, a lifelong friend of Andrew Mellon, owner of a coke oven factory and partner in Carnegie Steel Company (the forerunner of U.S. Steel). The club was founded in 1879 at the urging of Benjamin Ruff. The South Fork Fishing and Hunting Club purchased an old reservoir site and dam that was originally built between 1838 and 1853 as part of the Pennsylvania Main Line canal system. When the club purchased the property, the "lake" or Western Reservoir was not much more than a pond about ten feet deep. Local farmers grazed animals on the overgrown, parched reservoir bed. Club members changed the name of the Western Reservoir to Lake Conemaugh when they created a lake that was two miles long, one mile wide, and about sixty feet deep behind the dam. They also built a clubhouse and sixteen private cottages around the lake (Earnest 2002; Johnstown Area Heritage Association 2009; McCullough 1987: 51, 55; McGough 2002).

The club had sixteen charter members who purchased shares in the corporation at one hundred dollars a share (Earnest 2002). The club consisted of Pittsburgh's millionaires and other wealthy men. The club's most prominent members included Andrew Mellon, Andrew Carnegie, Henry Phipps (childhood friend of Carnegie and partner in Carnegie Steel), Henry Clay Frick, and Philander Knox (lawyer, attorney general, and U.S. senator). The club limited its membership to one hundred people, and membership cost eight hundred dollars annually (Johnstown Area Heritage Association 2009; Klein and Hoogenboom 1973: 380; McCullough 1987: 57).[6] The South Fork Hunting and Fishing Club contained many self-made men who came from modest means and made their own fortunes. However, by the time they joined the South Fork Fishing and Hunting Club, many of the members were millionaires who inhabited marble-floored mansions in Pittsburgh's East End. They summered in Europe and cultivated friendships with the most prominent people in New York (McCullough 1987: 61–62; McGough 2002).

The South Fork Fishing and Hunting Club was very secretive. It acquired the land for the club and began repairing the dam and building its clubhouse without disclosing the name of the club to local residents or discussing the plans for the resort with them. The club's membership list was not made public until a disaster forced the club to release it (McCullough 1987: 56–58).

Since some area residents desired a mountain resort and the South Fork Hunting and Fishing Club provided many jobs, locals were somewhat accepting of the secretiveness of club members. Club members depended on locals to perform work around the club but were irritated by the fact that area residents helped themselves to the fish stocked in the lake and streams whenever the opportunity arose. Despite posted signs on club grounds warning against poaching, local men and boys entered the grounds surreptitiously at night and fished. The club erected fences over the best trout streams, but these disappeared as fast as they were erected. The club threatened to shoot anyone caught fishing on the property, but this did not slow down the poaching. Club members also bickered with a neighboring farmer, Lehy, when floodwaters from the lake submerged his property in 1885. The enterprising Lehy promised to rent out fishing spaces on his submerged land, and the club ordered him to cease and desist or they would take him to court. Lehy was not intimidated and carried out his plan. The club responded by purchasing Lehy's farm for four thousand dollars (McCullough 1987: 62–63).

The South Fork dam collapsed on May 31, 1889, at around 3:10 p.m. after three days of torrential rain. Eight inches of rain fell in what has been called "the Great Storm of 1889" in Johnstown. The town was flooded even before the dam broke. The broken dam released about 20 million gallons of water, inundating the Little Conemaugh River Valley. The water rushed through South Fork, Mineral Point, East Conemaugh, Woodvale, and Johnstown, about fourteen miles away. The floodwaters were between thirty-five to forty feet high when it hit Johnstown, and it was moving at a speed of about forty miles per hour. It ravaged the town of roughly ten thousand inhabitants in about ten minutes. As the floodwater receded, the thirty-acre pile of debris lodged against the stone bridge caught fire, killing more people. In all 2,209 people were killed, sixteen hundred homes were destroyed, and the flood caused about $17 million in property damage. The high-water mark was eighty-nine feet above river level (Earnest 2002; Johnstown Area Heritage Association 2009; Klein and Hoogenboom 1973: 380; McCullough 1987: 64–67, 90–92; National Park Service 2009b; Pitz 2006).

Several factors contributed to the dam collapse, flooding, and high death toll. Heavy and sustained rains raised the level of the reservoir, eroded the hillsides, and swelled area streams. The narrowing of the stream channel to accommodate buildings and bridges were also contributing factors. In addition, the dam was not inspected by local or state authorities; its operation was left to a private club. The attitude of members of the South Fork Fishing and Hunting Club also played a role. As wealthy owners of a private club, they felt they had a right to do what they wanted on their property. Consequently, the welfare of the greater community was given a lower priority in decision making. Though three warnings were sent to Johnstown that the dam might fail, dispatchers did not sound the general alarm. To complicate matters, local residents did not take the message that the dam was breaking seriously, since they had joked about it for years and thought it was just another rumor (Klein and Hoogenboom 1973: 380; McCullough 1987: 95–97).

Only about six club members were on the premises when the dam broke, and they left the resort immediately after the catastrophe. A small group of angry town residents went to the club, broke into buildings, and ransacked them. After the flood, many club members abandoned their resort cottages, and some

Johnstown residents rendered homeless by the flood resided in them. Referring to themselves as the "Johnstown Colony," residents lived in the cottages until 1907. Outraged town residents blamed club members for failing to maintain the dam. Victims filed lawsuits but did not receive any compensation because the courts viewed the dam failure as an act of God. The dam was never rebuilt, and the club ceased to function after the flood. A few club members, including Robert Pitcairn, served on the relief committee, while about half of them made contributions to the disaster relief efforts. Andrew Carnegie donated ten thousand dollars and later rebuilt the Johnstown library. The club sold off the six-hundred-acre property in separate parcels in the twelve years following the flood. Coal was discovered in the former lake bed, and in 1907 the Maryland Coal Company bought thirty-one acres and began mining (Earnest 2002; Johnstown Area Heritage Association 2009; Klein and Hoogenboom 1973: 380; Pitz 2006).

The South Fork Fishing and Hunting Club was the playground of industrial giants seeking to escape the pollution of Pittsburgh. Town residents felt that the club members were not held accountable for the disaster; some saw the incident as a case in which the robber barons were grossly negligent and got away with it (Johnstown Area Heritage Association 2009). The incident brought into question the actions of wealthy industrialists and what kinds of social standards they were going to be held accountable to.

Game Protection in the West

Though wildlife protection organizations were becoming commonplace in the late nineteenth century, these organizations were in the East. Activists soon noted that little was being done to protect animals in the West. The following section chronicles the rise of two organizations that focused on protecting big game in the West: the Boone and Crockett Club and the American Bison Society.

THE BOONE AND CROCKETT CLUB

In an 1887 editorial in *Forest and Stream*[7] George Bird Grinnell suggested that an organization be formed to develop and pass state and federal conservation policies and laws (see also Reiger [1975] 2001: 49–51). Earlier that year Theodore Roosevelt's and Grinnell's dreams of becoming cattle barons came crashing down around them. The winter of 1886–1887 was ferocious, and Roosevelt lost about half of his herd; Grinnell suffered extensive losses too. By the time

Roosevelt returned to New York in 1887, he had decided he could not succeed as a cattle rancher. But he did not remain idle for long. Shortly after returning to New York, Roosevelt convened a meeting of the nation's leading big game hunters, writers, explorers, military men, scientists, and political leaders to discuss game and park issues in the West. Roosevelt called a dinner meeting, and before the diners parted ways for the evening, the sportsmen, all of whom had traveled extensively in the West, formed the Boone and Crockett Club. Named after Daniel Boone and Davy Crockett, two revered symbols of European American frontier manliness, the Boone and Crockett Club was an organization aimed at promoting manly sport with the rifle; travel and exploration in the wild, unknown, or little-known parts of the country; conservation of large game through the legislative process; recording and observing the habits and natural history of wild animals; and exchanging ideas on hunting, travel, and exploration. Exclusivity was a hallmark of the club, so it limited its membership to one hundred members and twenty-five to forty associates. The Boone and Crockett Club modeled itself after the New York Association for the Protection of Game. However, it differed from existing conservation clubs in two significant respects; its focus was on both western and eastern parks, and it concentrated on the protection of both game and national park environs rather than focus on wildlife refuges alone. The Boone and Crockett Club helped to establish the Adirondack Reserve and to protect Yellowstone National Park (Boone and Crockett Club 2014; Brands 1997: 208–210; P. Burroughs 1995: xxvii; *Forest and Stream* 1888: 124; Graham 1990; 43; Grinnell 1913: 435–436; Reiger [1975] 2001: 151–152; Trefethen 1975: 111).

To qualify for regular membership one had to be a wealthy white male who had "killed with the rifle in fair chase, by still-hunting or otherwise, at least one individual of three of the various kinds of American large game." Elite men who were not big game hunters were eligible only for honorary membership. The members of the club were graduates of Ivy League colleges, primarily from New York, and had well-respected family names. Club meetings were held at elite social clubs—the Union, Metropolitan, Cosmos, Century, or University clubs (*Forest and Stream* 1888: 124; see also Reiger [1975] 2001: 151–153).

Despite the efforts of Boone and Crockett members, between 1889 and 1894 the number of bison in Yellowstone dropped precipitously. The bison were still the prime targets of market hunters, since a bison could fetch as much as fifteen thousand dollars in the 1890s. Before passage of the Lacey Act, the punishment for a hunter caught killing a bison was minimal. But after the bill passed in 1894, violators could be fined one thousand dollars and/or sentenced to two years in prison. The Lacey Act, which will be discussed in more detail below, really targeted market hunters, so men who could afford to pay ranchers a fee continued to hunt bison without sanctions or limitations (Isenberg 2000: 179–180).

THE AMERICAN BISON SOCIETY

The efforts of the American Bison Society, founded in 1905, to save the buffalo highlights the conservationists' complex motives for protecting the animal and the ambivalence they felt about its destruction. Recognizing the effectiveness of the business environmentalism pioneered by the urban park advocates—that is, getting wealthy businessmen to fund and spearhead an effort—conservation organizations emulated this model and recruited businessmen to their causes (Taylor 2009: 223–337). Like other leading conservation organizations of the time, the American Bison Society recruited prominent, wealthy businessmen (Hornaday 1908; Isenberg 2000: 166). The American Bison Society membership included Theodore Roosevelt (the honorary president), Gifford Pinchot, and Andrew Carnegie. Though J. Pierpont Morgan (Carnegie's business partner) wasn't a member, he supported the organization. In 1910, he enclosed a 20,000-acre parcel of land in Colorado and stocked it with bison (Isenberg 2000: 169).

Though the American Bison Society leaders tried to recruit in the South, most of the organization's members lived in the northeastern and mid-Atlantic states. In 1908, 79 percent of the general members and 85 percent of the life members lived in New York, New Jersey, Pennsylvania, and New England. More than 85 percent of the members were men; female members were the wives and relatives of male members. Men occupied all of the organization's important leadership positions. Even though women helped to manage some of the bison ranches, conservationists tended to portray bison conservation as a manly endeavor (Isenberg 2000: 169, 172).

Though they were saddened by the slaughter of the bison, some of the leading conservationists and preservationists of the time believed the commercial exploitation of the bison was necessary for American economic development and westward expansion. For instance, John Muir wrote, "I suppose we need not go mourning the buffaloes. In the nature of things they had to give place to better cattle, though the change might have been made without barbarous wickedness" (Muir [1901] 1981: 335). Though he wrote in 1873 that the slaughter of the bison was not sustainable, Grinnell was ambivalent about the animal's destruction. He maintained that the decimation of the bison was "necessary" for economic growth. Theodore Roosevelt thought the buffalo had to be removed to make room for white settlers (Grinnell 1925: 219–220; Roosevelt 1994: 245; [1885] 1996: 242). He believed that extirpating the buffalo was crucial to gaining control of the Plains tribes and opening the area up to settlement and cattle grazing. Though he was saddened by the buffalo's loss, he thought the decimation of the bison was essential for long-term nation-building efforts (Roosevelt [1893] 1996: 343).

With the bison almost exterminated and white settlers firmly entrenched in the West, activists persuaded the government to restock Yellowstone with bison in the early 1900s. They also founded bison preserves in Oklahoma, Montana, South Dakota, and Nebraska between 1905 and 1914. It should be noted that the bison protectors envisioned the survival of the animal under strictly controlled conditions; they did not intend to have wild herds roaming freely on the Plains again. Thus they focused on establishing bison reserves and stocking Yellowstone, state parks, and zoos. The activists did not question the ranchers' choice to replace the buffalo with domesticated cattle. In fact, one impetus for saving the buffalo was the goal of engineering a cattle-buffalo hybrid, the cattalo (those efforts have not met with encouraging results). Buffalo conservationists also wanted to ensure that there was a supply of bison, reared on private grounds, for sport hunting and tourist attractions. Tourist interest also provided a rationale for funding restocking programs. Therefore, the conservationists installed the bison in a few easily accessible reserves that covered a minuscule portion of the animal's former range. Reserves were established on sites close to rail and other transportation routes. Once the bison were established in these locations, interest in bison conservation waned (Isenberg 2000: 165–167).

Ranchers raising bison to supply the zoos, reserves, parks, circuses, and restaurants worked with the American Bison Society to provide animals for stocking programs. The American Bison Society rarely purchased bison directly from ranchers; rather, it usually acted as an intermediary connecting zoos and other buyers to ranchers wanting to sell the animals. The American Bison Society even solicited customers for ranchers who were providing sport hunters with opportunities to hunt bison. By 1920, the American Bison Society was convinced that the buffalo would survive. That year the organization did not oppose a Utah ranch owner who disposed of his herd of over two hundred bison by selling the right to hunt them. In fact, Hornaday wrote that since the owners "find them [the bison] an unbearable nuisance and an interference with their cattle-growing operations, what else is to be done than to get rid of them." Similarly, in 1922 the American Bison Society stood by as surplus bison were killed at Yellowstone. The organization disbanded and stopped collecting dues in 1936. However, in 2005 it was relaunched by the Wildlife Conservation Society (Isenberg 2000: 178, 186; Wildlife Conservation Society 2015).

New Sporting Ethics and Class Conflicts

The rising popularity of fenced and guarded game preserves and exclusive hunting and angling clubs heightened class distinctions and conflicts between wealthy urbanites and poor rural residents. As the above cases show, fences were erected around these parks and clubs to keep the game in and to keep out locals looking for access to well-stocked woods, lakes, ponds, and streams. Some clubs such as Blooming Grove were patrolled by armed security guards; others were fortified with high fences. Managers of the South Fork Fish and Game Hunting Club threatened to sue and shoot locals. In some instances, the relationship between the sportsmen's clubs and local communities had a town-and-gown feel. The bag limit of forty-two trout per day per member at Blooming Grove Park fostered the perception of "haves" and "have-nots." Though wealthy club men valued their privacy and felt they could set and operate by their own rules in the private clubs, the fact that the clubs had working-class staff drawn from local communities to cater to their whims meant that residents of host communities were well aware of the ease with which one could hunt and fish there. Thus community residents were cognizant of the disparities in access to fish and game between club members and locals.

Wealthy sportsmen expected to have fish and game readily available to them when they went to rural resorts. Jay Cooke of Philadelphia, banker and financier of the Northern Pacific Railroad and a founding member of the Oquossoc Angling Association, was a case in point. Oquossoc, founded in 1869 in northern Maine, accepted only genteel men as members (Reiger [1975] 2001: 129). When Cooke decided that the state was not doing enough to ensure that sport hunters had access to game, he wrote a letter to the Maine fish commissioner pointing out the economic power that recreational users had in the state and the dependence of the state's economy on men like him (Judd 1997: 208). Cooke's logic reveals some of the complex motives sportsmen had for advocating wildlife protection; they wanted to see animals protected so that they could be certain there was something to hunt and fish for. They were also becoming aware that wildlife protection had larger societal benefits.

As more elites summered in resorts or small rural towns, conflicts arose over access to and use of resources, monitoring and administration, and recreation styles. When conservationists, who favored fly-fishing, stalking, and still hunting, proposed a ban on plug fishing, jacking, and hounding or dogging, irate farmers and rural residents thought the bans were meant to reinforce class distinctions that privileged the views and practices of the wealthy "who come to waste," while constraining the activities of local subsistence hunters and anglers (Judd 1997: 214).

During the nineteenth century, the changing attitudes of the elite sport hunters led them to define new sporting codes and reinforce existing ones. They also used their influence to get state game commissioners to change the rules to reflect elite sporting ethics. Sport hunters and anglers, unconcerned about long working days on the farm and the need to hunt or fish in ways that generated a large catch relatively quickly for subsistence purposes, began to place emphasis on the chase, on the skill, expertise, and expense involved in a successful hunting or fishing trip, as important elements of each sport. Sport hunters thought of animals in more humane ways, so they wanted to kill or capture animals in less brutal ways. The idea that the animal should have a chance to escape became an important element of these sports. Because the new techniques were costlier, the introduction of these techniques and the attempt to craft rule changes around them deepened the class divide and stoked resentments that had been simmering for decades. Some rural residents also objected to the shortened hunting season advocated by conservationists, which coincided with the busy fall harvesting season. Rural residents feared that the game would be inaccessible to them once the rich hunters had returned to the cities. This led one resident to proclaim that "the rich have, for reasons best known to wardens, been allowed to kill, to waste, while poor men who have killed to feed their families have been arrested." He also objected to "calling the men who . . . kill our game in the summer and waste it, 'true sportsmen,' and calling other . . . good men 'thieves and poachers,' if later they kill what they need to eat." Rural residents feared that New England was being turned into a game preserve for the wealthy (Judd 1997: 216; Reiger [1975] 2001: 5–44). Though subsistence hunters were concerned about the disappearance of game and fish too, time and money constraints made them adopt different hunting and fishing techniques from the elites.

Consequently, the class implications of the wildlife rhetoric and laws emanating from elite sportsmen clubs did not go unnoticed or unchallenged by subsistence and rural hunters and anglers. Heated exchanges took place in New England and other parts of the country as wealthy urbanites recreated in places such as Vermont, Maine, and New Hampshire. For many local residents, subsistence hunting and fishing was necessary to sustain life; but sport hunting and fishing was reminiscent of idleness. Resentment of sport hunters and anglers mounted as the sport hunter ranks swelled with wealthy, out-of-state urbanites bent on changing local and state fish and game laws. Locals thought some laws gave elite conservationists an advantage (Judd 1997: 208). For instance, a letter to the editor of *Forest and Stream* referred to the sportsmen as "aristocratic trespassers" invading the farms of East Rockaway in New York. The writer claimed the sportsmen got away with hunting on and destroying the property of farmers because the sport hunters were wealthy. This was seen as an infringement "upon the liberties of the people" (*Forest and Stream* 1880a: 319). Similar letters complained that sportsmen were exploiting farmers. Critics also grumbled that the game laws were being enacted to benefit the rich (*Forest and Stream* 1881: 139).

In 1837 one local hunter from Wisconsin published an article in the *Wisconsin Territorial Gazette* in which he mocked the game law that had been passed in the territory.[8] Perceiving the law as beneficial to elite sportsmen while punishing poor hunters, the writer made scornful references to terms like "rules and regulations," "bagged," and "poached." He also boasted that his friend had killed a deer in violation of the law and that the meat was delicious. Gideon Smith, then editor of *American Turf Register*, thought the article was a sneer at sportsmen and the game laws. Smith argued that had it not been for the game laws of England, there wouldn't be any game left in that country. He contended that the same could be said for the densely populated parts of the United States, where wildlife was disappearing rapidly (quotes from Reiger [1975] 2001: 33–34).

Sportsmen were aware of the growing divide and animosity between themselves and the poor. However, as the events that unfolded at the South Fork Fishing and Hunting Club highlight, wealthy sportsmen weren't necessarily sympathetic to the concerns of the poor. Henry William Herbert tried to articulate the elite sportsmen's view and bridge the gulf between sport hunters, farmers, and the poor. Herbert thought that rural residents saw the game laws as "feudal rights, individual privileges, and nominal distinctions" being imposed by wealthy sportsmen. To counter the rising resentments, Herbert suggested that sportsmen unite in their efforts to convince farmers that game laws were important and beneficial to all. Herbert wrote, "If they [the farmers] could now be brought as a body to understand that the provisions of these laws are not arbitrary and intended to suit the wishes of [the upper] classes [exclusively], they might be induced to lend their hand to the good work of game-preservation" (Forester 1849: 18–19).

However, some sportsmen and conservationists did not always seek to employ a collaborative approach. For example, in his magazine, *Forest and Stream*,

Grinnell called on sportsmen to scorn the pot hunter and "trout hog" (Grinnell 1881: 379; 1882: 223). Grinnell also sought to deny the charge that *Forest and Stream* was aristocratic or "favored measures which would make the enjoyment of legitimate sport by the poor man difficult." Grinnell tried to counter the arguments of critics of game laws by contending that it was actually the poor who benefited from the passage and enforcement of game laws. Grinnell wrote, "The rich man can travel to distant fields where game is plenty, and can have his shooting whether the laws are enforced or not. With the poor man it is not so; he has to take his day or half day in the field when he can get it, and has neither the time nor the money to travel far in search of game. It is, therefore, the man of modest means who is or should be interested in game preservation even more than he whose fortune is ample" (*Forest and Stream* 1881: 39).

Though he acknowledged that there was a relationship between social class and access to game, Grinnell was adamant that class should not be the focus of the debate. He argued that the question of class or wealth should not even enter into the discussion of game preservation. He sought to reinforce this point and frame the sportsmen's message in populist terms, arguing that "laws prohibiting the destruction of game in its breeding season and of fish on their spawning grounds are not for the advantage of any narrow class or clique. They are for the good of us, the people." Foreshadowing the wise-use utilitarian conservation discourse that drove a wedge between conservationists and preservationists decades later in the Hetch Hetchy controversy (discussed in chapter 10), Grinnell argued that, in the matter of fish and game conservation, *Forest and Stream* promoted "the greatest good for the greatest number" (*Forest and Stream* 1882: 503).

Grinnell was also more forceful than other activists in pushing for the enforcement of game laws. While groups such as the New York Sportsmen's Club worked on advancing game laws, Grinnell saw a need for greater enforcement of existing laws. Consequently, he proposed the development of a warden system (he called wardens "county game constables"). Grinnell also proposed a revolutionary idea: the warden system should be funded out of fees levied against hunters. The states regulated the wardens by appointing them (*Forest and Stream* 1880b: 1010; Reiger [1975] 2001: 92–93). Like the bird-protection advocates, sportsmen were part of a cadre of ethical elites asserting order in the area of wildlife policy making. They identified acceptable and unacceptable practices. They determined which practices should be expunged if possible. They felt it was their job to define and guard the code of appropriate behavior.

BLAMING WOMEN, IMMIGRANTS,
AND MINORITIES FOR BIRD DESTRUCTION

Recognizing the Problem

While some activists focused on big game, others were advocates for their feathered friends. Conservationists turned their attention to bird protection as it became clear that many avian species were going extinct. Ordinary citizens helped to focus attention on birds by debating their value. Some farmers saw birds as beneficial, while others perceived them as depredators, intruders, and thieves that should be destroyed. During the mid-nineteenth century, farmers began classifying the birds around their farms as "useful," "noxious," and of "doubtful utility." States began promulgating bird-protection legislation in the early eighteenth century, but it wasn't until the latter half of the nineteenth century that there was real momentum in the development of effective legislation. In the 1880s, urban activists began national bird-protection campaigns. They sought to protect beneficial birds, and by 1887, twenty-one states had instituted some kind of bird-protection legislation (Bell [1783] 1791: 118–119; Doughty 1975: 106–107; Judd 1997: 79–80, 83; Trefethen 1975: 106).

The debate about useful, beneficial, and noxious birds filled the pages of newspapers, conservation magazines, academic presses, farmers' and grangers' journals, and sporting journals. Consequently, more people took an interest in birds, and as a result birds were transformed into a valued species in the pastoral landscapes of the ruralized suburbs. During this period, bird-watching and nature studies became important pastimes for those living beyond the urban fringe (Doughty 1975: 41, 152; Judd 1997: 83–84).

The bird-protection discourse evolved over time. What began as an appeal to stop the slaughter of birds quickly morphed into a campaign that blamed women for the destruction of birds. While market hunters were blamed for the demise of big game, women bore the brunt of the culpability for the decline in birds. Poor whites, immigrants, minorities, boys, and cats were also implicated in the slaughter of birds. Interestingly, bird protection was one wing of the emerging conservation movement in which women were active and took on leadership roles. Nonetheless, female bird-protection activists held other women responsible for the massacre of birds.

The Feather Craze: Making Matters Worse

Despite the number of statewide wildlife protection ordinances and favorable court rulings upholding those regulations, some bird-protection activists grew more concerned about the decimation of birds as the market for birds kept growing. They were used in the millinery industry and the restaurant and hotel industry, to name a few. So when Mademoiselle Harris displayed black velvet promenade bonnets decorated with purple bird plumes in her exclusive New York store, no one quite envisioned the explosion in demand for birds this fashion innovation would generate (*New York Times* 1860: 1). In 1860 people predicted that plumes would be the future of hat trim, yet no one foresaw how popular this fashion trend would become and the major conservation battles it would ignite.

George Perkins Marsh decried the new trend in 1864, but his plea was ignored (Marsh [1864] 1965: iii). By then, newspapers were featuring articles instructing women on how to choose the right feathers for their hats, how to reuse and dye them, and how to get them at bargain prices. Throughout the 1870s, hundreds of newspaper advertisements and articles pointed women to the finest millinery establishments, listed opening days for the display of spring and fall hats, and provided guides to the latest fashions in feathers, hats, and apparel (*New York Times* 1870: 8).

Bird Protection Gets under Way

As the demand for bird feathers increased, activists began to organize conservation groups to help protect birds. One of the early bird-protection groups was the Nuttall Ornithological Club, founded in Cambridge, Massachusetts, in 1873 by a small group of distinguished ornithologists committed to protecting nongame birds. However, Nuttall members did not play a very active role in the conservation campaigns. So a decade after he founded the club, William Brewster, a curator of the Museum of Comparative Zoology at Harvard University and the Boston Society of Natural History, started a new organization designed to be more proactive.[1] In 1883 he invited ornithologists from the United States and Canada to a convention in New York; twenty-one people attended this meeting, the founding convention of the American Ornithological Union. The new organization took over Nuttall's journal, the *Bulletin*, and later renamed it the *Auk*. The *Bulletin*'s editor also edited the *Auk* (Doughty 1975: 45–48, 53, 100, 105–108; Orr 1992: 22–23, 67–68; Trefethen 1975: 129).

Bird-protection campaigns began in earnest the following year, after Brewster expressed his dismay at the large number of birds being slaughtered for use on women's hats. The American Ornithological Union's cofounder, Joel Allen, also identified other causes of bird destruction. Allen thought that excessive use of firearms by sport hunters, deforestation, drainage, and egging were also contributing to the decline of birds. The American Ornithological Union appointed a bird-protection committee to collect data on the millinery industry and develop legislation to protect plume and nongame birds. Some of the best-known conservationists of the time ended up working on this committee, including Brewster, Grinnell, William Dutcher, and T. Gilbert Pearson, all of whom also headed the Audubon Society at some point. The committee began working on a model bird-protection law; in 1886 New York and Massachusetts became the first two states to adopt it. By 1909, forty-three states adopted some version of that bird-protection law (J. A. Allen 1876: 53–60; Doughty 1975: 45–48, 53, 100, 105–108; Graham 1990: 6–7; Orr 1992: 22–23, 67–68; Trefethen 1975: 129).[2]

The intent of the model law was to develop uniform standards for defining game and nongame birds.[3] The law prohibited anyone from taking or destroying the eggs or nest of any bird except for the purposes of scientific collection. The American Ornithological Union's appeals reached well beyond the small group of ornithologists and soon involved other groups that supported bird protection, like Bands of Mercy. Founded in England in 1875, Bands of Mercy focused on getting children and adults to pledge to be kind to harmless living creatures and protect them from cruelty. Bands of Mercy was an important organization to collaborate with because in 1886 it had about four hundred thousand members in the United States and Canada (J. A. Allen 1876: 53–60; Doughty 1975: 45–48, 53, 100, 105–108; Graham 1990: 6–7; Orr 1992: 22–23, 67–68; Trefethen 1975: 129).

The model law met with immediate opposition. Though the committee tried to deflect conflict by excluding traditional game birds from the law's protection, the fact that all other native birds fell under the reach of the law resulted in much outrage. Some taxidermists claimed that the law would ruin their businesses. Leading ornithologists, fearing restrictions on scientific collecting, also opposed the law. This led ornithologist Charles B. Cory to proclaim, "I don't protect birds, I kill them" (Graham 1990: 7).

SUSAN FENIMORE COOPER AND OLIVE THORNE MILLER: BIRD PROTECTION

Susan Fenimore Cooper began her campaign to protect birds in the 1870s. She identified boys' attitudes toward birds as one source of bird destruction. In an 1878 *Appleton's Journal* article she wrote, "Young boys, scarcely old enough, one would think, to carry a gun, are allowed to shoot the birds with impunity in the spring, when they are preparing to build, or even when their eggs are actually in the nest." She called for better enforcement of existing bird-protection laws to halt this practice. She contended that the consumption of birds, particularly in the South, was also a factor in their decline. However, she was most troubled by the use of dead birds on women's hats and considered it a major reason for bird destruction. She implicated women of all ages in the bird slaughter and spoke directly to them (Cooper 1878a: 530).

Olive Thorne Miller was another outspoken critic of the use of birds to adorn women's hats. She referred to the adornments as "feather monstrosities with which milliners disfigure their hats" (O. T. Miller 1892: 217; see also O. T. Miller 1885: 22). Miller also discussed the beneficial characteristics of birds in her writings. She argued that the blue jay was useful in the economy, as it was efficient in disseminating the seeds of plants on which it fed (O. T. Miller 1887: 187).

THE AUDUBON MOVEMENT BEGINS

George Bird Grinnell got the idea of founding the Audubon Society while living at the Hemlocks, his father's house in Audubon Park. Grinnell was growing more concerned about the plight of the songbirds, waterfowl, and game birds that were in high demand in the millinery industry. He began his crusade by urging his sisters and friends to stop buying and wearing hats adorned with feathers. He also wrote about the slaughter of birds in *Forest and Stream* in 1886 (P. Burroughs 1995: xxx).

By this time Grinnell was actively involved with the work of the American Ornithological Union's bird-protection committee. In February 1886, as a way of strengthening the work of the committee, Grinnell founded the Audubon Society. The organization was named for both Lucy Audubon, who had a strong influence on Grinnell, and her late husband, John James Audubon (J. A. Allen 1897: 6; *Audubon Magazine* 1887: 3–5; Grinnell 1886: 41; Reiger 1972: 22–23).

The 1886 issue of *Forest and Stream* that announced the formation of the Audubon appealed to "those who are willing to aid us in our labors" to establish Audubon chapters in their communities. In it Grinnell argued that the wearing of feathers and bird skins as a fashion statement was abominable. He reasoned that the fashion trend would be frowned upon and decline in popularity. He also claimed that farmers were being hurt by the destruction of the birds, since birds ate insects that were harmful to crops (*Forest and Stream* 1886: 41).

Almost immediately, women emerged as the target of the Audubon Society's campaigns and the objects of disdain. Though elite men wore fedoras trimmed with feathers, they were not targeted in the campaigns aimed at reducing the use of feathers on hats (Erlich, Dobkin, and Wheye 1988). Soon after Grinnell announced the formation of the organization, writer Charles Dudley Warner sent Grinnell a congratulatory note that said, "A dead bird does not help the appearance of an ugly woman, and a pretty woman needs no such adornment." The poet John Greenleaf Whittier also noted, "I heartily approve of the proposed Audubon Society [and] could almost wish that the fashionable wearers of their feathers might share the penalty which was visited upon the Ancient Mariner who shot the Albatross" (Graham 1990: 9–13, 18, 25–26, 61; Orr 1992: 37). John Burroughs added, "False taste in dress is as destructive to our feathered friends as are false aims in science . . . Think of a woman or girl of real refinement appearing upon the street with her head-gear adorned with the scalps of our songsters" (Burroughs 1886: 214). That same year Frank Chapman claimed that on two strolls through Manhattan's shopping districts, he counted hundreds of women wearing hats festooned with feathers. This prompted him to start delivering a speech titled "Woman as a Bird Enemy" at Audubon events (Chapman 1886: 84).

Soon after the Audubon Society was formed, upper-class women's clubs such as the Ladies' Christian Union of New York began collaborating with it. At the May 1886 meeting, Mrs. Thompson Hollister and Mrs. Frank Bottome called members' attention to the destruction of birds. This generated much interest in the group. Elizabeth Curtis Grinnell (George Bird Grinnell's wife), a member of the group, spoke about the Audubon Society's history and goals. The group voted unanimously to join forces with the society (*New York Times* 1886: 8).

The Milliners' Response. Milliners moved quickly to counter the effect of the Audubon Society's rhetoric and reframe the issue from a business perspective. A prominent milliner in Washington, DC, gave a newspaper interview in which the reader was assured that the trade in birds was what the public wanted. The milliner said, "Birds are in great demand, and in fact about the only thing asked for in the way of bonnet ornaments." When asked if women were objecting to the use of birds on bonnets, the milliner responded, "Very few. Now and then there is one, but it is an oddity; perhaps one in fifty or sixty may object to them, but then they only do it to please their husbands and not because they care." The milliner said he believed the movement was being orchestrated by upper-class ladies (*Washington Post* 1886b: 2).

Others, such as Dr. F. Langdon of Cincinnati, countered the Audubon's claims more directly. Langdon argued that all the talk about the extermination of songbirds to meet fashion demands was "mere sentiment without a foundation." Claiming to have researched the matter thoroughly, Langdon asserted that the North American birds used most frequently on hats were gulls, terns, herons, and others—not songbirds or species beneficial to farmers. Langdon argued further that the most desirable songbirds—thrushes, wrens, greenlets, and finches—were in limited demand because of their plain colors. Furthermore, the most brightly plumed birds hailed from South America and other foreign countries. Langdon also argued that it was possible that enough predatory species were being slaughtered to more than compensate for the few songbirds killed (*Washington Post* 1886c: 2).

Rapid Growth and Decline of the Original Audubon. Grinnell was unprepared for the avalanche of new supporters who showed interest in the Audubon. Members could join by signing a pledge; there were no fees or dues. The organization grew rapidly; by December 1888 it had 48,862 members in the United States, Canada, England, Turkey, India, Germany, Switzerland, and the West Indies (*Audubon Magazine* 1887: 20–284; 1888: 20–262). Men and boys promised not to kill any wild birds (except for food) or pillage or damage any birds' nests, while women and girls promised not to use bird feathers for ornaments or household decorations. The American Ornithological Union and the Audubon worked closely together to direct their appeals to hunters, eggers (men and boys who raided birds' nests for eggs), and women of "bird-wearing age." Despite the group's apparent success, Grinnell, feeling overwhelmed by administrative tasks, stopped publishing the *Audubon Magazine* in December 1888 and shut the society down shortly thereafter (*Audubon Magazine* 1887: 19; Doughty 1975: 10, 102; Nash 1982: 46, 150–153; Orr 1992: 7–31; Trefethen 1975: 129–130).

Over the years there has been some discussion about why Grinnell discontinued the operations of the Audubon Society. Several factors may have played a role. First, the Audubon did not have the administrative staff needed to run an organization that had registered almost forty-nine thousand members in less than three years. The organization was also in debt, and though its magazine, the *Audubon Magazine*, had about fifty thousand subscribers, the periodical was a financial drain. The organization's leadership also thought the magazine was not essential to the bird-protection cause. In addition, the Audubon resembled its sister organization, the American Ornithological Union, in form and function, so there were questions about the need for a duplicate organization. Moreover, though the Audubon grew rapidly at first, leaders noticed that its rate of growth slowed considerably in 1888. Some argue that the organization failed because, apart from Grinnell, the Audubon did not openly recruit and enlist prominent citizens. The society had a list of prominent honorary members; *Audubon Magazine* listed fifty honorary vice presidents in its inaugural issue (*Audubon Magazine* 1887: 20, 262; P. Burroughs 1995: xxx; Doughty 1975: 98, 102–103; Welker 1955: 207).

PLUMAGE, STATUS, AND THE DECIMATION OF BIRDS

During the nineteenth century, plumage became a symbol of high status and wealth in France, Britain, and the United States. The demand for feathers increased in the late 1800s fueled by the conspicuous, trend-setting displays of movie stars, fashion houses, fashion magazines, and home journals. Wealthy women were encouraged to jump on the plumage bandwagon, and demand skyrocketed as urban, fashion-conscious women wore feathers on their hats, dresses, belts, boas, and coats or used them to decorate fans, the home, and so on. Feathers were also used on costumes, parasols, muffs, gowns, and capes (Doughty 1975: 1–16; *New York Times* 1886: 8; 1887: 8; *Washington Post* 1883: 3). The demand contributed to mass slaughters of birds like the one Audubon witnessed and described in 1813. Audubon estimated that about 1.1 billion pigeons passed overhead as he watched. Audubon noted that as the birds flew over Louisville, armed residents crowded onto the banks of the Ohio River and shot at them

(Audubon 1832: 320–321). Audubon also witnessed another mass slaughter of pigeons in 1816. Passenger pigeons had a tendency to fly in large groups, and Audubon described how quickly they could be killed when massive numbers of them flocked in a location (J. J. Audubon 1832: 323–324; L. B. Audubon 1869: 36–37).

When Margaret Fuller visited Rock River, Illinois, in 1843, she described the flocks of pigeons that flew in each evening. She described the scene thus: "One beautiful feature was the return of the pigeons every afternoon to their home. Every afternoon they came sweeping across the lawn, positively in clouds, and with a swiftness and softness of winged motion, more beautiful than anything of the kind I ever knew" (Fuller 1843: 47). Susan Fenimore Cooper also described the large flocks of pigeons and the indiscriminate shooting of them that she witnessed in and around her New York village. In 1850 Cooper noted that even though the flocks were still enormous, the number of birds was declining (Cooper 1850: 17–18).

There is no question that the millinery trade and indiscriminate market hunting took a heavy toll on birds and that focusing attention on this industry would reduce the slaughter of birds. Estimates vary, but conservationists calculate that about 200 million birds were killed annually for their feathers at the beginning of the twentieth century (Doughty 1975: 84; Orr 1992: 27, 38, 150; Trefethen 1975: 64). The wanton slaughter of birds resulted in significant declines. William Hornaday estimated that the bird population had declined by about 46 percent in twenty-six states between 1883 and 1898 (Doughty 1975: 82). However, most of the male conservationists of the time were slow to recognize the extent to which their own actions as sport hunters and collectors depleted wildlife stocks. For instance, John James Audubon ranted against eggers and market hunters, referring to them as "the pest of the feathered tribes," yet Audubon admitted to shooting hundreds of red-winged starlings (also known as marsh blackbirds) one afternoon even though he did not think they were very appetizing. He also described shooting Canada geese until the "number of geese obtained would seem . . . so very large that . . . [I] shall not specify it" (Audubon 1839: 350; Doughty 1975: 38).

Elliott Coues's advice to ornithologists in 1874 illustrates the extent to which bird destruction was a part of bird-watching and ornithology even in the late nineteenth century. Coues advised birders to spare no expense in acquiring a gun because "THE DOUBLE-BARRELLED SHOT GUN is your main reliance. Under some circumstances you may trap or snare birds, catch them with bird-lime, or use other devices; but such cases are exceptions to the rule that you will shoot birds, and for this purpose no weapon compares with the one just mentioned." He noted that the main purpose was the "destruction . . . of small birds, at moderate range, with the least possible injury to their plumage" (Coues 1874: 5). Coues also advised ornithologists to "begin by shooting every bird you can, coupling this sad destruction, however, with the closest observations upon habits" (Coues 1874: 29). Though Grinnell urged sport hunters to limit their kill, he reserved most of his disdain for market and plume hunters (Doughty 1975: 99; Grinnell 1884: 21; Trefethen 1975: 132–133).[4] The views of elites such as Coues went largely unchallenged for many decades.

SETTING THE STAGE: WOMEN AS BIRD ENEMIES

From the outset, the bird-protection discourse framed women as birds' enemy. George Perkins Marsh was one of the first activists to articulate this view. In 1864 Marsh wrote about the killing of birds and the use of feathers as a feminine decoration (Marsh [1864] 1965: iii). Before long, women and their actions were framed in more sinister terms: women were said to murder innocent birds to satisfy their superficial tastes. For example, Isaac McLellan wrote in 1883, "Should die that Youth should win another grace / To nod above the witchery of her face! / Ah! she [sic] forgets that to enhance her bloom, / A sweet bird dies to yield its purple plume" (McLellan 1883: 143).

The framing appealed even to college students. In 1892, T. Gilbert Pearson— who collected eggs, hunted, and stuffed birds—used one of Grinnell's flyers in a speech to the student body of Guilford College in North Carolina. Pearson argued, "It is bad enough for any cause, to see such sights; but when we know all this is done that women yes, even Christian women,—may decorate themselves with plumes, it becomes infinitely worse." He concluded his speech by declaring, "O fashion! O women of America, how many crimes are committed in your name!" (Pearson 1937: 31, 34).

Some journals played a duplicitous role in the bird-protection campaigns. On the one hand, the articles, fashion displays, and advertising in the publications encouraged women to wear plumage, but on the other, the magazines' editors berated women for wearing feathers. For instance, in 1884 *Harper's* suggested that women should keep abreast of fashion trends by rearranging the old bird pieces they had in a grotesque fashion to present a rustic, unkempt look. Yet in 1896 the magazine complained, "Feathers and plumes still wave from edifices which women wear on their heads, and it really seems as though it were time a crusade were organized against the lavish use of feathers, for some of the rarest and most valuable species . . . will soon be exterminated if the present craze continues" (*Harper's Bazaar* 1896: 663). The *Ladies' Home Journal* also included statements against killing birds to decorate hats (Doughty 1975: 14–15, 22–23, 81).

The framing of woman as bird enemy was enormously successful, and soon the sight of feathers on hats or dresses aroused indignation. Women wearing feathers or birds were seen as defiant, arrogant, and cruel. The plume became the Audubon Society's rallying cry in its campaign for bird protection. However, men who hunted large quantities of birds or eggs for sport were not accused of slaughtering birds or berated publicly. Instead, they were seen as masterful; some were even rewarded by having their collections displayed in museums.

AN IDEA GAINS A FOOTHOLD:
DEFENSELESS BIRDS AND CRUEL WOMEN

The Master Narrative. From the start the Audubon developed a master narrative that the bird-protection movement was aimed at stopping the destruction of birds that were being killed to provide fashion accessories for women. The media latched onto this framing. For instance, a newspaper article announcing the formation of the Audubon described how "hideous" and "irredeemably ugly" stuffed birds on a woman's hat looked. The article did not chastise the hunter or taxidermist for their acts, but it attacked women's use of birds to adorn their hats and apparel and outlined a strategy to get women to cease their acts of bird destruction. The article argued that women wearing hats decorated with feathers seldom thought about the fact that the bird was once a living thing. It urged the Audubon Society to educate young women about bird destruction and prevail upon them to rid themselves of the relic of "barbarism" that still connected them to their "painted ancestors" (*Washington Post* 1886a: 4).

The Audubon and American Ornithological Union bird-protection discourses framing women's behavior as a major source of the problem were effective in rallying both men and women to the movement. Fashionable women and milliners were cast as the main bird killers. Though some women were sport hunters, male hunters were more numerous (Merchant 2010: 5). In casting women as bird enemies, activists shifted the moralistic, guilt-laden discourse from men's actions to women's actions. By inviting pledges, they offered those implicated in wildlife destruction an easy way to reform themselves and participate in a nationwide movement. Pledging was also a way of getting women and children involved in the movement (through symbolic participation) without letting women share real power in the organizations. The bird-protection organizations remained spaces of masculine prowess, power, and dominance.

Women's Moral Duty to Protect Birds. Bird protectors implored women to take action to protect birds. In a speech before the American Ornithological Union in 1897, William Dutcher argued forcefully that women were responsible for the protection of birds. He stated that the salvation of birds was in the hands of women. Dutcher came to this conclusion after describing the hypocrisy and/or ignorance of women who, on the one hand, could be sympathetic to philanthropic causes but, on the other, wear hats festooned with plumes and feathers "obtained by acts of the greatest cruelty" (*New York Times* 1897a: 2).

The rhetoric of immorality and rectitude were common in the discourse. Heeding the pleas of the American Ornithological Union and the Audubon Society, women like Celia Thaxter, Irene Rood, Mabel Osgood Wright, and Harriet Hemenway became crusaders for the Audubon cause. They too framed the issues in terms of women's moral duty to care for and protect defenseless birds from cruel treatment and death. Thaxter, a renowned poet and an honorary vice president of the Audubon, attacked women for wearing birds in her poem "Woman's Heartlessness." She recounted her argument with a vacuous high-fashion woman who thought "a great deal of sentiment [was being] wasted on the birds." An exasperated Thaxter reported that the woman "went her way, a charnel house of beaks and claws and bones and feathers and glass eyes upon her fatuous head" (*Audubon Magazine* 1887: 20; Thaxter [1886] 1887: 13–14). Other women, such as the female members of the American Ornithological Union, were also disdainful of females wearing feathers (Doughty 1975: 100).

Women Revive the Audubon

After Grinnell allowed the Audubon to lapse in 1888, nothing happened with the organization until 1895. In the meantime, large numbers of birds were destroyed for a variety of purposes. Though a *Los Angeles Times* correspondent reported that there was a noticeable decline in the use of birds on hats for spring 1894—that feathers were being replaced by flowers—this does not appear to have been a widespread phenomenon (Florette 1894: 4). The newspapers and fashion magazines continued to advertise feathered hats.[5]

THE CHICAGO AUDUBON SOCIETY

There is some confusion about when and where the Audubon Society was reincarnated. Though Frank Graham's (Graham 1990: 14–23) history of the Audubon Society and Stephen Fox's account of the conservation movement (Fox 1981: 152–153) report that the rebirth of the Audubon occurred in 1896 with the formation of the Massachusetts Audubon Society, there is evidence that the Audubon was rejuvenated in Chicago in 1895. Graham indicates the Illinois chapter was founded in 1897. To confound matters even more, Reiger ([1975] 2001: 101) not only reports that the Audubon was revived in 1896 but also gives the credit for reviving it to William Brewster.

However, multiple sources report that in early 1895, members of a women's club formed the Chicago Audubon Society (later renamed the Illinois Audubon Society). The group chose Mrs. E. Irene Rood as its president. In March the organization had forty-four members, most of whom were women. The Audubon was formed for the protection of birds and to condemn the use of birds for millinery purposes. The women of the organization practiced what they preached: they did not wear birds in their bonnets. However, they still wore ostrich plumes, because the taking of ostrich plumes did not necessitate the killing of the bird. The Chicago Audubon Society vowed to pass bird-protection legislation and help strengthen Illinois game laws (*New York Times* 1895: 26; Nobles 1897: 18; *Washington Post* 1895: 22).[6] Another important event also occurred in 1895: Mabel Osgood Wright published her influential book *Bird Craft*.

THE MASSACHUSETTS AUDUBON SOCIETY

In February 1896, Harriet Hemenway, whose husband was the treasurer of Harvard College and trustee of the Boston Museum of Fine Arts, formed the Massachusetts Audubon Society after reading accounts of the destruction of heron habitats (J. A. Allen 1897: 6; Graham 1990: 14–15). Harriet Hemenway enjoyed watching birds on her thousand-acre farm in Canton and on her other properties on Cape Cod and in New Hampshire. After reading about the massacre of birds to obtain their feathers, Hemenway and her neighbor and cousin Minna Hall began organizing among society ladies. They used *The Boston Blue Book* (the social register) to identify recruits. Seeking to rectify what they perceived as women's destructive behavior, Hemenway and Hall sent circulars to the women asking them to join a society to protect birds and to discourage their friends and servants from wearing feathers. At the first meeting, held at Hemenway's home, attendees included members of prominent New England families like the Agassizs, Brewsters, Lowells, Cabots, Bangs, and Minots. Charles Minot, then president of the American Society of Naturalists, was elected chair of the board of directors. The following week William Brewster was elected president of the society; fifty honorary vice presidents were also named (Doughty 1975: 31, 101; Orr 1992: 204).[7] Many children also joined the organization (Graham 1990: 83–87, 96).[8]

Both the Chicago Audubon and the Massachusetts Audubon set about publicizing the work of the organizations and reestablishing the master narrative of women destroying birds to satisfy frivolous fashion tastes. Women were also framed as ignorant, thoughtless, moving closer to a savage state (not civilized), and immoral for using feathers, birds, wings, and so on as decorations. Male hunters and collectors, ornithologists, explorers, and female converts to the Audubon cause played a prominent role in propagating these ideas.

For instance, Caroline B. Hoffman, secretary of the Massachusetts Audubon, wrote an article in the organization's pamphlet evoking imagery of femininity, motherhood, nurturing, and purity. She argued that the female herons, which grow the white aigrettes only during breeding season, are usually killed while raising their baby birds. Once the mother is dead, the young birds usually starve to death—all, Hoffman says, for feminine vanity. She continued, "Equally guilty of this barbarous custom is every purchaser of these birds, martyrs unto death . . . may women at length reflect and acknowledge that there is something better, nobler, more to be desired than this foolish style, which is bought with the blood and life of creatures fashioned by the God of love." Hoffman also focused on the benefits of having birds around. She argued that birds consumed destructive insects and that the forests would disappear without the presence of birds to keep such pests in check. Hoffman concluded that, sentiments aside, the knowledge that one's actions resulted in the destruction of the forests, orchards, and fields should be sufficient to deter women from participating in the destruction of birds (*New York Times* 1897b: 14).

It was a common practice for bird-protection advocates to refer to Native American cultural and ceremonial use of feathers as acts of "savagery." For instance, in 1898, the year she founded the Connecticut Audubon, Mabel Osgood Wright coauthored a book with Edward Coues (who had urged ornithologists to shoot as many birds as they could) in which they wrote, "In an evil moment some woman, imitating the savages, used a bunch of these feathers to make a tuft upon her headgear" (Wright and Coues 1898: 370–371). The perceived cruelty of killing the female heron while she was nursing to get her delicate white plumes dominated the bird-protection discourse (see, for example, *New*

York Times 1897b: 14; Wright and Coues 1898: 370–371). The white feather—which became a potent symbol of the campaigns—represented the violation of the female body, the destruction of innocent newborns, and interference with the female reproductive and nurturing capacity.

In addition to categorizing most birds as beneficial, the Audubon Society also categorized some birds as neutral and a very few as injurious. The Audubon Society thought one could make appeals about beneficial birds based on their economic value to society. Regarding birds classified as neutral, the organization focused on their aesthetic appeal while trying to evoke humanistic responses (J. A. Allen 1897: 6). Audubon leaders sharpened their message by juxtaposing the narrative of birds as beneficial and beautiful creatures with that of women as bird enemies. They put out a steady barrage of newspaper and magazine articles describing how women's mindless obsession with fashion trends caused the destruction of birds (*Los Angeles Times* 1898a: 11). Men like the Reverend Henry Van Dyke took turns berating women and expressing their indignation at seeing women wearing hats adorned with birds. Van Dyke gave a speech at the New York Audubon's annual meeting (where several women wearing hats with bird wings were in attendance) that contained this line: "The sight of an aigrette fills me with a feeling of indignation and pity, and the skin of a dead songbird stuck on the hat of a timeless woman makes me hate the barbarism which lingers in our so-called civilization" (*New York Times* 1899c: 7). Newspaper articles reinforced the themes of barbarism and savagery. For instance, one article declared, "All women who sacrifice bird life for personal adornment show savage instincts" (*Washington Post* 1899b: 7).

The Audubon Society was composed of fashionable ladies willing to heed aristocratic women's moral appeal, and sportsmen interested in bird protection and changing women's attitudes about birds as a fashion symbol. Though many of the new Audubons were founded by wealthy women who directed their campaigns primarily toward other affluent women, the organizations were often led by men. This was true of the Massachusetts Audubon (Graham 1990: 15–18) and the branch in Washington, DC. Even though accomplished female bird-protection advocates such as Florence Merriam Bailey were among the founding members of the Washington Audubon, General George Sternberg was chosen as president, while two women, Mrs. John Patten and Miss Wescott, were chosen as secretary and treasurer, respectively (AAUW 2010; *Washington Post* 1897a: 7; 1897b: 10). Women founded the New Orleans Audubon and took care of the behind-the-scenes operations, but at the meetings, males made the speeches to largely female audiences (Nobles 1897: 18). A woman was named president of the Chicago Audubon, but men were also featured prominently on the programs (*New York Times* 1895: 26; *Washington Post* 1895: 22). Women tended to fill auxiliary roles such as secretary and event coordinator. In 1899, virtually all of the secretaries in the various Audubons were female (*New York Times* 1899: 24).

Furthermore, some of the women funded the Audubons out of pocket. For example, Mary Fluker Bradford, who founded the New Orleans Audubon, began contributions to the Audubon memorial by using five hundred dollars of her own money to open a bank account for the project (Nobles 1897: 18). Hemenway funded the Massachusetts Audubon Society in its early years but did not join the board of directors until 1910 (Graham 1990: 15–18). However, Hemenway used her social location as a wealthy woman connected to an influential family and powerful New England institutions to be the driving force behind the scenes. She worked with similarly positioned women in her social and cultural network: these women were fashion trendsetters who could use their personal influence and financial clout to influence the millinery industry. Similarly, Mary Bradford, one of New Orleans' leading society ladies, networked among women of similar social class and convinced them to join her in forming the Audubon.

Wealthy women were targeted as potential Audubon members or admonished to stop wearing feathers because feathers and hats were expensive. Ostrich plumes cost as much as nine dollars apiece, and aigrettes could sell for about thirty-five dollars per ounce. Most women wearing hats with the most elaborate bird and feather trimmings were well off. But the millinery industry depended on the labor of poor women to produce the merchandise that the wealthy consumed. In 1900, the headwear industry hired about eighty-three thousand people, most of them women (Doughty 1975: 17, 23; *Lawrence v. Everett* 1890). Though the laborers worked under poor conditions, worker health, workplace safety issues, and job alternatives were not considered part of the agenda of the Audubon or other bird-protection organizations.

The Audubon idea caught on the second time around, and by 1901 chapters were operating in thirty-one states and the District of Columbia. The new Audubons reestablished close ties to the American Ornithological Union. The Ornithological Union helped form new chapters of the Audubon, and the organizations worked closely together and held joint meetings. For instance, Brewster was the president of the Massachusetts Audubon at the same time he was a member of American Ornithological Union's bird-protection committee (Graham 1990: 15–18; Nobles 1897: 18).

Though local groups developed their own agendas, most used the same master frames and focused on the core Audubon theme of women as bird enemies and the core goals of passing bird-protection legislation and stopping the destruction of birds for millinery purposes. Leaders of the society wrote numerous newspaper articles and gave many talks similar to ones discussed above. This frame was so effective, so potent a symbol of shame, that in 1904 an Audubon member named Charles Skinner circulated flyers proposing a city ordinance that would require all disorderly women to wear hats with stuffed birds as a form of punishment (*New York Times* 1904b: 8). Women were so thoroughly associated with bird destruction that the proposed punishment did not extend to men.

THE AUDUBON'S BASE OF SUPPORT WIDENS

The Audubon kept up the attack on women who were seen as vain and barbaric in their choice of personal adornment. Influential European women supported the cause: in 1906 Queen Alexandra of England spoke disapprovingly about the use of plumage to decorate hats and feminine fashion. Queen Alexandra announced that she never wore aigrettes and looked disapprovingly upon those who did (*Washington Post* 1906a: SM7). Shortly after the queen's declaration, Theodore Roosevelt wrote: "Permit me, on behalf of both Mrs. Roosevelt and myself, to say how heartily we sympathize, not only with the work of the Audubon societies generally, but particularly their efforts to stop the sale and use of the so-called 'aigrets'—the plumes of the white herons" (Roosevelt 1906: 1).

The statements from a queen and the president of the United States had an impact. Within months women in groups such as the Corona Women's Improvement Club voted to stop wearing aigrettes and support the Audubon's cause (*Los Angeles Times* 1906b: 16). Members of the General Federation of Women's Clubs also pledged to stop wearing aigrettes. General Federation of Women's Clubs president Sarah Platt Decker wrote a letter in the *Federation Bulletin* labeling women who wore dead birds "vain" and "selfish." She accused such women of allowing the milliners to do the thinking for them and implored women to use their own tastes and ideas to shape their fashion sense. Club women were also influenced by Audubon representatives like T. Gilbert Pearson, who wrote about the destruction of heron habitats (Dutcher 1904a: 38; *Los Angeles Times* 1907a: V21).

Audubon activists continued their relentless attack on women by announcing that they would confront society women who wore aigrettes, even if this might cause a rift among social elites. At this juncture, the Civic Association joined forces with the Audubon. In 1909, the eighty-three thousand members of the Grangers also joined the Audubon cause; so did members of the Humane Society (*Los Angeles Times* 1908: 119; *New York Times* 1909b: 8).

In 1897, Massachusetts passed a law making it illegal to wear feathers; a similar law passed in New York's House and Senate, but the governor refused to sign it (*New York Times* 1897c: 14). This prompted the milliners to challenge the Audubon's claims publicly. Charles Farmer, editor of the *Millinery Trade Review*, claimed in an editorial that the New York Audubon had "overreached" because of its focus on "the wearing of birds, bird wings, and plumage" as trimming. Farmer argued that the state's game laws referred only to the protection of wild birds within the state. He argued that the law made no reference to wearing imported birds, wings, or plumage, or to possessing or selling them. He also argued that much of the plumage being worn was imported and that wearing it was not a violation of New York's game laws (Farmer 1897: 4).

Frank Chapman, chair of the New York Audubon's Executive Committee, responded to Farmer by contending that wearing feathers or dead birds violated the statute which stated that "wild birds shall not be killed at any time, or possessed, living or dead" (Chapman 1897: 4). Milliners asked whether there was any harm in killing owls for use on women's hats. Bird-protection activists responded to this by citing work done by C. Hart Merriam of the U.S. Department of Agriculture showing that a bounty on hawks and owls in Pennsylvania resulted in the killing of more than one hundred thousand of the birds and resulted in a loss of nearly $5 million in an eighteen-month period (*Washington Post* 1897c: 6).

Though milliners continued to manufacture hats trimmed with birds and feathers, by 1899 they began advertising hats that had no birds on them. These were popular with Audubon members (*Washington Post* 1899c: 5; 1899d: 4). Milliners collaborated with the Audubon to produce Audubonnets—hats that were not trimmed with birds (*Washington Post* 1900: 7; 1903a: 7; 1903b: 2).

The milliners also tried other tactics to win over public opinion and keep their businesses viable. They published newspaper articles quoting workers who claimed they were using only plumage from domestic fowls and game birds. The milliners also used the "jobs versus environment" argument: they pitted the interests of poor women against those of wealthy women arguing that a reduction in the use of feathers meant that thousands of workers— most of them poor women—would lose their jobs. Frank Chapman rebutted these claims by arguing that workers were ignorant about what they were doing and were not knowledgeable about birds. He also contended that the workers were being duped into thinking that they were actually using chicken feathers when they weren't. Finally, Chapman maintained that if the millinery industry switched to using artificial feathers rather than cutting jobs, larger numbers of workers could be employed in the industry (Chapman 1900: 24).

Milliners tried to reinforce the point that their industry hired poor female workers. They also took aim at sportsmen. Charles Farmer, secretary and treasurer of the Millinery Merchants' Protective Association, directly challenged George Shields, president of the League of American Sportsmen, arguing that Mr. Shields took a strong position against the use of plumage, yet went around the country "with a gun on his shoulder looking for birds to kill for sport." Farmer asked Shields why he was being so inconsistent and duplicitous: why did he think it was sinful for women to wear hats trimmed with birds, though he did not consider it a problem to shoot and kill the very birds women were being implored to save (Farmer 1900: 21)?

The milliners tried another tactic after the Hallock Bill was signed into law. The bill amended the game law by making it unlawful to possess the plumage or skins of wild and songbirds for commercial purposes (*New York Times* 1900a: 6). The milliners promised to abide by the law and try to remain in the good graces of the bird-protection organizations. However, Charles Farmer held an informal meeting with leading bird-protection activists Frank Chapman and William Dutcher in 1900. Chapman and Dutcher toured several millineries to inspect their facilities. Farmer's Millinery Merchants' Protective Association, which controlled more than 90 percent of the bird trade, also drew up a resolution to counter the Hallock Bill in the hope of reaching an agreement with the Audubon on how the industry would operate under the new regulations. The milliners indicated that they wanted to exhaust their inventory of birds and feathers. They promised not to use the plumage of domestic birds except fowls and game birds killed for food during the legal hunting season. They promised not to use any North American birds of similar species to those whose use was prohibited in the United States. And they pledged to refrain from using similar birds from other "civilized" countries also (Graham 1990: 39–40; *New York Times* 1900b: 6; 1900c: 9; 1900d: 12).

The Millinery Merchants' Protective Association racialized the discourse and added a North-South dynamic by seeking permission for its members to use birds from Asia, India, Africa, and "islands where no white man except hunters penetrate." Moreover, the milliners proposed that they would police their own industry and fine members violating the agreement. The Millinery Merchants' Protective Association also said it would abide by the agreement as long as the Audubon and other bird-protection associations did nothing to constrain the industry further. Dutcher and Chapman and other leaders wanted to accept the milliners' proposal, but decided to bring the resolutions to the larger Audubon membership for ratification. Chapman urged Audubon members to give consideration to the proposal in an editorial in *Bird-Lore*. If the membership agreed, then the Millinery Merchants' Protective Association, Audubon, and American Ornithological Union would work out a new bill that would be presented to lawmakers. However, Mabel Osgood Wright was very critical of the proposal and used her column in *Bird-Lore* to critique it. She also reminded Audubon members that the proposal would prevent the Audubon from enacting laws that the organization had pledged to put in place. As a result, Audubon members rejected the proposal (Graham 1990: 39–40; *New York Times* 1900b: 6; 1900c: 9; 1900d: 12).

A year later, a survey of the fall fashion hats on display in Washington, DC, found large numbers of hats trimmed with birds, wings, and feathers. Multiple birds were found on many hats. Journalist May Manton speculated that the milliners were showing their defiance of the Audubon through the styling of the hats (Manton 1901: 28). Ella Lowery Moseley surveyed the millinery fashions later that fall and reported fewer hats with birds on them (Moseley 1901: 33). But this finding could be a function of women purchasing the hats trimmed with birds faster than those devoid of bird trimming.

The milliners brought another proposal to the Audubon in 1903. In it the milliners agreed to refrain from importing, manufacturing, purchasing, or selling gulls, terns, grebes, hummingbirds, and songbirds regardless of their origin. The milliners also agreed to cease the importation, manufacture, purchase, or sale of plumage from egrets, herons, and all species of American pelicans. It was the responsibility of the Millinery Merchants' Protective Association to notify milliners of what birds could be used legally. In return the Audubon agreed to stop its wardens from harassing milliners who were complying with the law. The Audubon also agreed not to push for legislation that would place more stringent restrictions on the importation, manufacture, and sale of fancy feathers obtained from domestic fowls or foreign birds other than those specifically mentioned. Mabel Osgood Wright supported the proposal this time; so did Audubons in thirteen states. The agreement was scheduled to go into effect until 1906 (Graham 1990: 40; *Washington Post* 1903a: 7; 1903c: 12).

The Millinery Merchants' Protective Association was concerned about the actions of wardens because of the potential for bribery and corruption. As the milliners pointed out, in some states (Ohio, for instance), half of the wardens' wages were derived from the fines they collected. This created an incentive for overzealous wardens to harass traders regardless of whether they were in compliance with the law (*New York Times* 1903a: 24).

The Millinery Merchants' Protective Association was not able to deliver on its promise of getting its members to abide by the new agreement. The three largest importers of aigrettes announced that they would continue importing aigrettes. They issued a statement to their customers saying that they intended to meet the demand for feathers and that after consulting with their lawyers, they believed it was lawful to import aigrettes (*New York Times* 1903a: 24).

So, in 1904, the milliners conceded the fight. In January, the Millinery Merchants' Protective Association called a special meeting to announce that the organization was abandoning the fight against state and federal bird laws. Though they thought the Lacey Act (discussed later) was unconstitutional and had planned to mount a challenge to it, they decided they were not going to pursue that course of action. The merchants reached this conclusion after an assessment of the state of the bird trade indicated that the public supported the law and any further opposition by milliners would be injurious to the industry. They made it clear that they were taking this position out of deference to public opinion because they were fed up with being cast as the villains. The milliners went on to say that they had virtually ceased to use most wild birds on hats in the preceding two years. Instead they dyed and used the feathers of domestic fowls or used artificial feathers instead. The industry had also voluntarily abandoned the use of seagull wings after the birds almost went extinct. The milliners pointed out that they were responsible for about half the destruction of birds; they argued that other culprits, such as pot hunters and rapacious Italian hunters, were responsible too. The milliners did vow to continue their fight against corrupt wardens interfering with legal trade (*New York Times* 1904a: 24).

LEFT OUT OF THE EQUATION:
WORKING-CLASS WOMEN IN THE MILLINERY INDUSTRY

The Audubon's campaign to eliminate the use of feathers on hats illustrates the way in which early conservationists focused on harm to wildlife but overlooked the condition of the poor even when poverty and terrible work conditions were intimately connected to their campaign. The feather campaign also showed conservationists' disinterest in collaborating with the poor even when such collaboration could have enhanced the effectiveness of the campaign.

The millinery industry traditionally hired a lot of women in the hat-making factories, yet bird-protection activists did not engage the feather workers in their campaigns except to cast them as ignorant pawns in the bird-destruction tragedy (see, for example, Chapman 1900: 24). However, feather workers had knowledge of the industry that could have been useful to conservationists. Feather workers were also engaged in struggles of their own that bird-protection activists remained oblivious to. The feather workers earned low wages, and their working conditions were harsh. The conservationists did not call attention to the inhumane conditions in the millinery factories as part of the campaigns. This meant that feather workers tried to seek justice on their own. Thus in 1888, striking feather workers held a mass meeting at the Cooper Institute. Mary McGinley, a forewoman at Lowenstein and Grey's feather factory, led the meeting. She encouraged the women to strike for higher wages and improved working conditions. Feather workers had experienced pay cuts, but one manufacturer, T. H. Woods, argued that there was no need to cut wages and encouraged the women to organize to prevent further wage reductions (*New York Times* 1888a: 2).

The women formed a Feather Workers' Union and began striking. They estimated that around five hundred women were working at "starvation wages" in the industry and around two hundred thousand women in the city barely earned enough to live on. An important milliner, Isidor Cohnfeld, met with the strikers and promised to pay the women working in his factory their old wages, and those workers returned to work immediately (*New York Times* 1888b: 2; 1888c: 2). Feather workers walked off the job at other factories to protest wage cuts. Owners indicated they would rehire the workers at their old wage scale only if they returned as nonunionized workers. At a hearing of the State Board of Arbitration some women testified that they were fired because of their union activities (*New York Times* 1888d: 3; 1888e: 3).

At the time of the unrest, feather workers earned up to $12 per week during the busy season. During the off-season, workers were either laid off or worked at two-thirds time. Some made as little as $0.45 per day. Wages in the industry had been falling steadily for about two decades. Feather workers earned about $25 per week in 1869, but in 1888 weekly wages averaged around $9 to $11. Several Lowenstein & Gray workers testified that they used to earn as much as $30 per week during the busy season four years earlier, but in 1888, many of the women's wages had been reduced to less than $13.50 per week in the busy season. Workers also pointed out that the price of the goods they manufactured remained high, yet their wages were being cut (*New York Times* 1888e: 3; 1888f: 8; *Washington Post* 1888a: 4; 1888b: 1).

Strikes, lockouts, wage rollbacks, and attempts to unionize continued for the next two decades (*Los Angeles Times* 1913a: V17; *New York Times* 1899a: 8; 1889a: 5; 1889b: 2; 1889c: 8; 1889d: 3; 1889e: 4; *Washington Post* 1889a: 2). But none of these well-publicized actions drew the attention or sympathy of Audubon activists. Yet, incorporating the feather workers into the debate would have helped the conservationists gain an appreciation of the complexity of the problem and the broader dimensions of human-nature relations.

Spreading the Blame: The New Villains

FELINE BIRD MENACE

In time, the Audubon Society began to shift their framing and expand the list of those seen as villains in the bird-destruction campaigns. As the use of feathers on women's hats waned, the organization reduced its attacks on women wearing bird-trimmed hats and the millinery industry. Instead they now blamed bird massacre on cats, immigrants, pot hunters, minorities (blacks, Indians, and Japanese), and boys. In 1905, the Audubon identified cats as a menace to birds. As a *Los Angeles Times* article noted, "Cats, foreigners, boys with rifles and air-guns, and ignorant ranchers are the principal cause of the destruction of non-game birds" (*Los Angeles Times* 1909a: 111).

Audubon activists argued that there were too many cats and their population should be controlled. The organization suggested that cats should be licensed and forced to wear a numbered collar at all times. Strays should be rounded up and cat owners held responsible for their pets' actions (*New York Times* 1905b: 9). In proposing these measures, Audubon leaders argued, "There is nothing so destructive to the bird as the cats, and we should set our faces against the increase of their tribe" (*Washington Post* 1905a: A1). As Elizabeth Brown, chair of the New York Audubon's program committee, stated, cats have not been rounded up by dog catchers—except on a few occasions—but "the great movement of the Audubon societies in the near future will be in the feline line." Brown also announced that the Audubon planned to raise twenty-five thousand dollars for this purpose (*Washington Post* 1905b: MP4). As late as 1909, the California Audubon Society called for the licensing of cats to keep their numbers in check. Maria R. Audubon, granddaughter of John James Audubon, supported California's position, arguing that each cat killed about fifty birds per year (*Los Angeles Times* 1909a: 111).

As might be expected, there was strong opposition to the Audubon proposal. Lucia Grieve, referring to Audubon members as "cranks and faddists," argued that the organization was being inconsistent. She questioned their logic of waging war on one species to save another. Grieve also asked why the cat was being singled out when other animals also preyed on birds. Grieve contended that the number of birds killed by cats was insignificant when compared to the number of birds preyed upon by other birds. She also contended that birds and cats were beneficial because they kept the vermin population in check and that, like birds, cats were beautiful to look at, interesting to study, and friendly. Grieve concluded by reminding Audubon activists that cats might catch a stray bird or two, but rats and mice gnaw at birds' nests and suck their eggs (Grieve 1905: 8).

The Humane Society was drawn into the controversy. In 1904, they disposed of more than thirty-seven hundred cats, but ceased doing so that year. The Humane Society injected a note of reality into the debate by warning that it would be difficult for the Audubon to round up stray cats or to hold owners responsible for the actions of cats that strayed from the backyard and caught and killed a bird (*Washington Post* 1905c: 12).[9] In 1912, sportsmen and sports clubs joined the Audubon's chorus of implicating cats as the primary menace to birds. Cats were portrayed as "an army of hunting felines . . . roaming everywhere in the breeding season, searching for nests and young birds." William Minot estimated that approximately 150,000 cats on Massachusetts farms killed about 7.5 million birds annually (*New York Times* 1912: 35). More than a decade later, noted ornithologist E. H. Forbish asserted that cats destroyed more than 10 million songbirds annually (*New York Times* 1923b: 18).

POT HUNTERS, ITALIANS, BLACKS, AND NATIVE AMERICANS

Subsistence hunters were also blamed for destroying wildlife. The Audubon's bird-protection committee reported that in the South, "the native conchs [poor whites] and negroes, many of whom are desperate characters, can, by watching the wardens' movements, visit the rookeries with impunity and make wholesale depredations on the young herons, ibises, and even cormorants for food. Several expeditions of this kind have already been broken up by the judicious employment of negro spies, who have kept the warden informed" (Dutcher 1904b: 130). However, Susan Fenimore Cooper viewed the relationship between blacks and birds in a more generous light. She noted, "The negroes were great allies of the birds. Many were the ingenious devices of their own contrivance for enticing the little creatures to build about the dwelling which was their own home as well as that of their masters" (Cooper 1878b: 164–167). Finney (2014) documents the complex relationships blacks in the South had with national parks, wildlife refuges, and wilderness areas. Subsistence hunting and angling was a component of blacks' interactions with nature. This was not well understood by late nineteenth- and early twentieth-century wildlife activists.

Bird-protection activists also vented their ire on Italians and other southern Europeans who hunted to feed their families. Pearson, like Chapman and William Hornaday, espoused strong anti-immigrant and nativist views (Graham 1990: 55). The perception that market and pot hunters were responsible for the decimation of wildlife was one of the driving forces behind the passage of the Lacey Act. Advocates for the bill, which made no distinction between pot hunters and market hunters, argued that since state laws were being circumvented by pot hunters killing and shipping game and birds across state lines illegally, a federal law was needed. The bill stated, "The pot hunter in Iowa, Missouri, or Kansas kills quails out of season and in violation of the laws of those States. He does not merely kill a few for his own use, but he slaughters or traps them indiscriminately for the purpose of sending them for sale in the market. He avoids State law by secretly shipping them to a market beyond the State" (U.S. House of Representatives 1900: 1–3).

In 1911, the Audubon Society estimated that about $1 billion in increased prices for goods could be attributed to bird slaughter. Prices increased because birds were being destroyed instead of being left alone to control rodents and insects. The Audubon lay the blame for the bird destruction and rising costs on the pot hunter, who was described as "the man who kills all and several that come within range of his gun." The Audubon claimed the public should hold the pot hunter responsible for rising costs. Feather hunters were also implicated (*New York Times* 1911a: XX8).

Native Americans too were blamed for the decimation of birds. Elizabeth and Joseph Grinnell attacked tribal cultural practices such as the ceremonial use of feathers. They argued, "Some barbarous peoples possess a rude taste for the beautiful plumage of birds, decorating their bodies in feathers of softest and brightest tints." They went on to say that few tribes delighted in birdsong (Grinnell and Grinnell 1901: 9). Others also criticized the tribal use of feathers (Moseley 1901: 33).

Around the time the Lacey Act was passed, Dutcher learned that millinery companies were supplying tribes in Maine with guns and ammunition to kill gulls and terns. There were no laws prohibiting the hunting of coastal birds at the time, so Dutcher arranged to have wardens and lighthouse keepers guard the coastline and nesting islands off the coast. After obtaining permission of landowners, he asked the wardens and guards to post No Trespass signs in the hope of prosecuting Indians for trespassing. William Stanley, a lighthouse keeper on Great Duck Island off Mount Desert Island, described his encounter with Native Americans in a letter to Dutcher. Stanley saw a group of Native Americans on the island hunting birds and collecting eggs. He read the No Trespass notice and asked them to leave, but they refused to. Frustrated, Stanley claimed that he wanted a camera so that he could take pictures, but he also said he would rather shoot the Native Americans than take pictures of them.

Stanley eventually persuaded the Indians to leave the island (Graham 1990: 27–29). Indians and sportsmen also had numerous conflicts over hunting in New Mexico and Wyoming (Warren 1997: 71–171).

BOYS' MISCHIEF

Though the Audubon continued to pressure milliners, they began focusing attention on wildlife slaughter in the South and West. When they looked at the South, the hunting activities of boys came to the fore. In New Orleans, for instance, boys with air guns were seen killing birds in numerous locations in the city. Black boys and men were also accused of slaughtering birds in the city (*Los Angeles Times* 1901: 5).

In 1910, members of the Audubon in Pasadena censured young boys using air guns and catapults. The Audubon issued a flyer in which the air gun and slingshot were described as dangerous and illegal contrivances. The circular also quoted a city ordinance stating that it was illegal to discharge these contraptions within city limits. Violation of the ordinance could result in a fine or imprisonment. Warnings were also placed in the newspapers (*Los Angeles Times* 1910a: 117).

JAPANESE SUBSISTENCE HUNTERS

The Japanese were also held responsible for the bird slaughter. The Audubon claimed to have received numerous complaints of Japanese shooting songbirds on Sundays in the countryside around Pasadena. The Japanese allegedly used silent blowguns to shoot meadowlarks and mockingbirds, which they used to supplement their diet. According to a *Los Angeles Times* article, "Their epicurean tastes are satisfied with anything that wears feathers, and they seem to have no compunction whatever in regard to robbing the atmosphere of its sweetest songs and most brilliant plumage." Believing that Japanese residents were not aware of the state's bird laws, Audubon activists posted flyers printed in Japanese to inform Japanese hunters of the laws. The Audubon also warned that if Japanese were caught violating the laws, they could be jailed or fined (*Los Angeles Times* 1906a: 119).

SUPPRESSING IMMIGRANT HUNTERS

Recent immigrants were blamed for bird destruction and were targeted by Audubon campaigns on the East and West Coasts. At the beginning of the twentieth century, conservationists and native-born farmers in the East expressed their resentment of Italian hunters by collaborating with elite sportsmen to develop game laws that severely restricted the hunting activities of immigrants and the poor and levied heavy fines on them. Although elite sportsmen and conservationists such as Grinnell did not believe the wildlife conservation campaigns had a class dimension worthy of discussion, the game laws being instituted had differential impacts on poor and rich hunters. The tensions brought on by these laws resulted in violence.

The anti-immigrant, anti-Italian rhetoric gained currency as attacks on women subsided. In 1905, the Audubon urged its members to "do all they can to suppress the alien gunner and bring him to justice" (Graham 1990: 87). The following year, pot hunters were blamed for the destruction of ducks in the lakes along the Oregon-California border (*Washington Post* 1906b: B3). The Audubon was not alone in shifting attention to immigrants. Prominent sportsmen and their organizations also began focusing on immigrant pot and market hunters. The rapid growth in the immigrant population, the high levels of poverty among recent immigrants, and the need for subsistence hunting to supplement meager wages fueled the conflicts.

On the East Coast, Italian hunters were singled out as immigrants whose hunting activities should be curtailed. This idea was expressed in a 1906 *Washington Post* article claiming that Italians had "invaded" the United States and had become a "growing menace to the woods and fields of America." Asserting that "hordes" of Italians were "swarm[ing] through every region of the United States" killing thousands of birds, the Audubon gave strong support to bills aimed at controlling "alien hunters." The Audubon's president, Dutcher, called for the licensing of immigrants and stiff penalties to be levied against those running afoul of game laws (*Washington Post* 1906c: 3).

Confrontations between Italian immigrants and game wardens grew more frequent, and one incident resulted in the murder of Seeley Houk, the deputy game protector of Lawrence County in western Pennsylvania. As soon as Houk's bullet-riddled body was found weighted down with boulders in the Mahoning River, suspicion fell on the Italian immigrants who worked at the quarries and lived in segregated towns nearby. After a game warden, Guy Bradley, was killed in Florida in 1905, the number of deadly conflicts between game wardens and hunters increased steadily. In Pennsylvania alone, four game wardens were killed in shootouts with hunters in 1906 (*Commonwealth v. Racco* 1909; Nelli 2003: 86–87; Trefethen 1975: 136; Warren 1997: 14, 21).

By the late nineteenth century sportsmen and conservationists realized that they could spread the wildlife-protection message, pass wildlife legislation more effectively, and get better enforcement of said laws by enlisting rural allies in their campaigns. Farmers and the rural gentry were the obvious choice for activists. Though farmers had gone through a period of killing birds they deemed noxious, in the latter half of the nineteenth century conservationists had broadened their message to show how birds and other wildlife benefited farmers. Conservationists also argued that the destruction of birds cost farmers large sums of money. This made farmers more receptive to the conservation message and more involved in conservation issues. Farmers were also eager to take steps to protect their land from hunters who tramped around on their property and damaged crops and fences (Judd 1997: 79–83; Warren 1997: 48–50).

But farmers and conservationists were not in complete agreement on everything. Farmers routinely hunted for subsistence purposes, and some sold a portion of what they killed on the market to generate extra income. Farmers also saw wildlife that ate crops and caused other damage as nuisances to be disposed of. For instance, some farmers perceived the female deer as a gluttonous animal that wreaked havoc on farm crops and produced fawn that followed in her footsteps, but to conservationists the doe was an aesthetically pleasing symbol of femininity that should remain untouched by the hunt. As a result, farmers were uncomfortable with some of the hunting restrictions sportsmen were advocating and with the general vilification of market and pot hunters. Sportsmen were more interested in saving wildlife than farms per se; the alliance with farmers and other rural landholders was a means to an end (Forester 1849: 18–19; Judd 1997: 79–83; Warren 1997: 48–50). Thus urban and rural elites collaborated with each other and created a state enforcement mechanism that directed its actions against the most marginalized rural residents, such as Italian immigrants. In the South conservationists tried to restrict the hunting activities of blacks, while in the West the emphasis was on Japanese immigrants, Mexican Americans, and Native Americans.

Anti-Italian Hysteria, Rising Tensions, and Game Laws. In the first two decades of the twentieth century, the wildlife protection battles in Pennsylvania took center stage and typified other battles between upper-class conservationists, rural gentry, state authorities, and low-income and minority hunters going on elsewhere. The case of Seeley Houk, appointed in 1903, illustrates some of the tensions between wildlife conservation and social inequality that nature protection advocates were either ignorant of or oblivious to. The case also demonstrates how insisting on the passage of conservation and preservation laws without fully considering their social and economic ramifications sometimes led to deadly outcomes.

Like other states, Pennsylvania instituted laws to protect wildlife during the late nineteenth century. These laws gradually converted year-round subsistence hunting and angling into seasonal, recreational activities. In 1883, Pennsylvania passed a game law aimed at preventing dogs from chasing elk, deer, or fawns. Dogs caught chasing this wildlife could be killed and the owner fined ten dollars for each game animal killed by the dog (Act 1883). An 1897 law restricted the hunting season to November and prohibited the use of dogs in hunting these animals. Anyone caught violating the statute would be fined one hundred dollars for each offense or be jailed one day for each dollar of penalty imposed (Act 1897; *Commonwealth v. Frederick* 1905).

By 1900, the state had set bag limits, established closed seasons, and banned the hunting of many species of songbirds. At first these laws were enforced by local police but in 1895, the state appointed the first game warden. When it became clear that it was impossible for the ten wardens to enforce game laws effectively, the Game Commission lobbied to create an auxiliary force of wardens called deputy game protectors. The deputy game protectors were bonded and had the same powers as the wardens. Deputy game protectors earned their wages by collecting half the fines levied against people caught violating wildlife laws (Act 1903; *Alms v. Indiana County* 1911; Commonwealth of Pennsylvania 1903: 10, 26, 32; Warren 1997: 23).[10]

There was a strong relationship between the increased surveillance power of the state through the appointment of deputy game protectors, the tightening of restrictions on immigrant hunting activities, and increased fines being levied against violators of the game law. The act allowing counties to appoint deputies was passed on April 11, 1903, and on April 14 Pennsylvania passed a law stipulating that every "non-resident" and "unnaturalized foreign-born resident" of the state were required to purchase a hunting license for $10 before they could hunt in the state (*Commonwealth v. Canon* 1906). Since most immigrants could not afford the fee, they were effectively barred from hunting legally. It also meant that immigrants who did not buy a hunting license could be convicted for merely carrying a gun in the state. Violators were fined $25 or jailed for twenty-five days. Furthermore, violators caught with game were assessed $10 for each illegally hunted bird in their possession. Sunday hunting was banned, and violators were fined an additional $25 for hunting on that day. Hence the arrest of an immigrant for violating the game laws typically resulted in a fine of $60 or more (Commonwealth of Pennsylvania 1903: 33; Warren 1997: 29).

Seeley Houk's murder occurred near Hillsville, a rural farming community. The farmers were native-born English speakers but the ethnic balance in the community changed as large numbers of Italian immigrants moved into the area to work in the quarries and mines at the end of the nineteenth century. They earned about $1.65 per day in wages. There had been a rapid increase in the number of immigrants from eastern, central, and southern Europe arriving in America since the 1880s. There were many Italians among these new arrivals. Between 1900 and 1910 more than 2.1 million Italians immigrated to the United States, and many settled in Pennsylvania. Thus in 1906, about 900 of the 1,500 people in Hillsville were Italians (Warren 1997: 22–23, 26–27).

Prior to the arrival of the Italians, locals hunted a variety of animals on the farms and in the fields. However, there was a common understanding among longtime residents and mutual regulation of hunting behavior among community members. For instance, one was allowed to hunt on the farmland of others if one sought permission first or if one knew the landowner personally and had developed a relationship with them. Residents of small, tight-knit villages such as Hillsville were wary of strangers. When the railroads made such villages more accessible, rural residents complained about criminals, vagrants, poachers, and other urban pariah they thought the trains deposited on their doorsteps. Increasingly rural landowners complained about trespassers, damaged fences and crops, and maimed and injured animals left in the wake of hunting sprees. The arrival of the Italians in Hillsville and surrounding communities intensified those complaints and increased the antipathy toward newcomers. Hence the presence of a large group of armed, non-English-speaking hunters who were strangers was threatening to longtime community residents. The Italians, unaware of all the nuances of local customs, did not seek permission to hunt on particular farms, roamed the countryside at will killing rabbits, groundhogs, and songbirds. The cultural practices of the Italians also irked longtime residents. The Italians considered songbirds a delicacy and hunted them as well as game. Because native-born residents did not hunt and eat groundhogs and songbirds, it was easy for them to stereotype and portray the hunting practices of the Italians as depraved (Warren 1997: 22–29).

The anti-Italian and anti-immigrant stereotypes of the native-born Hillsville residents matched those of the conservationists. For instance, renowned conservationist Congressman John Lacey said in a speech in the House of Representatives, "The man or the woman who does not love songbirds should be classed with the person who has no love for music—fit only for treasons, stratagems, and spoils" (quoted in Warren 1997: 25). Thus in the framing of the wildlife discourse, Italians emerged as a major threat to birds because they hunted and consumed them (Warren 1997: 26). For this reason, Hornaday implored communities to be vigilant, and in so doing, his inflammatory rhetoric contributed to anti-Italian, anti-immigrant hysteria. He said, "Let every state and province in America look out sharply for the bird-killing foreigner; for sooner or later, he will surely attack your wildlife. The Italians are spreading, spreading, spreading. If you are without them to-day, to-morrow they will be around you" (Hornaday 1913: 102).

Hornaday also argued in lectures at the Yale School of Forestry that "the destruction of insectivorous birds of many species by the Italians of the North and the negroes of the South, and in some localities by white men calling themselves sportsmen but lacking anything even remotely resembling a code of ethics in shooting" was a major cause of the problem. He reiterated the point: "I am quite certain that their [the birds] disappearance has been caused by the slaughter of them for food, in the North by the Italians, and in the South by negroes." He supported his claim by saying that in 1905, two game wardens of the New York Zoological Society arrested two Italians who had forty-three insectivorous birds in their possession in New York City. He also stated, "All the members of the lower classes of southern Europe are a dangerous menace to our wildlife" (Hornaday 1914: 16–17, 61).

Many of the Italians migrating to the United States hunted in their homeland. In America they carried on this tradition, which allowed men to bond with each other while on hunting trips. Hunting was also important because it provided a respite from the drudgery of the mines, mills, and factories. The women cooked the songbirds the same as chicken, while the groundhogs were made into a hearty stew. Italian immigrants also hunted to supplement their income; they were both pot and market hunters, since they ate some of what they killed and sold the rest on the market. The Italians weren't the only ones practicing these small-scale market exchanges; farmers and other rural residents sold their excess meat on the market too. For many rural landholders, the cash generated in these exchanges helped to keep their farming operations solvent (Warren 1997: 27–28).

These activities caught the attention of deputy game protectors. One in particular, Seeley Houk, had many enemies. He had developed a reputation of being an overly zealous deputy who exceeded his authority, brought many Italian immigrants to court for violating game laws, roughed up suspects in his custody, and killed one of their hunting dogs. An Italian immigrant with alleged mafia ties, Rocco Racco was convicted, tried, and hanged for Houk's killing. The murder prompted Pennsylvania to pass even more restrictive anti-immigrant hunting laws. As Rocco Racco's trial drew to a close in 1909, Pennsylvania passed the Alien Gun Law, which made it illegal for unnaturalized foreign-born residents to possess shotguns or rifles or to kill wild game except in self defense or defense of property. On the day Racco was hanged, authorities arrested and fined eight Italian hunters for violating the gun laws. Five paid their fines, while the other three went to jail. The guns of all eight were confiscated. The new law virtually excluded all Italians and other immigrants from hunting in Pennsylvania. Consequently, some turned to subsistence fishing and trapping instead. However, immigrants continued to resist game laws that denied them access to resources. For decades after the murder of Seeley Houk and the hanging of Rocco Racco, the Game Commission reported almost two hundred arrests per year for violations of the gun law (*Commonwealth v. Racco* 1909; *Patsone v. Pennsylvania* 1914; Warren 1997: 32–33, 44–46).[11]

In the aftermath of the killings, murdered wardens were lionized as martyrs of the conservation cause, and their deaths were usually followed by outrage by conservationists, renewed efforts to strengthen game laws, efforts to hire additional wardens, and more stereotyping of racial and ethnic groups suspected in the killings (Trefethen 1975; Warren 1997: 44–45). However, the underlying tensions and resulting conflicts that led to their tragic deaths tended to go unresolved—which is not too surprising, given that elite conservationists insulated themselves from the poor quite effectively so they had little understanding of their ideas and needs and what factors influenced their behavior. Though many poor people hunted and angled, they had no input in the process of developing the game laws. Hence elite conservationists from urban areas developed and campaigned for conservation policies, passed legislation, and set up enforcement mechanisms without taking into consideration the circumstances of all of the affected stakeholders. Moreover, conservationists were not the ones on the front lines of enforcement. It was white men of modest means such as Seeley Houk and Guy Bradley, in need of jobs and seeking power and prestige, who took these jobs—and in some cases lost their lives—for the conservation cause.

Challenging the Anti-immigrant Gun Law. Pennsylvania's gun law passed in May 1909, and by September huge stacks of guns and rifles confiscated from unnaturalized residents of Pennsylvania were shipped to the State Game Commissioner. In addition, violators of the law were fined heavily. The game commissioners planned to sell the confiscated guns. A newspaper article reported that the guns were seized because of complaints that many "foreigners" were "wantonly slaughtering game out of season" with their guns (*Washington Post* 1909: ES4). Hornaday praised the gun law (Hornaday 1914: 61; *Patsone v. Pennsylvania* 1914).

However, an Italian immigrant, Patsone, challenged the law in a case that went to the U.S. Supreme Court. Patsone's suit argued that the law violated the Fourteenth Amendment, depriving him of liberty and property without due process. He also maintained that the law violated the 1871 treaty between the United States and Italy pertaining to the status and treatment of Italian citizens living in the United States. Patsone argued that the gun law was discriminatory in that it forbade only unnaturalized residents of the state from owning shotguns and rifles, thus depriving them of a means of protecting themselves. Patsone also argued that the law prevented unnaturalized residents from owning rifles and shotguns they could use to hunt on their own property or in other states. The Supreme Court ruled against Patsone. In affirming the lower court ruling, the Supreme Court argued that the states had a right to pass laws to protect wildlife and preserve it for their own citizens. To this end, the states had the power to identify the source of the "danger" to wildlife and regulate it. The court argued further that the state needn't identify all of the sources of danger in its attempt to protect wildlife (*Patsone v. Pennsylvania* 1914).

Despite this ruling, Italian immigrants continued to hunt surreptitiously around Hillsville. They also brokered a truce with some landowners. The farmers ceased to complain as long as the hunters remained out of sight and did not damage their property. This compromise was inevitable because Italian workers filled an important niche in the community—their labor was needed in the quarries and mines. Moreover, as the immigrants gained a foothold, earned better wages, and acquired property, they ceased hunting groundhogs, birds, and rabbits. Eventually, their children became recreational hunters who formed sportsmen clubs, such as the Mahoning Sportsmen's Association, that aimed to enhance game propagation efforts by teaching gun safety and educating others about sportsmanlike hunting (Warren 1997: 46–47).

Anti-immigrant Gun Laws Elsewhere. New Jersey adopted a law similar to Pennsylvania's in 1915. However, the New Jersey statute differed from Pennsylvania's in two significant respects: if unnaturalized residents owned real estate valued at two thousand dollars or more, they were exempt from the law; and under the New Jersey law, game wardens were empowered to search homes to look for evidence of violations (*New York Times* 1915: C4). Wyoming had a statute prohibiting unnaturalized foreign-born residents (referred to as "alien enemies") from obtaining firearms without a state license. In 1918 the State Game Board seized more than one hundred firearms from unnaturalized residents (*Christian Science Monitor* 1918: 8). In 1927, a California court struck down a law that penalized unnaturalized residents more heavily for violation of the anti-gun-toting law than naturalized and native-born residents. The court ruled in favor of Jose Vargas, an unnaturalized resident, after he was given a felony conviction for violating the law (*Los Angeles Times* 1927: A2).

Conservation Groups Develop Their Own Warden System

Though there were some state laws on the books to protect wildlife, enforcement was limited throughout the nineteenth century. As a result, the Audubon Society and the American Ornithological Union developed a warden system of their own to help curb the slaughter of wildlife. Abbot H. Thayer, artist and bird enthusiast, paid for the wardens. Thayer funded four positions in 1900, but by 1904 the number had grown to thirty-four wardens in ten states (Doughty 1975: 110–111). In addition to bird sanctuaries and wildlife reserves, wardens patrolled the streets of urban areas, where they raided millinery establishments and seized illegal birds, wings, heads, and feathers (*Los Angeles Times* 1898b: 8).

Thus in the absence of effective government regulation and management of natural resources, conservation clubs assumed public law enforcement roles where they found it lacking. However, not all members of the public accepted these roles. Like Boone and Crockett, wardens in Yellowstone, the Audubon Society and American Ornithological Union wardens worked in dangerous situations; some were killed challenging hunters and poachers. The milliners also paid a great deal of attention to what the wardens were doing. For instance, when wardens seized all the local birds in one dealer's store in Chicago and brought the case to court, the trial was attended by most of the city's bird dealers. The judge ruled against the defendant. Emboldened by the court decision, the wardens continued to seize dealers' birds and bring those violating the laws to trial (*Los Angeles Times* 1898b: 8).

Blameless Sportsmen and Collectors

Though elite sportsmen sought to make clear distinctions between themselves, pot hunters, and market hunters, the distinction between the three types of hunting was fuzzy. Though they didn't hunt primarily for subsistence or market purposes, it was common for sport hunters to sell their excess catch on the market. Audubon himself is an example of how easily these lines could be blurred. Audubon mixed scientific collection with pot and market hunting. Audubon had a penchant for hunting birds, killing and illustrating them, then either mounting them permanently or consuming them (Rhodes 2004: 41). Beginning in 1810, Audubon lived in and operated a shop in Henderson, Kentucky. He hunted and fished to provide both food for his table and goods that he could sell in his store (Rhodes 2004: 70).

Though sport hunters sometimes shot hundreds of birds while trapshooting, bagged large quantities of wildlife, killed large amounts of big game for trophies, and so on, conservationists did not focus on these actions. The general sentiment among elite sportsmen was summed up in an 1894 *Forest and Stream* editorial arguing that "the sportsman, who hunts for the sake of hunting, has had an effect so trivial, that in comparison with that of the market hunter, it need not be taken into consideration. The game paucity of today is due to the skin hunter, the meat killer [and] the market shooter" (*Forest and Stream* 1894a: 89).

Some sportsmen believed that the game belonged to them and that hunting was their domain. Referring to big game sport hunters, Theodore Roosevelt wrote while on a tour of Yellowstone, "It is to such men as he that the big game legitimately belongs" (Burroughs 1906: 7). One irate Audubon member finally questioned the wisdom of the organization's bag limits policy. He indicated that as late as the 1920s, the organization supported bag limits so high that a sport hunter could shoot over two thousand ducks and eight hundred wild geese in a single year (Graham 1990: 107).

Other acts of wildlife destruction by activists warranting scrutiny included the membership requirements of some clubs. For instance, to become a member of the Boone and Crockett Club, men needed to show three trophy heads (Nash 1982: 150–153). Collectors took a heavy toll on wildlife as well. Wildlife collecting has a long history in America. Both the establishment of private and public museums and the expanding recreation pursuits of the gentry fueled the desire to collect wildlife. In 1806, for instance, Audubon described the extensive animal collection he viewed in Willson Peale's Philadelphia Museum. The museum's Long Room had more than seven hundred American birds on display (C. C. Sellars 1980: 24–28). The twenty-one-year-old Audubon too, after living in America for only three years, already had an impressive private collection (Herrick [1917] 1938: 111–112).

Pearson, who came from a modest Quaker farming background, had an extensive egg collection that he traded for an education at Guilford College. While at Guilford he hunted and collected specimens all over the Southeast to build the college's museum collections. Similarly, Dutcher, an Audubon president, amassed a large collection of birds from the Long Island and New

Jersey shores. Likewise, George Sennett, a wealthy manufacturer and member of American Ornithological Union's bird-protection committee, had an extensive collection of birds' nests that he placed in the collection of the American Museum of Natural History. Since the male conservationists were themselves hunters and collectors, they sought to protect wildlife, preserve their sport, and direct attention to what they perceived as more egregious acts of wildlife destruction committed by others (Graham 1990: 20; Orr 1992: 7–31; Trefethen 1975: 29–30).

8

CHALLENGING WILDLIFE REGULATIONS
AND UNDERSTANDING THE
BUSINESS-CONSERVATION CONNECTIONS

As the nineteenth century progressed, it became evident to activists that wildlife conservation required more than developing fenced game parks and making rules to govern members' behavior. Consequently, some conservation organizations—for example, the Audubon Society, the Boone and Crockett Club, the American Ornithological Union, and the American Bison Society—focused on passing and implementing state and national game laws and policies. Though many of their members were birders, anglers, and hunters, they also concentrated on legislation, policymaking, and governance.

Legal Challenges to Game-Protection Laws

Opponents of wildlife-protection laws were quick to challenge such legislation in the courts. Litigants questioned whether states had authority to set and enforce closed seasons for killing or possessing game. Litigants also questioned whether wild animals belonged to the state or to the individuals who hunted or caught them, and whether state game laws interfered with the Interstate Commerce Clause.

In 1865, Vermont passed a statute banning the killing, harming, or harassment of deer for a ten-year period. Violators were fined fifty dollars plus the costs of prosecution (Act 1865). In 1870, Solomon Norton was charged with chasing and killing a deer. Norton argued that the statute was invalid on the grounds that it violated the state constitution, which gave residents of the state the right to hunt and fowl in season on their property or on unenclosed public lands. The judge argued that the rights secured in the constitution were not intended to be absolute and unconditional, but were governed and controlled by regulations made by the general assembly. The general assembly had the power to determine the hunting, fowling, and fishing seasons. The Supreme Court of Vermont upheld the lower court ruling against Norton (*State v. Solomon* 1873).

In 1871, New York passed an act specifying a closed season for quail, partridge, and prairie chickens that extended from January 1 to October 20 of each year (Act 1871: 1669). In 1873, Joseph Racey was charged with trying to sell quails and prairie chickens in March. Racey argued that the birds had been killed in December during the open season and that they were actually killed in Minnesota and Illinois, where it was legal to hunt them. He argued further that he had them in his possession during the closed season only because he had invented a device to preserve them. Racey also argued that the New York game preservation statute interfered with interstate commerce. The Court of Appeals of New York upheld the lower court ruling against Racey by arguing that regardless of the time and place where the game was killed, the 1871 statute prohibited its sale at the time Racey was selling them (*Royal Phelps v. Racey* 1875).

Missouri passed a game law in 1874 that prohibited anyone from catching, killing, injuring, or pursuing, or selling prairie chickens from February 15 to August 15 (Act 1874). In 1876, David Randolph, a St. Louis restauranteur, was charged with serving prairie chickens in his establishment during the closed season. Randolph argued that the prairie chickens in question were shipped from Kansas. If he was convicted for serving prairie chickens killed in another state, then the Missouri statute was invalid, as it was interfering with interstate commerce. Using arguments similar to those made in *Royal Phelps v. Racey*, the judge argued that the game law would be ineffectual if game could be imported from other states during the closed season, because it would be difficult to tell if game found in someone's possession during the closed season was killed in Missouri or in a neighboring state. The Court of Appeals of Missouri upheld the lower court decision in ruling against Randolph (*State of Missouri v. Randolph* 1876; see also *Royal Phelps v. Racey* 1875).

In another Missouri case, W. Judy of St. Louis was charged with having a quail and a prairie chicken in his possession during the closed season. He argued that the birds were killed in the open season but he had preserved them in a refrigerator he built. Judy was charged with violating an 1877 game law that made it illegal for anyone to have such birds in their possession during the closed season. The Court of Appeals of Missouri ruled against Judy, arguing that the time when the birds were killed is immaterial—that only the possession during the closed season was significant. The judge argued that making the possession of game during the closed season illegal was valid, since using refrigeration to preserve meat could make the game law ineffectual: it would be difficult to tell which game was killed during the open season and which was killed illegally during the closed season (*State of Missouri v. Judy* 1879). The Court of Appeals of Missouri also ruled against Joseph Farrell, who was charged with possessing and selling prairie chickens during the closed season in St. Louis in 1886 (*State of Missouri v. Farrell* 1886).

Illinois also developed a game law in 1879 that established closed seasons for several game species (Act 1879). John Magner, owner of a game market in Chicago, was charged with selling quails in 1880 during the closed season. Magner argued that some of the quail in his possession were killed in Kansas, therefore prohibiting their sale in Illinois was restricting interstate commerce. The judge in the case argued that the Illinois statute did not completely ban the possession or sale of game killed beyond the limits of the state. However, by banning possession of game from other states in the closed season, the Illinois law prevented people from circumventing the law. The judge also argued that the game in Magner's possession was killed in violation of Kansas laws, thus it was never a legitimate article of commerce. For these reasons Illinois Supreme Court upheld the lower court ruling against Magner (*James Magner v. The People* 1881). A similar ruling was made in Ohio (*Roth v. State* 1894).

In 1891 Minnesota passed a game law that prohibited anyone from catching, killing, or having in their possession fawn, moose, caribou, or antelope during the closed season (*Laws* 1891; *Laws* 1893). C. Rodman of St. Paul was indicted on January 9, 1894, for having prairie chickens, white-breasted grouse, and deer in his possession. R. Cobb of St. Paul was indicted on the same day for having deer in his possession. Both Rodman and Cobb argued that the game in their possession were hunted and killed in the open season. They also argued that the animals were wild and fugitive by nature and thus lacked the essential elements of property; consequently, they could not be the subjects of control or possession. The Supreme Court of Minnesota ruled against the defendants, arguing that wild animals were the property of the state and could be regulated by the state legislature (*State of Minnesota v. Rodman. Same v. Cobb* 1894).

In May 1889 Emma Fishbough of Brooklyn was charged with possessing and selling yellow-birds in violation of an 1879 statute. Fishbough argued that the statute was ambiguous because it wasn't clear whether possession of or exposure for sale of birds meant live birds or dead birds. The Supreme Court of New York ruled against her (*Forest, Fish and Game Law* 1879; *People v. Fishbough* 1890).

THE INTERSTATE COMMERCE
CLAUSE AND TRANSPORT OF GAME

Many challenges to the game laws were based on the Interstate Commerce Clause, which states that "Congress shall have power to regulate commerce with foreign nations, among the several states, and with Indian tribes"; it was common for those caught with game in the closed season to claim that the wildlife found in their possession was from another state. Policymakers sought to fix this issue by banning the shipment of game from one state to another. To this end, Kansas enacted a game law in 1876 that prohibited anyone from transporting prairie chickens from Kansas to other states (Act 1876: 183–184). In 1876, C. Saunders, an agent of the Adams Express Company, was charged with shipping prairie chickens from Kansas to Chicago, even though the birds were not caught and killed in violation of any laws. The plaintiff argued the prohibition on transporting the birds out of state was unconstitutional because it interfered with the Interstate Commerce Clause. The judge found the Kansas law invalid on the grounds that it allowed the prairie chickens to be caught and killed, thereby becoming an article of commerce, but prohibited anyone from transporting it from Kansas to other states. Using this argument, the Supreme Court of Kansas struck down the lower court ruling and found in favor of Saunders (*State of Kansas v. Saunders* 1877).

The Connecticut game law of 1888 prohibited anyone from killing or having in their possession woodcocks, partridge, quail, or gray squirrel with the intent of transporting them across state lines during the closed season (*General Statutes of Connecticut* 1888). Mr. Geer was charged with possessing woodcocks, ruffed grouse, and quail in 1889 in New London. It was further charged that Geer intended to ship the game out of the state of Connecticut. The Supreme Court of United States ruled against Geer, arguing that the state had the right to regulate and declare closed seasons on game within its boundaries (*Geer v. Connecticut* 1896).

New Jersey approved a game law in 1878 that placed greater restrictions on hunting and stiffer fines for violations on out-of-state residents than residents of the state (Act 1878). In the case of *Allen v. Wyckoff*, William Allen contended the statute was unconstitutional and an unwarranted exercise of legislative power. The lower courts and the Supreme Court of New Jersey ruled against him (*William L. Allen v. Lewis C. Wyckoff* 1886).

Comprehensive Bird Legislation and Enforcement

THE LACEY ACT

As the legal challenges to state game laws grew more common, it was clear that more comprehensive legislation was needed. Consequently, senators crafted legislation to help curb the trade in birds. Thus in 1898, Senator George Hoar of Massachusetts introduced a bill in Congress aimed at preventing plumes from being imported or shipped into or sold in the United States. Hoar's bill prompted the *Millinery Trade Review* to call on its members to fight the measure vigorously; the bill was defeated. The American Ornithological Union did not support Hoar's bill either, because the organization thought that some factions of the bird-protection movement were being overly zealous in promoting it (Graham 1990: 22).

However, two years later the American Ornithological Union, the Audubon Society, the Boone and Crockett Club, the League of American Sportsmen, and several other conservation organizations worked with Congressman Lacey, to pass the first federal bird-protection legislation—the Lacey Act of 1900. The Lacey Act, which was similar to the bill Hoar tried to pass, had three main goals. First, the bill permitted the secretary of agriculture to authorize the introduction and restoration of game, song, and insectivorous birds in some parts of the country where species were endangered or nearing extinction. Second, the bill sought to foil the introduction of foreign birds or animals; and third, it supplemented state bird-protection laws (Fox 1981: 148–153; U.S. House of Representatives 1900: 1–3).

The bill was intended to halt the interstate movement of illegal bird and game and deal with the question of interstate commerce that had been the subject of many lawsuits. Framers of the bill argued that state laws were being evaded by hunters and that bird and game were being killed and shipped across state lines to be sold on the open market. Because state laws had no extraterritorial force, federal legislation was needed. The Lacey Act prohibited the interstate commerce in game and birds killed or caught in violation of local laws. It also made any game imported into a state subject to that state's laws. The bill gave wardens the power to confiscate illegal game and birds and make arrests (U.S.

House of Representatives 1900: 1–3). Violators could be fined up to two hundred dollars for each violation of the act. The Lacey Act also banned the importation of foreign wild animals or birds by anyone without a special permit from the Department of Agriculture (Lacey Act 1900: 187–189). The act permitted the importation of specimens for museums and scientific collections. To help enforce the Lacey Act, many Audubon Society members patrolled local markets in the hopes of spotting illegal merchandise (Doughty 1975: 109; Trefethen 1975: 129–133).

CHALLENGING THE LACEY ACT

The passage of the Lacey Act did not stop the legal challenges to game laws. Several cases raised questions about the relationship between the Lacey Act and the various state game laws. For example, Jacob Bootman and his partners were charged with possession of about forty-eight thousand wild birds during the closed season of 1901. The group was fined almost $1.2 million for violating the law. Bootman took the case to court, arguing that the birds in question were hunted legally and imported into New York from other states during the open season. The state argued that the passage of the Lacey Act made the game subject to New York's game laws once the game was brought into the state. The Court of Appeals overturned the lower court ruling and dismissed the charges against the defendants, arguing that though the state's Forest, Fish and Game Law and the Lacey Act were both passed in 1900, the state law was passed first, thus the game in question was legally killed and imported into New York. In addition, the Buffalo Fish Company decision (also decided in 1900, and discussed in further detail below), which ruled that the states could not prohibit people from importing into their jurisdictions fish caught legally in a foreign country, gave legal support to the defendant's actions. The judges ruled that the Lacey Act, which would have made the imported birds subject to New York's game laws, did not apply, since the act was passed after the state's game law. The judges also argued that the New York game law was a very punitive statute and therefore had to be construed narrowly (*Forest, Fish, and Game Law* 1900; Lacey Act 1900: 187–189; *People v. Bootman* 1904; *People v. Buffalo* 1900).

August Silz's challenge to the New York game law eventually went to the U.S. Supreme Court. In March 1905, August Silz and his partner, John Hill, had imported birds in their possession during the closed season. They imported the birds legally through the U.S. customs. Silz and Hill argued that because the imported game was not subject to the state's game laws, they had committed no violations. The Supreme Court of New York agreed with them and ruled in their favor (*People v. Hesterberg* 1905). Silz and Hill argued in the Court of

Appeals that the New York law applied solely to game shipped between states, not to game that was imported. They also argued that if the Congress allowed foreign game to be imported and duties collected on that importation, then it could not allow the property imported to be confiscated. The Court of Appeals ruled against Silz and Hill on the grounds that the New York game law was not unconstitutional, was applicable to imported game, and represented a valid exercise of the state's police powers. The Lacey Act stipulates that imported game was subject to state laws and it is the citizen's responsibilities to avoid violating local laws. Silz and Hill were remanded to custody (*People v. Hesterberg* 1906). The case went to the U.S. Supreme Court, and the high court upheld the decision of the Court of Appeals (*New York v. Hesterberg* 1908).

Questions arose about whether game bred in private parks was subject to the same rules as animals hunted in the wilds. Charles Dieterich owned and maintained a fenced park in Millbrook where he bred deer, which breed rapidly and have to be culled annually. The only market for the venison was in New York City, and the only express company operating between Millbrook and the city was the American Express Company. In 1904, the game commissioner advised the American Express Company that venison from deer bred in captivity could be transported by the company as long as it was clearly marked. However, in 1906, the game commissioner reversed himself, on the pretext that since the law did not address the issue directly, the company could not transport the venison. When the American Express Company refused to take venison from Dieterich, he sued the company. The case was originally dismissed, but Dieterich appealed. The Court of Appeals of New York ruled in Dieterich's favor, arguing that the game commissioner had made the right decision in 1904—that the Forest, Fish and Game Law did not apply to venison from deer raised in captivity. The court ruled further that if the venison is clearly marked, there is no reason to prohibit the transportation and sale of such meat during the open season (*Charles Dieterich v. Fargo* 1909).

THE UNDERWOOD TARIFF ACT

Activists secured passage of three other significant pieces of bird-protection legislation in the early twentieth century. In 1913, the Underwood Tariff Act stopped the importation of feathers of foreign wild birds into the United States. That same year, the Migratory Bird Act helped to limit the species available for trade in the United States and Canada. In 1916, the Treaty with Great Britain was signed; this further constrained the market in feathers and birds (Doughty 1975: 83, 125–131; Underwood Tariff Act 1913; Act of July 2, 1916: 755–757). The Migratory Bird Treaty Act of 1918 implemented the 1916 Convention between the United States and Great Britain (signing on behalf of Canada) that was aimed at protecting migratory birds. Employees of the Department of Agriculture were empowered to enforce the act and arrest anyone violating it (Act of July 2, 1916: 755–757; Migratory Bird Treaty Act 1918).

Enforcement of the bird-protection legislation led to the confiscation of personal property. This burden fell heavily on women. Wealthy women weren't amused when customs agents confiscated their hats, boas, belts, and other personal items decorated with birds or feathers that they wore or brought home from trips abroad (Doughty 1975: 132–133, 145–146; Pearson 1937: 267). Despite passage and some enforcement of bird legislation, merchants were able to exploit loopholes in the laws and bring feathers to market. For instance, the 1913 Tariff Act allowed merchants to continue using any plumage secured before the passage of the act to be sold legally and were given six years to deplete their exempted inventory. In addition, feathers intended for use as fishing flies or for scientific use were not restricted. Hence, merchants continued to import feathers under the guise that they were being used for fly-fishing or scientific purposes (Doughty 1975: 147–149, 154).

THE MILLINERS OPPOSE BIRD-PROTECTION BILLS

The Audubon Society and the millinery industry continued to trade blows in the ongoing feud over birds. A lot was at stake for the milliners. In 1909, the trade in plumes amounted to $3 million a year in New York alone. Estimates of the number of birds killed annually for the millinery industry ran as high as 300 million. At the same time, however, the market for artificial feathers, flowers, and hat trimmings was around $50 million annually; three-fourths of this business was conducted in New York (Haskin 1909: 4; *New York Times* 1909c: 4).

The Eastern Millinery Association and the National Fancy Feathers Association fought the new bird-protection bills vigorously. They reiterated the argument that the Audubon's actions would ruin the industry and cost thousands of women working in the millinery industry their jobs. The Audubon's aggressive actions also made the organization vulnerable to the charge that they had become the fashion police, dictating what women should wear. As a result, William Dutcher and other prominent Audubon Society leaders began to respond to this charge during the 1910 campaign to pass bills aimed at stopping the sale and use of plumage of most birds. Dutcher denied the claim in some newspaper reports that the Radcliffe Bill, passed by the New Jersey House of Representatives, would make wearing aigrettes a misdemeanor (*Christian Science Monitor* 1910: 9; *New York Times* 1910a: 1; 1910b: 5). He also stressed that "the Audubon Society does not now nor has it ever attempted to interfere with the personal liberty of women ... It has confined itself to educating them to the horrors of bird slaughter for millinery use" (*New York Times* 1910b: 5; see also *New York Times* 1910c: 8). Andrew Meloy, vice president of the Long Island Game Protective Association, made a similar argument soon after the Shea Bill passed in New York (Meloy 1910: 10; see also *New York Times* 1910d: 9).

Even though the Audubon Society did not pay much attention to the actions of sport hunters, by the early 1900s some viewed the Audubon Society as a radical organization that threatened the sport. Even T. Gilbert Pearson, the new president of the Audubon Society, thought the Audubon had gone too far in attacking sport hunting and went to great lengths to highlight the wildlife-protection work of hunters like Grinnell, Brewster, Chapman, Dutcher, and Theodore Roosevelt. He argued that the antihunting brigade in the organization had made no such contributions (Graham 1990: 76–77). This internal rift weakened the effectiveness of the organization somewhat.

Fish Protection Legislation

American fish-conservation efforts date back to the early eighteenth century. Civic leaders were concerned about the fishing practices or urban residents, so in 1734 New York City passed an ordinance to restrict fishing in the Fresh Water Pond (the Collect) to "angling with angle-rod, hook, and line" (Goodspeed 1939: 30). Despite the ordinance, New Yorkers conserved neither the pond nor the fish over the long haul (Anbinder 2001: 14–15; Burrows and Wallace 1999: 32–33).

Other northeasterners passed fish protection laws as well. In 1788, residents living on the Upper Connecticut River in New Hampshire petitioned the legislature to halt the destructive commercial fishing activities at Bellows Falls. Similar petitions elsewhere in the region resulted in statewide regulations aimed at protecting shad and salmon on the Connecticut and Merrimack Rivers. In the early 1800s, New Englanders initiated other fish-conservation efforts. Communities concentrated on fish propagation, stocking, migration routes, and breeding grounds. Hence, in 1803, residents of Damariscotta, Maine, stocked a local pond with alewives and constructed a stone fishway through a previously inaccessible section of stream that emptied into the ocean. The town also appointed a Fish Committee to oversee matters. A century later, the Damariscotta River was the largest producer of alewives in New England. Several towns in Maine developed similar programs by stocking ponds with pickerel (Judd 1997: 50, 125).

In 1822, Daniel Webster introduced a bill in the Massachusetts legislature stating that trout could be caught only with hook and line. Webster's bill became law (Reiger [1975] 2001: 16–17). Because local towns still managed their fisheries, they also promulgated laws to protect their resources. Hence, in 1824, residents of Lincoln, Massachusetts, petitioned the legislature to pass a law prohibiting anglers from using more than one hook at a time in any of the town's ponds. Soon residents of other New England towns passed laws banning the use of multiple hooks and prohibiting out-of-towners from fishing in local ponds (Judd 1997: 51–53).

In 1829, a new journal—the *American Turf Register and Sporting Magazine*—began to publish angling news and information. George Gibson, who angled near Carlisle, Pennsylvania, wrote one of the magazine's earliest articles on trout fishing. Gibson expressed his concerns about the disappearing fish and the practice of netting, which he thought depleted stocks more rapidly. He mentioned a closed season for trout and advocated greater protection for fish (Reiger [1975] 2001: 17–18).

The concern of sport anglers about netting and other commercial methods of catching fish led to the formation of angling clubs such as the Cincinnati Angling Club, formed in 1830. Twenty-four prominent citizens of the state, including the governor, belonged to this club, which campaigned against commercial netters operating on the Great and Little Miami Rivers. Despite its success at curbing the activities of netters, the club was dormant by 1854 (Greve 1904: 651; Reiger [1975] 2001: 18).

Other notable fish-conservation activists include Frank Forester, who promoted fish-stocking programs to extend the quantity and range of game fish (Forester 1851, 1859). The work of George Perkins Marsh was also important in making people more aware of the need for fish conservation. Marsh, the fish commissioner of Vermont, was asked by the state to study the reasons for fish decline. Marsh's 1857 report linked fish decline to overfishing, angling during the spawning season, water pollution from sawmills, deforestation, and erosion that polluted and clogged streams (Marsh 1857: 8–15). Marsh's report is seen as a precursor to his seminal 1864 book, *Man and Nature*. Another important book published in 1864 was *The American Angler's Book*, by Thaddeus Norris. Like Marsh, Norris discussed environmental factors that contributed to fish decline, such as netting, dams, and industrial pollution (Norris 1864: 459–460).

Because local authorities were the main actors in developing fish-conservation laws, by 1869 there were literally hundreds of fish laws on the books in each state. Hence during the 1860s, states attempted to develop statewide laws. In 1867,

Vermont developed state codes that established closed seasons on various species of fish and regulated certain kinds of fishing equipment and stocking practices. The game commissioners were also granted the authority to close ponds when necessary (Judd 1997: 145–147, 174). In the 1870s the federal government also began to take an interest in fisheries. The U.S. Commission of Fish and Fisheries was formed in 1871; it later merged with the U.S. Fish and Wildlife Service (Reiger [1975] 2001: 28).

CHALLENGING THE STATES'
POWER TO REGULATE FISHERIES

As it became clear that dams were disrupting the passage of fish in waterways, many jurisdictions passed ordinances requiring dam owners to build passageways for the fish. In 1709, for example, Massachusetts passed a law prohibiting the construction of dams that hindered the passage of fish. Existing dams were grandfathered, so in 1746 a new law was passed that required sluiceways on all dams. Despite these laws, people continued to build dams that hindered the migration of fish in streams. Hence in 1789 the towns of Staughton, Sharon, and Canton passed an ordinance that required owners of dams on the Neponset River to modify the dams to provide passage for the fish over or around the barricades. Private dam owners were assessed three-fourths of the cost of modifying the dams. Edmund Baker and Daniel Vose challenged the ordinance, and the Supreme Court of Massachusetts ruled in their favor. Baker and Vose did not object to the idea of providing fish passages, only to the fact that they were not given enough time to alter their dam and that the town committee sent in their own contractor to construct the sluiceway. Consequently, they refused to pay their portion of the repair cost. The Supreme Court of Massachusetts noted that, in the public interest, a "reasonable and sufficient passage-way should be allowed for the fish" and the government had the right to erect such fish passages on the defendant's property. Nonetheless, they ruled in favor of Baker and Vose because they thought the defendants should have been given more time to do the job (*Inhabitants* 1808).

Similar laws were passed and cases were filed in New York and Maine (Act 1800; Judd 1997: 145; *People v. Platt* 1819; *Shaw v. Crawford* 1813; *Statute* 1801). For instance, in 1818 Zephaniah Platt was charged with maintaining a dam that obstructed the passage of salmon up the River Saranac. Platt took his case to court, and the Supreme Court of New York ruled in his favor. The judges argued that Platt had private ownership of the river above the dam, so there was no public right to take fish above the dam. As a result, he could not be forced to build a sluiceway to ensure the passage of fish over the dam (*People v. Platt* 1819).

Despite the many court rulings stipulating that legislative bodies had the power to regulate the taking of fish or pass laws to protect fish, people continued to challenge such laws late into the nineteenth century. As fish stocks dwindled, ordinances were passed to establish closed seasons. This prompted a new round of lawsuits. For instance, Elliott Gentile challenged an 1867 Indiana law that outlawed the catching of fish in any waters in the state for two years. After that there was an annual closed season and violators were fined (Act 1867). The Supreme Court of Indiana decided that the state had the power to pass such a law to regulate fishing within its boundaries (*Gentile v. the State* 1868).

FISHING REGULATIONS AND INTERSTATE COMMERCE

Laws were also passed to ban the interstate shipment of fish. In *Territory v. Evans*, Thomas Evans was charged with violating an 1890 Idaho law that banned the export of fish from the territory. The case examined the question of whether states had the power to regulate commerce across state lines. The Supreme Court of Idaho argued that the statute prohibiting the interstate shipment of articles of commerce was unconstitutional (*Territory v. Evans* 1890).

A similar case was heard in the Arkansas courts in 1892 with different results. The case arose when Mr. Organ, a steamboat operator, was charged with transporting a barrel of fish illegally from Arkansas to Tennessee in violation of an 1889 Arkansas statute. Organ argued that the Arkansas statute was unconstitutional since only Congress had the power to regulate interstate commerce. The Supreme Court of Arkansas ruled against Organ, arguing that game laws may indirectly affect interstate commerce without impinging on congressional prerogative (*Organ v. State* 1892).

In 1894, the Minnesota courts decided a case questioning whether the state's fish and game preservation statutes of 1891 and 1893 interfered with interstate commerce. Minnesota's statutes were crafted similarly to those in Arkansas. The Northern Pacific Express Company was charged with intent to ship fish caught in Minnesota out of the state. The Supreme Court of Minnesota ruled against Northern Pacific Express, arguing that the Minnesota statute was constitutional (*State of Minnesota v. Northern Pacific* 1894).

The case of the Buffalo Fish Company challenged another aspect of the Interstate Commerce Clause. This case challenged an 1892 New York law that forbade anyone from possessing specified fish during the closed season. The law applied to fish taken from waters in the state as well as those imported from a foreign country (*Fisheries* 1892). The Buffalo Fish Company was charged with having fish during the closed season in violation of the state statute.

The company argued in court that the fish in question were freshwater fish caught legally in Ontario and Manitoba, Canada, purchased from dealers and imported into the United States through the customs department. The company paid duties on the fish to import them. The company argued that the state's attempts to charge it with violating its statutes interfered with the commerce clause. The judges argued that the New York statute was valid when construed reasonably and fairly with reference to its purpose and object. The Court of Appeals upheld a lower court ruling in favor of the defendant. The judges argued that Congress had permitted the company to import the fish into the country and the company had complied with federal regulations and paid applicable dues. However, once the fish were imported into New York, state authorities stepped in to forbid the company from possessing and selling the fish. This created a direct conflict between federal and state regulations. When this occurs, federal regulations have supremacy over the state regulations. The justices stated further that the state had no power to extend its police powers to the transaction and no right to forbid what the Congress had expressly permitted (*People v. Buffalo* 1900).

The Lacey Act was going through Congress at the time the Buffalo Fish Company case was being argued. Supporters of the act crafted it to respond to the decision. Consequently, the Lacey Act stipulated that imported bird, fish, or game was subject to the game laws of the state into which it was imported (Lacey Act 1900: 187–189).

REGULATING COASTAL FISHERIES

States also began to regulate the way fish were caught. In 1886 Massachusetts passed a law that prohibited anglers from drawing, setting, or stretching "any drag net, set net or gill net, purse or sweep seine of any kind for taking fish" in coastal waters (Act 1886). Arthur Manchester challenged this statute when he was charged with illegally setting a purse seine in Buzzard's Bay. He was convicted and fined one hundred dollars. The Supreme Court affirmed the lower court ruling, arguing that the state's attempt to protect the fisheries in its bays was constitutional (*Manchester v. Massachusetts* 1891).

Eliminating the Markets for Wildlife

During the wildlife-protection campaigns, conservationists accomplished several goals: they developed effective framing of the message; educated themselves and the public about wildlife slaughter; identified villains and directed their campaigns toward them; developed policies, laws, and enforcement mechanisms to curb wildlife destruction; and heavily regulated the market for birds and game. They attacked the market for wildlife trade along the whole supply chain.

However, in the discourse about market hunters, conservationists lumped all kinds of market transactions into one category. Hence the poor rural hunter who killed a few animals per week and might have a few pounds of extra meat to trade on the market for cash was considered and characterized the same way as large-scale market hunters like Buffalo Bill, Orlando Brown, and Josiah Mooar, who killed scores of buffalo per day. Such commercial hunters took a few marketable parts and left most of the animal to rot. Although conservationists used different terms to distinguish between pot and market hunters, the two groups were demonized in similar ways in conservation discourses. Once the pot hunter entered the market exchange system, he or she was treated in the same fashion as the large-scale game killers, because most conservationists did not distinguish between the magnitudes of market transactions that pot and market hunters engaged in.

The development of the game commissions and the warden system was one of the most effective tools conservationists used to curb the trade in wildlife. Activists effectively framed the problem as one of wanton market and pot hunters running amok, depleting the game while leaving little or none for the sport hunter. To establish this view, sportsmen journals such as *Forest and Stream* and *In the Open* published articles alerting readers to the threat of market hunting. An editorial printed in a Pennsylvania journal in 1912 opined: "It is evident that so long as city dealers hold out temptation to the poor mountaineers and the country boys in the shape of alluring prices for grouse and quail, that the birds will be both shot and trapped in violation of law, and that the only way to stop the traffic is to have sufficient wardens to watch for illegal shipments and sales of game" (*In the Open* 1912: 45). Another article in the journal declared, "The law is being violated every day in the mountain sections and will continue to be violated until such time as the mountaineers are made to feel its power" (*In the Open* 1912: 28).

The call for enforcement was so ubiquitous and the warden system so popular that by 1911, thirty-four states required hunting licenses. The hunting licenses generated a cash windfall that was used to develop the game commissioners' offices and provide for salaried wardens. For instance, in 1913 Pennsylvania game commissioners took in three hundred thousand dollars from the sale of hunting licenses (Warren 1997: 57).

Elite sportsmen were willing to buy hunting licenses because they knew the money went to fund the game commissioners and wardens who protected the game and monitored and prosecuted those violating the game laws. The warden system provided some assurance that there would be game for the sportsmen to hunt after they purchased a license. Conservationists were able to get the cooperation of the rural gentry in this scheme because when farmers objected to paying for a license to hunt, the game laws were amended to allow them to hunt on their own property without paying a fee. Farmers did not lose out on the opportunity to generate cash from wildlife either: they were allowed to charge hunters to hunt on their property. While the game laws made it difficult, if not impossible, to kill and sell the meat of wildlife on the open market, farmers were buffered from any cash shortfalls by being able to charge others for the hunting opportunities they provided. Thus the development of the game laws represented a shift from market hunters being able to trade the game they killed for cash to the state and private landholders being able to trade the opportunity to hunt wildlife for a fee (Warren 1997: 55–60).

Hence conservationists effectively eliminated the wildlife market in which the poor and rich could generate cash from game animals and replaced it with one in which the state and private landowners could generate cash by trading in the opportunity to hunt and fish. In creating the new game market, conservationists did not interfere with the activities of private sports clubs. For decades private sports clubs traded in the wildlife market by providing hunting privileges to members or selling licenses to hunters and helping to provide targets to hunt. Such market transactions escaped the scrutiny and reform efforts of the conservationists. Similarly, the segment of the wildlife market that dealt in the manufacture of arms and hunting gear largely escaped the scrutiny of the conservationists.

Debt, Arms Manufacturers, and Ties to Conservation Organizations

The relationship between conservationists and businesspeople isn't always acrimonious. Though groups like the Audubon Society and the American Ornithological Union locked horns with the milliners, conservation groups developed a cozy relationship with gun manufacturers. While no one challenged this at first, by the 1920s the ties between gun manufacturers and conservation groups had become very contentious. The remainder of this chapter will examine the relationship between gun manufacturers and two influential conservation organizations that were forced to deal with this issue publicly: the Audubon Society and the Izaak Walton League.

The Audubon Society, like the other major conservation organizations, got much of its funding from wealthy individuals and corporations. Nonetheless, debt plagued some of the organizations, and that led them to accept funding from corporate moguls and gun manufacturers. Though the Audubon received a generous contribution from George Vanderbilt in 1902, it was heavily in debt two years later. The organization received a donation from John Thayer in 1904, but its financial woes continued. Thayer, who came from a family of wealthy financiers, was an Audubon board member and one of the wealthiest men in New England (Fox 1981: 154; Orr 1992: 145). That same year, the organization was bailed out by a wealthy New York merchant and insurance broker, Albert Willcox, who paid off all the Audubon's debt and promised it money in his will if the organization agreed to be incorporated as a national association working not only for the protection of birds but also for the benefit of useful mammals. He also stipulated that the organization should use the gift for fundraising purposes, not for general operating expenses. When Willcox died a few years later, his brother, David, president of the Delaware and Hudson Coal Company, allowed the Audubon to take its share of the estate (almost $333,000) in 1907. Despite the large gift, the organization ran an $8,000 deficit a year later. Though Mrs. Russell Sage, whose husband was a financier, donated $15,500 to the Audubon in 1910 to conduct public education campaigns in the South and to establish a fund to protect robins, the organization was still mired in debt (Fox 1981: 154; *Los Angeles Times* 1907b: 112; *New York Times* 1907: 9; 1910e: 1).

In 1911, Harry Leonard, vice president of the Winchester Repeating Arms Company, approached the Audubon's secretary, T. Gilbert Pearson, and tried to woo him away from the Audubon to head a new conservation organization Winchester was planning to start. As company representatives put it, Winchester was interested in slowing the slaughter of wildlife because the company felt that "as the game decreases our business grows less." Winchester promised to assign sales agents to the new organization to enroll new members. Pearson, who had assumed the responsibilities of the ailing Audubon president William Dutcher, declined the offer but suggested that Winchester find out whether other gun manufacturers were interested in supporting conservation efforts. If they were, they should pool their resources and give the money to the Audubon instead. Soon several gun manufacturers offered the Audubon a combined $25,000 a year for five years. Leonard also suggested in the gift letter to the Audubon that Pearson's salary be increased from $3,000 to $6,000 annually. The gun company donation doubled the organization's annual operating budget, and the Audubon accepted it. Since the organization had already accepted funding from an ammunition manufacturer—the U.S. Cartridge Company—in the past without controversy, the new gun company money did not seem problematic (Dutcher 1906, 1907; Dwight 1911; Fox 1981: 155–156; Graham 1990: 20–23, 45–47, 87–89; Grinnell 1911a, 1911b; Orr 1992: 94, 140–145, 160, 210–212, 223–230; Pearson 1937; Trefethen 1975: 135–136, 177–179).

Pearson brought the matter to the board, and six of them voted to accept the gift, while three wanted to reject the offer.[1] On hearing about the gift, prominent activists such as George Shields, Andrew Meloy, William Hornaday, and Henry Fairfield Osborn publicly expressed their objections to it (*New York Times* 1911b: 11; 1911c: 3; 1911d: 6). Critics argued that the gun manufacturers had approached other prominent conservationists and officers of sportsmen's clubs (for instance, Hornaday, Meloy, and Shields) with similar offers and were rejected. Hornaday produced a letter showing previous attempts by the gun manufacturers to strike a deal with him and Meloy. Shields indicated that he too was approached and turned down the gun manufacturers' offer. These critics claimed (and the letter Hornaday produced indicated) that in exchange for their donations, gun companies expected that any organization taking funds from them would not advocate for legislation that would ban the use of automatic guns in hunting. Critics argued that the gun manufacturers' gift to the Audubon was intended to buy the organization's silence on the question of automatic or pump guns. Opponents also pointed out that though several organizations, such as the New York Zoological Society, League of American Sportsmen, and the New York State Forest, Fish and Game League (of which Hornaday, Shields, and Meloy were leaders), had been actively fighting the use of pump guns for hunting, the Audubon had not joined the campaign. Groups opposed the use of automatic guns because such guns could kill vastly more birds and other wildlife than conventional guns and were already being used by market hunters. Another critic, Chapman, also argued that such a large donation earmarked for work on game birds would divert the organization from its traditional mission of protecting songbirds (*New York Times* 1911b: 11; 1911c: 3).

The Audubon responded to the critics by stating emphatically that the gun manufacturers' gift was unconditional and by publishing excerpts from a letter the board sent to the gun manufacturers, which stated, "It is expressly understood the acceptance of this fund does not commit the National Association [Audubon] to any policy for or against the use of any particular gun" (*New York Times* 1911d: 6). One board member who voted in favor of the gift pointed out that the Audubon was not on record as saying it opposed automatic guns (*New York Times* 1911d: 6). However, Hornaday published excerpts from a

1906 letter in which Dutcher wrote, "I beg officially to state that the National Associations of Audubon Societies is absolutely opposed to either the manufacture, sale, or use of such firearms, and therefore, hope that the meritorious bill introduced by the New York Zoological Society will become a law" (*New York Times* 1911e: 10).

Audubon board members also indicated that though Leonard's letter suggested a salary increase for Pearson, the board voted for the increase not because it was suggested by Leonard, but because Pearson had worked hard on behalf of the organization (*New York Times* 1911d: 6). The Audubon Society also received hundreds of letters from indignant members and friends of the association objecting to the funding from the gun manufacturers. As a result, two weeks after receiving the gift, the organization called a special meeting at which they decided to return the gun manufacturers' money (*New York Times* 1911c: 3; 1911f: 12; *Washington Post* 1911: 5). After the Audubon returned their donation, the gunmakers wrote a scathing article in the *New York Times* stating that Hornaday was prone to error and accused him of thwarting the plan for starting a game-protection division in the Audubon. According to the article, Hornaday's actions prevented the Audubon from carrying out "the most comprehensive and practical movement for real game protection ever conceived" (Winchester Repeating Arms Company 1911: 12).

The gun companies responded by forming their own conservation group—the American Game Protective Association. Despite the controversy surrounding its founding, leading Audubon activists got involved with the new organization. For instance, Grinnell suggested John Burnham,[2] deputy commissioner of the fish and game division of the state of New York, for the presidency of the organization. In addition, several prominent Audubon members, such as Grinnell, C. Hart Merriam, William Brewster, John Thayer, and the author John Burroughs, joined the American Game Protective Association. The American Game Protective Association modeled itself on the Audubon and adopted many of its objectives, such as protecting insectivorous birds and wildlife refuges, developing uniform game laws, prohibiting the sale of native game, and supporting bag limits. In addition, Theodore Roosevelt endorsed the American Game Protective Association, and Grinnell worked diligently to strengthen relations between the American Game Protective Association and the Boone and Crockett Club. Grinnell rationalized his actions by arguing that the gun manufacturers were trying to protect game so that their customers would have targets to hunt. Grinnell indicated that as long as the game was protected, how it was used did not matter (Fox 1981: 156; Graham 1990: 88–89; Orr 1992: 232; Trefethen 1975: 150–151).

Because the organizations shared members who had influential positions in both organizations, the Audubon and the American Game Protective Association worked together on the passage of the Weeks-McLean Bill in 1913 and on other campaigns. The bill attempted to regulate hunting seasons and protect some species. Henry Ford, an avid birder, supported the bill. He also urged his six hundred car dealerships to write letters of support to their congressional representatives. After intense political maneuvering, the bill was signed by President Taft in 1913 (Fox 1981: 157; Graham 1990: 91–93; Trefethen 1975: 152–153).

BIRD FIGHT: THE AUDUBON ON EDGE

An Unexpected Challenge. Thirty-four years after women revived the Audubon, another woman, Rosalie Edge, challenged the organization's policies and practices. However, this time the reformer did not target women to get them to change their behavior; instead she challenged men, along with the core Audubon values and practices, and forced the resignation of one of the society's most influential presidents. As the 1920s drew to a close, some members of the Audubon Society and other environmental groups grew increasingly uncomfortable with the relationship between environmental organizations and gun manufacturers. In 1929, Willard Gibbs Van Name, an accomplished field ornithologist, Audubon member, and curator of marine invertebrates at the American Museum, published a pamphlet titled *Crisis in Conservation*. The document criticized unnamed conservation groups for their problematic alliances and "deplorable and astonishing indifference to bird destruction and extermination." He warned nature lovers that if they believed the "self-congratulatory reports of bird-protection organizations," then they would be in for a "rude awakening" when they learned about the state of wildlife protection in America (Edge 1999; R. L. Taylor 1948: 31–45).[3] The pamphlet listed some species as very hard to find, sixteen species as "possibly within the realm of saving," ten species as "more or less in danger," and several others as "beyond saving" (Edge 1999).

Rosalie Edge, born in 1877 into a wealthy Gramercy Park family, grew up birding in the Ramble in Central Park. Before she and her husband separated, she also birded at their four-acre Long Island home. She was an avid birder, life member of the Audubon, prosperous New York socialite, and activist in the suffragist movement who got a copy of Van Name's pamphlet while traveling with her two children in Paris. On receiving it, she packed and returned to New York immediately. She arrived in the city in September 1929, and that year the Audubon's annual meeting was held in late October, a few days after Black Friday on the New York Stock Exchange. The annual meetings, which

242 ◆ Chapter 8

were usually held at the American Museum of Natural History, were informal gatherings where new members were elected to the board of directors, officers made speeches, a movie was shown, and luncheon was served. The meetings were attended almost exclusively by the Audubon staff; members rarely attended. Consequently, Edge created quite a kerfuffel when she showed up late and unexpectedly, seated herself in the front of the room, and demanded a response to Van Name's pamphlet. The officers, who had earlier decided that the document was not worthy of discussion, had considered the matter closed. Edge's questions sparked a heated exchange between her and T. Gilbert Pearson, Frank Chapman, and Robert Cushman Murphy. Edge reported that Pearson expressed his dissatisfaction with her because her interruptions spoiled the meeting (Edge 1999; R. L. Taylor 1948: 31–45).

The Formation of the Emergency Conservation Committee. Determined to continue her fight, Edge founded the Emergency Conservation Committee in 1930. It remained active until Edge died in 1962. The management of the American Museum—which had strong ties to the leaders of the Audubon Society—ordered Van Name to refrain from making public attacks on the Audubon, so he criticized the organization in publications distributed by the Emergency Conservation Committee. At first the Emergency Conservation Committee's office was located in the servant's sitting room of Edge's brownstone, but later it moved to a small office on Lexington Avenue. Davis Quinn (coauthor of *Crisis in Conservation*) served as secretary for a short time. Edge served as secretary from 1930 to 1933. From then on Edge gave herself the title of Chairman. Irving Brant, editor of the *Star Times*, a St. Louis newspaper, was treasurer of the Emergency Conservation Committee for as long as it operated. William Hornaday was also affiliated with the Emergency Conservation Committee. The organization operated on an austere budget that did not exceed ten thousand dollars a year. It did not make general appeals for funds. However, a contribution slip was placed in every pamphlet distributed and supporters sent the group small donations. Over its lifetime, the Emergency Conservation Committee distributed over a million pamphlets (Edge 1999).

Disrupting Meetings and Proxy Fights. The Audubon tried to isolate Rosalie Edge and suppress her efforts to make institutional changes. However, she used the fact that most of the men in the organization did not take her seriously or were uncomfortable dealing with a female critic to her advantage. She used the Emergency Conservation Committee's publications to frame the issues. Shortly before the 1930 annual meeting, Irving Brant wrote and the Emergency

Conservation Committee distributed a new pamphlet: *Compromised Conservation, Can the Audubon Society Explain?* Edge also wrote a letter to the officers and directors of the Audubon demanding that they discuss the charges in *Compromised Conservation*. The pamphlet and letter detailed the relationship between the Audubon, sportsmen, and commercial sporting interests. The documents alleged that Pearson was catering to wealthy sportsmen and the gun companies and that the Audubon's actions and policies were too strongly influenced by these groups. The pamphlet and letter attacked what the Emergency Conservation Committee saw as too much overlap between the secretary of agriculture, the board of the Audubon, and leaders of the American Game Protective Association, the American Wildfowlers, the Campfire Club, and the Boone and Crockett Club. The Emergency Conservation Committee sought to weaken the ties between the Audubon and these groups (Edge 1999; *New York Times* 1930a: 11; *Time* 1930: 34).

The Emergency Conservation Committee documents also claimed that Pearson and the Audubon were opposing the establishment of permanent, inviolate bird refuges and instead advocating the development of "interchangeable refuges" that later would be used as public shooting grounds. Edge and the Emergency Conservation Committee also criticized the *Bulletin No. 6*[4] distributed to Audubon members; it opposed the proposal to reduce the daily bag limit on wild ducks to 15. Hornaday expressed agreement with the Emergency Conservation Committee's position, stating that the Audubon was guilty of bird slaughter in "supporting the organized and unorganized game hogs of North America in their excessive killing privileges" (quoted in *Time* 1930: 34; see also Edge 1999; Fox 1981: 177–179; *New York Times* 1930a: 11; 1930b: 17).

Emergency Conservation Committee activists also criticized the Audubon for being on both sides of many conservation issues. The Emergency Conservation Committee argued that "they [the Audubon] are on both sides, and they collect money from both sides, and the man at the head of the organization [Pearson] gets a percentage of what is collected." Since the 1911 incident with the gun manufacturers' donation to the Audubon specifying that Pearson's salary should be doubled, there had been a cloud of suspicion over Pearson's fundraising activities and salary. The issue of Pearson's salary emerged again in the 1930s. However, a few days before the annual meeting, Pearson responded, "I am sure that any criticism of the policies of the Audubon Society is due to a misapprehension of the facts by the critics. There is certainly nothing in them that could be objected to by fair-minded and unprejudiced persons" (*New York Times* 1930a: 11).

Hornaday and Edge went to the 1930 Audubon annual meeting and demanded a response to the Emergency Conservation Committee charges. In addition, Emergency Conservation Committee activists made a motion to elect Edge, Hornaday, and Van Name to the board of the Audubon instead of the nominees already on the ballot. The meeting was boisterous as Audubon leaders registered their objections to Edge and Hornaday's ideas and the Emergency Conservation Committee activists were soundly defeated in their bid to be elected (*Christian Science Monitor* 1930: 4; *New York Times* 1930b: 17). Pearson told those attending the meeting that the Audubon collaborated with sportsmen because they were the most energetic advocates of conservation. After hearing the Audubon leaders' objections to the proposed bag limits, Pearson put the matter to a vote. Once again, the Emergency Conservation Committee's proposal was voted down. The Audubon Society's secretary, Robert Cushman Murphy, also addressed what he described as the "fallacies circulated" about Pearson's salary. Murphy explained that Pearson got a fixed salary (of $6,000) and the remainder of his salary varied with the organization's budget, but his total salary had not exceeded $14,500 (*New York Times* 1930b: 17).

Even though most of the Emergency Conservation Committee's motions were rejected, the Audubon did decide to create an independent three-man committee to investigate the organization's activities. The committee was composed of Chauncey Hamlin of Buffalo; Alexander Ruthven, president of the University of Michigan; and Thomas Barbour, director of the Harvard University Museum (*Christian Science Monitor* 1930: 4; *New York Times* 1930b: 17).

After the meeting Edge decided to distribute Emergency Conservation Committee publications to the entire Audubon membership. Since fewer than 150 members attended the annual meeting, Edge wanted to get more members involved in the decision making. She asked for the Audubon's mailing list, which had about twenty thousand names on it, but her request was denied. Edge asked the American Civil Liberties Union for help. Roger Baldwin, its director, was sympathetic to Edge's case and referred her to Charles Dickerman Williams, who took the case. A lawsuit was filed in June 1931. The central question in the case hinged on whether members of a voluntary, charitable organization like the Audubon had the same rights to the names and contact information of other members as the shareholders of a business have vis-à-vis other shareholders (Edge 1999; *New York Times* 1931a: 18). The court made it clear that the Audubon needed to show why the list could not be released to a member of the organization. During the hearing before Justice Carew of the Supreme Court of New York, the Audubon argued that they wanted to keep their mailing list private so as not to run the risk of annoying their members. The Audubon also argued that it had about eleven thousand members, not twenty thousand. The organization took the opportunity to refute Edge's claims that it promoted bag limits. Pearson also argued that the Audubon was withholding its list from Edge because of her attacks on the Biological Survey and the U.S. Department of Agriculture as well as the Audubon. Pearson also discussed his salary structure, explaining that in addition to his base salary, he got a commission on contributions brought into the organization; his commission for the preceding year had been $8,500 (*New York Times* 1931b: 18).

About two months before the 1931 meeting, the independent committee created a year earlier returned with its findings. The committee (which consisted only of Barbour and Hamlin because Ruthven withdrew) praised the Audubon's work. Referring to criticisms of the Audubon as a "long and rather turgid tirade," the committee said it was not worth the time to analyze and discuss the charges. They addressed the issue of bag limits and concluded that this problem was administrative, not executive. The committee also noted that George Sherwood, director of the American Museum of Natural History, had discredited the charges in the Emergency Conservation Committee pamphlet (*New York Times* 1931c: 14).

Edge did eventually get the Audubon's mailing list, and shortly before the annual meeting she sent out flyers urging members to attend the meeting or to send her proxies to vote on their behalf. The Audubon also collected proxies. Though fewer than one hundred people attended the 1931 annual meeting, Edge went to the meeting armed with 1,646 proxies, while the Audubon had 2,801. Edge and the Emergency Conservation Committee raised the same concerns they had raised a year earlier. Pearson responded by analyzing the contributions of the previous twenty-one years in his report. Pearson argued that 350,000 donations had been received, for a total receipt of $4 million. Of that amount, sportsmen's organizations had donated a total of $2,180, and gun manufacturers and powder makers had contributed $230. Pearson also discussed his salary and the sliding scale of base salary and commission put in place in 1925. He claimed that though the organization's income had grown in recent years, his salary had not exceeded $14,500. Once again, Edge and the Emergency Conservation Committee lost the vote on the motions they proposed (*Christian Science Monitor* 1931: 6; *New York Times* 1931d: 21). Though the Audubon characterized Edge and her supporters as a "zoophile cult," Edge's base of support could not be ignored (Fox 1981: 177–179).

Edge also scrutinized the Audubon's financial records, and her accountants discovered that between 1929 and 1932 the Audubon had received about $100,000 from the Rainey Wildlife Sanctuary in Louisiana. Hunters using the sanctuary were setting steel traps—sometimes baited with birds—to catch muskrats for their pelts. The payment was the Audubon's portion of the proceeds from the fees collected (Orr 1992: 131, 146; see also *Time* 1930: 34).[5] Over the years Edge built up a mailing list of about sixteen thousand wildlife enthusiasts. Edge published a pamphlet on the sanctuary issue and mailed it to Audubon members and her growing list of supporters. She also collected proxy votes for upcoming annual meetings. The Audubon prepared for the 1932 annual meeting by sending out nine thousand letters signed by Mrs. Theodore Roosevelt, Mrs. J. D. Rockefeller Jr., Mrs. Thomas A. Edison, and other notable women. The Audubon letter made reference to repeated attacks on the Audubon without mentioning Rosalie Edge or the Emergency Conservation Committee by name (*New York Times* 1932a: 36). The same scenario played out at this annual meeting as at the two previous ones: Edge lost the proxy vote. This time Edge had collected much fewer proxies than the previous year: she had 524 proxy votes, compared to the Audubon's 4,107. The Audubon also refused to stop the trapping on the Rainey Sanctuary (*New York Times* 1932b: 19; *Washington Post* 1932: 9).

Edge attended the 1934 annual meeting and continued to challenge the Audubon's policies and actions. However, the big news of the meeting was the resignation of T. Gilbert Pearson after twenty-four years at the helm of the organization.[6] Though Edge said her opposition to Pearson was not a battle directed against him personally, she acknowledged that she approved of the resignation. Edge believed the problems she identified in the Audubon were also rooted in the board, not just the president (*Christian Science Monitor* 1934: 4; *New York Times* 1934a: 21). In 1934, in addition to the resignation of its embattled president, the Audubon Society also stopped trapping in the Rainey Wildlife Sanctuary (Graham 1990: 102–105, 112–114; Trefethen 1975: 160).

By this time the Audubon was in trouble: its membership had plummeted to about 3,400. It should be noted, however, that the Audubon was not the only organization with a declining membership. The economic crisis brought on by the Great Depression affected membership in the Sierra Club and other conservation organizations too (Edge 1999; Fox 1981: 179–180; Graham 1990: 102–105, 112–114; Sierra Club 1960: 82–93; R. L. Taylor 1948: 31–45; Trefethen 1975: 160).

THE TIES THAT BIND

Irene Rood, Harriet Hemenway, Mabel Osgood Wright, Mary Fluker Bradford, and a host of other women revived the Audubon Society in the 1890s. However, they tended to elect men as the organizations' presidents and spokespersons. Even when they financed the organizations from their own funds, they remained in the background and took on the auxiliary roles. More than three decades later, Edge was different: she helped to transform the Audubon because she understood how to use her status and privilege to make the social and political changes desired. She did not work in the shadows of men. On the contrary, men did some of the behind-the-scenes work of the Emergency Conservation Committee, while Edge was its brainchild and unabashed spokesperson. All the aforementioned women had the cultural capital (Bourdieu 1977: 487–511; 1984, 1990) to penetrate and operate within the inner circle of male power and privilege. But Edge, shaped by the activism of the suffrage movement, was better placed to question the Audubon openly. These factors helped Edge to chart a different course and embrace the role of challenger (Lo 1992: 224–247). Because of her wealth, extensive travel, family background, organizational memberships, stature as a bird expert, and inability to take no for an answer, Edge demanded an opportunity to air her grievances. She was both an insider and an outsider. She used her insider's perspective (derived from her social class, life membership in the Audubon, and extensive knowledge of birds) to gain the information she needed, then used her outsider's role (a woman eschewing stereotypical female roles and her limited connections to wildlife networks) to raise questions about and critique the practices of the Audubon Society.

Edge also used her prior social movement experience in the suffragist movement to establish her position as an outsider or challenger. Edge mastered the art of framing. She had a simple and effective master frame (Taylor 2000: 508–580; 2010: 3–28) and rhetorically evoked themes of immorality and rectitude. She focused on the immorality of a conservation organization taking money from gun manufacturers. She also called attention to an organization getting money from practices that harmed the very birds it was supposed to be saving. She also called on the organization to change its ways by changing its ideology, internal structure, and practices.

The Izaak Walton League

Despite the growth in the number of conservation and preservation organizations during the late nineteenth and early twentieth centuries, most of these organizations and their members were in the northeast corridor. For instance in 1920, 72 percent of the Audubon's membership lived in New England, New York, New Jersey, and Pennsylvania. Most Boone and Crockett members lived in the Northeast, while Sierra Club members were primarily on the West Coast. However, a vibrant new organization arose in the Midwest that jolted the established conservation organizations (Fox 1981: 159–162; Trefethen 1975: 182–183).

WALTONISM AND THE CREATION OF A MASS FOLLOWING

In 1922, fifty-four anglers and hunters met for lunch at the Chicago Athletic Association. These middle-class sportsmen held business and professional jobs, but they were not connected to any of the major conservation or preservation groups. In March, they established the Izaak Walton League, and contributions flowed in from around the Midwest. Beginning in 1923, the League published *Outdoor America*, one of the most comprehensive conservation magazines of the time. The league's leader, Will Dilg, used his advertising background to brand and promote the group. He recruited members by framing his message around themes of manliness, conquest, nostalgia, nature worship, brotherhood, and a fraternal atmosphere of male bonding and fellowship. Members were encouraged to be raucous while camping and fishing. Appropriating the recruiting methods and style of the rapidly growing fraternal organizations, such as the Kiwanis and Rotary Clubs, and hiring an ex-Kiwanis office manager (and agents who recruited members for a commission), Dilg shaped a new type of conservation organization. The Izaak Walton League was organized to look like a fraternal order of anglers; it did not copy the style of any of the existing conservation or preservation organizations. The league appropriated the nineteenth-century language of manliness and used it to appeal to machismo rather than to genteel tastes (Fox 1981: 159–162; Trefethen 1975: 182–183).

During the 1920s, when the memberships of the Audubon, Sierra Club, and American Game Protective Association hovered around 10,000 or less, the membership of the Izaak Walton League was skyrocketing. By 1924, the organization had 1,200 chapters in forty-two states. The largest chapter (located in Kansas City) had 2,700 members. The organization reported having 160,000 members in 1926 at its fourth annual convention, and 3,000 chapters by 1927. The league, which began recruiting women to the organization heavily in 1926, knew there was potential to create a large organization. At the time, there was an estimated 10 million anglers in the country, and all indications were that the sport would continue to grow. From the outset, the Izaak Walton League attempted to create a conservation organization with a mass membership. It was not comprised of patricians or parvenus carefully guarding the membership. Though the Audubon Society had opened their membership to the public and its junior Audubon programs were popular, its adult membership was modest

(*Christian Science Monitor* 1926: 4A; J. M. Dickinson 1927: 23; Folds 1927: 32–33; Izaak Walton League 1928a: 44; *Los Angeles Times* 1924: 9; *New York Times* 1926: X18).

Modeling a new organization on the fraternal template was not too far-fetched. In fact, unions such as the Knights of Labor were organized like fraternal organizations. According to some estimates by the 1890s, fraternal organizations enrolled between one in five and one in eight American males (Clemens 1996: 216–217). The Izaak Walton League hoped to capitalize on the popularity of the fraternal model to help build their organization rapidly. Though the League was formed at a time when linking recreation and conservation politics was in vogue, the organization adopted a strategy that promoted cross-class male solidarity by creating apolitical settings where middle- and working-class men could bond (Izaak Walton League 1928b: 2, 40; Lammon 1937: 8–9). However, the promotion of cross-class male solidarity over political action were lines of tension that sent inconsistent messages to members of organizations adopting this model. For instance, the Knights of Labor would alternately advise their members to "let political parties and political clubs, of whatever name, severely alone"; at the same time, members were being urged to "organize, co-operate, educate until the stars and stripes wave over a contented and happy people" (Fink 1983: 24–25).

The fraternal model blurred lines of class and political conflicts on both the cultural and organizational levels. Consequently, elite and working-class men could boast membership in these organizations. The fraternal model enabled men of considerable social distance to view each other as brothers, thereby expressing their unified interests and common identity (Carnes 1989; Clawson 1989; Clemens 1996: 217; Izaak Walton League 1937: 8–9). Thus in 1937 "Dad" Lammon encouraged chapters to develop "a ritual or form of initiation ceremony." Chapters were encouraged to share their rituals or initiation ceremonies with other Waltonians. He thought some of the members, alienated by the "Ike beer parties," might find initiation rituals more interesting (Izaak Walton League 1937: 8–9).

The league tried to portray itself as an apolitical organization, but its actions and messages to members were ambiguous. On the one hand, Waltonian leaders engaged in conservation politics nationally and locally and urged their membership to be active, but on the other, they went to great lengths to show that the organization was a "nonpolitical" group that separated the political inclinations of individual members from those of the organization. For example, *Outdoor America* declared, "It should be understood once and for all, that *the Izaak Walton League has no political affiliations of any sort.* Distinguished men who are or have been officers or members of the League are regarded by Waltonians *entirely apart* from any political opinions or religious doctrines they may profess" (Izaak Walton League 1928c: 8, 25).

The league wanted members to abide by its policies on political involvement and its conservation agenda. Thus the organization called on members who were "involved politically" with the league or aligned against its policies to "come out flat footed and *state his position as for or against the League's one and only platform of Conservation*" (Izaak Walton League 1928b: 26, italics in original; 1928c: 25). The league also operated like a fraternal club or religious sect in its attempts to reprimand members for violating its code of conduct. The league stated outright that it "makes no apology for its advocacy of the decent, moderate and sportsmanlike killing of game." Hence, *Outdoor America* cursed "game hogs," publicized their wrongdoings, and promised to root out and disgrace offenders. One issue of the magazine proclaimed, "The League abhors game hogs and would punish them to the fullest extent." The article went on to say that when such members were found they were "treated with unsparing scorn" (Izaak Walton League 1928b: 26; 1928c: 25).

The league, which printed endorsements from presidents Coolidge and Hoover in its magazine, attracted members by framing its brand of conservation as "Waltonism"—a fervent moral "march" against the evils that threatened game, sport fishing, and hunting. Waltonians developed a map proclaiming "the conquest of Waltonism" that showed the spread of the league and its activities across the country (Izaak Walton League 1928c: 8). Waltonians were urged to recruit new members.[7] To encourage current members to recruit new ones, members were awarded bronze, silver, or gold watch fobs depending on how many new Waltonians they recruited or how many new chapters they started. In addition, the names (and sometimes pictures) of members receiving fobs were printed in *Outdoor America* under a list titled "Waltonian Merit Men." One member recruited 356 new members, and one new chapter opened with 233 people seeking membership (Folds 1927: 32–33; Izaak Walton League 1927: 2, 58, 74; 1928c: 2, 40, 51; 1928d: 2, 32; 1928e: 40).

THE IZAAK WALTON LEAGUE
AND THE ARMS MANUFACTURERS

The league did not stay out of conservation politics for long: wildlife controversies took center stage during the 1920s. As changes in the post–World War I economy brought shorter work weeks, more vacation time, more disposable income, increased housing construction, and more cars, migratory waterfowl and other wildlife faced increased threats from habitat loss, overexploitation, and pollution. In the early 1920s, the American Game Protective Association and other wildlife organizations tried to push a game refuge bill through Congress that would permit hunting on public lands. At the time, employees of gun manufacturers held prominent positions in the conservation organizations promoting this bill. For instance, in 1921 seven of the twelve members of the board of the American Game Protective Association were employed by gun and ammunition companies. That same year, 77 percent of the organization's income came from contributions made by the arms industry. Winchester, Remington, and Du Pont each contributed five thousand dollars (Fox 1981: 165).

The bill, drafted by John Burnham of the American Game Protective Association and E. W. Nelson of the Biological Survey,[8] proposed the development of a series of refuges located along the flyways of ducks, geese, and other migratory waterfowl. The refuges, which would be under the control of the Biological Survey, were to be used as public hunting grounds. The one-dollar-a-year hunting license was expected to fund the acquisition of additional land for the refuges and the administrative costs of the Biological Survey. At the time this bill was drafted, no hunting was allowed on existing federal refuges. Thus the new bill sought to redefine the nature and purpose of federal game refuges (Fox 1981: 164–169; Graham 1990: 111; Trefethen 1975: 182–185).

Some conservationists opposed the bill because of its provision allowing hunting on federal wildlife refuges, but groups such as the Audubon Society supported it. However, the bill was voted down in Congress each year it came up. This stalemate continued for several years, even as opinion polls showed that there was almost no public support for federal game refuges that allowed hunting. In addition, other suggestions to ease the wildlife crisis—like cutting bag limits in half (from twenty to ten ducks per day)—were not seriously considered. The bag-limit proposition was downplayed by the American Game Protective Association as it pressed vigorously for the passage of its own game refuge bill. Reducing bag limits ran counter to the interests of the gun companies funding the American Game Protective Association, as it could mean decreased sales of ammunition (Fox 1981: 164–169, 173; Graham 1990: 111; Trefethen 1975: 182–185).

It was Will Dilg who stepped forward with a bold plan to break the stalemate. In 1923, Dilg learned of plans to drain a three-hundred-mile stretch of Upper Mississippi bottomlands (in Minnesota, Iowa, Missouri, Wisconsin, and Illinois) to make way for development. This area served as the spawning grounds for bass and provided habitats for large numbers of birds. Dilg proposed that Congress appropriate $1.5 million to fund a wildlife refuge. Though he was given little chance of success, Dilg, with the backing of Izaak Walton League members and the General Federation of Women's Clubs, sought and received key congressional support. The following year Congress approved the proposal and President Coolidge signed it (*Christian Science Monitor* 1923: 6; Fox 1981: 164–169, 173; Graham 1990: 111; Izaak Walton League 1924a: 3; *New York Times* 1923a: B4; Trefethen 1975: 182–185).

Meanwhile, Hornaday continued to press for bag limits, and in 1925 he questioned what he regarded as a corrupt relationship between the American Game Protective Association and the Biological Survey. The American Game Protective Association went on the offensive, but by 1926 the gun companies were losing interest in the American Game Protective Association because of its limited achievements. In addition, some senators began probing into the relationship between the Biological Survey and American Game Protective Association. Hearings demonstrated that the game refuge bill would increase the slaughter rather than conserve wildlife. The congressional inquiry had an impact. In late 1926, the American Game Protective Association decided not to sponsor the game refuge bill anymore. It was only then that the issue of bag limits emerged as a viable possibility. The inquiry also led to leadership changes in the Biological Survey, and bag limits were finally approved in 1929: the limits were reduced to fifteen ducks and four geese per day. That same year a new federal game refuge bill was passed that established several wildlife refuges; no hunting was allowed on them (Fox 1981: 171–172; Grinnell 1924a, 1924b; Trefethen 1975: 194).

The success of the Izaak Walton League attracted the attention of prominent conservation organizations as well as the gun manufacturers. However, as it rose to prominence, the League found itself in financial difficulties. By 1924, the league had a deficit of $118,000. That same year Remington and other gun companies began advertising in *Outdoor America*. As many as twenty-five different arms, ammunition, and accessories companies advertised in a typical issue of the magazine (Fox 1981: 169–170; Izaak Walton League 1927: 74). Remington enrolled its traveling salesmen in the league; they helped to start new chapters. Though Dilg proclaimed that he did not want the Izaak Walton League to have ties to commercial interests, Remington's money materialized at a time when the league was mired in debt. As with the Audubon, funding from gun manufacturers created turmoil within the league. Consequently, in 1925 Dilg was removed as the group's head, and a new group of leaders—some with closer ties to eastern conservation organizations—took control (Fox 1981: 169–170; Madsen 1926; see also Izaak Walton League 1922, 1924b).

PART IV
GENDER, WEALTH, AND FOREST CONSERVATION

RURAL BEAUTIFICATION AND FOREST CONSERVATION
Gender, Class, and Corporate Dynamics

Among the first edicts that Peter Stuyvesant put forth when he became governor of New Amsterdam (New York) in 1647 was that all owners of vacant lots had to fence their properties and improve them (Abbott [1873] 2004: 126). The idea of neatly fencing and improving land spread beyond the city to the countryside and became a key part of the rural beautification movement that swept America two centuries later. The nineteenth-century sanitary reform and City Beautiful movements, which resulted in cleaner streets and more aesthetically pleasing urban areas, had an effect on rural towns and farms as well. The rural beautification and village improvement movement started around the same time that activists began agitating for landscaped urban parks (Taylor 2009: 199–250). In fact, one of the leading advocates of urban park development, Andrew Jackson Downing, also played a significant role in initiating the rural beautification movement.

The shabbiness of rural areas was an issue that concerned many. For instance, in 1870 Reverend J. Davis spoke to his congregation about the desolation that characterized Laramie, Wyoming. He complained about the dirt and garbage dumps and wondered what could entice anyone to visit the town, much less stay in it. In 1872, Cheyenne, Wyoming, was also described as a dusty, muddy town where pigs and cows roamed the streets and litter was everywhere (T. A. Larson 1965: 196). The conditions of towns like these prompted activists to promote rural and village beautification.

As more elites vacationed or lived in the countryside, they became frustrated with the unkempt farms, scruffy front yards, littered roadsides, and drab towns. Increasingly, articles appeared in the press lamenting the farms' derelict conditions and praising the charming rural villages that had undertaken rural beautification projects. As the railroads carried large numbers of urban tourists and summer residents familiar with the romantic aesthetic and pastoral scenery of landscaped parks into rural communities, the clash of cultures helped to fuel the rural beautification movement. Furthermore, suburban residents also wanted a picturesque, Arcadian landscape. Thus affluent tourists, suburbanites, and the rural gentry joined forces to create pastoral and picturesque vistas in farm country and on the fringes of wilderness.

Cultivating Rural Taste

There was great enthusiasm for gardening and other landscaping activities during the nineteenth century. While wealthy men became gentlemen farmers, genteel women took up gardening because it was a socially acceptable form of recreation for upper-class ladies. Such women, traditionally cloistered in their homes, found they could enjoy the freedom of gardening on their estates or around their yards without being criticized the way women who engaged in more strenuous outdoor recreational activities were. As urban sprawl engulfed small villages, Victorian women were urged to turn their homes and yards into bucolic refuges that were intended to serve as an antidote to the frenetic pace of urban life. Women and men botanized. They collected and learned about plants. Plant enthusiasts also formed horticultural societies that played important roles in rural beautification. In addition, women moving to the West took bulbs, seeds, and cuttings with them to beautify their new surroundings (Jenkins 2004: 385–388). This was the case with Caroline Kirkland when she moved to Pinckney, Michigan, in 1837. Though Kirkland brought seeds with her to start a garden, she found it challenging because stumps (grubs) were everywhere and had to be removed first before any gardening could begin (Clavers 1839: 133).

By the middle of the nineteenth century, landscape architects, gentlemen farmers, and rural estate owners were popularizing the notion of rural gentility and taste. Gentility spread to rural areas in part because many wealthy urbanites—already practicing genteel living and recreation in the cities—owned rural estates. They wanted to practice a genteel lifestyle at their country homes too, and brought these expectations to the villages. Moreover, Americans who traveled to Europe and saw how the European rural gentry lived wanted to emulate that lifestyle in the American countryside.

Andrew Jackson Downing played a leading role in this effort by introducing Americans to beautifully landscaped grounds and to techniques in cultivating orchards, gardens, and farms to create pastoral vistas. Downing was influenced by the romanticism of the Hudson River School artists living and painting in and around Newburgh, New York, and the Hudson River (Beveridge and Rocheleau 1998: 16; Rosenzweig and Blackmar 1992: 30). By the 1840s Downing's reputation was so great that he was commissioned to design the grounds of important government buildings such as the Smithsonian and the Capitol. He was also called on to design the grounds of Alverthorpe, Brookwood, and the Medary, three mansions in Philadelphia (Geffen 1982: 332).

Andrew Jackson Downing became one of the first Americans to articulate how well-designed landscapes can serve important civic functions. Downing argued that urban parks could play an important role in social control. He argued that parks could promote temperance, improved taste, civility, and refinement among the masses. He framed parks as works of art and convinced civic leaders and the public that art was necessary in a modern city and that investing in art was a critical component of nation building (Beveridge and Hoffman 1997: 75–78, 347–348; Blodgett 1976: 869–889; Peterson 1976: 76).

Downing played a similar role in the rural beautification movement. He believed refinement, gentility, and civility were needed in rural areas and could be taught to rural dwellers. In 1845 he published an influential book on rural landscape design, *The Fruits and Fruit Trees of America*. Downing adhered to Van Mons's theory of ameliorating the species and landscapes he worked with. Downing focused on domesticating various species of plants, hence he taught others about developing and caring for their domesticated plants. According to Downing, the garden varieties of fruits were not natural forms, but artificial productions of a particular culture (Downing [1841] 1860, [1845] 1864; Richardson 1995: 433–434). Periodicals like the *Horticulturalist* and the *Journal of Rural Art and Rural Taste* also helped to popularize the idea of rural beautification.

Downing's writings influenced many wealthy Americans to take up rural living as an antidote to urban living. He also encouraged them to build villas with expansive gardens. Though Downing admitted that villas really belonged on properties of several hundred acres, he thought that one could build smaller villas if they were grouped together around a common park in a romantic suburb. Downing died in a steamboat accident on the Hudson River in 1852 when he was only thirty-six years old. After his death, Downing's friend Alexander Jackson Davis continued his campaign for rural living; Davis helped to build several large country estates in rustic settings (Burrows and Wallace 1999: 718).

A group of wealthy New Yorkers also decided to experiment with Downing's idea of a romantic suburb in the 1850s. Alexander Jackson Davis helped Llewellyn Haskell, a wealthy drug merchant, begin work on Llewellyn Park in New Jersey in 1852. Llewellyn Park was a collection of villas set on curvilinear drives that ringed a fifty-acre park called the Ramble. Located in the foothills of the Orange Mountains, the elaborately landscaped development was a success. Modeled on the country estate aesthetic, homes were placed in a parklike setting by eliminating the hedges and fences between lots (Burrows and Wallace 1999: 718; Jenkins 2004: 385–388). Other entrepreneurs also developed planned communities. For instance, retail baron A. T. Stewart founded Garden City, Long Island, in 1869 (Scobey 2002: 116).

In some cases the development of country estates resulted in public benefits. In 1819, Henry Shaw, a wealthy Englishman, settled in St. Louis. While developing the gardens of his country estate, Tower Grove, he decided to turn the property into a botanical garden that he bequeathed to the public. This became the Missouri Botanical Garden in St. Louis. The garden was designed by Sir Joseph Hooker, director of the Royal Botanic Gardens at Kew in England, and Dr. George Englemann, Shaw's physician, who was also a trained botanist (Moore and Freame 2004: 125–128).

OLMSTED'S RURAL SUBURBS

Frederick Law Olmsted was involved in planning subdivisions and suburbs in the second half of the nineteenth century. Olmsted, the firstborn of a successful dry goods merchant in Hartford who belonged to one of the city's founding families, was steeped in the European park-building tradition. Born in 1822, he got early and frequent exposure to European parks and gardens from the prints his father kept around their Connecticut home, trips to the White Mountains, and other New England tours the family took each summer. Olmsted was first introduced to landscape gardening through works by two English writers on landscapes and agriculture: William Gilpin's *Remarks on Forest Scenery* (1794) and Uvedale Price's *An Essay on the Picturesque* (1796). Olmsted made several lengthy trips to Europe in the 1850s; he was also influenced by Downing (Beveridge and Rocheleau 1998: 30; Beveridge and Schuyler 1983: 1–48; Chadwick 1966: 49–53; Olmsted and Kimball 1922: 45–57; Rybczynski 1999: 23, 29, 40; Sutton 1997: 2–4).

Like Downing, Olmsted placed homes and buildings in a parklike setting to create a sense of openness. Olmsted also tried to define how a suburb should look. In his 1866 plan for the College of California at Berkeley, Olmsted argued that a suburb should provide "domestic seclusion" in parklike spaces that should serve as the "social rendezvous of the neighborhood." Olmsted pointed out that if there were undesirable features close by (e.g., dirty roads, ugly buildings, noisy taverns, or the haunts of drunken or undesirable people), then such features could be obscured by the strategic planting of trees and shrubs (Olmsted, Vaux and Company 1866b; Ranney, Rauluk, and Hoffman 1990: 546–573; Schuyler and Censer 1992: 28–29).

Olmsted's plan for a subdivision around Berkeley was never adopted; neither was his plan for Long Branch, New Jersey (Schuyler and Censer 1992: 29). Finally, Olmsted realized his goal of planning a suburban community when he helped to develop Riverside, Illinois, in 1868. He worked on the Riverside plan during the same time he was developing Central Park. Olmsted believed the "essential qualification of a suburb is domesticity." In his report to the Riverside Improvement Company, Olmsted stressed that there was a "vast increase" in the value of properties located close to public parks. He also argued that the density of urban dwellings is a "prolific source of morbid feebleness or irritability and various functional derangements" among urban dwellers. Olmsted thought urbanites could cure this condition by moving to suburban communities. In planning Riverside, located nine miles from Chicago, Olmsted suggested laying out the streets with "gracefully curved lines, generous spaces, and the absence of sharp corners." Dispensing with the grid pattern and right-angled corners, Olmsted wanted to use the curvilinear roads and oblique-angled intersections to "imply leisure, contemplativeness and happy tranquility" (Olmsted, Vaux and Company 1868; see also Schuyler and Censer 1992: 289).[1]

Olmsted was also concerned about undesirable land uses that might crop up to mar the aesthetic appeal of residential communities. He argued that shabby and ill-proportioned buildings were incompatible with taste and refinement. In an effort to control the aesthetic appeal of the community, the houses were set back from the sidewalks, and homeowners were required to plant trees in their front yards. Olmsted also recommended that some part of the subdivision be held open as public grounds. He thought the community should be designed with village greens, commons, and playgrounds rather than an enclosed park. Olmsted wanted openings large enough for a natural grouping of trees at regular intervals on each road. At such points Olmsted suggested placing croquet or ball grounds, sheltered seats, and drinking fountains (Olmsted, Vaux and Company 1868).

Village Improvement and the Rise of Rural Beautification

CAROLINE MATILDA KIRKLAND AND
MARY HOPKINS: THE BIRTH OF A MOVEMENT

Caroline Kirkland was an early advocate of rural beautification. In particular, she was concerned about the lack of development of village squares and parks. In 1842, she wrote about the lack of development of the public open space in Pinckney, Michigan, and about village residents' indifference to the need to beautify the settlement (Kirkland 1842: 42).

Women played key roles in village improvement projects that were aimed at ameliorating entire communities rather than just the estates of the wealthy. One of the first groups to be concerned about village improvement, the Laurel Hill Association, was formed in Stockbridge, Massachusetts, in 1853. The association was founded by Mary Gross Hopkins, a member of a prominent family. Hopkins got the idea of starting the association after reading Catherine Maria Sedgwick's book about her travels in England. Catherine Sedgwick, an urban park advocate, friend of Hopkins and Stockbridge native herself, was impressed by the way the English beautified the grounds around their homes and villages by planting flowers and shrubs, and she urged Americans to do likewise (Garner 2000: 50–51).

Hopkins raised money to plant trees along the streets and transform the local cemetery into a pastoral retreat replete with flowering shrubs. In addition to working to improve the image of Stockbridge, Hopkins traveled around New England encouraging other small communities to address conservation issues and enhance their communities through the formation of village improvement associations. Some communities hired landscape architects to help plan and enhance their towns. Observers noted that when village improvement initiatives and the urban park movement were compared, villages were expressing the same enthusiasm for beautification and exhibiting the same pride that urbanites exuded while developing their parks (Garner 2000: 50–51; *New York Times* 1878a: 5; 1914: X1).

The Laurel Hill Association developed a model for a successful association that was replicated around the country. By 1914, there were twelve hundred village improvement associations nationwide. In its first year of operation, the Laurel Hill Association planted 423 trees. Prominent citizens donated money for prizes. Rewards were also given to anyone reporting acts of vandalism. Children were incorporated into village improvement activities to give them a sense of pride and ownership of the activities. Trees were named after boys who tended them for two years (the same was not done for girls). Children were paid to remove litter from the village. Stockbridge residents also built a town library and got the railroad to set aside land around the station to be beautified (*Los Angeles Times* 1895: 8; *New York Times* 1914: X1).

SUSAN FENIMORE COOPER:
EXPANDING THE VILLAGE IMPROVEMENT IDEA

Susan Fenimore Cooper was another important figure in the village improvement movement. She argued that though nineteenth-century American villages were equipped with all the latest technology being deployed in cities and were somewhat orderly, there was still room for improvement. She lauded the work of the village improvement societies for helping to preserve the rural character of settlements. Cooper went on to suggest many ways that villages could be improved by blending the goals of the village improvement and sanitary reform movements. At the time village improvement got under way, sanitary reform advocates in cities were campaigning to clean up urban areas and develop adequate infrastructure to improve the residents' health. As a result, Cooper argued that emphasis should be placed on securing a clean and reliable water supply for consumption, hygienic purposes, and fire protection in villages. She urged municipalities to drain areas that had stagnant water. In addition, she thought attention should also be paid to the proper ventilation of public buildings (Cooper 1869: 359–366; see also Taylor 2009: 199–220).

Cooper also encouraged villages to fix their sidewalks, roadways, and wharves. Bridges should be made of stone, she said, and designed to be picturesque. She wanted to see trees and flowers planted, plank sidewalks replaced with pavements, and lawns in private yards and in public spaces trimmed. Cooper also wanted to see benches placed in the shade and in picturesque locations in villages. At the time Cooper was writing, urban park activists had been articulating their ideas about park design and functions for more than two decades. Cooper incorporated some of these ideas into her campaign for village improvement: for example, she argued that every village should have a green, park, or common of between fifteen and fifty acres for residents to congregate and breathe fresh air. She indicated that the park should be landscaped, even if it was only an acre. Not only should the park be a repository for trees; it should also serve associative functions by including monuments to commemorate local events. Cooper was influenced by the cemetery movement as well. She proposed that villages develop neat, well-kept cemeteries to replace weed-choked family graveyards. Recognizing that villagers might want to take excursions to the countryside, Cooper suggested that villages acquire land on their fringes and turn them into landscaped summer picnic grounds (Cooper 1865: 1–2; 1869: 359–366; Taylor 2009: 223–337).

Cooper also expressed her ideas about farm animals. She suggested that insect pests be eradicated and that pigs, cattle, and poultry be confined so that they couldn't roam the streets. Cooper wanted to avoid scenes like the one she described in 1850 when she vied for space on the street with the cows on her evening ramble. She wrote, "Came home from our walk with the village cows, this evening. Some fifteen or twenty of them were straggling along the road, going home of their own accord" (Cooper 1850: 153). She thought a "fierce war" of "extermination" should be waged against weeds growing in the streets, on embankments, and in yards. Cooper urged villages to use tasteful names for their streets. She spurned the use of numbered streets, arguing that in small villages numbering made little sense. Instead she advised that villages look to nature for their inspiration when choosing street names. She thought streets should be named after local trees, birds, animals, and natural landscape features, though she acknowledged that the names of founding families would also be appropriate (Cooper 1865: 1–2; 1869: 359–366).

Cooper exhorted readers to protect birds for their beauty and aesthetically pleasing songs and to aid in the control of noxious insects. However, Cooper had an elitist view of village improvement societies. She suggested that such groups should be organized by prominent people, "men and women of good sense [and] good taste," and that these groups should ignore any opposition that arose. The organizations should add members slowly, eventually inviting "the very poor and ignorant" to join. She organized a village improvement society in Cooperstown in 1870 (Cooper 1869: 359–366).

THE PINCHOTS: COMING FULL CIRCLE

James Pinchot, father of Gifford Pinchot, was an early convert to the village beautification cause. Beginning in 1863, he began to gentrify Milford, Pennsylvania. He tore down a building beside the family's store and built a post office. He urged his father, who had extensive landholdings in the area, to purchase additional village real estate so he could control the pace, type, and quality of construction in the town. The Pinchots also made plans to build a church and a library. James Pinchot grew even more motivated to enhance the aesthetic appeal of Milford after he toured the English countryside in 1871. A cultural nationalist, he was active in the National Academy of Design and the American Museum of Natural History. He wanted to bring some cultural enlightenment to Milford. He was impressed by the cleanliness and neat fences of the English countryside and grew increasingly perturbed by Milford's bedraggled appearance. He wished everyone in Milford had a chance to see the rural towns of Britain to get an idea of how they could improve the village. While touring Ireland and Italy, James Pinchot also began to associate ugly and squalid conditions with lower-class lifestyles. He was convinced that refinement in the landscape went hand in hand with gentility and refinement in the people (C. Miller 2001: 27–31).

Like other elites of the time, the Pinchots took the notion of gentility and refinement seriously. During the mid-1880s, they began work on their Norman-Breton bluestone manor. Renowned architect Richard Morris Hunt—who built Vanderbilt's Biltmore mansion in Asheville, North Carolina, and other mansions in New York City and Newport—was commissioned to build the Pinchot manor. Grey Towers, as the forty-four-room house was called, was built on a commanding eminence overlooking the town of Milford and the Delaware River. It dominated the physical and social landscape of the town. When Grey Towers was originally built, it sat atop a bare hillside. However, the lifestyle of the Pinchots came full circle when James Pinchot read the works of George Perkins Marsh. Moved to action by Marsh's appeal to halt the degradation of the environment, Pinchot decided to reverse the family's tradition of logging in Pennsylvania and to begin reforesting the hills around Grey Towers. By 1886, the dreary hillside had been replanted and the family had made plans to reforest hundreds of additional acres (C. Miller 2001: 28–29, 55–56).

Farmscaping: An Integral Part of Village Improvement

GEORGE PERKINS MARSH: THE CATALYST

During the 1820s gentlemen farmers began organizing agricultural societies in New England, the South, and Midwest (Kyle 2004: 12–15). However, it was George Perkins Marsh, senator and statesman from Vermont, who began to link rural beautification with farming. In a speech before the Agricultural Society of Rutland County in 1847, Marsh encouraged farmers to improve the aesthetic appeal of their farms. He urged them to build "a better style of domestic architecture"—that is, farmhouses that were warm, attractive, and equipped with conveniences. According to Marsh, a well-proportioned building is no costlier than a "mishapen disjointed structure." Marsh told farmers to paint their buildings, as this would help to preserve them. He also encouraged them to plant shade trees around their buildings to keep the structures cool in the summer and protect against blasts of cold winter air. The trees could also be used for fuel if necessary (Marsh [1847] 1848: 20).

Marsh also made a connection between domestic order and disciplined agricultural operations. He contended that domestic order, comfort, and neatness influenced the way in which farm operations were conducted. Marsh argued that a farmer with a neat and well-ordered house will have neat and proper lodging for his well-cared-for farm animals. Such a farmer will remove the stumps from his land, rid the farm of briars and bushes, and have a sturdy fence. Marsh also reasoned that the order instills a comfort in the farmer, which in turn fosters a feeling of homeliness and attachment to home and place. As Marsh saw it, making the home desirable, attractive, and warm was the most effective means of compensating for living in a harsh climate (Marsh [1847] 1848: 20).

Marsh thought that making rural Vermont more aesthetically pleasing would also help to keep rural people in the area. If locals made their homes and farms attractive, then they would not find the "slovenly husbandry" and "rickety dwellings" of the southern planter attractive or admire the "tame monotony of a boundless prairie." Neither would they be enticed by the "rude domestic arrangements, the coarse fare and the coarser manners" of westerners. Marsh was concerned about the out-migration of youths from rural Vermont. He argued that a youth is unlikely to leave the orchards, shrubs, and trees he or she planted and nurtured. If youths had a cheerful place to call home, well-tilled fields, carefully placed clumps of trees, and purling brooks to look at, they would not want to leave such enchanting landscapes (Marsh [1847] 1848: 20–21).

COLONEL GEORGE WARING: THE REINFORCER

George Waring was another important figure in the rural beautification movement. However, he was no stranger to civic improvement. He orchestrated a garbage collection scheme in New York City and built sewer systems in several towns (Taylor 2009: 202, 550). In 1877, Waring also began to address the issue of village improvement and farmscaping. He published a volume, *Village Improvements and Farm Villages*, that discussed drainage, sewerage, and the beautification of farming areas. Echoing Marsh's ideas, Waring contended that improved design and aesthetics of farms would slow the exodus of young people from farming villages. He also suggested clustering farmhouses together so that families, particularly the women and girls, could interact more easily. Waring also discussed ways of making villages attractive to residents and tourists alike. Using the examples of Stockbridge and Lenox, Massachusetts, Waring described how villages could go about improving their roads and pathways, removing unsightly debris from their towns, and planting trees and shrubs to beautify the municipality (Waring 1877).

GENTLEMEN FARMERS GET INVOLVED

Waring's publication prompted some farmers to take immediate action. In 1878, forty gentlemen farmers from the Bedford Farmers' Club of Westchester County met at the old John Jay homestead to form a village improvement society. The Bedford men researched the topic of village improvement and listened to a report delivered by the Honorable John Jay himself. The report, strongly influenced by Waring's ideas, urged the formation of civic improvement associations to improve townships' health, comfort, convenience, and attractiveness. It advised that such associations focus on improving paths and roads and drainage; planting trees, shrubs and flowers; abating nuisances; developing open spaces; placing seats and water fountains around the village; planning rural architecture; constructing sturdy gates and fences; building reading rooms, libraries, and lecture halls; and preserving historic buildings, trees, and open spaces. In addition, all residents of the village should be prevailed upon to participate by maintaining their own premises, including the street, sidewalks, grass, and shrubbery, in an orderly fashion. Residents were also asked to help plant trees along the streets and highways. Before adjourning, the men decided to add women to the committees (*New York Times* 1878b: 2).

Beautification efforts intensified between 1870 and 1910 as activists transformed rural landscapes into sylvan retreats. Once the lawn mower was invented in 1869, it became easier and more economical for middle-class families to tend to their grass regularly and cut their lawns at an even height. Before this, only wealthy families who could afford to hire groundskeepers or stock grazing animals were able to maintain lawns. The backyard was also transformed from a utilitarian domestic space to a more aesthetically pleasing one. The outhouses were removed, barns were replaced by garages, and the woodsheds gave way to furnaces, and the henhouses disappeared. Thus manicured lawns and gardens replaced shabby outbuildings (Jenkins 2004: 385–388).

But farms continued to be a focal point of the rural beautification efforts. Pointing to the clutter still present on many farms as visually unappealing, reformers urged farmers to clear swamps, eliminate stagnant water, and seed their farms with lawn grass. Farmers heeded the advice and began draining bogs; removing boulders, stumps, exposed roots, fallen trees, and branches; and smoothing the surface of the landscape by cutting the hard grassy tussocks from the meadows and mowing the grass. Farmers also tried to make the swamps more productive. Farmscaping also meant that farmers cleaned up their yards by removing equipment and junk from general view, mending stone and wooden fences, and trimming trees and hedges. Farmscaping was elevated to the level of "rural art" by some activists. Those in the forefront of the movement debated what mix of trees, rolling hills, and smooth open grassland created the optimal view in picturesque landscapes. Villagers were encouraged to turn unsightly highways into beautiful country lanes. The railroads also got involved by beautifying the train stations with flowers and grass and by planting trees along rail lines. Competitions were held, and awards were given to the best-maintained yards, gardens, cottage adornments, and so on (Garner 2000: 51; Judd 1997: 75–78).

Gentlemen farmers were also quite active in creating and maintaining rural charm. After the Revolutionary War, many gentlemen farmers in New England became interested in the practice of experimental agriculture. Their foray into this new type of agriculture helped to transform the perception and identity of gentlemen farmers. Their experimentation with new crops, livestock, tools, and techniques gave them an opportunity to create an identity of undertaking a gentlemanly pursuit for the public good. They amplified the frame of public good when they began studying crop diseases. They encouraged experimentation and innovation by founding agricultural societies, publishing farmers' journals, and organizing agricultural fairs. However, by the late nineteenth century, gentlemen farmers from New York who built their country estates in New England shifted away from the more utilitarian type of farming to planting and developing ornamental trees and elaborate formal gardens (Karr 2005b: 214–215; Macieski 2005: 193; P. Thornton 2005: 42).

BROADENING THE SCOPE OF VILLAGE IMPROVEMENT

Some village improvement associations framed their activities as efforts to foster community cohesion and facilitate nation building. Hence the Bedford Farmers Club saw the village improvement associations as the soul of progress, while the Pasadena Village Improvement Society saw the association as a means of uniting the whole community (*Los Angeles Times* 1883: 04; *New York Times* 1878b: 2). The Alhambra Village Improvement Society in California also saw the association as a means of getting homeowners to plant trees along the public highways as well as planting and caring for trees in front of their property (Yusuf 1887: 6).

The media played an important role in encouraging public participation. For instance, the *Washington Post* heaped praises on James G. Borden, a wealthy New Yorker who spent his winters in Green Cove Springs, Florida. In February 1889, Borden announced a prize of one thousand dollars that was awarded to the Florida city deemed the cleanest. The newspaper also encouraged other southern states to launch similar competitions and other wealthy people to sponsor them (*Washington Post* 1889b: 4).

Village improvement associations also launched antipollution campaigns, but they weren't always successful in getting industrial facilities to reduce hazardous emissions. For instance, the Village Improvement Association of New-Brighton (Staten Island) thought that abating the smoke and fumes from the nearby copper and sulfur factories was a critical element in village improvement. However, when residents complained of the dense smoke emanating from the Standard and Tidewater Companies that blanketed the community, the Bayonne Board of Health toured the facilities and told residents that the smoke was not a nuisance and posed no health risks. In fact, Mayor Farr assured residents that the sulfur and copper emissions benefited the health and sanitary condition of the arid area where trees did not grow. He also argued that thousands of healthy men worked in the facilities (*New York Times* 1892: 20).

Early Timber Conservation Efforts

Interest in greening the landscape and promoting conservation behavior spread from the villages, farms, and country estates to more remote forests. This transformation occurred as Americans began to realize that deforestation was related to environmental degradation, poor water quality, and the disappearance of wildlife. During his presidency (from 1825 to 1829), John Quincy Adams, who had an interest in the management and sustainability of natural resources, established a thirty-thousand-acre tract of live oaks on Santa Rosa Island in Pensacola Bay, Florida. Though Adams thought about the reserve in a utilitarian conservationist manner, it did not survive the onslaught from opponents. Adams expected that the reserve would provide timber to make hulls and masts for U.S. Navy ships. However, Andrew Jackson successfully framed the issue as one of the federal government overextending its powers. Jackson thought the federal government had infringed on the rights of the local people by sequestering their resources and preventing them from using the timber in whatever ways they pleased. Consequently, the reservation was nullified during Jackson's presidency (W. R. Adams 1972: 129–142).

Nonetheless, forest conservation continued to interest some Americans. Thus in 1833 John Weeks of Middlebury, Vermont, began an experiment in forest management when he discovered a patch of small white pines growing in his pasture. In 1839 he thinned the patch, and by 1850 had a healthy stand of trees (Judd 1997: 86). However, during the nineteenth century, people were more inclined to clear-cut the land than to experiment with selective cutting and other reforestation techniques.

Concern over dwindling timber resources led Massachusetts to conduct the first statewide inventory of its forests in 1830 (Cameron 1928: 180; Labau et al. 2007: 5). Nonetheless, forest destruction was rampant up to the end of the nineteenth century because Americans relied heavily on the forests to supply most of their energy needs. The forests also provided raw materials for furniture, housing, transportation, and so on. More than half a million acres of New England's forests had been cleared by 1700, and a century later most of the woodlands in the region had been cut. With the disappearance of the woodlands, New Englanders noticed that some terrestrial and aquatic species had completely disappeared or were on the brink of extinction (Worster 1994: 67–69).

GEORGE PERKINS MARSH ON FOREST DESTRUCTION AND CLIMATE CHANGE

Thinkers such as George Perkins Marsh helped lay the groundwork for Americans to change their attitudes about forests. In 1847 Marsh delivered a seminal speech to farmers in which he argued that humans had a right to use but not to abuse nature or deplete its resources. He hypothesized that climate change was being influenced by human action. The draining of wetlands and clear-cutting of the forests affected the amount of moisture in the air, evaporation, sunlight reaching the soil, heat, and wind action. Marsh noted that the mean temperature in cities such as London was higher than that of the surrounding countryside. He contended that human action also increased the likelihood of fires (Marsh [1847] 1848: 8, 11–12).

Marsh urged farmers not to see trees as encumbrances. He argued that trees not only were valuable as fuel and timber but also sheltered and protected the undergrowth. Furthermore, the decomposing remains of trees provided fertilizer that nourished the soil. Trees held the soil in place, thereby limiting erosion. Marsh explained that the forests acted like sponges, retaining excess moisture during the rainy seasons then releasing that moisture slowly during times of drought. In effect, forests helped to moderate the flow of water through the system, preventing sudden and large flows of water over the surface. Marsh warned that deforestation resulted in exhausted, degraded soil, floods, and erosion. He urged his listeners to reforest barren lands and to cut timber at widely spaced intervals to allow for the necessary regeneration of the forests. He also promoted the idea of sustained yield—using and replenishing the resources in perpetuity (Marsh [1847] 1848: 17–19).

RISING CONSCIOUSNESS

In many ways, Marsh was a man ahead of his time. It took decades for people to fully comprehend Marsh's insights and heed his advice. As a result, many states depleted their forest resources. In 1881, the New Hampshire legislature created a temporary commission to study forest destruction and watershed protection. The commission concluded that at least half of the state's land area should be perpetually devoted to wood and timber production (Judd 1997: 92, 97). Eventually activists realized that simply campaigning to stop the slaughter of wildlife wasn't enough to protect them; their habitats had to be protected too. This was part of the motivation for sportsmen's organizations such as the Bisby Club to begin to protect and plant trees and manage them at the same time they were protecting game. The Boone and Crockett Club also focused on game and national park protection.

Timber conservation emerged as a major concern by the late 1800s. The timber industry was a wasteful one: lumbermen cut trees and abandoned land rapidly and moved on to new forested tracts. Timber men did not utilize the resources efficiently; they cut the most valuable trees, leaving second-grade timber to waste. The destruction of the forests had catastrophic effects, as fire, disease, and wasteful logging practices decimated supplies. A series of devastating forest fires brought the issue of timber harvesting and forest cover into the conservation discourse. During the 1880s in Wisconsin, twenty-five hundred separate fires burned half a million acres each year. Fueled by the dry tops and slash left behind by logging crews, fire often burned unabated to consume stands of uncut forests. Floods and soil erosion followed in the wake of fires when the rains came. Wildlife and people were often endangered. It was in this context that Governor Sterling Morton of Nebraska and the activists who later participated in the American Forestry Association instituted Arbor Day in 1872. The goal was to plant tree lots and shelterbelts. The idea spread across the country rapidly. The following year, Franklin B. Hough of New York gave a presentation on American forests before the American Association for the Advancement of Science. This led the organization to form a committee to study the timber cultivation and forest preservation. Hough chaired the committee and produced an influential series titled *Reports on Forestry*. In 1874 the House of Representatives recommended the creation of a Commissionership of Forestry to compile statistics on timber, but the bill failed to pass. The following year activists formed the American Forestry Association to address the problem. They focused on arboriculture, public education and forest appreciation, plant research, the establishment of forest reserves, and the development of parks (Hays [1959] 1999: 27–28; Labau et al. 2007: 5; Trefethen 1975: 94–95; Wilkins 1995: 180).

In 1876, Congress appropriated two thousand dollars for the Commissioner of Agriculture to do a study of the rate of forest consumption and strategies to enhance forest renewal. Franklin Hough was commissioned to conduct the study, and he produced the *Report upon Forestry 1877*. From 1879 onward the Department of the Interior and the U.S. Geological Survey collected data on the state of the nation's forests (Labau et al. 2007: 5–6; Reiger [1975] 2001: 107).

Forest lands were also lost as they were taken from the public domain by poachers and speculators. Large companies, timber barons, and small-time entrepreneurs got in on the act. For instance, Daniel Muir—John Muir's father—was said to have poached timber from lands surrounding the family's Hickory Hill farm in Wisconsin. Ralph Waldo Emerson also earned a handsome profit buying up cheap land on the western frontier and later selling the parcels at a much higher price (Turner 1985: 280, 306). However, timber companies appropriated federal lands on a grand scale, amassing large profits in the process. Timber poaching was so widespread that it was considered a frontier tradition rather than theft. The appropriated timber was seen as a reward for the labor pioneers put into developing the country. In 1850, for instance, Wisconsin and Michigan produced an estimated 90 million board feet of timber, about half of which was stolen or obtained through deception. Poachers had no incentive to reforest the lands they denuded, and timber theft went unchecked until the latter part of the nineteenth century (Turner 1985: 306).

In the second half of the nineteenth century, some government officials responded to the demands to protect and expand the nation's forests. Secretary of the Interior Carl Schurz took tentative steps toward protecting the forests when he took office in 1877. His efforts were buttressed by John Wesley Powell's 1878 report on the arid lands of the West. The report pointed to the dangers of fires and the need for greater forest protection. A Division of Forestry was created in the U.S. Department of Agriculture in 1881. The following year,

Charles Sprague Sargent of Harvard's Arnold Arboretum began urging state legislatures to pass laws to protect eastern forests. Sargent also urged the federal government to remove lands from the public domain in the West and designate them as permanent preserves to protect them. In 1886, a professional forester, Bernhard Fernow, was appointed to run the Division of Forestry. Though the Division of Forestry was created, it operated on a pittance. As late as 1886, the annual appropriation for the division did not exceed ten thousand dollars (Pinchot [1947] 1998: 153; Wilkins 1995: 180–181). This made it difficult for the office to enforce any policies nationwide or even to understand the scope of the problem.

Establishing Forest Reserves

Eventually presidents took action to preserve forests. On March 2, 1891, in the waning hours of the legislative session, the Sundry Civil Service Act passed through the House and Senate with an unnoticed rider. The rider, which gave the president the authority to create forest reserves by executive order, drew little debate and few objections. Also known as the Forest Reserve Act, the measure was strongly supported by the Boone and Crockett Club, whose members wanted to see Yellowstone expanded and other reserves created (Fox 1981: 113; Hays [1959] 1999: 47; Trefethen 1975: 96–98; Wilkins 1995: 180–181).

President Harrison signed the bill and immediately took advantage of the rider to set aside more than 1.2 million acres in Wyoming as the Yellowstone Forest Reserve, and almost 1.2 million acres as the White River Forest Reserve in Colorado. On Valentine's Day in 1893, in the last days of his administration, Harrison set aside an additional 13 million acres of forest reserves, including 4 million acres for the Sierra Forest Reserve. Harrison was urged to create these forest reserves (especially the one in the Sierras) by the secretary of the interior, John Noble, who had been influenced by John Muir's writings on the state of the Yosemite Valley. Robert Underwood Johnson, editor of *The Century*, lobbied Noble personally on behalf of Muir and Yosemite. In all, Harrison created fifteen forest reserves before leaving office (Wilkins 1995: 182–183).

However, all was not well with the system of forest reserves that President Harrison had created. When Congress passed the Forest Act, it failed to specify the purposes to which such lands could be put. Moreover, when the reserves were created, no considerations were given for how they should be managed, except for the stipulation that they should be under the jurisdiction of the secretary of the interior. No steps were taken to protect the reserves from fire, timber theft, overgrazing, mining, and so on, hence many destructive practices continued unabated in them. For instance, about five hundred thousand sheep continued to graze in the Sierra Forest Reserve despite its status as a federal reserve (Wilkins 1995: 183).

THE FORESTRY COMMISSION

Though Pinchot is widely credited with being the first to practice wise-use forestry, both Marsh and Grinnell suggested this idea several years before Pinchot experimented with it at the Biltmore Estate. In 1884, Grinnell noted that the timber practices were very destructive and wasteful. At the time, about fifty young trees were destroyed and a great slash left behind in the process of harvesting one mature tree. Grinnell supported the utilitarian-conservationist approach of wise use. He urged the government to appoint a trained, professional Forestry Officer to develop a "forest conservancy" program, create state and federal forestry commissions, and establish reforestation programs. Grinnell also discussed European forestry techniques and encouraged Americans to adopt them (*Forest and Stream* 1884a: 2; 1884b: 161; 1884c: 301; 1885a: 461–462; 1885b: 482; 1885c: 502; Marsh [1864] 1965). As discussed above, the Blooming Grove Club also began practicing wise-use and sustained yield years before Pinchot did (Cart 1971).

During the 1890s, activists began paying more attention to sustained yield and other long-range forest management techniques aimed at producing a continuous supply of timber—that is, making sure annual cutting does not exceed reforestation rates. Furthermore, timber companies were expected to utilize waste materials from logging and take steps to reduce the damage from fire and disease (Hays [1959] 1999: 28).

As these ideas of scientific forestry caught on, pressure mounted for a comprehensive survey of the nation's forests. Consequently, in 1896, Gifford Pinchot, Robert Underwood Johnson, and Charles Sargent (a wealthy Boston Brahmin) organized an industry-endorsed,[2] government-sponsored National Forestry Commission to survey the western forests. At the time, a Public Land Service report calculated that about $37 million worth of forests were lost each year to illegal timber harvesting, grazing, and fire. Though Congress was reluctant to create the commission, the Forestry Commission was formed, and Congress appropriated $25,000 to fund its work. The commission's members served without pay. Pinchot, Johnson, and Sargent had worked together previously in helping to establish the Adirondack Forest Reserve. In the Adirondacks, Sargent and Johnson surveyed the forests to identify incursions by timber companies; it was this earlier collaboration and shared experience that led the three to propose the formation of the National Forestry Commission. In addition to Pinchot and Sargent, other members of the Forestry Commission included William Brewer of Yale; General Henry Abbott, an engineer and hydrologist; Alexander Agassiz of Harvard; and Arnold Hague of the U.S. Geological Survey. John Muir was asked to join the six-man commission in an advisory capacity (Hays [1959] 1999: 29–31, 36–40; Pinchot [1947] 1998: 91–92; Turner 1985: 300–301; Wilkins 1995: 191–193; Wolfe 1945: 268).

The Forestry Commission was asked to assess the state of the forests in the public domain. Millions of acres of such forests had been given away as grants to the railroads, sold for very little to special interests and unscrupulous land agents, or stolen. The aim of the commission was to catalog the remaining forests, evaluate their status, and recommend what should be done with them (Wilkins 1995: 193).

THE FORESTRY COMMISSION REPORT

Forestry Commission members agreed on the extent of forest destruction they witnessed but they disagreed on how the forests should be used, developed, protected, and administered in the future. In the Black Hills of South Dakota, for instance, they saw hillsides stripped bare by mining operations, fires, and illegal timber harvesting. Similarly, in the Big Horn Mountains of Wyoming they found forests reduced to charred stumps. The Continental Divide was shrouded in smoke from the fires set by prospectors, and they were greeted by large-scale logging operations in the Priest River Basin in the Bitterroot Mountains. They also found that the railroads were avaricious and extremely destructive. Edward Harriman's Northern Pacific Railroad, already subsidized by a huge land grant, not only devastated the forests and lands in the right of way, but also appropriated large swaths of timber on either side of the tracks. Sheep grazing at Oregon's Crater Lake stripped the land of so much vegetation that it took decades for the region to regain some of its flora even after the area was put under federal protection. The commission saw slashed and burned forest throughout California. They also found mines operating within the Grand Canyon in Arizona, even though it was one of the reserves set aside by President Harrison (Wolfe 1945: 270–271).

While commission members were working and writing their report, the differences between Muir's and Sargent's preservationism and Pinchot's utilitarian conservationism surfaced. Muir had first met Pinchot at a dinner party hosted by James Pinchot, Gifford's father, in their Gramercy Park home when Pinchot was still a young man studying forestry. Though Muir and Pinchot were friendly toward each other when they began their work on the Forestry

Commission (they even camped together away from other members of the commission), by the time the final report was issued, their ideological differences had turned them into bitter enemies and rivals (Turner 1985: 295; Wilkins 1995: 193–195). The Muir-Pinchot ideological divide was a harbinger of things to come: rifts between preservationists and conservationists kept surfacing for many years.

Once the Forestry Commission finished its travels, members met in exclusive social clubs such as the Brevoort House and the Century Club in New York City to write the report. Muir remained in California but kept in touch with the other commission members (Wilkins 1995: 195). The preservationists (Sargent, Muir, and Abbott) wanted to establish inviolate reserves. They argued that the reserves should be patrolled by the army to prevent abuse because the military would be less likely to succumb to political pressure. Muir had witnessed firsthand the results of army patrols of Yosemite and Yellowstone and was pleased with the results (Dilsaver 1994: 101–102; Fox 1981: 113; Muir [1901] 1981: 40; Wilkins 1995: 195).

Pinchot opposed military oversight. While studying in Germany, he had seen a civilian guard system that he wanted to replicate in America. He also believed that western politicians and other interest groups would oppose inviolate reserves. Instead he proposed regulated use of public lands under the supervision of trained civilian foresters. The trained forester could help to control fires, tackle diseases plaguing the forests, and supervise the felling and sale of timber. Brewer and Hague agreed with Pinchot. The conservationists thought this approach would protect the forests while maximizing the benefits people could obtain from them (Fox 1981: 109–113, 131; Hays [1959] 1999: 36; Trefethen 1975: 99–100; Turner 1985: 302–303; Wilkins 1995: 195; Wolfe 1938: 359–364; 1945: 271–272).

Sargent chaired the commission during the report-writing phase, and Pinchot had little respect for his ideas or leadership style. Pinchot described Sargent as a "dominating chair" who did not understand forest issues. Pinchot wrote that "he couldn't see the forest for the trees." Pinchot elaborated, "Sargent doesn't fish or hunt or know anything about the mountains. It is hard to understand him" (Pinchot [1947] 1998: 95, 101). Despite Pinchot's lack of confidence in the chair, Sargent was able to broker a compromise between the conservationists and preservationists on the question of who should manage the forests. The report recommended that military men supervise the reserves until an authorized, trained, and organized Forest Corps was ready to assume administrative responsibilities for the reserves. Consequently, the military patrolled the reserves and national parks until 1914 (Dilsaver and Tweed 1990: 101–102; Wilkins 1995: 196–198; Wolfe 1945: 271–272). The report, which was strongly influenced by the conservationist perspective, suggested banning sheep grazing in the reserves but left open the possibility of timber harvesting and mining in the forests. The report also recommended that existing mining and timber legislation that encouraged fraud be banned or repealed and that the forests be managed to ensure permanent sustained yields of timber (Fox 1981: 109–113, 131; Hays [1959] 1999: 36; Wilkins 1995: 196; Wolfe 1938: 359–364).

IMPEACHING THE PRESIDENT FOR
ESTABLISHING FOREST RESERVES

In January 1897, a draft[3] of the commission's report was sent to President Cleveland in the waning days of his administration. The report recommended the creation of thirteen new reserves in eight western states and of two national parks, Grand Canyon and Mount Rainier; the modification or repeal of existing timber and mining laws; and forest management aimed at maintaining a permanent timber supply (National Forestry Commission 1897).

Cleveland took the advice of the commission and used the Forest Reserve Act to set aside 21.3 million acres to create the new forest reserves and national parks. This resulted in a dramatic increase in the acreage in the forest reserve system. Prior to Cleveland's action, the area of existing forest reserves totaled 17.6 million acres. But in one stroke of the pen, Cleveland more than doubled that acreage. Cleveland's sudden move caught would-be opponents off guard. Sargent had gone out of his way to keep the commission's work a secret, and the report went to the president without fanfare or public scrutiny. As Pinchot described it, "The creation of thirteen new Reserves in seven states came like a thunderclap" (Pinchot [1947] 1998: 107–109).[4] Timber, mining, and grazing interests and western politicians were incensed. Telegrams whizzed back and forth across the country. Lobbyists for these industries were active in Washington; some had appointments in the General Land Office, where they could monitor federal action on public land issues. Opponents of the reserves protested what they saw as the "useless protection of dead timber" by a "few zealots, Harvard professors, sentimentalists, and impractical dreamers" of the East who advised the president (Fox 1981: 113; Hays [1959] 1999: 47; Wilkins 1995: 196–197; Wolfe 1945: 268, 272).

The reserves were designated at a sensitive time. Cleveland created the forest reserves a few years after the 1893 depression, which had wrought severe economic hardships on the West. During the depression, some state governments hovered on the brink of bankruptcy. They blamed federal monetary policies for hampering the growth of the silver mining industry. Thus many westerners saw the creation of the forest reserves as a federally imposed act that impounded resources, limited public access, and reduced the states' tax bases. They also feared the reserves would make the cash-starved states of the West more vulnerable and harm the grazing, timber, railroad, and mining industries (Wilkins 1995: 197–198). Opposition was so great that a mass meeting in Deadwood, South Dakota, drew thousands of people who protested the creation of the Black Hills reserve. Meeting participants argued that the federal government's actions would result in the region's depopulation (Fox 1981: 113; Turner 1985: 303–304; Wilkins 1995: 198; Wolfe 1945: 272).

Consequently, the Senate tried to impeach President Cleveland for establishing the reserves. When those efforts failed, senators tried to attach riders to bills in the hopes of annulling the reserves. Six days after Cleveland created the reserves, Senator Clark of Wyoming put forward an amendment to the Sundry Civil Appropriation Bill that attempted to overturn Cleveland's actions. Clark took this step because he thought the reserves were created without consultation with the relevant stakeholders. Clark argued that as a result of the president's actions, people would lose access to timber or mineral resources. He felt that the forest reserves were created at the behest of scientific gentlemen whom he described as "ornament[s] to the country" and who had not been near any of the reserves they recommended. Other western senators supported Clark. The three main objections to the reserves were that utilitarian activities were banned, there was no prior notice or consultation before the reserves were set aside, and lands set aside were not adequately inspected and evaluated before being designated as reserves. Clark's amendment passed the Senate. In response, John Lacey of Iowa drafted a substitute bill for the House to consider. The Lacey amendment allowed for the sale of timber, mining, and other domestic uses of the forest reserves. The Lacey amendment was debated vigorously and attacked by western representatives and their eastern supporters. Lacey's amendment passed the House, and both bills went to conference. Unable to craft a compromise except for an amendment giving the president the power to keep or cancel all or any part of the reserves, the Sundry Civil Appropriations Bill went to President Cleveland on March 4, 1897, the last day of the congressional session and his administration. Sensing that the amendment could give other presidents the power to cancel the reserves, Cleveland refused to sign the bill (Pinchot [1947] 1998: 109–113).

SUSPENDING THE RESERVES

Soon after taking office, President William McKinley called a special session of Congress to discuss the forest reserves. No action was taken on them, however. On June 4, 1897, the Congress passed a Forest Management Act. The measure suspended the forest reserves until March 1, 1898. Only the two reserves in California—Stanislaus and San Jacinto—were allowed to stand because both senators from the state requested it. Once the reserves were suspended, there was a massive resource grab as timber, mining, and grazing speculators filed claims and took control of resources in the suspended reserves. Mining and grazing were also allowed in the reserves. A day after the Forest Management Act was signed, Pinchot was quoted in the newspapers as saying sheep did not damage the forest reserves if allowed to graze in them. This comment alarmed preservationists, because Pinchot made this remark while in the state of Washington assessing the status of the commercial resources in the suspended reserves (Wilkins 1995: 201; Wolfe 1945: 273–276).[5] Nonetheless, the Forest Management Act did establish the principle that while timber from the reserves could be sold, the land itself could not be (Fox 1981: 114; Wilkins 1995: 196–199, 201).

In 1898, as the term of suspension of the forest reserves neared, the Senate passed an amendment to the Sundry Civil Appropriations Bill to abolish the reserves completely. But by this time, public opinion favored protecting the forests. Consequently, the bill failed by a wide margin (Wolfe 1945: 277).

Pinchot, Roosevelt, and Conservationism

DEFINING THE PURPOSE OF THE FORESTS

Still the question remained: What was the purpose of the reserves and what should be done about them? The Forest Management Act gave the secretary of the interior the power "to regulate the occupancy and use" of the forest reserves. This clause later provided Pinchot with the mandate he needed to practice utilitarian conservationism in the national forests. The measure also helped to define the purpose of the forests. Though the act did not specify that grazing and commercial activities were permitted in the forests, it did not prohibit these activities either. Instead the measure allowed the agency administering the forests to interpret the act and make decisions on a case-by-case basis. In their attempts to thwart efforts by preservationists to prohibit logging in the forest reserves, mining companies succeeded in inserting a clause in the Forest Management Act that permitted the logging and sale of dead or downed timber in said reserves. In addition, mining interests succeeded in getting the right to stake claims and take out patents on lands within the reserves. Consequently, the Forest Management Act set the stage for the development of the national forests in a manner that permitted grazing, commercial logging, hydropower development, and mining (Hays [1959] 1999: 37).

The secretary of the interior placed the forest reserves under the jurisdiction of the Division of the General Land Office in 1897. The division developed a rational conservation program that included fire prevention and suppression, timber sales, tree planting, and grazing. Pinchot was named chief of the Division of Forestry in 1898. The General Land Office remained in charge of the reserves until 1905. The Bureau of Forestry was created out of the Division of Forestry in 1901. Two years later it had a budget of three hundred thousand dollars (Hays [1959] 1999: 37).

THE FORMATION OF THE U.S. FOREST SERVICE

From the outset, Pinchot was convinced that the General Land Office was incapable of overseeing the forest reserves effectively. Consequently, he began campaigning for the creation of the Forest Service to administer all matters related to the reserves. He also wanted to transfer forest-related matters to the Department of Agriculture. Pinchot built support for his position by recruiting railroad, lumber, and mining corporations to speak out in favor of creating a Forest Service in the Department of Agriculture. The plan was also endorsed by a Forest Congress that Pinchot convened in Washington, DC, and by irrigation advocates such as George Maxwell and the National Board of Trade (Hays [1959] 1999: 38–39).

Pinchot was also able to convince Theodore Roosevelt to support his plan. Theodore Roosevelt became president after McKinley was assassinated on September 14, 1901. Once in office, Roosevelt wasted no time espousing his administration's conservation ideology. Roosevelt's first speech on the country's resources was written by Gifford Pinchot, F. Newell, George Maxwell, and W. McGee (Pinchot [1947] 1998: 188). In this speech, delivered on December 2, 1901, Roosevelt asserted, "The fundamental idea of forestry is the perpetuation of forests by use. Forest protection is not an end in itself; it is a means to increase and depend upon them. The preservation of our forests is an imperative business necessity." He stated that the forest reserves were of "practical usefulness" to the mining, grazing, irrigation, hydropower, and other interests. He concluded, "The forest and water problems are perhaps the most vital internal questions of the United States" (quoted in Pinchot [1947] 1998: 190–191).

Despite strong public support, Pinchot's first attempt to create a forest service bureau in the winter of 1901–1902 resulted in a resounding defeat in Congress. After this, Pinchot concentrated on garnering the support of influential western congressmen by emphasizing that commercial activities would be allowed in the forest reserves. Pinchot took this approach because the stipulation that the commercial development of the forest reserves should be minimized resulted in considerable opposition in Congress. In particular, stockmen wondered whether the forests were going to be treated like national parks, where grazing was kept to a minimum and other forms of commercial exploitation were banned. However, Pinchot had to walk a tightrope and execute a delicate balancing act. On the one hand, he wanted ranchers, miners, loggers, and hydropower developers to believe their interests would be protected, but on the other, he did not want to see the national forests turned into hunting and breeding reserves. Hence Pinchot fought off proposals to convert the forests into game reserves. For example, the Boone and Crockett Club (to which both Roosevelt and Pinchot belonged) tried unsuccessfully to carve out portions of the forests to be used exclusively for breeding game. However, when Secretary Lane prohibited grazing in the reserves in Arizona in 1900, Pinchot toured the area and recommended that grazing be allowed. He convinced the secretary that limited grazing would not pollute the water (Hays [1959] 1999: 39–41; Pinchot [1947] 1998: 177–182).

Pinchot also continued to promote the idea that the national forests were, first and foremost, places for utility and rational development. In a speech before the Society of American Foresters in March 1903, Pinchot said: "The object of our forest policy is not to preserve the forests because they are beautiful . . . or because they are refuges for the wild creatures of the wilderness . . . but . . . [for] the making of prosperous homes . . . Every other consideration comes in secondary" (quoted in Hays [1959] 1999: 41–42). This argument also represents an attempt by Pinchot to distinguish the national forests from the national parks.

In 1903 and 1904 Pinchot tried again to pass the forest service bill. He received help from John Lacey and Frank Mondell of Wyoming, but neither succeeded in getting the bill through Congress. Mondell's bill met with strong opposition from the Homestake Mining Company because company executives were afraid of losing access to timber in the Black Hills Forest Reserve of South Dakota (Hays [1959] 1999: 43–44). As part of the final push to pass the forest service bill, the American Forestry Association sponsored an American Forest Congress, which was held from January 1905. More than two thousand people, including representatives from mining, timber, grazing, irrigation, and railroad businesses, attended the event. Its purpose was "to establish a broader understanding of the forest in its relation to the great industries depending upon it; to advance the conservative use of forest resources for both the present and future need of these industries; [and] to stimulate and unite all efforts to perpetuate the forest as a permanent resource of the nation." The keynote speaker, Theodore Roosevelt, proclaimed that "for the first time, the great business and forest interest of the nation have joined together . . . to consider their individual and common interest in the forest" (as quoted in Chepesuik 2004: 14, 16–19). To improve the chances of passage, the forest service bill, known as the Transfer Act, was modified to take the Homestake Mining Company's objections into consideration. This time the bill passed Congress easily, and it became law on February 1, 1905 (Hays [1959] 1999: 43–44).

That same day, the secretary of agriculture, James Wilson, sent a letter to Pinchot outlining the parameters that would guide the management of the forest reserves. Wilson focused on the forest's utility and on scientific management. He did not express any concerns about the forest's aesthetic and recreational potential (Dana 1956: 82). Wilson wrote, "It must be clearly borne in mind that all land is to be devoted to its most productive use for the permanent good of the whole people, and not for the temporary benefit of individuals or companies. All the resources of the reserves are for use, and this use must be brought about in a thoroughly prompt and businesslike manner." Wilson reasoned that the forest reserves were vitally important to the industries in the western states and that the resources should be managed to ensure continued prosperity in the region. He noted that "where conflicting interests must be reconciled the question will always be decided from the standpoint of the greatest good for the greatest number in the long run" (Dana 1956: 82).

Roosevelt continued where Cleveland left off in setting aside lands for forest reserves and parks. When Roosevelt took office, there were forty-one reserves totaling 46.4 million acres of land. In the first year of his presidency he added 15.5 million more acres, and by 1907 he had increased the total to almost 151 million acres. In addition to enlarging Yosemite National Park, Roosevelt created fifty-three wildlife reserves, sixteen national monuments, and five new national parks (Fox 1981: 113; Hays [1959] 1999: 47; Trefethen 1975: 96–98).

The Forest Service quickly became the central platform from which Pinchot orchestrated his national conservationist agenda. However, perceiving the expanding reserve system as a form of western land grab, Congress opposed the expansion of the forest reserve system and in 1907 passed a bill stipulating that Congress had to approve any new reserves designated in six western states. However, while that bill was awaiting Roosevelt's signature, the president added another 75 million acres to the forest reserve system in the form of new reserves or expansion of existing ones (Fox 1981: 128–130; Hays [1959] 1999: 5–6, 135; Trefethen 1975: 126–127; Wilkins 1995: 203, 218).

When Pinchot became the head of the Division of Forestry, he set out to spread the conservation doctrine by educating the timber corporations about scientific forest management techniques. By 1905, Weyerhauser, Kirby, and other major corporations had all applied for technical assistance in scientific forest management; representatives from timber companies had also become active in the American Forestry Association. The association funded the Bureau of Forestry when Congress neglected to fund it; it also funded an endowed chair at the Yale School of Forestry and made its facilities available to Yale students for field training. In addition, the association provided support enabling Pinchot to stave off attacks on the Forest Service. As mentioned above, Pinchot also courted and got help from mining, railroad, trade, and livestock interests (Hays [1959] 1999: 29–31, 39–40).

THE GOVERNORS' CONSERVATION CONFERENCE

In 1908, the last year of his presidency, Theodore Roosevelt hosted a Governors' Conservation Conference. The idea for the conference first arose in a speech given by Roosevelt before the Society of American Foresters in 1903. In that speech Roosevelt said that forest preservation was not an end in itself but a mechanism to ensure the prosperity of the nation. The idea surfaced again in other Roosevelt speeches, and it became a topic of conversation during the 1907 Inland Waterways Commission trip along the Lower Mississippi River. Commission members decided to hold a conservation conference in Washington the following year. It would be first and foremost a conference of governors, and secondarily a meeting of experts who could shed light on conservation issues nationwide (*Proceedings of a Conference of Governors* 1908).

The conference, which convened in May 1908, worsened the rift between the conservationist and preservationist wings of the emerging environmental movement. While Pinchot, who financed the conference,[6] and other conservationists took center stage, Muir, Sargent, and other leading preservationists were ignored. Muir's friend Robert Underwood Johnson was the only prominent preservationist invited to the conference, and he was there as a member of the press, not as a preservationist. J. Horace McFarland of the American Civic Association was also allowed to speak in favor of preservation. All of the Supreme Court justices, fifty governors (each with three aides or advisers), many members of Congress, representatives from seventy national organizations, university presidents, and hundreds of conservation experts were in attendance (Fox 1981: 128–130; Hays [1959] 1999: 5–6, 135; Pinchot [1947] 1998: 344–347; *Proceedings of a Conference of Governors* 1908; Trefethen 1975: 126–127; Wilkins 1995: 230–231; Wolfe 1945: 315).

The conference reflected Pinchot's and Roosevelt's vision of rational planning and efficient development of natural resources. The agenda focused on minerals, soils, forests, sanitation, reclamation, grazing and stock raising, rail and water transportation, hydropower, and conservation as national policies. Despite the limited preservationist perspective, the conference was a success in that it catapulted conservation issues to national prominence. As conference participants recommended, a National Conservation Committee was formed to compile and inventory the nation's natural resources. The group planned a follow-up conference, which was held in December 1908 (Pinchot [1947] 1998: 355–360; *Proceedings of a Conference of Governors* 1908; Wilkins 1995: 231).

Water Companies, Citizen's Initiatives, and National Forests

Conservationists intensified efforts to create state, regional, and local forest reserves as the nineteenth century progressed. For example, activists such as Grinnell were instrumental in creating the Adirondacks Forest Reserve. Though DeWitt Clinton suggested preserving the Adirondack forests in 1822 and Samuel Hammond reiterated the idea again in 1857, the Adirondack Forest Reserve did not become a reality until 1885. Shortly after the establishment of the 715,000-acre reserve, the New Hampshire Forestry Commission began accepting donations of land. Citizens' initiatives also helped to create the White Mountain National Forest in New Hampshire. In the late 1800s, as logging activities escalated, New Hampshire residents, tourists, and resort owners expressed their concern about forest destruction. In 1901, the Society for the Preservation of New Hampshire Forests was formed. The group pushed for a national forest reserve in the White Mountains. The issue was brought before Congress, but it stalled. In 1909, a bill calling for federal funds to help create the reserve was put before Congress by Representative Weeks. The bill, which passed in 1911, was significant in accelerating the trend toward public ownership of the forests. The White Mountain National Forest was finally created in 1918 (Judd 1997: 109–110; Reiger [1975] 2001: 116–121; Turner 1985: 281; Wilkins 1995: xxv).

In the West, some water companies interested in watershed protection also played important roles in helping to establish national forests. For example, in the early 1890s, urban residents collaborated with water companies to lobby President Harrison to create the San Bernardino National Forest. Led by Adolph Wood, president of the Arrowhead Reservoir Company, who organized the California Water and Forest Association in 1899, the coalition pushed for state laws to protect the forests, encouraged tree planting in denuded watersheds, and urged that available water resources be quantified. The group also funded part of the U.S. Geological Survey's work, opposed grazing in the forests, and supported the exclusion of livestock from the reserves. The group teamed up with other organizations to lobby Cleveland, McKinley, and Theodore Roosevelt to establish reserves in California. Similar alliances were formed in states such as Colorado and Arizona (Hays [1959] 1999: 23–24).

Despite efforts to create forest reserves, these entities were not well maintained and protected. As late as the 1920s, the forest reserves were still under threat from overuse and degradation. This led Arthur Masten of the Tahawus Club to write, "No place is too remote for the tourist nor . . . for the poacher," hence the Adirondacks was overflowing with "neither sportsmen nor forest lovers, who regard the woods much as they would Coney Island" (Masten c. 1935: 186–187). Masten also complained that New York was managing the forests more for recreational purposes than for forest preservation (E. Comstock 1990: 35). It was well into the twentieth century before state and federal governments developed effective management plans for the reserves.

Class Conflicts in the Forest Reserves:
Poaching and Open Defiance

The forest reserves were the sites of many conflicts between conservationists, elite urban recreationists, and rural residents of modest means. Clashes between local residents and conservationists manifested themselves in the form of illegal hunting, timber poaching, arson, and other acts of defiance. Nowhere was this more evident than in the Adirondacks. The Adirondack Forest Reserve, composed of an amalgam of public lands and private parks, was the scene of many class disputes. By 1893 the reserve had expanded to include sixty private parks covering 940,000 acres as well as 730,000 acres of public lands. Like the wealthy sportsmen in the Adirondack League Club, affluent industrialists such as William Rockefeller built private parks and country estates in the area. Private clubs and property owners stocked their ponds and streams with fish, and forests with deer and imported exotic game (Comstock and Webster 1990: 12; *Forest and Stream* 1894b: 552; Ives 1898: 406; Jacoby 2001: 39–40; New York Forest Commission 1893: 9–10; *Recreation* 1901: 263–265). For instance, the industrialist William Seward Webb built a 112,000-acre private park, Ne-Ha-Sa-Ne, on his estate in 1891. Webb, owner of the Adirondack and St. Lawrence Railroad Company, had built the controversial rail line that ran from Utica to Montreal. He surveyed and fenced his property, which lay adjacent to the Adirondack League Club's holdings, and hired about sixteen men to guard his estate (more than twenty guards patrolled the Adirondack

League Club's forests). He posted signs at frequent intervals along the eight-foot-high barbed-wire fence forbidding trespassing, fishing, hunting, felling trees, cutting timber, and lighting fires (Jacoby 2001: 40; Kaiser 2003: 40–41; *Lelia E. Marsh . . . v. Ne-Ha-Sa-Ne* 1897; New York Forest Commission 1893: 154; *New York Times* 1891a: 1; 1891b: 8).

As private parks proliferated in the Adirondacks, tensions escalated between conservationists, wealthy landowners, and local residents who found their access to fish, game, and other forest resources impeded by barbed-wire fences, armed guards, and No Trespassing signs. The private parks—which defied a long-standing tradition of leaving undeveloped forests open for hunting, fishing, and foraging—became the source of rural people's ire. Policymakers couldn't ignore the conflict. Consequently, in 1899 an investigative committee of the New York State Assembly noted that poor rural residents were complaining that the forest lands were being bought up by private owners who employed guards to keep locals away from the resources (New York State Assembly 1899: 9).

Local residents responded to the private parks and estates in the Adirondacks by burning them, ripping down the No Trespassing signs, cutting holes in the fences, and firing at the guards. In 1888, there were reports of fires destroying the woods, so guards were hired to watch the woods at night. The following year, forestry officials noted that the number of fires had increased; they were also alarmed that the fire wardens had difficulty getting local men to help fight the fires. They believed the men were reluctant to help because many had been fined and otherwise punished for infractions of conservation laws (*New York Times* 1888g: 5; 1889f: 6; 1899b: 5). Refusal to fight fires was a form of everyday resistance[7] that local men used to communicate their displeasure to authorities who had penalized them for hunting, fishing, or harvesting timber.

Tensions were so high that Rockefeller, of Standard Oil, always traveled with armed body guards. Shots were often fired into the opulent lodge on his fifty-thousand-acre Bay Pond estate, so he installed bright floodlights. He had acquired the land for his estate in 1899 and posted 1,508 signs around the property that read, "NOTICE! PRIVATE PARK. All persons are hereby warned not to hunt, fish, camp or in any manner trespass upon the following described premises or any stream or body of water within their boundaries, or disturb or interfere in any way with the fish or wild birds or wild animals upon said premises, under strict penalty of the law, as the premises described now constitute a private park for the protection, preservation and propagation of fish, birds and wild animals" (*William Rockefeller v. Oliver Lamora* 1903). Snipers fired at his guards so frequently that some of them quit. Much of Rockefeller's park was burned by several fires in 1903. Reports are that Rockefeller hired a team of about 150 firefighters to battle the blaze, which lasted almost a month; Rockefeller himself also helped fight the fire (Adirondack League Club 1899: 24; 1904: 15; Jacoby 2001: 41–43; *New York Times* 1903d: 5; 1903e: 1; 1904c: 8; 1904d: 1). The forest fires of 1903 also threatened the estates or "camps" of J. P. Morgan and Alfred G. Vanderbilt (*New York Times* 1903f: 1; *William Rockefeller v. Oliver Lamora* 1903).

At times, wealthy landowners enclosed people within their parks. Rockefeller purchased lands surrounding the small town of Brandon to create his estate. Though most town residents sold their properties to him only to watch as he demolished their homes, fourteen families refused to sell. Rockefeller simply built and fenced in his private park around them. A series of long-running court battles ensued, as residents were prohibited from using any of the resources in the park. Local residents ignored the No Trespassing signs and continued to hunt, fish, cut timber, and forage for resources in the woods. Rockefeller took one resident, Oliver Lamora, to court because he continued to fish in the streams. Lamora argued that he had a right to fish in Rockefeller's park because the stream was stocked with fish by the state, therefore the stream was open to the public. However, the Appellate Court ruled against Lamora, concluding that Lamora had not proven his case and that the stream was private (*William Rockefeller v. Oliver Lamora* 1903, 1904, 1905, 1906).

Before working-class men vented their frustrations about discriminatory conservation laws and enforcement by murdering the game wardens such as Guy Bradley in Florida and Seeley Houk in Pennsylvania, poor men in the Adirondacks turned their guns on a wealthy landowner to show their displeasure at having their access to forest resources curtailed. On September 20, 1903, Orrando Perry Dexter, a wealthy lawyer and landowner who had sued local men who poached timber from and set fire to his property, was shot to death on his five-thousand-acre estate. He was driving his carriage on what used to be a public road when he was killed; he had privatized the road by enclosing it. Dexter was also in a bitter dispute with locals after he purchased land around and enclosed a stream on which area residents had floated logs to the mills for years. Dexter was a forty-nine-year-old Oxford-educated bachelor and Columbia Law School graduate who collected hunting trophies. Convinced his son had been killed by a timber poacher, Dexter's father, the millionaire founder of the American News Company, called in the Pinkerton Detective Agency and offered a reward of five thousand dollars, but no arrests were made. After Dexter's death, the new owners of the estate allowed locals to hunt and fish on the tract (Burdick 1982: 23–49; *New York Times* 1903b: 3; 1903c: 14; 1905c: 5).

A 1904 Bureau of Forestry report concluded that many of the fires occurring in the Adirondacks were deliberately set. The report noted that fires were also caused by natural causes, carelessness, fallow burning (fires set in the spring and fall to burn the fields before and after the planting season), and railroad operations. The report estimated that seventy-five thousand acres of private parks had been burned. However, the report also blamed the fires on the high wages paid to firemen (who allegedly set fires so there would be work to do) and on local residents who believed the laws prevented them from using timber for subsistence purposes (Adirondack League Club 1899: 24; 1904: 15; Jacoby 2001: 41–43; *New York Times* 1903d: 8; 1903e: 1; 1904c: 8; 1904d: 1).

Many rural residents resented the state foresters, but they disdained private park owners and wealthy out-of-town sportsmen even more. There was also a lingering feeling that the wealthy recreationers did not abide by the rules and were not being punished for infractions of the laws. Consequently, local residents provided tips to foresters and game wardens to help bring affluent landowners and sportsmen who violated conservation laws to justice. John Hunkins recalled how challenging it was for foresters to work in the reserves. He reported, "On my first trip [to St. Lawrence County] I was unable to obtain a boat or any accommodations from these people for any consideration. Our lives were in constant jeopardy, either from those we had prosecuted or from those who feared being called to account for their many misdeeds" (New York Fisheries Commission 1894: 158).

However, as time went on, local people gave Hunkins and other foresters information about the infractions of sport hunters and wealthy landowners. For instance, local residents made foresters aware that Lieutenant Governor Woodruff was violating the hounding law by keeping a pack of deer-hunting dogs in his private park. Some of J. Pierpont Morgan's employees also informed game protectors that Morgan fished out of season on the streams in his private park. Morgan was fined $155 for thirteen trout found at his camp that were caught out of season. Oliver Lamora, Rockefeller's nemesis in court, also helped to secure the arrest of two of Rockefeller's employees for hounding deer. Rockefeller's superintendent, John Redwood, and one of the gamekeepers, Harry Melville, were fined $100 each. Local residents were so intent on exposing the misdeeds of rich sportsmen and estate owners—and to dispel the myth that only poor rural residents broke the game and timber laws—that a group of Tucker Lake residents formed the Adirondack Game and Fish Protective Association in 1903 to "fight Rockefeller men" (*Forest and Stream* 1906: 547; Jacoby 2001: 62–63; Van Valkenburgh 1979: 72). In so doing, local residents inserted themselves into the conservation discourse as more than just poachers; they adopted the role of wildlife and forest protectors and law enforcers. They did this by mimicking the name of conservation organizations and by appropriating the discourse of conservationists. By forming such a group, local residents were also putting game protectors and foresters to the test to see whether they would prosecute affluent people who violated conservation laws.

The tensions between locals and the owners of private parks and estates were so great that by 1897 the state's legislature created a fund to purchase land to expand the public forest preserve. Four years later, the state owned more than a million acres of land. But this did not stop affluent men from having significant control over the resources. Arguing that "the Adirondack preserve is largely for the benefit of the millionaires who own large estates in that section," in 1904 Senator Burton pushed the state legislature to appropriate funds to acquire more lands in the reserve for public use (Jacoby 2001: 46–47; *New York Times* 1904e: 8). By 1906, the state owned roughly 1.52 million acres of land (New York Forest, Fish, and Game Commission 1907: 8).

However, putting more forests in the hands of the state did not solve one vexing problem in the region: access to timber. Because the woodlands were essentially under state control or in the hands of private estate and park owners, many local people had no access to wood for firewood or building materials. As a result, they regularly resorted to timber poaching. While forestry officials and private landowners saw their actions as theft, locals didn't perceive it this way. They saw the cutting of timber for subsistence purposes as a necessity to ensure their survival, not a criminal act (Jacoby 2001: 51–52; New York Forest, Fish, and Game Commission 1895: 760–761). The challenges faced by the Adirondack Forest Reserve were not unique. During the late nineteenth and early twentieth centuries, many of the forest reserves and state parks faced similar challenges and class conflicts, which made managing these reserves a difficult task.

PRESERVATION, CONSERVATION, AND BUSINESS INTERESTS COLLIDE

Many activists preferred vast, untamed landscapes to the cities and countryside. Those activists took solace in remote areas; wilderness was the landscape that held the greatest attraction for them. Like the development of rural cemeteries, urban park building, conservationism, and rural beautification, the idea of wilderness preservation originated among the eastern literati.

Cultural Nationalism and the Idea of National Parks

Early wilderness appreciation and advocacy was closely linked to the emerging cultural nationalism and romanticism that elites espoused. Appreciation for vast, open, remote, and solitary places, promoted by the likes of Muir and Thoreau, resulted in the romanticization of the wilderness and a desire to see and preserve it. American elites, feeling that their country's civility and cultural attainment lagged behind Europe's, began searching for ways to enhance the prestige of American culture at home and abroad. Thus they set their sights on developing and promoting art; cultural and educational institutions such as museums, galleries, and universities; and large landscaped parks. They also sought to identify natural wonders that had no counterparts in Europe or exceeded European landscapes in aesthetic and dramatic appeal. In addition, during the nineteenth century, gentility spread from the upper class to the middle class. That meant more Americans collected books and artwork, hired tutors for their children, toured Europe, attended theaters and museums, and joined literary clubs. In addition, communities built elaborate churches, libraries, athenaeums, and civic institutions. Americans also began to preserve artifacts and to recognize unique and dramatic landscapes as important national and cultural symbols (Curtis 1855: 124–125; Downing 1848: 138–146; 1851: 147–153; Nash 1982: 1–83; Rosenzweig and Blackmar 1992: 23; Rybczynski 1999: 31).

Landscape painters—most notably Thomas Cole and Winslow Homer of the Hudson River School, and Albert Bierstadt and Thomas Moran of the Rocky Mountain School—played a significant role in raising people's consciousness about the beauty and uniqueness of the American landscape. These artists were ardent cultural nationalists. Beginning in the 1820s, Hudson River School artists such as Cole, steeped in the romantic tradition, began painting and publicizing the forest and wilderness scenes of the Catskills and other eastern mountains. By the 1850s, Bierstadt, Moran, and other artists had begun painting the Sierra Nevadas, Rockies, and other western landscapes on gigantic canvases. In addition to artwork revealing stunning, mysterious, and breathtakingly beautiful landscapes, explorers and naturalists regaled the public with tales of their outdoor explorations. Early European settlers viewed the wilderness negatively; it was feared, associated with damnation, or seen as an obstacle to be tamed, conquered, or manicured. But by the mid-nineteenth century, Americans were starting to view the wilderness more positively. This changing perception of wilderness coincided with the elites' desire to take pride in being American. In their frequent travels to Europe and correspondence with their European contemporaries, they were often stung by the criticism that America was uncultured and backward. In addition, when they compared America to Europe, America came up wanting. The United States lacked Europe's grand cathedrals, museums, landscaped parks, and mountain retreats like the Alps. Eventually the literati came to realize that the American wilderness had no counterpart in Europe. Thus wilderness was transformed from a liability to an asset, and the vast mountains became its crowning glory (Dilsaver 1994: 7; Nash 1982: 1–83).

Americans wrote about wildlands more frequently in positive terms during the nineteenth century than ever before. For instance, Audubon wrote that he gazed all day at the grandeur and beauty of the scenery as he and his wife glided down the Ohio River by boat in 1808 (Audubon 1832: 29). William

Cullen Bryant, one of the earliest and most ardent urban park advocates, was an early wilderness advocate too. In 1811, he paid homage to forested landscapes in a poem. Four years later Bryant, a lover of the picturesque and a romantic expressing Rousseauesque sentiments, urged those who had experienced the stress and cares of the civilized world to go to the wilds and see nature (Bryant and Parke 1883: 19, 23, 228–232; Nash 1982: 74–75; Runkle 1872: 31–52). Also in 1815, Thomas Jefferson argued that government should protect places of beauty for the public. When he refused to sell the land around the Natural Bridge in Virginia, he justified his decision thus: "I view it in some degree as a public trust and would on no consideration permit the bridge to be injured, defaced or masked from the public view" (Jefferson 1815). During the 1820s, Audubon wrote about the destruction of the forests to feed the lumber mills while he traveled the Ohio Valley in search of bird specimens (Audubon 1926: 4, 9–10). In 1929, Audubon complained about the degradation of the landscape and disappearing wildlife around the Ohio River. Audubon also saw the early signs of industrialization and sprawl as the woods gave way to new towns and villages. He noted that native tribes were being displaced to accommodate the changing land uses and settlements (Audubon 1831–1839: 31–32). Romantics like James Fenimore Cooper, Thomas Cole, Washington Irving, and Francis Parkman expressed similar sentiments (Nash 1982: 75–115). Caroline Kirkland, too, was critical of forest practices that resulted in deforestation and degradation of the environment (Kirkland 1842: 43).

The painter and explorer George Catlin was one of the first people to articulate the idea of a national park. In 1832, after spending time with Native Americans hunting buffalo on his travels through South Dakota, he wrote that forest destruction was endangering entire ecosystems and that the wildlife and tribes would not survive (Catlin [1841] 1965: 260). He suggested the establishment of a national park to preserve native tribes and the buffalo. According to Catlin such a park would promote refinement in the citizenry. Catlin wanted a pristine "magnificent park" where "refined citizens" could see "the native Indian in his classic attire, galloping his wild horse, with his sinewy bow, and shield and lance, amid the fleeting herds of elks and buffaloes" (Catlin [1841] 1965: 261–262). It should be noted that Catlin wanted to see a national park in which elites (the "refined citizens") could view both wildlife and Indians on display. Moreover, with this conceptualization Catlin establishes the idea that national parks should be pristine. They should also be places where the effects of time could be suspended and natural and human curiosities preserved in perpetuity. In 1832, Congress set aside Hot Springs in Arkansas because of its medicinal value; the springs were not preserved because of unique scenery (Runte 1987:

26).[1] After that, preservation and open-space development efforts ground to a halt for about a decade.

During the 1840s Thomas Cole expressed his concern over the disappearance of wilderness and saw the need for saving and perpetuating its features (Noble [1853] 1964: 299), while in 1851 Horace Greeley of the *New York Tribune* urged Americans to "spare, preserve and cherish some portion of... [their] primitive forests" (Greeley 1851: 39). Henry David Thoreau, a friend of Greeley, also expounded on these themes. He argued that wildness was an essential component of life. Thoreau wrote, "Life consists with wildness. The most alive is the wildest. Not yet subdued to man, its presence refreshes him" (Thoreau 1982: 611). He stressed that humans are intimately connected to nature (Thoreau 1982: 592).

Throughout the 1840s and 1850s Thoreau campaigned to halt the destruction of the wilderness. He also refined Catlin's park idea. He estimated the size of a viable park and introduced the idea of public, inviolate sanctuaries. Thoreau suggested that each Massachusetts township should develop a park of five hundred to one thousand acres to preserve the trees and wild animals (Thoreau 1893: 208; 1982: 78–79, 613–614). As Thoreau saw it, "trees made an admirable fence to the landscape, skirting the horizon on every side" (Thoreau 1982: 195).

Thoreau recognized that there were class disparities in access to open space. He noted that the upper class had access to private parks and were willing to abuse their power to secure, maintain and privatize those resources. Consequently, he suggested developing public parks that everyone could have access to. In 1853, he proposed that America should have national preserves (Thoreau 1982: 88–108). Thoreau had spent time in the forests of Maine, whose government had begun setting aside small pockets of public lands throughout the state (D. B. Botkin 2001: 147). The jurist and naturalist Samuel Hammond also proposed that the government establish large parks. He wanted to create a reserve in New York's Adirondack Mountains. Hammond declared that he would "mark out a circle of a hundred miles in diameter, and throw around it the protecting aegis of the constitution" (Hammond 1857: 82–84).

Yosemite as a Symbol of Cultural Nationalism

The idea of national parks and wilderness protection in America did not originate with any one person; rather, it evolved over half a century as various activists formulated and refined it. Though Yellowstone is recognized as the nation's first national park, it was in Yosemite that the idea first took shape. Early visitors to Yosemite saw the area's potential to become a national symbol. They wrote about the valley in glowing cultural nationalistic terms. These descriptions helped to publicize the valley and create the impetus to preserve it. For instance, Horace Greeley wrote after his 1859 visit to Yosemite, "The big trees have been quietly nestled for I dare not say how many thousand years . . . they were of very substantial size." Greeley also described the valley as "the most unique and majestic of nature's marvels . . . no single wonder of nature on earth" could surpass it (Greeley 1860: 306–307, 311–312).

Awestruck by Yosemite, Reverend Thomas Starr King of Boston wrote an article in the *Boston Evening Transcript* describing the area's "stupendous rock scenery." He declared that nothing "among the Alps, in no pass of the Andes," could rival Yosemite, except "the awful gorges of the Himalayas" (King 1861: 1). Samuel Bowles, publisher of the *Springfield (Massachusetts) Republican*, traveled across the country with a party of explorers during the summers of 1865 and 1866. He met Frederick Law Olmsted in Yosemite. On seeing the valley Bowles wrote, "It is not too much to say that no so limited space in all the known world offers such majestic and impressive beauty. Niagara alone divides honors with it in America. Only the whole of Switzerland can surpass it,—no one scene in all the Alps can match this" (Bowles 1869: 375). He was also impressed with the Three Brothers, Cathedral Rocks, and Cathedral Spires and thought they outshone the Gothic cathedrals of Europe (Bowles 1868: 226–227). Clarence King, famed explorer of the Sierras, also wrote about the region in cultural nationalistic terms (King [1872] 1970: 43–44).

Some early visitors were less concerned about cultural nationalism, focusing instead on Yosemite's potential for tourism. James Mason Hutchings, one of the earliest Anglo visitors to the valley, hired an artist to sketch the valley on his first visit in 1855; in 1859 he also became the first to hire a photographer to take pictures of the valley. With an eye toward capitalizing on tourism, he began publishing romanticized sketches and engravings of Yosemite in his *Hutchings's Illustrated California Magazine* and *Scenes of Wonder and Curiosity in California*. Carleton Watkins photographed the valley in 1862, and the following summer Albert Bierstadt spent seven weeks sketching the valley. The thirty-three-year-old Bierstadt, who was hosted by Hutchings, used bold colors (in contrast to the Hudson River painters, who were fond of pastel shades) to dramatize the scenes, making the valleys appear deeper, the cliffs higher, and the sunlight more vivid. These paintings garnered wide publicity (Hutchings 1871; Runte 1990: 16).

The decisive push to turn the Yosemite Valley into a park did not come from the budding preservationists of the time; it came from businessmen and political elites. The businessmen benefited from their support of preservation efforts, hence some park supporters had mixed motives for wanting to see Yosemite turned into a park. In February 1864, Israel Raymond, the California state representative of the Central America Steamship Transit Company of New York, sent a letter to one of California's senators, John Conness, urging him to preserve the Yosemite Valley and the Mariposa Grove of giant sequoias. Raymond enclosed photographs of the valley in his letter. Raymond's plea to save the valley did not rest solely on the aesthetic appeal of the valley or its intrinsic worth; he thought the valley should be preserved because it did not appear to be commercially exploitable except for tourism. He wrote that the summits were composed of bare granite rocks, and elsewhere the ground was covered by pine trees that "can never be of much value." Raymond urged Conness to take steps to prevent private parties from taking ownership of or destroying the valley, since the best use would be to make it a public recreational resort that was "inalienable forever." However, he argued that portions of the valley could be leased for up to ten years (Farquhar 1965: 123; Roper 1973: 268; Runte 1990: 19).[2]

Raymond's valuation of the valley did not take into consideration the use value that Native American tribes ascribed to their homeland (W. Harding 2014; Solnit 2000). It ascribed worth only to developmental value or civil rights potential. Worth derived from natural rights was not considered. The settler colonial practice of ignoring the value tribes placed on their territories was evident in the campaign to establish Yellowstone and other national parks.

Senator Conness forwarded Raymond's letter to the General Land Office. In May, the Senate Committee on Public Lands responded favorably to the proposed bill. According to the Senate, the bill sought to preserve lands "that are for all public purposes worthless, but which constitute, perhaps, some of the greatest wonders of the world." In addition to assuring fellow senators that the valley was a scenic wonderland that did not hold anything of commercial value, Conness also evoked cultural nationalistic arguments. He reminded his colleagues that the British had originally denied the existence of the giant sequoias. He argued that when sections of a fallen giant sequoia were displayed at the London World's Fair, some viewers declared it to be a "Yankee invention," because people did not believe that such large trees grew in America. To counter this skepticism, a grove of large sequoias should be saved as proof of their existence. Yosemite and the giant sequoias were symbols to be used to defend America's pride and patriotism. The bill requested that the Yosemite Valley and Mariposa Grove be given as a grant to the state of California to be administered by "gentlemen" appointed by the governor. Noting that the application for protection had come from "various gentlemen of California, gentlemen of fortune, of taste, and of refinement," Conness urged Congress to grant the valley to the state. The measure passed, and on June 30, 1864, President Abraham Lincoln signed the Yosemite Park Act into law (Act 1864; Roper 1973: 268, 282; Runte 1990: 19–21).

OLMSTED AND YOSEMITE'S FIRST MANAGEMENT PLAN

Once Yosemite Valley was declared a park, the state of California had jurisdiction over it. However, at the time the park was established, the ecology of the valley was not well understood (Runte 1990: 7). Consequently, the park boundaries were too small to protect all the sensitive ecosystems that needed protection. In September 1864, Frederick Law Olmsted,[3] then head of the floundering Mariposa Mining Company, was appointed by Governor Frederick Low to chair the eight-man commission[4] charged with managing the valley and grove (Censer 1986: 4, 59; Ranney, Rauluk, and Hoffman 1990: 29; Roper 1973: 268). One of Olmsted's first tasks was to oversee James Gardner and Clarence King as they conducted a survey of the park boundaries. In August 1865, shortly before returning to New York to resume work at Central Park, Olmsted outlined the goals and functions of a park of this nature in his first commissioner's report (Ranney, Rauluk, and Hoffman 1990: 22–23; Roper 1973: 287).

In the management plan, Olmsted wrote that places like Yosemite should be public parks for all to enjoy. It is to the advantage of the commonwealth, he maintained, to possess objects that cannot be removed from the public domain. Furthermore, the parks should never be privatized. He argued that the main (if not sole) duty of the government was to provide the means for citizens to pursue happiness and to protect them from the whims of those likely to hinder said pursuits. Olmsted noted that the wealthy could build, and have throughout history built, private parks, hunting preserves, and clubs; in countries such as Britain, he pointed out, the "choicest natural scenes in the country and the means of recreation connected with them" are monopolized by the wealthy. Therefore he urged the government to take steps to ensure that Yosemite did not become a private preserve for the rich. Olmsted was also familiar with how wealthy American urbanites had built private parks and hunting grounds for themselves while the masses lacked access to open space. After years of working as the superintendent of Central Park, Olmsted was well versed in the art of making arguments in support of public parks and in framing them as democratic instruments that reduced social inequality.[5] Thus Olmsted contended that women and the agricultural class were less likely to have access to recreation, yet were in greater need of the reinvigoration that exposure to places like Yosemite could bring. Democratic arguments notwithstanding, Olmsted hastened to argue that the "civilized" (middle and upper) classes were more likely to appreciate places like Yosemite than "savages" (Olmsted 1865). He explained, "The power of scenery to affect men is, in a large way, proportionate to the degree of their civilization and the degree in which their taste has been cultivated. Among a thousand savages there will be a much smaller number who will show the least sign of being so affected than among a thousand persons taken from a civilized community" (Olmsted 1865: 8).

Here Olmsted completely misunderstood or refused to appreciate the extent to which Native Americans shaped the very landscape he admired and was trying to preserve. There is no indication that he knew how fire and other practices by the tribes resulted in the open meadows and other landscape features that he admired and sought to protect (W. Harding 2014; Olwig 1995; Solnit 2000). In fact, he fretted about the Native American use of fire in the valley (Olmsted 1865).

Olmsted concluded that it was the duty of the government to guard and manage Yosemite "for the free use of the whole body of the people forever." Noting that the valley was being degraded rapidly, he suggested that laws be enacted and enforced to protect it from unjust uses (such as the cutting or burning of trees) by individuals (Olmsted 1865).

Olmsted was not the first to express the idea that the government should preserve places of unusual beauty for the benefit of the whole population; Jefferson had made the argument half a century earlier (T. Jefferson 1815). The urban parks too provided a model of public ownership of open spaces. However, Olmsted refined Jefferson's argument in applying it to Yosemite. Olmsted read the report before the other commissioners and invited guests such as Samuel Bowles to attend. After hearing the report, Bowles suggested that reservations modeled after Yosemite should be established at Niagara Falls, in parts of the Adirondacks, and in the lake-and-woods regions of Maine. Bowles's observations appeared in his book describing his 1865 cross-country trip (Bowles 1868: 231; Roper 1973: 287).

The idea that it was possible to establish national parks in America was born with the establishment of the Yosemite Valley and Mariposa Grove Reserve, but the national park idea was first fully realized in Yellowstone eight years later.

YELLOWSTONE AND CULTURAL NATIONALISM

Whites may have visited Yellowstone between 1806 and 1810, when John Colter was said to have traversed the area. Though it is doubtful that Colter actually saw Yellowstone, the evidence is stronger that James Bridger saw the territory by the 1830s. Soon after gold was discovered in the nearby Montana Territory, miners began to relay stories about the area to the public. As the legend of Yellowstone grew, an expedition was organized in 1869. The Cook Expedition reported on the existence of canyons, lakes, geysers, and thermal basins in the area. The Washburn-Langford-Doane Expedition was organized the following year. Henry Washburn served two terms in Congress, after which he was appointed surveyor-general of Montana. The nineteen-man expedition consisted primarily of easterners who had attained some prominence as politicians, lawyers, reporters, and military men (Runte 1987: 34–37). In describing the Upper Geyser Basin to Congress, Lieutenant Gustavus Doane highlighted the superiority of the American geysers to any in Europe (Doane 1871: 142). Nathaniel Langford called the geysers the "most remarkable feature in our scenery and physical history" and said they were "found in no other countries but Iceland and Tibet" (Langford 1871b: 127). In his report to Congress, Representative Dunnell, a member of the Committee on the Public Lands, repeated Doane and Langford's description of the geysers and added his own glowing descriptions of the hot springs (Dunnell 1872: 1–2).

THE PARK IDEA TAKES HOLD

While camping in Yellowstone, members of this expedition discussed the region's future. Some members wanted to stake claims to lands around the features that were most prominent or had the most potential for commercial exploitation. However, Cornelius Hedges, a miner, lawyer, and correspondent for the *Helena Herald*, disapproved of those plans (Runte 1987: 41–42). According to Langford, Hedges suggested that there shouldn't be any private ownership of the area; instead, the land should be set aside as a national park, and expedition members should campaign to make this happen. Others agreed with him, and a plan of action was set in motion (Langford 1872: 117–118). Though it is doubtful that the campfire discussants used the term "national park" in 1870, the men did help to get Yellowstone designated the nation's first national park (Runte 1987: 42).

During the winter of 1870–1871, the Northern Pacific Railroad paid Langford to make presentations on the expedition in Washington, New York, and Philadelphia. In Washington, Ferdinand Hayden, a geology professor at the University of Pennsylvania and director of the U.S. Geological Survey, heard Langford's talk and became interested in Yellowstone. Hayden immediately made plans to mount an expedition to Yellowstone in 1871. Congress appropriated forty thousand dollars to fund the survey team. A military reconnaissance mission also set out for a Yellowstone expedition at the same time the Hayden team departed. The Hayden Expedition included a large number of scientists, along with artist Thomas Moran and William Jackson, a frontier photographer who captured images of the Southwest and Yellowstone. Like Bierstadt, who grew famous from his Yosemite drawings, Moran became famous for his Yellowstone paintings (Runte 1987: 39).

MORE WORTHLESS LAND

It is quite likely that activists used the Yosemite grant as the model for promoting the idea that Yellowstone should be designated a public park (the enabling legislation of Yellowstone did not even refer to a national park). However, unlike Yosemite, which was ceded to the state of California, the federal government retained control of Yellowstone because Wyoming was a territory, not a state, at the time the proposal was being made. Proponents of the park described the area as picturesque, but they wished to see some developments in the region that would facilitate tourism (Act 1864; Runte 1987: 42–44; Yellowstone Act 1872: 32–33).

By the time the Hayden Expedition got to Yellowstone in 1871, two speculators were already cutting poles so that they could fence off and privatize the geyser basins along the Firehole River. Northern Pacific Railroad financier Jay Cooke and officials of that railroad, which provided the sole passenger rail service to the area, played a role in the passage of the Yellowstone Park bill. Cooke was interested in government ownership and administration of Yellowstone because he thought it would be more expedient for the railroad to deal with the government than with private landowners. He indicated that turning the area into a federal reservation or park would prevent "squatters and claimants" from privatizing the most scenic spots. Cooke wanted the government to assume control of the area as quickly as possible (Runte 1987: 44–46; Sellars 1997: 9).

Hence Northern Pacific Railroad not only sponsored Langford's lecture series, but also funded Thomas Moran to travel with the Hayden survey team. In October 1871, a Northern Pacific Railroad agent asked Hayden to lobby on behalf of the park proposal. Hayden's report strongly recommended that the House Committee on Public Lands turn the area into a public park. Congress asked Hayden to suggest an appropriate boundary for the park. He drew the boundary large enough to protect Yellowstone's curiosities, but not necessarily the larger wilderness surrounding them (Runte 1987: 44–46; Turner 1985: 282–283).

In the meantime activists worked hard to secure passage of the Yellowstone Park bill. They distributed four hundred copies of Langford's articles in *Scribner's Monthly* to Congress (Langford 1871a: 10; 1871b: 127–128; Runte 1987: 46). Jackson's photographs and Moran's watercolors and sketches were also prominently displayed at the Capitol. In 1872, Congress bought one of Moran's renditions, *The Grand Canyon of the Yellowstone*, for ten thousand dollars and hung it in the lobby of the Senate. In addition, Hayden and others also met with individual legislators to persuade them to vote in favor of the bill. But before Congress approved the bill, its members wanted to ascertain whether the area had any future economic potential. Hayden argued persuasively that the land was useless except for tourism (Runte 1987: 39, 46–54; U.S. Congress 1872: 1–2).

Promoting Yellowstone as a place with the potential of becoming a "resort for all classes of people from all portions of the world," Representative Dunnell tried to convince Congress that the area was in immediate need of protection because entrepreneurs and vandals would ruin the park. Dunnell argued, "Persons are now waiting for the spring to open to enter in and take possession of these remarkable curiosities, to make merchandise of these beautiful specimens, to fence in these rare wonders so as to charge visitors" (Dunnell 1872: 1–2). Finally convinced that the area was generally worthless but in immediate need of protection, Congress passed the bill. On March 1, 1872, President Ulysses S. Grant signed the Yellowstone Park Act into law (Yellowstone Act 1872).

Though Dunnell's report mentioned the words "national park," the Yellowstone Park Act did not. The area was designated as a "public park, or pleasuring ground for the benefit and enjoyment of the people." As with Yosemite, leases were granted for the construction of buildings for terms not exceeding ten years. In addition, all persons who were considered trespassers in Yellowstone would be removed from the park (Act 1864; Dunnell 1872: 1; Yellowstone Act 1872).

Once Yellowstone National Park was created, Langford became its superintendent. In a letter from the acting secretary of the Department of the Interior,
Langford was told that the department was not interested in any attempts to
beautify or adorn the park. His duty was simply to protect the park from "injury or spoliation" of the timber, mineral resources, and curiosities. Congress
did not appropriate any funds to administer Yellowstone, so Langford acted as
superintendent without pay until appropriations were made (Cowen 1872: 1).

Almost a year after taking the superintendent's job, Langford compiled a
report on the park in which he noted the need to enhance access to the park by
constructing roads. He noted that several individuals had applied for permits to
build access roads to the park. There was also considerable interest from people
wanting to build hotels at the main tourist attractions in the park. Others applied for permits to build sawmills. Langford indicated that he spent much of
the first year dealing with squatters' claims, establishing and enforcing rules to
protect wildlife, and reducing timber poaching (Langford 1873: 3).

The removal clause in the Yellowstone Act was a major factor in the park's
management. It affected Native Americans whose ancestral lands lay within
the park boundaries. The establishment of the park meant the tribes lost access
to traditional hunting and gathering grounds and religious sites. The removal
clause was also aimed at squatters and speculators who had taken up residence
in the vicinity shortly before it was declared a national park. The speculators
tried to establish squatters' rights to land around the greatest points of interest
in the park in the hope that they would preempt the Yellowstone Act and be
granted private property rights in the park. Some of those speculators applied
for recognition of their property rights during the first year the park was in operation. Langford recommended that all such claims be denied (Langford 1873:
4; Yellowstone Act 1872).

POACHING, ARSON, AND THE BOONE

AND CROCKETT CLUB'S PARK ADVOCACY

Boone and Crockett members began campaigning to improve the condition of
Yellowstone National Park soon after it gained park status.[6] But some senators,
such as John Ingalls of Kansas, saw the park as irrelevant and expensive. An
opponent of making appropriations for the upkeep of the park, Ingalls argued
that the government should not get into "show business." Instead he urged that
the government survey the area and sell it off (Nash 1982: 113).

At the time it was established, the park and its wildlife were coming under severe pressures from the increasing numbers of visitors touring the site (about five thousand annually), the construction of hotels and roads in the park; the rapid growth of border towns; the activities of timber thieves, poachers, and vandals; mining interests; real estate speculators; and plans to build a rail line through it. Without any federal laws or enforcement mechanisms to support them, park superintendents were left on their own to manage and protect park resources. Senator George Vest of Missouri came to Yellowstone's defense. During the urban parks campaign activists had argued that parks were necessary because they were breathing spaces or the lungs of the city. Co-opting this argument, Vest argued that Yellowstone was a "mountain wilderness" that acted "as a great breathing-place for the national lungs" (Nash 1982: 111, 114; Taylor 2009: 223–250).[7]

In 1883, the Yellowstone Park Improvement Company sought to lease 640 acres of parkland to build hotels, stores, and stage and telegraph lines; raise cattle; and have unlimited access to water, timber, and arable lands. Initially the company's request was approved. However, while Senator Vest fought to protect Yellowstone through congressional action, Grinnell used *Forest and Stream* to publicize what was happening in the park. Grinnell published articles arguing that to complete the six-hundred-room hotel the Yellowstone Park Improvement Company planned to build at Mammoth Springs, the company wanted to build a sawmill to harvest the timber from the park. That same year Vest tried to pass a bill (the Vest Bill) aimed at making the park an inviolate wildlife sanctuary; each time the bill was introduced, however, it was opposed by hunters, trappers, real estate speculators, miners, and railroad companies. The Vest Bill also proposed increasing the size of the park to about 3,344 square miles, adding station troops to guard the park, and fining poachers. The bill passed the Senate in 1884, but failed in the House. Moreover, the Cinnabar and Clark's Fork Railroad Company had also succeeded in attaching riders to the bill that would have granted them right-of-way access across the park (Nash 1982: 114; Reiger [1975] 2001: 135–145).

The Cinnabar and Clark's Fork Railroad Company did not give up when the bill failed to pass. They tried to get right-of-way across the park on their own in order to facilitate mining ventures during the mid-1880s. Representative Lewis Payson of Illinois thought granting the railroad's wishes would not harm the park's geysers and hot springs. He believed that the mine would generate millions of dollars, so the railroad's request was reasonable. A railroad representative, speaking before Congress, indicated that to deny the railroad the right-of-way would be to "yield to . . . a few sportsmen bent only on the protection of a few buffalo." Undaunted, park supporters continued to campaign hard for the park; they spoke about its "marvelous scenery" and the need to preserve a public park with "inspiring sights and mysteries of nature." Congress eventually voted to deny the railroad access to the park (*Congressional Record* 1886: 150).

In 1892 the railroad lobby managed to introduce a bill (the Segregation Bill) in Congress that sought to remove 622 square miles in the northern portion of the park from the national park boundaries. Grinnell and the Boone and Crockett Club campaigned vigorously to oppose the bill. Grinnell was adamant that the northeastern corner of the park should not be opened to what he saw as the "depredations" of hunters, trappers, and prospectors. Though the Segregation Bill was defeated, the park and its managers were still threatened. On some occasions poachers killed park patrollers. Even when they were arrested, poachers were often released soon afterward because there were no laws governing park offenses. Thus the Boone and Crockett Club decided to take action to protect park resources. *Forest and Stream* published a steady barrage of articles on the violence and poaching problems in the park, and Grinnell sent photographers to document these activities. Soon after a photographer caught a notorious poacher, Howell (responsible for killing eighty buffalo and damaging between two thousand and five thousand dollars' worth of park property), in the act of killing a buffalo, Congressman Lacey, a member of the Boone and Crockett Club, introduced his version of the Vest Bill in Congress. The story of the poacher was reported in newspapers across the country, and that aroused public indignation (E. Hough 1894: 1–6; *Forest and Stream* 1894c: 243). Early park superintendents also documented the degradation of the park. This included graffiti, removal of artifacts, throwing logs into the geysers, and washing laundry in the hot springs (Oberhansley 1938: 1).

As with the forest reserves, rural residents and Native American tribes did not see hunting and killing of the wildlife in the national parks for subsistence purposes as poaching or criminal activities. Indeed, hunting was so well established in the park that the first superintendent, Langford, proposed that hunting in the Yellowstone be restricted to subsistence hunting for local residents and park visitors. However, laws prohibiting hunting in the park remained (Oberhansley 1937: 4). A later superintendent, Captain Moses Harris, discussed the widespread poaching in the park. Harris also reported that some of the fires burning in the park were deliberately set by local residents angry at his predecessor, Superintendent Wear. Harris noted that though some of the fires may have been started by careless campers, others were started by "unscrupulous hunters, who, being prevented from hunting in the Park, resort to this method of driving the game beyond the Park limits." Harris also blamed Bannock Indians from the Lembi Reservation for setting fires deliberately (M. Harris 1886: 7).[8] According to Harris, "The Park is surrounded by a class of old frontiersmen, hunters and trappers, and squaw-men. As the game diminishes outside the Park [they] increase their efforts and resort to all sorts of expedients to get possession of that which receives the protection of law" (U.S. Department of the Interior 1886: 2). Superintendent Wear noted that these things went on because of the "entire inadequacy of the laws to provide punishment to violations of the regulations for the protection of the Park" (Wear 1886: 2).

Hornaday blamed both market hunters and subsistence hunters for decimating the game in the park and expressed his outrage that neither were caught nor convicted (Hornaday 1914: 21–22). As in the Adirondacks, there was apparent local support for poaching and arson as a means of protesting national park rules. Hornaday, who saw such acts as contempt for the law, was exasperated with this way of thinking. He argued that both judge and jury were sympathetic to those charged with these acts and often let them go free because they were hunting to feed their families. He warned, "Any community which tolerates contempt for law, and law-defying judges, is in a degenerate state, bordering on barbarism; and in the United States there are literally *thousands* of such communities! The thoroughness with which one lawless individual who goes unwhipped by justice can create a contempt for law and demoralize a whole neighborhood is both remarkable and deplorable. That way lies anarchy" (Hornaday 1914: 188–190, italics in original).

Hornaday wrote about the resistance to conservation and preservation laws in the West. He stated that, "Out West, there is said to be a 'feeling' that game and forest conservation has 'gone far enough' . . . Many men of the Great West,—the West beyond the Great Plains,—are afflicted with a desire to do as they please with the natural resources of that region" (Hornaday 1913: 335). One westerner living in Wyoming summed it up this way: "When you say to a ranchman, 'You can't eat game, except in season,' you make him a poacher, because he is neither going hungry himself nor have his family do so . . . More than one family [here] would almost starve but for the game" (Letter to the Editor 1895: 141).

The infamous Yellowstone poacher Howell added his perspective to the debate. He sent letters to the newspaper in which he argued that he hunted buffalo in the park because of the skill and bravery involved. For instance, he and his hunting party planned their forays into the park in great detail. They were aware of animal behavior and knew the terrain and how to identify good hunting grounds. He also indicated that it was thrilling to outwit the park employees and execute a successful hunt. Howell thought that more people would brave the heavy snowfall, subzero temperatures, and military patrols to hunt in the park if they weren't so timid (*Forest and Stream* 1894d: 444; Howell 1894a, 1894b). Though elite hunters and conservationists framed men like Howell as worthless, greedy, and ignorant market hunters bent on decimating wildlife, Howell did not see himself as such. In his reflections on why he hunts (to show bravery, take risks, demonstrate skill and knowledge, overcome natural elements, and outwit patrols or avoid ambush), he identifies reasons similar to the ones that motivate elite sportsmen. Manliness was another overarching theme that connected elite sportsmen and poachers. Both saw hunting as a manly activity to provide food for the table, earn money, or demonstrate mastery over wild animals.

Many of the poachers in the park were working-class men who labored in agriculture or in the nearby quartz and coal mines (U.S. Department of the Interior 1908: 12; 1907: 24). It should be said that not all locals around Yellowstone were poachers or wanted to be considered such. In fact, some local residents provided tips about poaching activities to park employees. Others made it clear that they did not want to be lumped together with poachers (Anonymous n.d., Document No. 696; Anonymous n.d., Document No. 2553; Doyle 1901). This was evident in 1899 when residents of Jackson Hole, Wyoming, collected money to hire an extra game warden to track down elk poachers in the adjacent Grand Tetons. In 1902, they formed a Game Protective Association, and in 1906, they started a citizens' committee to identify poachers and seek their prosecution (Betts 1978: 181–184; E. W. Hayden 1971: 22–36, 64; Simpson 1898a: 468; 1898b: 485; *United States v. Binkley* 1906: 220).

The Boone and Crockett Club's campaign to protect Yellowstone gained public support. Letters and petitions expressing outrage at the lack of protection for Yellowstone's resources poured into Congress. In 1894, Lacey drafted a bill to protect wildlife in Yellowstone and halt the slaughter of bison in the park. The Lacey Bill "to protect the birds and animals in Yellowstone National Park, and to punish crimes in said park" was signed by President Cleveland. The bill also made it illegal for convicts to seek refuge in the park and for individuals or trains to transport wildlife taken from the park. It mandated jail sentences for anyone killing wildlife, removing mineral deposits, or destroying timber, and it specified that the vehicles and equipment of park offenders could be confiscated. In addition, the bill authorized funds to build a jail at the park's headquarters (Lacey 1894: 73; Trefethen 1975: 82–90).

With the designation of the nation's first reserve and national park, interest in wilderness as well as romantic and picturesque scenery soared. In 1872 and 1874, the publication of William Cullen Bryant's two-volume *Picturesque America* brought a rich variety of descriptions and illustrations of wilderness areas into the living rooms of upper- and middle-class Americans. In the preface of the first volume, Bryant argued that there was no need for Americans to go overseas to see the grandest mountains, valleys, precipices, or rocky pinnacles, since the West offered scenery that surpassed any in Europe (Bryant 1872: preface; 1874). As Americans flocked to these places, the move to preserve them grew stronger.

The Sierra Club

The popularity of wilderness exploration and mountaineering led to the formation of alpine clubs in the late nineteenth century. For instance, the Williamstown Alpine Club was formed in 1863. The White Mountain Club was formed a decade later, and the Appalachian Mountain Club in 1876 (Turner 1985: 290). Toward the end of the nineteenth century, East and West Coast elites, with the help of activists in organizations such as the Sierra Club, launched a more concerted effort to define and preserve wilderness. When John Muir met with a group of men in 1889 to explore the possibility of establishing an alpine club, the select group included Berkeley professors, the president of Stanford University, and an attorney who would later become the mayor of Oakland. The Sierra Club was founded in 1892 at the urging of Robert Underwood Johnson, member of the Appalachian Mountain Club and the editor who had published Muir's Yosemite articles in *The Century* (Cohen 1988: 21–22, 66; Colby 1947: 4; Easton 1969: 13–15; Fox 1981: 107; Schrepfer 1983: 10–11; Sierra Club 1960: 4–5; Turner 1985: 291; Wilkins 1995: 177–178). Club members dedicated themselves to "exploring, enjoying and rendering accessible the mountain regions of the Pacific Coast, and to enlist the support and co-operation of the people and the government in preserving the forests and other features of the Sierra Nevada Mountains" (Publications of the Sierra Club 1892).

Only 5 of the original 182 charter members were women; 25 were professors, 12 were doctors, 1 was a university president, and 4 had the word "Honorable" in their titles. While twenty-eight of the charter members were affiliated with the University of California at Berkeley, 9 were affiliated with Stanford,

6 belonged to the California Academy of Sciences, 2 were with the Stock Exchange, and 2 were with the U.S. Geological Survey. The Sierra Club did not want a mass membership. In fact, Johnson urged Muir to control the size of the membership. Notwithstanding, the club attracted some public interest in the first year of its founding. Two hundred fifty people attended the first general meeting, and about six hundred attended the second (Publications of the Sierra Club 1893: 23–24; *Sierra Club Bulletin* 1893a: 16–20; 1893b: 25–29).

Unlike the Audubon Society, which organized branches in many states and nationalized its agenda from the outset, the Sierra Club remained one organization with a specific focus on the protection of the Sierra Nevada Mountains. Hence five years after its founding, the Sierra Club had only about three hundred members and was contemplating opening its first branch in Los Angeles. If the club organized branches, the impulse was still to locate them in California (*Los Angeles Times* 1897: 7). While the Audubon targeted children and got them involved in Audubon activities soon after its founding, the Sierra Club did not consider forming a junior Sierra Club until 1913 (*Los Angeles Times* 1913b: 118). Nonetheless, the Sierra Club emerged to play major roles in campaigns to expand Yosemite and place it under federal control, and to stop the damming of the Hetch Hetchy Valley.

The Federal Government and Preservation Efforts

THE CAMPAIGN FOR THE EXPANSION OF YOSEMITE

Though preservationists were pleased that the Yosemite Valley / Mariposa Grove area was a reserve, they quickly realized that the original grant was too small to preserve the ecosystem it was intended to protect and that California was unable to manage the valley effectively. Thus activists such as John Muir began campaigning to expand the boundaries of the park and to place it under federal protection. However, arguments based purely on aesthetic appeal and scenic preservation did not sway lawmakers. It took an intervention from Southern Pacific Railroad and the irrigators of the San Joaquin Valley to accomplish this feat. The two groups joined forces with preservationists when the irrigators realized they needed to protect the sources of freshwater in the mountains and the railroad realized the profits that could be made from promoting tourism and transporting tourists in the Sierra Nevadas. The Yosemite Park Commission endorsed the proposal to expand the park in 1881 by using arguments that blended preservationism and utilitarian conservationism. They supported the expansion not only to protect the valley and preserve water flow, but also because they wanted to sustain the area's mines (Runte 1990: 45–46).

In its 1882 and 1884 reports, the Park Commission also supported the enlargement of the park. Despite the growing movement to expand Yosemite, the Interior Department began selling off lands on the perimeter of the Yosemite Grant to timber and mining companies. As a result, about sixty thousand acres of forests fell into private hands between 1881 and 1890 (Runte 1990: 46, 49). The Northern Pacific Railroad, which began promoting Yellowstone National Park in 1883, demonstrated how railroads could capitalize on the synergistic effects that existed between railroads and tourism in the newly designated national parks. The Southern Pacific Railroad, which was also responsible for irrigated farms and other land developments in California's Central Valley, grasped the significance of protecting watersheds for tourism and development needs. Thus when John Muir and Robert Underwood Johnson turned to the railroad for help in expanding Yosemite, Southern Pacific was only too willing to assist (Runte 1990: 54).

In March 1890, Representative William Vandever of Los Angeles introduced a bill in Congress to establish a national park around the 1864 land grant. At first the bill attempted to increase the size of the park from 58 square miles to 288 square miles. Muir and other preservationists were dismayed, as the proposed boundary was a lot smaller than they campaigned for and left many critical watersheds unprotected. Vandever's bill was backed by Daniel Zumwalt, a land agent for the Southern Pacific Railroad, and it passed easily. But on the last day of the legislative session, a new Yosemite bill was introduced by Vandever. The new bill, which called for adding 1,512 square miles to the original 58 square miles of the grant, passed the House and Senate easily. President Harrison wasted no time signing the measure into law. On October 1, 1890, he signed the bill establishing a new preserve around the original grant. Thus Yosemite National Park was born. However, the 1864 land grant area still remained under the jurisdiction of California. Following the precedent established at Yellowstone in 1886, Yosemite was placed under the protection of the U.S. Cavalry in 1891. Troops patrolled the park until 1914, when they were replaced by civilian rangers (Act 1890; Farquhar 1965: 202–203; Runte 1990: 45, 55–57, 84).

THE CAMPAIGN TO REDUCE THE SIZE OF YOSEMITE

Opponents of Yosemite immediately began lobbying to reduce the size of the park. In 1891, they called for a removal of all the sugar pine forests from the western boundary and all the mining and grazing districts from the southern portion of the park. The Sierra Club opposed any reduction in the size of the park. However, the opponents kept reiterating their demands until finally, in 1905, Congress approved a bill that eliminated about 542 square miles of territory from the park.

The lands removed were in the foothills—well outside the core scenic areas of the park. Moreover, to compensate for land eliminated, Congress extended the boundary of the park northward to incorporate an additional 113 square miles of mountainous terrain. But although the area eliminated was not as scenic as that which remained in the park, it served as significant wildlife habitat: it was the breeding ground and winter refuge of some of the park's fauna. In addition, the lands removed contained some of the park's oldest trees. Thus in many ways, while scenic beauty was preserved, the biological integrity of the park had been compromised. President Theodore Roosevelt signed the bill redrawing the boundaries of Yosemite (*New York Times* 1893: 4; Runte 1990: 67–68, 76).

Ironically, while lands were being withdrawn from Yosemite, Yellowstone was actually enlarged twice. When Yellowstone was created in 1872, it covered 3,344 square miles. By 1897, when it was enlarged a second time, it had almost doubled in size (Muir [1901] 1981: 39).

THE CAMPAIGN FOR THE RECESSION OF THE VALLEY

Around the time the debate over the size of Yosemite reached a fever pitch, another debate was also nearing its crescendo. The Sierra Club and the Southern Pacific Railroad supported the recession of the original Yosemite Grant to the federal government. They thought unified management and control would be best for the park. Supporters of recession also believed that federal control would provide additional funding and would reduce the corruption and mismanagement that had plagued the original grant. At the time, the Yosemite Park Commissioners were unpaid, and the Yosemite Valley and Mariposa Grove had an operating budget that didn't exceed fifteen thousand dollars per year. Thus preservationists argued that the state could not care for the valley properly (Runte 1990: 84–85).

Though the Sierra Club urged the federal government to undertake projects that promoted tourism, the concessionaires and local developers opposed recession because they believed the state was more amenable to a wider range of commercial developments in the valley than the federal government would be. However, the Southern Pacific Railroad realized that its own interest in tourism and passenger traffic would be facilitated if the federal government appropriated funds to build the infrastructure in and around the park. In January 1905, John Muir appealed to his friend Edward Harriman (who controlled Southern Pacific Railroad) to help with the passage of the recession bill. Harriman and Southern Pacific were enormously influential in California politics, and later that year the California legislature approved a bill transferring the land grant back to the federal government. Harriman also helped preservationists win congressional acceptance of California's gift. In June 1906, President Roosevelt signed a joint resolution by the House and Senate recognizing California's decision to reconvey Yosemite Valley and Mariposa Grove to the federal government. But there was a catch: an amendment to the resolution accepting Yosemite Valley and Mariposa Grove from California further reduced the size of the park by about 16.33 square miles (Runte 1990: 85–86).

The Antiquities Act: A New Vehicle for Preservation

The Antiquities Act was an important piece of legislation enacted in 1906 that bolstered preservation efforts. Under the act a president could declare lands of historic value, historic and prehistoric structures, and objects of historic or scientific interest situated on government-owned or controlled lands to be national monuments. Furthermore, anyone who appropriated, evacuated, injured, or destroyed any historic or prehistoric ruin or monument or any object of antiquity found on government-owned land without permission could be convicted, fined, or jailed. The Antiquities Act also allowed the secretary of the interior to accept private donations on behalf of the government (Act 1906).

Originally the Antiquities Act was envisioned as one that would protect mostly prehistoric tribal ruins and artifacts on federal lands in the West. However, after it was passed Theodore Roosevelt interpreted the act broadly and used it to protect eight hundred thousand acres of the Grand Canyon and similar areas. In three years, Roosevelt used the Antiquities Act to protect eighteen monuments. President Taft used the Act in a similar fashion; by 1911 he protected ten additional monuments. It wasn't until 1943 that this broad interpretation and use of the Antiquities Act was challenged (National Park Service 2004). The Antiquities Act quickly became an alternative vehicle that preservationists used to protect land of significant cultural, historical, and scientific interest. The act provided protection for landscapes that weren't as large or spectacular as Yosemite or Yellowstone but nevertheless had unique features worth preserving.

MUIR WOODS

Although there had been great strides in protecting wildlands, preservation conflicts continued to simmer in the West. By the late nineteenth century most of the stands of redwoods in and around the San Francisco area had been logged. However, a stand of old-growth redwoods was left untouched in Marin County on the southern flank of Mount Tamalpais in an area known as Redwood Canyon. These redwoods were spared because the slopes where they grew were rugged and inaccessible. Sightseers started visiting the area in the 1870s to see the giant trees. The San Francisco–based Bohemian Club took an interest in the area and considered buying the property as a retreat for club members. But the club abandoned the idea soon after spending a cold, foggy night in the canyon in 1892. After the Bohemian Club lost interest in the Mount Tamalpais property, it was sold (Evarts and Popper 2001: 132).

As early as 1900, Muir was asked to help preserve the redwoods on Mount Tamalpais, but nothing much came of it. Efforts to preserve the canyon gained momentum in 1903 when Congressman William Kent met with local preservationists in nearby Mill Valley to create the Mount Tamalpais National Park Association. Kent's friend Gifford Pinchot also attended the meeting. The goal was to create a twelve-thousand-acre national park to help protect Redwood Canyon (also known as Sequoia Canyon). Kent also owned property on Mount Tamalpais and stood to benefit from the creation of a national park on the mountain. Activists knew that the Tamalpais Land and Water Company, owner of the land, was interested in selling the property. They were also aware that a new railroad near the property would make it more accessible and vulnerable to logging. Kent was reluctant to purchase the parcel at first but decided to buy 611 acres of the land in the canyon for forty-five thousand dollars in 1905. Kent's purchase was fortuitous, since it is quite likely the canyon would have been logged the following year in the aftermath of the San Francisco earthquake and fire, which resulted in a dramatic increase in the demand for wood (Evarts and Popper 2001: 132; Fox 1981: 134–135; National Park Service 2002).

Kent considered turning the property into a private resort, but before he could finalize those plans, the redwoods were threatened again. In 1907, the North Coast Water Company of Sausalito went to court to obtain the right to dam Redwood Creek and flood most of Redwood Canyon. Part of Kent's property containing giant redwoods was condemned to make room for the dam and reservoir. In response, Kent contacted officials in Theodore Roosevelt's cabinet and offered the land as a gift to the nation. Kent's hope was that Roosevelt would take advantage of the Antiquities Act and accept the land under the aegis of this legislation. In addition to establishing national monuments, the Antiquities Act allowed the president to accept gifts from private citizens without congressional approval. With the aid of spectacular photographs of the canyon and Pinchot's lobbying, Kent convinced Roosevelt to accept the gift (Evarts and Popper 2001: 132; National Park Service 2002).

Consequently, in December 1907, William Kent and his wife, Elizabeth, donated a 295-acre portion of their property on Mount Tamalpais to the federal government. The transfer, signed by Theodore Roosevelt, was officially completed on January 9, 1908, and the property was named Muir Woods National Monument in honor of John Muir. Muir Woods, the tenth National Monument designated, was the first created from land donated by a private citizen. A day before his death in 1928, Kent donated an additional two-hundred-acre parcel of land that helped provide the core of Mount Tamalpais State Park—a steep ravine bordering Muir Woods (Act 1906; Evarts and Popper 2001: 133; *Los Angeles Times* 1928: 9; National Park Service 2002).

ACADIA NATIONAL PARK

Wealthy families on the New England coast reacted to perceived threats to their property in much the same way that the Bay Area elites did. By the 1870s, Mount Desert, an island off the coast of Maine, was an established, exclusive vacation destination for aristocrats. Mount Desert was about fourteen miles long and eight miles wide. In 1896, the Seal Harbor Water Supply Company acquired property for pipelines and a reservoir on the island through condemnation proceedings. In 1901, wealthy families (including the Vanderbilts, Danas, Dorrs, and Eliots) living or summering on Mount Desert met to discuss how the island was being developed. The families formed a nonprofit land trust, the Hancock County Trustees of Public Reservations, to prevent further subdivision of the land. The land trust was chartered by the state to accept private gifts of land and hold them, tax-free, for public recreational use in perpetuity. Development on the island intensified in 1909 when real estate companies began building cottages on Eagle Lake above Bar Harbor, thereby threatening the water supply. The following year, Rockefeller bought a home at Seal Harbor on Mount Desert Island (Bunce 1872b: 1–17; Dorr 1938, 1940; Dutcher 1907; Eliot 1915; Fox 1981: 136–138; Judd 1997: 199; *Sieur de Monts* 1916: 1785–1791).

Both the Bar Harbor Water Company and the land trust group opposed the Eagle Lake development. The water company responded by condemning the lakefront property and then acquiring the property through the land trust. Incensed, local real estate developers countered by introducing a bill in the state legislature to rescind the land trust's charter. In response, the leader of the land trust lobbied the Speaker of the House (one of his good friends) intensely and managed to defeat the bill. However, the land trust wanted a more permanent way to preserve land. Hence in 1913, George Dorr, whose ancestors had made a fortune from the China trade, met with Secretary of the Interior Lane to get support for preservation efforts on Mount Desert Island. Two years later, Dorr had asked Charles Eliot, president of Harvard University, to find out whether Rockefeller would make a contribution toward preservation efforts on the island. Rockefeller donated $17,500. He followed this with a gift of twenty-seven hundred acres of land to the trust. However, Rockefeller reserved the right to build roads across and ride his horses on the land he donated. Using the Muir Woods model pioneered by Kent, the land trust offered about five thousand acres of Mount Desert land to the federal government to establish a national monument. In July 1916, President Woodrow Wilson accepted the gift. It was named Sieur de Monts National Monument.[9] The monument was renamed Lafayette National Park in 1919 and Acadia National Park in 1929. In 1935, Rockefeller donated another 3,935 acres to Acadia, and again he reserved and exercised the right to build three more road projects in the park (Albright and Schenck 1999: 269–271; Fox 1981: 137–138, 220–221; Lafayette National Park 1919: 1178–1179; *Sieur de Monts* 1916: 1785–1791).

Damming Hetch Hetchy

Preservationists weren't fully aware of it yet, but while they fought for the valley, another gargantuan battle was brewing over the fate of Yosemite. The conflicts around resource use, access to water, energy development, and wilderness preservation soon came to a head in the Hetch Hetchy controversy. Thus far conservationists had successfully challenged the millinery industry, as well as hoteliers,' restaurateurs,' and furriers' use of birds, fish, and game. They were also successful in halting commercial development in Yellowstone. Hetch Hetchy became one of the first major environmental battles where conservationists and preservationists openly challenged each other over the development of a wilderness resource. The controversy pitted two of the leading ideological thinkers of the time—Pinchot and Muir—against each other and thus played an important role in the rise of the conservation movement.

As San Francisco grew, civic leaders began searching for a cheap, reliable water supply. In 1877, Colonel George Mendel of the Army Engineering Corps conducted a study for the city in which he identified fourteen potential sources that could provide adequate water. The city's interest in Hetch Hetchy began when an 1879 report by the State Geologists of California suggested that Lake Eleanor and Hetch Hetchy (the Tuolumne River Valley), both of which lay in Yosemite National Park, would be the most appropriate sources of water for San Francisco. In 1883, a corporation was formed to investigate the possibility of bringing Hetch Hetchy water to the city (*New York Times* 1909d: 8; Vilas 1915: 1–12). A 1900 city charter stipulated that San Francisco must develop its own water supplies and storage facilities. That year, the city engineer Colonel Mendel began assessing fourteen potential reservoir sites, and in 1901 Mendel and Manson submitted a report that recommended developing the Tuolumne River valley (Branson 1909: 3–5; Committee on Public Lands 1908: 6; Vilas 1915: 10).[10]

The Tuolumne Valley, which lies 3,700 feet above sea level, drained 1,501 square miles of the western slopes of the Sierra Nevada Mountains. The proposed Hetch Hetchy Valley site was about 160 miles east of San Francisco. Water from the valley could reach the city through a 183-mile conduit. By the time the report was completed, the engineers had spent fifty thousand dollars studying the feasibility of getting Hetch Hetchy and Lake Eleanor water to San Francisco. About seventy-nine square miles of tributaries drain into Lake Eleanor, which lies about eight miles northwest of Hetch Hetchy and is about one thousand feet higher in elevation. The lake drains into the Tuolumne River (Committee on Public Lands 1908: 6; Fox 1981: 139; Rosekrans et al. 2004: vii; Vilas 1915: 7–10; Wilkins 1995: 226–227).

According to the engineers' report, Hetch Hetchy and Lake Eleanor were the best sources of water. Despite the distance from San Francisco, the Tuolumne Valley was preferred over other sites because the water was pure and abundant. There were ample storage sites, and the valley was unencumbered by water rights claims. It also had the potential for hydropower development. The Board of Public Works approved the report soon after it was submitted, and in July 1901, Mayor Phelan submitted a claim for ten thousand miner's inches of water from the Tuolumne River for irrigation, manufacturing, power generation, and domestic use (Vilas 1915: 10–11).

San Francisco's water supplier was the Spring Valley Water Company. One could say the city and the water company grew up together. The Spring Valley Water Company had a storage reservoir on Pilarcitos Creek, located about twenty-five miles from San Francisco. Though the Spring Valley Water Company charged high fees for water, their service was poor. At the time the city began to investigate alternative sources of water, San Francisco was consuming about 50 million gallons of water per day. Of that amount, the Spring Valley Water Company provided about 41.5 million gallons (Vilas 1915: 18). Because the city was dissatisfied with the water company, civic leaders were on the lookout for a new water source and were anxious to gain access to Hetch Hetchy water.

THE PASSAGE OF THE RIGHTS-OF-WAY ACT

San Francisco got one step closer to damming Hetch Hetchy when Congress passed a Rights-of-Way Act in 1901 that made it possible to build dams in national parks, forests reserves, and on other public lands. Nine months after the Rights-of-Way Act was passed, San Francisco's mayor, James Phelan, applied for the water rights in both Hetch Hetchy Valley and Lake Eleanor. The city then applied for a permit to build dams at both sites in 1903. In December of that year, Secretary of the Interior Ethan Hitchcock, rejected the proposal on the grounds that it violated the 1890 law creating Yosemite National Park, which guaranteed the park's integrity. Though the city did not file another petition right away, it questioned the legal right of the secretary of the interior to decide on right-of-way petitions. In 1905, the attorney general ruled that the secretary of the interior had full discretionary powers to make decisions on requests to grant rights-of-way in national parks (Committee on Public Lands 1908: 6–7; Rights of Way Act 1901: 790–791; Runte 1990: 76; Wilkins 1995: 226–227).

EARTHQUAKE AND FIRE: A NEW IMPERATIVE

The 1906 earthquake and subsequent fire catapulted water to the top of San Francisco's agenda. Shortly after the disaster, San Francisco bonded itself for $6 million. The city also constructed a reservoir at an elevation of six hundred feet, a pumping station that drew salt water from the bay, and a high-pressure water system that supplied about seventy-two miles of pipes. The city also attempted to purchase the Spring Valley Water Company (Vilas 1915: 18).

Civic leaders also revived plans to dam Hetch Hetchy. Mayor Phelan used the hysteria caused by the devastating earthquake and fire to his political advantage. He argued that had his earlier applications to dam the valley been approved, San Francisco would have had enough water to fight the fire. Phelan obfuscated the facts: once a permit is granted to build a dam, it takes several years before the dam is operational, so even if the permit had been approved in 1903, the city still would not have had access to Hetch Hetchy water in 1906. Second, Phelan glossed over the fact that lack of water was not what caused the fire to spread throughout the city. There was adequate water, but the earthquake broke the water mains, thus water drained from broken pipes, creating a muddy slush (Wilkins 1995: 227–228).

In the meantime Pinchot was working behind the scenes to help San Francisco. By 1906 it was more widely known that a secretary of the interior could grant permission to build dams at Hetch Hetchy and Lake Eleanor without congressional approval. As long as Hitchcock or any other secretary of the interior with similar ideological views was in office, this was not a possibility. But the winds of political change shifted in San Francisco's favor. That year James Garfield (son of the former president) was appointed as secretary of the interior. Pinchot, a friend of Garfield's, did not waste any time informing San Francisco that the time was right to reapply for the permit (Wilkins 1995: 228). Pinchot made his intentions clear in a letter to Marsden Manson: "I hope sincerely that in the regeneration of San Francisco its people may be able to make provision for a water supply from the Yosemite National Park . . . I will stand ready to render any assistance which lies in my power" (Pinchot 1906; quoted in Wolfe 1945: 312).

DAM HEARINGS IN SAN FRANCISCO AND
AN ILL-TIMED TRIP TO THE HIGH SIERRAS

Though San Francisco's petition to dam Hetch Hetchy was closed in 1903 after the Hitchcock ruling, city officials proceeded as if they still had an open petition before the Department of the Interior. Thus on the evening of July 24, 1907, while Sierra Club members (the most vocal opponents of the dam) were away on their annual outing to Yosemite, hearings about the proposed dams were held in San Francisco. Since no one appeared to oppose the dam, plans for the project moved forward. However, that fall the opponents of the dam—Muir, the Sierra Club, and other preservationists—began soliciting support from other like-minded activists across the country. They sought and got support from groups such as the Appalachian Mountain Club and the General Federation of Women's Clubs. They also published articles in influential magazines such as *Outlook* and *Century Magazine* and in leading newspapers. Ironically, the preservationists and the local water company—the Spring Valley Water Company—were on the same side. This did not help the preservationists' cause, since the water company was reviled by many of the city's inhabitants (Nash 1982: 161).

In 1908 John Muir appealed directly to President Roosevelt to try to save Hetch Hetchy. Muir, who first saw Hetch Hetchy in 1871, argued that all the water needed by San Francisco could be obtained from sources outside Yosemite. Muir's appeal led Roosevelt to suggest to Garfield that he grant a permit for Lake Eleanor alone (Muir 1988: 18, 192). Roosevelt wrote to Garfield that he thought it was "unnecessary to decide about the Hetch Hetchy Valley at all at the present. Why not allow Lake Eleanor, and stop there? . . . There seems to be no reason why we should take action on the Hetch Hetchy business now" (Roosevelt 1908, quoted in Wolfe 1945: 313).

In 1908 San Francisco again filed for a petition to build dams in Hetch Hetchy and Lake Eleanor. Though the city did not have an active petition before the Department of the Interior, Garfield treated the case as if the city's petition had never lapsed and the 1908 petition simply meant a continuation of an ongoing case (Committee on Public Lands 1908: 11–15). On May 11—four days after receiving the city's petition—Garfield issued a "revocable permit" to San Francisco for the reservoir rights of Lake Eleanor and Hetch Hetchy. The permit imposed no condition on which the government would be compensated for property valued at about $200 million that would be affected by the dams. The permit stipulated that the Lake Eleanor site should be developed first to its full capacity, that San Francisco residents had to accept the gift, and that Congress had to ratify it. Two days after Garfield issued the permit, Pinchot and Roosevelt hosted the Governors' Conference on Conservation at the White House (Committee on Public Lands 1908: 11–15; Wilkins 1995: 228–230; Wolfe 1945: 314). The conflict continued to escalate.

On November 12, 1908, a referendum on the Hetch Hetchy question was held in San Francisco; residents favored six to one taking the government grant of land at Hetch Hetchy Valley and Lake Eleanor for the purposes of constructing a dam (Committee on Public Lands 1908: 31–33). After the referendum, the dam opponents stepped up their national campaign. They argued, "We do not believe that a great national property preserved for the enjoyment of the people of the entire nation should be thus unnecessarily sacrificed and diverted from its dedicated purposes for the mere pecuniary benefit of a local interest" (Fox 1981: 142; Muir 1908c). Meanwhile, letters commenting on the proposed dam poured in from all over the country; most were from outside California. Muir, the leading dam opponent, wrote, "[The] most precious and sublime feature of the Yosemite National Park, one of the greatest of all our natural resources for the uplifting joy and peace and health of the people, is in danger of being dammed and made into a reservoir to help supply San Francisco with water and light, thus flooding it from wall to wall and burying its gardens and groves one or two hundred feet deep" (Muir 1988: 192).

The dam's opponents wanted to preserve the land, not use it in a utilitarian manner. They wanted to leave it untouched for future generations. They were also motivated to stop the Hetch Hetchy dam because between 1905 and 1906 Yosemite National Park had lost about 558 square miles of territory. They thought the removal of lands violated the 1890 Park Act, and they were reluctant to see the park violated again (Runte 1990: 7, 85–86). Framing Yosemite as "the people's park," Muir attacked the conservation ideology by claiming it was supported by those seeking immediate gratification and commercial gain from the park's destruction. He also argued that the degradation of the park was couched in the language of nation building. He argued that the parks "have always been subject to attack by despoiling gainseekers and mischief-makers of every degree from Satan to Senators, eagerly trying to make everything immediately and selfishly commercial, with schemes disguised in smug-smiling philanthropy, industriously, shampiously crying, 'Conservation, conservation, panutilization,' that man and beast may be fed and the dear Nation made great" (Muir 1988: 193). Muir referred to the lake that would be created behind the dam as "the beautiful sham lake"; he said it would be an eyesore and a dismal blot on the landscape (Muir 1988: 195–196).

Likewise, conservationists publicly criticized and belittled the preservationists. The dam's proponents—the City of San Francisco, Gifford Pinchot, and many western legislators—argued that Muir and his colleagues were being selfish. Dam supporters embraced the conservationist position: they claimed that they intended to use the land wisely and sustainably. They argued that the good of the many (providing water for approximately 750,000 people in metropolitan San Francisco) and the current generation should prevail over the good of a few. For them, utility had supremacy over intrinsic worth (Committee on Public Lands 1908; Fox 1981: 139–141; Holway Jones 1965: 90; Nash 1982: 161–167; Pinchot 1906; Roosevelt 1907). Dam supporters also argued that Hetch Hetchy was not unique—at least not in the way preservationists claimed it was. Conservationists described the valley as a mosquito-infested meadow that would be improved by damming, as the valley floor would be transformed into a beautiful lake after the reservoir was completed. In fact, they argued, if Hetch Hetchy was another Yosemite Valley (as preservationists contended), and only a paler version of its better-known counterpart, then the less spectacular of the two valleys could be dammed (Runte 1990: 81; Wilkins 1995: 227).

Though preservationists were drawn to the solitude and wildness of Hetch Hetchy, conservationists seized on its remoteness as yet another reason to utilize the site as a dam and reservoir rather than a tourist destination. The preservationists' own description of the remoteness of Hetch Hetchy was used to justify damming the valley. Take for instance Edmund Whitman's description of Hetch Hetchy and Pinchot's reaction to the valley. Whitman, a Boston lawyer and president of the Society for the Protection of National Parks, said of Hetch Hetchy, "I cannot attempt to describe to you the character of the country. It is some of the roughest God ever made. You do find little places here and there with grass and water, but the largest part of the country is the roughest sort, where camping is as impossible as it would be on the top of this table . . . There are only three places in the entire park where you can take care of horses" (quoted in Vilas 1915: 8). This led Pinchot to conclude that Hetch Hetchy's scenic beauty was "altogether unimportant compared with the benefits to be derived from its use as a reservoir" (Wilkins 1995: 229–230).

The preservationists were also referred to as "hoggish and mushy esthetes," an opposition composed largely of "short-haired women and long-haired men" (Committee on Public Lands 1909: 16; Manson 1910). The conservationists considered the preservationists gullible and thought they were being used as mouthpieces for the water company. Kent, a Sierra Club member and the man who donated land for Muir Woods, maintained that the campaign against the dam was being orchestrated by private water power interests who were using "misinformed nature lovers" to speak on their behalf (W. Kent 1913a). J. Horace McFarland responded to conservationists who referred to the preservationists as "nature fakers" by accusing the city of San Francisco of spending hundreds of thousands of taxpayers' money to promote the dam project and maintain lobbyists in Washington (J. H. McFarland 1913: 12).

Conservationists also directed public criticisms and personal attacks directly at Muir. They sought to portray him as a selfish zealot and loner willing to sacrifice everything to save the park. San Francisco's Mayor Phelan argued, "John Muir loves the Sierras and roams at large, and is hypersensitive on the subject of the invasion of his territory" (Phelan 1907), and "I am sure he would sacrifice his own family for the preservation of beauty. He considers human life very cheap, and he considers the works of God superior" (Wolfe 1938: 316). Even Kent supported the dam and criticized Muir. In a letter to Representative Sydney Anderson of Minnesota, Kent wrote, "I hope you will not take my friend, Muir, seriously, for he is a man entirely without social sense. With him it is me and God and the rock where God put it, and that is the end of the story. I know him well and as far as this proposition is concerned, he is mistaken" (W. Kent 1913b).

In December 1908, the House Committee on Public Lands held a hearing on Hetch Hetchy. Most of the members of the House and Senate committees were from western states (Muir 1909b: 21). Activists on both sides of the controversy sent letters or testified before the committee. John Muir argued in his letter that "most of our forests have already vanished in lumber and smoke," hence it was important to save Hetch Hetchy because "beauty plays an important part in human progress." Muir continued, "Every national park is besieged by thieves and robbers and beggars with all sorts of plans and pleas for possession of some coveted treasure of water, timber, pasture, rights-of-way, etc. Nothing dollarable is safe, however guarded." He thought the San Francisco board of supervisors and "monopolizing capitalists" were trying to ruin Hetch Hetchy for private gain. To Muir, the damming of the Tuolumne Valley would amount to a monumental public loss. To stave off the criticism that preservationists cared more about nature than the lives of the people, Muir made the case in another letter submitted to the committee: "We [the dam's opponents] hold life more sacred than scenery, than even great natural wonderlands" (Committee on Public Lands 1908: 31–33).

Muir heaped scorn on opponents, whom he referred to as "these temple destroyers" and "devotees of ravaging commercialism" who "seem to have a perfect contempt for Nature." According to Muir, "instead of lifting their eyes to the God of the mountains" they "lift them to the Almighty Dollar." He uttered in disgust, "Dam Hetch Hetchy! As well dam for water-tanks the people's cathedrals and churches, for no holier temple has ever been consecrated by the heart of man" (Muir 1988: 196–197). Muir also argued that dam supporters believed destroying Hetch Hetchy was the only option (Muir 1908d: 211–220).

Muir and other dam opponents made constant references to the similarities between Hetch Hetchy and Yosemite—a line of argument that was turned against them during the campaign. In his earliest article on Hetch Hetchy, written in 1873, Muir began the essay by referring to Hetch Hetchy as "one of a magnificent brotherhood of Yosemite Valleys." He described several similarities between the two valleys and asserted that "the world is so rich as to possess at least two Yosemites instead of one" (Muir 1873: 2). Muir made similar comparisons in other publications (see for example Muir 1908c; 1908d: 211–220). Robert Underwood Johnson and Allen Chamberlain also submitted statements to the Committee on Public Lands that describe Hetch Hetchy as being similar to Yosemite, but "less wonderful" (R. U. Johnson 1908) and "a little inferior" (Chamberlain 1908). Similar comparisons were made in *Yosemite against Corporate Greed* (Branson 1909: 7).

When conservationists argued that the less spectacular of the twin valleys could be dispensed with, Muir rebutted by describing Hetch Hetchy as a high-lying natural landscape garden with unique features that were rare and beautiful. Drawing comparisons to Central Park, Muir pointed out that to argue that damming Hetch Hetchy would enhance its beauty was akin to saying that same thing about Central Park (Committee on Public Lands 1908: 31–33). Muir used the urban park movement to strengthen his case: he brought in the "landscaped garden" theme, evoking Americans' love for elegant urban parks. He contended, "Landscape gardens, places of recreation and worship, are never made beautiful by destroying and burying them." Muir argued that this thirst for nature could be seen "displayed in poor folks' window-gardens made up of a few geranium slips in broken cups, as well as in the costly lily gardens of the rich, the thousands of spacious city parks and botanical gardens, and in our magnificent National Parks" (Muir 1908d: 211–220). However, even after the Committee on Public Lands hearings where opponents described Hetch Hetchy as an underutilized, expendable Yosemite lookalike, Muir still continued to refer to Hetch Hetchy as a "wonderfully exact counterpart of the great Yosemite" (Muir 1909b: 2).

Conservationists wishing to refute the argument that the Hetch Hetchy Valley was used by large numbers of people pointed out that though roughly seven thousand people visited Yosemite annually, only about three hundred visited Hetch Hetchy (Vilas 1915: 8). To support this point, Colonel Cosby of the Board of Engineers testified that only two groups of people used Hetch Hetchy—those who were unusually wealthy and those who were unusually strong and healthy (Vilas 1915: 24).

Muir also tried to dispel the notion that Hetch Hetchy had the purest water and was the only adequate source of water for the city of San Francisco. He argued that the water was not the cleanest because a campground used by hundreds of visitors and their animals drained into the river. Muir noted that the engineers' report indicated that there were many other potential sources of water. Muir also questioned the fact that only the residents of the city of San Francisco and county were allowed to vote on whether Hetch Hetchy should be dammed even though damming the Tuolumne River affected residents in other counties as well (Committee on Public Lands 1908: 31–33).

In a circuit court case in northern California Pinchot contended that San Francisco's water supply was "inadequate and unsatisfactory" and that the "Tuolumne supply offered the best and most available supply for the city." However, William Colby, recording secretary of the Sierra Club, also submitted a letter to the Committee on the Public Lands noting that Gifford Pinchot also admitted there were other sources of water that San Francisco could use. Colby's position was supported by engineers who testified in the circuit court case. Colonel Mendel identified fourteen potential reservoir sites; in addition, Mr. C. Grunsky indicated that the Spring Valley Water Company supplied high-quality water to the city. Several engineers testified that the company could expand its capacity to as much as 250 million gallons per day. Moreover, Professor C. Marx of Stanford University testified that drainage areas capable of supplying 200 million gallons per day were available on several streams in the Sierras (Committee on Public Lands 1908: 33–35; Muir 1909b: 4–5).

Secretary of the Interior James Garfield also testified before the committee. Garfield said that the city of San Francisco had acquired landholdings in the Hetch Hetchy Valley and in the surrounding park and forest reserve. The city planned to exchange its landholdings outside the park, acre for acre, for those it planned to appropriate from within. Garfield said he had weighed both sides of the issue and decided to grant a revocable permit to San Francisco because damming the valley would not destroy it—the reservoir would create a beautiful, accessible lake where the meadow once stood. Garfield also thought that a reservoir was the best use of the water, giving San Francisco pure water and the ability to generate cheap electricity. Garfield was also convinced that Hetch Hetchy wasn't unique. He argued that though the valley was great and beautiful, Yosemite—a more wonderful, beautiful, and accessible valley—was close by. He thought the reservoir would convert a "beautiful but somewhat unusable meadow floor" into "a lake of rare beauty" (Committee on Public Lands 1908: 11–15).

TAFT AND HETCH HETCHY

In 1909, William Taft became president of the United States. He appointed Richard Ballinger of Seattle to replace Garfield as the secretary of the interior. Consequently, things moved quickly on the Hetch Hetchy front. The hearings continued, and the Spring Valley Water Company used the forum to complain about San Francisco's plan to acquire the company either by condemnation or by eminent domain. On February 1, by a vote of 8 to 7, the House Committee on Public Lands granted the city and county of San Francisco the rights to dam Hetch Hetchy Valley and Lake Eleanor. Of the representatives voting against the Hetch Hetchy resolution, only F. Mondell of Wyoming came from a western state (*Los Angeles Times* 1909b: 14; 1909c: 14; Wilkins 1995: 232–234).

Muir was optimistic when he was invited to tour Yosemite with Taft in October. On the trip Taft told Muir that he was opposed to the dam. At Taft's behest, Ballinger also toured Hetch Hetchy with Muir. Ballinger, like Taft, was impressed by the valley. The visit led President Taft to appoint a board of engineers to study the feasibility of using Lake Eleanor as the sole source of water for San Francisco. If that were possible, then there would be no need to dam Hetch Hetchy. The board reported that Lake Eleanor would be sufficient to supply San Francisco's water needs. Ballinger then scheduled a hearing in which San Francisco was asked to justify why the Hetch Hetchy Valley water was needed. But San Francisco was in no hurry to justify its plans. The city procrastinated and repeatedly asked for more time for fact finding. In all, five extensions were granted, and the stalemate continued for the duration of the Taft administration (Wilkins 1995: 232–234; Wolfe 1945: 316, 322–325).

In November 1909 city residents passed a resolution that allowed San Francisco to issue a bond for $600,000 to acquire land and water rights at Hetch Hetchy and Lake Eleanor. Once the resolution passed, San Francisco purchased 720 acres of land in the Hetch Hetchy Valley—comprising two-thirds of the valley floor—for $174,311. The city also spent around $400,000 to acquire the land and water rights from private owners living around Lake Eleanor (Vilas 1915: 11–12).

President Taft dismissed Pinchot in January 1910 after the latter had a public feud with Ballinger about opening up public lands for commercial activity (Pinchot [1947] 1998: 451). Around the same time, San Francisco county residents voted to approve a $45 million bond measure to cover the cost of building the Hetch Hetchy system, but they rejected the proposal to buy the Spring Valley Water Company for $35 million (*Los Angeles Times* 1910b: 13).

THE PRESERVATIONIST CAMPAIGNS CONTINUE

Preservationists continued to publicize the dam controversy and write favorably about Hetch Hetchy. For instance, Branson circulated one thousand copies of his booklet. Framing Hetch Hetchy in cultural nationalistic terms, Branson described the valley as "the most splendid scenery of the world." He also said Hetch Hetchy surpassed in beauty the natural wonders of Europe. Branson wrote: "Neither Switzerland nor the whole of Europe has anything in gorge and water-fall scenery to compare with the Hetch-Hetchy Valley and the Tuolumne 'Grand Canyon' much less match them" (Branson 1909: 10).

In 1909, the Sierra Club and the Appalachian Mountain Club also developed and distributed a booklet titled *Let Everyone Help to Save the Famous Hetch-Hetchy Valley and Stop the Commercial Destruction Which Threatens Our National Parks*. In it Muir pointed out that 90 million Americans were being defrauded so that San Francisco could save money. Muir argued that "our great national wonderlands should be preserved unmarred as places of rest and recreation for the use of all people" (Muir 1909b: 1). Similar editorials appeared in *Outlook*. One reader wrote, "While the Yosemite National Park might very properly be sacrificed to save the lives and health of the citizens of San Francisco, it ought not to be sacrificed to save their dollars" (*Outlook* 1909: 234–236). Preservationists also tried to expose what they called "the beautiful lake fallacy." Activists said the "slimy sides" of the reservoir would be visible, along with the "gathered drift and waste, death and decay." It contended that the reservoir would be a "rough imitation of a natural lake" for a few months in the spring and an "open mountain sepulcher" for most of the year. John Noble—former secretary of the interior—said granting the permit to dam Hetch Hetchy signified "a return to the idea that the nation has nothing that cannot be appropriated" (Muir 1909b: 9).

THE SIERRA CLUB DIVIDED

Though John Muir and the Sierra Club were the most vocal opponents of the dam, within the organization support for the preservationist position was not unanimous. This caused such a rift in the club that William Colby and Muir formed an ad hoc group called the Society for the Preservation of National Parks to fight the dam. Because the issue was so divisive for its members, the Sierra Club held a referendum in December 1909. Of those casting ballots, 589 opposed the dam, while 161 favored it. About fifty club members, including Warren Olney, one of the founders, resigned over the conflict. Dissension wracked the sixteen-hundred-member club for almost as long as the controversy lasted. In 1912, the organization went on record as opposing the dam, prompting the resignation of more members (Cohen 1988: 27, 43; Fox 1981: 139–144; *Los Angeles Times* 1912: 14; Nash 1982: 170–179; Sierra Club 1909; Wilkins 1995: 234).[11]

THE FINAL VOTE

As the debate continued, preservationists began to ask whether the driving force behind the quest to dam Hetch Hetchy was the potential for profits from hydroelectric power distribution. Consequently, Congress added an amendment to the Raker Bill ordering that the power generated from Hetch Hetchy be distributed to consumers directly, not through private utilities such as the Pacific Gas and Electric Company (Raker Act 1913; Wilkins 1995: 237–238; Wolfe 1945: 337). The profits from Hetch-Hetchy-generated power were expected to help pay for the project's construction (Wilkins 1995: 237–238; Wolfe 1945: 337).

In March 1913, the newly elected president, Woodrow Wilson, appointed Franklin Lane, the city attorney of San Francisco, as his secretary of the interior. The appointment of Lane ensured that the Hetch Hetchy project remained viable. Lane moved quickly to clear the remaining hurdles to the dam's construction. During June, the House Committee on Public Lands held more hearings on the dam. San Francisco's city engineer, M. O'Shaughnessy, testified before the committee that the city needed 75 million gallons of water per day to meet its needs and that about a third of the city did not have water. Some city residents and businesses relied on wagons to supply their water. O'Shaughnessy also testified that the water shortage was hampering the city's development (Albright and Schenck 1999: 20; Vilas 1915: 18; Wilkins 1995: 237–238; Wolfe 1945: 337).

On September 3, the Raker Bill, which would transfer Hetch Hetchy to San Francisco, was brought to a quick vote in the House while many of the representatives opposing the bill were not in Washington. The bill passed easily. Supporters of the bill rushed it through on the pretext of an impending drought. However, a water shortage was not imminent: the city had about a two-year supply of water on hand (Badè 1914; Nash 1982: 175–176).

Throughout the campaign, John Muir and other dam opponents were linked to the water company that had given city residents overpriced service for years. Residents of San Francisco hated the Spring Valley Water Company and saw opposition to dam construction as a nod of support for the company. Some also feared that Pacific Gas and Electric desperately wanted to seize control of water in Hetch Hetchy to generate electricity; they maintained that by gaining control of the valley, San Francisco could stymie Pacific Gas and Electric's plans. Some dam supporters argued that it was important for the public, rather than private corporations, to have control over power-generating sources such as Hetch Hetchy and thought that Muir and the dam opponents were either being duped by the water and power companies into doing their bidding or were in collusion with them. The preservationists were never able to completely shake themselves free of these suspicions (Righter 2005: 6).

As the Senate vote neared, farmers in the San Joaquin Valley, fearing that there wouldn't be enough water left over for irrigation purposes after San Francisco drew its allotment from Hetch Hetchy, vigorously expressed their opposition. Senator Works argued that 99 percent of the irrigators in the San Joaquin Valley opposed the Hetch Hetchy bill. Preservationists and other opponents of the dam bombarded the Senate with letters from influential people. Thousands of leaflets encouraging people to write letters to save Hetch Hetchy were sent out. Everyone listed in *Who's Who in America* received a flyer urging them to participate in the letter-writing campaign. Senators estimated they each received about five thousand letters opposing the dam. Secretary Lane also received thousands of letters opposing the dam. William Randolph Hearst, newspaper magnate and publisher of the *San Francisco Examiner*, joined the fracas on the other side. Not only did he send a reporter to Washington, DC, to cover the issue; he also published a special sixteen-page Washington edition of the paper supporting the dam that was placed on the desk of every senator. The special edition also printed a telegram from farmers in Modesto and Turlock Irrigation Districts informing senators of their change of heart and their decision to support the dam project. On December 6, 1913, the Senate voted overwhelmingly in favor of the dam, and on December 19, President Wilson approved the Hetch Hetchy grant. San Francisco got water power rights to 420,000 acres of the Hetch Hetchy Valley floor (Albright and Schenck 1999: 20; Fox 1981: 139–144; Vilas 1915: 6–7; Wilkins 1995: 234, 240; Wolfe 1945: 339, 344–345).

The month after the passage of the Hetch Hetchy bill, William Badè published a scathing editorial in the *Sierra Club Bulletin* in which he warned that the bill "must be regarded as the first act in a movement to break down our national park policy, and to expose the parks to commercial exploitation by municipal politicians and engineers." Badè argued that developing the agricultural capacity of the Central Valley was vital to the development of California and that after San Francisco drew its share of the water from the Tuolumne River, there wouldn't be enough left over for farmers. Badè also raised the issue of states' rights, questioning federal action that took precedence over local and state management of the river. With great foresight, Badè predicted that one of the lasting legacies of the Hetch Hetchy controversy would be that it would make it "more difficult if not impossible" to get projects like the Hetch Hetchy dam approved in the national parks in the future (Badè 1914).

Once the Hetch Hetchy bill passed, San Francisco initiated condemnation proceedings against Spring Valley Water Company. Eventually, in 1930, San Francisco purchased the Spring Valley Water Company for $40 million. The city also moved ahead with plans to build a 300-foot-high dam in the Hetch Hetchy Valley. Construction began in the spring of 1914. The dam flooded 1,930 acres. The "lake" created by the reservoir was about eight miles long and about a mile and a half wide at its widest point. The Hetch Hetchy dam had the capacity to supply the city with up to 500 million gallons of water per day. The city also had permission to build a 150-foot-high dam at Lake Eleanor; this dam flooded about 1,443 acres (San Francisco Public Utilities Commission 2004; Vilas 1915: 19). This meant that a total of 3,373 acres of Yosemite was flooded to create the two reservoirs. Of the area to be flooded, the city owned 1,300 acres. The city of San Francisco had to return 1,843 acres of land outside the national park to the federal government to accommodate almost all the acreage flooded in the national park that was not owned by the city (Vilas 1915: 19).

The dam itself was completed in 1924, but the remainder of the system was not completed until a decade later. The first water from Hetch Hetchy finally arrived in San Francisco in 1934. But the cost of the dam soared over time. At the time of the 1908 referendum, the city had estimated it would cost about $43 million to acquire all the rights, purchase the distribution system, and build the transmission lines. When the Hetch Hetchy bill was approved in 1913, the cost was estimated at around $77 million. However, by the time the water got to San Francisco in 1934, it cost about $100 million (Fox 1981: 139–144; *Los Angeles Times* 1934: A4; Nash 1982: 170–179; Wilkins 1995: 234, 240; Wolfe 1945: 339, 344–345). In 1935, the final estimate for the project was about $128 million (*Los Angeles Times* 1935: A4). Because of the dam's spiraling cost, San Francisco was unable to fund it and eventually lost control over the water and power from Hetch Hetchy (Righter 2005: 7).

In the mid-1920s, Oakland and East Bay communities, tired of waiting for Hetch Hetchy water, purchased the rights to the Mokelumne River. They built a dam in four years at a cost of about $36 million. Ironically, it was the Mokelumne River, which had been rejected as a source or water in favor of Hetch Hetchy, that supplied San Francisco with water in 1931 when the city experienced water shortages (San Francisco Public Utilities Commission 2004; Wolfe 1945: 344–345). The Modesto and Turlock Irrigation Districts also built the Don Pedro dam, which holds six times the capacity of Hetch Hetchy. Both of these were options that San Francisco eschewed in favor of Hetch Hetchy (Righter 2005: 8).

NATIONAL PARK PRESERVATION, RACISM, AND BUSINESS RELATIONS

National Parks: The Floating Orphans

The national park idea caught on slowly and grew in fits and starts until the early twentieth century. After the Yosemite Reserve was created in 1864, the first entity in the national park system—Yellowstone National Park—was not created until 1872. Congress created a second national park—Michigan's Mackinac National Park—in 1875, but this fact is not widely known: unlike Yosemite and Yellowstone, Mackinac was a small park, covering only a thousand acres. The army, already on the island to manage a fort, managed Mackinac National Park until 1895, when they were withdrawn. Since then, Michigan has managed it as a state park. No other national parks were created until 1890, when Sequoia and Yosemite were designated national parks (Sellars 1997: 11).

Park creation and administration proceeded in a piecemeal fashion for several more years, as the passage of the Antiquities Act in 1906 allowed smaller areas to be designated national monuments. However, the Hetch Hetchy controversy exposed the vulnerability of the national parks and brought the issue of park protection to the fore. Feeling that the national parks were threatened and that existing bureaus would not adequately protect the integrity of these natural areas, activists pursued other solutions. Around 1910, the Sierra Club and the American Civic Association started lobbying for a bureau to manage the national parks. Under the Roosevelt-Pinchot regime, the Forest Service was well organized and financed and the forest reserves were numerous, while the national parks were few, underfunded, and not well protected. In a 1910 report Secretary of the Interior Ballinger, influenced by Muir and other preservationists, recommended that a National Park Service be created (Russell [1959] 1992: 158; Wolfe 1945: 343).

In many respects the drive to establish the park service resembled the campaign to create the U.S. Forest Service. As Forest Service advocates had done, park bureau advocates clarified the framing of what made national parks unique, their purpose, their utility to the public, and their contribution to nation building. Park advocates also succeeded in differentiating the national parks from the national forests. They rallied around key activists and a charismatic, influential, and persuasive spokesperson who championed the cause tirelessly. Parks bureau advocates took advantage of political opportunities and found key western congressional allies to guide the legislation through Congress. They also collaborated with corporate partners and made concessions to business interests in exchange for their support. Both campaigns also used conferences to generate and endorse policies and support the creation of the bureaus.

RE-FRAMING THE NATIONAL PARKS: FROM USELESS LANDS TO SCENIC WONDERS

Originally the national parks were set aside on the premise that they were worthless as lands but breathtaking as landscapes, and hence worthy of being preserved. The Hetch Hetchy controversy raised the issue of utility again. Conservationists successfully framed Hetch Hetchy as an underutilized, inaccessible valley that was not unique. From the conservationist perspective, Hetch Hetchy could be used more efficiently and serve the needs of more people if it were dammed.

The challenge for preservationists, then, was to show that national parks were being utilized, but they wanted to do so in a way that kept dams or other commercial and industrial development at bay. They also wanted to advocate for development in a way that did not view waterways as potential dams, timber as a harvestable crop, grass as grazing lands, and rocks and minerals as potential mines. Scenery was an obvious resource that could be commodified and consumed in a nonextractive manner. By popularizing scenery, park advocates hoped that Americans could be encouraged to visit the parks to marvel at them without extracting from them. Consequently, park advocates promoted the parks as scenic wonderlands—the nation's playgrounds.

Though this approach to park preservation contrasted with that of the conservationists, it was still a utilitarian tack. That is, far from leaving the parks unmodified for future generations, preservationists promoted commercial development, increased accessibility, and expanded tourism in the parks. Though preservationists objected to dams and other industrial facilities in the national parks, they did not think the development of tourist facilities was incompatible with preservation. So from around 1908 onward the Sierra Club, John Muir, and William Colby advocated for the development of trails and roads in Yosemite and its surroundings. In particular, the *Sierra Club Bulletin* called for road improvements in Yosemite and the purchase and repair of Tioga Road (Carr 1916: 19). Robert Sterling Yard, Stephen Mather, and others in the Department of the Interior also expressed this view (Department of the Interior 1915; Sellars 1997: 28–29; Yard 1916: 10–11).

KEY PARK BUREAU ADVOCATES

The campaign to establish a parks bureau was greatly influenced by J. Horace McFarland, Stephen Mather, Horace Albright, Robert Sterling Yard, and Frederick Law Olmsted Jr., and the framing of the debate reflected their biases. J. Horace McFarland was a prominent horticulturalist, landscaper, urban planner, and leader in the City Beautiful movement. Olmsted Jr.—who followed in his father's footsteps as a landscape architect—was also primarily concerned about aesthetics and landscaping. Both McFarland and Olmsted Jr. played key roles in drafting the park service bill (Sellars 1997: 30).

McFarland drafted the 1910 proposal for the creation of a parks bureau. Secretary Ballinger used parts of this draft in the parks bureau proposal he presented to President Taft. The national parks were framed as resorts managed by administrators and guards—recreational spaces and manipulated gardens overseen by guardians of taste and civility. When Taft addressed Congress on this matter, he focused on the national parks' recreational potential, increased accessibility, and utility. He urged Congress to allocate funds to establish a bureau of national parks to ensure the effective management of "those wondrous manifestations of nature" and "bring all these natural wonders within easy reach of the people" (Schneider-Hector 2014: 647; Sellars 1997: 30).

As part of the campaign for a national parks bureau, the Department of the Interior sponsored a series of parks conferences. The first took place in Yellowstone National Park on September 11–12, 1911. The sixty-nine men in attendance were government employees in park-related jobs, concessionaires already operating in the parks, transportation company representatives, journalists, and representatives of other organizations interested in park matters. Participants focused on transportation and accessibility, concessions, and management challenges. Louis Hill of the Great Northern Railroad Company argued that Americans were traveling to Canada to see the Rockies instead of going to the American West. He believed that the railroads could collaborate with the national parks to increase visitation to American parks (*Proceedings Held at Yellowstone* 1912: 1–4). The "See America First" campaign, which sought to lure middle- and upper-class white American tourists to the wonderlands of the West, was gaining momentum. Though railroad executives were very interested in promoting national park visitation, they insisted that conditions in the parks had to be improved for the campaign to be effective. As Thomas Cooper of the Northern Pacific Railway argued, "The majority of the people who can afford a trip to the national parks are of a class who are used in their daily life to a reasonable degree of comfort, and no matter how ardent their love of nature may be they will not make the park trip unless it can be done with a reasonable degree of comfort and safety" (*Proceedings Held at Yellowstone* 1912: 7).

The national park publicist, L. H. Schmeckebier, reported that the Department of the Interior was promoting the parks by asking Americans "to see America first before seeing the sights of the Old World" (*Proceedings Held at Yellowstone* 1912: 105). Attendees also discussed the deplorable conditions of the parks and the need for high and uniform standards of lodging, service, maintenance, staffing, and financial accountability (*Proceedings Held at Yellowstone* 1912: 1–4).

A second conference was held in Yosemite National Park on October 14–16, 1912. The one hundred delegates in attendance included three women and congressional members (*Proceedings Held at Yosemite* 1913: 5–7). There were no ethnic minorities at either of the conferences even though Yosemite had had a black superintendent and black soldiers had helped with construction and management there and at other national parks. Asians, too, helped to build the main road that traverses Yosemite from 1882 to 1883. Moreover, Native Americans lived around several parks during the time of the conferences (National Park Service n.d., 2014; Shellum 2010: 136–159; Shu 2015).

Corporate delegates—especially from the railroads—were well represented at the second conference too. Hence delegates had lengthy discussions about the role railroads could play in facilitating access to and improving service in the national parks. Representatives from automobile associations and stage-coach delegates were also present at the conference, and each group advocated for better roads in and around the parks (*Proceedings Held at Yosemite* 1913).

Robert B. Marshall,[1] chief geographer of the U.S. Geological Survey, suggested that park management should be standardized. He also thought that management of the parks would be more effective if the park staff were considered civil service employees and compensated based on wage scales similar to those in the private sector; if each park had a superintendent and assistant and was patrolled by rangers or guards; and if a national parks bureau was created, headed by a superintendent to oversee the entire system (*Proceedings Held at Yosemite* 1913: 108–119; Schneider-Hector 2014: 649–650).

BUILDING SUPPORT AND MOMENTUM

Parks bureau bills were introduced in Congress in 1911 and again in 1912 by Senator Smoot and Representative Raker, respectively. Despite support from the president, the bills died in committee. A similar fate met the parks bureau bill that Raker introduced in 1913 (Albright and Schenck 1999: 124–125).

Nonetheless, activists continued to agitate for a parks bureau. The government took tentative steps in that direction with the appointment of Adolph Miller, a former economics professor at the University of California, Berkeley, as an assistant to Secretary of the Interior Franklin Lane in 1913. Miller invited Horace Albright, a twenty-two-year-old Berkeley law student, to be his assistant. At the time, the Hetch Hetchy controversy was nearing an end. In 1913, the national monuments were under the auspices of the Forest Service (they had been transferred from the Department of the Interior to the Forest Service in 1905), and there were only eight inspectors to administer Interior's operations. Miller created a National Parks field office and asked Mark Daniels to head the entity that would oversee the national parks and monuments. In 1914 Daniels, a landscape architect and urban planner and the wealthy owner of the architectural firm Daniels and Wilhelm, was appointed as the first general superintendent of the national parks. The superintendent's office was located in San Francisco—an indicator of the parks' marginality and the lack of support the office received from the federal government. As Albright viewed it, the national parks were the "floating orphans" in the Department of the Interior— they were not attached to any bureau. Albright also found out quite quickly that the parks did not generate much interest in Congress, hence the failure of earlier efforts to create a parks bureau (Albright and Schenck 1999: 16, 18–28; A. C. Miller 1914: 9; Schneider-Hector 2014: 660–662).

Adolph Miller resigned his position at the Department of the Interior in early 1914 and was succeeded by a longtime friend from Berkeley, Stephen Tyng Mather. Despite his connection to Miller, Mather got the position in a roundabout way. He sent a letter to Secretary Lane in fall 1914 that was particularly critical of conditions in the national parks. Mather's letter stood out, and Lane took notice. In his letter Mather expressed his outrage at the decrepit, filthy, and unsanitary state of the parks, lodging, food, and facilities. He was also angered by the exploitation of the parks, the conspiracy of businessmen to appropriate land with stands of giant sequoias, and the government's laissez-faire attitude toward it all. Intrigued by the letter, Lane arranged a meeting with Mather (Albright and Schenck 1999: 31, 41).

Mather had some prior involvement with preservation efforts: in 1912 he had traveled to Washington, DC, to oppose the construction of the Hetch Hetchy dam. But though he was friends with Miller and with well-known preservationists such as William Colby and Joseph Le Conte and had met John Muir, he was unknown to Lane. Lane met Mather twice and offered him a job in the Department of the Interior. Mather began working for the Department of the Interior in January 1915, and Albright became his assistant (Albright and Schenck 1999: 33–38).

Stephen Mather, a Sierra Club member since 1904 and a wealthy borax manufacturer, organized a branch of the California Club in Chicago. When he decided to work for the Department of the Interior on the parks, he was following a well-established tradition of businessmen taking the lead on major environmental issues. Mather, born in 1867 in San Francisco, graduated from Berkeley in 1887. He and a friend, Thomas Thorkildsen, founded the Thorkildsen-Mather Company in 1904. He was also president of the Sterling Borax Company and owner of borax mines in the West. Mather, a Chicago millionaire, was also president of the Brighton Chemical Company of Pennsylvania (Albright and Schenck 1999: 31–33, 49, 197–198; Cohen 1988: 40; Russell [1959] 1992: 162–163; Sellars 1997: 31; Shankland 1970: v, 9).

At the time Mather began working at Interior, there were fourteen national parks and thirty monuments. He expressed his philosophy about the parks and exerted his will immediately. Mather, a mountaineer, was a strong advocate of building roads to the national parks to improve access to them. He believed that if tourists did not visit the parks, there wouldn't be enough political support to create a parks bureau, and he did not waste any time taking action to achieve those goals. His skills complemented those of McFarland and Olmsted Jr. Mather was suave and at ease with the rich. He was also an enthusiastic fundraiser who got others to contribute to the national parks cause. Mather's assistant, Horace Albright, also proved to be an influential person in the campaign for national parks and in the administration of the park service once it was established (Cohen 1988: 39–48; Mackintosh 1999; Sellars 1997: 31).

As soon as he accepted the Department of the Interior position, Mather began spending his own money to support the national parks. Within six months he raised Albright's wages by eight hundred dollars per year, paying for the salary increase himself (at the time it was legal for government employees to receive payments from private sources). Mather also realized that the parks needed a publicist, so he hired an old friend, Robert Sterling Yard, the Sunday editor of the *New York Herald*. As with Albright's wage increase, Mather paid Yard's annual salary of five thousand dollars out-of-pocket. Mather also proposed that the government accept private donations of land and money for the national parks. The proposal passed in March 1915 (Albright and Schenck 1999: 38, 43–44, 59, 61).

Mather had a knack of getting his wealthy associates to donate money to the parks. His modus operandi was to invite unsuspecting recruits to dinners, parties, and mountaineering trips and after making his pitch for the parks, either ask them to donate money or suggest a sum they could donate. This is how he acquired funding for the Old Tioga Road. Having discussed strategies for buying the road with Sierra Club officers over lunch one day at the Bohemian Club, Mather invited six friends to dinner that night at the Palace Hotel in San Francisco in March 1915. He got pledges from all six men, and one did the legal work to close the deal free of charge. When some of the men later reneged on their promises, Mather found other people to contribute (Albright and Schenck 1999: 48–49, 65–66).

THE THIRD NATIONAL PARK CONFERENCE

Two park conferences had already occurred before Mather and Albright joined the Department of the Interior. When Mather began working at the agency, most of the people running the national parks were political appointees. Mather was convinced that the parks needed to be publicized, facilities needed improvement, and park supervisors needed to be evaluated. A third conference provided the opportunity to work on those goals. The conference also provided a chance for Mather to meet and consult with park supervisors. Mather also took advantage of the two expositions already under way in California (to celebrate the opening of the Panama Canal and San Francisco's recovery after the fire) to promote the parks. Mather thought that making the media aware of the high-level contingent of government officials and parks personnel visiting the expos would provide publicity for the parks and elevate the status of the conference. He was also interested in encouraging the development of distinctive architectural buildings in the national parks and believed the expos would provide some inspiration for this. The conference was attended by seventy-one men and two women. In addition to park personnel, attendees included concessionaires, transportation and railroad companies, representatives of the Forest Service and the Bureau of Entomology, officers of the Sierra Club, and several members of Congress. Female members of the Sierra Club hosted a dinner for conference attendees (Albright and Schenck 1999: 43–53; *Proceedings Held at Berkeley* 1915: 4–5).

The Park Village Concept Emerges. One important idea discussed at the conference was the concept of developing small villages or even cities in each park. The idea came from General Superintendent Mark Daniels, who believed the parks should be used to stimulate cultural nationalism, encourage greater education and health, and encourage domestic travel. Hence Daniels thought that a visitor's area resembling a village should be created in each park. The park village should offer all the amenities visitors required or wanted. Additional villages could be added to the parks as needed. Mather, seeing the potential to develop the parks this way, was enthusiastic about the idea of villages, but much more skeptical about developing actual cities in the parks. Albright, who was lukewarm about the concept of villages, was strongly opposed to developing cities in the parks. Even before the conference concluded, and without much further consultation, Mather decided to pick a park—Yosemite, his favorite—and develop a model village that could be replicated in other parks. Eventually, the grand hotel built at Glacier National Park by the Great Northern Railroad would become the model for the national parks' signature lodges (Albright and Schenck 1999: 50, 54, 102–110; Daniels 1916: 1; *Proceedings Held at Berkeley* 1915: 15–20).

Concessions in the Parks: Regulated Monopolies. Park concessions was another significant topic discussed at the conference, centering on the question of whether there should be competition for the concessions or they should instead be monopolies. Ford Harvey raised the issue and argued in favor of regulated monopolies. Harvey ran the hotels (including El Tovar) and restaurants at Grand Canyon and dining cars for the Santa Fe Railroad (Albright and Schenck 1999: 55). Mather was enthusiastic about the concept of regulated monopolies. However, David Curry, who operated a large campsite in Yosemite, objected to the monopolies idea. Curry, fearing that his camp would have to close if a monopoly was permitted to run Yosemite's concessions, argued that there should be different "classes" of concessions based on the visitors' ability to pay. Mather, who found the regulated monopolies idea more convincing than competing concessions, had dinner with a group of wealthy men at the end of the conference. During dinner they formed the Desmond Park Service Company and pledged $250,000 to begin operations in Yosemite. Mather invested in the Desmond Company, despite the obvious conflict-of-interest questions that such an investment raised. Joseph Desmond, a supplier of camp equipment and competitor to Curry's camp, was chosen to run the company (Albright and Schenck 1999: 55–56).

The National Monuments. The conference highlighted the precarious status of the national monuments, which were even more neglected than the national parks. Superintendents of the national monuments were compensated one dollar a month for their work. Though Mather sympathized with the superintendents and paid their travel costs to the conference, he was not particularly interested in the monuments. He felt they were not scenic wonders and did not quite measure up to the grandeur of the national parks (Albright and Schenck 1999: 51).

By the end of the conference, Mather had resolved that no new parks should be established until the existing ones were improved. He thought this was the best way to win approval for the creation of a national parks bureau. Mather was also reluctant to establish national parks in the eastern part of the country: he was convinced the wonderlands were in the West. So while Mather focused on national parks in the West, the Forest Service acquired lands and developed national forests all over the country. With the exception of Sieur de Monts (designated in 1919), the Park Service did not start developing eastern parklands until the mid-1920s (Albright and Schenck 1999: 51, 57, 269–271).

THE ROLE OF THE FOREST SERVICE

At the time of the campaign to create a national parks bureau (1910–16), the U.S. Forest Service already managed an expansive forest system of more than 151 million acres. In comparison, the national park system comprised about 4.6 million acres. However, recognizing that a new parks bureau could mean competition, the Forest Service opposed the plan. As a result, Forest Service officials said the national parks and forests should be managed with the same principles in mind. Gifford Pinchot was a staunch opponent of the creation of a parks bureau. Arguing that a national parks bureau was "no more needed than two tails to a cat," Pinchot stifled efforts to create such a bureau—even after he was relieved of his duties at the Forest Service. During his campaign to create the Forest Service in 1904, he had proposed that national parks be transferred to his jurisdiction and administered by the same agency as the national forests. Pinchot prepared bills to this effect, but they were opposed by Congressman Lacey, then chair of the House Public Lands Committee. Secretary of the Interior James Garfield supported Pinchot's position all along. Garfield argued that the parks and forests were "practically the same" and should be managed by the Forest Service (Albright and Schenck 1999: 41; Department of the Interior 1907: 55–56; Hays [1959] 1999: 47, 195–196; Pinchot 1911; Sellars 1997: 35–36).

Pinchot and the Forest Service also tried to obstruct the creation of new national parks. For instance, when Glacier National Park was originally proposed, it made no provisions for commercial exploitation excepting the removal of dead, downed, or decaying timber. The Forest Service prepared a rival bill that permitted the logging of mature timber, the development of hydropower, and railroad construction in the park. Similarly, Pinchot developed a counterproposal to the measure to set aside the Calaveras Big Trees Grove: his proposal permitted logging any timber except the Big Trees themselves. And in 1916 the Rocky Mountain National Forest was extended to cover an area that park advocates had hoped to include in Rocky Mountain National Park (Hays [1959] 1999: 195–196).

Pinchot's successor at the Forest Service, Henry Graves, took a more nuanced approach to the establishment of a parks bureau. At the first parks conference, Graves highlighted the connections between national forests and national parks and urged cooperation between the two. He contended, "The problems of administration of the national parks have a very intimate relation to those of the national forests, which are under my direction. Most of the parks themselves are great forests. Many of them are entirely surrounded by national forests or are adjacent to national forests with very similar physical conditions. It is absolutely necessary that those in charge of the parks and the forests work in close, practical partnership" (*Proceedings Held at Yellowstone* 1912: 66).

Graves supported the idea of establishing a bureau to manage the scenic wonders but believed a clear distinction should be made between the national parks and the national forests. He thought that if the two entities were not clearly defined, the establishment of the "so-called parks" might result in the "hybridizing" of the units. Graves did not object to creating national parks exclusively for promoting their scenic features and recreational potential, and he worried that hybridization would occur if logging, mining, grazing, and hydropower development were allowed in the parks. Graves agreed with Pinchot that the creation of a parks bureau would duplicate functions and services already being performed by the Forest Service. However, he focused on making clear distinctions between the parks and forests and urged national forest proponents to resist proposals to establish parks on lands that had value for purposes other than scenic preservation. Under Graves's leadership, representatives from the Forest Service participated in the national park conferences and offered suggestions for managing the parks more effectively (Graves 1916; *Proceedings Held at Yellowstone* 1912: 66–68; Schneider-Hector 2014: 651–653; Sellars 1997: 36).

McFarland also tried to make clear distinction between the national forests and parks by framing the national forests as "the nation's woodlot" and the national parks as "the nation's playground." McFarland believed that the two required different management philosophies and styles (J. H. McFarland 1911; Sellars 1997: 37).

CREATING THE NATIONAL
PARK SERVICE: THE FINAL PUSH

Increasing Publicity and Accessibility and Establishing Monopolies. After the 1915 parks conference, Stephen Mather and Robert Sterling Yard concentrated on publicizing the parks. World War I was making it difficult for Americans to vacation overseas, so park activists aimed their publicity at travelers who would normally be heading to Europe. They also wanted to dissuade them traveling to the Canadian wonderlands. To this end, national park activists contacted media outlets and got them to publish articles and photographs about the American parks. For example, in early 1916 the *National Geographic* published a special issue on national parks containing full-page and fold-out color pictures of the parks. A copy was delivered to every member of Congress (Albright and Schenck 1999: 143; *Annual Report of the Director* 1917: 17–18; Schneider-Hector 2014: 670–671). That year Yard produced *The National Parks Portfolio*, which contained pictures and pamphlets. Mather donated more than five thousand dollars to produce the photographic plates, then persuaded twenty-one western railroad companies to cover the remaining forty thousand. Scribner's produced more than 350,000 portfolios and distributed them to libraries, travel agencies, editors, and government employees. The General Federation of Women's Clubs provided the mailing list for distribution. Scribner's also produced 2.7 million copies of a smaller edition, *Glimpses of Our National Parks*, which was sold in bookstores (Albright and Schenck 1999: 60; Sellars 1997: 42; Yard [1916] 1917).

Park activists continued to publicize the parks and endeavored to make them more accessible. Yellowstone, Yosemite, and Mount Rainier were opened to automobiles between 1915 and 1916; the remaining national parks were opened to automobile traffic in 1918. Mather continued to pay for the expenses of influential men to accompany him on mountain party trips (Albright and Schenck 1999: 63–91, 98; Carr 1916: 19; Mackintosh 1999). Though Mather did not overtly evoke themes of manliness and a strenuous lifestyle in the parks campaigns, they were present subliminally.

Mather combined the mountain parties with publicity, efforts to improve conditions in the parks, and moves to install concession monopolies therein. In August 1915, having toured Crater Lake and seen the horrid condition of the park, Mather met with a group of businessmen in Portland. He persuaded R. Price, manager of the Multnomah Hotel, to buy out the Crater Lake Company, build improved accommodations, and provide better services. The Southern Pacific Railroad also agreed to build a new rail spur to the park. Mather did the same with the concessions at Mount Rainier: he convinced a group of businessmen to form the Rainier National Park Company to buy out the existing concessionaires and replace dilapidated camps with an elegant hotel (Albright and Schenck 1999: 87–92).

Mather also made a significant administrative change: he removed Mark Daniels from the post of general superintendent of the national parks and in December 1915 replaced Daniels with Robert B. Marshall. With this move, the office of the superintendent was now located in Washington, DC (Schneider-Hector 2014: 665).

Legislative Maneuvers. Despite the past defeats, Congressman Raker wanted to submit another parks bureau bill in 1916. However, Raker was not the best sponsor for this bill. Some in Congress thought he was being disingenuous by simultaneously pushing for the construction of the Hetch Hetchy dam and advocating for a parks bureau to protect the national parks. Others felt that Raker, feeling some remorse about Hetch Hetchy, was working on the parks bureau bill to restore his reputation. So McFarland asked William Kent to sponsor a parks bill in the House of Representatives. Though Kent supported Hetch Hetchy, he had more credibility than Raker. Kent wasn't a lead actor in the Hetch Hetchy controversy, and he wasn't simultaneously promoting a parks bill and the dam. Second, Kent had demonstrated his support for national parks years earlier by donating Muir Woods to the government and by donating money to buy the Old Tioga Road in Yosemite. Reed Smoot of Utah was asked to sponsor the Senate version of the bill. So Raker and Kent presented parks bureau bills in the House at the same time; the bills were eventually combined (Albright and Schenck 1999: 125–126; Sellars 1997: 42–43).

Park supporters debated whether to keep the bill's language vague or be specific about the purpose and functions of the national parks and the parks bureau. They recognized the paradox of promoting the parks' use while trying to keep resources unimpaired for future generations. Deciding that too much specificity might constrain management options in the future, they decided to word the bill vaguely. For example, the statute made no mention of provisions for roads, and there was a general reference to concessions that could be granted twenty-year leases. There was also no language in the bill to protect the parks from degradation by lessors. Furthermore, the parks bill did not try to amend the Rights-of-Way Act that paved the way for the Hetch Hetchy dam (this right was finally withdrawn by Congress in 1920). The parks bureau bill passed the House Committee in May 1916 (Albright and Schenck 1999: 126–128; Sellars 1997: 44).

The bill was then debated in the full House, with some members opposing Kent's amendment to allow grazing in the national parks. The bill also allowed for logging to control pests. Fearing that they wouldn't be able to graze their livestock on national park lands, western ranchers opposed the formation of a parks bureau. Consequently, Kent—who owned a ranch in Nevada and had friends who were ranchers—struck a compromise: he showed his support for the parks by sponsoring the parks bill, and he showed his support for the ranchers by allowing grazing in the parks. He argued that grazing did not interfere with scenic preservation and could reduce fire hazards in the parks (W. Kent 1916: 16; Sellars 1997: 37).

Though Yard, McFarland, and Albright were opposed to grazing in the parks, Mather was ambivalent about it. Mather's indecisiveness stemmed from the fact that he needed Kent's support for the bill and was afraid that strong opposition to grazing would lose him that support and stall the bill. The parks bill passed the House on July 1 and the Senate on August 5. A compromise bill passed the House and Senate later that August and was signed by the president (Act to Establish a National Park Service 1916; Albright and Schenck 1999: 128–130, 145).

APPROVAL OF THE NATIONAL PARK SERVICE

J. Horace McFarland coined the slogan "1916, the year to win." He was right: the National Park Service bill was approved on August 25, 1916. The parks were framed as spaces to protect scenery and promote recreation. The purpose of the parks, monuments, and reservations was to "conserve the scenery and the natural holistic objects and the wild life therein and to provide for the enjoyment of the same in such a manner and by such means as will leave them unimpaired for the enjoyment of future generations." The park act also allowed for the cutting of timber to control insects and conserve scenery or natural or historic objects, the granting of permits for concessions not to exceed twenty years, and the granting of permits to graze livestock within park boundaries (Act to Establish a National Park Service 1916; Albright and Schenck 1999: 125; Sellars 1997: 42–43).

The National Park Service was woefully underfunded; its budget of $19,500 wasn't appropriated until the spring of 1917 and had to cover the salaries of five employees. Mather removed Superintendent Robert B. Marshall from his post in December 1916. Mather himself became the first director of the National Park Service in May 1917. Early on, the park service was staffed almost entirely by Californians with close ties to the University of California at Berkeley and the leaders of the Sierra Club (Albright and Schenck 1999: 177; Cohen 1988: 39–48; Russell [1959] 1992: 161–164; Sellars 1997: 48–49).

Because of the paltry funding allocated to the national parks, preservationists solicited private donations to acquire parklands and cover the bureau's administrative costs. Shortly after Mather started working for the Department of the Interior, he began using his own money to acquire and manage parklands. In 1915 he and other wealthy donors bought the Old Tioga mining road in Yosemite, and he also purchased an inholding in Glacier for eight thousand dollars (Albright and Schenck 1999: 100–101; Cohen 1988: 39–48). Donors such as John D. Rockefeller Jr. contributed millions of dollars through the purchase of land. For instance, in 1930 Rockefeller purchased about forty thousand acres of land in Jackson Hole, Wyoming, for about $1.5 million. He then donated the land to the federal government to form the Grand Teton National Park (Russell [1959] 1992: 160).

Saving the Redwoods

The creation of the National Park Service did little to protect the redwoods. Despite the fact that preservationists were concerned about saving the giant Sequoias, most of the stands of redwoods remained unprotected outside the national parks. It wasn't until the early twentieth century that a vibrant movement emerged to protect them.

EARLY ATTEMPTS TO PRESERVE THE REDWOODS

The earliest efforts to preserve redwoods in the United States did not meet with much success. When California gained statehood in 1850, most of the lands on which the coastal redwoods grew were in the public domain. In 1852, Assemblyman Henry Crabb of San Joaquin County introduced a joint resolution recommending that the federal government prohibit settlement of redwood lands in the public domain. Crabb also argued that the redwoods should not become an article of commerce. Not long after Crabb's resolution failed, redwood forests began to move into private hands. This process intensified with the passage of the Homestead Act of 1862 and the 1878 Timber and Stone Act, which authorized the sale of federal lands for $2.50 per acre (Evarts and Popper 2001: 124–126).

Asa Gray delivered a keynote address on the sequoias at the American Association for the Advancement of Science in 1872, and John Muir gave a presentation about the sequoias before the same body in 1876. Nonetheless, the destruction of the redwood forests was so evident that in 1879 Secretary of the Interior Carl Shurz worried that the redwoods would be completely destroyed if steps were not taken to protect them. He proposed that forty-six thousand acres in two townships in the Coast Range be set aside, but this proposal was ignored. Others were taking an interest in the redwoods too. During the 1880s, journalist and businessman Alfred Noyes called for the management of forest resources through "timber culture": he urged the government to subsidize tree propagation efforts (Evarts and Popper 2001: 124–125).

In 1867, Joseph Welch brought property near Felton in Santa Cruz County that had a redwood forest on it. He developed the property into a resort with cabins, dance pavilions, and a dining hall. The South Pacific Coast Railroad, completed in 1880, ran through the property. Welch's Big Tree Grove, as the resort was called, became a major tourist destination. Presidents Benjamin Harrison and Theodore Roosevelt visited the resort. When the Welch family decided to sell the property in the late 1920s, activists urged the county to buy it and establish a public park on the site. The county purchased 120 acres of the property and renamed it the Santa Cruz County Big Trees Park. In 1954, when Samuel Cowell decided to give the state 1,600 acres surrounding the park, a condition of the gift was that the county must donate the original 120 acres to the state. The new park became known as the Cowell Redwoods State Park (Evarts and Popper 2001: 127).

Despite the fascination with the redwoods, by the late nineteenth century the rush to extract "sequoia gold" devastated coastal stands of redwoods (Evarts 2001: viii). In 1886, Ralph Sidney Smith, editor of the *Redwood City Times and Gazette*, suggested that a twenty-thousand-acre tract of old-growth redwood forest located near the headwaters of Pescadero and Butano Creeks be preserved as a park and resort. Prominent residents of California supported Smith's idea, but the legislature ignored the suggestion, and the area was logged shortly afterward. Undeterred, Smith began campaigning to preserve the upper watershed of nearby Waddell Creek in the area known as Big Basin. Other activists supported the cause. Unfortunately, Smith was murdered in 1887, and after his death the movement to preserve Big Basin dissipated. However, fate intervened: Big Basin might have been spared because of the Panic of 1893. The economic depression, which lasted until around 1898, devastated the logging industry and the region as a whole. During that time, William Dudley, a professor of botany at Stanford and one of the Sierra Club's founding members, began studying the region and campaigning to save the trees (Evarts and Popper 2001: 128).

THE SEMPERVIRENS CLUB

While Dudley made a compelling argument for saving Big Basin, it was an incident that occurred at Welch's Big Trees Grove in early 1900 that reignited the movement to save Big Basin. That year Andrew Hill, an artist and photographer from San Jose, visited Welch's to photograph the grove for a magazine article. When Welch learned that Hill had taken snapshots, the incensed owner demanded the photographic plates and told Hill that the public was not allowed to take pictures of the property. Hill refused to hand over the plates and left the property, vowing to turn it into a public park. Hill encouraged his friends and colleagues to publicize the issue by writing articles about it. Hill also called a meeting to discuss the status of Big Basin, and fourteen people attended. In addition, twenty-six men and a woman traveled to Big Basin by train and wagon. While the group sat around a campfire, they decided to form the Sempervirens Club to help make the Big Basin Redwood Park a reality. The group got local newspapers to print supportive articles along with photographs of the area (Evarts and Popper 2001: 128–130; Schrepfer 1983: 11).

The land the Sempervirens Club was interested in converting to Big Basin Park was owned by the Pescadero Lumber Company and others. The property owners told club members that the area would be logged in 1902. Though some speculated that the lumber companies were dangling the threat of logging before the preservationists to get a better offer on the property, club members did not want to risk finding out that the property owners were not bluffing. Club members wanted to establish a park of between thirty thousand and sixty thousand acres that would connect old-growth forests in the Santa Cruz Mountains. However, they scaled their plans back when it became clear that the legislature wouldn't appropriate the funds to acquire so much property. In 1901, the legislature appropriated $250,000 to purchase about twenty-five thousand acres to create the California Redwood State Park (later renamed Big Basin Redwood State Park). One property owner, M. Middleton, donated eight hundred acres of chaparral and five hundred acres of previously logged and burned land to the park (Evarts and Popper 2001: 130; Schrepfer 1983: 11).

SAVE THE REDWOODS LEAGUE

The Southern Pacific Railroad supported the acquisition of Big Basin because, in addition to the lumber they already transported to Santa Cruz, the trains could take passengers to the park as well. Governor Gage, who signed the bill approving the park's purchase, had been the legal counsel for Southern Pacific before becoming governor. Furthermore, the first Redwood State Park commissioner was a railroad land agent. Enthusiasm for the redwoods spread, and other California groups petitioned for redwood parks to be established along the new rail line of the Northwestern Pacific Railroad or on one of the new motor roads (Schrepfer 1983: 12).

Representatives Kent and Raker continued to play both sides of the conservationist-preservationist coin depending on the issue and the constituents involved. In 1911, Raker introduced legislation to examine the feasibility of a redwood national park, but his attempt failed. In 1913, Kent sponsored a congressional resolution calling for a redwood national park, but his efforts too were unsuccessful. The redwoods were still in danger, because the Sierra Club focused on protecting redwoods in the Sierra Nevadas, while the Sempervirens Club focused on Big Basin. That meant that most of the coastal redwoods were still unprotected. Recognizing the problem, a new organization emerged to advocate for protection of remaining stands of redwoods. The issue of redwood preservation came up in 1917 at the annual retreat of the Bohemian Club. Among those discussing the topic were Madison Grant of the New York Zoological Society, Henry Fairfield Osborn of the American Museum of Natural History, and John Campbell Merriam of the University of California, Berkeley. The three were anxious to see the redwoods, and after the retreat they headed north on the redwood highway to see the stands in northern California. On the trip they witnessed both the majestic redwoods and the intense logging; this impelled them to form an organization to help protect the trees. The following year, they founded the Save the Redwoods League. Grant and Merriam convinced Franklin Lane, then secretary of the interior, to serve as the league's president. Save the Redwoods League members also enlisted the support of wealthy people from both coasts (Evarts and Popper 2001: 138–139; Schrepfer 1983: 12).

When it became clear that the federal government would not provide funding to create a new national redwood park, the Save the Redwoods League decided to acquire stands of redwoods by soliciting contributions of private individuals. The league therefore got wealthy citizens to donate land or money to the cause. Mather, Kent, and the Sierra Club were strong supporters of the league and donated generously, as did several others. In addition, in 1921 Governor Stephens signed a Redwood Preservation Bill that allocated three hundred thousand dollars of state funds to acquire redwoods (Evarts and Popper 2001: 1, 39; Schrepfer 1983: 12–13).

The Save the Redwoods League worked closely with timber companies, and the corporations responded by contributing land (*Christian Science Monitor* 1924: 6). The league also relied heavily on getting private donations and leveraging state funds for its land purchases, and it was quite successful: by 1927, it had acquired thousands of acres of redwoods. In 1931 the fundraising efforts of the Save the Redwoods League got a major boost when John D. Rockefeller donated $2 million. Around the same time, Edward Harkness donated $500,000 to the campaign. These donations, along with $1.8 million in state park bond funds, were used to buy 13,629 acres of redwoods from Pacific Lumber Company and adjacent landowners (Evarts and Popper 2001: 142; *New York Times* 1931e: 1).

Though men were the public face of the organization, women were also quite involved in Save the Redwoods League activities. The Women's Clubs of California worked hard for the redwood cause. In 1919, about seven hundred women formed the Women's Save the Redwoods League of Humboldt County. Five years later, when the Save the Redwoods League's membership was around five thousand, the seventy thousand members of the California State Federation of Women's Clubs launched a campaign to raise sixty thousand dollars to purchase a grove of redwood trees. Save the Redwoods League also got support from the General Federation of Women's Clubs, which had about 3 million members at the time. Women also donated hundreds of acres of redwoods or publicized the cause through their newspaper articles (Save the Redwoods League 2004).

At first the Save the Redwoods League had a limited membership because Merriam had suggested that the organization screen prospective members and admit only those whose status would strengthen the cause. First and foremost, Merriam wanted the league to be composed of a small group of "influential men"; later the public could be instructed on how others could "attach themselves" to Save the Redwoods League (Schrepfer 1983: 13–20; Wilkins 1995: 186). However, the organization eventually opened up its membership to activists concerned about saving the redwoods.

During the early part of the twentieth century, preservationism and conservationism were sometimes tinged with the racist discourse of nativists and eugenicists. One of the most blatant instances could be found in the Save the Redwoods League. Eugenics, the "science" which seeks to improve the qualities of a particular race, stresses human improvement and status reinforcement through selective breeding. The eugenics movement reached its apogee of influence in the United States with the passage of the restrictive immigration acts in 1917, 1921, and 1924. Eugenicists took a special interest in saving the redwoods. At least eleven influential men in Save the Redwoods League subscribed to eugenics principles. Four of them—Grant, Osborn, Charles Goethe, and Vernon Kellogg—were widely published eugenicists. William Kent and George Lorimer (of the *Saturday Evening Post*) also campaigned with Grant and Goethe to get Congress to pass the restrictive immigration bills that effectively barred all but northern Europeans from entering the United States for a period of time. Madison Grant was the vice president of the Immigration Restriction League for many years. He was also one of eight members of the International Committee of Eugenics. Other members of the Save the Redwoods League—such as Major Frederick Burnham; Harold Bryant of the Park Service; Benjamin Wheeler, president of Berkeley; and Newton Drury, the organization's publicist—were also known eugenicists (Galton 1904: 1–25; Grant 1930; Schrepfer 1983: 4, 13–14, 43–45).

Eugenicists were also connected to the National Park Service. As late as 1930, four of the six members of the Park Services' Educational Advisory Board were eugenicists. Madison Grant, a prominent conservationist, argued that the Nordic race would go extinct because of interbreeding with inferior stock. Goethe, a wealthy Sacramento Valley resident, articulated a relationship between preservation and eugenics. He donated heavily to redwood causes and the national parks because he thought there was a relationship between "conservation of humans" and "conservation of other members of the environment." He felt that Americans of Nordic heritage were superior individuals who should be made to survive. He believed natural selection should be replaced with artificial selection because the former was too slow and because the superior man's breeding habits (i.e., bearing offspring with those of inferior stock) often caused his extinction. Goethe wanted to spread this message to the public, and he regarded conservation and preservation education as one of the best ways of doing this. Consequently, he was one of the earliest sponsors of park naturalist programs. Goethe thought naturalist programs made people more "biologic-minded." He felt that knowledge of the laws of evolution, and exposure to ecosystems that were centuries old, would increase public awareness of biological selection processes, promote selective breeding, and garner support for the passage of immigration laws. This was the logic that undergirded the eugenicists' interest in the redwoods. In the eugenic-preservationist discourse, the redwoods were often referred to as the fittest of their species, the survivors of a master race (Goethe 1949, 1955; Grant 1916; Schrepfer 1983: 4, 13–14, 43–45).

Advocating for Mesa Verde

Upper- and middle-class women were very active in other preservation efforts as well. They also launched major campaigns to protect the Anasazi cliff dwellings at Mesa Verde in Colorado. The first non-Indian explorer to see Mesa Verde may have been Don Juan Maria de Rivera, who led an expedition from New Mexico into the area of the cliff dwellings in 1765. The area was explored again in 1859 by J. Newberry, who conducted a geological study there. Other geologists explored the site in the 1870s. As details about the site leaked out, large numbers of artifacts were removed and sold (Torres-Reyes 1970).

In 1886, an editorial in the *Denver Tribune Republican* called for the area to be designated a national park. Alice Fletcher and Matilda Stevenson emerged as leaders in the campaign to protect Mesa Verde. In 1887, arguing that the ruins should be set aside as a "national reserve," they asked the American Association for the Advancement of Science to help. They surveyed the site and identified more than forty ruins, including Chaco Canyon, Canyon de Chelly, and Mesa Verde, that they thought needed immediate protection. However, their efforts did not pay off for some time. In 1890 another article in the *Durango Herald* called for a national park at Mesa Verde. The following year a team of Swedish scientists led by Baron Gustaf Nordenskiold visited Mesa Verde; they collected about six hundred items there and sent them to Sweden (Kaufman 1996: 27).

Around the same time Fletcher and Stevenson were trying to protect Mesa Verde, Virginia McClurg and a women's club, the Cliff Dwelling Association of Colorado, launched a similar effort. McClurg, a writer for the *New York Daily Graphic*, and Mrs. George Sumner first visited the cliff dwellings in 1882. McClurg's first visit took place a year after Richard Wetherill saw the ruins and began leading tours. The tourists and gold hunters desecrated the ruins, digging up burial sites and stealing artifacts. The local Native Americans objected to the activities at Mesa Verde, but to no avail. Therefore, as tourism increased, tribes began collecting tolls from tourists. In the meantime, McClurg lectured widely on the need to protect the ruins. The Cliff Dwelling Association paid for the mapping of Mesa Verde and the construction of a wagon road to the ruins (Kaufman 1996: 28; Keller and Turek 1998: 32–33).

The Cliff Dwelling Association activists wanted to protect the ruins while the Native Americans still lived in their ancestral home. Thus they wanted to lease the land from the affected tribes. Consequently, McClurg and a friend, Alice Bishop, visited the Southern Ute Reservation in 1899 to meet with tribal leaders. McClurg made a proposal to lease the site for thirty years at three hundred dollars a year; the Utes would retain grazing rights and would police the park. The Cliff Dwelling Association wanted to build a toll road and guest house and market the park to tourists. The tribe's leader, Ignacio, demanded that the entire nine thousand dollars be paid at the beginning of the lease. Caught by surprise and lacking the money, McClurg and Bishop left the reservation. Bishop and four women from Durango returned to the reservation a year later and secured a tentative agreement, but the secretary of the interior nullified it by claiming that private citizens had no authority to negotiate agreements with tribes. Another agreement was submitted to the Department of the Interior in 1901, but it too was rejected. Cliff Dwelling Association activists sought and got permission from Congress to negotiate with tribes, but by then the Utes refused to sell or lease Mesa Verde (Kaufman 1996: 28–29; Keller and Turek 1998: 33–34).

The first proposal to turn Mesa Verde into the Colorado Cliff Dwellings National Park was introduced before Congress in February 1901. The bill failed that year and again in 1903. The Mesa Verde bill was introduced in Congress again in 1905. Meanwhile, Mesa Verde activists joined forces with those pushing for the passage of the Antiquities Act and with political elites such as John Lacey who supported their cause. However, as support for a national park gathered steam, McClurg and some members of the Cliff Dwelling Association decided they wanted Mesa Verde to become a state park instead, under the control of women. McClurg argued that the federal government would not be a good caretaker of the ruins, since it would allow museums and universities to excavate the ruins for scientific purposes. Other prominent women in the Cliff Dwelling Association, such as Lucy Peabody and the General Federation of Women's Clubs, continued to campaign for a national park (Act 1906; Kaufman 1996: 29–30; Keller and Turek 1998: 34–35; D. A. Smith 1988: 40–62).

The Mesa Verde National Park came into being under the Antiquities Act. The Mesa Verde park bill was signed by President Roosevelt in June 1906. The Mesa Verde Park Act called for the protection of the ruins and prohibited anyone from collecting artifacts from the park, but allowed museums and universities to collect items for the purposes of archeological analyses. Unauthorized persons caught collecting specimens could be fined as much as one thousand dollars and/or imprisoned for up to twelve months. Unauthorized collectors would also be required to return objects to their original site if possible. Ironically, when the 42,000-acre park was created, its southern border stopped just shy of the ruins it was intended to protect. An amendment passed two weeks later added 175,000 acres containing the ruins. Grazing and mining were also allowed in park territory. No money was appropriated for administering it until 1907 (Mesa Verde National Park 1906; Robertson 1990: 61–72; Torres-Reyes 1970).

NATION BUILDING, RACIAL EXCLUSION, AND THE SOCIAL CONSTRUCTION OF WILDLANDS

The Evolution of Wildlands Framing

For much of the nineteenth and early twentieth centuries, the forests and wilderness were important entities in nature protection campaigns. Why were they such a vital part of the discourses of preservationists and conservationists? These discourses framed forests and wilderness as places unspoiled by development and industrialization and largely untouched by human hands. They were areas where people could escape the urban ills and transcend their earthly concerns. Wildlands were antidotes to the worst of human instincts; they were refuges to which people could turn.

Early in the Industrial Revolution, Emerson began juxtaposing "the ugliness of towns" and evils of the city with the virtues of unspoiled nature. He extolled solitude and called attention to nature's ability to renew and refresh people. He argued that nature's restorative powers were unparalleled and that the woods made us feel less fearful (Emerson 1883). Similarly, Thoreau saw wildlands as spaces that reinvigorated society. For him the woods was an elixir generating liveliness and vigor (Thoreau 1982: 258–572). He wrote, "In Wildness is the preservation of the World. Every tree sends its fibers forth in search of the wild . . . The founders of every state which has risen to eminence have drawn their nourishment and vigor from a similar wild source" (Thoreau 1982: 609–610).

Muir believed that going to the mountains was akin to going home and that the parks were fountains of life that rejuvenated the body (Muir 1898: 15–28). Isabella Bird was similar to Thoreau and Muir in that she reveled in solitude. She explained that the Rocky Mountain scenery inflamed her imagination and energized her. Though sublime landscapes could sometimes be overwhelming when one was alone in them, Bird proclaimed that she preferred the solitude over the distractions of companions (Bird [1879] 1893: 97–98, 157–158). Sarah Orne Jewett also loved the woods and saw a natural vitality in the trees (Jewett 1881: 167–171). Edith Matilda Thomas suggested intense communication with nature as a way to understand its secrets (Thomas 1886: 5), while Margaret Fuller wrote that sublime landscapes evoked lofty emotions in her (Fuller 1843: 11).

Thoreau also saw in nature something that protects and refines the citizenry (Thoreau 1982: 50). Thoreau made this argument around the same time that urban park advocates were urging cities to develop public parks. The notion that parks civilized the masses was articulated by the likes of Andrew Jackson Downing and William Cullen Bryant (Downing 1851: 147–153). At the time he made these arguments, Thoreau was living in New York City and interacting with Horace Greeley, an urban park advocate. It is likely he would have encountered these arguments there as they were espoused by urban elites.

The wildlands were also places where one could be deliberate and thoughtful. Thoreau went to Walden Pond for this reason. He used his time there to live simply and intentionally. He wrote, "I went to the woods because I wished to live deliberately, to confront only the essential facts of life, and see if I could not learn what it had to teach" (Thoreau 1982: 343). Another mid-nineteenth-century American who used the woods to escape the trappings of everyday life and live simply was Elizabeth Wright (E. C. Wright 1860: 9–20).

From earlier discussions we see that not all elites perceived the wildlands the same way. While Thoreau and Muir went to the wilds for spiritual renewal, Audubon, Roosevelt, and Grinnell saw the frontier woods and frontier lifestyle as valid and highly desirable types of living. The latter group explored entrepreneurial ventures during their time on the frontier. Catlin used his frontier experiences to study Native American culture and depict landscapes. Muir, who grew up on a Wisconsin frontier farm, did not see the frontier as true wilderness, so he sought out wilder landscapes. He shunned the agrarian lifestyle to plunge deep into the uncultivated lands with less human manipulation. Thoreau also sought out remote landscapes beyond Concord and Walden Pond.

He took trips to the Maine woods for that reason. Working-class men such as Cody and Brown eked out a living on the frontier as market hunters.

The American forests and wilderness did not always have a positive image. Until the mid-nineteenth century, wilderness was viewed as savage, barren, desolate—a wasteland. Biblical references to wilderness describe it as a place where people were banished to wrestle with evil or atone for their wrongdoings (Cronon 1995: 69–73; Nash 1982: 8–43; Oelschlaeger 1991). However, from the early nineteenth century on, explorers and thinkers began to write about the American wilderness in positive terms. For instance, Audubon began writing about the positive features of the woods and wilderness in the early 1800s. His illustrations of birds also fascinated people (Audubon 1832, 1835; Rhodes 2004). Moreover, landscape painters such as George Catlin, Thomas Cole, and Winslow Homer depicted captivating scenery on their canvases in the early nineteenth century (Nash 1982: 23–83). By the middle of that century Thoreau, Muir, and others were writing about the virtues of wildlands (Muir [1911a] 1972, 1917, 1938; Thoreau 1982: 138–227). Consequently, places like Niagara Falls, the Adirondacks, Catskills, Grand Canyon, Yellowstone, and Yosemite became "must see" stops on the affluent traveler's itinerary. And given the scarcity that resulted from the decimation of wildlife in settled areas, the frontier and wilderness were the premier repositories of fish and game for those interested in hunting and angling. The creation of national forests and parks hastened the transformation of wildlands from desolate wastelands into stands of trees to be managed sustainably or repositories of natural wonders.

Several bodies of thought have had significant influence on our understanding of American wildlands and helped to transform them from wastelands to national treasures. Among these are cultural nationalism, romanticism, Transcendentalism, and frontierism. These ideas converged to construct potent and persistent images of wildlands. Earlier discussions show that cultural nationalism played a critical role in helping Americans view wild and natural landscapes as valued resources. As romantics, Transcendentalists, and frontierists reframed natural areas in a positive light, they imbued them with some of the deepest cultural values of the society that endowed them with sacredness. Wildlands were thought to develop in people characteristics essential for nation building. They helped citizens to understand that civility and order was necessary in society. They fostered self-reliance, a strenuous lifestyle, and civic pride.

Transcendentalism is important in the transformation of wild landscapes because adherents believed that natural objects reflected universal truths and that such truths were most evident in forests (Emerson 1883; Nash 1982: 84–86;

Paul 1952; Thoreau 1893). According to Emerson, nature emanated beauty and perfection and represented a higher spiritual element. Emerson also believed that nature was a driver of thought and intellect; it expressed a truth that was emancipatory (Emerson 1883). Emerson saw Transcendentalists as idealists, thinkers who gained a higher level of intellect and consciousness than materialists. Idealists used information provided by their senses to guide their actions; they believe in their intuitions and nature's spirituality. For Emerson, nature was transcendental (Emerson 2000: 81–95).

Frederick Jackson Turner saw wildlands and the frontier as central to the construction of the American national identity—that is, a place for experiencing what it meant to be American. According to Turner, the frontier liberated people, decreased America's dependence on Europe, and fostered nationalism (Turner [1893] 1953: 22–27). However, frontier ideology was also rooted in the settler colonial notions of free, cheap, or appropriated land; slave labor; and servile indigenous peoples subjugated for the benefit of European Americans. The passing of the frontier meant the passing of a Euro-American identity built around taming wildland, animals, indigenous peoples, and slaves. Many looked back at this change with regret and nostalgia. Thus concern for the vanishing frontier became one factor that motivated some to preserve wildlands. Those who saw the frontier as vital to the development of the national character sought to save the last remaining stands of forests as a reminder of the past. As the frontier was vanishing, movements to establish national parks, wilderness, and wildlife sanctuaries gained momentum. Hence, enshrining the remaining frontier was an essential step in protecting one of the nation's most cherished creation myths.

Turner ([1893] 1953: 22–27) argues that wildness was essential to American culture, a fundamental component of and formative influence on the national character. Efforts to recapture such essential experiences led prominent leaders like Theodore Roosevelt to write about the "vigorous manliness" that the wilds promoted and to warn that the modern American was in danger of becoming an "overcivilized man, who has lost the great fighting, masterful virtues." Theodore Roosevelt urged people to overcome the trend toward "flabbiness" and "slothful ease" by keeping in touch with the frontier and leading a "life strenuous of endeavor." This principle motivated him to organize the Boone and Crockett Club. Theodore Roosevelt urged "every believer in manliness . . . every lover of nature, every man who appreciates the majesty and beauty of wilderness and of wild life" to support wilderness (Roosevelt 1910).

While elites in the latter half of the nineteenth century agreed that visiting the wilds was desirable, there was no consensus about how tourists should experience these places once they got there. Three competing views of tourist recreation emerged that are relevant to this discussion: frontierism, wilderness Transcendentalism, and pastoral Transcendentalism.

FRONTIERISM

Theodore Roosevelt, Grinnell, Audubon, and others of that ilk advocated the strenuous frontier experiences of hunting, living on the fringes of developed areas, being exposed to the dangers (human and natural) of the environment, overcoming the elements, and exerting manhood and power. Roosevelt and others also stressed the need to control indigenous people and the working class (Grinnell 1911c; Roosevelt [1885] 1996, [1888] 2000, [1893] 1996).

WILDERNESS TRANSCENDENTALISM

Frontierism has some overlap with Transcendentalism. The Transcendentalist approach to recreation required expenditure of energy through sauntering, arduous hikes, and mountain climbing to gain access to sublime and romantic peaks, river valleys, glaciers, and so on. The difference between the Transcendental and frontierist approaches is that for the affluent frontierist living in remote areas, the thrill of the chase, the conquest of fauna through hunting or fishing, and stuffing and mounting trophies to show prowess is the primary goal. The enjoyment of nature for nature's sake is secondary. For the working-class person living on the frontier, subsisting and transforming the wilderness to make a living are the primary goals. For the Transcendentalist, simply being in the wilds and getting a deeper connection to and understanding of nature is the raison d'être. Though some Transcendentalists did hunt, the thrill of the chase was not the primary rationale for connecting with nature. John Muir and Thoreau practiced and espoused the Transcendentalist approach (Muir 1875: 489–496; 1909a; 1915; Thoreau 1893). Mather was a hybrid: though he experienced the exhilaration of climbing remote mountains and conquering new heights, he was not obsessed with or focused on hunting or trophy collections.

The female nature lovers tended to enjoy the wilds as they hiked, rode, or studied the forests. Though some, including Isabella Bird, Hannah Taylor Keep, and Esther Jones, reveled in ascending mountain peaks, they did not seek conquest over the wildlife in the places they hiked. They did not plan their mountaineering adventures around hunting and fishing trips; their climbs were adventures in and of themselves (Bird [1879] 1893: 97–98, 157–158; Waterman and Waterman 1989: 122–124, 162). Margaret Fuller's travels on the prairies epitomized the Transcendentalist approach to wildland recreation (Fuller 1843: 7–11).

Olmsted and Muir represented the pastoral approach. As part of the framing and social construction of urban parks, landscape architects adopted a muted form of Transcendentalism that I will refer to as pastoral Transcendentalism to distinguish it from the more intense or extreme form of wilderness Transcendentalism described above. Pastoral Transcendentalism attributed virtues to natural objects like trees, meadows, and brooks that could be replicated in parklike settings (Taylor 2009: 224–225, 266–267). Therefore, rather than developing parks around vast, dramatic natural landscapes that evoked fear, urban landscape architects designed subtle landscapes for the gentle exercise of the mind and body. From the pastoral Transcendentalist perspective, the recreation experience is intended to put people into a contemplative mood and tranquilized state of mind. Through exposure to the scenery, users are expected to transcend their everyday stress and concerns (Olmsted, Vaux and Company 1866a, 1868).

Though Muir is best known for his romantic and Transcendental views of wilderness and preferred the most sublime landscapes, he also encouraged pastoral recreation in national parks with dramatic landscapes and vistas. In particular, tourists who were not very familiar with the wilderness or were not willing or able to undertake the laborious activities associated with the traditional Transcendentalist approach were encouraged to enjoy the pastoral aspects of the parks. For instance, Muir recognized that not all visitors to national parks were ready for the sublime experiences like delighting (as he did) in earthquakes and wild storms while sitting atop swaying trees or clinging to mountaintops (Muir 1875: 495–496; 1878: 55–59). So Muir suggested instead that the less experienced tourist might enjoy pastoral landscapes.

Parks, Wilderness, and Indian Removal

The movement to establish national parks, forests, and wilderness areas gained momentum as the last of the Indian Wars drew to a close. Even before the last Native American tribes were forced onto reservations, national parks, forests, and wilderness areas were established on "empty," "pristine," land "untouched by human hands" that were formerly tribal lands. In many cases the reserves were established to preserve "virgin forests."

THE MARIPOSA BATTALION AND
INDIAN REMOVAL FROM YOSEMITE

The establishment of some of the early national parks and forests coincided with efforts to remove tribes from their homelands. For instance, Yosemite was the home of the Ahwahneechees and Yosemites until tensions between Indians and whites escalated during the gold rush. In 1850, Indians who had lost much of their hunting and gathering grounds to white miners, prospectors, and traders tried to assert their claim to Yosemite Valley and the surrounding region by engaging in small-scale battles with whites. They ambushed explorers, raided trading posts and camps, and in some instances killed settlers. Whites were quick to avenge theft and killings, whether real or rumored. Early in 1851, after a series of skirmishes between settlers and local tribes, traders who feared the conflicts would escalate called in reinforcements, and a volunteer militia, the Mariposa Battalion, was activated. The battalion rounded up Indian tribes and placed them on reservations along the Fresno River. However, several bands of Indians refused to sign treaties or settle on reservations and instead fled to the High Sierras. The Mariposa Battalion gave chase, thus its members became some of the first whites to set eyes on the Yosemite Valley. Though the battalion did not capture the Indians right away, they were intent on removing all of them from the valley. The Ahwahneechee Indian tribe, which had been decimated by what was believed to be smallpox in 1800, never regained its full pre-epidemic strength, so its members were no match for the well-armed Mariposa Battalion hunting them down. The battalion consisted of 204 men, while there were about 200 members in the tribe. After months of tracking, capturing, maiming, and summarily executing the Indians; pursuing a scorched-earth policy of burning their villages to starve or freeze them into submission; and coercing captured Indians to spy on and reveal the secret hideouts of their tribes and other tribes,' the battalion finally captured the last members of the Yosemite tribe at Lake Tenaya. The captured Indians were removed from Yosemite and placed on reservations. Eventually some were permitted to leave the reservation; they returned to Yosemite, while other members of the tribe escaped to rejoin their compatriots. Yosemite was declared a state park in 1864 and a national park in 1890 (Bunnell [1880] 1990; Farquhar 1965: 36; Runte 1990: 9–11; Russell [1959] 1992: 1–8, 196–201).

The removal of Indians from Yosemite can also be viewed in the context of settler colonialism. That is, whites—some of whom had been in California for a very short time—took it upon themselves to hunt down native peoples and force tribes onto reservations. The removal was also an attempt to exclude tribes from having access to land, valuable resources, and emerging labor markets. In the case of Yosemite, Indians were excluded from the region by whites who wanted exclusive access to and control of the land, water, and mineral resources. The few Indians who remained in the region were either completely shut out of the labor market or confined to the secondary labor market as low-wage menial workers, guides, interpreters, porters, or panners (for gold).

Places such as Yosemite were by no means empty; yet after the tribes were subjugated, preservationists depicted them as such. Tourism began in Yosemite in 1855. That year James Mason Hutchings, a failed gold miner, began exploring the possibility of settling in Yosemite and developing the tourist trade in the valley. Hutchings hired an artist to sketch the valley so he could publicize it; he, the artist, and two Indian guides entered the valley in 1855. Forty-two tourists entered the valley that year; some were led by former members of the Mariposa Battalion. In 1856, the first permanent structure constructed by whites—the Lower Hotel—was built in the valley, and other tourist facilities and settlers' abodes soon followed. Hutchings's articles attracted well-to-do tourists from as far away as the East Coast (Farquhar 1965: 117–118; Runte 1990: 13–17, 22–23; Russell [1959] 1992: 54).

Both settlers and early park activists expressed a deep discomfort with the few Indians who continued to inhabit Yosemite and, as time went on, declared that they did not belong in the park. For instance, the writings of Bunnell, a member of the Mariposa Battalion, expressed the feeling that landscapes like Yosemite were best enjoyed without an Indian presence. He detailed how he was mesmerized by Yosemite's awe-inspiring scenery at the same time that he was orchestrating plans to kill or remove all of the area's Indians (Bunnell [1880] 1990; Dilsaver 1994: 8; Nash 1982: 161–181).

INDIAN REMOVAL FROM YELLOWSTONE
AND OTHER NATIONAL PARKS

Indians were also removed from Yellowstone to make it a safer space for whites to travel. The first whites in the area were trappers, hunters, campers, and other explorers. Several tribes, including the Lakota, Shoshone, Crow, Bannock, Nez Percé, Flathead, and Blackfoot, used the area. Though the 1851 Fort Laramie Treaty recognized Blackfoot and Crow claims to the area, later treaties nullified these claims. Thus the act establishing Yellowstone declared that "all persons who shall locate or settle upon or occupy the same [Yellowstone] or any part thereof . . . shall be considered trespassers and removed therefrom . . . All persons trespassing upon the same [Yellowstone] after the passage of this act [shall] be removed therefrom." Hence Native Americans were expelled from the park shortly after it was created in 1872. However, whites were allowed to open concessions, profit from their commercial operations, and dwell at those concessions in the park (Keller and Turek 1998: 22; Yellowstone Act 1872).

Indian removal occurred in other places too to make way for the national parks and forests. The "crown jewels" of the national park system—Yosemite, Yellowstone, Mt. Rainier, Crater Lake, Mesa Verde, Olympic, Grand Canyon, Glacier, and Rocky Mountain—are located in places that were Indian territories in the 1850s. However, by 1920 several national parks were established on Indian lands. Indian removal from national parks and wilderness areas continued well into the twentieth century (Keller and Turek 1998: 19–21).

UNUSED LAND, SUPERSTITIOUS INDIANS

Once Indians were removed from national parks and forests, activists and adventurers perpetuated the myth that Indians had not been present in the area—that the area was empty. Such reserves were depicted as virgin territory. The tribes' rights were ignored, and many of the traditional uses of land and resources in the designated park and forest areas were banned. Stories were also propagated to foster the notion that Indians did not use the land before these areas were incorporated into the national park or forest system because they were superstitious and fearful of certain landforms. For example, Gustavus Doane, who explored Yellowstone in 1871, wrote, "We saw, however, no recent traces of them [the tribes]. The larger tribes never enter the basin, restrained by superstitious ideas in connection with the thermal springs" (Doane 1871: 26). Likewise, in an essay in *Picturesque America*, Bunce wrote, "For years, marvelous stories have been rife among the hunters of the Far West of a mysterious country in the heart of the Rocky Mountains, which the Indians avoided as the abode of the evil spirits" (Bunce 1872b: 294). A similar story was told about Mesa Verde. According to Horace M. Albright, the Ute Indians were happy to trade Mesa Verde for other lands because they rarely used it. Albright thought they had a superstitious feeling that it was "accursed" and "was a land of the spirits" (Albright and Schenck 1999: 252).

REMOVING LANDS FROM RESERVATIONS

When Native Americans weren't being expelled from areas to create national parks and forests, their lands were being appropriated for such purposes. For instance, Theodore Roosevelt was firmly committed to the idea that the bison had to be exterminated to bully the Indians into submission and to make way for the greater settlement of the West. However, once the animal was hunted to near extinction, Roosevelt was an enthusiastic supporter of the idea of placing the bison on reserves. Since Roosevelt was also committed to the idea that Indians had no greater claims to the land than whites, it was not surprising that he removed 18,500 acres of land from the Flathead Indian Reservation in 1908 to create the National Bison Range. The Confederated Salish and Kootenai Tribes received only $50,700 for the land (E. S. Morris 1998; Roosevelt [1885] 1996: 9–11, 25–26, 243). Native Americans objected to the removal of lands from their reservations elsewhere too. Between 1933 and 1937, when Robert Marshall, ardent wilderness advocate and founder of the Wilderness Society in 1935, was director of forestry for the Bureau of Indian Affairs, he created sixteen wilderness areas on Indian reservations (Fox 1981: 209; Keller and Turek 1998: 5–6).

Wildlands and Elite Perceptions of Native Americans

Bunnell wrote disparagingly about Native Americans as he pondered how he and his battalion would effectuate their removal from the Yosemite Valley (Bunnell [1880] 1990). Olmsted, who became the head of the Yosemite Commission three months after the park was established, did not view the local Native Americans around Yosemite positively either (Ranney, Rauluk, and Hoffman 1990: 22). In notes written while he lived in Bear Valley, Olmsted expressed the view that the indigenous peoples were feeble-minded, malleable, and unable to resist the will of others (Olmsted 1860). In outlining the policies he thought should be adopted to protect the park, Olmsted did not necessarily advocate the removal of Indians from Yosemite. However, he also did not endorse Catlin's vision of making the preservation of Indians and aspects of their culture an explicit part of park policy (Olmsted 1865). The artist James Smillie wrote in a similar light to Olmsted and Bunnell. He argued that Indians in Yosemite "straggle vagrant and worthless through the region, hopelessly debauched and demoralized . . . They are dirty and disagreeable" (Smillie 1872: 483–484).

Elites exploring the wilds often expressed their fear of Native Americans. Samuel Bowles expressed his anxieties of being attacked by Indians as he traveled across the country to Yosemite and other western wonders in 1865 and 1866. He argued that the "long dominant thought in the East against the use of force and its incident policy of treating the Indians as of equal responsibility and intelligence with Whites, are unphilosophical and impracticable." Bowles also suggested that the government should stop making treaties with tribes; instead he thought that more reservations should be established and that force should be used to place tribes on them and keep them there (Bowles 1869: 155–157).

Such incendiary language and paternalistic views of Native Americans greatly influenced conservation and preservation policies during the nineteenth and early twentieth centuries. The antipathy toward the tribes was common among those administering land and natural resources policies. Therefore it is not surprising that there was consensus among policy elites about turning tribal homelands into forests, parks, and game reserves. John Muir is one prominent nature protection activist and thinker who documented his attitudes and perceptions of Native Americans quite extensively. An analysis of some of Muir's writings shows how complex these reactions were; they also show how activists of his time viewed wildlands and the place of Native Americans within them.

Muir, one of the strongest advocates of preserving Yosemite, also wrote disparagingly about the Indians he encountered in and around the reserve. Muir was uncomfortable around Native Americans and thought they did not belong in wilderness areas such as Yosemite. Thus Muir strayed even further than Olmsted from Catlin's conceptualization of a national park. Though he stops short of advocating Indian removal, Muir expressly states that the Native Americans have no rightful place in the wild environment. Though Muir is saddened by the death of Chief Tenaya (which occurred when the Mariposa Battalion rounded up the last of the Ahwahneechees), he is not generally remorseful over the disappearance of the Indians. Olmsted is not remorseful either. Though Catlin sees Indians as savages, he, like his contemporary Thoreau, also sees beauty in the Indians and expresses remorse at their disappearance. Grinnell too spent time among and studied Native American tribes and worried about their plight. Though Muir sometimes expressed admiration for the Indians' ability to leave minimal impact on the landscape, more often than not he expressed his revulsion at their presence (Catlin [1841] 1965; Grinnell 1873b, 1923; Muir 1913). For example, Muir observed the semi-nomadic hunter-gatherer tribes in and around Yosemite. He wrote, "A strangely dirty and irregular life these dark-eyed, dark-haired, half-happy savages lead in this clean wilderness—starvation and abundance, deathlike calm, indolence . . . Two things they have that civilized toilers might well envy them,—pure air and pure water . . . These go far to cover and cure the grossness of their lives" (Muir [1911a] 1972: 277–278).

In Muir's writings, Native Americans are often framed in animal imagery or equated with them: if Indians are seen as wild animals, then the lands can be framed as areas untouched by human hands once the Native Americans are removed. For instance, Muir wrote about clashes between whites and Indians when he visited the lava beds that were the site of the Modoc War in 1874. He was sympathetic to the white soldiers who died in battle, but wrote in unflattering terms about the "begrimed" and "devilish" Indians, who repelled him (Muir 1874: 358–363; 1938: 65–67).

One day Muir encountered a group of Mono Indians as he walked through the Sierras admiring the sounds of the birds. He records the meeting in his diary:

> As I was gazing eagerly about me, a drove of gray hairy beings came in sight, lumbering toward me with a kind of boneless, wallowing motion like bears. I never turned back, though often so inclined, and in this particular instance, amid such surroundings, everything seemed singularly unfavorable for the calm acceptance of so grim a company. Suppressing my fears, I soon discovered that although as hairy as bears and as crooked as summit pines, the strange creatures were sufficiently erect to belong to our own species. They proved to be nothing more formidable than Mono Indians dressed in the skins of sage-rabbits . . . Occasionally a good countenance may be seen among the Mono Indians, but these, the first specimens I had seen, were mostly ugly, and some of them altogether hideous . . . Somehow they seemed to have no right place in the landscape, and I was glad to see them fading out of sight down the pass . . . and as I drifted toward sleep I began to experience an uncomfortable feeling of nearness to the furred Monos. (Muir [1894] 1991: 92–93; see also Muir [1911a] 1972: 293–295)

Reflecting on his encounters with Native Americans, Muir noted, "Perhaps if I knew them better I should like them better. The worst thing about them is their uncleanliness. Nothing truly wild is unclean" (Muir [1911a] 1972: 303–306).

Until the end of the Indian Wars in the 1890s, travel to the wilds could entail bloody encounters with tribes. Thus explorers often armed themselves or traveled with military escorts. The skirmishes between whites and Indians provided a rationale for whites to push for the expulsion of Native Americans from designated park, forest, and wilderness areas. Muir understood that whites' fear of confrontations with Indians would lead some to avoid visiting the wilds, so he went to great lengths to assure them that the Indian "threat" had been removed from the national parks. In several instances Muir told his readers not to be fearful of Native Americans because they didn't inhabit the parks anymore. In this way he helped to perpetuate the myth that the national parks, forests, and wilderness areas were Indian-free zones. He wrote, "The Indians are dead now . . . Arrows, bullets, scalping-knives, need no longer be feared; and all the wilderness is peacefully open" (Muir [1901] 1981: 14–15). He also said, "Yet it is far safer to wander in God's woods than to travel on Black highways or to stay at home . . . As to Indians, most of them are dead or civilized into useless oblivion" (Muir [1901] 1981: 28). On another occasion Muir wrote,

> When an excursion to the woods is proposed, all sorts of exaggerated or imaginary dangers are conjured up, filling the kindly soothing wilderness with colds, fevers, Indians, bears, snakes, bugs, impassable rivers, and jungles of brush, to which is always added quick and sure starvation . . . The Indians are seldom found in the woods, being confined mainly to the banks of the rivers where the greater part of their food is obtained. Moreover, the most of them have been either buried since the settlement of the country or civilized into comparative innocence, industry, or harmless laziness. (Muir 1918: 312)

Like Muir, Susan Fenimore Cooper propagated the notion that Native Americans had vanished from the wilderness. She equated the indigenous peoples with the animals of the forests, and noted that though the tribes were extinct, the trees had survived. In a 1878 essay she wrote, "The red-man, and all the larger animals who haunted that region a thousand years ago, have passed away, have vanished almost entirely. But the trees of that grand forest, and the birds who haunted them, are here to-day" (Cooper 1878c: 273–277). Isabella Bird also wrote disparagingly about the native tribes she encountered in the Sierras and promoted the idea that they were becoming extinct (Bird [1879] 1893: 4).

Theodore Roosevelt's views on Native Americans are also very important given his position as president and the enormous influence he wielded over conservation policies. Even though his political career overlapped with the Progressive Era (1880s–1920s), the censorious tone Roosevelt used when he wrote about Native Americans recalls that of the activists discussed above. Roosevelt was not sympathetic to arguments that Native Americans had lost their land by unfair or fraudulent means. He argued, "During the past century a good deal of sentimental nonsense has been talked about our taking the Indians' land. Now, I do not mean to say for a moment that gross wrong has not been done to the Indians, both by government and individuals . . . But as regards taking the land, at least from the western Indians, the simple truth is that the latter never had any real ownership in it at all" (Roosevelt [1885] 1996: 25).

Believing that the semi-nomadic hunter-gatherer lifestyle of the Plains tribes negated any claims to ownership of the land, Roosevelt argued that the tribes "had no stronger claim" to the land "than that of having a few years previously butchered the original occupants." Hence the white hunters' title to the land "was quite as good as that of most Indian tribes to the land they claim; yet nobody dreamed of saying that these hunters owned the country." He wrote, "The Indians should be treated in just the same way that we treat the white settlers. Give each his little claim [of 160 acres], and if they refused to farm it, then they should "perish from the face of the earth which he cumbers." He also evoked the-good-of-the-few versus the-good-of-the-many argument that was used so effectively in Hetch Hetchy and other resource conflicts: "It does not do to be merciful to a few, at the cost of justice to many" (Roosevelt [1885] 1996: 25–26).

Black Regiments and National Park Protection

It was because of military oversight of the national parks that Colonel Charles Young was able to rise through the ranks and become the first black superintendent in a national park unit—Sequoia National Park. Charles Young was born into slavery in 1864 in May's Lick, Kentucky. His father escaped slavery in 1865 and enlisted in the Fifth Regiment. The Young family moved to Ripley, Ohio, where Charles grew up. On graduating with honors from high school, Charles was refused admission to West Point despite having the second highest score on the entrance examination. He was finally admitted in 1884. When he graduated in 1889 he was stationed in the West; he was also a distinguished faculty member at Wilberforce University in Ohio. In 1903, Colonel Young was appointed the superintendent of Sequoia National Park. He and the segregated black cavalry (Buffalo Soldiers) stationed at the Presidio in San Francisco were ordered to care of Sequoia for the summer. Though Sequoia had been designated a national park thirteen years earlier, in 1903 it showed signs of neglect and was difficult to reach. Although road construction had begun in the park in 1900, when Young and his troops arrived in the park barely five miles of road had been built. Young and his crew worked feverishly, and in one summer they added more new road to the system than had been built in the previous three years. They also managed, maintained, and patrolled the park (National Park Service 2014; Shellum 2010: 136–159). When Young and his regiment was sent to the park in 1903, it wasn't the first time black soldiers had been asked to monitor the park. Buffalo Soldiers had also patrolled Sequoia and General Grant (Kings Canyon) and Yosemite in the summer of 1899 (National Park Service n.d.).

Well into the twentieth century, American wildlands were perceived as unspoiled, pristine areas with great restorative powers. The wildlands were also believed to have the ability to enhance manliness and promote strength, vigor, and individual transformations. In a similar way, the Civilian Conservation Corps, a work relief program aimed at alleviating poverty, was couched in the language of manliness, self-reliance, civic responsibility, and nation building; but the program was rife with class, racial, and gender conflicts.

The Great Depression was the catalyst that set in motion the events that resulted in the creation of the Civilian Conservation Corps (CCC). The Depression forced governing elites to confront the economic crisis by devising programs that blended social and conservation policies. The work relief idea was first put in practice in America when the urban poor were put to work chopping wood in exchange for food and other kinds of aid during the depressions and harsh winters of the nineteenth century in New York and other cities (Taylor 2009: 43–68). During the late 1850s, New York City government officials put thousands of unemployed white men to work clearing land in what was then described as the Manhattan wilderness to build Central Park (Taylor 1999: 420–477; 2009: 251–337). The idea resurfaced again in a 1910 essay by Harvard philosopher William James:

> Instead of military conscription a conscription of the whole youthful population to form for a certain number of years a part of the army enlisted against Nature . . . The military ideals of hardihood and discipline would be wrought into the growing fibre of the people . . . Our gilded youths [would] be drafted off . . . to get the childishness knocked out of them, and to come back into society with healthier sympathies and soberer ideas. They would have paid their blood-tax, done their own part in the immemorial human warfare against nature; they would tread the earth more proudly, the women would value them more highly, they would be better fathers and teachers of the following generation. (Quoted in McDermott 1967: 669)

Five years later George Maxwell of the National Irrigation Association proposed that the government develop a national construction corps comprised of young men who would do conservation work in the forests and on the Plains (Salmond 1967: 4–5). Franklin Delano Roosevelt put the idea of a youth conservation work program into practice and popularized it in America. Franklin Roosevelt grew up at Springwood, his family's twelve-hundred-acre estate along the Hudson River in Hyde Park, New York. That property, which had been in the family since the early nineteenth century, had become badly eroded by the time the twenty-eight-year-old Franklin Roosevelt began managing it in 1910. Large gullies on the property widened with each rainfall. But Roosevelt knew that this kind of erosion and deterioration of the property was preventable because he had seen well-managed forests in Germany in 1891. He began reforesting Springwood shortly after becoming manager, and by 1945 he had planted more than half a million trees on 556 acres of the property. Franklin Roosevelt managed Springwood's forest as a practical business endeavor—he made a profit by selling fuelwood, sawlogs, and cross-ties to the railroad (Maher 2008: 18, 20–24; Nixon 1957: 118–119).

Franklin Roosevelt was governor of New York in 1931 when he set up a temporary emergency relief administration that hired unemployed people to work on conservation projects: clearing underbrush, fighting fires, doing reforestation and insect control, constructing roads and trails, improving forests, enhancing lakes and ponds, and developing recreational facilities. Similar programs were established in other states (Gibbs 1932: 633; 1933: 195, 160–161, 173).

THE CIVILIAN CONSERVATION CORPS AND WORK RELIEF

One of the major challenges facing the cities during the Great Depression was the vast number of unemployed people in their midst. Consequently, wildland enhancement projects were used to reduce unemployment and alleviate poverty during the 1930s. Soon after Franklin Roosevelt took office in 1933, working-class people participated in some of the largest public works projects ever undertaken in this country. Many of these were enhancements of forests, parks, playgrounds, and wilderness areas. President Franklin Roosevelt's New Deal made funds available for conservation work from relief programs such as the Works Progress Administration, the Public Works Administration, and the Civilian Conservation Corps. Authorized by the Emergency Conservation Act of March 1933, the CCC undertook road-construction projects such as Skyline Drive in Shenandoah National Park, as well as the construction of numerous visitor facilities. Eventually, the CCC was also used to develop a nationwide system of state parks (Sellars 1997: 133–140).

The CCC employed single, young male American citizens who were out of school and had no criminal convictions. Many of these men were recruited in the cities and sent to work in remote locations. The recruits, who were housed in quasi-military camps, were between the ages of eighteen and twenty-five. The program grew rapidly, and by July 1933—three months after its inception—three hundred thousand men were enrolled in CCC camps in forty-seven states. Within a year, the program had enrolled six hundred thousand men. Most of the camps were supervised by the Forest Service, the Park Service, the Bureau of Indian Affairs, and the War Department. The men worked eight-hour days five days per week, and about five-sixths of their wages were sent home to their families each month. Eventually camps were also established on Alaska native reservations and in Puerto Rico (Cole 1999: 2–3; *New York Times* 1933a: 12; 1934b: 18).

The Forest Service operated thirteen hundred camps, most of which were located in national forests. CCC enrollees also lived in camps located in 94 national parks and monuments and 881 state, county, and municipal parks. Army camp commanders administered the day-to-day operations of the camps, while the National Park Service or Forest Service administered the conservation projects. There was a camp superintendent for every two hundred men. A foreman was assigned to supervise work crews composed of forty to fifty men. At times the recreation activities of the men ran afoul of park norms. Park administrators found the boxing matches and vaudeville shows particularly irritating and urged enrollees to take remedial courses and engage in more traditional park recreation activities. CCC men also sometimes vandalized the camps and harassed park wildlife (Dilsaver and Tweed 1990: 16, 188; Maher 2002: 435–462; Sellars 1997: 100–101, 141).

Race and the Civilian Conservation Corps. The CCC was established according to the official principle that men should be admitted without regard to their race, color, or creed. However, Native Americans were not eligible for the program when it first started; they were admitted later and placed under the jurisdiction of the Bureau of Indian Affairs (Emergency Conservation 1933). From the outset, several southern states barred blacks and other minorities from enrolling in the program. In Georgia, for instance, only whites were allowed to enroll in the Corps in its early weeks of operation. Georgia began enrolling blacks only after the CCC headquarters in Washington, DC, threatened to stop all enrollment in the state unless minorities were admitted to the program (Cole 1999: 4, 14–17, 46–47).

Moreover, the program encouraged segregation of the units. The following excerpt from a memorandum written by Robert Collins, adjunct general of the War Department, indicates that segregation was commonplace: "Colored personnel will be employed to the greatest extent practical in colored units within their own states of origin. In the future segregation of colored men by company, while not mandatory, will be the general rule and earnest effort will be made to reduce the total number of colored men in White units" (Collins 1934).

Racism and discrimination was rampant in the CCC, and not only were blacks and other minorities discriminated against during the enrollment process; they also faced discrimination once admitted to the program. At first black enrollees were dispersed throughout predominantly white units, but in 1935 the CCC developed a policy of segregating black and white camps except in states where there weren't enough blacks to create all-black camps. Blacks were also stationed in the state where they registered or on military reservations. In states such as California, men of Japanese, Chinese, Filipino, and Mexican ancestry enrolled in the program (Baldridge 1971; Cole 1999: 46–47; C. Johnson 1972: 82; *Report of the Chief of Staff* 1935: 1).

Reports from African American CCC participants indicate that the army officers running the program routinely referred to black recruits as "niggers" and "black boys." According to John Howard, a twenty-one-year-old black male from Gary, Indiana, who joined the program in 1933, his camp in Fort Knox, Kentucky, was segregated into four groups: African Americans from the North, whites from the North, African Americans from the South, and whites from the South. While the northern blacks and whites became allies, the southern whites tried to assault the northern blacks. Southern blacks did not take sides and tried to stay out of the clashes. On one occasion army troops with bayonets drawn stepped in to separate southern whites from northern blacks. When Howard left the CCC in 1934, his honorable discharge papers described him as being "as black as coal" (Needleman 2003: 68–70).

Race riots also broke out at Camp Osborne Springs, Idaho, after blacks complained about poor treatment and being called derogatory names. Conditions were so oppressive that black enrollees wrote to President Franklin Roosevelt requesting to be moved from the camp. The army investigated the matter and responded by dismissing the black enrollees from the program. Blacks were also dismissed from a camp near Chico, California, after racial conflicts erupted there. At Camp Palomar Mountain in the Cleveland National Forest, some enrollees donned white sheets and attacked other corpsmen who associated with blacks (Cole 1999: 19, 24).

Not only did the CCC segregate blacks into all-black camps; in cases where blacks were placed with predominantly white units, camp administrators also organized along racial lines the tasks enrollees had to perform. The army supervisors assigned the most menial tasks to blacks. A common practice was to have blacks serve as cooks and dishwashers. These practices weren't the work of rogue racists in the corps—they adhered to a directive that came from the top. In 1835, in response to complaints about blacks being placed in white units, program director Robert Fechner said that placing a limited number of blacks in white camps was tolerable "because of the natural adaptability of Negroes to serve as cooks." A few months later Fechner argued that "the small group of Negroes will be assigned to kitchen police or similar camp duties" (Gower 1976: 123).

The use of kitchen duties to segregate the enrollees meant that black enrollees did not eat with or interact with the white work crews doing the fieldwork. This was also a way of making blacks invisible to the communities objecting to their presence. This practice had other detrimental effects on black enrollees. Though blacks tried to gain leadership positions in the CCC, very few became leaders. Racism aside, it would have been difficult for anyone assigned solely to kitchen duties to rise to leadership positions on work crews where they had to supervise work they were not trained for. Furthermore, because kitchen work did not teach enrollees conservation skills, some black enrollees reported leaving the CCC without marketable skills that could help them obtain jobs or work for conservation agencies (Cole 1999: 5, 20–21, 64–67; Gower 1976: 123–135; C. Johnson 1972: 82–87). Mexican Americans enrolled in camps in Arizona, Texas, and New Mexico reported widespread discrimination; those stationed in camps in Utah and other states seemed to encounter less discrimination (Baldridge 1971).

Women and the Civilian Conservation Corps. Even though many of the wage earners who lost their jobs during the Depression were female, the CCC was only for males. This didn't go unnoticed, and within a month of the founding of the CCC, female activists began lobbying for a work relief program for women. Despite the vocal support of prominent advocates such as First Lady Eleanor Roosevelt and Secretary of Labor Frances Perkins, the CCC continued to provide relief work for men only. Consequently, in June 1933 Eleanor Roosevelt and Frances Perkins joined forces to open a camp for two hundred jobless women. While the CCC program had millions of dollars, the women's camp began operation with a $4,200 grant from the Federal Emergency Relief Administration. The women's camps were not established on the same premise as the CCC work camps: for example, female campers did not receive any wages. Women helped with chores around the camp and learned sewing and other domestic skills while they were enrolled. The camps were also intended to provide rest and relaxation for the women. Eventually thirty-one camps were established in several states. These camps accommodated about three thousand women from eighteen to thirty-five years old, and two of them—located in

Georgia and Maryland—served black women (Maher 2002: 438–462; McIntosh 2001: 23–28; *New York Times* 1933b: 1; 1933c: 18).

THE RESPONSE OF WILDERNESS ADVOCATES
TO RELIEF WORK IN NATIONAL PARKS

New Deal funds meant a massive infusion of cash into the National Park Service coffers. Though the Forest Service dwarfed the Park Service in the number of camps administered and amount of the appropriations, CCC funds became a way for the Park Service to build both the physical and human infrastructure of the bureau (Sellars 1997: 133, 140). However, not everyone was happy with the work being done in the national parks and forests. Despite the vast sums of money pouring into the National Park Service and Forest Service to rehabilitate and develop parks and forests, some wilderness advocates opposed relief work. Critics of relief work noted that road building, trail construction, the building of administrative and visitor facilities, and the development of water and sewage facilities resulted in extensive alteration of the natural environment. They also objected to forestry projects in which non-native species were used to reforest areas and trees were planted in straight rows. Critics contended that the projects being undertaken were not always in the best interest of the parks, as they conflicted with the development of farsighted projects that had minimal impacts on natural ecosystems. Critics also contended that the crews worked on projects that were utilitarian in focus. That is, the projects being undertaken focused primarily on the wise use of the parks' scenic resources and the utilitarian concerns of park users (Maher 2008: 8–9; Sellars 1997: 100–101, 126–127, 129–131).

Wilderness advocates like Robert Marshall, a wealthy New Yorker who grew up summering in the Adirondack Mountains, and Rosalie Edge and environmental groups such as the newly formed Wilderness Society weighed in on the issue too. They saw the relief workers as a threat to the wilderness. Opponents of relief work contended that the projects were being undertaken to employ large numbers of people rather than to make improvements that were necessary in protected areas. They also feared that the projects would make wilderness areas too accessible to too many people, which in the long term would threaten these areas' integrity (Fox 1981: 209–211; G. Marshall 1951: 44–45; R. Marshall 1930: 141–148; 1935). For instance, Edge wrote, " 'Build a road!' Apparently this is the first idea that occurs to those who formulate projects for the unemployed . . . often without consideration of whether the road is needed at all." She continued, "There is a thrust upon the Park Superintendents the necessity to employ . . . CCC men, whether or not their services are needed; and the wilderness goes down before these conquerors" (R. Edge [1936] 1994: 137, 139). Robert Marshall, while working as director of forestry for the Bureau of Indian Affairs in 1935, wrote to Ferdinand Silcox, head of the Forest Service, saying, "The bulldozers are already rumbling up the mountain. Unless you act very soon . . . eager . . . CCC boys will have demolished the greatest wildernesses which remain in the United States" (R. Marshall 1935). Critics also objected to the work being done in the national forests. They opposed the development of recreational facilities in some forests. Renowned ecologist Aldo Leopold was a leading critic of the corps' attempts to stock forests with deer and streams with fish. Though Leopold initially supported the stocking programs, he later criticized them as upsetting the ecological balance of the areas where the programs were being implemented (Maher 2008: 9).

Professor Merrit Fernald of Harvard also chastised the CCC. In a lecture delivered at a science conference, Fernald argued that the "misguided and enthusiastic young men" of the CCC, under the guidance of "highly trained and overcultured landscapist[s]," had embarked on a course of misguided conservation. Fernald thought the CCC had destroyed the "natural equilibrium of nature" because of their activities in the forest. He explained that the construction of artificial ponds, roads, bridges, and beaches and the introduction of trees and shrubs is not conservation, since these activities disrupt an ecosystem's natural equilibrium. He proclaimed, "If vast regiments of otherwise unemployed young men are to be encouraged to hew, rake and burn the forests, they will unconsciously become destroyers of the natural equilibrium of nature" (*New York Times* 1938: 1).

VIGOR, CIVIC VIRTUE, AND THE RHETORIC OF THE CIVILIAN CONSERVATION CORPS

During the Great Depression, young people accounted for approximately a third of the unemployed. This is an important reason the CCC was such an integral part of the president's work relief agenda. The CCC was seen as an effective mechanism for putting idle young men to work (Cole 1999: 9). The program's rhetoric combined romanticism with militaristic and late nineteenth-century notions of manhood propagated by men such as Theodore Roosevelt, who wrote about the vigorous manliness that the wilderness promoted. Roosevelt had warned that modern Americans were in danger of losing their masterful virtues and urged people to lead a "life strenuous of endeavor" by keeping in touch with the frontier (Fox 1981: 140–141; Nash 1982: 146–153; Roosevelt 1910).

Evoking this tradition, the work and accomplishments of the CCC were framed to highlight the ways that military discipline, rigorous outdoor labor, and fresh air restored the enrollees' manliness, vigor, and vitality. According to Franklin Roosevelt, program administrators, and supporters, the CCC enabled thin, pale, sickly, unemployed, and hungry recruits—many plucked from unhealthy urban environments where they languished, unable to care for themselves and their families—to blossom into civic-minded, patriotic, healthy, tanned, and muscular men with work experience and skills to help them fare better in the labor force. While in the CCC they provided for their families by sending money home. The camps provided the job training they received, while also fostering patriotism. The CCC was seen as an effective means of emptying the cities and rural villages of hordes of young, potentially volatile, unemployed men, and channeling their energies into nation-building activities. The group's administrators linked the health of the enrollees with the health of the forests and nation. According to the CCC, as the men regained their health and vitality, they were capable of being more productive. That productivity was directed toward making the nation's forests and parks healthier. On being discharged from the corps, men were given a certificate attesting to the completion of their "Tour of Duty" in "that magnificent Army of Youth and Peace that put into action the Awakening of the People to the facts of Conservation and Recreation" (*Certificate Issued to Youths*, n.d.; Maher 2002: 435–462; *New York Times* 1933d: xx2; 1936: 2). In essence, the CCC was as much about muscular conservation as about environmental protection.

A MISSED OPPORTUNITY: WILDLAND ACTIVISTS AND THE CCC

Some wildland advocates were so focused on protesting the work of the CCC and the young men involved in the program that they might have missed a golden opportunity to recruit millions of working-class men and their families into conservation and preservation organizations. During the Depression, many of these organizations lost membership. In addition, at the time, these organizations drew their members almost exclusively from the upper and middle classes (Taylor 2000: 504–580).

With the advent of the CCC, millions of working-class men from a range of racial and ethnic backgrounds were drawn into conservation work. Many of these young men admitted to knowing little or nothing about conservation and environmental stewardship before entering the corps. But while in service, they learned about the environment, and some took an interest in it. Some men were so influenced by their experiences in the program that they enrolled in university forestry and conservation-related programs after leaving the CCC. Others went on to work in the Forest Service and Park Service.

Some even founded their own conservation organizations, like the Citizens for Conservation and Trustees of the Earth, American Conservation Enrollees, and the National Association of CCC Alumni (Maher 2002: 435–462). Therefore, had nature protection activists been keener to draw working-class whites, blacks, Native Americans, Puerto Ricans, Alaskans, Japanese, Filipinos, Latinos, and Pacific Islanders into their organizations or work collaboratively with enrollees, they could have tapped into a pool of 3 million CCC enrollees and their families. Some criticisms of the CCC by conservationists and preservationists were valid; yet their focus on vilifying the enrollees and the work they did served to alienate many CCC men from the environmental groups.

Racial Exclusion and Access to Outdoor Recreation

Despite the fact that people of color helped to build and maintain national and state parks and forests, these were—at times—segregated entities that barred blacks and other people of color from using all or parts of the facilities. National parks and other outdoor recreation areas have a long and complex history of segregation.

BLACKS AND THE DESIRE FOR WILDLAND RECREATION

Most of the effort to exclude people of color from outdoor recreation opportunities was directed at blacks but this did not deter African Americans from going to rural and wild areas to recreate. Several factors—some of them similar to those motivating whites to travel to the wilds—influenced blacks to travel to such places. Throughout the nineteenth and early twentieth centuries, blacks increasingly found themselves living in crowded, polluted, and unhealthy urban environments with no access to open space. Racially restrictive zoning laws and covenants[1] prevented them from moving to desirable neighborhoods in many cities and suburbs (Taylor 2014: 147–227). Once slavery was abolished, Jim Crow laws—prohibiting blacks from using facilities or transportation at the same time or in the same manner as whites—proliferated in the South and were instituted in the North as well. Consequently, blacks using urban parks risked violent attacks like the one that killed Eugene Williams[2] and triggered a five-day race riot in Chicago in 1919 (Drake and Cayton [1945] 1993: 104; Taylor 2009: 332–337: Tuttle, 1980: 3–10, 35–37, 199, 234–235).

Like their white counterparts, black elites in the Midwest, on the East Coast, and in parts of the South extolled the virtues of escaping the cities and visiting the countryside. They used black newspapers like the *Chicago Defender*,[3] the *Whip*, and multiracial magazines like the National Association for the Advancement of Colored People's *Crisis* to reach blacks from all walks of life to encourage them to go to the wilds to refresh and renew themselves, connect with nature, explore their spirituality, engage in "respectable" recreation, and escape segregated neighborhoods and urban violence. The growing black middle class also resorted to the wilds to recreate and network with other black elites (Chatelain 2008: 199–255; Fisher 2005: 62–76; Foster 1999: 131–132; Taylor 2009: 332–337). For instance, Dr. William Wilberforce—the health editor of the *Chicago Defender*—explained to readers that a summer resort was "a place where . . . and one may get close to nature, to view the beauties of nature and get a larger vision of nature" (W. Williams 2014b: 8). He explained further,

> We desire that you should get the habit of camping out . . . it will do you good . . . [we] hope that you will get the habit of treating yourself and family to a delightful summer outing in a camp . . . There is an ever increasing demand, for us to get out, and away from the city—to get close to nature—to commune with the running brooks, trees, and singing birds and all the growing vegetation—to get far away from the heat, the dust, the hurry, the bustling marts and the streets of overcrowded, jostling municipality and find some cool, shady spot to camp where one may find rest for the mind and body with nature's purest food, water and air . . . And do not forget to take along our fishing tackle. (W. Williams 1914b: 8)

African Americans were also drawn to and actively participated in the back-to-nature movement. Black elites, businesses, religious, and community institutions played key roles in encouraging black families to enroll their children in the Young Men's Christian Association and the Young Women's Christian Association, and in outdoor clubs like Boy Scouts (founded in 1910), Girl Scouts (founded in 1912), and the Camp Fire Club of America[4] (founded informally in 1910 and formalized in 1912). The Camp Fire Club was formalized by leading conservationists William Hornaday, Dan Beard, and Ernest Thompson. Theodore Roosevelt was an early, ardent, and influential member of the club (Camp Fire Club 2015; *The Chicago Defender* 1916: 11; Chatelain 2008: 199–255; 2015).

Blacks did not separate race and class inequalities from conservation issues and experiences. Hence, the participation in leisure and nature experiences was part of a larger agenda of racial uplift that was salient in black communities. Racial uplift refers to a belief in mutual aid as well as to a slate of programs and services that middle class blacks developed to help acculturate and facilitate the upward mobility of poor blacks (Chatelain 2008: 3–4; Du Bois 1921: 158–160; Gaines 1996: 4). Despite the fact that afore-mentioned youth organizations were segregated, as early as 1916 *The Chicago Defender* promoted the Camp Fire Club and urged its readers to join (*The Chicago Defender* 1916: 11).

SEGREGATING THE WILDLANDS

At the same time blacks were seeking to expand their access to outdoor leisure activities and supporting the conservation and preservation messages of exploring the wilds and connecting to nature, efforts to segregate the national parks, historic preservation sites, and national forests intensified. At times private entrepreneurs operating concessions on public lands orchestrated the segregation, at other times it was senior government employees who enacted and executed segregationist policies. For instance, the issue of segregating facilities came up almost immediately after the George Washington Birthplace National Monument was designated in Virginia in 1930 (Bruggeman 2008: 153–157; Shumaker 2006: 20–21). In 1931, Arthur Demaray, a high-ranking administrator in the Department of the Interior, corresponded with Horace Albright, then director of the National Park Service, about the desire to segregate facilities at the monument. Demaray wrote,

> There is another matter which should be mentioned at this time. If the recreational area is developed at Pope's Creek and the Wakefield Memorial Association places their proposed recreational building at this location, there will be need of another recreational area where colored people can go. When we were at Wakefield this time, we went down to the old wharf on the Potomac River beyond the burial ground and found colored people bathing there. I understand that more and more this area is being utilized by colored people. I think this situation should be frankly met by encouraging the colored people to go to this point and by providing tables and other picnicking facilities for limited use by colored people. (Demaray 1931: 2)

In 1933 a comfort station in the Wakefield section of the monument was designated for "use . . . by colored people." The comfort station was constructed by the CCC (Shumaker 2006: 22). Sister Dominica describes the appalling conditions she encountered in 1938 when she took a group of black schoolchildren to the monument and was forced to use the Wakefield picnic grounds. She sent an angry letter to Arno Cammerer, the third director of the National Park Service.[5] In it she wrote,

I was amazed when we reached the gates yesterday and were told by the superintendent that it was the law that colored people should be segregated from the whites on the picnic grounds. He then jumped into his car and escorted us to the place he claimed that was set aside for colored. It was about a mile from the mansion, and if we had gone much further we should have been in the water. There were no tables or benches such as you would expect to find in a picnic ground or any other conveniences. The superintendent returned later and brought two old and dirty buckets of water for us to drink from, also an old dirty dipper, and trashcan. He told us that if we left any trash he could, according to law, compel us to come back and clean it up. . . . Then too, at the tea room we were told that they did not sell soft drinks or ice cream, a statement which was untrue, but that we could get both at the Post Office . . . I should like to state as a criticism that you should choose a superintendent who is not steeped in prejudice and who is at least a gentleman. We are contemplating another trip to Wakefield and if the same thing happens I shall refer the matter directly to Secretary Ickes. (Dominica 1938)

In response to Sister Dominica's complaint, Superintendent Philip Hough corresponded with Director Cammerer. Hough explained the situation as such:

All that happened was due to the fact that they were segregated for their lunch only. All I can say is that that is the way it's done in Virginia. If I did wrong, I'm sorry—but then again if I had let them in the regular picnic ground we would no doubt be having complaints from the white visitors. This matter may become a real problem. I would say off-hand that not more than one percent of our visitors are colored and it does not seem justifiable to maintain a special picnic ground for them, and if we did we would soon be swamped with colored people. That kind of news travels fast . . . I fully realize that this place is open to all people, under definite regulations. We have never drawn any line except in the matter of their eating. We do not ignore colored visitors. We answer their questions civilly and try to give them the essential information about the place—but we do not go out of our way to encourage them to come here. (P. Hough 1938: 3)

Cammerer responded to Hough and reinforced the idea of creating separate facilities for blacks and whites. Cammerer argued that building segregated facilities was already de rigueur in some national parks and the practice should be continued. He wrote,

In the Shenandoah and Great Smoky Mountains National Parks we have set aside picnic areas for colored people which will be further expanded as the demand increases. At Fort Pulaski National Monument and other areas we have separate comfort stations for colored people. It is our policy, depending upon the demand, to have equal accommodations for colored people and for white people. Since there apparently is a demand for this type of service at Wakefield, you should develop a picnic area for colored people that will be of equal character and attractiveness to the one provided for white people . . . If you make arrangements above as outlined, I think you will have no further trouble. (Cammerer 1938: 1)

Blacks were not welcomed as visitors at nearby Mount Vernon either. While blacks were hired to work at Mount Vernon, black visitors could not take the whites-only excursion steamer to the site. The few blacks who made it to the site by other means (on segregated street cars), were not allowed to use the facilities. Moreover, the River Queen, which carried black passengers, could not dock at Mount Vernon (Kahrl 2008: 62–63). The remainder of this section provides more examples of the segregation and exclusionary activities that occurred in these public entities. Despite their claims of protecting nature for the public good, conservationists and preservationists were silent as these discriminatory and inhumane practices were put in place and maintained for years.

Hot Springs, Arkansas. Native Americans (the Choctaws, Cherokees, Quapaws, and other tribes) once used the land now called Hot Springs. They used it for about eight thousand years calling that portion of the Ouachita Mountains, Valley of the Vapors. Native Americans quarried the area and made tools from the rocks; they also bathed in the water from the forty-seven geothermal springs that dot the area. An 1818 treaty forced the Quapaw tribe to cede the area to the U.S. government. Two years later a proposal was made to create a protected area at the site. The removal of native tribes from the area in the 1830s meant that site was stripped of Indian presence. Hot Springs reserve was created in 1832 and white settler-entrepreneurs were allowed to establish private facilities in the reserve (Hot Springs National Park n.d.; Paige and Harrison 1987: 21–22).

Until the early 1870s, blacks served as service workers at the 265-acre Hot Springs Reservation. They were also allowed to bathe alongside whites in the indoor and outdoor bathing facilities. However, during the Reconstruction era segregation laws proliferated and this led to the constriction of bathing privileges at the facility. When the federal government built a free bathhouse at the "mud hole" for the public in 1878, it was segregated by race and gender.

The segregationist policy continued in 1898 when it was remodeled. The other bathhouses at Hot Springs were also segregated. By this time Hot Springs had become an internationally known spa and blacks wanted to experience the curative powers of its waters. With newspapers like the *Chicago Defender* singing its praises, blacks traveled from around the country to visit the reserve. For instance, Representative Arthur Wergs Mitchell, the only black person in the U.S. Congress, traveled by train from Chicago to Hot Springs for a two-week vacation. He was prompted to file a law suit because he was evicted from the first-class cabin of the train as soon as he reached Arkansas. In response to the African American demands for bathing accommodations, black entrepreneurs began building bathhouses for blacks at Hot Springs in 1904; these were physically segregated also—they were located on the edge of the black business district, not on the main bathhouse row as the other bathing facilities. Park Service director, Stephen Mather, visited Hot Springs in 1916 and became very interested in developing the reserve. As a result, Hot Springs received national park designation in 1921[6] (Hot Springs National Park 2006 1–4; *A. Mitchell v. United States et al.*, 1941; Paige and Harrison 1987: 74, 92–93, 135–137; Shugart 2003: 8; 2006; Shumaker n.d. 16–20).

Harpers Ferry. The first slave was brought to Harpers Ferry, West Virginia in the 1750s. Since then blacks have been a part of the tapestry of this site. In 1859, the abolitionist John Brown and 21 men—including five blacks—launched an ill-fated raid on the armory at Harpers Ferry.[7] In 1867, Storer College, an integrated institution aimed at educating freed slaves opened on Camp Hill in Harpers Ferry; Frederick Douglass was a trustee of Storer. The college was such an important symbol among blacks that the Niagara Movement, the forerunner of the National Association of the Advancement of Colored People, held its second national gathering there in 1906. W. E. B. Du Bois, one of the leaders of the movement, participated in the conference (Gordon 1961: 445–449; Kahrl 2008: 57; Moore 1999; Whitman 1972: 46–84).

Harpers Ferry and Storer College served important commemorative, associative, and recreational functions for many African Americans. By the 1880s, urban blacks traveled by train to visit Harpers Ferry and the college, pay their respects to those who participated in the rebellion, have picnics, go bird watching, hike the mountain trails, or stroll along the banks of the Shenandoah and Potomac rivers. During the summers, African Americans repaired to the countryside at Harpers Ferry. In 1881, Storer College decided to open its dorms to black and white visitors. By the following year, black newspapers in the mid-Atlantic region began publicizing the availability of housing for black travelers to Harpers Ferry (Kahrl 2008: 57–59). In imploring blacks to visit Harpers Ferry, newspaper articles drew on the significance of the site in black liberation and the promise of freedom. One article said:

The spirit of freedom has always been dwelt among the mountains, and when old John Brown looked upon the mountains which rise in majesty round about the place, the spirit of liberty stirred afresh within him, here he resolved to do and dare and die, if need be, that his fellow man might come forth from the chattel house of bondage. (*Washington Bee* 1888: 1)

Black elites from the Niagara Movement raved about Harpers Ferry in the newspapers. The Baltimore & Ohio railroad also advertised their weekend excursions to African Americans; the railroad also urged black churches and other organizations to hold events at Harpers Ferry. For some black middle class families on extended stay, mothers and children stayed for weeks at a time while the fathers joined their wives and children on the weekends. Beginning in 1883, black entrepreneurs opened guest houses and hotels at Harpers Ferry (Kahrl 2008: 57–59, 64–68; *Washington Bee* 1888: 1).

Shenandoah National Park. The Shenandoah Valley and surrounding Blue Ridge Mountains were occupied by Native Americans[8] who farmed, hunted, fished, reared cattle, and participated in the fur trade. The containment of native tribes in the region began during the eighteenth century. In 1722 the Iroquois signed the treaty of Albany that stipulated that they should cede their lands east of the Blue Ridge Mountains and confine themselves to the west of the mountains. This made way for European settlers to gain control of land in the fertile valley. However, the frequent conflicts between the indigenous peoples and the settlers led to the signing of a second treaty. The Lancaster Treaty of 1744 also mandated that the tribe cede their lands and stay to the west of Blue Ridge. Blacks were enslaved in the Shenandoah Valley; they were used to grow tobacco, cotton, and fruit trees on the plantations (Hofstra 2004; Kappler 1904: 659; Rountree 1993: 195–196).

From around 1740 to the time of the civil war, a portion of the land that Virginia's Shenandoah National Park occupies was dotted with plantations. In the late nineteenth century entrepreneurs built resorts such as Skyland to lure vacationers to the area. As early as the 1880s, mention was made of building a large park in the Southern Appalachia. Once the National Park Service was established, Stephen Mather and other park activists began to look for suitable sites in the eastern part of the country to create parks. The search began around

1920 and in 1923 Mather outlined he plan to create such a park in his annual report. Five prominent men were also chosen to serve on the Southern Appalachian National Park Committee charged with helping to identify a site to establish a park. The owner of the Skyland Resort, Hugh Naylor, became an enthusiastic supporter of establishing a national park in the Blue Ridge area. He formed a Northern Virginia Park Association to promote the idea. President Herbert Hoover, who built a retreat—the Rapidan Camp (also called Camp Hoover)—on 164 acres in the area in 1924 also supported the park idea. Hoover used the camp during his presidency. Congress authorized the park in 1926 and Shenandoah became a national park in 1935. The CCC helped to build the park and Skyline Drive which snakes through it (Hunter 1931; Lambert 1989: 38, 67–68, 177–178, 193–196; Updyke 2004; Weaver 1987).

Not even the presence of a presidential abode in Shenandoah could spare blacks from unequal treatment if they visited the park. Arno Cammerer, recognizing that a park so close to Washington, D.C., and other cities with large black populations would be frequented by blacks, thought the park should be segregated. Hence, in 1932—three years before the park was opened—Cammerer sent a note to the National Park Service Director Albright calling for "Provision for colored guests" (quoted in Shumaker n.d.: 24). Arthur Demaray expounded on this idea in a 1936 document:

> The program of development of facilities . . . for the accommodation and convenience of the visiting public contemplates . . . separate facilities for white and colored people to the extent only as is necessary to conform with the generally accepted customs long established in Virginia but not to such an extent as to interfere with the complete enjoyment of the park equally by all alike. . . . To render the most satisfactory service to white and colored visitors it is generally recognized that separate rest rooms, cabin colonies and picnic ground facilities should be provided. (Demaray 1936)

In 1937 Lewis Mountain, a site seven miles south of Big Meadows, was chosen to build a picnic area, campground, lodge, and cabins to accommodate blacks. The facilities at Dickey Ridge, Elkwallow, Skyland, and Big Meadows were reserved for the exclusive use of whites. Notwithstanding, blacks were flocking to the park—between 1938 and 1940, ten thousand African Americans visited Shenandoah (Engle 1996; Lambert 1989: 259–266; Shumaker n.d.: 24–25). Demaray continued to promote the separate but equal doctrine arguing that, "the Park Service must insist upon early provision for Negro accommodations equal to facilities for white persons . . . so that charge cannot be made that we are not furnishing at least the same type and character of facilities that are provided for whites" (Demaray 1939).

Secretary Ickes of the Department of the Interior also insisted on separate but equal dining facilities in the park but he wanted to experiment with integration. He mandated that the Pinnacles Picnic Grounds should be open for use by blacks and whites. The secretary also prohibited park staff from mentioning the segregationist practices in park materials or in presentations to visitors. All of the park's picnic areas were integrated in 1941; however, the restaurants remained segregated until 1945. In 1945 the federal government issued a directive that ordered the National Park Service concessioners to desegregate all their facilities in the national parks. The gradual desegregation of the remainder of Shenandoah continued through 1946 and 1947; Lewis Mountain was integrated in 1947 (Engle 1996; *Federal Register* 1945: 14866; Lambert 1989: 259–266; Shumaker n.d.: 24–25).

The Great Smoky Mountains National Park. Similar segregationist policies and practices were established in the Great Smoky Mountains National Park (created in 1934 on the border of North Carolina and Tennessee). The park's master plan called for three black campgrounds. After much debate in 1941 it was suggested that the word "colored" be removed from descriptions of the campgrounds but plans for the segregated facilities should move forward. The facilities designated for whites and blacks were not publicly designated but park staff enforced segregation in the operation of the park. All-white CCC crews began construction on the park facilities. There was opposition on the park staff and in surrounding communities when four black CCC companies were assigned to work on the park. In response, white units were brought in to replace the black companies (*The Regional Review* 1938: 42; Shumaker n.d.: 32–34).

THE RISE OF BLACK RESORTS AND RURAL GETAWAYS

Like their white counterparts, African Americans gained more free time and disposable income during the late nineteenth and early twentieth centuries. Consequently, many sought to travel to resorts and the wilds. So in the 1870s and 1880s black aristocrats from Louisiana, Detroit, Memphis, and Boston vacationed at Saratoga Springs. Some resorts in other places like Newport, Rhode Island; Cape May, New Jersey; and Martha's Vineyard, Massachusetts also extended their services to the growing cadre of prosperous black vacationers. But as the number of blacks traveling to leisure destinations grew, so did the discomfort of white recreationers. This resulted in the institution of Jim Crow segregationist policies that permeated the leisure and travel industries.

However, some excursion companies saw the business potential and advertised to black clients. Notwithstanding, by the 1890s blacks were forced to stay at black-owned inns or those catering exclusively to a black clientele in resort locations (Foster 1999: 132–133; Haizlip 1996: 12–14; Jefferson 2007: 23–24; Nelson 2005).

Blacks responded to the violence, exclusion, segregation, unequal treatment they encountered when they tried to recreate in the outdoors by developing rural getaways and outdoor recreation areas. They also patronized recreation sites specializing in catering to black vacationers. Hence beaches, ranches, and resort development catering to blacks proliferated. By the beginning of the twentieth century, black resorts and retreats were developed all over the country. In California alone, Lake Elsinore, Bruce's Beach in Manhattan Beach, Santa Monica Beach near Pico Boulevard (also pejoratively known as "the Ink Well"), Val Verde in the Santa Clarita Valley, and Murray's Dude Ranch in Apple Valley–San Bernadino County catered to blacks (Foster 1999: 130–137; Jefferson 2007: 1–2). In addition to Hot Springs and Harpers Ferry discussed above, black retreats could also be found in the Poconos Mountains of Pennsylvania; Silcott Springs, Backroe Beach, Bay Shore, and Mark Haven in Virginia; Sag Harbor on Long Island in New York; Oak Bluffs on Martha's Vineyard; Freeman Beach in Wilmington, North Carolina; Buck Eye Lake near Columbus, Ohio; Arundel-on-the-Bay (also called Highland Beach) near Annapolis, Maryland; Barrett Beach in Port Monmouth, New Jersey; Lake Ivanhoe in Wisconsin; Fox Lake near Angola, Indiana; the Gullah Sea Islands in South Carolina and Georgia; American Beach in Florida; and Gulfport near Biloxi, Mississippi (Cromwell 1984: 2–35; Dresser 2010; Foster 1999: 136–140; Holland 1991: 3–26; Jefferson 2007: 25).

Two rural retreats were developed in Michigan. Blacks found out about destinations like these through word-of-mouth and through descriptions in newspapers like the *Chicago Defender*. For instance a 1915 article described one of the resorts as such:

> The West Michigan Resort [in Benton Harbor] easily ranked as the pride of the colored citizens of Chicago and the Mississippi valley . . . it is understood that it was never the purpose of the management to make money out of this enterprise . . . They are perfectly willing to break even, provided they can give the people a nice, quiet, clean resort, away from the dust, flies, heat and noise of the city, where the people may go and find awaiting them quiet rest, good pure food, splendid bathing facilities, fresh air, and get close to nature and nature's heart; where they may

regain and rebuild that which they have lost and torn down during their busy life in the city. (W. Williams 1915: 8)

Idlewild—located about seventy miles north of Grand Rapids—was Michigan's most famous retreat. The 2,700-acre property consisting of previously logged forest containing Lake Idlewild was purchased by four white developers in 1912. They sold lots to blacks wanting to purchase sites for their camps or cabins; blacks took control of the property in 1921. Those staying at Idlewild went hiking, horseback riding, boating, swimming, and fishing. By the 1940s the summertime residents of Idlewild numbered around twenty-two thousand (Foster 1999: 138–139). W. E. B. Du Bois, who purchased lots in Idlewild, said "For sheer physical beauty, for sheen of water and golden air, for nobleness of tree and shrub, for shining river and song of bird and the low, moving whisper of sun, moon and star . . . and all the wide leisure of rest and play—can you imagine a more marvelous thing than Idlewild?" (Du Bois 1921: 158–160).

Oak Bluffs was another renowned black resort. Blacks were living on Martha's Vineyard as early as 1765. Some of these black residents intermarried with the Chappaquiddick and Wampanoag Indians. Throughout the nineteenth century blacks settled in and vacationed in Oak Bluffs. Increasingly black vacationers from Boston, New York, and Washington, D.C., flocked to Oak Bluffs (Cromwell 1984: 2–35; Dresser 2010; Kenan 1999: 34–35).

For much of their history conservationists and preservationists either ascribed to or promoted discriminatory policies or remained blind to them. These actions made it challenging for people of color and the working class to engage in environmental activities on an equal footing with the white middle class or to collaborate with them.

Conclusion

The Rise of the American Conservation Movement describes the movement of elites from teeming, polluted, and disorderly cities to the urban fringes and rural suburbs, and eventually to remote areas. This outward movement occurred for a variety of reasons, including concerns about safety, status, and taste; quest for cleaner environments; improved health and well-being; the need for more space; access to greater recreational opportunities; dwindling wildlife stocks; and westward expansion. Those most likely to go searching for wild nature were affluent, well educated, or well connected socially and politically. Some of the outward bound were also ideological thinkers who openly criticized industrialism and promoted rural and wilderness lifestyles as antidotes to the perceived ills of the city.

In America, the Transcendentalists were among the first to openly express their concerns about creeping industrialization and environmental degradation and suggest people turn away from the cities as a means of combating the conditions brought on by unfettered industrial growth. They tried to attain the idealized lifestyle they wrote about by moving from cities and relocating in villages and small towns. Though Transcendentalism captured the imagination of some of the leading thinkers in New England, the movement was constrained by its focus on theoretical ideas and individual action as the key to societal transformation. Transcendentalists published journals and newsletters, but these were not aimed at a mass audience. Likewise, there were some collective efforts among Transcendentalists to build utopian communities, but these were short lived and not particularly successful.

Other elites moving away from the cities who became active in environmental issues tried more practical approaches. They attempted to accomplish change on two fronts—through personal transformations as well as through collective efforts. Hence, at the same time there was a focus on changing behaviors (such as ethical hunting and improvements in the way estates and farms are constructed and maintained), there was also a focus on building organizations to either meet the needs of members, challenge the system, or remedy perceived problems. This group not only identified problems, but also began to build institutions and develop regulations to resolve these issues as they saw fit.

Competing Frames: Conservation versus Preservation

The environmental consciousness that arose in America during the nineteenth century reflected elements of settler colonialism, cultural nationalism, and frontierism as well as Transcendental and romantic thought. It was also influenced by pioneer experiences, the politics of environmental governance, the desire to protect natural resources, the emphasis on genteel tastes and lifestyles, racial attitudes, class tensions, and gender relations. By the 1930s, the early conservation movement had taken form. Ideologues, birdwatchers, sport hunters, mountaineers, anglers, gardeners, natural history buffs, collectors and trophy seekers, businessmen, scientists, government agencies, lawmakers, policymakers, resource managers, nature writers, outdoor enthusiasts, and farmers participated in activities that gave rise to the movement.

The environmental discourses of the late nineteenth and early twentieth centuries established the frames of manliness, virtue, prowess, mastery of nature, nation building, civility, gentility, spirituality, wise use of resources, and nature's intrinsic worth. Moreover, in the first two decades of the twentieth century activists began to distinguish between conservation and preservation. In the wildlife conflicts, conservationists saw the problem as one of morality, religion, rectitude, and crass commercialism. For instance, the bird-protection movement argued that it was the moral duty of Christian women to protect birds and that those who wore feathers should atone by joining the Audubon's cause.

However, the Hetch Hetchy controversy was one of competing frames between conservationists and preservationists. Religious imagery was prominent during the Hetch Hetchy controversy. Preservationists frequently used religious and moral rhetoric; their framing also invoked lack of reason, loss of nature and culture, future generations, and the public good. The wilderness was portrayed as a blameless victim being plundered and sacrificed. The conservationists framed the conflict in terms of rationality, efficiency, entitlement, and fairness: for example, they argued that the people of San Francisco were entitled to a reliable source of inexpensive water, hence it was fair to use Hetch Hetchy water. Conservationists also stressed the efficiencies of their scheme to dam the valley and listed many potential uses for the water.

The conservationists gained ground in putting forward an environmental vision that blended utilitarianism with pro-environmental concerns, market applications, and nation-building rhetoric. This approach was more attractive and less threatening to politicians and business leaders than the purely preservationist approach. Many feared that preservation implied absolute protectionism (i.e., preventing the commercial exploitation of resources by sequestering them in perpetuity). However, to pass legislation and put policies in place, both conservationists and preservationists found themselves striking deals and making concessions with corporate and commercial interests to get what they wanted.

Activists communicated and recruited quite effectively through their dense interpersonal and organizational networks of friends. These ties stemmed from their participation in similar forms of outdoor recreation; exclusive social clubs; elite churches; conservation and preservation organizations; business enterprises; community organizations; intermarriage, family, and friendship networks; expeditions; travel to Europe, fashionable resorts, and the West; living in exclusive residential enclaves; as well as memberships in artistic, literary, and academic institutions. For instance, Theodore Roosevelt, Grinnell, and Pinchot grew up in elite residential enclaves in New York City, attended Ivy League universities, knew each other well, and belonged to similar organizations. To form conservation organizations, they recruited friends from college, business partners, family members, and friends who were similarly socialized.

In general, the nineteenth- and early twentieth-century environmental activists placed great emphasis on recruiting through their social and business networks. The sportsmen's clubs and early environmental clubs—the Boone and Crockett Club, Sierra Club, and Save the Redwoods League—made deliberate attempts to limit their membership. It wasn't until the Izaak Walton League was formed in the 1920s that this mold was broken and mass recruitment of the wealthy and working class became more commonplace. But even then, the Waltonians used the institutional framework of fraternal organizations as their model of recruitment. Some thought the original Audubon folded because it was not exclusive enough. However, it should be noted that though the Audubon sent out mass mailings and got pledges, these were symbolic acts of participation. The organization's full members were still recruited from elite social networks.

Taking Action

Activists were frequently faced with the challenge of responding to political leaders and governance structures that were either nonexistent or ineffective. They also found it challenging to get Congress and the other branches of government to be proactive on environment-related issues. For much of the nineteenth century, scientists, sportsmen, and amateur naturalists wrote about the destruction of the natural environment and the seeming inability of the government to halt the degradation. The public believed areas such as Yellowstone and Yosemite that had been placed under government control were not subject to commercial exploitation, but during the preservation and conservation battles, they discovered that these areas were not being protected effectively—that destruction was still occurring. This fostered a diminished sense of trust in the government and its ability to protect lands and resources in its jurisdiction; it also raised questions about the efficacy of administrators. Consequently, citizens decided to organize themselves and develop their own policies and institutional infrastructures to ameliorate conditions and prepare for future contingencies.

Hence, the Boone and Crockett Club, American Ornithological Union, and the Audubon Society took the drastic steps of developing wildlife protection legislation and hiring their own game wardens as they assumed the role of patrolling and managing federal game reserves and national parks at their own expense. Private sports clubs and reserves also purchased land, put timber and game management plans in place, and hired their own wardens. One private citizen, Stephen Mather, financed preservation efforts and moved to Washington to help administer the national parks.

However, the impotence of governing bodies sometimes coincided with political opportunities that activists recognized and took advantage of. One such opportunity arose when Theodore Roosevelt became president. During this period there was a growing rift between conservationists and preservationists, yet Theodore Roosevelt (like Grinnell, Lacey, Kent, and Raker) embraced both ideas and occupied a middle ground between the two factions. Both sides took advantage of having Theodore Roosevelt in office by promoting forest conservation, wilderness preservation, and wildlife protection. For instance, members of the Boone and Crockett Club, whose founder was now in the White House, successfully used the opportunity to advocate for the legal protection of Yellowstone National Park and its resources and the designation of other national park areas. Similarly, other clubs, such as the Audubon Society and the American Ornithological Union, used Grinnell's affiliation with both clubs (as well as the Boone and Crockett) and his close friendship with Theodore Roosevelt to facilitate the establishment of wildlife refuges. By 1909, when Theodore Roosevelt left office, he had created scores of bird sanctuaries. Though there were times when it was difficult to get bills through Congress, activists identified and used elite political allies such as Congressmen Lacey (a Boone and Crockett member), Weeks, and Kent to secure the passage of wildlife, national park, and national forest legislation.

Though the preservationists lost the Hetch Hetchy dispute, the enormous publicity the controversy generated served to educate many people about the environment and arouse their interest. Publicity from other conservation battles too, such as the Audubon's campaign to reduce the slaughter of birds, helped to raise people's consciousness. Generally speaking, conservation and preservation issues gained a higher profile when Theodore Roosevelt was in office because he helped to elevate the issues to national prominence. Not only did he preside over major conservation conferences and disputes; he also visited and camped in Yosemite with John Muir. In approving the formation of the Forest Service, Theodore Roosevelt helped to make room for the government appointment of a pool of scientifically trained, professional civil servants who were interested in and worked on conservation issues. Though other bureaus and divisions dealing with such issues existed before the Forest Service was formed, the Forest Service elevated the profile of wildlands and natural resources at the federal level. In short, the Forest Service represented the institutionalization of forest protection at the highest levels of government.

The passage of key wildlife bills in the early 1900s captivated the interests of those seeking greater protection of game and nongame animals. Activists interested in bird-watching and extractive recreational pursuits such as fishing and hunting also developed an interest in broader conservation issues. Nonetheless, at the beginning of the twentieth century some conservation and preservation organizations were little more than social clubs for people who enjoyed outdoor adventures together. This led Grinnell to complain that the Audubon Society heard lectures and met twice a year for dinner, while individual members pursued initiatives they were interested in. The Sierra Club also seemed to be floundering. Muir fretted that the club was losing influence because members held meetings and wrote letters to Congress but did little else (Fox 1981: 108, 119–120). However, as wildlife bills, forest preservation matters, dam conflicts, and other natural resources issues surfaced, these clubs adopted a more deliberate and overtly political approach. Recognizing that haphazard lobbying and politics was not always efficient or beneficial, they began developing more calculated political strategies and positions. Recreation and conservation or preservation politics became inseparable as people who enjoyed the outdoors realized that their continued recreation hinged on sophisticated and sustained political activism.

Power Elites

This analysis points to the existence of power elites who advocated for the environment: primarily they were white male hunters, birders, anglers, naturalists, hikers, and mountaineers concerned about nature protection. Because these activists were primarily from wealthy backgrounds, they had the cultural capital and the social networks to facilitate their activist agenda. As the movement coalesced, the power elites grew more influential and were able to make significant decisions and enact policies with major implications for the nation-state.

Within this network of activists, one can identify central network actors (Theodore Roosevelt, Grinnell, Lacey, Pinchot, Brewster, Weeks, James Garfield, Pearson, Kent, and Mather), central network organizations (the Audubon Society, American Ornithological Union, and Boone and Crockett Club), central government entities (the White House, U.S. Forest Service, and Department of the Interior); and central industries (the railroads and gun manufacturers). The network actors had multiple, interlocking network ties in the central network organizations. In addition, they had interlocking ties to government and business partners. They assumed leading roles in conservation and preservation conflicts; they pushed for legislation and policies beneficial to their causes, raised funds, and monitored and managed natural resources. Most of them were not only economic elites but also policy and implementation elites. Some, including Pinchot, Theodore Roosevelt, and Grinnell, emerged as ideological elites as well. Theodore Roosevelt was also a political elite.

The power elites were experts at organizing and mobilizing resources. Because of their social location and the tremendous resources at their disposal, the power elites weren't always interested in expending large amounts of time and effort courting widespread grassroots support. In fact, several of the organizations discussed above restricted their membership to a small number of wealthy, influential members with multiple and powerful institutional and interpersonal ties. Women had memberships in the organizations, but only a few, like Anna Botsford Comstock, Harriet Hemenway, Mabel Osgood Wright, and Rosalie Edge, emerged as real powerbrokers. For the most part, the movement was male dominated.

The General Federation of Women's Clubs also emerged as a powerful organization. Though strictly speaking it was neither a conservation nor preservation organization, it was one of the most powerful women's groups and had millions of members. The federation and its affiliates sponsored and supported many conservation and preservation activities. During its heyday, a variety of activists sought the support and endorsement of the General Federation of Women's Clubs.

While some historical accounts portray John Muir as the central actor in early twentieth-century environmental activism (see for example Fox 1981; Limbaugh 1993: 3–13; Turner 1985), this analysis questions that assumption. There is no question that Muir played a pivotal role in publicizing natural resource issues and laying an ideological foundation for the rise of environmental consciousness; however, the above discussion indicates that Muir and the Sierra Club were peripheral network actors in the early twentieth century. Michael Cohen (1984: 277) too argues that scholars mistakenly cast Muir as a central figure in the conservation movement; according to Cohen, an analysis of conservation history that looks at a broad range of events supports a different conclusion.

At the time the power elites were consolidating their power, Muir and the Sierra Club were framed as radical extremists. To further exaggerate its marginality, the Sierra Club was a California-based organization oriented toward statewide wilderness issues. Unlike the Audubon, which spread its influence by developing branches all over the country soon after its revival, the Sierra Club remained a single organization; not until many years after its founding did it begin forming branches, and then only in California. Moreover, the Sierra Club was spatially separated from the other powerful and influential conservation and preservation organizations, all based on the East Coast. Muir, who lived in California, was not well connected to either the East Coast activists or the government. Though Muir met many elite power brokers on his trips to the East Coast or when eastern elites visited California, those meetings were fleeting and acquaintances casual. He did not belong to the social clubs (such as the Cosmos, Century, or Metropolitan) or conservation clubs of the East Coast elites; attend church, theater events, and lectures with them; or go to the same schools they did. In fact, Muir did not even graduate from college: though he received honorary degrees, he left the University of Wisconsin–Madison after attending it for two years.

Muir's marginality showed during the Hetch Hetchy controversy. Muir viewed Theodore Roosevelt as an ally who had taken the time to seek out his opinion on environmental issues and spend time with him (Turner 1985: 324–328; Wolfe 1945: 288–293). It is not surprising that Muir, somewhat cloistered in California, misread the extent to which Theodore Roosevelt saw things the way he did. Muir also underestimated Roosevelt's commitment to dam and irrigation development. In fact, Roosevelt, who once owned two ranches in South Dakota, expressed great interest in federal water development projects. He supported the National Irrigation Congress and twenty-four dam projects that were under way in 1910. Theodore Roosevelt saw water development projects as an integral part of nation building. Muir also misunderstood the extent to which water development projects were central to the conservation ideology of efficient use of resources, scientific decision making, and multiple uses of resources. Finally, Muir underestimated the depth of Roosevelt's commitment to Pinchot's view of natural resource management (Hays [1959] 1999: 5, 14–15).

Institutional ties are also indicators of centrality. While Grinnell, Pinchot, and Theodore Roosevelt belonged to several environmental organizations, Muir belonged to (and served as president of) the Sierra Club; its derivative, the Society for the Preservation of National Parks; and the American Alpine Club (Wilkins 1995: 248). Furthermore, Muir was away on extended world travels during the period when Hetch Hetchy and some of the other major conservation and preservation battles were at their peak (Muir 1911c, 1915). Though Muir spent time with Theodore Roosevelt in Yosemite, it was a very brief encounter (Turner 1985: 324–328; Wolfe 1945: 288–293). Consequently, he did not have as much influence on Theodore Roosevelt as Grinnell and Pinchot did—a fact that played an important role in the Hetch Hetchy controversy. Muir simply did not have as many ties to government as Pinchot and the other leading East Coast environmentalists did.

Though Muir was a member of the Forestry Commission team, he joined the Commission partway through its travels and returned to California at the end of the site visits. He was not present for much of the writing of the report, so Pinchot was able to insert his ideas into the report more effectively than Muir was. Muir could not wield as much influence on the report as Pinchot, because Muir kept in touch with the team only intermittently, while Pinchot was very involved with the writing process.

Furthermore, Muir and the Sierra Club, with their emphasis on wilderness preservation in California, focused on an aspect of nature protection that differed from the interests of the other groups. Many of the major conservation organizations of the time were engrossed in game- and bird-protection struggles. Moreover, organizations working on bird and game issues found a great deal of overlap in their interest, tactics, and strategies. They often supported each other's campaigns (for example, passing model laws). The Hetch Hetchy controversy did not fit this mold or have the same salience for the wildlife activists. The focus on dam construction, water supply, and hydropower overshadowed other aspects of natural resource protection within the conflict. Though wildlife was affected in the Hetch Hetchy case, the controversy was not framed as a wildlife-protection battle. Moreover, Hetch Hetchy was located in a national park, so regardless of the outcome of the controversy, the area would not be opened to extractive sports such as hunting and fishing. Consequently, sport hunters and anglers found this controversy less compelling than other ongoing battles that involved wildlife protection and access to game.

The game and bird protectors were much more closely aligned to Pinchot's timber conservation policies than Muir's wilderness preservationism, which meant a limit on recreational pursuits such as hunting and fishing on public lands. Muir, who had hunted very little (he hunted as a youth in Wisconsin, and accompanied friends on a hunting trip in the Mount Shasta region in 1874), strongly opposed hunting and was somewhat critical of angling (Wolfe 1945: 292; S. H. Young [1915] 1990: 171). Muir and Pinchot had an irreparable ideological and policy split dating back to 1897 (Fox 1981: 143–144; Nash 1982: 166). A similar ideological rift surfaced in 1899 between Muir and Grinnell while discussing the fate of Alaska's natural resources as they traveled on the Harriman Expedition. Muir believed that the Alaskan wilderness should be left untouched, while Grinnell thought that laws should be put in place to regulate and use the resources wisely (P. Burroughs 1995: xvii). The conservation groups had closer ties to Pinchot and Grinnell than to Muir, whose publicized rifts with leading conservationists limited his effectiveness in those circles.

Business Environmentalism

This analysis also indicates that conservationism and preservationism did not arise from popular grassroots discontent and grievance; rather, they arose because a peculiar set of business, recreation interests, and political opportunities converged. As Samuel P. Hays argues, "Conservation neither arose from a broad popular outcry, nor centered its fire primarily upon the private corporation. Moreover, corporations often supported conservation policies . . . One must discard completely the struggle against corporations as the setting in which to understand conservation history" (Hays [1959] 1999: 1–2). Though

Hays's analysis focused on the political structure and the decision-making contexts in which resource policies were made and executed, his analysis supports the claim that there was limited grassroots mobilization in the early years of the conservation movement.

Some scholars, such as John Reiger ([1975] 2001: 2–3), argue that upper-class sportsmen were responsible for the formation of the conservation movement. Reiger's account overstates the case—he ignores or downplays the role of women and other activists who weren't sportsmen in the formation of the movement—but his general point that elite outdoor recreationists were influential in movement formation is well taken. Louis Warren's (1997) analysis also indicates that elites were the dominant force in the formation of the movement and that there was no grassroots mobilization to speak of. Kenneth Prewitt and Alan Stone (1973) too contend that the conservation movement was a Progressive Era, elite-driven movement orchestrated by business, political, and scientific actors. According to Hays ([1959] 1999: 1–2), businessmen joined forces with sympathetic applied scientists and engineers and political and governmental elites to sponsor conservation legislation. Consequently, federal policies for mineral extraction were strongly influenced by prospectors; natural resource policies by timber, tourism, and real estate development interests; and so on. Popular participation in the formulation and promulgation of these policies was uncommon. The public was asked to take part only occasionally, to legitimize policies or campaigns. Thus the activists discussed in this book were a true power elite.

Business environmentalism was attractive to many activists. Many of the wealthy conservationists who became political or financial backers of conservation and preservation initiatives were from the business community, so it is not surprising that they were more comfortable with this kind of environmentalism than with more radical forms. Business leaders knew that some kind of environmental intervention was needed to sustain their recreational pursuits and enable them to profit from environmental ventures. From their perspective, it was a matter of how best to protect nature without completely stifling business interests.

The late nineteenth century was also a time when the wealthy were being pressured to give back some of their wealth to the less fortunate, contribute to social causes, and help in nation building. In response, some contributed to charities, while others established philanthropic institutions (Burrows and Wallace 1999). The environment emerged as one of the worthy causes to which the rich began to donate time and money. In this spirit Kent, Rockefeller, and Mather donated land and money to help create national parks and monuments. Harriman launched a major scientific expedition, while other wealthy businessmen donated money toward acquiring land for parks and forests.

Women also donated money and land to conservation and preservation causes. Hemenway, Fluker, and Edge used their own funds to help build bird-protection organizations. Mrs. Russell Sage also contributed a large sum to the Audubon. In addition, women donated land and money to organizations like the Save the Redwoods League and to campaigns like the one to protect the ruins at Mesa Verde.

The preservationist position was vulnerable on several other fronts. Though business leaders were often able to wring concessions from preservationists, business interests found preservationism more threatening than conservationism. Commercial interests such as logging, mining, and grazing feared that if preservationists got their way they would severely curtail access to valuable resources. However, the preservationists were not as effective as they could have been because they did not have as many strong ties to government and environmental policymakers as the conservationists. Consequently, preservationists lost the Hetch Hetchy battle and ended up with policies that allowed grazing in the national parks. They did not even get a Park Service bill passed until eleven years after the Forest Service was created. Once the Park Service was created, it was so underfunded and understaffed that it had difficulty managing the parks effectively or acquiring additional park lands for several more years.

Business ties also made it difficult to develop a large base of support for the purely preservationist position. In fact, John Muir, the leading preservationist of the time, was himself a businessman at one time. He also had friends like the railroad magnate Harriman, with whom he worked closely (Fox 1981: 127–128; Wilkins 1995: 219; Wolfe 1945: 319–320). Others, such as Stephen Mather and William Kent, were wealthy businessmen who embraced both the preservationist and conservationist perspectives. The Sierra Club, the leading preservationist organization, had many businesspeople among its membership. Though the conservationists were always more inclined to consider a wider range of commercial activities as resource management tools than preservationists, some preservationists either opposed or supported commercial development on a case-by-case basis. Neither Kent nor Raker, for example, was committed to a strict policy of prohibiting commercial exploitation of resources. Kent, a Sierra Club member who went to extraordinary lengths to preserve Muir Woods, took a position similar to Theodore Roosevelt and Grinnell when he supported the construction of the Hetch Hetchy dam a few years after preserving the stand of old-growth trees. Similarly, Raker was promoting the Hetch Hetchy bill at the same time he was advocating for the creation of the National Park Service.

And Rockefeller, who donated money to purchase redwood groves and inhold-ings in Yosemite, and gave substantial amounts of land to help create Acadia National Park and the Grand Tetons, was one of the leading business tycoons of his time (Fox 1981: 220–221; Russell [1959] 1992: 160). Such ambivalence eroded the preservationists' position, making them vulnerable to utilitarianism and compromises with corporate elites. Over time, those adopting the strict preservationist approach were not strong enough to overcome the more utili-tarian, probusiness form of environmentalism that was evolving.

Conservationists working for the government courted business leaders to garner support for their environmental policies and legislation. The relation-ships between Pinchot and various business groups have already been explored. Another case in point: in 1898, George Maxwell courted commercial and indus-trial interests to gain support for his irrigation policies. He convinced business interests that more irrigation in the West would increase production and lead to expanded markets and sales in the East. Thus the National Board of Trade, National Businessmen's League, and the National Association of Manufactur-ers supported Maxwell's irrigation policies. Pinchot and Frederick Newhall of the U.S. Geological Survey also collaborated with business interests to secure passage of irrigation policies (Hays [1959] 1999: 10, 13).

Race, Class, Gender, and Activism

In general, early action around conservation and preservation issues created spaces for upper- and middle-class white male activism, politics, and recreation. Nonetheless, upper- and middle-class white women also found ways to be-come actively involved in nature protection. Their discourse focused on bird and game protection, rural beautification, access to outdoor recreation, tim-ber and resource conservation, and wilderness preservation. Though most of the conservation and preservation clubs operated in the teeming northeastern urban centers where many of their members lived, activists were often divorced from the harsh realities of the cities. Their recreational pursuits took them to the wilds, refuges, sanctuaries, and private clubs they created. Few worked on urban environmental issues, though Theodore Roosevelt and Kent worked with urban reformers and Olmsted developed urban parks.

From the outset, conservationism and preservationism were divorced from the inequities prevalent in society. That is, the activists discussed in this book did not tend to connect their understanding of the environment with social is-sues. They did not challenge social injustices such as slavery, the appropriation of land from indigenous people, the expulsion of Native Americans from their traditional territories, the creation of the reservation system, widespread poverty, and rising inequalities. Emerson, Thoreau, and other Transcendentalists opposed slavery, yet they took only limited steps to articulate how the racism and discrimination arising from colonial practices such as slavery manifested itself in environmental inequalities (such as lack of housing, poor living conditions, poor health, and denial of the right to own land, etc.). Muir's response to the question of slavery is ambiguous at best—he is not on record as either supporting or opposing it. He fled to Canada to avoid the Civil War draft. Shortly after returning to the United States Muir embarked on a walk from Indiana to the Gulf, and while on this walk he wrote disparagingly about blacks and expressed his fear of them. He also wrote matter-of-factly about staying with southern slaveholders who still had slaves on their property after the war ended. Toward the end of his life he traveled to Brazil, where he was again hosted by plantation owners (including some from the United States who had fled to Brazil to continue their slaveholding practices) with throngs of slaves on their plantations (Muir 1916: 60–61; 1911c). Audubon owned and traded in slaves (Rhodes 2004: 114–115, 125), as did many other southern elite sportsmen, naturalists, and environmental thinkers.

Catlin, Thoreau, and Grinnell lived among Native Americans and expressed sympathy for their plight. Early female preservationists also expressed concern for native tribes and tried to help them protect their lands. However, this "protection" generally involved turning Native American land into parks for tourists to visit. As earlier discussions show, on the more fundamental questions of Native American rights to land and resources, the wars with tribes, the inhumanity of the reservation systems, the appropriation of territory from Latinos, and the establishment of national parks and forests on indigenous lands, some of the leading environmental thinkers and activists either remained silent or supported harsh treatment of Native Americans.

The adherence of early activists to the dominant social dogmas of their time is reflected in the nature of the conservation and preservation organizations they established. The organizations were not established as multiracial or cross-class institutions. Many of these were established for wealthy and powerful male citizens only, and some excluded women. In many cases, western European ancestry was a prerequisite for membership. During the late nineteenth century, conservationism and preservationism began to receive national attention and many organizations were formed. Coincidentally, this was also the time period when Jim Crow segregationist policies were being put in place, the last of the Native American tribes were being relegated to reservations, and Asians were being subjected to restrictive immigration laws. When minorities made it into the conservation and preservation discourses, they were often portrayed as landless vagrants or menial and servile laborers who were out of place in the environment and were the root cause of environmental ills (wildlife slaughter, degradation, disease, crime, poverty, etc.).

The alienation of nature-protection activists from the poor and minorities led to the passage of policies that discriminated against the poor and caused severe hardships for them; consequently, there was a backlash against some of those policies. The callous behavior of wealthy sports and businessmen of the South Fork Fishing and Hunting Club—who operated a poorly constructed and inadequately maintained dam that broke and flooded a poor rural community, killing more than two thousand people—widened the rift between wealthy outdoor recreationers and local residents in host communities.

The wealthy could build private preserves or join exclusive clubs that provided access to fish and game whenever it was desired, while the poor had little or no access to such resources. The conversion of rural lands into private sportsmen's clubs and game reserves, virtual armed camps designed to keep game, fish, and timber resources in and local residents out, stoked class resentments that led to deadly conflicts. As a result, the establishment of forest reserves in areas such as the Adirondacks turned poor rural residents into poachers and criminalized their subsistence activities. Because land was tied up either in government holdings or in private hands, local residents had little or no access to the timber, fish, or game they had traditionally subsisted on. Cut off from vital resources, locals resorted to poaching, arson, assassinations, vandalism, and surveillance of the wealthy. Conservationists and preservationists left the impression that they were not very concerned about the poor, blamed them for environmental degradation when possible, and devised laws to criminalize and punish them. Many conflicts resulted, and the poor challenged environmental laws when possible.

The lack of understanding of land uses that predated the establishment of national parks, and the lack of concern for indigenous peoples and other subsistence dwellers, were also evident in the laws governing the establishment and use of these lands, which stipulated that there should be no permanent inhabitants. Park rules also prohibited hunting and gathering in their confines. The establishment of national parks on Native American tribal lands instantly turned many indigenous peoples into squatters and poachers. Their traditional hunting and gathering behaviors were also criminalized under new park rules.

Though wildlands have played a significant role in the cultural landscape of America and in nation-building efforts, the discomfort with the role of minorities and the white working class in this domain was evident as late as the 1930s, with the controversy over the role of CCC in conservation work. The CCC was envisioned as a way of alleviating economic hardships by employing poor, unemployed youths to contribute to the development of the nation-state by performing conservation work. Though the program had strong support in political circles and among the general public, some prominent conservation and preservation advocates openly opposed it; they attacked the work the young men were doing and questioned whether the wilderness and parks should be used for work relief or developed to attract large numbers of visitors. In so doing, these critics showed little empathy for the plight of the destitute CCC enrollees and provided no alternative economic solutions or opportunities for them.

Despite the goal of relieving poverty and unemployment, the CCC program was built on sexist and racist principles. It was framed and developed as a program from men to recover their manliness, develop character, and build the nation. Even when female activists called for a similar program for women, females were not incorporated into the CCC. Only a paltry sum was provided to develop a skeletal women's program—and this was focused primarily on white women. Racism was rampant in the CCC too. Because the program had contradictory policies on racial equity, African Americans were at a severe disadvantage.

IT SHOULD BE NOTED that not all nineteenth- and early twentieth-century reformers were oblivious to social inequalities. As detailed in my earlier book, *The Environment and the People in American Cities*, some urban activists working on environmental issues made the city their arena of reform. There they were forced to confront gender, class, and racial inequalities. Though they weren't always sensitive to the plight of the poor or racial minorities, urban reformers made attempts to collaborate with them.

The legacy of race and class discrimination and the practice of separating environmental issues from those of social inequality are challenges that the conservation movement has had a difficult time overcoming. Discussions and conflicts about these issues still occur regularly even today.

Notes

CHAPTER 1. *Key Concepts in Early Conservation Thought*

1 Though no author is attributed to the document, it has been widely attributed to Winthrop; there is correspondence from Winthrop to family members referencing the drafting of the document. See Winthrop [1629] 1846: 277–278.
2 This book was originally written and published in 1689, but the first edition bore a 1690 publication date.
3 See Locke [1690] 1824: 147–158 for more about Locke's views on natural rights and private property.
4 Most African slaves were taken to Brazil.
5 The fifteen slave-holding states were Alabama, Arkansas, Delaware, Florida, Georgia, Kentucky, Louisiana, Maryland, Mississippi, Missouri, North Carolina, South Carolina, Tennessee, Texas, and Virginia.
6 Arizona, California, Colorado, New Mexico, Nevada, and Utah as well as parts of Kansas, Oklahoma, and Wyoming were formed from land that was formerly in Mexican territory.
7 The preservationist stance was not necessarily antibusiness, but it did seek to pose more restrictions on business operations than the conservationist position did. It should also be noted that business leaders also took part in the preservationist movement and belonged to preservationist groups such as the Sierra Club.

CHAPTER 2. *Wealthy People and the City*

1 In 1640, war broke out between Indians and whites; hostilities continued for several years.

2 London-born Sir Edmund Andros was the royal governor of the province of New York and New Jersey from 1674 to 1681.

3 New Amsterdam was renamed New York after the British took control of the territory.

4 In 1640 Boston, with a population of twelve hundred, was the largest town in the country.

5 During the 1840s and 1850s, the city sold off some of its public lands—and some of that land had to be repurchased to build Central Park. See *Journal of Commerce* 1851a for slightly different estimates of park acreages and the value of park property.

CHAPTER 3. *Wealth, Manliness, and the Outdoors*

1 This work has been attributed to Berners. The original publication date of the treatise is uncertain.

2 S. D. Bruce published seven volumes through 1896. From 1898 on, the Jockey Club purchased the rights to the book's later volumes.

3 Audubon was born out of wedlock. His mother, a chambermaid, died shortly after his birth.

4 The Emerson home, built in 1828 by J. J. Coolidge, was originally named Coolidge Castle. The Emersons renamed it Bush. See Emerson 1883 for a reprint of *Nature*.

5 Unlike Audubon, who embraced the idea of being an American (while remaining proud of his French heritage) and filed for citizenship three years after immigrating to the United States, John Muir did not become a naturalized citizen until 1903, fifty-four years after he migrated. The primacy of his Scottish identity is evident in his writings.

6 Muir's father became a citizen of the United States shortly after moving to Wisconsin. His brother David also became a citizen before John did.

7 Grinnell's unpublished autobiography, written in 1915, covers his life up to 1883.

8 The Grinnells' property was located between 155th and 158th streets near Bloomingdale Road (now close to Amsterdam Avenue). Grinnell's father was a partner of Cornelius Vanderbilt, "the Commodore." George Bird Grinnell grew up hunting muskrats in the Harlem River but spent his summers in the West hunting buffalo.

9 Grinnell dissolved the brokerage business his father turned over to him in 1874. He later acquired *Forest and Stream*.

10 Gifford's grandfather had denuded these same hillsides to make the family's fortune. The copy of Marsh's book Pinchot got was an updated version.

11 There are no records that show Muir was ever drafted.

CHAPTER 4. *Wealth, Women, and Outdoor Pursuits*

1 The term *oecologie* was coined by Ernst Haeckel, a German disciple of Darwin, to denote the emerging field of science that concerned the study of the relations of living organisms to the external world, their habitat, and customs. *Oecologie* comes

from the Greek word *oikos*, which originally referred to the family household, a place of conflict, competition, and mutual aid.

2 The book was attributed to "A Lady" when it was first published.

3 She later reentered Cornell and earned a degree in natural history in 1885.

4 Caroline Kirkland wrote under the pseudonym Mary Clavers.

5 There is some controversy as to whether whites first saw the valley in 1833 or in 1851.

6 By the time she was a teenager, Floy (Florence) became a guide; Mount Florence is named after her. Cosie (Gertrude) worked in Yosemite concessions and taught at Wawona.

CHAPTER 5. *People of Color*

1 From 1777 to 1871 the federal government signed hundreds of treaties with various Indian tribes. Treaty provisions varied greatly, but they frequently included a guarantee of peace; an outline of the boundaries of territories being negotiated; a transfer of lands from tribes to the federal government; a guarantee of Indian hunting, gathering and fishing rights (this applied to ceded lands too); reserved water rights for Indian reservations, etc.; a statement indicating that the tribe recognized the authority of or placed itself under the protection of the United States; an agreement regarding the regulation of trade and travel of people in Indian territory; a provision for punishment of crimes between Indians and non-Indians; and provisions for health care and education. Indian treaties are treated the same as treaties with foreign nations. They take precedence over any conflicting state laws and are the exclusive prerogative of the federal government. Treaties are seen as "contracts among nations" that represent the "supreme law of the land." As such the protection of treaty rights is a critical part of the federal–Indian trust relationship.

2 The ordinance was passed to pacify Indians threatening to repudiate treaties and confederate the tribes as a way of ending American rule. It promised that "the utmost good faith shall always be observed toward the Indians; their land and property shall never be taken from them without their consent; and in their property, rights and liberty, they never shall be invaded or disturbed, unless in just and lawful wars authorized by Congress; but laws founded in justice and humanity shall, from time to time, be made, for preventing wrongs being done to them, and for preserving peace and friendship with them."

3 Congress has special authority over Indian affairs under the Indian Commerce Clause of the Constitution (art. 1, §8, Cl. 3), which allows for the national legislature to regulate commerce with foreign nations, among the several states, and with the Indian tribes.

4 The Georgia gold rush began in 1828.

5 New Echota refers to the Cherokee capital located near present-day Elton, Georgia.

6 This pro-treaty group was known as the "ridge party" or the "treaty party."

7 At the time the federal government paid a minimum of $1.25 per acre for land. The

payout to the tribe for ceded land was well below this minimum (Gregg and Wishart 2012: 425).

8 Internment camps or "emigration depots" were located in southeast Tennessee, southwest North Carolina, and northern Georgia at Fort Cass, Red Clay, Bedwell Springs, Chatata, Mouse Creek, Rattlesnake Springs, Chestuee Creek, and Calhoun.

9 On surplus land that was later sold, the mineral rights were given to either the tribe or the federal government.

10 See Camille Dungy's 2009 book, *Black Nature: Four Centuries of African American Nature Poetry* for a collection of 180 poems about nature written by African American writers.

11 See Stewart (2006: 9–36) for more details.

12 After six years of putting forward bills (all of which failed) to create a national monument in honor of Harriet Tubman, in 2013 President Barack Obama took executive action: he created the Harriet Tubman Underground Railroad National Monument at the Blackwater National Wildlife Refuge on Maryland's Eastern Shore. In December 2014 a bill was passed that authorized the creation of the Harriet Tubman National Historical Park in Maryland and the Harriet Tubman National Historical Park in Cayuga County, New York (R. Harding 2014; *Star Democrat* 2014).

CHAPTER 6. *Sport Hunting and Wildlife Protection*

1 The book was published anonymously in New York, but authorship is attributed to Charles Bell.

2 Though the book is published anonymously, it is attributed to Dr. Jesse Y. Kester.

3 Henry William Herbert, a British nobleman who moved to New York in 1831, went by the pen name Frank Forester.

4 Jacking is the act of setting a light on the bow of a canoe or boat and floating slowly and quietly along the shoreline. Hunters kill the deer as they are drawn to the light.

5 Originally founded as the Colony in Schuylkill, the Schuylkill Fishing Company bills itself as the oldest social club in the English-speaking world. The Fort St. David's Fishing Club merged with the Schuylkill Fishing Company in the 1760s.

6 The Johnstown Area Heritage Association lists seventy members of the South Fork Fishing and Hunting Club on its website. See www.jaha.org/FloodMuseum/history.html.

7 *Forest and Stream* was founded in 1873 by Charles Hallock. Grinnell purchased the magazine in 1880 and used it to promote his conservation ideas. Grinnell retained control of the magazine until 1911.

8 Wisconsin became a state in 1848.

1 Nuttall is still in existence today. The organization focuses on scholarly publications; its membership criteria are still very rigorous. See www.nuttallclub.org.

2 New York's law was later repealed.

3 Ducks, geese, rail, coot, shorebirds, turkey, grouse, pheasant, and quails were classified as game birds. All other birds except the English sparrow were considered nongame birds.

4 One exception was George O. Shields, founder of the League of American Sportsmen, who criticized the excessive catches of hunters and anglers in his magazine *Recreation*. He instituted a monthly "game hog" and "fish hog" award for proud sportsmen who submitted photographs of themselves with the strings of dead birds, game, or fish they had killed. Instead of praising them for their prowess, he embarrassed and ridiculed them by printing their pictures with the caption "These men are hogs!"

5 Aigrettes are the long, delicate dorsal plumes taken from adult herons or egrets in breeding season.

6 Irene Rood was a member of the American Ornithological Union and chair of the Women's Committee for the 1893 Congress on Birds (*Auk* 1893: 386–387).

7 In addition, the society had life and sustaining members. These were primarily wealthy men who donated a fixed amount to the organization annually. Women and children tended to have regular and junior memberships. Only a few women, such as Mabel Osgood Wright, head of the Connecticut Audubon, rose to prominence in the organization.

8 The Audubon recruited children heavily by registering them in the Junior Audubons, sending them Audubon materials below cost, and providing materials for schoolteachers whom Dutcher described as "Audubon Auxiliaries" or "imbuers," who "imbued" the children with the Audubon message. By 1917, there were 260,000 Junior Audubonists registered in over six thousand classes.

9 Most of the cats the Humane Society disposed of were cats brought in by people wanting to exterminate them.

10 Wardens received a regular salary of up to two dollars per day. Before 1901 game wardens were compensated in a similar fashion to the deputy game protectors.

11 A second man, Jim Murdock, was also charged in Seeley Houk's murder in 1922 (*New York Times* 1922: 2).

1 Pearson, Grinnell, J. A. Allen, Mabel Osgood Wright, William Brewster, and F. Lucas approved the gift, while W. Grant, Frank Chapman, and Henry Chapman opposed it.

2 Burnham once worked for Grinnell at *Forest and Stream*.

3 Van Name was the nephew of Willard Van Gibbs, a renowned mathematical physicist at Yale.

4 The document was published anonymously by the Audubon but is attributed to Charles Shelton of the American Wild Fowlers.

5 The Audubon had received funds from hunters for renting the organization's boat and from fees collected for hunting licenses for a long time.

6 When Pearson was secretary, he assumed many of the duties of Dutcher, the ailing president.

7 Though earlier membership drives had been orchestrated by an ex-Kiwanis office manager and by arms manufacturer salesmen, within a few years of its founding members were called upon to recruit others.

8 This was the federal bureau overseeing wildlife issues; it was later reorganized and renamed the Fish and Wildlife Service.

CHAPTER 9. *Rural Beautification and Forest Conservation*
_____

1 Though this report is signed as an Olmsted and Vaux collaboration, there is strong evidence that Olmsted wrote this report and drew the design of Riverside on his own, since Vaux was traveling in Europe at the time it was being written. Olmsted made the site visit and worked on the report.

2 In the early planning phases of the commission, Pinchot sought and obtained endorsement from business groups like the New York Board of Trade and Chamber of Commerce.

3 The final report was submitted on May 1, 1897, early in the McKinley presidency.

4 The reserves created were the Black Hills Reserve in South Dakota (967,680 acres), Big Horn Reserve in Wyoming (1,198,080 acres), Teton Forest Reserve in Wyoming (829,440 acres), Flathead Reserve in Montana (1,382,400 acres), Lewis and Clark Forest Reserve in Montana (2,926,080 acres), Priest River Forest Reserve in Idaho and Washington (645,120 acres), Bitterroot Forest Reserve in Montana and Idaho (4,147,200 acres), Washington Forest Reserve in Washington (3,594,240 acres), Olympic Forest Reserve in Washington (2,188,800 acres), Mount Rainier Forest Reserve in Washington (1,267,200 acres), Stanislaus Forest Reserve in California (691,200 acres), San Jacinto Forest Reserve in California (737,280 acres), and Unita Forest Reserve in Utah (705,120 acres).

5 Pinchot's comments reportedly sparked a public confrontation between him and Muir (although it is uncertain whether such a confrontation actually occurred). They happened to be staying in the same hotel the day the story was reported in the papers, and Muir was said to have approached Pinchot in the lobby and asked if he was correctly quoted. When Pinchot said yes, Muir told Pinchot that he did not want to have anything to do with him again.

6 By the time this conference was convened, Congress was bitterly opposed to Roosevelt's natural resource policies. Because Congress did not appropriate any funds for the conference, Pinchot funded it out of pocket.

7 For more on everyday resistance see Scott 1985.

1 The area became a national park in 1921.

2 Runte (1987) argues that Raymond might have picked up the term *inalienable forever* from conversations he might have had with Olmsted about the fate of the valley. Farquhar (1965) also argues that Olmsted helped Raymond to formulate the bill. But Roper (1973), a noted Olmsted scholar, found no evidence that Olmsted helped Raymond to craft his argument or write the Yosemite bill.

3 During the Civil War Olmsted left Central Park and went to the South to work as a member of the Sanitary Commission. After the war he went to California to work at the Mariposa Mining Company. It was during this time that he was invited to help oversee the management of Yosemite.

4 Other members of the commission included Josiah Whitney, William Ashburner, Israel Raymond, E. Holden, Alexander Deering, George Coulter, and Galen Clark.

5 Olmsted and other park advocates made these arguments even though Central Park and others like it were designed and managed by the middle and upper classes primarily to benefit those users. The working classes had limited access to these parks, and their use was severely restricted. See Taylor 1999: 420–477; 2004: 92–99; 2009: 296–337.

6 Three Yellowstone Park superintendents—all military men—were members of the Boone and Crockett Club.

7 The idea of creating Yellowstone National Park was first proposed in 1870 by Cornelius Hedges while on an expedition to the area. A year later, Jay Cooke and Company, financiers of the Northern Pacific Railroad, began campaigning for the park's creation. The railroad company was interested in seeing Yellowstone become a vacation destination like Niagara Falls; the company hoped to transport tourists to the park.

8 Harris thought Native Americans "were allowed entirely too much liberty" and were "a constant source of annoyance."

9 Samuel de Champlain, traveling under the authority of Sieur de Monts, explored Mount Desert Island and the Maine Coast in 1604. The monument was named in honor of this expedition.

10 The other thirteen sites were the Stanislaus River, Eel River, San Joaquin River, Sacramento River, Lake Tahoe, Yuba River, Feather River, American River, Mokelumne River, Cosumnes River, Clear Lake, Bay Shore Gravels, and the Spring Valley Water Company system.

11 Other organizations opposing the Hetch Hetchy dam included the Society for the Preservation of National Parks, American Civic Association, American Scenic and Historic Preservation Society, Playground Association of America, General Federation of Women's Clubs, American Alpine Club, Appalachian Mountain Club, Mazamas, Mountaineers of Seattle, Chicago Geographical Society, and Saturday Walking Club of Chicago (Muir 1909b: 3).

1   This is not the same Robert Marshall who is a cofounder of the Wilderness Society.

1   These are deed restrictions placed on property that prohibit certain racial or ethnic groups from purchasing, renting, leasing, or living on the property.

2   Williams and his friends, who were playing in the water in the segregated black section of Lake Michigan, inadvertently crossed over into the white section. White beach goers hurled rocks at the children. One rock struck and killed Eugene.

3   *The Chicago Defender* was founded in Chicago but became a national newspaper with a distribution of 125,000 in 1918. Circulation grew to 160,000 in 1945. Copies of the paper were shipped by rail to more than 1,500 southern cities and towns (J. Botkin 2006).

4   Originally named Campfire Club, the name was changed to Camp Fire Boys and Girls Club in 1975 and finally to Camp Fire USA in 2001.

5   Stephen T. Mather was the first and Horace Albright was the second director of the National Park Service.

6   The Hot Springs National Park is 5,500 acres in size. The 1.8 million acre Ouachita National Forest was created around Hot Springs in 1926.

7   Harriet Tubman had agreed to participate in the raid but was ill at the time and could not take part. Frederick Douglass was asked to participate but declined the invitation. Henry David Thoreau—who had made donations to John Brown—and Ralph Waldo Emerson wrote to Brown expressing their support for him while he was in jail awaiting execution (Whitman 1972).

8   Several tribes, namely the Piedmont Siouans, Catawbas, Shawnee, Delaware, Cherokees, Susquehannocks, and the Iroquois were said to have lived in the area. The Iroquois comprised six nations—the Mohawks, Oneidas, Onondagas, Cayugas, Senecas, and later Tuscaroras.

References

AAUW (American Association of University Women). 2010. "Florence Merriam Bailey: Pioneer Naturalist." St. Lawrence County, NY: AAUW.

Abbott, John S. C. [1873] 2004. *Peter Stuyvesant the Last Dutch Governor of New Amsterdam.* Whitefish, MT: Kessinger.

Act for the Preservation of American Antiquities. 1906. 34 Stat. 225. Approved June 8.

Act for the Preservation of Game. 1874. General Assembly of Missouri. Approved February 7.

Act for the Preservation of Salmon in Certain Rivers Running on Lakes Ontario, Erie and Champlain. 1800. Sess. 23, ch. 74. March 28.

Act for the Protection of Birds. Laws of 1876, 183–184.

Act for the Protection of Game and Game Fish. 1878. Pamph. L. 293. Approved April 4.

Act for the Protection of the Fisheries in Buzzard's Bay. 1886. Laws of 1886. C. 192. Approved May 6.

Act of April 11, 1903. An Act to Provide for the Appointment of Deputy Game Protectors for the Commonwealth of Pennsylvania. Pub. L. 163.

Act of 1871 for the Preservation of Game. Chap. 721. Laws of 1871, 1669.

Act of June 4, 1897. Pub. L. 123.

Act of June 27, 1883. Pub. L. 163.

Act of June 30, 1864. An Act Authorizing a Grant to the State of California of the "Yosemite Valley," and the Land Embracing the "Mariposa Big Tree Grove." 13 Stat. 325.

Act of July 2, 1916. An Act to Give Effect to the Convention between the United States and Great Britain for the Protection of Migratory Birds Concluded at Washington, August Sixteenth, Nineteen Hundred and Sixteen, and for Other Purposes. July 2. S. 1553. Pub. Act No. 186. Stat. Vol. 40, part 1, chap. 128, 755–757.

Act of October 1, 1890. An Act to Set Apart Certain Tracts of Land in the State of California as Forest Reservations. 26 Stat. 650.

Act of November 8, 1865. An Act for the Protection of Deer. Gen. Stat. 891.

Act to Establish a National Park Service, and for Other Purposes. 1916. 39 Stat. 535. August 25.

Act to Provide for the Preservation of Fish. 1867. Acts 1867, 128. Approved March 9.

Act to Revise and Consolidate the Several Acts Relating to the Protection of Game, and for the Protection of Deer, Wild Fowl and Birds. Game Law of 1879. Approved May 14.

Acuna, Rodolfo. 1988. *Occupied America: A History of Chicanos*. 3rd ed. New York: Harper and Row.

Adams, John Quincy. 1903. *Life in a New England Town: 1787, 1788. Diary of John Quincy Adams, While a Student in the Office of Theophilus Parsons at Newburyport*. Boston: Little, Brown.

Adams, William R. 1972. "Florida Live Oak Farm of John Quincy Adams." *Florida Historical Quarterly* 51: 129–142.

Adirondack League Club. 1890. "Notice." Old Forge, NY: Author; O. L. Snyder, secretary.

Adirondack League Club. 1894. *Adirondack League Club Hand-Book for 1894*. Old Forge, NY: Author.

Adirondack League Club. 1899. *Annual Report*. Old Forge, NY: Author.

Adirondack League Club. 1904. *Annual Report*. Old Forge, NY: Author.

Agassiz, Elizabeth Cary, ed. 1887. *Louis Agassiz: His Life and Correspondence*. Boston: Houghton Mifflin.

Agbayani-Siewert, Pauline, and Linda Revilla. 1995. "Filipino Americans." In *Asian Americans: Contemporary Trends and Issues*, edited by Pyong Gap Min, 134–168. Thousand Oaks, CA: Sage.

Aguirre, Adalberto, Jr., and Jonathan H. Turner. 1998. *American Ethnicity: The Dynamics and Consequences of Discrimination*. 2nd ed. Boston: McGraw-Hill.

Akers, Donna L. 1999. "Removing the Heart of the Choctaw People: Indian Removal from a Native Perspective." *American Indian Culture and Research Journal* 23, no. 3: 63–76.

Albright, Horace M., and Marian Albright Schenck. 1999. *Creating the National Park Service: The Missing Years*. Norman: University of Oklahoma Press.

Allen, Joel A. 1876. "Decrease of Birds in Massachusetts." *Bulletin of the Nuttall Ornithological Club* (September): 53–60.

Allen, Joel A. 1897. "An Ornithologist's Plea." *New York Times*, November 25.

Allen, Martha Mitten. 1972. "Women in the West: A Study of Book Length Travel Accounts by Women Who Traveled in the Plains and Rockies with Special Attention to General Concepts That the Women Applied to the Plains, the Mountains, Westerners and the West in General." PhD diss., University of Texas at Austin.

Allen, William Francis, Charles Pickard Ware, and Lucy McKim Garrison. 1867. *Slave Songs of the United States*. Bedford, MA: Applewood Books.

Alms v. Indiana County. 1911. 45 Pa. Super. 137.

Alpern, Stanley B. 2013. "Did Enslaved Africans Spark South Carolina's Eighteenth-Century Rice Boom?" In *African Ethnobotany in the Americas*, edited by Robert Voeks and John Rashford, 35–66. New York: Springer.

Alves, Susan. 2005. "Literature of Industrialism." In *The Encyclopedia of New England*, edited by Burt Feintuch and David H. Watters, 1004–1006. New Haven, CT: Yale University Press.

Ambler, Marjane. 1990. *Breaking the Iron Bonds: Indian Control of Energy Development*. Lawrence: University Press of Kansas.

Ambrose, Stephen E. 1996. Introduction to *Hunting Trips of a Ranchman and the Wilderness Hunter*, by Theodore Roosevelt. New York: Modern Library.

American Sportsman. 1873. "Fall Sport at Blooming Grove Park." 3: 85.

Anbinder, Tyler. 2001. *Five Points: The Nineteenth-Century New York City Neighborhood that Invented Tap Dance, Stole Elections, and Became the World's Most Notorious Slum*. New York: Free Press.

Anderson, Irving W. 1999. "The Sacagawea Mystique: Her Age, Name, Role, and Final Destiny." *Columbia Magazine* 13, no. 3 (fall): 3–7.

Anderson, Lorraine, and Thomas S. Edwards. 2002. *At Home on This Earth: Two Centuries of U.S. Women's Nature Writing*. Hanover, NH: University Press of New England.

Anderson, William L., ed. 1991. *Cherokee Removal: Before and After*. Athens: University of Georgia Press.

Anna, Timothy E. 1978. *The Fall of the Royal Government in Mexico City*. Lincoln: University of Nebraska Press.

Annual Report of the Director of the National Park Service. 1917. Washington, DC: Government Printing Office.

Anonymous. n.d. Document No. 696. "A-E, January 1, 1882–December 31, 1894." Item 4. Yellowstone National Park Archives.

Anonymous. n.d. Document No. 2553. "F-K, January 1, 1895–December 31, 1899." Item 11. Yellowstone National Park Archives.

Aragón y Ulibarrí, Daniel. 1999. *Devil's Hatband*. Santa Fe, NM: Sunstone Press.

Archer, Christon I., ed. 2003. *The Birth of Modern Mexico*. Wilmington, DE: SR Books.

Atkinson, James R. 2004. *Splendid Land, Splendid People: The Chickasaw Indians to Removal*. Tuscaloosa: University of Alabama Press.

Auchincloss, Louis. 2001. *Theodore Roosevelt*. New York: Henry Holt.

Audubon, John James. 1832. *Ornithological Biography, or an Account of the Habits of the Birds of the United States of America; Accompanied by Descriptions of the Objects Represented in the Work Entitled "The Birds of America," and Interspersed with Delineations of American Scenery and Manners*. Volume 1. Philadelphia: E. L. Carey and A. Hart.

Audubon, John James. 1835. *Ornithological Biography, or an Account of the Habits of the Birds of the United States of America; Accompanied by Descriptions of the Objects Represented in the Work Entitled "The Birds of America," and Interspersed with Delineations of American Scenery and Manners*. Volume 2. Edinburgh: Adam Black.

Audubon, John James. 1839. *Ornithological Biography, or an Account of the Habits of the Birds of the United States of America*. Vol. 5. Edinburgh: A. and C. Black.

Audubon, John James. 1926. *Delineations of American Scenery and Character*, with introduction by Francis Hobart Herrick. New York: G. A. Baker.

Audubon, John James. 1999. *John James Audubon, Writings and Drawings*. Edited by Christopher Irmscher. New York: Library of America.

Audubon, Lucy Bakewell. 1808. Letter to Euphemia Gifford dated May 27. John James Audubon Collection, Manuscripts Division, Department of Rare Books and Special Collection. Princeton, NJ: Princeton University Library.

Audubon, Lucy Bakewell. 1869. *The Life of John James Audubon, the Naturalist*. New York: G. P. Putnam.

Audubon Magazine. 1887. 1 (February): 1–284.

Audubon Magazine. 1888. 2 (February): 1–262.

Auk. 1893. "Notes and News." 10 (October): 386–387.

Austin, Allan W. 2007. "Eastward Pioneers: Japanese American Resettlement during World War II and the Contested Meaning of Exile and Incarceration." *Journal of American Ethnic History* 26 no. 2 (winter): 58–84.

Austin, Mary Hunter. 1903. *Land of Little Rain*. Boston: Houghton Mifflin.

Badè, William F. 1914. "The Hetch-Hetchy Situation." *Sierra Club Bulletin* 9, no. 3 (January), www.sierraclub.org/ca/hetchhetchy/bade_jan_1914_scb.html.

Bailey, Florence Merriam. 1889. *Birds through an Opera Glass*. Boston: Houghton, Mifflin and Company.

Bailey, Florence Merriam. 1894. *My Summer in a Mormon Village*. Boston: Houghton, Mifflin and Company.

Bailey, Florence Merriam. 1896. *A Birding on a Bronco*. Boston: Houghton, Mifflin and Company.

Bailey, Florence Merriam. 1898. *Birds of Village and Field*. Boston: Houghton, Mifflin and Company.

Bailey, Florence Merriam. 1902. *Handbook of Birds of the Western United States*. Boston: Houghton Mifflin and Company.

Bailey, Florence Merriam. 1919. "Olive Thorne Miller." *Auk* 36, no. 2 (April): 163–169.

Bailey, Florence Merriam. 1928. *Birds of New Mexico*. Santa Fe: New Mexico Department of Game and Fish.

Bailey, Florence Merriam. 1939. *Among the Birds in the Grand Canyon National Park*. Washington, DC: National Park Service.

Baker, Anne. 2003. "Margaret Fuller." In *Writers of the American Renaissance: An A to Z Guide*, edited by Denise D. Knight, 130. Westport, CT: Greenwood.

Baker, Anne. 2005. "Transcendentalist Writers." In *The Encyclopedia of New England*, edited by Burt Feintuch and David H. Watters, 1032–1033. New Haven, CT: Yale University Press.

Baldridge, Kenneth. 1971. "Nine Years of Achievement: The Civilian Conservation Corps." PhD diss., Brigham Young University.

Bankston, Carl, III. 1995. "Filipino Americans." In *Asian Americans: Contemporary Trends and Issues*, edited by Pyong Gap Min, 180–202. Thousand Oaks, CA: Sage.

Barbara (Mabel Osgood Wright). 1901. *The Garden, You, and I*. New York: Macmillan.

Barr, Alwin. 2000. Introduction to *Black Cowboys of Texas*, edited by Sarah Massey, 1–10. College Station: Texas A&M University Press.

Bartram, William. 1958. *The Travels of William Bartram: Naturalist's Edition*. Edited by Francis Harper. New Haven, CT: Yale University Press.

Bauman, John F. 2000. "Introduction: The Eternal War of the Slums." In *From Tenements to the Taylor Homes: In Search of an Urban Housing Policy in Twentieth-

Century America, edited by Roger Biles, Kristin M. Szylvian, and John F. Bauman, 1–20. University Park: Pennsylvania State University Press.

Bedigian, Dorothea. 2013. "African Origins of Sesame Cultivation in the Americas." In *African Ethnobotany in the Americas*. Edited by Robert Voeks and John Rashford, 67–120. New York: Springer.

Beecher, Catharine E. 1842. *Treatise on Domestic Economy for Use of Young Ladies at Home and at School*. Boston: Thomas H. Webb.

Beecher, Catharine E., and Harriet Beecher Stowe. 1869. *The American Woman's Home*. New York: J. B. Ford.

Beecher, Jonathan. 1996. *Charles Fourier: The Visionary and His World*. Berkeley: University of California Press.

Bell, Charles. [Anonymous (A Gentleman)]. [1783] 1791. *The Sportsman's Companion, or, An Essay on Shooting: Illustriously Shewing in What Manner to Fire at Birds of Game, in Various Directions and Situations*. Burlington, VT: Isaac Neale.

Bennett, John E. 1897a. "Should the California Missions Be Preserved?—Part I." *Overland Monthly* 29, no. 169 (January): 9–24.

Bennett, John E. 1897b. "Should the California Missions Be Preserved?—Part II." *Overland Monthly* 29, no. 170 (February): 150–161.

Bennett, Lerone, Jr. 1993. *The Shaping of Black America: The Struggles and Triumphs of African-Americans, 1619 to the 1990s*. New York: Penguin.

Berlin, Ira, Joseph P. Reidy, and Leslie S. Rowlands, eds. 1982. *Freedom: A Documentary History of Emancipation, 1861–1867*. 5 vols. Cambridge: Cambridge University Press.

Berners, Dame Juliana. 1496. "The Treatyse of Fysshynge with an Angle." In *Boke of St. Albans*, edited by Wynkyn de Worde. St. Albans, UK: St. Albans Press.

Best, Joel. 1987. "Rhetoric in Claims-Making." *Social Problems* 34, no. 2: 101–121.

Betts, Robert B. 1978. *Along the Ramparts of the Tetons: The Saga of Jackson Hole, Wyoming*. Boulder: Colorado Associated University Press.

Betts, Robert. 1985. *In Search of York: The Slave Who Went to the Pacific with Lewis and Clark*. Boulder: Colorado Associated University Press.

Beveridge, Charles E., and Carolyn Hoffman. 1997. *The Papers of Frederick Law Olmsted, Supplementary Series, Writings on Public Parks, Parkways, and Park Systems*. Baltimore: Johns Hopkins University Press.

Beveridge, Charles E., and Paul Rocheleau. 1998. *Frederick Law Olmsted: Designing the American Landscape*. New York: Universe.

Beveridge, Charles E., and David Schuyler. 1983. *The Papers of Frederick Law Olmsted: Creating Central Park, 1857–1961*. Vol. 3. Baltimore: Johns Hopkins University Press.

Bird, Isabella Lucy. [1879] 1893. *A Lady's Life in the Rocky Mountains*. New York: G. P. Putnam's Sons.

Bittner, Steve. 2008. "Maryland Hunters: A Legacy of Support for Conservation." *National Wild Turkey Federation* 2 (fall): 10–11.

Blackmar, Elizabeth. 1989. *Manhattan for Rent: 1785–1850*. Ithaca, NY: Cornell University Press.

Blassingame, John W. 1979. *The Slave Community: Plantation Life in the Antebellum South*. New York: Oxford University Press.

Blauner, R. 1969. "Internal Colonialism and Ghetto Revolt." *Social Problems* 16 (spring): 393–408.

Blauner, R. 1972. *Racial Oppression in America*. New York: Harper and Row.

Blauner, R. 1982. "Colonized and Immigrant Minorities." In *Classes, Power and Conflict: Classical and Contemporary Debates*, edited by A. Giddens and D. Held, 501–519. Berkeley: University of California Press.

Blockson, Charles L. 1987. *The Underground Railroad: First Person Narratives of Escapes to Freedom in the North*. New York: Prentice Hall.

Blodgett, Geoffrey. 1976. "Frederick Law Olmsted: Landscape Architecture as Conservative Reform." *Journal of American History* 62: 869–889.

Blooming Grove Township Comprehensive Plan. 2008. Blooming Grove Township, PA: Community Planning and Management.

Board of Indian Commissioners. 1902. *Annual Report*. Washington, DC: Bureau of Indian Affairs.

Bode, Carl, ed. [1947] 1982. *The Portable Thoreau*. New York: Penguin Books.

Bolnick, D. A., and D. G. Smith. 2003. "Unexpected Patterns of Mitochondrial DNA Variation among Native Americans from the Southeastern United States." *American Journal of Physical Anthropology* 122: 336–354.

Bonner, Thomas D. 1856. *The Life and Adventures of James P. Beckwourth: Mountaineer, Scout, and Pioneer and Chief of the Crow Nation of Indians*. Memoirs dictated by Beckwourth to Thomas D. Bonner. New York: Harper and Row.

Boone and Crockett Club. 2014. "Big Game Records Program." Missoula, MT: Boone and Crockett Club. Available at www.boone-crockett.org/bgRecords/records _overview.asp?area=bgRecords (accessed May 10, 2015).

Boonville Herald. 1893. "Adirondack Clubs Consolidate." May 25.

Botkin, Daniel B. 2001. *No Man's Garden: Thoreau and a New Vision for Civilization and Nature*. Washington, DC: Island.

Botkin, Joshua. 2006. "Chicago Defender." *Encyclopedia of African-American Culture and History*. Available at http://www.encyclopedia.com/topic/Chicago_Defender .aspx (accessed July 20, 2015).

Bourdieu, Pierre. 1977. "Cultural Reproduction and Social Reproduction." In *Power and Ideology in Education*, edited by Kerome Karabel and A. H. Halsey, 487–511. New York: Oxford University Press.

Bourdieu, Pierre. 1984. *Distinction: A Social Critique of the Judgment of Taste*. London: Routledge and Kegan Paul.

Bourdieu, Pierre. 1990. *The Logic of Practice*. Cambridge: Polity.

Bowden, Jocelyn Jean. 1969. "Private Land Claims in the Southwest." MA thesis, Southern Methodist University.

Bowles, Samuel. 1868. *Across the Continent: A Summers' Journey by the Rocky Mountains, the Mormons and the Pacific States*. Springfield, MA: S. Bowles.

Bowles, Samuel. 1869. *Our New West. Records of Travel between the Mississippi River and the Pacific Ocean*. Hartford, CT: Hartford Publishing Company.

Boyer, Paul. 1978. *Urban Masses and Moral Order in America, 1820–1920*. Cambridge, MA: Harvard University Press.

Bradford, Sarah H. [1869] 1981. *Harriet Tubman: The Moses of Her People*. Gloucester, MA: Peter Smith.

Bradley, Richard. 2005. "Nativism and Anglo-Saxonism." In *The Encyclopedia of New England*, edited by Burt Feintuch and David H. Watters, 388–389. New Haven, CT: Yale University Press.

Bradstreet, Anne. 1678. "The Four Seasons of the Year." In *Several Poems*, 59–68. Boston: John Foster.

Bradstreet, Anne. [1657] 1898. "As Spring the Winter Doth Succeed." May 13. In *An Account of Anne Bradstreet, the Puritan Poetess, and Kindred Topics*, by Luther Caldwell, 53. Lynn, MA: Nicholls Press.

Brands, Henry William. 1997. *T. R.: The Last Romantic*. New York: Basic Books Brands.

Branson, Isaac Reichelderfer. 1909. *Yosemite against Corporate Greed: Shall Half of Yosemite National Park Be Destroyed by San Francisco?* Aurora, NE: I. R. Branson, Publisher.

Brewster, William. 1878. Letter dated December 15. In the Howard Jones Papers at the Ohio Historical Society. Columbus, OH.

Bridges, Amy. 1984. *A City in the Republic: Antebellum New York and the Origins of Machine Politics*. New York: Cambridge University Press.

Brodess, Eliza Ann. 1849. "Three Hundred Dollars Reward." *Cambridge Democrat*. October 3.

Bronner, Edwin B. 1982. "Village into Town, 1701–1746." In *Philadelphia: A 300-Year History*, edited by Russell F. Weigley. New York: W. W. Norton & Company.

Brown, Amy Belding. 2005. *Mr. Emerson's Wife: A Novel*. New York: St. Martin's.

Brown, John. 1855. *Slave Life in Georgia: A Narrative of the Life, Sufferings, and Escape of John Brown, a Fugitive Slave, Now in England*. Edited by Louis A. Chamerovzow. London: W. M. Watts.

Brubaker, Rogers. 2009. "Ethnicity, Race, and Nationalism." *Annual Review of Sociology* 35 (August): 21–42.

Bruce, Philip Alexander. 1895. *Economic History of Virginia in the Seventeenth Century: An Inquiry into the Material Condition of the People, Based upon Original and Contemporary Records*. New York: Macmillan.

Bruce, Sanders Dewees. [1868] 1898. *American Stud Book*. New York: New York Jockey Club.

Bruggeman, Seth C. 2008: *Here, George Washington Was Born: Memory, Material Culture, and the Public History of a National Monument*. Athens: University of Georgia Press.

Bryant, William Cullen. 1844. "A New Park." *New York Evening Post*. July 3.

Bryant, William Cullen. 1872. *Picturesque America; or The Land We Live In*. Vol. 1. New York: D. Appleton.

Bryant, William Cullen. 1874. *Picturesque America; or The Land We Live In*. Vol. 2. New York: D. Appleton.

Bryant, William Cullen, and Parke Goodwin, eds. 1883. *The Poetical Works of William Cullen Bryant*. Vol. 1. New York: D. Appleton.

Buettner, Cynthia K. 2004. "Parties, Police, and Pandimonium: An Exploratory Study of Mixed-Issue Campus Disturbances." PhD diss., Ohio State University.

Bunce, O. B. 1872a. "Our Great National Park." In *Picturesque America; or, The Land We Live In*, edited by William Cullen Bryant, 300–301. New York: D. Appleton.

Bunce, O. B. 1872b. "On the Coast of Maine." In *Picturesque America; or, The Land We Live In*, edited by William Cullen Bryant, 1–17. New York: D. Appleton.

Bunnell, LaFayette. [1880] 1990. *Discovery of Yosemite and the Indian War of 1851*. Yosemite National Park, CA: Yosemite Association.

Buntline, Ned. [1869] 1974. *Buffalo Bill and His Adventures in the West*. New York: Arno.

Burdick, Neal S. 1982. "Who Killed Orrando P. Dexter?" *Adirondack Life*. (May–June): 23–49.

Bureau of Indian Affairs. 1999. July. *Report on Tribal Priority Allocations*. Washington, DC: Department of the Interior.

Bureau of Indian Affairs. 2012. "BIA." Washington, DC: U.S. Department of the Interior, Indian Affairs. Accessed September 5, 2012. www.bia.gov/WhoWeAre/BIA/index.htm.

Burlingame Treaty. 1868. 16 Stat. 739 1848–1871. July 28.

Burns, Bree. 1992. *Harriet Tubman and the Fight against Slavery*. New York: Chelsea House.

Burroughs, John. 1886. *Signs and Seasons*. Boston: Houghton, Mifflin.

Burroughs, John. 1902. *Harriman Alaska Series*. Vol. 1. New York: Doubleday, Page.

Burroughs, John. 1906. *Camping and Tramping with Roosevelt*. Boston: Houghton Mifflin.

Burroughs, Polly, ed. 1995. "George Bird Grinnell, Pioneer Conservationist." In *Grinnell, George Bird. Alaska 1899: Essays from the Harriman Expedition*, xiii–xvi. Seattle: University of Washington Press.

Burrows, Edwin G., and Mike Wallace. 1999. *Gotham: A History of New York City to 1898*. New York: Oxford University Press.

Busman, William G. 2005. "Local Ornithology in the Nineteenth and Early 20th Century." Accessed July 10, 2010. www.scvas.org/pdf/local ornithology.pdf.

Butterworth, Hezekiah. 1887. *A Zigzag Journey in the Sunny South; Wonder Tales of Early American History*. Boston: Estes and Lauriat.

Byrd, William. 1901. *The Writings of "Colonel William Byrd of Westover in Virginia Esqr."* Edited by John Spencer Bassett. New York: Doubleday, Page.

Cameron, J. 1928. *The Development of Government Forest Control in the United States*. Baltimore: Johns Hopkins University Press.

Cammerer, Arno. 1938. Letter to Philip Hough. June 20. "1950s Reading File," folder A3615, NPS Records Box 9 of 25, George Washington Birthplace National Monument Archives.

Camp Fire Club of America. 2015. "Conservation." Chappaqua: Camp Fire Club of America. Accessed July 10, 2015. http://www.campfireclub.com/guest-welcome.

Cannadine, David. 2006. *Mellon: An American Life*. New York: Alfred A. Knopf.

Capers, Gerald M. 1939. *The Biography of a River Town: Memphis, Its Heroic Age*. Chapel Hill: University of North Carolina Press.

Cardova, Fred. 1983. *Filipinos: Forgotten Asians*. Dubuque, IA: Kendall/Hunt.

Carlson, Leonard A. 1981. "Land Allotment and the Decline of the American Indian Farming." *Explorations in Economic History* 18: 128–154.

Carlson, Leonard A., and Mark A. Roberts. 2006. "Indian Lands, 'Squatterism,' and Slavery: Economic Interests and the Passage of the Indian Removal Act of 1830." *Explorations in Economic History* 43, no. 3 (July): 486–504.

Carnes, Mark C. 1989. *Secret Ritual and Manhood in Victorian America*. New Haven, CT: Yale University Press.

Carney, Judith A. 2001. *Black Rice: The African Origins of Rice Cultivation in the Americas*. Cambridge, MA: Harvard University Press.

Carr, Larry. 1916. "Yosemite Wide Open to Motor Car Owners." *Los Angeles Times*, February 27, 19.

Carretta, Vincent. 2011. *Phillis Wheatley: Biography of a Genius in Bondage*. Athens: University of Georgia Press.

Cart, Theodore W. 1971. "The Struggle for Wildlife Protection in the United States, 1870–1900: Attitudes and Events Leading to the Lacey Act." PhD diss., University of North Carolina.

Cary, Richard. 1962. *Sarah Orne Jewett*. New Haven, CT: Twayne.

Catlin, George. [1841] 1965. *North American Indians: Being Letters and Notes on Their Manners, Customs, and Condition, Written during Eight Years' Travel amongst the Wildest Tribes of Indians in North America*. London: George Catlin.

Catlin, George. [1844] 1973. *Letters and Notes on the Manners, Customs, and Conditions of the North American Indians: Written during Eight Years' Travel (1832–1839) amongst the Wildest Tribes of Indians in North America*. New York: Dover.

Caton, John Dean. 1877. *The Antelope and Deer of America: A Comprehensive Scientific Treatise upon the Natural History, Including the Characteristics, Habits, Affinities, and Capacity for Domestication of the Antilocapra and Cervidoe of North America*. New York: Forest and Stream Publishing Company.

Censer, Jane Turner. 1986. *The Papers of Frederick Law Olmsted: Defending the Union, the Civil War and the U.S. Sanitary Commission, 1861–1863*. Baltimore: Johns Hopkins University Press.

Certificate Issued to Youths Who Completed Civilian Conservation Corps Training within National Park Service Camps. N.d. RG 79, NA.

Chadsey, Mildred. 1915. "Municipal Housekeeping." *Journal of Home Economics* 7 (February): 53–59.

Chadwick, George F. 1966. *The Park and the Town: Public Landscape in the Nineteenth and Twentieth Century*. New York: Praeger.

Chamberlain, Allen. 1908. "Appalachian Mountain Club." Statement submitted to the Committee on Public Lands of the House of Representatives. House Joint Resolution 184—Part 8. December 16.

Champagne, Duane. 1992. "Economic Culture, Institutional Order, and Sustained Market Enterprise: Comparisons of Historical and Contemporary American Indian Cases." In *Property Rights and Indian Economies*, edited by Terry L. Anderson, 195–213. Lanham, MD: Rowman and Littlefield.

Chapman, Frank M. 1886. "Birds and Bonnets." *Forest and Stream* 26 (February 24): 84.

Chapman, Frank M. 1897. "Birds for Millinery: Audubon Society Refers to Laws Governing the Subject." *New York Times*, July 16, 4.

Chapman, Frank M. 1900. "Destruction of Birds." *New York Times*, April 22, 24.

Charles F. Dieterich v. James C. Fargo. 1909. 194 N.Y. 359; 87 N.E. 518; 1909 N.Y. February 23.

Chatelain, Marcia. 2008. *"The Most Interesting Girl of this Country is the Colored Girl": Girls and Racial Uplift in Great Migration Chicago, 1899–1950.* PhD diss., Brown University.

Chatelain, Marcia. 2015. *South Side Girls: Growing Up in the Great Migration.* Durham, NC: Duke University Press.

Chepesuik, Ron. 2004. "The Centennial Congress." *Forest Service Centennial.* Tampa: Faircount.

Cherokee Nation v. Georgia. 1831. 30 U.S. (5 Pet.) 1.

The Chicago Defender. 1916. "Seen and Heard Along the North Shore." September 30, 11. Accessed October 10, 2015. http://search.proquest.com.proxy.lib.umich .edu/hnpchicagodefender/docview/493374620/D37C5D08E76E402CPQ/13 ?accountid=14667.

Chiff, Judith A. 1981. "The Social History of New Haven." In *New Haven: An Illustrated History*, edited by Floyd Shumway and Richard Hegel, 95–114. Woodland Hills, CA: Windsor.

Chin, Art. 1992. *Golden Tassels: A History of the Chinese in Washington, 1857–1977.* Seattle: Self-published.

Chomsky, Aviva. 2008. *Linked Labor Histories: New England, Colombia, and the Making of a Global Working Class.* Durham, NC: Duke University Press.

Christian Science Monitor. 1910. "Must Wear Birdless Hat." March 24, 9.

Christian Science Monitor. 1918. "Aliens' Guns Confiscated." May 14, 8.

Christian Science Monitor. 1923. "Izaak Walton League after Refuge on Mississippi." December 26, 6.

Christian Science Monitor. 1924. "California Begins Redwood Planting." April 4, 6.

Christian Science Monitor. 1926. "Women Sought to Aid League." April 12, 4A.

Christian Science Monitor. 1930. "Golf Club Bird Sanctuaries Are Being Fostered." October 29, 4.

Christian Science Monitor. 1931. "Audubon Work Shows Advance in Many Fields." October 28, 6.

Christian Science Monitor. 1934. "Wild Duck Brought under Protection of Audubon Societies." October 31, 4.

Churchill, Ward. 1992. "The Earth Is Our Mother: Struggles for American Indian Land and Liberation in the Contemporary United States." In *The State of Native America: Genocide, Colonization and Resistance*, edited by M. Annette Jaimes, 139–188. Boston: South End Press.

City of Boston. 1990. *Boston Common Management Plan.* Boston: Boston Parks and Recreation Commission.

City of Centralia. 2009. "George Washington Park." Accessed November 12, 2009. www.cityofcentralia.com/ Page.asp? NavID=60.

Clark, Ella E., and Margot Edmonds. 1979. *Sacagawea of the Lewis and Clark Expedition.* Berkeley: University of California Press.

Clark, William, and Meriwether Lewis. 2003. *The Journals of Lewis and Clark*. Edited by Frank Bergon. New York: Penguin.

Clarke, Charles G. 1970. *The Men of the Lewis and Clark Expedition*. Glendale, CA: Arthur H. Clark Company.

Clarke, Robert. 1973. *Ellen Swallow: The Woman Who Founded Ecology*. Chicago: Follett.

Clausen, J. A., and S. M. Nishi. 1983. Preface to the *Proceedings of Research Conference on Social and Psychological Effects of Exclusion and Detention*. Washington, DC: Commission on Wartime Relocation and Internment of Civilians.

Clavers, Mary (Caroline Kirkland). 1839. *A New Home, Who'll Follow? or Glimpses of Western Life*. New York: C. S. Francis.

Clawson, Mary Ann. 1989. *Constructing Brotherhood: Class, Gender, and Fraternalism*. Princeton, NJ: Princeton University Press.

Clemens, Elizabeth S. 1996. "Organizational Form as Frame: Collective Identity and Political Strategy in the American Labor Movement: 1880–1920." In *Comparative Perspectives on Social Movements: Political Opportunities, Mobilizing Structures, and Cultural Framings*, edited by Doug McAdam, John D. McCarthy, and Mayer N. Zald, 205–226. Cambridge: Cambridge University Press.

Clinton, Catherine. 2004. *Harriet Tubman: The Road to Freedom*. New York: Little, Brown.

Cohen, Michael. 1984. *The Pathless Way: John Muir and the American Wilderness*. Madison: University of Wisconsin Press.

Cohen, Michael. 1988. *The History of the Sierra Club: 1892–1970*. San Francisco: Sierra Club Books.

Colby, William E. 1947. "The Story of the Sierra Club." In *The Sierra Club: A Handbook*, 1–5. San Francisco: Sierra Club.

Cole, Olen, Jr. 1999. *The African-American Experience in the Civilian Conservation Corps*. Gainesville: University of Florida Press.

Collins, Robert L. 1934. Letter to all commanding generals. September 10. Washington, DC: National Archives and Record Service. RG 35, entry 6.

Colorado State Archives. 2001. "Spanish-Mexican Land Grants." Accessed September 9, 2010. www.colorado.gov/dpa/doit/archives/mlg/mlg.htm1.

Committee on Public Lands. 1908. "San Francisco and the Hetch Hetchy Reservoir." Committee on the Public Lands of the House of Representatives. December 16. H.J. Res. 184, 6.

Committee on Public Lands. 1909. 60th Congress, 2nd session. House Report 2085. February 8, 16.

Commonwealth. 1863. "Interview with Harriet Tubman." July 17, 1.

Commonwealth of Pennsylvania. 1903. *Digest of Game and Fish Laws*. Harrisburg, PA.

Commonwealth v. Canon. 1906. 32 Pa. Super. 78. November 11.

Commonwealth v. Frederick. 1905. 27 Pa. Super. 228. January 17.

Commonwealth v. Racco. 1909. 225 Pa. 113; 73A. 1067. May 24.

Comstock, Anna Botsford. 1903. *Ways of the Six Footed*. Harlow, UK: Ginn.

Comstock, Anna Botsford. 1905. *How to Keep Bees: A Handbook for the Use of Beginners*. Garden City, NY: Doubleday, Page and Company.

Comstock, Anna Botsford. 1911. *Handbook of Nature Study*. Ithaca, NY: Comstock Publishing Company.

Comstock, Anna Botsford. 1916. *Trees at Leisure*. Ithaca, NY: Comstock Publishing Company.

Comstock, Edward. 1990. *To Have and to Hold: The Role of Private Preserves in the Adirondack Park*. Old Forge, NY: Privately printed.

Comstock, Edward, and Mark C. Webster, eds., 1990. *The Adirondack League Club, 1890–1990*. Old Forge, NY: Adirondack League Club.

Comstock, John Henry, and Anna Botsford Comstock, eds. 1904. *How to Know the Butterflies: A Manual of the Butterflies of the Eastern United States*. New York: D. Appleton.

Comstock Publishing Associates. 1953. *The Comstocks of Cornell: John Henry Comstock and Anna Botsford Comstock*. Ithaca, NY: Comstock Publishing Associates.

Congressional Record. 1886. 49th Congress, 2d sess., December 11, 94; December 14, 150.

Connecticut Women's Hall of Fame. 2010. "Mabel Osgood Wright." Accessed September 15, 2010. www.cwhf.org/browse_hall/hall/people/wright.php.

Cookingham, H. J. 1883. "The Bisby Club and the Adirondacks." *American Field* (formerly *Field and Stream*) 18 (March 10): 172.

Coolidge, Susan [Sarah Chauncy Woolscy]. 1873. "A Few Hints on the California Journey." *Century* (May): 25–31.

Cooper, Susan Fenimore. 1850. *Rural Hours*. New York: George P. Putnam.

Cooper, Susan Fenimore. 1865. "The Church-Yard Humming-Bird." July 20. Cooperstown, NY: Cooperstown Christ Episcopal Church. Accessed September 10, 2010. http://external.oneonta.edu/cooper/susan/ hummingbird.html.

Cooper, Susan Fenimore. 1869. "Village Improvement Societies." *Putnam's Magazine* 4, no. 21 (September): 359–366.

Cooper, Susan Fenimore. 1878a. "Ostego Leaves I: Birds Then and Now." *Appleton's Journal* 4, no. 6 (June): 529–530.

Cooper, Susan Fenimore. 1878b. "Ostego Leaves II: The Bird Mediaeval." *Appleton's Journal* 5, no. 2 (August): 164–167.

Cooper, Susan Fenimore. 1878c. "Ostego Leaves III: The Bird Primeval." *Appleton's Journal* 5, no. 3 (September): 273–277.

Corbett, Michael R. 1995. "Meatpacking." In *The Encyclopedia of New York City*, edited by Kenneth T. Jackson, 745–746. New Haven, CT: Yale University Press.

Cordova, Fred. 1983. *Filipinos: Forgotten Asian Americans—A Pictorial Essay: 1763–1963*. Dubuque, IA: Kendall/Hunt.

Corey, Steven H. 2005. "Waste Management." In *The Encyclopedia of New England*, edited by Burt Feintuch and David H. Watters, 620–621. New Haven, CT: Yale University Press.

Corfield, Penelope J. 1990. "Walking the City Streets: The Urban Odyssey of Eighteenth-Century England." *Journal of Urban History* 16: 132–174.

Cortesi, Laurence. 1972. *Jean Du Sable: Father of Chicago*. Philadelphia: Chilton.

Coues, Elliott. 1874. *Field Ornithology Comprising a Manual of Instruction: Procuring, Preparing and Preserving Birds*. New York: Dodd and Mead.

Coues, Elliott. 1880. *Bulletin of the Nuttall Ornithology Club* 5, no. 1 (January): 39.

Coues, Elliott. 1882. *Bulletin of the Nuttall Ornithology Club* 7: 112.

Coulter, Robert T. 1978. "Seminole Land Rights in Florida and the Award of the Indian Claims Commission." *American Indian Journal* 4, no. 3: 22–27.

Cowen, B. R. (Acting Secretary, Department of the Interior). 1872. Letter to N. P. Langford, May 10. Washington, DC: Department of the Interior.

Cromwell, Adelaide M. 1984. "The History of Oak Bluffs as a Popular Resort for Blacks." *The Dukes Count Intelligence* 26, no. 1 (August): 2–35.

Cronon, William. 1995. "The Trouble with Wilderness; or, Getting Back to the Wrong Nature." In *Uncommon Ground: Toward Reinventing Nature*, edited by William Cronon, 69–73. New York: W. W. Norton.

Crosby, A. W. 2004. *Ecological Imperialism: The Biological Expansion of Europe.* New York: Cambridge University Press.

Crouse, Jamie S. 2005. "'If They Have a Moral Power': Margaret Fuller, Transcendentalism, and the Question of Women's Moral Nature." *American Transcendentalist Quarterly* 19 (December): 259–279.

Crowley, Walt. 1998. *National Trust Guide Seattle.* New York: John Wiley.

Cruickshank, Dan, and Neil Burton. 1990. *Life in the Georgian City.* London: Viking.

Cunliffe, John, and Guido Erreygers. 2001. "The Enigmatic Legacy of Charles Fourier: Joseph Charlier and Basic Income." *History of Political Economy* 33, no. 3 (fall): 459–484.

Curry, Mary. 1995. "Harriman, Edward H(enry)." In *The Encyclopedia of New York City*, edited by Kenneth T. Jackson, 529. New Haven, CT: Yale University Press.

Curtis, George W. 1855. "Editor's Easy Chair." *Harper's Magazine*, June, 124–125.

Czudnowski, Moshe M. 1983. *Political Elites and Social Change.* DeKalb: Western Illinois University Press.

Dana, Samuel T. 1956. *Forest and Range Policy.* New York: McGraw-Hill.

Daniels, Mark. 1916. *Annual Report of the Superintendent of National Parks.* Washington, DC: Government Printing Office.

Daniels, R. 1988. *Asian America: Chinese and Japanese in the United States since 1850.* Seattle: University of Washington Press.

Davis, David Brion. 2006. *Inhuman Bondage: The Rise and Fall of Slavery in the New World.* New York: Oxford University Press.

Davis, John (One Who is Considered Nobody). 1835. *Essays on Various Subjects. Written for the Amusement of Everybody.* New York: J. W. Bell.

Dawes Act. 1887. 25 U.S.C. § 331 et. seq.

Demaray, Arthur E. 1931. Letter to Horace Albright. August 6. Folder "d32 landscaping," National Park Service Records Box 9 of 25, George Washington Birthplace National Monument Archives.

Demaray, Arthur E. 1936. Letter to L. E. Wilson. September 18. Washington, DC: Department of the Interior.

Demaray, Arthur E. 1939. Memorandum for the Director. February 11. Enclosure 1911136. Washington, DC: Department of the Interior. Accessed June 12, 2015. http://www.nps.gov/shen/learn/historyculture/upload/Demaray_1939_segregation_memo.pdf.

Department of the Interior. 1895. *Report on Population of the United States at the Eleventh Census: 1890.* Part 1. Washington, DC: Government Printing Office.

Department of the Interior. 1907. *Reports of the Department of the Interior. I.* Washington, DC: Government Printing Office.

Department of the Interior. 1915. *National Park Conference: Proceedings.* Washington, DC: Government Printing Office.

DeRosier, Arthur H., Jr. 1970. *The Removal of the Choctaw Indians.* Knoxville: University of Tennessee Press.

Dewey, Scott Hamilton. 2000. *Don't Breathe the Air: Air Pollution and U.S. Environmental Politics, 1945–1970.* College Station: Texas A&M University Press.

Dickinson, Anna E. 1879. *A Ragged Register (of People, Places and Opinions).* New York: Harper and Brothers.

Dickinson, Jacob M. 1927. "A Call to Arms." *Outdoor America* 6, no. 2 (September): 23.

Dilsaver, Larry M. 1994. *America's National Park System: The Critical Documents.* Lanham, MD: Rowman and Littlefield.

Dilsaver, Larry M., and William Tweed. 1990. *Challenge of the Big Trees: A Resource History of Sequoia and Kings Canyon National Parks.* Three Rivers, CA: Sequoia Natural History Association.

Dippe, Brian, Christopher Mulvey, Joan Carpenter Troccoli, and Therese Thau Heyman. 2002. *George Catlin and His Indian Gallery.* Washington, DC: Smithsonian American Art Museum and W. W. Norton.

Dixon, Melvin. 1987. *Ride out the Wilderness: Geography and Identity in Afro-American Literature.* Urbana: University of Illinois Press.

Doane, Gustavus C. 1871. *The Report of Lieutenant Gustavus C. Doane upon the So-Called Yellowstone Expedition of 1870.* S. Ex. Doc. 51, 41st Congress, 3d sess. March 3.

Dobyns, H. F. 1993. "Disease Transfer at Contact." *Annual Review of Anthropology* 22: 273–291.

Dominica, Sister M. Letter to Arno Cammerer. June 15, 1938. "1950s Reading File," folder A3615, National Park Service Records Box 9 of 25, George Washington Birthplace National Monument Archives.

Dorr, George B. 1938. December 22. Manuscript fragment. Dorr Papers. Bar Harbor: Maine Historical Society.

Dorr, George B. 1940. January 26. Manuscript fragment. Dorr Papers. Bar Harbor: Maine Historical Society.

Doughty, Robin W. 1975. *Feather Fashions and Bird Preservation: A Study in Nature Protection.* Berkeley: University of California Press.

Doughty, Thomas. [1830] 1930. "Characteristics of a True Sportsman." *Cabinet of Natural History and American Rural Sport* 1: 8.

Downing, Andrew Jackson. 1848. "A Talk about Public Parks and Gardens." *Rural Essays* (October): 138–146.

Downing, Andrew Jackson. 1851. "The New York Park." *Rural Essays* (August): 147–153.

Downing, Andrew Jackson. [1841] 1860. *A Treatise in the Theory and Practice of Landscape Gardening Adapted to North America with a View to the Improvement of Country Residences.* New York: C. M. Saxton.

Downing, Andrew Jackson. [1845] 1864. *The Fruits and Fruit Trees of America*. New York: John Wiley.

Doyle, Helen McKnight, to Pitcher. July 7, 1901. Document No. 3759, "Letters Received. A-E, January 1, 1900–December 31, 1902." Item 15. Yellowstone National Park Association.

Doyle, Helen McKnight. 1939. *Mary Austin: Woman of Genius*. New York: Gotham House.

Drake, St. Clair, and Horace R. Cayton. [1945] 1993. *Black Metropolis: A Study of Negro Life in a Northern City*. Chicago: University of Chicago Press.

Drenning, June. 1950. "Black Pioneers of the Northwest." *Negro Digest* 8: 65–67.

Dresser, Thomas. 2010. *African Americans of Martha's Vineyard: From Enslavement to Presidential Visit*. Charleston: The History Press.

Dubofsky, Melvyn. 1996. *Industrialism and the American Worker*. 3d ed. Wheeling, IL: Harlan Davidson.

Du Bois, William Edward Burghardt. [1899] 1996. *The Philadelphia Negro: A Social Study*. Philadelphia: University of Pennsylvania Press.

Du Bois, William Edward Burghardt. 1921. "Hopkinsville, Chicago and Idlewild. *The Crisis* 22, no. 4 (August): 158–160.

Duncan, Barbara R., and Brett H. Riggs. 2003. *Cherokee Heritage Trails Guidebook*. Chapel Hill: University of North Carolina Press.

Dungy, Camille T. 2009. *Black Nature: Four Centuries of African American Nature Poetry*, edited by Camille T. Dungy. Athens: University of Georgia Press.

Dunlap, Patricia Riley. 1995. *Riding Astride: The Frontier in Women's History*. Denver: Arden Press.

Dunnell, M. H. 1872. "The Yellowstone Park." Committee on the Public Lands. 42nd Congress, 2nd sess. Report no. 26. February 27.

Durham, Philip C., and Everett L. Jones. 1965. *The Negro Cowboys*. New York: Dodd.

Dutcher, William. 1904a. "The Snowy Heron." *Bird-Lore* 6: 38.

Dutcher, William. 1904b. "Report of the Committee on Bird Protection." *The Auk* 21: 130.

Dutcher, William E. 1906. Letter to Theodore S. Palmer. July 9. Theodore S. Palmer Papers. Washington, DC: Library of Congress.

Dutcher, William E. 1907. Letter to T. Gilbert Pearson. May 23. Audubon Papers. New York: New York Public Library Annex.

Dwight, Jonathan, Jr. 1911. Letter to Theodore S. Palmer. May 31. Audubon Papers. New York: New York Public Library Annex.

Earnest, Jason. 2002. "The South Fork Fishing and Hunting Club." Accessed May 12, 2009. www.nps.gov/archive/jofl/theclub.htm.

Easton, Ethel Olney. 1969. "Sierra Club Beginnings." *Sierra Club Bulletin* 54 (December): 13–15.

Eder, Klaus. 2009. "A Theory of Collective Identity Making Sense of the Debate on a 'European Identity.'" *European Journal of Social Theory* 12, no. 4: 427–447.

Edge, Peter. 1999. "A Most Determined Lady: Rosalie Edge, 1877–1962." Kempton, PA: Hawk Mountain Sanctuary.

Edge, Rosalie. [1936] 1994. "Roads and More Roads in the National Parks and National Forests." Reprinted in *America's National Park System*, edited by Larry M. Dilsaver, 137–139. Lanham, MD: Rowman and Littlefield.

Einhorn, Robin. 2005. "Lager Beer Riot." *The Electronic Encyclopedia of Chicago*. Chicago: Chicago Historical Society.

Eliot, W. Charles. 1915. Letter to Ellen Bullard. September 1. Dorr Papers. Bar Harbor: Maine Historical Society.

Elliott, William. [1846] 1859. *Carolina Sports by Land and Water: Including Devil-fishing, Wild-cat, Deer and Bear Hunting*. New York: Derby and Jackson.

Ellis, John H. 1992. *Yellow Fever and Public Health in the New South*. Lexington: University of Kentucky Press.

Ellisor, John T. 2010. *Second Creek War: Interethnic Conflict and Collusion on a Collapsing Frontier*. Lincoln: University of Nebraska Press.

Eltis, David, and David Richardson. 2010. *Atlas of the Transatlantic Slave Trade*. New Haven, CT: Yale University Press.

Emergency Conservation Work Bulletin 3. 1933. *Handbook for Agencies Selecting Men for Emergency Conservation Work*. Washington, DC: U.S. Government Printing Office.

Emerson, Edward Waldo. 1889. *Emerson in Concord*. Boston: Houghton Mifflin.

Emerson, Ralph Waldo. 1838. "Letter to Martin Van Buren, President of the United States: A Protest against the Removal of the Cherokee Indians from the State of Georgia." April 23. Accessed December 31, 2015. http://rwe.org/iii-letter-to-president-van-buren/.

Emerson, Ralph Waldo. 1862. "Eulogy of Henry David Thoreau: Biographical Sketch." Accessed December 8, 2008. http://hdt.typepad.com/about.html.

Emerson, Ralph Waldo. 1883. "Nature." In *Essays*, 161–188. Boston: Houghton Mifflin.

Emerson, Ralph Waldo. 2000. "The Transcendentalist." In *The Essential Writings of Ralph Waldo Emerson*, edited by Mary Oliver, 81–95. New York: Modern Library.

Engle, Reed. 1996. "Shenondoah: Segregation/Desegregation." Washington, DC: National Park Service. Accessed July 10, 2015. http://www.nps.gov/shen/learn/historyculture/segregation.htm.

Erlich, Paul R., David S. Dobkin, and Darryl Wheye. 1988. "Plume Trade: Frank Chapman's 1886 Feathered Hat Census." Accessed November 23, 2014. https://web.stanford.edu/group/stanfordbirds/text/essays/Plume_Trade.html.

Espiritu, Yen Le. 1997. *Asian American Women and Men*. Thousand Oaks, CA: Sage.

Estrada, Leonardo F., F. Chris Garcia, Reynaldo Flores Macias, and Lionel Maldonado. 1981. "Chicanos in the United States: A History of Exploitation and Resistance." *Daedalus* 2: 103–131.

Ethridge, Robbie Franklyn. 2003. *Creek Country: The Creek Indians and Their World*. Chapel Hill: University of North Carolina Press.

Evans, Estwick. 1819. *A Pedestrious Tour of Four Thousand Miles through the Western States and Territories during the Winter and Spring of 1818*. Concord, NH: Joseph C. Spear.

Evans, Howard Ensign. 1997. *The Natural History of the Long Expedition to the Rocky Mountains (1819–1820)*. New York: Oxford University Press.

Evarts, John. 2001. Introduction to *Coast Redwood: A Natural and Cultural History*, edited by John Evarts and Marjorie Popper. Los Olivos, CA: Cachuma Press.

Evarts, John, and Marjorie Popper, eds. 2001. *Coast Redwood: A Natural and Cultural History*. Los Olivos, CA: Cachuma Press.

Faiman-Silva, Sandra. 1997. *Choctaws at the Crossroads*. Lincoln: University of Nebraska Press.

Faragher, John Mack. 1979. *Women and Men on the Overland Trail*. New Haven, CT: Yale University Press.

Farmer, Charles W. 1897. "Birds, Wings, and Millinery: Law Still Permits This Kind of Trimming on Women's Hats." *New York Times*, July 14, 4.

Farmer, Charles W. 1900. "Killing, Eating, and Wearing Birds." *New York Times*, May 13, 21.

Farnham, Eliza. 1846. *Life in Prairie Land*. New York: Harper and Brothers.

Farnham, Thomas J. 1981. "New Haven, 1638 to 1690." In *New Haven: An Illustrated History*, edited by Floyd Shumway and Richard Hegel, 8–27. Woodland Hills, CA: Windsor.

Farquhar, Francis. 1965. *History of the Sierra Nevada*. Berkeley: University of California at Berkeley.

Farquhar, Francis. 1969. "Mount Whitney—The Early Climbs." *History of the Sierra Nevada*. Berkeley: University of California Press, 173–188.

Federal Register. 1945. "General Bulletin." 10 FR (December 8), 14866.

Federal Reporter. 1890. "In Lee Re Sing." 43: 358–361.

Federal Writers' Project. 1941. *Colorado: A Guide to the Highest State*. New York: Hastings House.

Fenelon, James V., and Clifford E. Trafzer. 2014. "From Colonialism to Denial of California Genocide to Misrepresentations: Special Issue on Indigenous Struggles in the Americas." *American Behavioral Scientist* 58, no. 1: 3–29.

Fetterley, Judith, ed. 1985. *Provisions: A Reader from Nineteenth-Century American Women*. Bloomington: Indiana University Press.

Fink, Leon. 1983. *Workingmen's Democracy: The Knights of Labor and American Politics*. Urbana: University of Illinois Press.

Finney, Carolyn. 2014. *Black Faces, White Spaces: Reimagining the Relationship of African Americans to the Great Outdoors*. Chapel Hill: University of North Carolina Press.

Fisher, Colin. 2005. "African Americans, Outdoor Recreation, and the 1919 Chicago Race Riot." In *To Love the Wind and the Rain: Essays in African American Environmental History*, edited by Dianne Glave and Mark Stoll, 62–76. Pittsburgh: University of Pittsburgh Press.

Fisheries, Game, and Forest Law. 1892. L. 1892. Ch. 488. Section 110, 112.

Fleck, Richard F. 1985. *Henry Thoreau and John Muir among the Indians*. Hamden, CT: Archon Books.

Florette. 1894. "Few Feathers on Hats." *Los Angeles Times*, March 27, 4.

Florida Department of State. N.d. *Florida Cuban Heritage Trail*. Tallahassee, FL: Division of Historical Resources.

Florida Indian Land Claim Settlement Act. 1982. 96 Stat. 2012.

Folds, Charles W. 1927. "Izaak Walton League Expansion Begins." *Outdoor America* 6, no. 3 (October): 32–33.

Forbes, Linda C., and John M. Jermier. 2002. "The Institutionalization of Bird Protection: Mabel Osgood Wright and the Early Audubon Movement." *Organization and Environment*. 15 (4): 458–465.

Forest and Stream. 1880a. "A Proposition to Gentlemen Sportsmen." 15: 319.

Forest and Stream. 1880b. "Should the Guns Be Taxed?" 13 (January 22): 1010.

Forest and Stream. 1881. "New Facts on Game Protection." 16 (March 24): 39.

Forest and Stream. 1882. Untitled. 17 (January 26): 503.

Forest and Stream. 1884a. "Forest Wealth." 22 (January 31): 2.

Forest and Stream. 1884b. "Unheeded Lessons." 22 (March 27): 161.

Forest and Stream. 1884c. Untitled. 22 (May 15): 301.

Forest and Stream. 1885a. "Forests and Forestry III." 23 (January 8): 461–462.

Forest and Stream. 1885b. Untitled. 23 (January 15): 482.

Forest and Stream. 1885c. "Forests and Forestry V." 23 (January 22): 502.

Forest and Stream. 1886. "The Audubon Society." 26 (February 11): 41.

Forest and Stream. 1888. "The Boone and Crockett Club." 30 (March 8): 124.

Forest and Stream. 1894a. "A Plank." 42 (February 3): 89.

Forest and Stream. 1894b. "Preserves in the Adirondack Park." 43 (December 22): 552.

Forest and Stream. 1894c. "A Premium on Crime." 42 (March 24): 243.

Forest and Stream. 1894d. "Park Poachers and Their Ways." 42 (May 26): 444.

Forest and Stream. 1906. "A Hounding Prosecution Threatened." 66 (April 7): 547.

Forest, Fish and Game Law. Laws of N.Y. 1879. Ch. 534, sec. 12.

Forest, Fish and Game Law. Laws of N.Y. 1900. Ch. 20.

Forester, Frank (William Herbert). 1849. *Field Sports of the United States and British Provinces of North America*. Vol. 2. New York: Stinger and Townsend.

Forester, Frank (William Herbert). 1851. "Trout and Trout-Fishing." *Graham's Magazine*, May, 394.

Forester, Frank (William Herbert). 1859. *Fish and Fishing of the United States and British Provinces of North America*. New York: Geo. E. Woodward.

Forester, Frank (William Herbert). 1881. *Sporting Scenes and Characters*. With Fred C. Pond and Will Wildwood. Philadelphia: T. B. Peterson and Brothers.

Forten, Charlotte. 1864. "Life on the Sea Islands." *Atlantic Monthly* 13 (May): 596.

Foster, Mark S. 1999. "In the Face of 'Jim Crow': Prosperous Blacks and Vacations, Travel and Outdoor Leisure, 1890–1945." *The Journal of Negro History* 84, no. 2 (spring): 130–149.

Fox, Stephen. 1981. *The American Conservation Movement: John Muir and His Legacy*. Madison: University of Wisconsin Press.

Franklin, John Hope, and Alfred A. Moss Jr. 1994. *From Slavery to Freedom: A History of African Americans*. New York: Alfred A. Knopf.

Freeman's Record. 1865. "Harriet Tubman." 1 (March): 34–38.

Fresonke, Kris, and Mark David Spence. 2004. *Lewis and Clark: Legacies, Memories, and New Perspectives*. Berkeley: University of California Press.

Friday, Chris. 1994. *Organizing Asian American Labor: The Pacific Coast Canned-Salmon Industry, 1870–1942*. Philadelphia: Temple University Press.

Friedman, Debra, and Doug McAdam. 1992. "Collective Identity and Activism: Networks, Choices and the Life of a Social Movement." In *Frontiers in Social Move-*

ment Theory, edited by Aldon D. Morris and Carol McClurg Mueller, 156–173. New Haven, CT: Yale University Press.

Frothingham, O. B. 1888. *George Ripley*. Boston: Houghton Mifflin.

Fuertes, Mary Boynton. 1956. *Louis Agassiz Fuertes*. New York: Oxford University Press.

Fuller, Margaret. 1843. *Summer on the Lakes, in 1843*. Boston: Freeman and Bolles.

Furlow, John W., Jr. 1976. "Cornelia Bryce Pinchot: Feminism in the Post-Suffrage Era." *Pennsylvania History* 43: 328–346.

Gaines, Kevin K. 1996. *Uplifting the Race: Black Leadership, Politics, and Culture in the Twentieth Century*. Chapel Hill: University of North Carolina Press.

Gallman, J. Matthew. 2006. *America's Joan of Arc: The Life of Anna Elizabeth Dickinson*. New York: Oxford University Press.

Galton, Francis. 1904. "Eugenics: Its Definition, Scope and Aims." *American Journal of Sociology* 10 (July): 1–25.

Gandolfo v. Hartman. 1892. 49 Fed. 181 (C.C.S.D. Cal.). January 25.

Garner, John S. 2000. "The Garden City and the Planned Industrial Suburbs: Housing and Planning on the Eve of World War I." In *From Tenements to the Taylor Homes: In Search of an Urban Housing Policy in Twentieth Century America*, edited by John F. Bauman, Roger Biles, and Kristin M. Szylvian, 43–59. University Park: Pennsylvania State University Press.

Garrison, J. Ritchie. 2005. "Agriculture." In *The Encyclopedia of New England*, edited by Burt Feintuch and David H. Watters, 4–5. New Haven, CT: Yale University Press.

Garrison, Tim Alan. 2002. *The Legal Ideology of Removal: The Southern Judiciary and the Sovereignty of Native American Nations*. Athens: University of Georgia Press.

Geer v. Connecticut. 1896. 161 U.S. 519. 16 S. Ct. 600. 40 L. Ed. 793. March 2.

Geffen, Elizabeth M. 1982. "Industrial Development and Social Crisis, 1841–1854." In *Philadelphia: A 300-Year History*, edited by Russell F. Weigley, 307–362. New York: W. W. Norton.

General Statutes of Connecticut. Revision of 1888. Section 2546.

Genovese, Eugene D. 1972. *Roll, Jordan Roll: The World the Slaves Made*. New York: Vintage.

Gentile v. The State. 1868. 29 Ind. 409. 1868 Ind. May.

Gibbs, John T. 1932. "Roosevelt and Forestry." *American Forests* 38 (December): 633.

Gibbs, John T. 1933. "Tree Planting Aids Unemployed." *American Forests* 39 (April): 160–161, 173, 195.

Gibson, Campbell J., and Emily Lennon. 1999. *Population Division Working Paper No. 29*. February. Washington, DC: U.S. Bureau of the Census.

Giddens, Anthony. 1994. "Elites and Power." In *Social Stratification: Class, Race and Gender in Sociological Perspective*, edited by David Grusky, 170–174. Boulder: Westview.

Gilje, Paul A. 1995. "Riots." In *The Encyclopedia of New York City*, edited by Kenneth T. Jackson, 1006–1008. New Haven, CT: Yale University Press.

Gilman, William H., et al. 1960–1982. *The Journals and Miscellaneous Notebooks of Ralph Waldo Emerson*. 16 vols. Cambridge, MA: Harvard University Press.

Gilmore, David D. 1991. *Manhood in the Making: Cultural Concepts of Masculinity*. New Haven, CT: Yale University Press.

Gilpin, William. 1794. *Remarks on Forest Scenery and Other Woodland Views*. London: R. Blamire.

Glenn, Evelyn Nakano. 1986. *Issei, Nisei, War Bride: Three Generations of Japanese Women in Domestic Service*. Philadelphia: Temple University Press.

Goethe, Charles M. 1949. *Seeking to Serve*. Sacramento, CA: Keystone Press.

Goethe, Charles M. 1955. *Garden Philosopher*. Sacramento, CA: Keystone Press.

Goetzmann, William H., and Kay Sloan. 1982. *Looking Far North: The Harriman Expedition to Alaska, 1899*. Princeton, NJ: Princeton University Press.

Goldstein, Eric A., and Mark A. Izeman. 1995. "Water." In *The Encyclopedia of New York*, edited by Kenneth T. Jackson, 1244–1246. New Haven, CT: Yale University Press.

Goodspeed, Charles Eliot. 1939. *Angling in America: Its Early History and Literature*. Boston: Houghton Mifflin.

Gordon, Vivian V. 1961. "Section E: A History of Storer College, Harpers Ferry, West Virginia," *Journal of Negro Education* 30, no. 4: 445–449.

Gottlieb, Robert. 1993. *Forcing the Spring: The Transformation of the American Environmental Movement*. Covelo, CA: Island Press.

Gower, Calvin W. 1976. "The Struggle of Blacks for Leadership Positions in the Civilian Conservation Corps: 1933–1942." *Journal of Negro History* 61, no. 2 (April): 123.

Graham, Frank, Jr. 1990. *The Audubon Ark: A History of the National Audubon Society*. Austin: University of Texas Press.

Graham, Shirley. 1953. *Jean Baptiste Pointe de Sable, Founder of Chicago*. New York: J. Messner.

Grant, Madison. 1916. *The Passing of a Great Race*. New York: Charles Scribner's Sons.

Grant, Madison. 1930. *The Alien in Our Midst; or, "Selling Our Birthright for a Mess of Pottage."* New York: Galton.

Graves, Henry S. 1916. Letter to J. Horace McFarland. Papers of the American Society of Landscape Architecture. March 30. Washington, DC: Library of Congress.

Grebler, Leo, Joan W. Moore, and Ralph C. Guzman. 1970. *The Mexican American People*. New York: Free Press.

Greeley, Horace. 1851. *Glances at Europe: In a Series of Letters from Great Britain, France, Italy, Switzerland, etc., during the Summer of 1851. Including Notices of the Great Exhibition, or World's Fair Glances at Europe*. New York: Dewitt and Davenport Press.

Greeley, Horace. 1860. *An Overland Journey from New York to San Francisco in the Summer of 1859*. New York: C. M. Saxton, Barker.

Greenwood, Grace [Sarah Jane Lippincott]. 1873a. *From New Life in New Lands: Notes on Travel*. New York: J. B. Ford.

Greenwood, Grace [Sarah Jane Lippincott]. 1873b. "Notes on Travel." *New York Times*, October 20, 5.

Gregg, Josiah. 1851. *Commerce of the Prairies or the Journal of a Santa Fe Trader during Eight Expeditions across the Western Prairies, and a Residence of Nearly Nine Years in Northern Mexico*. 5th ed. Vol. 1. Philadelphia: J. W. Moore.

Gregg, Matthew T. 2009. "Shortchanged: Uncovering the Value of Pre-Removal Cherokee Property." *The Chronicles of Oklahoma* 3: 320–335.

Gregg, Matthew T., and David M. Wishart. 2012. "The Price of Cherokee Removal." *Explorations in Economic History* 49, no. 4 (October): 423–442.

Greve, Charles Theodore. 1904. *Centennial History of Cincinnati and Representative Citizens*. Vol. 1. Chicago: Biographical Publishing Company.

Grieve, Lucia. 1905. "Plea for the Cat." *New York Times*, November 9, 8.

Grimké, Charlotte Forten. 1988. *The Journals of Charlotte Forten Grimké*. Edited by Brenda Stevenson. New York: Oxford University Press.

Grinder, Robert Dale. 1973. *The Anti-Smoke Crusades: Early Attempts to Reform the Urban Environment, 1893–1918*. Columbia: University of Missouri Press.

Grinnell, Elizabeth, and Joseph Grinnell. 1901. *Bird of Song and Story*. Chicago: A. W. Mumford.

Grinnell, George Bird. N.d. "William Cody." Grinnell File. Fairfield: Birdcraft Museum, Connecticut Audubon Society.

Grinnell, George Bird. 1873a. "Elk Hunting in Nebraska." *Forest and Stream* 1, no. 8 (October 2): 116.

Grinnell, George Bird. 1873b. "Buffalo Hunt with the Pawnees." *Forest and Stream* 1 (December 25): 305–306.

Grinnell, George Bird. 1876. Letter of Transmittal. In *Report of a Reconnaissance from Carroll, Montana Territory, on the Upper Missouri, to the Yellowstone National Park, and Return, Made in the Summer of 1875*, edited by William Ludlow. Washington, DC: Army Corps of Engineers, Government Printing Office.

Grinnell, George Bird. 1881. "The Order of Trout Hogs." *Forest and Stream* 17 (June 16): 379.

Grinnell, George Bird. 1882. "Pot-Hunters." *Forest and Stream* 18 (April 20): 223.

Grinnell, George Bird. 1884. "The Sacrifice of Songbirds." *Forest and Stream* 23 (August 7): 21.

Grinnell, George Bird. 1886. "The Audubon Society." *Forest and Stream* 26 (February 11): 41.

Grinnell, George Bird. 1892. Letter to F. G. Webber. Letter Book, 727. January 22. Fairfield: Birdcraft Museum, Connecticut Audubon Society.

Grinnell, George Bird. 1911a. Letter to Henry Fairfield Osborn. May 23. George Bird Grinnell Papers. Fairfield: Connecticut Audubon Society.

Grinnell, George Bird. 1911b. Letter to W. W. Grant. May 29. Audubon Papers. New York: New York Public Library Annex.

Grinnell, George Bird. 1911c. *Trails of a Pathfinder*. New York: Charles Scribner's Sons.

Grinnell, George Bird. 1913. *Hunting at High Altitudes: The Book of the Boone and Crockett Club*. New York: Harper Brothers.

Grinnell, George Bird. 1915. *Memoirs*. Unpublished manuscript. Grinnell File. Fairfield: Birdcraft Museum, Connecticut Audubon Society.

Grinnell, George Bird. 1923. *The Cheyenne Indians: Their History and Ways of Life*. New Haven, CT: Yale University Press.

Grinnell, George Bird. 1924a. Letter to Charles Sheldon. July 23. Fairfield: Connecticut Audubon Society.

Grinnell, George Bird. 1924b. Letter to T. Gilbert Pearson. October 13. Audubon Papers. New York: New York Public Library Annex.

Grinnell, George Bird. 1925. "American Game Protection: A Sketch." In *Hunting and Conservation: The Book of the Boone and Crockett Club*, edited by George Bird Grinnell and Charles Sheldon. New Haven, CT: Yale University Press.

Grinnell, George Bird. 1927. *Audubon Park*. New York: Trustees of Hispanic Society of America.

Griscom, John H. 1845. *The Sanitary Condition of the Laboring Population of New York*. New York: Harper and Brothers.

Griscom, John H. 1855. *Anniversary Discourse, before the New York Academy of Medicine*. Delivered in Clinton Hall, November 22, 1854. New York: New Academy of Medicine.

Groneman, Carol. 1995. "Collect." In *The Encyclopedia of New York City*, edited by Kenneth T. Jackson, 250. New Haven, CT: Yale University Press.

Groves, H. E. 1950–1951. "Judicial Interpretation of the Holdings of the United States Supreme Court in the Restrictive Covenant Cases." *Illinois Law Review* 45: 614.

Gwaltney, William W. 1994. *Beyond the Pale: African Americans in the Fur Trade West*. Fort Laramie, WY: National Park Service.

Haberly, Loyd. 1948. *Pursuit of the Horizon*. New York: Macmillan.

Habermas, Jurgen. 1975. *Legitimation Crisis*. Boston: Beacon Press.

Haizlip, Shirlee Taylor. 1996. "The Black Resorts." *American Legacy Magazine*, summer: 12–14.

Hallock, Charles. 1873. *The Fishing Tourist: Angler's Guide and Reference Book*. New York: Harper and Brothers.

Hallock, Charles. 1878. *Hallock's American Club List and Sportsman's Glossary*. New York: *Forest and Stream*.

Halter, Marilyn, and Robert L. Hall. 2005. "Ethnic and Racial Identity." In *The Encyclopedia of New England*, edited by Burt Feintuch and David H. Watters, 330–337. New Haven, CT: Yale University Press.

Hammond, Samuel H. 1857. *Wild Northern Scenes, or, Sporting Adventures with the Rifle and the Rod*. New York: Derby and Jackson.

Hamnett, Brian R. 1986. *Roots of Insurgency: Mexican Regions, 1750–1824*. New York: Cambridge University Press.

Hannan, Christopher W. 2001. "Indian Land in Seventeenth Century Massachusetts." *Historical Journal of Massachusetts* 29, no. 2 (summer). Accessed April 4, 2010. www .westfield.ma.edu/mhj/.

Harding, Robert. 2014. "Congress Gives Final Approval to Bill Creating Harriet Tubman National Historical Park in Cayuga County." *Auburn Citizen*, December 13. Accessed May 21, 2015. http://auburnpub.com/blogs/eye_on_ny/congress-gives -final-approval-to-bill-creating-harriet-tubman-national/article_657e0b24-8234-11e4 -a4dd-bb6df71996b5.html.

Harding, Walter. 1992. *The Days of Henry Thoreau*. Princeton, NJ: Princeton University Press.

Harding, Wendy. 2014. "Frederick Law Olmsted's Failed Encounter with Yosemite and the Invention of a Proto-Environmentalist." *Ecozon* 5, no. 1: 123–135.

Harper's Bazaar. 1896. Untitled. 29 (February): 663.

Harris, Moses. 1886. *Report of the Superintendent of Yellowstone National Park*. Washington, DC: United States Department of the Interior.

Harris, Thaddeus Mason. 1805. *The Journal of a Tour into the Territory Northwest of the Allegheny Mountains*. Boston: Manning and Loring.

Haskin, Frederic J. 1909. "The Millinery Business." *Washington Post*, November 6, 4.

Haverman, Christopher D. 2008. "Final Resistance: Creek Removal from the Alabama Homeland." *Alabama Heritage* 89 (summer): 9–19, 60.

Hawthorne, Nathaniel. [1845] 1860. "The Celestial Railroad; or, Modern Pilgrim's Progress after the Manner of Bunyan . . ." Boston: J. V. Hines.

Hayashi, Brian M. 2004. *Democratizing the Enemy: The Japanese American Internment*. Princeton, NJ: Princeton University Press.

Hayden, Dolores. 2003. *Building Suburbia: Green Fields and Urban Growth, 1820–2000*. New York: Pantheon.

Hayden, Elizabeth Wied. 1971. "Driving Out the Tusk Hunters." *Teton Magazine* (winter–spring): 22–36.

Hays, Samuel P. [1959] 1999. *Conservation and the Gospel of Efficiency: The Progressive Conservation Movement, 1890–1920*. New York: Atheneum.

Hazen, Henry A. 1881. *Necrology*. Boston: Beacon.

Hearn, Lafcadio. 1883. "The St. Malo Story." *Harper's Weekly*, March 31, 98.

Hechter, M. 1994. "Toward a Theory of Ethnic Change." In *Social Stratification: Class, Race, and Gender in Sociological Perspective*, edited by D. B. Grusky, 487–500. Boulder, CO: Westview.

Helweg, Arthur Wesley, and Usha M. Helweg. 1990. *The Immigrant Success Story: East Indians*. Philadelphia: University of Pennsylvania Press.

Herman, David Justin. 2001. *Hunting and the American Imagination*. Washington, DC: Smithsonian Institution Press.

Herrick, Francis Hobart. [1917] 1938. *Audubon the Naturalist; A History of His Life and Time*. New York: D. Appleton.

Hirabayashi v. United States. 1943. 320 U.S. 81.

Hoffman, Charles Fenno. 1835. *A Winter in the West*. New York: Harper and Brothers.

Hofstra, Warren R. 2004. *The Planting of New Virginia: Settlement and Landscape in the Shenandoah Valley*. Baltimore: Johns Hopkins University Press.

Hogan, Linda. 2015. "New Trees, New Medicines, New Wars: The Chickasaw Removal." *Canadian Review of Comparative Literature / Revue Canadienne de Littérature Comparée* 42, no. 1 (March): 121–129.

Holland, Jacqueline L. 1991. "The African American Presence on Martha's Vineyard." *The Dukes Count Intelligencer* 33, no. 1 (August): 3–26.

Homberger, Eric. 2002. *Mrs. Astor's New York: Money and Social Power in a Gilded Age*. New Haven, CT: Yale University Press.

Hornaday, William T. 1899. *The Extermination of the American Bison with a Sketch of Its Discovery and Life History*. Report to the U.S. National Museum, 1866–1877. Washington, DC: Smithsonian.

Hornaday, William Temple. 1908. Personal communication with H. S. Herring. October 3. Letterbooks, Box 273. Bozeman, MT: American Bison Society Papers.

Hornaday, William Temple. 1913. *Our Vanishing Wildlife: Its Extermination and Preservation*. New York: New York Zoological Society.

Hornaday, William Temple. 1914. *Wildlife Conservation in Theory and Practice: Lectures Delivered before the Forest School of Yale University*. New Haven, CT: Yale University Press.

Horvath, Ronald J. 1972. "A Definition of Colonialism." *Current Anthropology* 13, no. 1: 45–57.

Hot Springs National Park. n.d. "Hot Springs." National Park Service: Hot Springs National Park. Accessed October 15, 2015. http://www.nps.gov/hosp/learn /historyculture/upload/american_indians.pdf.

Hot Springs National Park. 2006. "Bath Houses of Hot Springs" 1 (summer): 1–15.

Hough, Emerson. 1894. "Account of Howell's Capture." *Forest and Stream* 49, no. 18 (May): 1–6.

Hough, Philip R. Letter to Arno Cammerer. June 16, 1938. "1950s Reading File," Folder A3615, NPS Records Box 9 of 25, George Washington Birthplace National Monument Archives.

Howe, Henry. 1896. "Edith M. Thomas." In *Historical Collections of Ohio: An Encyclopedia of the State*. Vol. 2. Norwalk, OH: Laning Printing.

Howell. 1894a. "Letter to the Editor." *Livingston (Montana) Post*, April 12.

Howell. 1894b. "Letter to the Editor." *Livingston (Montana) Post*, August 2.

Hult, Ruby E. J. 1962. *The Saga of George W. Bush*. Seattle: University of Washington Press.

Hummel, Richard. 1994. *Hunting and Fishing for Sport: Commerce, Controversy, Popular Culture*. Bowling Green, OH: Bowling Green State University Press.

Hummel, Richard. 2004. "Hunting." In *Encyclopedia of Recreation and Leisure in America*, vol. 1, edited by Gary S. Cross, 460–464. Farmington Hills, MI: Charles Scribner's Sons.

Hunter, Thomas Lomax. 1931. *The President's Camp on the Rapidan*. Richmond: Virginia State Commission on Conservation and Development.

Hutchings, James Mason. 1871. *Scenes of Wonder and Curiosity in California*. San Francisco: A. Roman.

Ichioka, Yuji. 1988. *The Issei: The World of the First Generation Japanese Immigrants: 1885–1924*. New York: Free Press.

Ingram, David. 1987. *Habermas and the Dialectic of Reason*. New Haven, CT: Yale University Press.

The Inhabitants of the Towns of Staughton, Sharon, and Canton, versus Edmund Baker and Daniel Vose. 1808. 4 Mass. 522; 1808 Mass. October.

In re Lee Sing. 1890. 43 F. 359 (C.C.D. Cal.). August 25.

In the Open. 1912. "Game Dealers Are Caught." 1, no. 6 (February): 45.

Irving, Washington. 1835. *A Tour on the Prairies*. Paris: Baudry's European Library.

Irving, Washington. 1873. *The Adventures of Captain Bonneville USA in the Rocky Mountains and the Far West, Digested from His Journal and Illustrated from Various Other Sources*. Chicago: Belford, Clarke and Company.

Isenberg, Andrew C. 2000. *The Destruction of the Bison*. New York: Cambridge University Press.

Ives, H. L. 1898. "Some Adirondack Preserves." *Forest and Stream* 50 (May 21): 406.

Izaak Walton League. 1922. *Outdoor America* 1 (May).

Izaak Walton League. 1924a. "The Drainage Crime of the Century." *Outdoor America* 3, no. 1 (July): 3.

Izaak Walton League. 1924b. *Outdoor America* 3 (November).

Izaak Walton League. 1927. "Index of Advertisers." *Outdoor America* 6, no. 4 (November): 2, 58, 74.

Izaak Walton League. 1928a. "Waltonian Activities: News of Izaak Walton League Chapters." *Outdoor America* 6, no. 6 (January): 44.

Izaak Walton League. 1928b. "Service" and "Waltonian Merit Men." *Outdoor America* 6, no. 7 (February): 2–40.

Izaak Walton League. 1928c. "Non-Political" and "How the Izaak Walton League has put Conservation on the Map." *Outdoor America* 6, no. 10 (May): 2, 8, 25, 40, 51.

Izaak Walton League. 1928d. "Waltonian Merit Men." *Outdoor America* 6, no. 8 (March): 2, 32.

Izaak Walton League. 1928e. "Waltonian Merit Men." *Outdoor America* 6, no. 9 (April): 40.

Izaak Walton League. 1937. *Outdoor America* 2, no. 4 (February): 8–9.

Jacklin, Kathleen. 1971. "Comstock, Anna Botsford." In *Notable American Women, 1607–1950*, vol. 2, edited by Edward T. James, Janet Wilson James, and Paul S. Boyer, 367–369. Cambridge, MA: Radcliffe College.

Jackson, Andrew. 1835. "To the Cherokee Tribe of Indians East of the Mississippi River." House Documents, Otherwise Publ. as Executive Documents: 13th Congress, 2d. Document No. 286: 40–43. March 16. Washington, DC: United States Congress, House.

Jackson, Donald, ed. 1962. *Letters of the Lewis and Clark Expedition, with Related Documents, 1783–1854*. Urbana: University of Illinois Press.

Jackson, Helen Hunt. 1872. *Ah-wah-ne Days; A Visit to the Yosemite Valley in 1872*. San Francisco: Book Club of California.

Jackson, Helen Hunt. 1878. *Bits of Travel at Home*. Boston: Roberts Brothers.

Jackson, Helen Hunt. 1883. *Glimpses of California and the Missions. With Illustrations by Henry Sandham*. Boston: Little, Brown.

Jackson, Helen Hunt. 1884. *Ramona: A Story*. Boston: Little, Brown.

Jackson, Helen Hunt. 1890. *A Century of Dishonor: A Sketch of the United States Government's Dealings with Some of the Indian Tribes*. Cambridge, MA: John Wilson and Son.

Jackson, Kenneth T., and David S. Dunbar. 2002. *Empire City: New York through the Centuries*. New York: Columbia University Press.

Jacoby, Karl. 2001. *Crimes against Nature: Squatters, Poachers, Thieves, and the Hidden History of American Conservation*. Berkeley: University of California Press.

Jaimes, M. Annette. 1992. "Federal Indian Identification Policy: A Usurpation of Indigenous Sovereignty in North America." In *The State of Native America: Genocide, Colonization and Resistance*, edited by M. Annette Jaimes, 123–138. Boston: South End Press.

James, Edward T., Janet Wilson James, and Paul S. Boyer, eds. 1971. *Notable American Women, 1607–1950: A Biographical Dictionary*, vol. 1, 67–69. Cambridge: Belknap Press.

James, Laurence P., and Sandra C. Taylor. 1978. "Strong Minded Women: Desdemona Stott Beeson and Other Hard Rock Mining Entrepreneurs." *Utah Historical Quarterly* 46, no. 2 (spring): 136–150.

James Magner v. The People of the State of Illinois. 1881. 97 Ill. 320. 1881 Ill. February 3.

Janvier, Thomas. [1894] 2000. *In Old New York*. New York: St. Martin's.

Jefferson, Alison Rose. 2007. "Lake Elsinore: A Southern California African American Resort Area During the Jim Crow Era, 1920s–1960s, and the Challenges of Historic Preservation Commemoration." Master's thesis. University of Southern California.

Jefferson, Thomas. 1815. Letter to William Caruthers. March 15. Vol. 203. Washington, DC: Library of Congress, Thomas Jefferson Papers.

Jeffrey, Julie Roy. [1979] 1998. *Frontier Women: "Civilizing" the West? 1840–1880*. New York: Hill and Wang.

Jenkins, Virginia Scott. 2004. "Gardening and Lawn Care." In *Encyclopedia of Recreation and Leisure in America*, edited by Gary S. Cross, vol. 1, 85–388. Farmington Hills, MI: Thomson Gale.

Jewett, Sarah Orne. 1877a. *Deep Haven*. Boston: James R. Osgood.

Jewett, Sarah Orne. 1877b. *The Night before Thanksgiving, A White Heron and Selected Stories*. Boston: James R. Osgood.

Jewett, Sarah Orne. 1881. *Country By-Ways*. Boston: Houghton Mifflin.

Jewett, Sarah Orne. 1896. *The Night before Country of the Pointed Firs*. Boston: Houghton Mifflin.

Jibou, Robert M. 1988a. *Ethnicity and Assimilation: Blacks, Chinese, Filipinos, Japanese, Koreans, Mexicans, Vietnamese, and Whites*. Albany: State University of New York Press.

Jibou, Robert M. 1988b. "Ethnic Hegemony and the Japanese in California." *American Sociological Review* 53: 353–367.

Johnson, Charles. 1972. "The Army, the Negro, and the Civilian Conservation Corps, 1933–1942." *Military Affairs* 35 (October): 82–87.

Johnson, Robert Underwood. 1908. "San Francisco and the Hetch Hetchy Reservoir." Statement submitted to the Committee on Public Lands of the House of Representatives. House Joint Resolution 184—Part 8. December 16.

Johnson, Rochelle, and Daniel Patterson, eds. 2002. *Essays on Nature and Landscape by Susan Fenimore Cooper*. Athens: University of Georgia Press.

Johnson v. McIntosh. 1823. 21 U.S. (8 Wheat.) 543.

Johnstown Area Heritage Association. 2009. "The South Fork Fishing and Hunting Club and the South Fork Dam." Accessed May 6, 2009. www.jaha.org/Floodmuseum/clubanddam.html.

Jones, Billy. 1984. *Cherokees: An Illustrated History*. Muskogee, OK: The Five Civilized Tribes Museum.

Jones, Genevieve, Eliza Shulze, Virginia Jones, and Howard Jones. 1879–1886. *Illustrations of the Nests and Eggs of Birds of Ohio*. Circleville, OH: Nelson E. Jones Family.

Jones, Holway R. 1965. *John Muir and the Sierra Club*. San Francisco: Sierra Club.

Jones, Howard. [1931] 1970. "Personal Reminiscences." *Pickaway Quarterly* (spring 1970): 14–19.

Josselyn, John. [1672] 1865. *New England Rarities: Discovered in Birds, Beasts, Fishes, Serpents, and Plants of That Country*. Introduction by Edward Tuckerman. Boston: Applewood Books.

Journal of Commerce. 1851a. "The Proposed Great Park." June 5, 2.

Journal of Commerce. 1851b. "The East River Park." June 24, 2.

Journal of Negro History. 1927. "Letters of George Bonga." 12: 41–54.

Judd, Richard W. 1997. *Common Lands, Common People: The Origins of Conservation in Northern New England*. Cambridge, MA: Harvard University Press.

Jung, Judy. 1995. *Unbound Feet: A Social History of Chinese Women in San Francisco*. Berkeley: University of California Press.

Kahrl, Andrew William. 2008. "The Political Work of Leisure: Class, Recreation, and African American Commemoration at Harpers Ferry, West Virginia, 1881–1931." *Journal of Social History* 42, no. 1 (fall): 57–77.

Kaiser, Harvey H. 2003. *Great Camps of the Adirondacks*. Boston: David R. Godine.

Kappler, C. J. 1904. *Indian Affairs: Laws and Treaties, vol. 2*. Washington, DC: Government Printing Office.

Karr, Ronald Dale. 2005a. "Boston Common." In *The Encyclopedia of New England*, edited by Burt Feintuch and David H. Watters, 212–213. New Haven, CT: Yale University Press.

Karr, Ronald Dale. 2005b. "Brookline, Mass." In *The Encyclopedia of New England*, edited by Burt Feintuch and David H. Watters, 214–215. New Haven, CT: Yale University Press.

Kastor, Peter J., and Conevery Bolton Valenčius. 2008. "Sacagawea's 'Cold': Pregnancy and the Written Record of the Lewis and Clark Expedition." *Bulletin of the History of Medicine* 82, no. 2 (summer): 276–309.

Katz, William Loren. 1971. *The Black West: A Documentary and Pictorial History of the African American Role in the Westward Expansion of the United States*. Garden City, NY: Doubleday.

Katz, William Loren. 1992. *Black People Who Made the Old West*. Trenton, NJ: Africa World Press.

Kaufman, Polly Welts. 1996. *National Parks and the Women's Voice: A History*. Albuquerque: University of New Mexico Press.

Keller, Robert H., and Michael Turek. 1998. *American Indians and National Parks*. Tucson: University of Arizona Press.

Kenan, Randall. 1999. *Walking on Water: Black American Lives at the Turn of the Twenty-First Century*. New York: Vintage.

Kent, James. 1828. *Commentaries on American Law*. New York: O. Halsted.

Kent, William. 1913a. Letter to Gifford Pinchot. October 8. Kent Family Papers, Box 26. New Haven, CT: Yale University Library.

Kent, William. 1913b. Letter to Sydney Anderson. July 2. Kent Family Papers, Box 26. New Haven, CT: Yale University Library.

Kent, William. 1916. Letter to the Secretary of Agriculture. April 7. House Committee on the Public Lands. *Hearings on H.R. 434 and H.R. 8668*.

Kester, Jesse Y. (A Gentleman of Philadelphia County). 1827. *The American Shooter's Manual, Comprising, Such Plain and Simple Rules, as are Necessary to Introduce the Inexperienced into a Full Knowledge of All That Relates to the Dog, and the Correct Use of a Gun; also a Description of the Game of This Country.* Philadelphia: Carey, Lea and Carey.

Kilpinen, Jon T. 2004. "The Supreme Court's Role in Choctaw and Chickasaw Dispossession." *Geographical Review* 94 (October 4): 484–501.

King, Clarence. [1872] 1970. *Mountaineering in the Sierra Nevada.* Lincoln: University of Nebraska Press.

King, Thomas Starr. 1861. "A Vacation among the Sierras." *Boston Evening Transcript,* January 26, 1.

Kirkland, Caroline Matilda. 1842. *Forest Life.* Vol. 1. New York: C. S. Francis.

Kiser, Joy M. 2012. *America's Other Audubon.* New York: Princeton Architectural Press.

Kitano, Harry H. L. 1969. *Japanese Americans: The Evolution of a Subculture.* Englewood Cliffs, NJ: Prentice-Hall.

Kitano, Harry H. L., and Roger Daniels. 1995. *Asian Americans: Emerging Minorities.* Englewood Cliffs, NJ: Prentice-Hall.

Klandermans, Bert and Dirk Oegema. 1987. "Potentials, Networks, Motivations and Barriers." *American Sociological Review* 52: 519–531.

Klein, Philip Shriver, and Ari Hoogenboom. 1973. *A History of Pennsylvania.* College Park: Pennsylvania State University Press.

Knight, Sarah Kemble. [1704] 1838. "The Journal of Madam Knight." In *The Puritans,* edited by Perry Miller and Thomas H. Johnson. New York: American Book Company.

Knowlton, Clark. 1980. "The Town of Las Vegas Grant: An Anglo-American Coup d'Etat." *Journal of the Southwest* 19, no. 3 (July): 12–21.

Kofalk, Harriet. 1989. *No Woman Tenderfoot: Florence Merriam Bailey, Pioneer Naturalist.* College Station: Texas A&M University Press.

Korematsu v. United States. 1944. 323 U.S. 214.

Kreiger, Alex. 2001. "Experiencing Boston: Encounters With the Places on the Maps." In *Mapping Boston,* edited by Alex Kreiger, David Cobb, and Amy Turner. Cambridge, MA: MIT Press.

Kyle, Gerard. 2004. "Agricultural Fairs." In *Encyclopedia of Recreation and Leisure in America,* vol. 1, edited by Gary S. Cross, 12–15. Farmington Hills, MI: Thomson Gale.

LaBastille, Anne. 1980. *Women and Wilderness.* San Francisco: Sierra Club Books.

Labau, Vernon J., James T. Bones, Neal P. Kingsley, H. Gyde Lund, and W. Brad Smith. 2007. *A History of the Forest Survey in the United States: 1830–2004.* Washington, DC: U.S. Department of Agriculture.

Lacey, Bill. 1894. An Act to Protect the Birds and Animals in Yellowstone National Park, and to Punish Crimes in Said Park and for Other Purposes. Stat. Vol. 28, 73. Approved May 7.

Lacey Act. 1900. An Act to Enlarge the Powers of the Department of Agriculture, Prohibit the Transportation of Interstate Commerce of Game Killed in Violation of Local Laws, and for Other Purposes. March 1. H.R. 6634. Pub. Act No. 119. Stat. Vol. 31, chap. 533, 187–189.

Lafayette National Park. 1919. An Act to Establish the Lafayette National Park in the State of Maine. U.S. Statutes at Large. February 26; 40 (1. S. 4957. Public Act No. 278): 1178–1179.

Lambert, Darwin. 1989. *The Undying Past of Shenandoah National Park*. Niwot, CO: Roberts Rinehart.

Lammon, Dad. 1937. "Password, Please, Brother Ike." *Outdoor America* 2, no. 4 (February): 8–9.

Lancaster, Jane Fairchild. 1986. "The First Decades: The Western Seminoles from Removal to Reconstruction, 1836–1866." PhD diss., Mississippi State University.

Langford, Nathaniel Pitt. 1871a. "The Wonders of Yellowstone, I." *Scribners Monthly* 2 (May): 10.

Langford, Nathaniel Pitt. 1871b. "The Wonders of the Yellowstone, II." *Scribners Monthly* 2 (June): 127–128.

Langford, Nathaniel Pitt. 1872. *The Discovery of Yellowstone National Park*. Lincoln: University of Nebraska Press.

Langford, Nathaniel Pitt. 1873. *Report of the Superintendent of the Yellowstone National Park for the Year 1872*. Washington, DC: 42nd Congress, 3d sess. Ex. Doc. No. 35. Feb. 4.

Lanman, Charles. 1847. *A Summer in the Wilderness: Embracing a Canoe Voyage up the Mississippi and around Lake Superior*. New York: D. Appleton.

Lapp, Rudolph M. 1977. *Blacks in Gold Rush California*. New Haven, CT: Yale University Press.

Larsen, C. S. 1994. "In the Wake of Columbus: Native Population Biology in the Postcontact Americas." *American Journal of Physical Anthropology* 37: 109–154.

Larson, Kate Clifford. 2004. *Bound for the Promised Land: Harriet Tubman, Portrait of an American Hero*. New York: Ballantine Books.

Larson, T. A. 1965. *History of Wyoming*. Lincoln: University of Nebraska Press.

Latimer, Margaret. 1995. "Bowling Green." In *The Encyclopedia of New York City*, edited by Kenneth T. Jackson, 132. New Haven, CT: Yale University Press.

Lawrence, Henry W. 1993. "The Greening of the Squares of London: Transformation of Urban Landscapes and Ideals." *Annals of the Association of American Geographers* 83, no. 1: 90–95.

Lawrence v. Everett. 1890. 11 N.Y.S. 881. 1890 N.Y. Misc. December 18.

Laws of 1891. Ch. 9, Section 11.

Laws of 1893. Ch. 124, Section 9.

Le Beau, Bryan F. 2005. "Transcendentalism." In *The Encyclopedia of New England*, edited by Burt Feintuch and David H. Watters, 806–808. New Haven, CT: Yale University Press.

Lebergott, Stanley L. 1966. "Labor Force and Employment, 1800–1960." In *Output, Employment, and Productivity in the United States after 1800*, edited by Dorothy S. Brady, 117–204. NBER Studies in Income and Wealth, 30. New York: Columbia University Press.

Lee, Catherine. 2003. "Prostitutes and Picture Brides: Chinese and Japanese Immigration, Settlement, and Nation-Building, 1870–1920." Working Paper No. 70. San Diego: University of California at San Diego, Center for Comparative Immigration Studies.

Lelia E. Marsh and George W. Ostrander v. Ne-Ha-Sa-Ne Park Association (Supreme Court of Hamilton County, March 1897, Civil Case No. 352, Hamilton County Court House), 33–34.

Leonard, K. I. 1994. *Making Ethnic Choices: California's Punjabi Mexican Americans.* Philadelphia: Temple University Press.

Letter to the Editor. 1895. *Recreation* 3 (September): 141.

Lewis, Monte Ross. 1981. "Chickasaw Removal: Betrayal of the Beloved Warriors, 1794–1844." PhD diss., University of North Texas.

Lewison, Laura. 1995. "Lawn Bowling." In *The Encyclopedia of New York City*, edited by Kenneth T. Jackson, 657. New Haven, CT: Yale University Press.

Library of Congress. n.d. "Immigration: Puerto Rico/Cuba." Washington, DC: Library of Congress. Accessed June 12, 2015. http://www.loc.gov/teachers /classroommaterials/presentationsandactivities/presentations/immigration/cuban3 .html.

Library of Congress. 2004. *Historical Comprehension: Buffalo Bill's Wild West Shows.* Washington, DC: Library of Congress.

Lillquist, Karl. 2010. "Farming the Desert: Agriculture in the World War II-era Japanese-American Relocation Centers." *Agricultural History* 84, no. 1 (winter): 74–104.

Limbaugh, Ronald H. 1993. "Introduction: John Muir's Life and Legacy." In *John Muir: Life and Work*, edited by Sally M. Miller, 3–13. Albuquerque: University of New Mexico Press.

Limerick, Patricia Nelson. 1992. "Disorientation and Reorientation: The American Landscape Discovered from the West." *The Journal of American History* 79, no. 3 (December): 1021–1049.

Lindberg, Richard C. 1999. "Jean Baptiste Point DuSable." *American National Biography* 7: 166–168. New York: Oxford University Press.

Lipson, Dorothy Ann. 1981. "From Puritan Village to Yankee City, 1690 to 1860." In *New Haven: An Illustrated History*, edited by Floyd Shumway and Richard Hegel, 28–43. Woodland Hills, CA: Windsor.

Littlefield, Daniel. 1991. *Rice and Slaves: Ethnicity and the Slave Trade in Colonial South Carolina.* Baton Rouge: Louisiana State University Press.

Lo, Clarence Y. H. 1992. "Communities of Challengers in Social Movement Theory." In *Frontiers in Social Movement Theory*, edited by Aldon D. Morris and Carol McClurg Mueller, 224–247. New Haven, CT: Yale University Press.

Locke, John. [1690] 1824. "An Essay Concerning the True Original, Extent, and End of Civil Government." Book 2. In *Two Treatises of Civil Government*. London: C. Baldwin Printers.

Longrigg, Roger. 1972. *The History of Horse Racing.* New York: Stein and Day.

Los Angeles Times. 1883. "Pasadena: The Village Improvement Society and Public Library." May 23, 0-4.

Los Angeles Times. 1895. "How a Village Was Beautified." March 14, 8.

Los Angeles Times. 1897. "Sierra Club." May 11, 7.

Los Angeles Times. 1898a. "Traffic in Birds." September 13, 11.

Los Angeles Times. 1898b. "Song Birds." July 2, 8.

Los Angeles Times. 1901. "Great Slaughter of Birds South." December 11, 5.

Los Angeles Times. 1906a. "Japs Slay Our Song Birds." April 2, 119.

Los Angeles Times. 1906b. "To Save the Birds." November 4, 16.

Los Angeles Times. 1907a. "Club Women Bar Aigrette." April 7, V21.

Los Angeles Times. 1907b. "Wills Cash to Protect Birds." May 4, 112.

Los Angeles Times. 1908. "Ladies Beware of Bird Cops." July 1, 119.

Los Angeles Times. 1909a. "Urges Tax on Cats to Save the Birds." June 20, 111.

Los Angeles Times. 1909b. "Favors Hetch Hetchy." February 2, 14.

Los Angeles Times. 1909c. "May Condemn Spring Valley." February 13, 14.

Los Angeles Times. 1910a. "Air Gun Warning." November 30, 1117.

Los Angeles Times. 1910b. "Hetch Hetchy Is Selected." January 15, 13.

Los Angeles Times. 1912. "Sierra Club Dissension." November 26, 14.

Los Angeles Times. 1913a. "The Strike News of This Uneasy World." April 6, V17.

Los Angeles Times. 1913b. "Junior Sierra Club Proposed." October 6, 118.

Los Angeles Times. 1924. "Asks Nation to Protect Wilds." August 24, 9.

Los Angeles Times. 1927. "Alien Gun Law Ruled Illegal." October 14, A2.

Los Angeles Times. 1928. "Family Given Kent Fortune." March 31, 9.

Los Angeles Times. 1934. "Hetch Hetchy Completed." October 30, A4.

Los Angeles Times. 1935. "Ickes Sifts Hetch Hetchy Power Sale." May 12, A4.

Loudon, John Claudius. 1838. *The Suburban Gardener, and Villa Companion.* London: J. C. Loudon.

Lovejoy, Arthur. 1955. *Essays in the History of Ideas.* New York: A. Braziller.

Lowry, Beverly. 2008. *Harriet Tubman: Imagining a Life.* New York: Anchor Books.

Macieski, Robert L. 2005. "Cities and Suburbs." In *The Encyclopedia of New England,* edited by Burt Feintuch and David H. Watters, 188–198. New Haven, CT: Yale University Press.

Mackintosh, Barry. 1999. *The National Park Service: A Brief History.* Washington, DC: Department of the Interior.

Madsen, David. 1926. Letter to T. Gilbert Pearson. April 13. New York Public Library Annex. Audubon Papers. New York, NY.

Magagnini, Stephen. 1998. "Fortune Smiled on Many Black Miners: Gold Dust Allowed Thousands to Gain Freedom, Influence." *Sacramento Bee,* January 18.

Maher, Neil M. 2002. "A New Deal Body Politic: Landscape, Labor, and the Civilian Conservation Corps." *Environmental History* 7, no. 3: 435–462.

Maher, Neil M. 2008. *Nature's New Deal: The Civilian Conservation Corps and the Roots of the American Environmental Movement.* New York: Oxford University Press.

Majumdar, R. D. 2006–2007. "Racially Restrictive Covenants in the State of Washington: A Primer for Practitioners." *Seattle University Law Review* 30, no. 4: 1095–1117.

Malloy, Elaine, Daniel Malloy, and Alan J. Ryan. 2002. *Hopedale: Images of America.* Charleston: Arcadia Publishing.

Manchester v. Massachusetts. 1891. 139 U.S. 240; 11 S. Ct. 559; 35 L. Ed. 159. 1891 U.S. March 16.

Manson, Marsden. 1910. Letter to G. W. Woodruff. Bancroft Library, University of California—Berkeley, Marsden Manson Correspondence and Papers.

Manton, May. 1901. "The Season's Hats." *Washington Post.* September 22, 28.

Marsh, George Perkins. [1847] 1848. *Address Delivered before the Agricultural Society of Rutland County*. Rutland, VT: Herald Office.

Marsh, George Perkins. 1857. *Report Made under Authority of the Legislature of Vermont on the Artificial Propagation of Fish*. Burlington, VT: Free Press Print.

Marsh, George Perkins. [1864] 1965. *Man and Nature: or, Physical Geography as Modified by Human Action*. New York: Charles Scribner.

Marsh, George Perkins. 1885. *The Earth as Modified by Human Action, a New Edition of Man and Nature*. New York: Charles Scribner's Sons.

Marshall, George. 1951. "Adirondacks to Alaska: A Biographical Sketch of Robert Marshall." *Ad-i-Ron-Dac* 15, no. 3: 44–45, 59.

Marshall, Megan. 2005. *The Peabody Sisters: Three Women Who Ignited American Romanticism*. Boston: Houghton Mifflin.

Marshall, Robert. 1930. "The Problem of Wilderness." *Scientific Monthly* (February): 141–148.

Marshall, Robert. 1935. Letter to Ferdinand Silcox. June 24. Washington, DC: Robert Marshall Papers, Wilderness Society.

Masten, Arthur H. 1935. *The Tahawus Club: 1898–1935*. Burlington, VT: Privately printed.

Matthiessen, Peter. [1959] 1995. *Wildlife in America*. New York: Penguin.

McChesney, Fred S. 1992. "Government as Definer of Property Rights: Indian Lands, Ethnic Externalities, and Bureaucratic Budgets." In *Property Rights and Indian Economies*, edited by Terry L. Anderson, 109–146. Lanham, MD: Rowman and Littlefield.

McCoy, Michael B. 2007. "Absconding Servants, Anxious Germans, and Angry Sailors: Working People and the Making of the Philadelphia Election Riot of 1742." *Pennsylvania History* 74, no. 4 (October): 427–451.

McCullough, David G. 1987. *The Johnstown Flood*. New York: Simon and Schuster.

McDermott, John M. 1967. *The Writings of William James: A Comprehensive Edition*. New York: Random House.

McFarland, J. Horace. 1911. Letter to Henry S. Graves, February 21. J. Horace McFarland Papers. Harrisburg: Pennsylvania State Archives.

McFarland, J. Horace. 1913. "Hetch Hetchy Lobby." *Los Angeles Times*. November 8, 12.

McFarland, Philip. 2004. *Hawthorne in Concord*. New York: Grove.

McGough, Michael. 2002. *The 1889 Flood in Johnstown, Pennsylvania*. Gettysburg, PA: Thomas.

McIntosh, Phyllis. 2001. "The Corps of Conservation." *National Parks* 75, nos. 9/10: 23–28.

McLellan, Isaac. 1883. "Spare the Swallows." *Forest and Stream* 21 (September 20): 143.

McLoughlin, William G. 1986. *Cherokee Renascence in the New Republic*. Princeton, NJ: Princeton University Press.

McMahon, Michael. 1997. "Beyond Therapeutics: Technology and the Question of Public Health." In *A Melancholy Scene of Devastation: The Public Response to the 1793 Yellow Fever Epidemic*, edited by J. Worth Estes and Billy G. Smith, 97–118. Canton, OH: Science History Publications/USA.

McMullan, Kate. 1991. *The Story of Harriet Tubman, Conductor of the Underground Railroad*. New York: Bantam Doubleday Dell.

McRae, Bennie J., Jr. 1996. *Black Cowboys*. Trotwood, OH: Lest We Forget Publications.

Meehan, Thomas A. 1963. "Jean Baptiste Point du Sable, the First Chicagoan." *Journal of the Illinois State Historical Society* 56: 439–453.

Melendy, H. Brett. 1984. *Chinese and Japanese*. New York: Hippocrene.

Meloy, Andrew D. 1910. "Value of Birds." *New York Times*, April 16, 10.

Melville, Herman. 1855. "The Paradise of Bachelors and the Tartarus of Maids." *Harper's Monthly Magazine* (April): 671–678.

Merchant, Carolyn. 1984. "Women of the Progressive Conservation Crusade, 1900–1916." *Environmental Review* 8 (spring): 57–85.

Merchant, Carolyn. 2010. "George Bird Grinnell's Audubon Society: Bridging the Gender Divide in Conservation." *Environmental History* 15 (January): 3–30.

Mesa Verde National Park. 1906. An Act Creating Mesa Verde National Park. U.S. Statutes at Large. June 8; 34, Part 1. Chap. 3607. H.R. 5998. Public Act No. 353: 616–617.

Migratory Bird Treaty Act. 1918. 16 U.S.C. 703–712; Ch. 128; July 13; 40 Stat. 755.

Miller, Adolph C. 1914. *Hearing before the Committee on the Public Lands*. House of Representatives, 63rd Congress, 2nd sess. on H.R. 104. Washington, DC: Government Printing Office.

Miller, Char. 2001. *Gifford Pinchot and the Making of Modern Environmentalism*. Covelo, CA: Island Press.

Miller, Michael. 2004. "Las Gorras Blancas: The Roots of NuevoMexican Activism." Santa Fe: New Mexico Office of the State Historian. Accessed March 15, 2012. www.newmexicohistory.org/filedetails.php?fileID=21344.

Miller, Olive Thorne [Harriet Mann Miller]. 1885. *Bird-Ways*. Boston: Houghton Mifflin.

Miller, Olive Thorne [Harriet Mann Miller]. 1887. *In Nesting Time*. Boston: Houghton Mifflin.

Miller, Olive Thorne [Harriet Mann Miller]. 1892. *Little Brothers of the Air*. Boston: Houghton Mifflin.

Miller, Olive Thorne [Harriet Mann Miller]. 1894. *A Bird-Lover in the West*. Boston: Houghton Mifflin.

Miller, Olive Thorne [Harriet Mann Miller]. 1897. *Upon the Tree-Tops*. Boston: Houghton Mifflin.

Miller, Olive Thorne [Harriet Mann Miller]. 1899. *The First Book of Birds*. Boston: Houghton Mifflin.

Miller, Robert J. 2006. *Native America, Discovered and Conquered: Thomas Jefferson, Lewis & Clark, and Manifest Destiny*. Westport, CT: Praeger.

Millner, Darrell M. 2003. "York of the Corps of Discovery." *Oregon Historical Quarterly* 104, no. 3 (fall): 302–333.

Mills, C. Wright. 1994. "The Power Elite." In *Social Stratification: Class, Race, and Gender in Sociological Perspective*, edited by David B. Grusky, 161–169. Boulder, CO: Westview.

Min, Pyong Gap, ed. 1995. *Asian Americans: Contemporary Trends and Issues*. Thousand Oaks, CA: Sage.

Ming, W. R. 1949. "Racial Restriction and the Fourteenth Amendment: The Restrictive Covenant Cases." *University of Chicago Law Review* 16, no. 2 (winter): 203–238.

Mitchell, Arthur Wergs v. United States et al., 1941. 313 U.S. 80.

Mitchell, Don. 2012. *They Saved the Crops: Labor, Landscape, and the Struggle over Industrial Framing in Bracero-Era California*. Athens: University of Georgia Press.

Mondragón-Valdéz, Maria. 2010. "Real Estate Speculation, Lawyers, and *Los Pobladores*: The Labyrinth of Land Loss on the Sangre de Cristo Land Grant." Santa Fe: New Mexico Office of the State Historian. Accessed August 10, 2010. www .newmexicohistory.org/filedetails.php?fileID=705.

Mooney, James E. 1995a. "Stuyvesant, Peter." In *The Encyclopedia of New York City*, edited by Kenneth T. Jackson, 1133–1134. New Haven, CT: Yale University Press.

Mooney, James E. 1995b. "Fox Hunting." In *The Encyclopedia of New York*, edited by Kenneth T. Jackson, 435–436. New Haven, CT: Yale University Press.

Moore, Glenn, and Jessica Freame. 2004. "Botanical Gardens." In *Encyclopedia of Recreation and Leisure in America*, edited by Gary S. Cross, 1:125–128. Farmington Hills, MI: Thomson Gale.

Moore, Jacqueline M. 1999. *Leading the Race: The Transformation of the Black Elite in the Nation's Capital, 1880–1920*. Charlottesville: University of Virginia Press.

Morris, Elizabeth S. 1998. *History of the National Bison Range*. Moiese, MT: U.S. Fish and Wildlife Service.

Morris, Glen T. 1992. "International Law and Politics: Toward a Right to Self-Determination for Indigenous Peoples." In *The State of Native America: Genocide, Colonization and Resistance*, edited by M. Annette Jaimes, 55–86. Boston: South End Press.

Morris, James S., and Andrea L. Kross. 2004. *Historical Dictionary of Utopianism*. Lanham, MD: Scarecrow Press.

Moseley, Ella Lowery. 1901. "Fashion Has No Soul." *Washington Post*. November 10, 33.

Moses, Marion. 1993. "Farmworkers and Pesticides." In *Confronting Environmental Racism: Voices from the Grassroots*, edited by Robert Bullard, 161–178. Boston: South End Press.

Mosher, Donald L. 1994. "Virility and Machismo." In *Human Sexuality: An Encyclopedia*, edited by Vern L. Bullough and Bonnie Bullough, 601–605. Philadelphia: Taylor and Francis.

Moulton, Gary E., ed. 1983–2001. *The Journals of the Lewis and Clark Expedition*. Lincoln: University of Nebraska Press.

Mount Shasta Companion. 2001. "Women Artists of Mount Shasta: 1860s–1930s." Accessed September 16, 2010. www.siskiyous.edu/shasta/art/wom.htm.

Muir, John. 1862. Letter to Frances Pelton. September 28. Series 1A, Reel 1. Stockton, CA: Stuart Library, University of the Pacific.

Muir, John. 1863. Letter to Sarah Muir Galloway and David Galloway. June 1. John Muir Papers, Series 1A, Reel 1. Stockton, CA: Stuart Library, University of the Pacific.

Muir, John. 1868. Letter from John Muir to David Muir. July 14. John Muir Papers, Series 1A, Reel 2. Stockton, CA: Stuart Library, University of the Pacific.

Muir, John. 1869. Letter from John Muir to John and Margaret Muir Reid. January 13. John Muir Papers, Series 1A, Reel 2. Stockton, CA: Stuart Library, University of the Pacific.

Muir, John. 1873. "The Hetch Hetchy Valley." *Boston Weekly Transcript*, March 25, 2.

Muir, John. 1874. "The Wild Sheep of California." *Overland Monthly* 12: 358–363.

Muir, John. 1875. "Flood-Storm in the Sierra." *Overland Monthly* 14, no. 6 (June): 489–496.

Muir, John. 1878. "A Wind Storm in Yuba." *Scribner's Monthly* 7, no. 1 (November): 55–59.

Muir, John. [1894] 1991. *The Mountains of California*. New York: De Vinne.

Muir, John. 1898. "Wild Parks and Forest Reservations of the West." *Atlantic Monthly* 1, no. 483 (January): 15–28.

Muir, John. [1901] 1981. *Our National Parks*. Boston: Houghton Mifflin.

Muir, John. 1903. John Muir Business and Legal Papers, Series 1C, Reel 22. Naturalization Certificate, April 28. Passport Letter, April 22. Passport, June 9. Stockton: Stuart Library, University of the Pacific.

Muir, John. 1908a. *Autobiography*. TCCMS Manuscript, Reel 45, no. 18. John Muir Paper Series IIIB. Stockton: Stuart Library, University of the Pacific.

Muir, John. 1908b. *First Draft Auto[biography], Pelican Bay Manuscripts*. Reel 46, TCCMS 2. Stockton: Stuart Library, University of the Pacific.

Muir, John. 1908c. "The Endangered Valley—The Hetch Hetchy Valley in the Yosemite National Park." Statement submitted to the Committee on Public Lands of the House of Representatives. House Joint Resolution 184—Part VIII. December 16.

Muir, John. 1908d. "The Hetch Hetchy Valley." *Sierra Club Bulletin* 6 (January): 211–220.

Muir, John. 1909a. *Stickeen*. Boston: Houghton Mifflin.

Muir, John. 1909b. *Let Everyone Help to Save the Famous Hetch-Hetchy Valley and Stop the Commercial Destruction Which Threatens Our National Parks*. Washington, DC: Library of Congress.

Muir, John. [1911a] 1972. *My First Summer in the Sierra*. Boston: Houghton Mifflin.

Muir, John. 1911b. *Edward Henry Harriman*. Garden City, NY: Doubleday, Page.

Muir, John. 1911c. "South America," "Africa Trip." August 12, 1911–March 27 Microfilm. John Muir Papers, Reel 30 TMS 7. Stockton, CA: Stuart Library, University of the Pacific.

Muir, John. 1913. *The Story of My Boyhood and Youth*. Boston: Houghton Mifflin.

Muir, John. 1915. *Travels in Alaska*. Boston: Houghton Mifflin.

Muir, John. 1916. *A Thousand-Mile Walk to the Gulf*. Boston: Houghton Mifflin.

Muir, John. 1917. *The Cruise of the Corwin*, edited by William Frederic Bade. Boston: Houghton Mifflin.

Muir, John. 1918. *Steep Trails*. Boston: Houghton Mifflin.

Muir, John. 1938. *John of the Mountains: Unpublished Journals of John Muir*. Edited by Linnie Marsh Wolfe. Boston: Houghton Mifflin.

Muir, John. 1954. *The Wilderness World of John Muir*. Edited by Edwin Way Teale. Boston: Houghton Mifflin.

Muir, John. 1988. "Hetch Hetchy Valley." In *The Yosemite*. Foreword by David Brower. San Francisco: Sierra Club Books.

Muir, John. 1993. *Letters from Alaska*, edited by Robert Engbert and Bruce Merrell. Madison: University of Wisconsin Press.

Muir, John. 2001. *Kindred and Related Spirits: The Letters of John and Jeanne C. Carr*, edited by Bonnie Johanna Gisel. Salt Lake City: University of Utah Press.

Museum Gazette. 1999, February. "George Washington Bush and the Human Spirit of Westward Expansion." Washington, DC: National Park Service.

Myres, Sandra L. 1982. *Westering Women and the Frontier Experience: 1800–1915.* Albuquerque: University of New Mexico Press.

Nabokov, Peter. 1991. *Native American Testimony: An Anthology of Indian and White Relations: First Encounter to Dispossession.* New York: Harper and Row.

Nasaw, David. 2006. *Andrew Carnegie.* New York: Penguin Press.

Nash, Roderick. 1982. *Wilderness and the American Mind.* 3d ed. New Haven, CT: Yale University Press.

Nathan, Walter L. 1940. "Thomas Cole and the Romantic Landscape." In *Romanticism in America*, edited by George Boas, 24–62. Baltimore: Johns Hopkins University Press.

National Academy of Public Administration. 1999. *A Study of Management and Administration: The Bureau of Indian Affairs.* Washington, DC: National Academy of Public Administration.

National Forestry Commission. 1897. *National Forestry Commission Report, Draft.* Washington, DC: U.S. Government.

National Park Service. n.d. "Buffalo Soldiers: Guardians of California National Parks." Accessed June 19, 2014. www.nps.gov/goga/planyourvisit/upload/folder-buffalo-low -res.pdf.

National Park Service. 1941. *Lassen Volcanic Guidebook.* Washington, DC: U.S. Department of the Interior.

National Park Service. 2002. *Cultural History of Muir Woods National Monument.* Washington, DC: National Park Service.

National Park Service. 2004. *Antiquities Act of 1906.* Washington, DC: Department of Interior.

National Park Service. 2009a. "York." Accessed May 15, 2013. www.nps.gov/jeff /historyculture/york.htm.

National Park Service. 2009b. "Johnstown Flood National Memorial." Accessed May 12, 2014. www.nps.gov/parkoftheweek/jofl.htm.

National Park Service. 2014. "Colonel Charles Young." Accessed May 2, 2014. www.nps .gov/chyo/learn/historyculture/colonel-charles-young.htm.

National Park Service. 2015. "Yosemite: Buffalo Soldiers." Accessed June 3, 2015. www .nps.gov/yose/learn/historyculture/buffalo-soldiers.htm.

National Park Service–National Register. n.d. "Utopias in America." Accessed December 29, 2015. http://www.nps.gov/nr/travel/amana/utopia.htm.

Nebraska State Historical Society. 2010. "George Bird Grinnell, 1849–1938." Accessed September 3, 2010. www.nebraskahistory.org/lib-arch/research/manuscripts/family /george-grinnell.htm.

Needleman, Ruth. 2003. *Black Freedom Fighters in Steel: The Struggle for Democratic Unionism.* Ithaca, NY: Cornell University Press.

Nelli, Humbert S. 2003. "The Black Hand from the Business of Crime." In *Wise Guys: Stories of Mobsters from New Jersey to Vegas*, edited by Clint Willis. New York: Thunder's Mouth Press.

Nelson, Jill. 2005. *Finding Martha's Vineyard: African Americans at Home on an Island.* New York: Doubleday.

New York ex rel. Silz v. Hesterberg. 1908. 211 U.S. 31. 29 S. Ct. 10. 53 L. Ed. 75. 1908 U.S. November 2.

New York Fisheries Commission. 1894. *Twenty-Third Annual Report, 1894.* Albany, NY: J. B. Lyon, State Printers.

New York Forest Commission. 1893. *Annual Report, 1893.* Vol. 1. Albany, NY: J. B. Lyon, State Printers.

New York Forest, Fish, and Game Commission. 1895. *Annual Reports of the Forest, Fish and Game Commission of the State of New York.* Albany, NY: J. B. Lyon, State Printers.

New York Forest, Fish, and Game Commission. 1907. *Annual Reports of the Forest, Fish and Game Commissioner of the State of New York for [1895]–1909.* Albany, NY: J. B. Lyon, State Printers.

New York Herald. 1899. "Many Scientists to Invade Alaska." April 23, 4.

New York State Assembly. 1899. *Report of the Special Committee Appointed to Investigate as to What Additional Lands Shall Be Acquired within the Forest Preserve.* Document No. 43.

New York Times. 1858. "Suicide of 'Frank Forrester.'" May 18, 1.

New York Times. 1860. "Fall Fashions." September 21, 1.

New York Times. 1869. "New-York Sportsmen's Club." November 11, 2.

New York Times. 1870. "All about Feathers." November 27, 8.

New York Times. 1874. "Field Sports: New-York Association for the Protection of Game." May 14, 2.

New York Times. 1878a. "Our Beauty Spots." October 29, 5.

New York Times. 1878b. "Village Improvement." September 28, 2.

New York Times. 1886. "Protecting the Birds." May 18, 8.

New York Times. 1887. "All about Feathers." November 27, 8.

New York Times. 1888a. "Feather Workers Meet." October 6, 2.

New York Times. 1888b. "An Armistice Declared." October 8, 2.

New York Times. 1888c. "Better Wages for Women." October 10, 2.

New York Times. 1888d. "Feather Workers Strike Again." October 31, 3.

New York Times. 1888e. "Feather Workers' Strike." December 7, 3.

New York Times. 1888f. "Isidor Cohnfeld Tricked." December 8, 8.

New York Times. 1888g. "Woods on Fire." July 18, 5.

New York Times. 1889a. "Girls Out on Strike." January 11, 5.

New York Times. 1889b. "Accepting Union Rates." January 13, 2.

New York Times. 1889c. "Feather Workers Win Their Fight." January 15, 8.

New York Times. 1889d. "Feather Workers Locked Out." January 26, 3.

New York Times. 1889e. "Feather Workers Return to Work." March 21, 4.

New York Times. 1889f. "Stealing Is Their Trade." October 4, 6.

New York Times. 1890. "The Bisby Club's Resort. Grand Sport in the Woods of Herkimer County." June 8, 12.

New York Times. 1891a. "The Big Forest in Danger." June 10, 1.

New York Times. 1891b. "By Permission of Dr. Webb He Controls Some of the Best Lands in the Adirondacks." June 29, 8.

New York Times. 1892. "Not a Nuisance: New-Brighton Must Put Up with Smoke and Fumes." December 25, 20.

New York Times. 1893. "A National Park in Danger." February 25, 4.

New York Times. 1895. "To Save the Birds: The Chicago Audubon Society the Only One of Its Kind." March 17, 26.

New York Times. 1897a. "To Protect the Wild Birds: Report of the Committee of the American Ornithologists' Union at Its Congress." November 12, 2.

New York Times. 1897b. "Plea for the Birds: Their Destruction Is Endangering the Forests and Orchards." April 4, 14.

New York Times. 1897c. "Feathers." July 18, 14.

New York Times. 1899a. "Feather Workers Gain Their Point." January 9, 8.

New York Times. 1899b. "Adirondack Fires Increase." August 18, 5.

New York Times. 1899c. "To Protect the Birds." March 24, 7.

New York Times. 1899d. "Paradise for Sportsmen: Records of the Blooming Grove Park Association. Lakes, Covers and Preserves." November 26, 14.

New York Times. 1900a. "Bird Protection Bill Signed." May 3, 6.

New York Times. 1900b. "Plumage of Birds on Hats." May 4, 6.

New York Times. 1900c. "Audubon Societies' Triumph." June 3, 9.

New York Times. 1900d. "Pleading for the Birds." June 3, 12.

New York Times. 1903a. "Millinery Trade at War." November 15, 24.

New York Times. 1903b. "Reward for Capture of Dexter's Slayer." September 21, 3.

New York Times. 1903c. "Clue to Dexter Murder: Man's Footprints on Road Where He Was Slain." September 22, 14.

New York Times. 1903d. "Adirondack Woods Ablaze." May 14, 5.

New York Times. 1903e. "William Rockefeller Now a Fire-Fighter." May 20, 1.

New York Times. 1903f. "Forest Fires Still Blaze. Adirondack Camps of J. P. Morgan and A. G. Vanderbilt Threatened." May 28, 1.

New York Times. 1904a. "Won't Attack the Bird Laws." January 24, 24.

New York Times. 1904b. "Here's a Scheme to Protect the Birds." December 18, 8.

New York Times. 1904c. "Many Big Adirondack Fires Were Incendiary." May 1, 8.

New York Times. 1904d. "Fire on Rockefeller Guards: Strenuous Protests of Adirondack Natives Against Game Preserves." November 23, 1.

New York Times. 1904e. "Adirondacks for the Rich." April 6, 8.

New York Times. 1905a. "Oldest Dining Club in the World." January 15. http://query .nytimes.com/mem/archive-free/pdf?res=9907E6D6173AE733A25756C1A9679C9 46497D6CF.

New York Times. 1905b. "War on Cats Declared by Audubon Society." November 1, 9.

New York Times. 1905c. "Dexter Tract Open to All: New Owners Will Not Forbid Hunting and Fishing." February 20, 5.

New York Times. 1907. "Get Willcox Bequests." March 4, 9.

New York Times. 1909a. "Famous Hunt Club Destroyed by Fire. Blooming Grove Hunting and Fishing Lodge in Pike County, Penn., a Total Loss." February 12, 20.

New York Times. 1909b. "The 'Aigrette' Plume." March 18, 8.

New York Times. 1909c. "Conflict over Bill to Save Birds." March 21, 4.

New York Times. 1909d. "Begin Fight to Save the Yosemite Park." January 17, 8.

New York Times. 1910a. "Must Wear Birdless Hats." March 24, 1.

New York Times. 1910b. "Oppose Anti-Plumage Bills." March 25, 5.

New York Times. 1910c. "Piffling Legislation." March 26, 8.

New York Times. 1910d. "Audubon Society Bill Passed." April 13, 9.

New York Times. 1910e. "Mrs. Sage Gives $15,000." June 12, 1.

New York Times. 1911a. "High Prices Laid to Bird Slaughter." May 28, XX8.

New York Times. 1911b. "Audubon Men Take Gunmakers' Gift." June 3, 11.

New York Times. 1911c. "Rejects Gun Money." June 17, 3.

New York Times. 1911d. "Audubon Defense of Gunmakers' Gift." June 4, 6.

New York Times. 1911e. "Hornaday Hits at Big Gunmakers." June 16, 10.

New York Times. 1911f. "Audubon People Give Back $25,000 from Gunmakers." June 17, 12.

New York Times. 1912. "Cats Kill Game Birds: Prowlers of Woods and Fields more Destructive than any other Animal." June 16, 35.

New York Times. 1914. "Amid Summer Scenes: Fine Work of Laurel Hill Association at Stockbridge Is Attracting Attention All over the Country." June 21, X1.

New York Times. 1915. "Puzzled by Alien Gun Law." April 25, C4.

New York Times. 1922. "Reopen 1908 Murder Case. Warrant Issued in Crime for Which Another Was Hanged in 1909." February 17, 2.

New York Times. 1923a. "A Call to Anglers." August 5, B4.

New York Times. 1923b. "Fears Extinction of the Game Bird." October 31, 18.

New York Times. 1926. "Anglers' Army Grows in Number." August 29, X18.

New York Times. 1930a. "Fights Game Policy of Audubon Society." October 23, 11.

New York Times. 1930b. "Audubon Societies Vote Down Critics." October 29, 17.

New York Times. 1931a. "Charges Hypocrisy to Audubon Society." June 12, 18.

New York Times. 1931b. "Audubon Society Defended in Court." July 30, 18.

New York Times. 1931c. "Audubon Societies Defended in Report." September 3, 14.

New York Times. 1931d. "Pearson Is Upheld by Audubon Groups." October 28, 21.

New York Times. 1931e. "Million Dollar Gift by Rockefeller Helps California Buy Parks." June 22, 1.

New York Times. 1932a. "Audubon Leaders Defend Dr. Pearson." October 3, 36.

New York Times. 1932b. "Alaska Bear Issue Stirs Audubon Row." October 26, 19.

New York Times. 1933a. "Forestry Values Enhanced by Civilian Conservation Corps." December 26, 12.

New York Times. 1933b. "Women's Forest Work Camps May Be Set Up if Enough Ask for Them, Says Mrs. Roosevelt." May 24, 1.

New York Times. 1933c. "Camp for Women to Cost $4,376 to Date." August 27, 18.

New York Times. 1933d. "Forests and Men Benefited by Civilian Conservation Corps." October 8, XX2.

New York Times. 1934a. "Audubon Member Split over 'Racket.'" October 31, 21.

New York Times. 1934b. "Judging Civilian Conservation Corps Results." February 14, 18.

New York Times. 1936. "Roosevelt Praises Work of Civilian Conservation Corps Men." April 18, 2.

New York Times. 1938. "Says Civilian Conservation Corps Upsets Nature's Balance." May 21, 1.

New York Tribune. 1893. "Adirondack League Clubhouse." February 19, 22.

Ngai, Mae M. 2015. "Chinese Gold Miners and the 'Chinese Question' in Nineteenth-Century California and Victoria." *Journal of American History* 101, no. 4 (March): 1082–1105.

Niles' Weekly Register (Baltimore). 1832. P. 480.

Nishi, Setsuko Matsunaga. 1995. "Japanese Americans." In *Asian Americans: Contemporary Trends and Issues*, edited by Pyong Gap Min, 95–133. Thousand Oaks, CA: Sage.

Nixon, Edgar. 1957. *Franklin D. Roosevelt and Conservation, 1911–1945*. Hyde Park, NY: Franklin D. Roosevelt Library.

Noble, Louis Legrand. [1853] 1964. *The Life and Works of Thomas Cole*. Cambridge, MA: Belknap Press.

Nobles, Katherine. 1897. "Audubonists: Popular Interest in the Great Naturalist Is Spreading." *Los Angeles Times*, May 16, 18.

Nord, David Paul. 1997. "Readership as Citizenship in Late-Eighteenth-Century Philadelphia." In *A Melancholy Scene of Devastation: The Public Response to the 1793 Yellow Fever Epidemic*, edited by J. Worth Estes and Billy G. Smith, 19–44. Canton, OH: Science History Publications/USA.

Norris, Thaddeus. 1864. *The American Angler's Book: Embracing the Natural History of Sporting Fish, and the Art of Taking Them*. Philadelphia: Porter and Coates.

Northern Prairie Wildlife Research Center. 2004. *Presettlement Wildlife and Habitat of Montana: An Overview*. Washington, DC: U.S. Geological Survey.

Nye, David E. 1998. *Consuming Power: A Social History of American Energies*. Cambridge, MA: MIT Press.

Oberhansley, Frank. 1937. "Buffalo in Yellowstone Park." *Yellowstone Nature Notes* 14, nos. 1–2 (January–February): 4.

Oberhansley, Frank. 1938. "Defacement of Thermal Areas by Vandals." *Yellowstone Nature Notes* 15, nos. 1–2 (January–February): 1.

Oehser, Paul H. 1952. "In Memoriam: Florence Merriam Bailey." *Auk* 69: 26.

Oelschlaeger, Max. 1991. *The Idea of Wilderness: From Prehistory to the Age of Ecology*. New Haven, CT: Yale University Press.

O'Fallon, Brendan D., and Lars Fehren-Schmitz. 2011. "Native Americans Experienced a Strong Population Bottleneck Coincident with European Contact." *Proceedings of the National Academy of Sciences of the United States of America* 108, no. 51 (December): 20444–20448.

Office of American Indian Trust. 2000a. *Legal Basis for Native American Consultation and Coordination: Overview of Indian Treaties*. Washington, DC: Department of the Interior.

Office of American Indian Trust. 2000b. *American Indians and Alaska Natives*. Washington, DC: Department of the Interior.

Office of Indian Affairs. 1832. *Report from the Office of Indian Affairs*. Department of War. 10 (2): 159–178.

Office of Indian Affairs. 1836. *Report from the Office of Indian Affairs*. Department of War, 1–49.

Office of Indian Affairs. 1838. *Report from the Office of Indian Affairs*. Department of War. 12 (1): 440–550.

Oldham, Kit. 2003. "George and Mary Jane Washington Found the Town of Center-ville (now Centralia) on January 8, 1875." HistoryLink.org Essay 5276. February 23. Accessed November 12, 2009. www.historylink.org/index.cfm?Display Page=output .cfm&File_Id=5276.

Oldham, Kit. 2004. "George W. Bush Settles with His Family at Bush Prairie near Tumwater in November 1845." History Link.org Essay 5646. February 1. Accessed November 12, 2009. www.historylink.org/index.cfm?DisplayPage=output .cfm&File_Id=5646.

Olmsted, Frederick Law. 1860. "A Pioneer Community to the Present Day." Frederick Law Olmsted Papers. Washington, DC: Library of Congress.

Olmsted, Frederick Law. 1861. "Park." *New American Cyclopaedia: A Popular Dictionary of General Knowledge* 2:768–775.

Olmsted, Frederick Law. 1864a. Letter to John Olmsted. March 11. Frederick Law Olmsted Papers. Washington, DC: Library of Congress.

Olmsted, Frederick Law. 1864b. Letter to John Olmsted. June 25. Frederick Law Olmsted Papers. Washington, DC: Library of Congress.

Olmsted, Frederick Law. 1865. *Preliminary Report upon the Yosemite and Big Tree Grove.* Frederick Law Olmsted Papers. Washington, DC: Library of Congress.

Olmsted, Frederick Law, Jr., and Theodora Kimball. 1922. *Forty Years of Landscape Architecture: Central Park*, 45–57. Cambridge, MA: MIT Press.

Olmsted, Vaux and Company. 1866a. *Preliminary Report to the Commissioners for Laying Out a Park in Brooklyn, New York: Being a Consideration of Circumstances and Site and Other Conditions Affecting the Design of Public Pleasure Grounds.* Submitted to the Board of Commissioners of Prospect Park. January 24. Frederick Law Olmsted Papers. Washington, DC: Library of Congress.

Olmsted, Vaux and Company. 1866b. *Report upon a Projected Improvement of the Estate of the College of California, at Berkeley, Near Oakland.* June 29. Frederick Law Olmsted Papers. Washington, DC: Library of Congress.

Olmsted, Vaux and Company. 1868. *Preliminary Report upon the Proposed Suburban Village at Riverside, Near Chicago.* Submitted to the Riverside Improvement Company. September 1. Frederick Law Olmsted Papers. Washington, DC: Library of Congress.

Olson, Sherry H. 1997. *Baltimore: The Building of an American City.* Baltimore: Johns Hopkins University Press.

Olwig, Kenneth R. 1995. "Reinventing Common Nature: Yosemite and Mount Rushmore—A Meandering Tale of Double Nature." In *Uncommon Ground: Toward Reinventing Nature*, edited by William Cronon, 379–408. New York: W. W. Norton.

O'Neale, Sondra A. 1986. "A Slave's Subtle War: Phillis Wheatley's Use of Biblical Myth and Symbol." *Early American Literature* 21 (September): 144–65.

Organ v. State. 1892. 56 Ark. 267. 19 S. W. 840. 1892 Ark. May 28.

Orr, Oliver H., Jr. 1992. *Saving American Birds: T. Gilbert Pearson and the Founding of the Audubon Movement.* Gainesville: University of Florida Press.

Osborne, William S. 1972. *Caroline M. Kirkland.* New York: Twayne.

Outlook. 1909. "Editorial." January 30, 234–236.

Ozawa v. United States. 1922. 260 U.S. 178.

Paige, Amanda L., Fuller L. Bumpers, and Daniel F. Littlefield, Jr. 2010. *Chickasaw Removal*. Ada, OK: Chickasaw Press.

Paige, John C., and Laura Soulliere Harrison. 1987. *Out of the Vapors: A Social and Architectural History of Bathhouse Row, Hot Springs National Park*. Washington, DC: U.S. Department of the Interior.

Palmer, Theodore Sherman. 1910. *Private Game Preserves and Their Future in the United States*. Washington, DC: Government Printing Office.

Palmer, Theodore Sherman. 1912. *Chronology and Index of the More Important Events in American Game Protection, 1776–1911*. Biological Survey Bulletin No. 41. Washington, DC: U.S. Department of Agriculture.

Parish, Peter J. 1989. *Slavery: History and Historians*. New York: Harper and Row.

Park, Yoosun. 2008. "Facilitating Injustice: Tracing the Role of Social Workers in the World War II Internment of Japanese Americans." *Social Science Review* 82, no. 3 (September): 447–483.

Parkman, Francis. 1947. *The Journals of Francis Parkman*. Vol. 1. Edited by Mason Wade. New York: Harper and Brothers.

Patsone v. Commonwealth of Pennsylvania. 1914. 232 U.S. 138; 34 S. Ct. 281; 58 L. Ed. 539. January 9.

Patterson, Daniel. 2008. "Elizabeth C. Wright." In *Early American Nature Writers: A Biographical Encyclopedia*, edited by Daniel Patterson, Roger Thompson, and J. Scott Bryson, 400–406. Westport, CT: Greenwood.

Paul, Sherman. 1952. *Emerson's Angle of Vision: Man and Nature in the American Experience*. Cambridge, MA: Harvard University Press.

Pearson, T. Gilbert. 1937. *Adventures in Bird Protection, an Autobiography*. New York: Appleton-Century.

Pease, Jane, and William Pease. 1990. *Choice and Constraint in Antebellum Charleston and Boston*. Chapel Hill: University of North Carolina Press.

Pena, Devon, and Joseph Gallegos. 1993. "Nature and Chicanos in Southern California." In *Confronting Environmental Racism: Voices from the Grassroots*, edited by Robert Bullard, 141–160. Boston: South End Press.

Pennsylvania Magazine of History and Biography. 1903. "The Mount Regale Fishing Company of Philadelphia." 27: 88.

People of the State of New York v. The Buffalo Fish Company, Limited. 1900. 164 N.Y. 93. 58 N.E. 34. 1900 N.Y. October 2; Lacey Act. 1900, 187–189.

People of the State of New York v. Jacob V. Bootman, et al. 1904. 180 N.Y. 1. 72 N.E. 505. 1904 N.Y. December 6.

People of the State of New York ex rel. August Silz v. Henry Hesterberg. 1905. 109 A.D. 295. 96 N.Y.S. 286. 1905 N.Y. App. Div. November.

People of the State of New York ex rel. John Hill v. Henry Hesterberg. The People of the State of New York ex rel. August Silz v. Henry Hesterberg. 1906. 184 N.Y. 126. N.E. 1032. 1906 N.Y. February 27.

People v. Fishbough. 1890. 12 N.Y.S. 24. 1890 N.Y. Misc. December 10.

People v. Platt. 1819. 17 Johns. 195. 1819 N.Y. October.

Perdue, Theda, and Michael D. Green. 2005. *The Cherokee Removal: A Brief History with Documents*. 2nd ed. Boston: Bedford St. Martins.

Perkins, Eli. 1877. "California's Big Trees." *New York Times*, June 17, 5.

Peterson, John Alvah. 1976. *The Origins of the Comprehensive City Planning Ideal in the United States, 1840–1911*. Cambridge, MA: Harvard University Press.

Pettus, T. 1948. "Seattle Is Blighted by Restrictive Covenants." *New World*. January 15, 1.

Phelan, James. 1907. Letter to Garfield, J. R. November 21. James Phelan Papers. The Bancroft Library. Berkeley: University of California at Berkeley.

Phillips, John C., and Lewis Webb Hill, eds. 1930. *Classics of the American Shooting Field: A Mixed Bag for the Kindly Sportsman 1783–1926*. Boston: Houghton Mifflin.

Phillips, Kate. 2003. *Helen Hunt Jackson: A Literary Life*. Berkeley: University of California at Berkeley.

Pinchot, Cornelia Bryce. n.d. Unpublished Manuscript. Cornelia Bryce Pinchot Papers. Washington, DC: Library of Congress.

Pinchot, Gifford. 1906. Letter to Marsden Manson. May 28. Gifford Pinchot Papers. Washington, DC: Library of Congress.

Pinchot, Gifford. 1911. Letter to James R. Garfield. November 22. Papers of James R. Garfield. Washington, DC: Library of Congress.

Pinchot, Gifford. 1936. *Just Fishing Talk*. New York: Telegraph Press.

Pinchot, Gifford. [1947] 1998. *Breaking New Ground*. New York: Harcourt Brace Jovanovich.

Pitz, Marylynne. 2006. "National Park Service to Acquire South Fork Club Which Was at the Heart of Johnstown Disaster." *Pittsburgh Post-Gazette*, July 18. Accessed May 15, 2012. www.post-gazette.com/life/lifestyle/2006/07/18/National-Park -Service-to-acquire-South-Fork-club-which-was-at-heart-of-Johnstown-disaster /stories/200607180113.

Porter, Kenneth Wiggins. 1971. *The Negro on the American Frontier*. New York: Arno.

Posadas, Barbara M. 1999. *The Filipino Americans*. Westport, CT: Greenwood.

Powell, John Harvey. [1949] 1993. *Bring Out Your Dead: The Great Plague of Yellow Fever in Philadelphia in 1793*. Philadelphia: University of Pennsylvania Press.

Prewitt, Kenneth, and Alan Stone. 1973. *The Ruling Elites: Elite Theory, Power, and American Democracy*. New York: Harper and Row.

Price, Uvedale. 1796. *An Essay on the Picturesque: As Compared with the Sublime and the Beautiful; and, On the Use of Studying Pictures, for the Purpose of Improving Real Landscape*. London: J. Robson.

Proceedings of a Conference of Governors. 1908. Washington, DC: Library of Congress.

Proceedings of the National Park Conference Held at the Yellowstone National Park. 1912. Washington, DC: Government Printing Office.

Proceedings of the National Park Conference Held at Yosemite National Park. 1913. Washington, DC: Government Printing Office.

Proceedings of the National Park Conference Held at Berkeley, California. 1915. Washington, DC: Government Printing Office.

Prucha, Francis Paul. 1975. *Documents on United States Indian Policy*. Lincoln: University of Nebraska Press.

Prucha, Francis Paul. 1986. *The Great Father: The United States Government and the American Indians*. Lincoln: University of Nebraska Press.

Publications of the Sierra Club. 1892. *Proceedings of the Sierra Club.* Vol. 1. San Francisco: Sierra Club.

Publications of the Sierra Club. 1893. *Proceedings of the Sierra Club.* 2: 23–24.

Punke, Michael. 2009. *Last Stand: George Bird Grinnell, the Battle to Save the Buffalo, and the Birth of the New West.* New York: HarperCollins.

Pusey, Michael. 1993. *Jürgen Habermas.* New York: Routledge.

Rabinovitch, Eyal. 2001. "Gender and the Public Sphere: Alternative Forms of Integration in Nineteenth-Century America." *Sociological Theory* 19, no. 3: 354–355.

Raker Act. 1913. 38 Stat. At L. 242, chap. 4.

Ramirez, Jan Seidler. 1995. "Greenwich Village." In *The Encyclopedia of New York*, edited by Kenneth T. Jackson, 506–509. New Haven, CT: Yale University Press.

Randolph, Peter. 1893. *Slave Cabin to the Pulpit. The Autobiography of Rev. Peter Randolph: The Southern Question Illustrated and Sketches of Slave Life.* Boston: James H. Earle, Publisher.

Ranney, Victoria P., Gerald J. Rauluk, and Carolyn F. Hoffman. 1990. *The Papers of Frederick Law Olmsted: The California Frontier: 1863–1865.* Baltimore: Johns Hopkins University Press.

Rea, Gene. 1961–1962. "Dr. Jones's Incredible Amateurs: Circleville Enthusiasts Produced a Work Rivaling Audubon's." *Ohioana Quarterly* 4 (winter): 98–119.

Recreation. 1901. "An Ideal Game Preserve." 14 (April): 263–265.

The Regional Review. 1938. "Negro Recreational Program Gains Momentum." 1, no. 4 (October): 42.

Reiger, John F. 1972. *The Passing of the Great West: Selected Papers of George Bird Grinnell.* New York: Winchester.

Reiger, John F. [1975] 2001. *American Sportsmen and the Origins of Conservation.* Corvallis: Oregon State University Press.

Reiss, Steven A. 1995. "Horse Racing." In *The Encyclopedia of New York City*, edited by Kenneth T. Jackson, 557–559. New Haven, CT: Yale University Press.

Remini, Robert V. 2001. *Andrew Jackson and His Indian Wars.* New York: Viking.

Report of the Chief of Staff, War Department. 1935. May 13. Official File 268, 3. Hyde Park, NY: Franklin D. Roosevelt Presidential Library.

Reynolds, Charles B. 1886. *Old St. Augustine: A Story of Three Centuries.* St. Augustine, FL: E. H. Reynolds.

Rhodes, Richard. 2004. *John James Audubon: The Making of an American.* New York: Alfred A. Knopf.

Richardson, Robert D., Jr. 1995. *Emerson: The Mind on Fire.* Berkeley: University of California Press.

Richardson, Robert D., Jr. [1986] 1996. *Henry Thoreau: A Life of the Mind.* Berkeley: University of California Press.

Richter, Daniel K. 2001. *Facing East from Indian Country: A Native History of Early America.* Cambridge, MA: Harvard University Press.

Rigg, Dorothy Mae. [1942] 1975. "George Washington—Founder of Centralia." In *Centralia: The First Fifty Years*, edited by Herndon Smith, 193–222. Tumwater, WA: H. J. Quality Printing.

Righter, Robert W. 2005. *The Battle over Hetch Hetchy*. New York: Oxford University Press.

Rights of Way Act. 1901. An Act Relating to Rights of Way through Certain Parks, Reservations, and Other Public Lands. H.R. 11973. Stat. Vol. 31, chap. 372. February 15, 790–791.

Riley, Glenda. 1980. "Not Gainfully Employed: Women on the Iowa Frontier, 1833–1870." *Pacific Historical Review* 49 (May): 237–264.

Rinehart, Mary Roberts. 1916. *Through Glacier Park: Seeing America First with Howard Eaton*. Boston: Houghton Mifflin.

Rinehart, Mary Roberts. 1918. *Tenting Tonight: A Chronicle of Sport and Adventure in Glacier Park and the Cascade Mountains*. Boston: Houghton Mifflin.

Rinehart, Mary Roberts. 1948. *My Story: A New Edition and Seventeen New Years*. New York: Rinehart.

Robertson, Janet. 1990. *The Magnificent Mountain Women: Adventures in the Colorado Rockies*. Lincoln: University of Nebraska Press.

Rodríguez, Clara E. n.d. "Puerto Ricans: Immigrants and Migrants." Accessed December 20, 2015. https://americansall.org/sites/default/files/resources/pdf/ethnic-and -cultural/9.9_Puerto_Ricans_Immigrants_and_Migrants.pdf.

Rogers, Elizabeth Barlow, with contributions from Marianne Cramer, Judith L. Heintz, Bruce Kelly, Philip N. Winslow, and John Berendt. 1987. *Rebuilding Central Park: A Management and Restoration Plan*. Cambridge, MA: MIT Press.

Rome Semi-Weekly Citizen. 1890. "The North Woods." July 12.

Ronda, James P. 1984. *Lewis and Clark among the Indians*. Lincoln: University of Nebraska Press.

Roosevelt, Robert Barnwell. 1884. *Superior Fishing or the Striped Bass, Trout, Black Bass, and Blue-Fish of the Northern States*. New York: Orange Judd.

Roosevelt, Theodore. [1885] 1996. *Hunting Trips of a Ranchman: Sketches of Sport on the Northern Cattle Plains*. New York: Random House.

Roosevelt, Theodore. [1888] 2000. *Ranch Life and the Hunting Trail*. New York: Century Company.

Roosevelt, Theodore. [1891] 2000. "Daniel Boone and the Founding of Kentucky." In *Hero Tales: How Common Lives Reveal the Heroic Spirit of America*, edited by Theodore Roosevelt and Henry Cabot Lodge. Nashville, TN: Cumberland House.

Roosevelt, Theodore. [1893] 1996. *The Wilderness Hunter: An Account of the Big Game of the United States and Its Chase with Horse, Hound, and Rifle*. New York: Random House.

Roosevelt, Theodore. 1906. "Against Use of Aigrettes." *Washington Post*. August 5, 1.

Roosevelt, Theodore. 1907. Letter to John Muir. September 16. John Muir Papers. Stockton, CA: Stuart Library, University of the Pacific.

Roosevelt, Theodore. 1908. Letter to James R. Garfield. April 27. Washington, DC.

Roosevelt, Theodore. 1910. *The Strenuous Life*. London: A. Moring, Limited.

Roosevelt, Theodore. 1994. "Hunting Trips of a Ranchman." In *Theodore Roosevelt: An American Mind*, edited by Mario R. DiNunzio. New York: Penguin.

Roper, Laura Wood. 1973. *FLO: A Biography of Frederick Law Olmsted*. Baltimore: Johns Hopkins University Press.

Rosekrans, Spreck, Nancy E. Ryan, Ann H. Hayden, Thomas J. Graff, and John M. Balbus. 2004. *Paradise Regained: Solutions for Restoring Yosemite's Hetch Hetchy Valley*. New York: Environmental Defense.

Rosenbaum, Robert J. 1981. *Mexicano Resistance in the Southwest: The Sacred Right of Self-Preservation*. Austin: University of Texas Press.

Rosenberg, Charles E. 1987. *The Cholera Years: The United States in 1832, 1849, 1866*. Chicago: University of Illinois Press.

Rosenkrantz, Barbara Gutmann. 1972. *Public Health and the State: Changing Views in Massachusetts*. Cambridge, MA: Harvard University Press.

Rosenzweig, Roy, and Elizabeth Blackmar. 1992. *The Park and the People: A History of Central Park*. Ithaca, NY: Cornell University Press.

Ross, Alan. 1977. Foreword. In *Rambles in King's River Country*, by John Muir. Ashland, CA: Lewis Osborne.

Roth v. State. 1894. 51 Ohio St. 209. 37 N.E. 259. 1894 Ohio. March 13.

Rountree, Helen C., ed. 1993. *Powhatan Foreign Relations, 1500–1722*. Charlottesville: University Press of Virginia.

Rousseau, Jean-Jacques. [1761] 1880. *Julie ou La Nouvelle Heloise*. Paris: Garnier Freres.

Rousseau, Jean-Jacques. [1762] 1974. *Emile*. Translated by Barbara Foxley. New York: Sutton.

Royal Phelps v. Joseph H. Racey. 1875. 60 N.Y. 10. 1875 N.Y. February 2.

Runkle, L. G. 1872. "Up and Down the Columbia." In *Picturesque America: or The Land We Live In*, edited by William Cullen Bryant, 31–52. New York: D. Appleton.

Runte, Alfred. 1987. *National Parks: The American Experience*. Lincoln: University of Nebraska Press.

Runte, Alfred. 1990. *Yosemite: The Embattled Wilderness*. Lincoln: University of Nebraska Press.

Russell, Carl Parcher. [1959] 1992. *One Hundred Years in Yosemite*. Yosemite National Park, CA: Yosemite Association.

Russell, Lynette, ed. 2001. *Colonial Frontiers: Indigenous-European Encounters in Settler Societies*. Manchester, UK: Manchester University Press.

Rybczynski, Witold. 1999. *A Clearing in the Distance: Frederick Law Olmsted and America in the Nineteenth Century*. New York: Touchstone.

Sachs, Aaron. 2006. *The Humboldt Current: Nineteenth-Century Exploration and the Roots of American Environmentalism*. New York: Viking.

Salmond, John A. 1967. *The Civilian Conservation Corps, 1933–1942: A New Deal Case Study*. Durham, NC: Duke University Press.

San Francisco Public Utilities Commission. 2004. *San Francisco Public Utility Commission History: Creation of the San Francisco Water Department*. Accessed March 4, 2010. www.sfwater.org/index.aspx?page=162.

Satz, Ronald. 1986. "The Mississippi Choctaw: From the Removal Treaty of the Federal Agency." In *After Removal: The Choctaw in Mississippi*, edited by Samuel J. Wells and Roseanna Tubby. Jackson: University Press of Mississippi.

Save the Redwoods League. 2004. *League Information*. San Francisco: Save the Redwoods League.

Schiff, Judith A. 1981. "The Social History of New Haven." In *New Haven: An Illustrated History*, edited by Floyd Shumway and Richard Hegel, 101. Woodland Hills,
CA: Windsor.

Schlesinger, Andrew B. 1971. "Las Gorras Blancas, 1889–1891." *Journal of Mexican-
American History* 1 (spring): 87–143.

Schneider, Mary Jane. 1994. *North Dakota Indians: An Introduction*. 2nd ed. Dubuque,
IA: Kendall/Hunt.

Schneider-Hector, Dietmar. 2014. "Forging a National Park Service: 'The Necessity for
Cooperation.'" *Journal of the Southwest* 56, no. 4 (winter): 603–641.

Schrepfer, Susan R. 1983. *The Fight to Save the Redwoods: A History of Environmental
Reform, 1917–1978*. Madison: University of Wisconsin Press.

Schuyler, David. 1996. *Apostle of Taste: Andrew Jackson Downing: 1815–1852*. Baltimore:
Johns Hopkins University Press.

Schuyler, David, and Jane Turner Censer. 1992. *The Papers of Frederick Law Olmsted:
The Years of Olmsted, Vaux & Company*. Baltimore: Johns Hopkins University Press.

Scobey, David. 2002. *Empire City: The Making and Meaning of the New York City
Landscape*. Philadelphia: Temple University Press.

Scott, James C. 1985. *Weapons of the Weak: Everyday Forms of Peasant Resistance*. New
Haven, CT: Yale University Press.

Scott, James C. 1990. *Domination and the Arts of Resistance: Hidden Transcripts*. New
Haven, CT: Yale University Press.

Sellars, Charles Coleman. 1980. *Mr. Peale's Museum: Charles Willson Peale and the First
Popular Museum of Natural Science and Art*. New York: W. W. Norton.

Sellars, Richard West. 1997. *Preserving Nature in the National Parks*. New Haven, CT:
Yale University Press.

Sernett, Milton C. 2007. *Harriet Tubman: Myth, Memory, and History*. Durham, NC:
Duke University Press.

Severance, Carol. n.d. "Cornelia Bryce Pinchot (1881–1960)." Milford, PA: Grey Towers National Historic Landmark.

Shankland, Robert. 1970. *Steve Mather of the National Parks*. New York: Alfred Knopf.

Shaw, et al. v. Crawford. 1813. 10 Johns. 236. 1813 N.Y. May.

Sheldon, Addison E. 1914. *History and Stories of Nebraska: With Maps and Illustrations*.
Chicago: University Publishing.

Shellum, Brian G. 2010. *Black Officer in a Buffalo Soldier Regiment*. Lincoln: University
of Nebraska Press.

Sheridan, Dick. 1971. "Out the Gate." *New York Daily News*. April 8.

Sheth, Manju. 1995. "Asian Indian Americans." In *Asian Americans: Contemporary
Trends and Issues*, edited by Pyong Gap Min, 169–198. Thousand Oaks, CA: Sage.

Shields, John C. 2010. *Phillis Wheatley and the Romantics*. Knoxville: University of
Tennessee Press.

Shirley, Gayle C. 2011. *More than Petticoats: Remarkable Montana Women*, 2nd Ed.
Guilford, CT: Globe Pequot Press.

Shook, B. A., and D. G. Smith. 2008. "Using Ancient mtDNA to Reconstruct the Population History of Northeastern North America." *American Journal of Physical Anthropology* 137: 14–29.

Shu, Julia. 2015. "What does Race have to do with this Yosemite Hike?" *Grist*. July 15. Accessed December 15, 2015. http://grist.org/article/what-does-race-have-to-do-with -this-yosemite-hike/.

Shugart, Sharon. 2003. "Hot Springs National Park: A Brief History of the Park." Hot Springs National Park: National Park Service.

Shugart, Sharon. 2006. "African Americans and the Hot Springs Baths." Exhibit at the Hot Springs National Park Visitors Center. Hot Springs: Hot Springs National Park.

Shumaker, Susan. n.d. "Untold Stories from America's National Parks: Segregation in the National Parks." Part 1, 15–36. Boston: Public Broadcasting Service.

Shute, Katharine H. 1877. "To the Pupil." In *The Night before Thanksgiving, A White Heron and Selected Stories*. Boston: James R. Osgood.

Sierra Club. 1909. *Let All the People Speak and Prevent the Destruction of Yosemite Park*. San Francisco: Sierra Club.

Sierra Club. 1960. *The Sierra Club: A Handbook*. San Francisco: Sierra Club.

Sierra Club Bulletin. 1893a. "Charter Members of the Sierra Club." 1, no. 1 (January): 16–20.

Sierra Club Bulletin. 1893b. "Letters from Honorary Members." 1, no. 2 (June): 25–29.

Sieur de Monts National Monument. By the President of the United States: A Proclamation. 1916. July 8. 34: 1785–1791.

Silva, C. 2009. "Racial Restrictive Covenants: Enforcing Neighborhood Segregation in Seattle." Seattle Civil Rights and Labor History Project. Seattle: University of Washington. Accessed June 10, 2015. http://depts.washington.edu/civilr/covenants _report.htm.

Simpson, William L. 1898a. "The Game Question in Jackson Hole." *Forest and Stream* 51 (December 10): 468.

Simpson, William L. 1898b. "The Jackson Hole's Situation." *Forest and Stream* 51 (December 17): 485.

Sky, Doris. 2009. "Helen Hunt Jackson." Denver: Colorado Women's Hall of Fame. Accessed September 16, 2010. www.cogreatwomen.org/jackson.htm.

Slack, Nancy G. 1993. "Botanical Explorations of California: From Menzies to Muir (1786–1900). With Special Emphasis on the Sierra Nevada." In *John Muir: Life and Work*, edited by Sally M. Miller, 221–223. Albuquerque: University of New Mexico Press.

Sletcher, Michael. 2004. *New Haven: From Puritanism to the Age of Terrorism*. Charleston, SC: Arcadia.

Smillie, James D. 1872. "The Yosemite." In *Picturesque America; or, The Land We Live In*, edited by William Cullen Bryant, 483–484. New York: D. Appleton.

Smith, Beatrice Scheer. 1994. "The 1872 Diary and Plant Collection of Ellen Powell Thompson." *Utah Historical Quarterly* 62 (spring): 104–131.

Smith, David C. 1997. *The Transcendental Saunterer: Thoreau and the Search for Self*. Savannah: Frederic C. Beil.

Smith, Duane A. 1988. *Mesa Verde National Park: Shadows of the Centuries*. Lawrence: University of Kansas Press.

Smith, Edward H. 1976. "The Comstocks and Cornell: In the People's Service." *Annual Review of Entomology* 21 (January): 1–26.

Smith, Herbert F. 1965. *John Muir*. New York: Twayne.

Smith, Nathaniel S. 1903. "Blooming Grove Park Association." *New York Times*, October 4, 14.

Smithsonian Institution Research Information System. 2010. "George Bird Grinnell Photograph Collection 1902–1904." Washington, DC: Smithsonian Institution.

Snow, Pamela. 2005. "Agriculture in the Precolonial and Colonial Eras." In *The Encyclopedia of New England*, edited by Burt Feintuch and David H. Watters, 23–24. New Haven, CT: Yale University Press.

Solnit, Rebecca. 2000. *Savage Dreams: A Journey into the Landscape Wars of the American West*. Berkeley: University of California Press.

Spady, Matthew. 2007. "Audubon Park: A Brief History." Accessed May 2, 2009. www.audubonparkny.com/AudubonParkBriefHistory.html.

Spann, Edward K. 1981. *The New Metropolis: New York City, 1840–1857*. New York: Columbia University Press.

Sprague, William Forrest. 1940. *Women and the West: A Short Social History*. Boston: Christopher.

Stansell, Christine. 1987. *City of Women: Sex and Class in New York 1789–1860*. Chicago: University of Illinois Press.

Star Democrat. 2014. "House OKs Tubman National Park." December 5, 1. Accessed May 21, 2015. www.stardem.com/news/local_news/article_92588783-e5eb-546d-a3fa-b111e91531c3.html.

State of Kansas v. C. A. Saunders. 1877. 19 Kan. 127. 1877 Kan. July.

State of Minnesota v. C. W. Rodman. Same v. R. E. Cobb. 1894. 58 Minn. 393. 59 N. W. 1098. 1894 Minn. July 25.

State of Minnesota v. Northern Pacific Express Company. 1894. 58 Minn. 403. 59 N. W. 1100. 1894 Minn. July 25.

State of Missouri v. David S. Randolph. 1876. 1 Mo. App. 15. 1876 Mo. App. January 31.

State of Missouri v. Joseph T. Farrell. 1886. 23 Mo. App. 176. 1886 Mo. App. October 26.

State of Missouri v. W. W. Judy. 1879. 7 Mo. App. 524. 1879 Mo. App. October 28.

State v. Solomon Norton. 1873. 45 Vt. 258; 1873 Vt. January.

State v. Townessnute. 1916. 89 Wash. 478, 154 Pac. 805. February 4.

Statute for the Preservation of Fish in Certain Waters. 1801. 1 K. & R. L. 420, Sess. 24, ch. 127. April 3.

Stevenson, Brenda. 1988. Introduction. *The Journals of Charlotte Forten Grimké*, edited by Brenda Stevenson, 3–56. New York: Oxford University Press.

Stevenson, Brenda. 1996. *Life in Black and White: Family and Community in the Slave South*. New York: Oxford University Press.

Steward, Austin. 1857. *Twenty-Two Years a Slave, and Forty Years a Freeman*. Rochester, NY: William Alling.

Stewart, John. 1975. *Winds in the Woods—The Story of John Muir*. Philadelphia: Westminster.

Stewart, Mart A. 2006. "Slavery and the Origins of African American Environmentalism." In *"To Love the Wind and the Rain": African Americans and the Environment*, edited by Dianne D. Glave and Mark Stoll. Pittsburgh: University of Pittsburgh Press.

Stiffarm, Lenore A., and Phil Lane. 1992. *The Demography of Native North America: A Question of American Indian Survival*. Boston: South End Press.

Stoddard, Seneca Ray. 1893. *The Adirondacks*. Glens Falls, NY: Seneca Ray Stoddard.

Stoddart, Anna M. 1907. *The Life of Isabella Bird (Mrs. Bishop)*. New York: E. P. Dutton.

Stoller, Marianne. 1980. "Grants of Desperation, Lands of Speculation: Mexican Period Land Grants in Colorado." In *Spanish and Mexican Land Grants in Colorado and New Mexico*, edited by John R. Van Ness and Christine M. Van Ness, 22–39. Manhattan, KS: Sunflower University Press.

Stoller, Marianne. 1985. "La Merced." In *La Cultura Constante de San Luis*, edited by Randall Tweeuwen, 12–17. San Luis, CO: San Luis Museum and Cultural Center.

Stowe, Harriet Beecher. 1873. *Palmetto-Leaves*. Boston: James R. Osgood.

Strouse, Jean. 1999. *Morgan: American Financier*. New York: Random House.

Stryker, Sheldon. 1968. "Identity Salience and Role Performance: The Relevance of Symbolic Interaction Theory for Family Research." *Journal of Marriage and the Family* 30: 558–564.

Stryker, Sheldon. 1981. "Symbolic Interactionism: Themes and Variations." In *Social Psychology: Sociological Perspectives*, edited by Morris Rosenberg and Ralph Turner, 23–24. New York: Basic.

Sublette, Ned, and Constance Sublette. 2016. *The American Slave Coast: A History of the Slave-Breeding Industry*. Chicago: Lawrence Hill Books.

Sung, Betty Lee. 1971. *The Story of the Chinese in America*. New York: Collier.

Sutton, Silvia Barry. 1997. Introduction. *Civilizing American Cities: A Selection of Frederick Law Olmsted's Writings on City Landscapes*, edited by Silvia Barry Sutton, 2–4. New York: Da Capo.

Takaki, Ronald. 1983. *Pau Hana: Plantation Life and Labor in Hawaii*. Honolulu: University of Hawaii Press.

Takaki, Ronald. 1989. *Strangers from a Different Shore*. Boston: Little, Brown.

Takaki, Ronald. 1993. *A Different Mirror: A History of Multicultural America*. Boston: Little, Brown.

Tauber, Alfred I. 2001. *Henry David Thoreau and the Moral Agency of Knowing*. Berkeley: University of California Press.

Tauber, Gilbert. 1995. "Lispenard Swamp." In *The Encyclopedia of New York City*, edited by Kenneth T. Jackson, 679. New Haven, CT: Yale University Press.

Taylor, Dorceta E. 1999. "Central Park as a Model for Social Control: Urban Parks, Social Class and Leisure Behavior in Nineteenth-Century America." *Journal of Leisure Research* 31, no. 4: 420–477.

Taylor, Dorceta E. 2000. "The Rise of the Environmental Justice Paradigm: Injustice Framing and the Social Construction of Environmental Discourses." *American Behavioral Scientist* 43, no. 4: 508–580.

Taylor, Dorceta E. 2004. "Park Movements." In the *Encyclopedia of Recreation and Leisure in America*, edited by Gary Cross, 92–99. New York: Charles Scribner's Sons.

Taylor, Dorceta E. 2009. *The Environment and the People in American Cities, 1600s–1900s: Disorder, Inequality, and Social Change*. Durham, NC: Duke University Press.

Taylor, Dorceta E. 2010. Introduction to *Research in Social Problems and Public Policy* 18: 3–28.

Taylor, Dorceta E. 2014. *Toxic Communities: Environmental Racism, Industrial Pollution, and Residential Mobility*. New York: New York University Press.

Taylor, Henry Louis. 1993. "John Mercer Langston and the Cincinnati Riot of 1841." In *Race and the City: Work, Community, and Protest in Cincinnati, 1820–1970*, edited by Henry Louis Taylor. Champaign: University of Illinois Press.

Taylor, Quintard. 1999. *In Search of the Racial Frontier: African Americans in the American West, 1528–1990*. New York: W. W. Norton.

Taylor, Robert Lewis. 1948. "Profiles: Oh, Hawk of Mercy!" *New Yorker*, April 7, 31–45.

Taylor, Ronald B. 1975. *Chavez and the Farm Workers: A Study in the Acquisition and Use of Power*. Boston: Beacon.

Teale, Edwin Way. 1954. *The Wilderness World of John Muir*. Boston: Houghton Mifflin.

Territory v. Evans. 1890. 2 Idaho 658. 23 P. 115. 1890 Ida. February 12.

Thaxter, Celia. [1886] 1887. "Woman's Heartlessness." Reprinted in *Audubon Magazine* 1, no. 1 (February): 13–14.

Thomas, Edith Matilda. 1886. *The Round Year*. Boston: Houghton Mifflin.

Thomas, Emma, Phil McGarty, and Kenneth I. Mavor. 2009. "Aligning Identities, Emotions, and Beliefs to Create Commitment to Sustainable Social and Political Action." *Personality and Social Psychology Review* 13, no. 3 (August): 194–218.

Thoreau, Henry David. 1893. *Excursions: The Writings of Henry David Thoreau*. Boston: Houghton Mifflin.

Thoreau, Henry David. [1906] 1962. *The Journal of Henry D. Thoreau*. 14 vols. Edited by Bradford Torrey and Francis Allen. New York: Dover.

Thoreau, Henry David. [1958] 1974. *The Correspondence of Henry David Thoreau*. Edited by Walter Harding and Carl Bode. New York: New York University Press.

Thoreau, Henry David. 1982. *The Portable Thoreau*. Edited by Carl Bode. New York: Penguin Books.

Thornton, Pamela Plakins. 2005. "Gentlemen Farmers." In *The Encyclopedia of New England*, edited by Burt Feintuch and David Watters, 42. New Haven, CT: Yale University Press.

Thornton, Russell. 1987. *American Indian Holocaust and Survival: A Population History since 1492*. Oklahoma City: University of Oklahoma Press.

Thornton, Russell. 1991. "The Demography of the Trail of Tears Period: A New Estimate of Cherokee Population Losses." In *Cherokee Removal: Before and After*, edited by William L. Anderson, 75–93. Athens: The University of Georgia Press.

Thornton, R. 1997. "Aboriginal North American Population and Rates of Decline, ca. AD 1500–1900." *Current Anthropology* 38: 310–315.

Thurman, Sue Bailey. 1952. *Pioneers of Negro Origin in California*. San Francisco: Acme Publishing Company.

Time. 1930. "Bird Fight." November 3, 34.

Tinkcom, Harry M. 1982. "The Revolutionary City, 1765–1783." In *Philadelphia: A 300-Year History*, edited by Russell F. Weigley, 109–154. New York: W. W. Norton.

Tong, Benson. 2000. *The Chinese Americans*. Westport, CT: Greenwood.

Torres-Reyes, Ricardo. 1970. *Mesa Verde National Park: An Administrative History: 1906–1970*. Washington, DC: Department of the Interior.

Townshend, Charles Hervey. 1900. *The Quinnipiack Indians and Their Reservation*. New Haven, CT: Tuttle, Morehouse and Taylor.

Trefethen, James B. 1964. *Wildlife Management and Conservation*. Boston: D. C. Heath.

Trefethen, James B. 1975. *An American Crusade for Wildlife*. New York: Winchester.

Turner, Frederick. 1985. *Rediscovering America: John Muir in His Time and Ours*. New York: Viking.

Turner, Frederick Jackson. [1893] 1953. *The Frontier in American History*. New York: Henry Holt.

Tuttle, William M. 1980. *Race Riot: Chicago in the Red Summer of 1919*. New York: Atheneum.

Underwood Tariff Act of 1913. Ch. 16, 38 Stat. 114, October 3.

United States v. William Binkley, Charles Purdy, and Oscar Adams. 1906. U.S. District Court, Ninth Circuit, Southern District of California. Available at the Yellowstone National Park Archives, 228.

Updyke, Gloria. 2004. "Restoring a National Historic Landmark: President and Mrs. Hoover's Rapidan Camp, Shenandoah National Park." Washington, D.C.: National Park Service.

U.S. Census Bureau. 1864. *Population of the United States in 1860, Compiled from the Original Returns of the Eighth Census*. Washington, DC: Government Printing Office.

U.S. Census Bureau. 1897. *Population of the United States, 1890*. Part 2. Washington, DC: Government Printing Office.

U.S. Census Bureau. 1975. *Historical Statistics of the United States: Colonial Times to 1970*. Part 2. Washington, DC: U.S. Department of Commerce.

U.S. Census Bureau. 1998. "Population of the Largest 100 Cities and Other Urban Places in the United States: 1790–1990." Prepared by Campbell Gibson et al. Population Division Working Paper No. 27. Released June 15. Accessed November 23, 2008. www.census.gov/population/www/documentation/ twps0027/twps0027.html.

U.S. Commission on Human Rights. 1992. *A Historical Context for Evaluation*. Edited by Fremont J. Lyden and Lyman H. Legters. Pittsburgh: University of Pittsburgh Press.

U.S. Congress, House Committee on the Public Lands. 1872. "The Yellowstone Park." H. Rept. 26 to accompany H.R. 764, 42d Cong., 2d sess. February 27; 1872 U.S. Congress, 1–2.

U.S. Department of the Interior. 1886. *Annual Report of the Superintendent of Yellowstone National Park*. Washington, DC: Government Printing Office.

U.S. Department of the Interior. 1907. *Annual Report of the Acting Superintendent of Yellowstone National Park*. Washington, DC: Government Printing Office.

U.S. Department of the Interior. 1908. *Annual Report of the Acting Superintendent of Yellowstone National Park*. Washington, DC: Government Printing Office.

U.S. House of Representatives. 1834. *Regulating the Indian Department*. 23d Congress 1st sess. May 20; 474: 1–129.

U.S. House of Representatives. 1900. *Enlarging the Powers of the Department of Agriculture, etc.* 56th Congress, 1st sess. March 1; 474: 1–3.

Utica Morning Herald and Daily Gazette. 1880. "Rome Matters." March 4.

Utica Weekly Herald. 1886. "Rod and Gun." November 9, 12.

Utica Weekly Herald. 1888. "Rod and Gun." February 14, 7.

Vallejo, Guadalupe. 1890. "Ranch and Mission Days in Alta California." *Century Magazine* 41, no. 2 (December). Accessed February 12, 2014. www.sfmuseum.org/hist2/rancho.html.

Van Valkenburgh, Norman J. 1979. *The Adirondack Forest Preserve: A Narrative of the Evolution of the Adirondack Forest Preserve of New York State.* Blue Mountain Lake, NY: Adirondack Museum.

Veracini, Lorenzo. 2010. *Settler Colonialism: A Theoretical Overview.* New York: Palgrave Macmillan.

Veracini, Lorenzo. 2011. "Introducing: Settler Colonial Studies." *Settler Colonial Studies* 1, no. 1: 1–12.

Veracini, Lorenzo. 2013. "Constructing 'Settler Colonialism': Career of a Concept." *Journal of Imperial and Commonwealth History* 41, no. 2: 313–333.

Vialet, Joyce. 1980. *Temporary Worker Programs: Background and Issues.* United States. Cong. Senate. Committee on the Judiciary. 96 Cong., 2 sess. S. Rept. Washington, DC: Government Printing Office.

Vilas, Martin Samuel. 1915. *Water and Power for San Francisco from Hetch-Hetchy Valley in Yosemite National Park.* San Francisco: Martin S. Vilas.

Vogel, Virgil. 1992. *This Country Was Ours.* New York: Harper and Row.

Wainwright, Nicholas B. 1982. "The Age of Nicholas Biddle, 1825–1841." In *Philadelphia: A 300-Year History,* edited by Russell F. Weigley, 258–306. New York: W. W. Norton.

Walcott, Frederic C. 1914. "Private Game Preserves as Factors in Conservation." In *Wildlife Conservation in Theory and Practice,* edited by William T. Hornaday, 195–222. New Haven, CT: Yale University Press.

Walker, Dale L. 1998. *The Boys of '98: Theodore Roosevelt and the Rough Riders.* New York: Tom Doherty Associates.

Walls, Michael D. 2015. "Rediscovery of a Native American Cultural Landscape: The Chickasaw Homeland at Removal." PhD diss., University of Kentucky.

Wang, Ning, Xiaodong Zhou, Filemon K. Tan, Morris W. Foster, Frank C. Arnett, and Ranajit Chakraborty. 2004. "Genetic Signatures of Pre-expansion Bottleneck in the Choctaw Population of Oklahoma." *American Journal of Physical Anthropology* 124: 373–379.

Waring, George E. 1877. *Village Improvements and Farm Villages.* Boston: James E. Osgood.

Warner, Sam Bass. 2001. "A Brief History of Boston." In *Mapping Boston,* edited by Alex Kreiger, David Cobb, and Amy Turner, 3. Cambridge, MA: MIT Press.

Warren, Louis S. 1997. *The Hunter's Game: Poachers and Conservationists in Twentieth-Century America.* New Haven, CT: Yale University Press.

Washington Bee. 1888. June 16, 1.

Washington Post. 1883. "The Fashions in France." July 22, 3.

Washington Post. 1886a. "The Audubon Society." April 4, 4.

Washington Post. 1886b. "Birds and Bonnets: Very Few Ladies Influenced by the Agitation." November 21, 2.

Washington Post. 1886c. Untitled. June 21, 2.

Washington Post. 1888a. Untitled. December 7, 4.

Washington Post. 1888b. "Girl Feather Workers." December 7, 1.

Washington Post. 1889a. "Girl Feather-Workers Resume Work." March 21, 2.

Washington Post. 1889b. Untitled. February 19, 4.

Washington Post. 1895. "To Save the Birds: The Chicago Audubon Society the Only One of Its Kind." March 31, 22.

Washington Post. 1897a. "To Save Feathered Songsters: Newly Organized Audubon Society Will Begin Active Work." May 24, 7.

Washington Post. 1897b. "Save the Song Birds: Audubon Society Will Oppose Fashion's Decrees." May 27, 10.

Washington Post. 1897c. "Owls and Pretty Hats." November 3, 6.

Washington Post. 1899a. "Hunting a Giant Bear." July 16, 19.

Washington Post. 1899b. "Social and Personal: Crusade of Audubon Society." March 25, 7.

Washington Post. 1899c. "Work of Audubon Society." February 1, 5.

Washington Post. 1899d. "Bonnets without Birds." March 26, 4.

Washington Post. 1900. "Protectors of the Birds." January 30, 7.

Washington Post. 1903a. "The Audubon Hat Show." October 16, 7.

Washington Post. 1903b. "Pretty Hats without Birds." October 18, 2.

Washington Post. 1903c. "Meeting of Audubon Society." May 1, 12.

Washington Post. 1903d. "The Audubon Hat Show." October 16, 7.

Washington Post. 1905a. "Proposes Cat Licenses." November 1, A1.

Washington Post. 1905b. "Will War on Tramp Cats." November 22, MP4.

Washington Post. 1905c. "Hard to Catch Cats." November 22, 12.

Washington Post. 1906a. "Will President's Plea Save the White Heron?" August 26, SM7.

Washington Post. 1906b. "Ducks Killed by the Ton." March 4, B3.

Washington Post. 1906c. "Italians Kill Song Birds." December 29, 3.

Washington Post. 1909. "Seizing Aliens' Guns." September 26, ES4.

Washington Post. 1911. "Rejects Gunmakers' $25,000." June 17, 5.

Washington Post. 1932. "Audubon Society Holds Hectic Ballot Session." October 26, 9.

Waterman, Laura, and Guy Waterman. 1989. *Forest and Crag: A History of Hiking, Trailblazing, and Adventure in the Northeast Mountains*. Boston: Appalachian Mountain Club.

Watson, John F., and Willis Hazard. 1884. "The Schuylkill Fishing Company." *Annals of Philadelphia, and Pennsylvania, in the Olden Time; Being a Collection of Memoirs, Anecdotes, and Incidents of the City and Its Inhabitants, and of the Earliest Settlement of the Inland Part of Pennsylvania*. Philadelphia: Edwin S. Stuart.

Wear, D. W. 1886. *Report of the Superintendent of the Yellowstone National Park*. Washington, DC: United States Department of the Interior.

Weaver, Warren, Jr. 1987. "Washington Talk: Presidential Retreats; The Camp that was Hoover's." *New York Times*. August 14. Accessed May 15, 2015. http://www.nytimes

.com/1987/08/14/us/washington-talk-presidential-retreats-the-camp-that-was
-hoover-s.html.

Weinberg, P. 1999. "Equal Protection." In *The Law of Environmental Justice: Theories and Procedures to Address Disproportionate Risks*, edited by M. B. Gerard, 3–22. Chicago: American Bar Association.

Welker, Robert Henry. 1955. *Birds and Men*. Cambridge, MA: Belknap Press.

Welter, Barbara. 1966. "The Cult of True Womanhood." *American Quarterly* 18 (summer): 151.

Whalen, Ken. 2013. "Driving with the Driven: A Re(-)view of the Trail of Tears in the Roadside Montage." *American Indian Culture and Research Journal* 37, no. 2: 207–232.

Wheatley, Phillis. 1783. *Poems on Various Subjects, Religious and Moral*. By Phillis Wheatley, Negro Servant to Mr. John Wheatley of Boston. London: Printed for Archibald Bell and sold in Boston by Cox and Berry.

Wheatley, Phillis. 1916. *Life and Works of Phillis Wheatley. Containing her Complete Poetical Works, Numerous Letters and a Complete Biography of This Famous Poet of a Century and a Half Ago*, edited by G. Herbert Renfro. Washington, DC: A. Jenkins.

Wheatley, Phillis. 1930. *The Poems of Phillis Wheatley, Edited with an Introduction and Notes*, edited by Charlotte Ruth Wright. Philadelphia: The Wrights.

White, Deborah. 1987. *Ar'n't I a Woman: Female Slaves in the Plantation South*. New York: W. W. Norton.

Whitman, Karen. 1972. "Re-evaluating John Brown's Raid at Harpers Ferry." *West Virginia History* 34, no. 1 (October): 46–84.

Wildlife Conservation Society. 2015. "The American Bison Society." Accessed June 20, 2015. www.wcs.org/saving-wildlife/hoofed-mammals/bison/the-american-bison -society.aspx.

Wilkins, Thurman. 1995. *John Muir: Apostle of Nature*. Norman: University of Oklahoma Press.

William L. Allen v. Lewis C. Wyckoff. 1886. 48 N.J.L. 90. 2 A. 659. 1886 N.J. February 15.

William Rockefeller v. Oliver Lamora. 1903. 85 A.D. 254; 83 N.Y.S. 289; N.Y. App. Div.

William Rockefeller v. Oliver Lamora. 1904. 96 A.D. 91; 89 N.Y.S. 1; N.Y. App. Div.

William Rockefeller v. Oliver Lamora. 1905. 106 A.D. 345; 94 N.Y.S. 549; N.Y. App. Div.

William Rockefeller v. Oliver Lamora. 1906. 186 N.Y. 567; 79 N.E. 1115; N.Y.

Williams, Jean Kinney. 2006. *Bridget "Biddy" Mason: From Slave to Businesswoman*. Minneapolis: Compass Point Books.

Williams, Raymond. 1973. *The Country and the City*. New York: Oxford University Press.

Williams, Wilberforce. 1914a. "Talks on Preventative Measures First Aid Remedies Hygienics and Sanitation: Summer Resort Health." *The Chicago Defender*, July 11, 8.

Williams, Wilberforce. 1914b. "Talks on Preventative Measures First Aid Remedies Hygienics and Sanitation: Camping Out." *The Chicago Defender*, July 25, 8.

Williams, Wilberforce. 1915. "Talks on Preventative Measures First Aid Remedies Hygienics and Sanitation: The West Michigan Resort. *The Chicago Defender*, June 26, 8.

Wilson, Sherrill D., and Larry A. Greene. 1995. "Blacks." In *The Encyclopedia of New York City*, edited by Kenneth T. Jackson, 112–115. New Haven, CT: Yale University Press.

Winchester Repeating Arms Company. 1911. "Gunmakers Roused against Hornaday." *New York Times*, July 9, 12.

Winter, Thomas. 2003. "Cult of Domesticity." In *American Masculinities: A Historical Encyclopedia*, edited by Brett E. Carroll, 120–122. Thousand Oaks, CA: Sage.

Winthrop, John. [1629] 1846. "General Considerations for the Plantations in New England, with an Answer to Several Objections." In *Chronicles of the First Planters of the Colony of Massachusetts Bay, from 1623 to 1636*, edited by Alexander Young. Boston: Charles C. Little and James Brown.

Wisconsin Territorial Gazette. 1837. Untitled. July 2.

Wolfe, Linnie Marsh. 1938. *John of the Mountains: Unpublished Journals of John Muir.* Boston: Houghton Mifflin.

Wolfe, Linnie Marsh. 1945. *Son of the Wilderness: The Life of John Muir.* Madison: University of Wisconsin Press.

Wolfe, Patrick. 1999. *Settler Colonialism and the Transformation of Anthropology: The Politics and Poetics of an Ethnographic Event.* London: Cassell.

Women in History. 2009. "Biddy Mason Biography." Lakewood Public Library. March 9. Accessed November 14, 2009. www.lkwdpl.org/wihohio/maso-bid.htm.

Wong, Morrison G. 1995. "Chinese Americans." In *Asian Americans Contemporary Trends and Issues*, edited by Pyong Gap Min, 58–94. Thousand Oaks, CA: Sage.

Wood, Peter H. 1975. *Black Majority: Negroes in Colonial South Carolina from 1670 Through the Stono Rebellion.* New York: Alfred A. Knopf.

Worcester v. Georgia. 1832. 31 U.S. (6.Pet.) 515.

Wordsworth, William. 1936. "The Prelude." In *The Poetic Works of Wordsworth*, Book 6, edited by Thomas Hutchinson. London: Oxford University Press.

Worster, Donald. 1994. *Nature's Economy: A History of Ecological Ideas.* 2nd ed. New York: Cambridge University Press.

Wright, Elizabeth C. 1860. "Into the Woods." In *Lichen Tufts, from the Alleghanies.* New York: M. Doolady.

Wright, Mabel Osgood. 1894. *The Friendship of Nature: A New England Chronicle of Birds and Flowers.* New York: Macmillan.

Wright, Mabel Osgood. 1895. *Birdcraft: A Field Book of Two Hundred Song, Game, and Water Birds.* New York: Macmillan.

Wright, Mabel Osgood. 1898. *Four-Footed Americans and Their Kin.* New York: Macmillan.

Wright, Mabel Osgood. 1901. *Flowers and Ferns and Their Haunts.* New York: Macmillan.

Wright, Mabel Osgood, and Elliott Coues. 1898. *Citizen Bird: Scenes from Bird-Life in Plain English for Beginners.* New York: Macmillan.

Wyatt, Victoria. [1901] 1995. "The Harriman Expedition in Historical Perspective." In *Alaska 1899: Essays from the Harriman Expedition*, edited by George Bird Grinnell, xxxvii–xxxix. Seattle: University of Washington Press.

Yamamoto, Kazuya. 2015. "Mobilization, Flexibility of Identity, and Ethnic Cleavage." *Journal of Artificial Societies and Social Simulation* 18, no. 2: 8–22.

Yard, Robert Sterling. 1916. "Making a Business of Scenery." *Nation's Business* 4 (June): 10–11.

Yard, Robert Sterling. [1916] 1917. *The National Parks Portfolio.* Washington, DC: Department of the Interior.

Yellowstone Act. 1872. An Act to Set Apart a Certain Tract of Land Lying Near the Headwaters of the Yellowstone River as a Public Park. U.S. Statutes at Large. Vol. 17, chap. 24, pp. 32–33. Approved March 1.

Yelverton, Thérèse. 1872. *Zanita: A Tale of the Yo-Semite.* New York: Hurd and Houghton.

Yenne, Bill. 2005. *Indian Wars: The Campaign for the American West.* Yardley, PA: Westholme.

Yick Wo v. Hopkins. 1886. 118 U.S. 356, 6 S.Ct. 1064, 30 L.Ed. 220.

Young, Phyllis. 1997. "Beyond the Water Line." In *Defending Mother Earth: Native American Perspectives on Environmental Justice*, edited by Jace Weaver, 85–98. Maryknoll, NY: Orbis Books.

Young, Samuel Hall. [1915] 1990. *Alaska Days with John Muir.* Salt Lake City: Gibbs Smith.

Yusuf. 1887. "Our Neighbors." *Los Angeles Times*, December 9.

Zanjani, Sally. 1997. *A Mine of Her Own: Women Prospectors in the American West, 1850–1950.* Lincoln: University of Nebraska Press.

Zinn, Howard. 1995. *A People's History of the United States.* New York: HarperCollins.

Index

382; sounds, 136, 143, 361; tribal use of feathers, 212; women's punishment, 204
bird sanctuary or refuge, 174, 221, 244, 252, 387
birdwatchers or birdwatching, 173, 190, 196, 200, 377, 384, 387
Bisby Club, 173, 177–178, 271
Bishop, Alice, 347–348
Bittner, Steve, 173
Black Codes, 129
Blackfoot tribe, 79, 107, 128, 357
Black Friday, 242
Black Hills, 275, 278
Blackmar, Elizabeth, 36, 38, 44, 47–48, 259, 291
blacks, 13, 38–39, 80, 84–86, 125, 128–131, 133, 137–138, 142, 154, 369, 373; abolitionists, 142; aristocrats, 380; Civilian Conservation Corps, 367–368; cowboys, 133; elites, 372–373, 378; gold miners, 130; national park construction and protection, 331, 365; newspapers, 373, 377; pioneers, 128–131; and slaughter of birds, 211, 213; trappers and fur traders, 128, 131; travel to national parks and resorts, 373–382
Blackwater National Wildlife Refuge, 135
Blassingame, John W., 14, 126–127, 134, 138
Blauner, Robert, 19–20
Blockson, Charles L., 135–136, 138–139
Blodgett, Geoffrey, 259
Blooming Grove Hunting and Fishing Club, 176, 185
Blooming Grove Park Association, 173, 175
Board of Indian Commissioners, 123
Board of Public Works, 314
Bode, Carl, 24, 60, 62–63, 138
Boeing Aircraft Company, 19
Bohemian Club, 311, 334
Bolnick, D. A., 113
Bonga, Pierre, 128
Bonner, Thomas D., 131
bonnets, 190, 194, 200
Boone, Daniel, 77, 80, 170, 182
Boone and Crockett Club, 181–182, 221–222, 224, 228, 241, 244, 248, 271, 273, 281, 301, 303, 305, 353, 385–388
Boonville Herald, 178
Bootman, Jacob, 229
Borden, James, 269
Boston Common, 32, 36, 44–45
Boston Museum of Fine Arts, 200
Boston Society of Natural History, 191
Botkin, Daniel B., 293
Bottome, Frank, Mrs., 193
Bourdieu, Pierre, 248

Bowden, Jocelyn Jean, 144
Bowles, Samuel, 68, 294, 297, 359–360
Bowling Green (New York), 44, 46, 70
Boyer, Paul, 36, 38, 98
bracero, 147
Bradford, Mary Fluker, 203, 247
Bradford, Sarah H., 99, 135–139
Bradley, Guy, 214, 219, 287
Bradley, Richard, 22, 37
Bradstreet, Anne, 95
Brandegee, Kate Curran, 104
Brands, Henry William, 38, 67, 73–75, 182
Branson, Isaac Reichelderfer, 314, 320, 323
Brant, Irving, 243
breeding season, 169, 188, 201, 211
Brevoort House, 276
Brewster, William, 90, 191, 200–201, 203, 232, 241, 388
Bridger, James, 298
Bridges, Amy, 36
Brighton Chemical Company, 333
British, 10, 13, 36, 101, 113–114, 295
Brodess, Eliza Ann, 135–137
Brodt, Helen, 99
Bronner, Edwin B., 38
Brook Farm, 59–60
Broughton, Hope, 100
Brown, Amy Belding, 59
Brown, Elizabeth, 210
Brown, John, 127, 377–378
Brown, Lucy, 59
Brown, Orlando, 237, 352
Brubaker, Rogers, 30
Bruce, Philip Alexander, 14
Bruce, Sanders Dewees, 52
Bruggeman, Seth C., 374
Bryant, Harold, 346
Bryant, William Cullen, 47–48, 64, 69, 292, 306, 351
Buettner, Cynthia K., 62
buffalo (bison), 182–184, 358–359
Buffalo Bill. *See* Cody, William Coyle
Buffalo Fish Company, 229, 235–236
Buffalo Soldiers, 363
Bulletin (Nuttall), 191
Bunce, O. B., 107, 312, 358
Bunnell, Lafayette, 101–102, 356–357, 359
Buntline, Ned, 68
Burdick, Neal S., 287
Bureau of Forestry, 280, 283, 288
Bureau of Indian Affairs (BIA), 20, 122, 359, 366, 370
Burlingame Treaty, 17

poach, 187, 272, 287; poachers, 168, 173, 186, 217, 221, 272, 275, 287–288, 302–305, 396; poaching, 52, 131, 166, 179, 272, 285, 289, 301, 303–305, 396

pollution, 1, 36, 42, 54, 87, 181, 251, 269; air, 2, 42, 127; industrial, 6, 41, 233; water, 41, 87, 233

Pope's Creek, 374

Porter, Kenneth Wiggins, 128

Porter, William, 172

Posadas, Barbara M., 149

poverty, 1, 33, 36–37, 59, 81, 89, 100, 140, 208, 214, 364–365, 395–397

Powell, Ellen, 104

Powell, John Harvey, 40

Powell, John Wesley, 104

praying towns, 115

Preemption Act, 116

preservation, 5, 24, 27, 58, 142, 162, 283, 286, 290, 293, 330, 346, 350, 384, 389, 392–394, 397; battles or conflicts, 311, 313, 386, 388, 390; campaigns, 307, 310, 323, 330, 333, 347, 386–387; definition, 27; and eugenics, 346–347; forest, 272, 280, 283, 285, 387; game, 172–173, 187–188; groups, clubs, or organizations, 163, 248–249, 371, 385, 389, 393–395; historic, 374; land, 311; laws, 215, 225, 235, 304; message, 374; park, 2, 5, 60, 318–319, 328, 330; politics, 388; redwoods, 344–345; scenic, 307, 338, 340; self-preservation, 11; wilderness, 290, 386, 390–391, 394

preservation movement, 54

preservationism, 2, 27, 31, 275, 307, 346, 391, 393–395; wilderness preservationism, 391

preservationist, 3, 27, 58, 68, 87, 135, 183, 276, 279, 283, 307–311, 313, 318–320, 323–325, 329–330, 333, 341, 343–344, 350, 384–386, 393, 395–396; battles or conflicts, 5, 318; cause, 313; criticism of the Civilian Conservation Corps, 372; and discrimination, 376, 382; discourse or ideology, 5, 60, 396; and native tribes, 357, 359–360; perspective, 5, 284, 385, 393–394; and solitude, 319

Prewitt, Kenneth, 28, 392

Price, Overton, 27

Price, R., 339

Price, Uvedale, 261

primitive forests, 293

primitive masculinity, 23

primitivistic or primitivism, 2, 26, 77, 98

pro-environmental: activities, 27; advocacy 30; behavior, 1; concerns, 385; thought, 21

Progressive Era, 362, 392

Prospect Park, 175

Prucha, Francis Paul, 115–116, 118, 121

Public Works Administration, 365

Pueblo Indians, 113

Puerto Ricans, 147–148, 372

Punjabi immigrants and farmers, 18

Punke, Michael, 71

Puritans, 24

Pusey, Michael, 28

Quakers, 38, 55, 100, 138, 222

Quapaws, 376

Quinn, Davis, 243

Quinnipiacs, 115

Rabinovitch, Eyal, 23

Racco, Rocco, 214, 218–219

race, 4–5, 9, 10, 17, 21, 96, 116, 120, 130, 133, 346–347, 351, 366, 373, 394, 397; master race, 347; race relations, 9, 21; race riots or wars, 37–38, 367, 372

Racey, Joseph, 225

racial mixing, 2, 22

racial uplift, 373–374

racism, 2, 4, 6, 9, 328, 367–368, 395, 397

racist, 346, 397

Radcliffe Bill, 231

railroads, 15–16, 27, 38, 107, 114, 126, 146–147, 150–153, 162, 164, 168, 177, 217, 258, 263, 268, 275, 278, 280–281, 283, 288, 299, 302–303, 307–308, 311, 331–332, 335, 337–338, 344, 365, 378, 388, 393

Rainey Wildlife Sanctuary, 246–247

Raker Act, 324

Ramirez, Jan Siedler, 43

Randolph, David, 225

Randolph, Peter, 140

Raney, Peter, 131

Ranney, Victroria P., 103, 261, 296, 359

Rapidan Camp, 379

Raymond, Israel, 295

Rea, Gene, 90

Recreation, 285

Redwood Canyon, 311

Redwood City Times and Gazette, 342

Redwood Creek, 311

redwoods, 311, 341–342, 344–347

Refugee Escape Act, 152

regulated monopolies in national parks, 335

Reiger, John F., 70–73, 165, 168–171, 173, 178, 181–182, 185–188, 193, 200, 233–234, 272, 284, 302, 392

Reiss, Steven A., 52

Remington Arms, 253